Acclaim for Jorge G. Castañeda's

UTOPIA UNARMED

"Destined to become a classic...an insightful, much-needed look at where Latin America's left is headed and how it must transform itself to remain a political player.... No one else has produced a similar work—despite the crying need."
—*Christian Science Monitor*

"Range[s] over enormous terrain, both physically and intellectually. Castañeda...has put a lifetime of learning into this volume.... Often vivid...the book reminds us, refreshingly, that the left has been alive in Latin America for a long time."
—*Washington Post Book World*

"*Utopia Unarmed* will be one of the most talked-about political books in decades in Latin America.... Castañeda brings to life some of the hemisphere's revolutionaries—the last great Quixotes around.... A brilliantly argued proposal for all sectors of the left." —*San Francisco Chronicle*

"Eminently humane and reasonable...this book deserves to be at the top of any reading list on Latin America. Jorge Castañeda, a well-known Mexican scholar, has written a timely, fascinating and skillfully crafted account of the impact of the end of the Cold War on the Latin American left." —*Foreign Affairs*

"Important...fascinating...Castañeda's expert reading of the Latin American left's turbulent currents should help readers understand the political ferment that undoubtedly lies ahead."
—*Business Week*

"*Utopia Unarmed* is a timely contribution...a devastating critique [by] a leading participant in many of the events which are narrated here...of the Latin American left from within—courageous and unsentimental, admirably free of cant, euphemism and evasion." —*Times Literary Supplement*

Jorge G. Castañeda

UTOPIA UNARMED

Jorge Castañeda was born and raised in Mexico City. He received his B.A. from Princeton University and his Ph.D. from the University of Paris. He has been a professor of economics and of international affairs at the National Autonomous University of Mexico since 1978. He has also been a Senior Associate of the Carnegie Institute for International Peace in Washington, and a visiting professor at Princeton University and the University of California, Berkeley.

Among the six books he has authored or co-authored is *Limits to Friendship: The United States and Mexico* (1988), with Robert Pastor. He is a regular columnist for the *Los Angeles Times, Newsweek International*, and the Mexican weekly *Proceso*.

BOOKS BY Jorge G. Castañeda

Utopia Unarmed

Limits to Friendship (with Robert Pastor)

UTOPIA
UNARMED

UTOPIA
UNARMED

■

The Latin American Left

After the Cold War

■

Jorge G. Castañeda

VINTAGE BOOKS

A Division of Random House, Inc.

New York

The Library of Congress has cataloged the Knopf edition
as follows:
Castañeda, Jorge G.
Utopia unarmed: the Latin American left after the Cold War / by
Jorge G. Castañeda.
p.   cm.
Includes index.
ISBN 0-394-58259-4
1. Latin America—Politics and government—1980-
2. New Left—Latin America—History.
3. Democracy—Latin America—History.
4. Latin America—Relations—United States.
5. United States—Relations—Latin America.
I. Title.
F1414.2.C38   1993
320.5'3'098—dc20   92-36213   CIP
Vintage ISBN: 978-0-679-75141-0

144903659

Contents

■

Acknowledgments

■

This book was made possible by a Research and Writing Grant from the Program on International Peace and Cooperation of the John D. and Catherine C. MacArthur Foundation. I am also deeply grateful to the Department of Political and Social Sciences of the National Autonomous University of Mexico, the institution I have belonged to since 1979, for its ongoing and generous support. I must also thank the Center for Latin American Studies at the University of California, Berkeley, for its hospitality. The Woodrow Wilson School of Public and International Affairs, the Program in Latin American Studies, and the Center of International Studies, all at Princeton University, also provided support during the final stages of the book's production.

Many friends and colleagues have taken the time to read parts or all of the manuscript, and to offer critical and helpful suggestions. I wish to acknowledge their contribution, and of course absolve them of any responsibility for the content of the book. My thanks to: Dudley Ankerson, Régis Debray, Jorge Domínguez, Richard Fagen, Mark Falcoff, Adolfo Gilly, Enrique Guatemala, Enrique Hett, Albert O. Hirschman, David Ibarra, Gwen Kirkpatrick, Casio Luiselli, Francis Pisani, Alan Riding, Jill Roberts, Victor Romeo, Salvador Samayoa, Paco Ignacio Taibo II, and Francisco Weffort.

Ash Green has, once again, been the perfect editor and, more important, a friend. Finally, and as always, thanks go to my family, and particularly to Miriam, without whom nothing is possible, and to Javiera, who read, typed, and researched reams of material.

J.G.C.

UTOPIA
UNARMED

Introduction

■

The Cold War is over and Communism and the socialist bloc have collapsed. The United States and capitalism have won, and in few areas of the globe is that victory so clear-cut, sweet, and spectacular as in Latin America. Democracy, free-market economics, and pro-American outpourings of sentiment and policy dot the landscape of a region where until recently left-right confrontation and the potential for social revolution and progressive reform were widespread. Today conservative, probusiness, often democratically elected and pro-U.S. technocrats hold office around the hemisphere. The United States spent nearly thirty years combating nationalist Marxist revolutionaries where the left was active, influential, and sometimes in control, and where it is now on the run or on the ropes. But then a question arises: If the left is either nonexistent or irrelevant in the post–Cold War era, why bother with it in Latin America at all, much less devote an entire book to it?

First, out of historical curiosity. How has a current of thought, action, and motivation that has in fact rarely and only briefly governed in Latin America, and that has been mostly subjected to repression, division, and enduring marginalization, generated as much intensity of feeling and as great a sense of peril in the United States, and so much interest and often sympathy elsewhere in the world? Secondly and much more important, the left remains relevant in Latin America because the end of the Cold War and the fall of socialism in Eastern Europe and the Soviet Union have not brought an end to the original causes that gave it birth. If anything, those causes today are more real, more compelling, than ever: poverty, injustice, gaping social disparities, and overwhelming daily violence.

Latin America is too modern and "westernized" for social change and political reform to seem meaningless as they do in Africa and parts of Asia, given the intractability of the problems and the mystery of the solutions. But it is also too poor and divergent from the West to join the postmodern, post–"left-right" world; an abyss separates it from First World modernity. The moment one looks beyond today's headlines and yesterday's disenchantments, the substance of the debates and divisions that have for many years polarized the region's socially segregated and economically backward societies persists. Only its terms have—inevitably—changed.

The left counts for yet another reason, perhaps the weightiest one. As this book attempts to demonstrate, over the past thirty years it has been universally present in Latin America. In its different ideological shades—populist, Communist, social-democratic, Castroist, and political-military—and its social expressions—the intellectual left, the grass roots left—it has figured prominently in the political equation of every Latin American nation. Although it has seldom attained power, much less kept it or done much with it, the left has exerted enormous influence on the shape of things in Latin America today.

With the exception of Cuba, it has failed miserably in its efforts to take power, make revolution, and change the world. As a nongovernmental actor, however, the Latin American left has probably been the most important domestic factor in the continent's political evolution. It has succeeded rotundly in an enterprise it never sought to pursue: making a difference by existing, fighting, pressuring, and provoking, sometimes for the worse, but mostly for the better. If Latin America today enjoys a degree of democratic rule that, however shallow, represents a huge improvement over the past, it is in part the result of the left's existence and struggle against the dictatorships of years gone by. As Jaime Wheelock of the Sandinista Front acknowledged in the course of an interview for this book: "If we had won the election of 1990, democracy in Nicaragua would not have advanced as much as it has with us in opposition." Likewise, if many nations created ramshackle, corrupt, and inefficient but at least partly functioning welfare states to protect part of the population from poverty, inequality, and exclusion, this was largely a by-product of the left's impact. If some governments apply neoliberal policies with greater concern than others and pay at least lip service to the idea of combating extreme poverty, this "kinder and gentler" approach can be partially attributed to the left. If in cities across the hemisphere, from Lima to São Paulo, from Caracas to Mon-

tevideo, grass-roots groups have organized, voted, and elected municipal authorities of the left, it is because there is a belief that they make
a difference. And if the rest of the world has noticed that south of the
Rio Grande there were peoples, cultures, and problems, it was often in
reaction to the threat or hope awakened by the left.

The left's impact on the region during the three decades since the
Cuban Revolution is due above all to the failures and weakness of the
alternative. Despite twenty years of aggregate economic growth (from
1960 to 1980), and a decade of democracy (1980 to 1990), Latin America today is not much better off overall than in the late fifties. In
absolute terms, undeniable progress has been made in many fields; but
the region has fallen further behind the industrialized world, its social
and economic disparities are greater than before, and, at least in the
short term, the hope for effective solutions to its problems is as dim as
ever.

Latin America paid a price for seeking a better way: the numbers of
killed, disappeared, and tortured during the past thirty years are terrifying. The hemisphere lived through illegality and authoritarian rule,
and the ravages of the bipolar rivalry: everything was either a symptom
or a consequence of the Cold War, which in turn justified every horror,
any excess. No wonder the forces for change survived repression, incompetence, and ideological discredit.

The purpose of this book is to ascertain whether the relevance of
the left in Latin America is intact. Even if many of its traditional
stances and outlooks have been rendered meaningless by the disappearance of the socialist paradigm, the classic traits of Latin American
society endure, and thus the need for social and economic change
remains. If the left, after an excruciating but unavoidable process of
self-analysis and critical revision, is able to rebuild itself and enter the
post–Cold War world without losing its way or its soul, it will have a
key role to play in effecting necessary change. The grounds for this
assessment begin with context and recent history.

The *regional economic, social, and political* context—in contrast
to the *international ideological* environment in which the Latin American left must carry out this aggiornamento—is uncommonly and paradoxically propitious. Since 1982, Latin America has undergone a
double transformation that has significantly altered the region's phys-
iognomy. During the 1980s and through the beginning of the 1990s,
the hemisphere suffered its worst economic and social crisis since the
Depression. In 1980, 120 million Latin Americans, or 39 percent of the
area's population, lived in poverty; by 1985 the number had grown to
160–170 million; toward the end of the decade it was estimated at the

appalling figure of 240 million. It was no surprise, then, that exit polls taken during the 1989 Brazilian elections showed that approximately 70 percent of the voters had no more than an elementary education; most had less. The ancestral injustice of Mexican society attained alarming proportions, making citizens unequal even in the face of death: according to the World Bank, life expectancy for the poorest 10 percent of the population was twenty years less than for the richest 10 percent. Half a century had elapsed since the continent had lived through such a sustained period of economic and social deprivation. Were it not for illegal drug exports, immigration, and an income-reducing but shock-absorbing informal economy, the outcome could have been far more tragic.

At the same time, Latin America was also living through its most substantive and broadly based process of democratization since the thirties. With the exception of the U.S.-supported, civilian-military regimes in Central America, where elections were held but often meant little, Mexico, where change continued to occur at a snail-like pace, and Cuba, democratization drives in most fields of political endeavor took place throughout the hemisphere. This trend went well beyond the simple celebration of elections. It included a newfound respect for human rights in the former Southern Cone dictatorships, and an opening up of the press, unions, and related sectors of civil society in Brazil and other nations.

At no time since the 1930s has the conjunction of these two developments—economic crisis and democratization—so greatly enhanced the relevance of social change and political shifts in Latin America. This in turn has maintained the left as a central actor in hemispheric politics, despite its apparent obsolescence in other regions of the world. The populist or center-left regimes of the mid-thirties and early forties that emerged during or just after the Depression and in the midst of a generalized clamor for more democratic rule throughout most of Latin America—Cárdenas in Mexico, Vargas in Brazil, Perón in Argentina, the Popular Front in Chile—bear eloquent testimony to an undeniable historical precedent.

In addition, the region's economic crisis—as it unfolded in an international context where socialism was unraveling, the welfare state was self-destructing, and a conservative, so-called neoliberal tidal wave engulfed the world—gave way to a peculiarly Latin blend of Reaganomics. Trade liberalization, enticing foreign investment, cutting subsidies, privatization, "leave it to the market," and the "end of the state" generated an unpredictable social dynamic. In the long term, it was foolish to discard the possibility of the neoliberal policies' success in triggering growth, employment, and competitiveness as well as reducing social disparities. But in the short and medium run, they aggravated inequality, deepened the gap between rich and poor, ripped the slender safety net, and bred resentment among the poor and poorer over the fortunes of the rich and richer. The backlash was waiting to hit, and it seemed almost inevitable that it would, if not everywhere, in many nations; if not immediately, in time. This book seeks to show what the Latin American left has been and what it could be today, and, if its day returns, what it would have done in the past and what it might do in the future.

1

Travels with Argentina:
Defining the Latin American Left

■

Argentina has always imported and exported revolutionaries. From independence leader José de San Martín, who marched interminably from Buenos Aires across the Andes and northward to Peru, then ended his days in Boulogne-sur-Mer, to Ernesto "Che" Guevara, who terminated his in the jungles of Bolivia, Argentines have mixed exile, revolution, and travel as have few others. They have also repeatedly defied all efforts of inclusion into any tidy classification of the hemisphere's leftist revolutionary or reformist currents. How could it be otherwise, with self-descriptions such as this one from Argentina's populist leader Juan Domingo Perón:

> If I have repeatedly been a central actor in history, it's because I contradicted myself. You have heard of Schlieffen's strategy. One has to change plans several times a day and unfold them, one by one, as necessary. The socialist fatherland? I invented it. The conservative fatherland? I keep it alive. I have to blow in every direction, like the cock on a weathervane.[1]

The conjunction of both trends, defying order and the penchant for political exports, has led to one of contemporary Latin America's stranger paradoxes. The Argentine armed left, insofar as it can be identified as such, has had a disproportionate—and rarely constructive—

---

1. Whether Perón ever actually uttered these words is in the last analysis irrelevant: he could have, he would have, and he probably did. Tomás Eloy Martínez, *La Novela de Perón* (Buenos Aires: Legasa Literaria, 1985), p. 28.

influence on the Latin American universe. The saga of the Argentine funds and revolutionaries that made their way across the continent, leaving behind them a wake of conspiracy, treason, and rebellion abroad, is thus a good starting point for any map of the Latin American left. It is also a story worth telling in its own right.

On September 19, 1974, in downtown Buenos Aires, Montoneros, the self-appointed armed wing of the Peronist movement, kidnapped Jorge and Juan Born, heirs and managers of the Bunge y Born grain fortune and conglomerate. Since the nineteenth century, when it was founded by a pair of Belgian émigré wheat merchants, the Bunge y Born empire had been a symbol of staid Argentine prosperity and world-class economic standing. Although in recent years it had moved much of its business abroad, Bunge y Born remained an Argentine company, whose executives were also distinguished Argentine citizens. They were also very wealthy, as demonstrated by the ransom they paid for the Born brothers: $64 million,[2] including approximately $40 million in stocks, bonds, and other negotiable documents and $2–3 million in goods—clothing, supplies, medicines, toys—given away by the kidnappers to their supporters in the shantytowns of Buenos Aires.

While the $64 million in ransom money was quickly spread throughout numerous banks in Europe, the United States, and Mexico, the Peronist urban guerrillas carried out at least two more highly lucrative operations, one for $4 million and another, involving a German businessman working for Mercedes Benz, for roughly the same amount.[3] The entire sum, amounting to well over $70 million,[4] was subsequently consolidated and stashed away in European banks. As it was held outside Argentina, the funds automatically came under the formal management of the organization's External Commission headed by Roberto "El Negro" Quieto. Predictably, this generated

---

2. Some sources give a slightly different aggregate figure ($60 million, "thirty million per brother"). See Dan Morgan, *Merchants of Grain* (New York: Penguin Books, 1980), p. 223. The figure of $64 million is quoted in Juan Gasparini, *Montoneros. Final de Cuentas* (Buenos Aires: Puntosur, 1988), pp. 77–78.

3. Gasparini, ibid., p. 74.

4. Richard Gillespie, *Soldiers of Perón: Argentina's Montoneros* (New York: Oxford University Press, 1982), p. 225. There are, of course, discrepancies over the exact amounts involved. Gillespie gives the figure of $5 million for the Mercedes Benz kidnapping; Juan Gasparini, in a different book from the one cited above, gives $4 million. A source close to the Montoneros gave the author a figure of $25 million for the third kidnapping, making the total value of the deals rise over $100 million. On Christmas Eve, 1989, Buenos Aires judge Alberto Piotti sequestered $13.5 million of Peronist financier David Graiver's surviving kin's assets, the equivalent, according to the judge, of the $4 million the Montoneros put in Graiver's hands for safekeeping. Juan Gasparini, *El Crimen de Graiver* (Buenos Aires: Grupo Editorial Zeta, 1990), p. 220.

frictions with the domestically based military wing, led by Roberto Cirilo Perdía. In order to reduce these tensions, Mario Firmenich— "El Pepe," the maximum leader of the group—who in fact controlled the money all along, decided to concentrate it in one country, so as to facilitate central control. The United States was deemed to be the ideal location.

To this end, a major financial operation was quickly set in motion. The man charged with this endeavor was a somewhat shady financier, David Graiver, a U.S.-Argentine Jewish banker from New York who put his apparently considerable pecuniary talents and presumed contacts with Israeli intelligence at the service of Perón. Through business contacts in Mexico, he made the Aztec nation his *plaque tournante*, developing excellent contacts with the infamous Mexican Federal Security Directorate. On August 7, 1976, during a business trip to Mexico, his plane disappeared en route to Acapulco, over the Sierra of Guerrero. His body was not definitively identified—only a decapitated trunk was found—and the money he was thought to be transporting never surfaced. According to some accounts, Graiver did not die; he simply took off with the money. Another theory holds that the plane was mistaken for a drug-trafficking flight and was shot down by Mexican drug-enforcement agents. Others surmised his plane was brought down by Mexican security forces who suspected he was carrying a huge sum of money—according to some accounts, up to $40 million in Montonero cash—and wanted to get their hands on it.[5] Another interpretation made Graiver responsible for keeping "only" 16,825,000 Montonero dollars, and accused the CIA of having sabotaged his private jet once it discovered that Graiver was "the Montoneros' banker."[6]

If any of these accounts are true, the Montoneros were left with

---

5. According to the most recent investigation of Graiver's disappearance, the banker was not carrying any Montonero money with him; see Gasparini's *El Crimen de Graiver*. A source close to the Montoneros gave the author the higher figure of $40 million. Richard Gillespie adopts an intermediate viewpoint, stating that "Graiver presumably had with him 17 million dollars . . . when the plane crashed." Gillespie, p. 306.

6. This is the basic thesis of Gasparini's recent research on the Graiver disappearance. He clearly had access to some State Department documents (the unclassified ones are reproduced in the book) and to information from sources close to the Mossad, which Graiver allegedly worked for. But the specific charges regarding the CIA, including the details he gives of how Graiver's jet was booby-trapped in Houston on its way to Acapulco, having been forced to land there through subterfuge, are not sourced or sustained in the book. What is evident from the documents published by Gasparini is that the United States Embassies in Buenos Aires and Mexico City showed an uncommon interest in the mystery surrounding an Argentine-Jewish banker who laundered Montonero money and moonlighted for the Mossad, or the other way around.

only part of the wealth they had originally amassed, but still a considerable sum. This portion remained in Europe. The frictions between factions intensified, but now the money was as much a symbol as a real source of tension. Differences surfaced over the importance of the armed struggle and the need to stress the political, less militaristic aspects of the fight for revolution. These disagreements intensified as the political and military tide in Argentina turned against the left after the 1976 coup d'état that overthrew the brutal, quasi-comic astrological regime of Isabelita Perón and José López Rega. Many of the Montoneros' cadres in charge of the money were captured. El Negro Quieto attempted to conciliate matters and divide the money between the domestic and external factions, but, fatally ill with cancer, he died in 1978 on a beach in Argentina literally fighting a helicopter—though some say the Army was tipped off by his comrades-turned-adversaries. Subsequently, the money was managed by operatives inside Argentina, though mainly in small amounts still kept separate from the large sums deposited in Europe. Accusations surfaced over missing sums, profligate ways, and extravagant expenditures.

Finally an agreement was reached.[7] The money would be handed over to a third party trusted by all others: the Cubans. Thus in 1976 and early 1977, the Cubans received just under $70 million in cash and documents—the sum left over after the Guerrero accident, minus the minor misappropriations, plus compound interest accrued.[8] The money was once again placed in American and European banks in long-term investments, but now under Cuban supervision, and with interest accruing to them. But as the Montoneros were being decimated in Argentina, and revolution in the entire Southern Cone was

---

7. In diplomatic circles in Buenos Aires during the early 1980s another version circulated, according to which the erstwhile Peronist head of the Argentine Navy, Admiral Emilio Massera, who always conserved ties with Firmenich, even when his Navy officers were torturing Montonero prisoners at the Navy Mechanic School in Buenos Aires, tried to get his hands on the money and began negotiations for that purpose through the Argentine Naval Intelligence office in Paris. It was said that an Argentine diplomat stationed in Paris, Elena Holmberg, found out about the exchanges and threatened to denounce the affair publicly. She was kidnapped in Buenos Aires on July 20, 1978. Her body was identified several months later. Massera claimed that he had her eliminated because she was about to accuse him of giving Firmenich $1.3 million in Paris; which of course makes little sense, unless it was the other way around. Claudio Uriarte, *Almirante Cero; Biografía no autorizada de Emilio Eduardo Massera* (Buenos Aires: Planeta-Espejo de la Argentina, 1992), pp. 224–225.

8. At this stage the numbers begin to get fuzzy. If Graiver disappeared with many millions, then either the Cubans did not receive what was thought or the Montoneros had more to begin with. Or, if Graiver was not carrying that much, there was more left over for later.

clearly on the wane, conflicting claims on the vast sum began to emerge. The survivors of the "dirty wars" of the South needed financing precisely to survive. But the Cubans were being pressed for aid and support by needy revolutionary groups elsewhere in Latin America, who could at this stage put the funds to far better political use than the Argentines. As the Central American guerrilla conflicts and insurrections heated up, the idle money left over from the Argentine debacle became increasingly coveted.

Toward the end of 1977, the Cubans asked the Montoneros to donate a significant sum to the Nicaraguan Sandinistas—a request they pressed vigorously and insistently. A meeting was held in Havana in November 1977, attended by Firmenich, Perdía, Fernando Vaca Narvaja, the third remaining member of the Montonero leadership, and Daniel and Humberto Ortega, representing the Sandinistas together with Jaime Wheelock. Also present were several Cuban officials, notably Manuel Piñeiro and Fernando Ravelo, respectively the head and deputy of the Cuban Communist Party's Central Committee Department of America. The Argentines objected, arguing that the funds were earmarked for the imminent final offensive and definitive victory of their revolution, and, in particular, for the disruption of the World Cup Soccer Finals, scheduled for June 1978 in Buenos Aires. Firmenich and his comrades contended that they had no money to waste on nickel-and-dime sideshows like Nicaragua. All of this was couched in abstract theoretical language stressing the importance of the larger Latin American countries, the weight of the proletariat in those societies, and the scant possibilities of revolution in small, backward, unindustrialized countries like the "banana republics" of Central America. The Cubans, upset over this Argentine arrogance, scolded Firmenich and his associates, insisting that the money be donated. Firmenich was summoned by Cuban vice president Carlos Rafael Rodríguez, who applied much more direct pressure and pointed out that the Argentines should recall how they were enjoying Cuba's wholehearted support and should feel obligated in turn to support the Nicaraguans.

Finally, the Montoneros agreed to hand over $1 million—but with a surprising condition. Firmenich explained that their combatants back home needed encouragement, and that one way to achieve this was to show them that their leaders were actively engaged in leading the revolution everywhere in Latin America. The Sandinistas were asked to cooperate by circulating pictures and stories of "El Pepe's" participation in the Sandinista insurrection. The most famous one appeared a year later in *Barricada* and *Granma*, respectively the Nicaraguan and

Cuban official party dailies, showing Firmenich getting off a plane in combat fatigues, "proving" that he had been fighting in Nicaragua and was leading the Sandinista struggle on the Southern Front.[9] However, the picture was false. Firmenich never fought in Nicaragua, and did not set foot in Managua until July 20, 1979, the day after the revolution had triumphed.[10] Numerous foreign correspondents witnessed this and other scenes and examples of Montonero fabrication and arrogance toward the Sandinistas, in some cases even after they had actually taken power.

Shortly thereafter, as the Montoneros disintegrated under the on-slaught of the Argentine Army's counteroffensive in 1979, each of its individual factions began to demand its share of the money. The divisions became institutionalized. Some leaders abandoned the organization; others, such as the professional military machinery, remained in the ranks of revolution, but split up. Under pressure to hand out money to all solicitors, the Cubans responded that they could not assume the responsibility for deciding whom it should be given to nor the identity of the legitimate owners of the money. However, while the Argentines worked out their differences, the Cubans would keep the funds.

During subsequent years they intermittently donated small sums to other Latin American groups and even to the Argentines themselves. Until 1981, the amounts remained modest, since the possibility existed that the Montoneros would resurface and claim the money. But by 1981, "Perón's soldiers" had been wiped out and the money began to be spread around more generously. The Salvadorean Farabundo Martí Liberation Front (FMLN) insurgents received $200,000 between December 1980 and February 1981, to partially finance their failed final offensive. The Guatemalan Unidad Revolucionaria Nacional Guatemalteca (URNG) guerrillas were offered a similar amount in 1981; likewise the Honduran Cinchonero and Lorenzo Celaya Fuerzas Populares Revolucionarias. Although the Chilean Movimiento de Izquierda Revolucionaria (MIR) was rumored to have received the larg-est sum, its ties with other Argentine organizations made it anathema

---

9. According to Gillespie, "Montonero support for the Sandinista struggle against Somoza included an economic contribution, the presence of Fernando Vaca Narvaja in Nicaragua during the last month of the war, and the dispatching of the 'Adriana Haidar' Health Brigade to treat the Sandinista wounded in Masaya." Gillespie, op. cit., p. 311.

10. The account of the Cuban, Nicaraguan, and Argentine encounters was provided by a former Central American guerrilla cadre intimately familiar with the details of the entire affair, in the course of several interviews with the author in Mexico City between February and November 1990, who requested to be identified only in the above terms.

to the Montoneros. In his more megalomaniacal moments, Firmenich was said to daydream how he was playing San Martín, while the MIR leader and nephew of President Salvador Allende, Andrés Pascal Allende, was a latter-day Bernardo O'Higgins, the father of Chilean independence. Yet according to Pascal Allende, Firmenich never gave his comrade-in-arms any money.[11]

This saga continued until early 1990, when the governor of the Cuban Central Bank traveled to Buenos Aires to try to settle the issue of the funds' rightful ownership once and for all. In the interim, Firmenich was captured in Brazil in 1988 and, after serving two years of a long sentence for the Born brothers' kidnapping, was released in December 1990 under President Carlos Saúl Menem's blanket pardon for crimes committed during the dirty war.[12] On February 20, 1991, weeks after Firmenich's release, Juan Martín Romero Victorica, the Argentine prosecutor in charge of the kidnapping case, filed an injunction in a Buenos Aires court demanding the freezing of 100 million Montonero dollars deposited in the National Bank of Cuba.[13] The Cuban Embassy in Argentina notarized the freeze, but rumors persisted that Fidel Castro would return the money only when the three Montonero factions—Firmenich, Vaca Narvaja, and Perdía—agreed on what should be done with it. One way or another, the money was possibly on its way back to Argentina, having wandered for fifteen years from Buenos Aires to Mexico, from Europe to New York, and from Havana to Managua, Santiago, Morazán, and Guatemala.[14] A long and secretive trip through the sometimes well-supplied, often empty, coffers of the Latin American armed left had come to an end.

The story of the Montoneros' money illustrates the Latin American left's extreme complexity, internal contradictions, and ongoing metamorphoses. The right wing of the left, as exemplified by Argentine Peronism, ended up funding, arming, or organizing the extreme left of

---

11. Andrés Pascal Allende, interview with the author, Mexico City, June 28, 1991.

12. The Argentine federal prosecutor, who resigned over Menem's pardon, declared, "I want the President to say he pardoned them because he cut a deal with the military or because Firmenich put up the money for his campaign." Gregorio Selser, Argentina: "El indulto a jefes de la guerra sucia," *La Jornada* (Mexico City), December 31, 1990.

13. "Busca Argentina repatriar 100 millones de dólares de ex Montoneros," *Excelsior* (Mexico City), February 21, 1991, pp. 2, 12.

14. According to one "final" and even more convoluted account, David Graiver's heirs and the Born family reached an agreement whereby Graiver's widow paid Jorge and Juan Born back nearly $50 million, equal to part of the ransom plus interest. The agreement was "blessed" by the judge in charge of the case. "Acuerdo con benedición de Romero Victorica: Graiver-Born." *Humor* (Buenos Aires), May 1992, p. 11.

the Central American revolutionary movement. Sometimes armed, sometimes not, on occasion Marxist, but usually opposed to any theoretical elaboration, mostly middle-class, but with a real working-class constituency, the Montoneros were an archetypal example of the varying shades and stages of the Latin American left. They constituted a distinct, almost reactionary, expression of frustrated Argentine nationalism: an expression of despair aroused in important sectors of the Argentine middle class over the ruling class's failure to give the country the place it merited on the world stage, the place Perón had promised. But they also came to portray an extreme version, almost a caricature, of the traits other variants of the left would acquire and then lose from 1959 to 1990.

These are the contradictions, the twisted tracks that must be followed to understand how thousands of the region's best young hearts and minds gave up their lives for a vision no one else outside their own circle really shared. In the same way that the Argentine guerrillas' influence across the continent vastly surpassed their authentic weight and numbers, the impact of the hemisphere's armed left was far greater than its actual political importance in any one country at any one time. For more than a decade, the urban, middle-class, university-educated, politicized youth of an entire continent was mesmerized by the armed struggle.[15] Isolated fiction attempted to capture this fascination; their authors either knew it well but weren't novelists, or wrote marvelously about a subject matter they were ultimately unfamiliar with.

The Latin American armed left of the sixties and early seventies was never the central player in the zone of the political spectrum it wished to occupy; virtually all of its card-carrying members of this period were destroyed. But the generation of Latin Americans affected by the armed struggle, and who did not die or disappear in the jungles, mountains, or torture chambers, gave way to the middle-aged activists, journalists, labor leaders, and environmentalists of today. They now work for votes and abandoned children in the shantytowns of Rio de Janeiro, and defend—like Fernando Gabeira—what is left of the city's

---

15. Even at the time many realized what was occurring: "An entire generation of Latin American revolutionaries, coming from the radicalized middle classes, chose the path of guerrilla warfare in the sixties, just as in the eighties of the last century a whole generation of Russian revolutionaries chose the road of terrorism. Like them, among the Latin Americans were the very best of the hemisphere's youth, and not only those for whom revolution was simply a youthful phase on the way to disenchantment or settling down in the society that they earlier wished to transform." Adolfo Gilly, La senda de la guerrilla (Mexico City: Editorial Nueva Imágen, 1986), p. 177.

environment. Many of them—like Antonio Navarro Wolff—helped draft a 1991 Constitution in the Colombian Constituent Assembly, and have held key positions—like Minister of Economics Carlos Ominami—in the management of the Chilean economy, attempting to combine social justice with sound economic policy. They—like Teodoro Petkoff and Freddy Muñoz—have legislated in the Venezuelan Parliament, accommodating their nationalism to the needs of a country that imports virtually everything it consumes. In Buenos Aires they helped found honest newspapers published by a new generation—*Página 12*—and splendid weeklies; have written best-selling novels—Miguel Bonasso's *Memorias de la muerte*; and have made blockbuster films—Fernando Solanas's *El viaje*—recounting the stories of guns and betrayal they lived when they were young.

That same generation also reflected the obsessions, frustrations, and persistence of a broad stratum of the hemisphere's society—stretching beyond the narrow confines of the Montoneros—that even today continues to define itself, after the Cold War and the passing of the socialist world, "to the left." Although it has become fashionable in a way that occurs every two or three decades, to discount the significance of terms such as "left" or "right" in "the new world order," this view is certainly not shared by all concerned. Largely because it is wrong. As Carlos Fuentes has phrased it:

> Far from being dissolved in the euphoria of triumphant capitalism, the meaning of the terms "left" and "right" is clearer than ever. . . . Where the distinction between "left" and "right" appears most necessary is in our Latin America.[16]

Dating back to the early days of the French Revolution, the use of the word "left" remains essentially topographical, as it was long before the Cold War and as it continues to be after the geopolitical and ideo-

---

16. Fuentes's definition of the left in Latin America in the post–Cold War era is succinct but revealing: "Free from the alienation of Soviet policy and Marxist dogma, the modern left in Latin America has before it the obligation of promoting and defending social justice in a continent where the absolute number of poor continues to grow as income distribution continues to deteriorate; where salaries shrink, jobs disappear, food becomes scarce, public services decline, security forces become autonomous and repressive in the name of the war on drugs, malnutrition and infant mortality rise dramatically. . . . If the left doesn't confront these problems, no one else will." Carlos Fuentes, *Excelsior* (Mexico City), December 18, 1990. Another simpler and briefer definition, but no less meaningful, is provided by one of Latin America's leading left-of-center intellectuals-cum-politicians, Brazilian senator, and later Foreign and Finance Minister, Fernando Henrique Cardoso: "The left means being against the existing social order, the right, in its favor. . . ." Fernando Henrique Cardoso, *Social Democracia: O que é, o que propóe para o Brazil* (pamphlet, São Paulo, 1990), p. 12.

logical confrontation that made it relevant to most of the world. The left can best be defined by the right, and by the stances taken by different groups in society on the major issues of the day. For years to come, both modern and traditional societies will find themselves divided over the choices they face. Each issue will present at least two major options and an infinite number of nuances.

On one side of those variations will be a right and on the other a left—obviously no longer Communist, Soviet-inspired, or even Marxist in doctrinal terms. Long before Communism, the Soviet Union, and Marx, there were a left and a right. They will best define themselves in contrast to the "Other," and by their aims as well as the means through which they choose to attain them. During traumatic transitions, such as the one currently under way in the formerly socialist world, the terms and topography may seem confusing and inverted—i.e., hardline, Marxist, Soviet ideologues constituting the "right," pragmatic, innovative reformers making up the "left"—but with time, matters will invariably be straightened out. In any case, for Latin America that type of transition, with its accompanying semantic dissonance, is still far removed.

A further broad definition of the Latin American left is more thematic or political. It concerns the importance that the left, in contrast to its peers or adversaries, attributes to certain issues. In the left today are parties, groups, movements, or political leaders who since the Cuban Revolution have stressed change over continuity; democracy and human rights over domestic security; and national identity and sovereignty over economic integration (free trade, foreign investment, etc.). In economic and social matters, the left tends to emphasize social justice over economic performance (subsidies over fiscal rigor, employment over efficiency, national control over natural resources and strategic sectors of the economy over "market-oriented," free-enterprise economic policies), income distribution over well-functioning markets, reducing inequalities over competitiveness, social spending over controlling inflation, the need to spend over the imperative of healthy government finances.

In an ideal world—and at certain times in parts of Western Europe—these multiple aims have not been construed as incompatible. Unfortunately, in Latin America today, as for the past fifty years at least, the inevitability of trade-offs among different purposes of this nature is largely established. The left and the right are defined chiefly by their respective stands on the opposing sides of a given trade-off. Not every sector of the left takes exactly the same stance or position; nor are all those who do support some of the left's positions necessarily part of the left. But broadly speaking, most elements of the Latin American left fall on the same sides of the aforementioned issues.

Often the best definition is a good description. It is also, however, a frequent symptom of a complex, partially unsolved problem. This is no exception. Defining the left in Latin America is no easy chore, and the contours sketched out here leave many questions unanswered. One in particular deserves to be mentioned: there is a theoretical threshold which, when crossed, divests groups, ideas, or individuals initially of the left, of their membership in good standing. Time, excess, or distortion can force a crossing of the threshold; the left is only the left up to the brink of that threshold.

For the left today, five key dates serve as descriptive milestones, though of course, as with all time frames, durations overlap and the markers are more symbolic than precise. The first, and by far the most important, is the Cuban Revolution and Fidel Castro's triumphal entry into Havana on January 8, 1959. The second and third reflect a six-year phase demarcated by the deaths of two of the left's martyrs: Ernesto "Che" Guevara in Bolivia on October 8, 1967, and Salvador Allende in the bombed and besieged presidential palace in Santiago de Chile on September 11, 1973. The next landmark event is the victory of the Nicaraguan Revolution on July 19, 1979. And the final turning point— pending the denouement of the Cuban drama—comes with those same Sandinistas' defeat in the February 25, 1990 elections in Nicaragua, when for the first time in the Latin American left's history a regime of its own was democratically removed from office.

In addition to these key periods, the Latin American left can be sorted according to two determining criteria, which may also become superimposed but nonetheless provide indications of fundamental differences. The first principle implies an ideological and political classification; the second is functional. Ideologically and politically, the Latin American left can be broken down into four groups: traditional Communist parties, the nationalist or populist left, the political-military organizations, and the region's reformists. Functionally, two groups can be added: the grass-roots and the intellectual left.

The old-school Communist parties were generally born in the 1920s. They were essentially urban-based, soon converted to the so-called "peaceful road to power," and possessed close, often servile ties to the Soviet Union. The nationalist or popular left, to which the imprecise but useful label of "populist" has often been attached, included a wide variety of leadership: from Brazil's Getulio Vargas from the 1930s to the early 1950s, and Lázaro Cárdenas in the 1930s, to Omar Torrijos in the 1970s. Beginning in the 1920s and until the Cuban Revolution, the central issue faced by the Communists and the populists was precisely the nature of their relationship: conflictive or cooperative, subservient or equal.

The political-military organizations sprang up throughout Latin America in the wake of the Cuban Revolution. They are chiefly characterized by their adherence to the "armed struggle" and their almost universal ideological affinity for Cuba and Fidel Castro. In addition, they frequently designated the United States as their "principal enemy." From 1959 onward, the key topic dividing the new political-military left was the way the two existing components—Communists and national-populists—would respond to the impact of the Cuban Revolution, and to the new organizations, tactics, and theories that it wrought.

The main features of the reformist left lie in a strong electoral vocation, an essentially urban, working-class following, a relatively nonaligned geopolitical stance—still critical of the United States and its role in Latin America, but with greater distances from the Soviet Union and Cuba—and a basically balanced emphasis on democracy, human rights, and social justice. For the period ranging from the fall of Salvador Allende to the Sandinistas' defeat in 1989, the burning question facing the left, and dividing it into different groups, factions, and coalitions, consisted of the relationship between reformism and "Marxism-Leninism." The Marxist-Leninists opposed both the moderate and "viabilistic" reformist left that sought above all to govern, and the radical left that placed a premium on principle and protest.

Beyond these categories, there is also a functional or organizational classification which is less precise but perhaps more easily recognizable. Though present in many countries of Latin America for some years now, the grass-roots left introduces a novel ingredient into the left's classical configuration. While often linked to the political left, it cannot be assimilated by it. Not only does it include traditional labor unions, peasant leagues and organizations, churches and comunidades eclesiales de base, cooperatives and organized urban marginals (pobladores, colonos, etc.), but it also has incorporated into its ranks the ecological, women's, and Indian groups as well as the human rights associations that have flourished in Latin America over the past two decades.

Finally, there is an intellectual left. In a region where a vacuum has been generated by the chronically weak institutions of civil society, the figure of "the intellectual"—writer, priest, journalist, academic, artist, activist—has often played a key role. The intellectual frequently articulates the perceived national, social, and democratic demands of the region's people through the press, academia, government, and from abroad. While consistently exposed to the charge of false or exaggerated representation, well-known and anonymous intellectuals alike are an essential part of the Latin American left. It often has "organic" links to the political or grass-roots left, but remains a distinct current.

A brief word is in order about some of the variations of the Latin American left that will not be dealt with. The most obvious are the Trotskyist organizations that acquired a degree of notoriety in certain countries of the hemisphere at given times (Mexico, Bolivia, Guatemala), and the Maoist factions. Among the latter, only Peru's Sendero Luminoso will be examined, but more in light of its importance as an armed movement and part of the second wave of guerrilla efforts, not as a consequence of its Maoism. As it did elsewhere, the Sino-Soviet conflict of the sixties led to multiple schisms within the Latin American left, as many Communist parties suffered splits to their left with a pro-Chinese inclination. The most important instances, outside of Sendero, were the Partido Comunista do Brazil, some of the pro-Chinese factions in Mexico, and various splinter groups in Chile.

Despite their generally marginal presence[17] and influence, the Trotskyists and the Maoists boasted several notable features that would be worth examining: the Trotskyists' generally perceptive analysis of Latin American reality, and the Maoists' particularly unrelenting militancy and devotion to "serving the people." It is nonetheless impossible to study every individual chapter of the Latin American left without losing sight of the broader picture. This is also the case for the politically organized Christian left, which must be distinguished from the Catholic grass-roots left examined below. From the outset, the emergence of the large Christian Democratic parties in many Latin American nations was accompanied by the proliferation of small, left-wing groups with a Christian vocation that subsisted as political parties, albeit marginal ones. The Chilean Izquierda Cristiana is an example.

But the mainstream left, and the one that had the greatest impact,

---

17. "In reality, most Latin American Maoists had little interest in applying the broad front and "protracted struggle" aspects of the Chinese experience (critical distinctions in a continent dominated by Castroist impatience) or had little idea how to work toward those Maoist objectives." William Ratliff, "The Future of Latin American Insurgencies," in Georges Fauriol, *Latin American Insurgencies* (Washington, D.C.: Georgetown University Center for Strategic and International Studies/National Defense University, 1985), p. 171.

is confined to the currents enumerated above; it is the left that made a difference. Its saga encompasses the histories of small shops and immigrant homes of the 1920s, of women's groups and high-tech factories in the Latin megalopolises of the century's end. It is at once an exhilarating and a traumatic story, a story of great hopes and of dashed expectations.

2

In the Beginning: Communists and Populists

■

Until the Cuban Revolution, the twentieth-century history of the Latin American left could be read as a chronicle of the differences, alliances, and conflicts between the region's Communist parties, and the so-called populist, nationalist, or "national-popular" movements. The latter were identified at varying times and places with charismatic leaders or mass organizations such as Cárdenas in Mexico, Perón in Argentina, Getulio Vargas in Brazil, and Haya de la Torre's APRA party in Peru. The hemisphere's Communist parties appeared on the scene in Latin America in the aftermath of the Russian Revolution and the formation of the Third International, or Comintern.[1] Today, with few exceptions, the Communist parties in Latin America have virtually vanished, either dissolving into other organizations, or being reduced to extreme marginality, splitting infinitely into politically irrelevant *grupitos*.

In their time, and in certain countries, the Communist parties achieved significant authority and considerable strength and following among urban or raw material workers, intellectuals, federal employees, and, on occasion, among the smaller peasantry in the countryside. In 1941 the Chilean Communist Party broke into the electoral arena when it received 12 percent of the vote.[2] Subsequently, the party av-

---

1. The two classic works on the region's Communist parties are Robert Alexander, *Communism in Latin America* (New Brunswick: Rutgers University Press, 1957), and Boris Goldenberg, *Kommunismus in Latein Amerika* (Stuttgart: Kolhammer, 1971).

2. Luis Durán B., "Visión cuantitativa de la trayectoria electoral del Partido Comunista de Chile: 1937–1973," in Augusto Varas, ed., *El Partido Comunista en Chile* (Santiago: Cesoc-Flacso, 1988), pp. 351, 354.

eraged nearly 15 percent of the vote in most elections, obtaining its highest total ever, 17 percent, in 1971. Its support originated in the nitrate fields, and soon extended into the copper mines, ports, and transportation industry, as well as among government employees, university students, and intellectuals. Similarly, in Brazil, at the peak of its electoral strength just after the Second World War, "the Partido Comunista Brasileiro emerged as (what was then) the strongest Communist Party in Latin America," with 9 percent of the vote, "securing a mass base" in the trade unions of São Paulo and Rio de Janeiro, as well as among the country's intellectuals.[3] In Uruguay, the agricultural processing industry and the sugar fields, together with the immigrant tradition from Mediterranean Europe, promised the party a long life and considerable sway over the labor movement, intellectuals, and students. This foundation was so strong that the Uruguayan Communist Party survived the crisis at the end of the 1980s better than any other, participating as a leading member of the coalition that in 1990 elected Tabaré Vázquez to the mayoralty of the capital, Montevideo, which contains almost half the country's population.

From the late twenties onward, the Cuban Communist Party became an important factor in political life, developing a mass constituency among the sugar mill workers and the urban population. Similarly, in the copper mines, northern sugarcane fields, and main ports of Peru, the Communist Party exerted considerable clout; among intellectuals, the works of José Carlos Mariátegui became classic reference points for any study or analysis of Peruvian society. Though it never consolidated a mass following, the Mexican Communist Party nonetheless also attained real strength and representation among the country's intellectuals from the twenties through the forties: many of Mexico's great painters of the time, including Rivera, Siqueiros, and Frida Kahlo, were members at one point or another. But by and large, for reasons explained below, with the exception of a few special cases, the region's Communist parties never developed the type of constituency or influence that analogous organizations achieved in France, Italy, Spain after 1936, or even Germany until 1933.

The founding of these parties was sometimes anecdotally interesting, though mostly uneventful. For example, the Mexican Communist Party, the first regional organization to actually join the Communist International, was created in 1918 by an Indian (Manabendranath Bha-

---

3. Thomas Skidmore, *Politics in Brazil. 1930–1964* (New York: Oxford University Press, 1965), pp. 64–66.

tachayra Roy), a Russian (Mijail Gruzenberg or Borodin), and an intelligence agent recruited by the American Embassy's military attaché in Mexico City.[4] Similarly, Abilio de Nequete, a Syrian immigrant, holds the honor of having founded the Brazilian Communist Party in 1922, and being elected its first Secretary-General.[5] The Cuban Communist Party was organized in August of 1925 by Julio Antonio Mella, who before his assassination in downtown Mexico City in 1929 was also known for his torrid, turbulent love affair with one of Latin America's great (for intellectuals) sex symbols—the Italian photographer and socialite Tina Modotti, in whose arms he died.

These exotic origins were not unrelated to the substantive original sin of Communism in Latin America. The foreign nationality of the Communist parties' founding fathers, even in countries with geographically circumscribed (Brazil) or nonexistent (Mexico) immigrant traditions, was a symptom of Marxism's congenitally alien character in Latin America. It was also a reflection of the transplanted nature of the parties themselves: not a home-grown, well-rooted product of local circumstances, but an imported variety. This was neither the first nor the last time that Latin America—mainly through its powerful and ubiquitous intellectual elite—would import ideologies from abroad and graft them on to the local physiology.

Like their counterparts in Europe, many of the initially large, mass-based parties traced their origins back to previously existing Socialist parties. The Uruguayan, Chilean, and Argentine Communist parties clearly fit this category. The first two survived as influential organizations in their countries until the late 1980s, whereas the Argentine party would flounder on the shoals of Perón and military rule. The Chilean Socialist Party suffered from the same trauma its European counterparts experienced, as the process of "Bolshevization" brought an erosion of votes and cadres, together with unconditional subordination to Moscow. Between 1921, the last election in which the old Socialist Party was on the ballot as such, and 1924, the first election in which the Communist Party participated, the organization lost 25 per-

4. "José Allen, the brand-new Secretary General of the Mexican Socialist Party (later to become the Mexican Communist Party) . . . was recruited by the military attaché of the American Embassy, Col. Campbell, to spy on the Mexican war industry. . . . Allen would be forced to rebuild the party, to have something to report on." Paco Ignacio Taibo II, *Bolchevikes: Historia narrativa de los orígenes del comunismo en México (1919–1925)* (Mexico City: Joaquín Mortiz, 1986), p. 45, 76.

5. Ronald H. Chilcote, *The Brazilian Communist Party, Conflict and Integration 1922–1972* (New York: Oxford University Press, 1972), p. 26.

cent of its constituency.[6] Other parties either emerged later or transformed themselves into significant factors several years after their founding. Thus, with the entry of the legendary leader of the Columna Prestes, Luis Carlos Prestes, the Brazilian Communist Party actually surfaced as a significant force on the political scene in the thirties, carrying out a military Mao-like Long March across Brazil in 1925 and the insurrection of 1935. Similarly, the Salvadorean Communist Party moved swiftly into history. Only months after he had formally founded the party, schoolteacher Augusto Farabundo Martí plunged it into a bloodily repressed insurrection in the spring of 1932.[7]

The Communist parties' first phase lasted from the formative years through the Seventh Congress of the Comintern in 1935. This was the meeting that shifted every party's tactics away from the disastrous sectarian "class against class" policy that culminated in the defeat of the German Communist Party and Hitler's victory in 1933. Subsequently, the International crafted the Popular Front policy that gave birth to important, though short-lived successes in France, Spain, and Chile. This tactic called for first "enlarging the alliances of the Communist parties with the working class parties, then with the middle classes, and in the end, even with the anti-fascist fringe of the bourgeoisie."[8] In Latin America the Seventh Congress's radical change in strategy did not have immediate effects. Indeed, the Prestes-led insurrection against the nationalist-populist Vargas government in Brazil rested exactly on a contrary approach.

But shortly thereafter, Communist parties everywhere in Latin America began forging alliances with nationalist, reformist, populist regimes. In Mexico the party supported President Lázaro Cárdenas from 1936 onward, persevering in its policy of "unity at any cost" even

---

6. Durán B., op. cit., pp. 345–346. "The affiliation of the Socialist Workers Party (POS) to the III International and its transformation into the Communist Party in 1922 did not mean an automatic and sudden conversion of founder Luis Emilio Recabarren's socialist convictions to Leninism. . . . But between 1921 and 1927 the Comintern formulated a policy for Latin America . . . and in consequence the region's Communist Parties tried to adjust themselves and follow those recommendations in order to repeat the model of victorious revolutionary parties." Augusto Varas, "Ideal socialista y teoría marxista en Chile: Recabarren y el Comintern," in Varas, op. cit., pp. 45–46.

7. This was an entirely homegrown affair: "The revolt of early 1932 was the first Communist insurrection in the Western hemisphere . . . the Comintern had practically nothing to do with it. As far as is known, it seems to have been a spontaneous initiative of the Salvadorean Communists." Manuel Caballero, *Latin America and the Comintern: 1919–1943* (Cambridge, Eng.: Cambridge University Press, 1986), p. 52.

8. Ibid., p. 110.

when Cárdenas chose a right-of-center successor who forsook his own reformist commitments. In Chile it led the party to endorse the Popular Front in 1938. Although it did not join the government, the party backed the center-left coalition even in the face of strikes and discontent among its own rank and file. In Cuba, this approach induced the party to associate itself with the first Batista regime as early as 1938. Eventually, two Communist cabinet ministers were appointed, including Carlos Rafael Rodríguez, the number-three man in Cuba as late as 1990.

Although this new strategy's formally stated purpose was to create a united front against fascism and imperialism, it was also directly inspired by the coming war in Europe, and then by its outbreak and vicissitudes. Many scholars of this period believe there was more to it than just domestic tactics:

> What was proposed actually in Latin America was a sort of United Front not *against* imperialism, but *including* American imperialism as an ally. . . . It has to be linked perhaps more to the understanding by Stalin of the fact that Franklin Delano Roosevelt was interested in intervening in the coming European war; that he was ready to fight against Germany, well before the outbreak of hostilities.[9]

The Comintern's real policy in Latin America, and the one virtually every member-party would adhere to, even after the International's dissolution in 1943, was one of a National Union against the Axis, not one of a labor-friendly Popular Front against local fascism and the right. The best proof of this lay in the Argentine party's virulently confrontational reaction to the rise of Perón in 1943, first to the Ministry of Labor, then to the presidency. Vittorio Codovilla, an Italian who, after an active role as one of the Comintern's most notorious envoys in Latin America, captained the Argentine party from the early forties, coined the memorable phrase "Nazi-Peronists" and developed a convoluted theory about Peronism's international links:

---

9. Ibid., p. 123. It is perhaps somewhat less certain than Caballero says what exactly Stalin understood. As archives in the former Soviet Union open up and are studied, there may be greater, and more accurate, light cast upon this problem. But there is a basic consensus that the popular-front policy in Latin America was essentially Soviet-inspired and -oriented: "If at the outset (1935–36), the popular front in Latin America had an anti-imperialist program, as the rapprochement between the USA and the USSR against Germany took place, this dimension tended to disappear. In a general fashion, the policy of the Communist Parties toward the United States in the thirties and forties would closely follow the thrust of Soviet foreign policy." Michel Lowy, *Le Marxisme en Amérique Latine*, Anthologie (Paris: François Maspéro, 1980), p. 36.

In order to stop the Nazi-Peronists from receiving too much support, we must present single candidacies (in the coming elections). The word must be: Not a single seat for the Peronists. . . . Only this way can we avoid the entry to parliament of the fascist Trojan horse. Look carefully at Peronism's "anti-imperialist" demagogy. . . . They speak of imperialism in general but they specialize in attacking "Yankee" imperialism. Why? Because the British trusts and monopolies dominate our country and largely support Peronism . . . whereas the democratic sectors of the government of the United States express their rejection of the Nazi-Peronist dictatorship, even through the speeches of some American diplomats.[10]

The Perón regime would survive the party's scathing criticisms and carry out the most important nationalistic and social reforms in that country's history, forever depriving the Communists of a working-class base, just as the National Revolutionary Party, and then the Party of the Mexican Revolution, the ancestors of the PRI, stripped the Mexican Communist Party of any proletarian constituency.

Once the Second World War was in full swing, the true extent and implications of the Comintern's policies in Latin America became more clearly perceptible. The term "Browderism," in honor of Earl Browder, was coined to describe the policies implemented during this period. Browder headed the U.S. Communist Party and moonlighted as the Comintern's delegate charged with supervising the Caribbean and Central American parties. Setting aside all ideological and political obstacles, he advocated as much cooperation with governments in power as possible, on the condition that those governments back the Allies' war effort. Browder later carried his approach even further. He developed a lengthy analysis of the nature of American capitalism, concluding that the very existence of a party in the United States was unnecessary. Although most Communist parties in the region were already toeing the line subsequently attributed to Browder, his name became irremediably entwined with these policies and their consequences. He was ultimately expelled from the party, but not before his influence in Cuba, Mexico, and Venezuela led to the decimation of local organizations.[11]

---

10. Vittorio Codovilla, *Batir el nazi-peronismo para abrir una era de libertad y progreso* (Buenos Aires, 1946), quoted by Lowy, ibid., p. 179.

11. Soviet scholars attribute Browder's positions and the CP USA's adhesion to them to the latter's withdrawal from the Comintern in 1940: "It is worth noting, nonetheless, that the withdrawal of the PC USA from the III International encouraged the opportunist and revisionist tendencies expressed by Earl Browder." It is also worth noting, though, that Browder's influence among the Latin American parties was largely of Soviet mak-

The Second World War period was characterized by years of class collaboration in Latin America. There was an overwhelming dilution of political and ideological differences, as well as the abandonment of any vestige of nationalism that implied criticism of, or antagonism against, the United States. The Chilean party illustrated the mood of the hour in an astonishing document whose interminable title was "Why Collaboration Will Be Possible Among All Progressive Forces of Capitalism in Every Country in Order to Increase Production and Raise the Standard of Living of the Working People":

> After the war and once the independence of every people is assured, instead of an open struggle within every nation for discharging the consequences of the war over a given class or social stratum . . . the reconstruction of economic life will be done upon the basis of collaboration and the common effort of the whole population and with the external aid of the economically stronger nations. In the colonial, semi-colonial and dependent countries—this is the case of Latin American countries—it will be carried out not by policies of increased colonization and dependence, but by policies of collaboration and aid tending to developing the national economy and full national independence.[12]

During this period, Communist parties either changed their names, tried to form more broadly based fronts and national unions, or found remarkably strange bedfellows among the local oligarchies (the Peruvian Communist Party in Manuel Pardo's Frente Democrático and the Liberal Party in Colombia).

By the time the U.S.-Soviet alliance disintegrated in 1947 and the Cold War broke out, almost all of Latin America's Communist parties were seriously weakened, divided, or divorced from their traditional or potential constituencies. In fact, the events surrounding the end of World War II facilitated the efforts of the newly emerged regimes to curtail the open political activities of the Communist Party. In 1947 and '48, the parties of Brazil, Chile, Mexico, and several other countries were declared illegal. Their papers were seized, their cadres thrown in jail, and their followers harassed, repressed, or exiled. During most of the 1950s, the parties reacted to these events with a policy that defended the Soviet Union in the context of the Cold War, and through class antagonism and radical confrontation, all the while maintaining the same theoretical scaffolding erected twenty years be-

---

ing. A. Sobolev et al., Institute of Marxism-Leninism of the Central Committee of the Communist Party of the Soviet Union, "La internacional comunista, Ensayo histórico sucinto," *Editorial Progreso* (Moscow), undated, p. 464.

12. Quoted by Caballero, op. cit., pp. 136–137.

fore. The Communist parties' central, long-term objective remained a national-democratic revolution, agrarian reform, and an alliance with the middle classes and the national bourgeoisie. But now, the principal enemy was once again imperialism, reduced to its barest expression: the government of the United States.

The only opportunity to put this posture into practice was presented to the Guatemalan Workers' Party (PGT) during the 1951–54 tenure of Colonel Jacobo Arbenz. The PGT achieved substantial influence during the Arbenz government, but rarely directed the course of events:

> With Arbenz's backing, the communists gained influence far beyond their numbers. The PGT leaders—Fortuny foremost—were Arbenz's closest advisers and constituted his kitchen cabinet, which discussed all major decisions. This was true of the agrarian reform as well as of the purchase of weapons from Czechoslovakia; when Arbenz decided to resign, on June 26, 1954, he consulted only the PGT.[13]

The personal relationship between its secretary-general, Juan Manuel Fortuny, and Arbenz himself, as well as the hard work and honesty of the Communist cadres in the agrarian reform effort and in Congress, explains why this political clout was disproportionate to their numbers and following. And although the PGT did play a key role in the attempt to purchase arms from Czechoslovakia and distribute them to workers' militias just before the June 1954 CIA-organized coup that deposed Arbenz, it was far from being an incendiary, rabble-rousing, or radicalizing force.[14] Even though the policy failed and the experiment ended in tragedy, other parties throughout the region persevered along the same line as if by sheer inertia.

---

13. Piero Gleijes, *Shattered Hope: The Guatemalan Revolution and the United States. 1944–54* (Princeton, N.J.: Princeton University Press, 1991), p. 182.

14. In the most recent and authoritative book on the Guatemalan Revolution—by Piero Gleijes—Bill Krieg, deputy chief of the American Embassy in Guatemala City between 1951 and 1954, is quoted to the following effect on the PGT: "The revolutionary parties were groups of bums of the first order; lazy, ambitious, they wanted money, were palace hangers-on. Those who could work, had a sense of direction, ideas, knew where they wanted to go, were Fortuny and his PGT friends; these were very honest, very committed. This was the tragedy: the only people who were committed to hard work were those who were, by definition, our worst enemies." Ibid., p. 193. The author argues convincingly that the PGT did play a key role in the entire process, and that Arbenz relied increasingly on it to push forward his program of land reform, introducing an income tax and fostering national independence. But Gleijes also argues that he had no choice but to do so: "Arbenz's party was the PGT. No other partner was possible, for no political party shared Arbenz's commitment to social reform and his willingness to put the interests of the nation before his own." Gleijes, p. 378. But all of this also guaranteed, at the time, the growing hostility of the United States.

The Latin American parties became essentially "tribunal" organizations, devoted to the defense of a domestic or foreign constituency, but no longer willing or able to struggle for power, much less revolution.[15] On the eve of the Cuban revolution, their epitaph could be justly written the way it was summed up years later by three students of the region:

> Working class parties, socialist or communist, had only a limited importance, in Latin America, with the exception of Chile. . . . Introduced late into the family circle, like a poor relative or a distant cousin that never got a word in edgewise, the Latin American communist movement had to espouse all of the twists and turns of the Communist International, but these shifts arose from changes in situations or modifications in the balance of forces in Europe and Asia. Latin America either followed too soon or too late (. . .) and the region's Communist Parties found themselves working against the tide of their own regional history . . . The history of the Latin American sections of the Communist International is the history of a failure. The revolutionary party had ceased to be revolutionary because it had relinquished the idea of world revolution. It had also ceased to be a party, because it had lost the *ressort* of all parties: the will to power.[16]

In the sixties and seventies, the Communist parties were split into those which exercised only a marginal, passive role and those that became active players in the political arena: Brazil in 1961–64, Chile in 1970–73, and, to a lesser degree, Uruguay in 1973–74. In Cuba, the Partido Socialista Popular (PSP, the name of the official Communist party) played a passive role. It eventually overcame its initial, troublesome conflicts with Fidel Castro's MR-26 de Julio, and as the need for accommodation with the Soviet Union grew, Fidel's rapprochement with the PSP became more tangible. But the old Stalinist apparatus never wielded any real power, neither during the prerevolutionary days in the Sierra Maestra nor in the course of the transition from guerrilla wars to the "building of socialism."

As the transition and process of state-building proceeded, however,

---

15. Or in the words of one of their fiercest critics: "The Communist Parties' true vocation . . . was not to promote an assault on power, but rather to resist assaults from power." Régis Debray, "Mémoire Populaire et Lutte Révolutionnaire," *Le Monde Diplomatique*, September 1979, p. 10. The term *parti tribunitien* or *function tribunitienne* was applied to the French Communist Party by several scholars, notably Georges Lavau.

16. The first quote is from Alain Touraine, *La Parole et le Sang* (Paris: Odile Jacob, 1988), p. 66; the second one is from Régis Debray, *La Critique des Armes. I* (Paris: Seuil, 1974), pp. 42–43; the last one is from Caballero, op. cit., pp. 150, 154.

Castro was forced to use PSP cadres as professionals fled the island en masse. And even after the purges of 1962 and 1968, PSP Communists filled positions of responsibility well beyond what their actual participation in the revolution entitled them to. Similarly, the policies Cuba followed domestically, particularly after 1968, came uncannily to resemble what the PSP would have called for if it had survived as a separate entity. But the Cuban Revolution never became the old Communists' revolution. With the exception of Carlos Rafael Rodríguez, who joined Castro in the Sierra Maestra early on, not a single member of the PSP made it into the newly founded Cuban Communist Party's first Politburo in 1965. Time, age, and unending pressure from Washington may have helped Fidel's *barbudos* transform themselves into Stalinist bureaucrats, but this could bring scant comfort at best to old PSP leaders watching from the sidelines.

Similarly, in Nicaragua, the Sandinistas' initial attempt to incorporate the Partido Socialista Nicaragüense into the 1979 government was quickly abandoned. After a brief stint as vice minister of foreign affairs, Alvaro Ramírez, the party's secretary-general, was shipped off to Berlin as ambassador. The Nicaraguan Communists proved ultimately unnecessary: too weak to be useful as cadres or an expedient channel to the Soviets; and too easily replaceable by the Cubans. In Nicaragua, Cubans and former Chilean army officers, economic technicians, and police instructors assumed the function the PSP had filled in Cuba—building a state out of nothing and working matters out with the Soviet Union. The Sandinistas needed the support: they mistrusted and soon lost their own local professionals and white-collar cadres, though for some time they retained a strong middle-class base.

In a sense, the 1979 Revolution came too soon, though had it been forced to wait, it would probably have never arrived at all. The Sandinistas simply did not have enough people to manage the new state—its ministries, Army, police, banks, and nationalized industrial and agricultural firms. They did not bring Cubans and Chileans into the process by choice; they called upon support from outsiders because there was no one else they could rely on. Given their ideological and political baggage, as well as the fear that a large part of the state bureaucracy was colluding with the ousted Somoza regime, they resisted handing over key posts to anyone they did not trust.

If the Communist parties were marginal actors at best where revolution triumphed—Cuba, Nicaragua, and, if only briefly, Grenada—they certainly played an important role where substantive reform was stymied or repressed. This was the case in Brazil (1961–64) and Chile (1970–73).

In Brazil the Communist Party, although not a central actor, contributed greatly to the widespread perception that the 1964 military coup against President João Goulart was carried out with broad, middle-class backing against the threat of chaos and a Communist takeover. This is ironic, considering that over the years, and especially after 1958, the party gradually exchanged its radical tradition of direct action for an espousal of electoral representation. The reason for this evolution went beyond changes in the world and in the international Communist movement. In the words of one scholar:

> From 1958 onward new themes emerged: instead of a critical, explosive and catastrophic situation, the Communists discovered new and broad opportunities for the country's development; instead of cohesive ruling classes insensitive to popular demands, they began to perceive divisions and gaps within the elites—permitting the hypothesis of attracting a ruling sector—the national bourgeoisie. In consequence, resorting to force gave way to electoral struggles, to the appreciation of existing political institutions, to the peaceful road for the transformation of Brazilian society.[17]

In fact, during the early 1960s the party adopted a prudent, perhaps overly cautious, stance in relation to other sectors of the left—particularly the Northeastern Peasant Leagues led by Francisco Julião, Miguel Arraes (the recently elected governor of Pernambuco), and the radical populist movement headed by Leonel Brizola (Goulart's brother-in-law). Various scholars of this period contrast the party's caution[18] with the confrontational stance adopted by Brizola, Arraes, and Julião, but also emphasize the radical postures assumed by the Brazilian student movement and the labor unions where Communist influence was greatest.[19]

---

17. Daniel Aarão Filho, *A Revolucão Faltou ao Encontro: Os Comunistas no Brasil,* (São Paulo: Editora Brasiliense, 1990), p. 23.

18. "The Moscow-line Communist Party (PCB), with its bitter experience of repression under the Estado Novo (1937–45), counseled caution." Thomas Skidmore, *The Politics of Military Rule in Brazil, 1964–85* (New York: Oxford University Press, 1989), p. 14.

19. In contrast to the Brazilian armed left of the 1970s, which never attained a working class base, the Communist Party counted numerous proletarians among its rank and file and mid-level cadres. In the fifties and early sixties, 46.9 percent of the State Committee leaders in the entire country were working class, and in 1961–64, 52 percent of the São Paulo state leaders were "lower class." Chilcote, op. cit., pp. 181, 191.

While no longer holding a monopoly on left-wing politics in Brazil, the party remained powerful at the same time it was becoming increasingly conservative—an ironic situation that has been thus neatly summed up:

> Thus the paradox: at the very moment when politics was seducing the young, the intellectuals and a sector of the working class, the Communists—traditionally the most enthusiastic supporters of the idea of revolution—were moderating their stance, talking about an alliance with the business sector, and the peaceful road for revolution. . . . But despite the growing questioning of its leadership, the Party conserved its hegemony in the unions until the coup.[20]

The Communists were probably not responsible for the 1964 coup, and they certainly exercised no great power in the Goulart regime, yet the coup was—rightly—perceived as a defeat for the left in general and for the party in particular.[21] The setback led to its decimation in union and student ranks and virtual elimination from the Brazilian political scene.

The problem lay in the Communists' inability to influence or unify the left. They were strong enough to serve as a useful scarecrow, uniting the Brazilian right with the middle classes, the business sector, and the American Embassy in a temporarily monolithic front, but too weak to mold the regional, nationalist, and populist left, the grass-roots Catholic movements, student movements, unions, and intellectuals into a coordinated, unified, and effective coalition. The party was too radical and pro-Soviet to avoid frightening large sectors of the Brazilian business community, middle classes, and the United States, but too moderate and prudent to control and orient the radicalized sectors of Brazil's highly polarized political left. It systematically overestimated both its strength within the popular movement and the government's capacity to forestall a military uprising. It counseled moderation in reform and the conservation of existing institutions, but "began to stimulate armed confrontations and land takeovers."[22] Once its moment passed, the party rapidly became marginal, splitting further into armed and reformist factions, pro-Soviet groups and more independent

---

20. Aarão Filho, op. cit., p. 591.
21. Thus Luis Carlos Prestes, its secretary-general, declared only days before the coup that "President João Goulart, through his deeds and words, told the Brazilian people that he assumed the leadership of a democratic process of development in the country. . . . We Communists think that all patriots, at this time, cannot but have a position of firm support for President Goulart." Ibid., p. 198.
22. Ibid., p. 32.

ones. Never again would it be a significant force in Brazilian politics, though the refreshing campaign of its candidate in the 1989 elections, Roberto Freire, would be widely acclaimed, if not voted for.[23]

The Chilean experience in 1970–73 was in many ways quite different. Although the Communist Party of Chile was only one member of a broad multiparty coalition, and it was not the political organization President Salvador Allende formally belonged to, it played a central role in the Popular Unity experiment. As with its Brazilian counterpart, most of the blame for the overwhelming defeat of the left in 1973 was foisted upon it. However, in this case, the responsibility went well beyond perceptions. Because the strongest, most popularly based Communist Party in Latin America did fill a key position in Chile's politics during the Allende presidency, the defeat of the Popular Unity was to a significant extent also the defeat of the Communist Party.

As in Brazil, the Chilean Communist Party exercised a moderating influence. It systematically tried to slow down the process of reform by controlling its impetus and neutralizing, or even eliminating, the more radical elements within the coalition, such as the left wing of Allende's Socialist Party and the Castroist Movimiento de Izquierda Revolucionaria (MIR). The Communists favored fewer nationalizations, resolutely resisted indiscriminate wage hikes and labor actions, and adamantly opposed the proliferation of workers' councils in the factories around Santiago. As early as 1971, and as late as hours before the fatal coup of September 11, 1973, the party sought a deal with the armed forces and with Chile's Christian Democrats.

Its influence within Allende's governing circle grew as its cohesion contrasted increasingly with the constant internecine conflicts that plagued other organizations:

> The defense of the "peaceful road" implied a defense of the popular government and disagreeing with anything that could weaken it or with an alternative form of political power. This meant sticking to the institutional course; in this way, the CP was absolutely faithful to the Popular Unity's program as far as remaining within the bounds of the law was concerned.[24]

Even well after the bloodshed of 1973, the party continued to argue that the origin of the Popular Unity's destruction lay in its radical

---

23. At its 9th Congress in Rio on June 3, 1991, the Brazilian Communist Party decided to abandon Marxism-Leninism other than as a historical reference, and embraced a program that included elections as the only means for achieving power, private property, and the market economy. *La Jornada* (Mexico City), June 4, 1991.

24. Alonso Daire, "La política del Partido Comunista desde la post-guerra a la Unidad Popular," in Augusto Varas, op. cit., p. 223.

nature and in the sectarian policies that impeded any realistic rapprochement with the Chilean armed forces.[25] But equally so, the 1973 coup was the result of the party's inability to impose its moderate approach on the rest of the Chilean left, and to convince the right, the Christian Democrats, and the middle classes that it was truly devoted to these policies and capable of implementing them.

The party understood two things about the Chilean process that remained incomprehensible to many others. The first was that the Allende government had an extraordinary emotional link with a large sector of the Chilean people, and that preserving its very existence was of the utmost importance, beyond what its survival actually implied in terms of specific policies. As late as September 4, 1973, nearly a million people marched in the streets of Santiago in support of Salvador Allende, despite the hardships and tensions the government, barely a week before its downfall, had at least partly contributed to. Their motivation could be largely summarized in one of the slogans painted on the walls of the city: "This government may stink, but it's mine."[26]

The Communists, together with the Radical Party, also grasped the fact that the Popular Unity had lost the middle classes because of the extreme attitudes of the grass-roots movements and the other members of the coalition. Scarcities, inflation, insecurity, and the daily devaluations of the currency had undercut Allende's middle-class support, which had been decisive in his 1970 election and as recently as the March 1973 congressional elections in which the governing alliance obtained 43 percent of the vote, 10 percent more than Allende received three years before. The party was sensitive to the obvious: worker takeovers of economically insignificant plants were alienating the population.[27]

But as many participants and students of the Chilean upheaval

---

25. "The Party criticized the Popular Unity period's policies, maintaining that the sectarian nature of some of the coalition's groups impeded it from giving breathing space to the progressive sectors of the Armed Forces." Tomás Moulián and Isabel Torres D., "¿Continuidad o cambio en la línea política del Partido Comunista de Chile?," in Varas, op. cit., p. 465. The most important document in this regard is CP secretary-general Luis Corvalán's Report to the Plenum of the Central Committee in August 1977. See "El Pleno de agosto de 1977 del Comité Central del Partido Comunista de Chile," Ediciones Colo-Colo, 1978, particularly pp. 11–42.

26. Rodrigo Atria et al., Chile: La memoria prohibida, vol. 1 (Santiago: Pehuén Editores, 1989), p. 22.

27. "At the heart of the struggle between the branches of government lay the lack of definition of the state-owned sector of the economy, that stimulated workers to take over all sorts of plants—at an exorbitant political cost among the middle class that had recently voted for Allende—many of which represented nothing more than problems for a socialized economy." Ibid., p. 37.

concluded later, the very idea of an alliance or understanding between the Christian Democrats, the Socialist Party, and the Communists was well ahead of its time. In what is perhaps the most insightful memoir written by a major player in the drama, Carlos Altamirano, the secretary-general of the Socialist Party, described the Communist dilemma the following way:

> There would never be an agreement between the Christian-Democrats and the Communists. Everything else is secondary, as I often told my Communist companions. Even if at that time the CP appeared to be the chief voice of moderation and realism, the fact was that the Communists were always the main stumbling block. Their presence within the Popular Unity was the main danger, both for important sectors of the country as well as for the government of the United States. The alliance between the Christian Democrats and the Socialists was not a major problem. . . . But with the Communists the problem was not their leadership; the problem was the party, its ideology, and its unconditional alignment with the Soviet Union.[28]

Deep disagreement persists among participants in and scholars of the Chilean experiment as to whether the final, tragic, bloody outcome was unavoidable. Most tend to believe that after the June 29 aborted coup and Allende's ensuing decision to respect the military hierarchy, there was literally no plausible alternative scenario.[29]

On the eve of the coup, Allende had decided to call a plebiscite on the issue of his remaining in office,[30] but it was probably too late. His own party, although not Altamirano, opposed this solution. If he had won, a coup, though more illegitimate than in the absence of a plebiscite, would have become inevitable; if he had lost, Allende had agreed to resign. The criticism most often leveled at the party—i.e., that it never contemplated the military problem of power, and the possibility of building a military component—is valid, but not necessarily relevant. Even if the Communists, along with others, had tried to either split the armed forces or construct their own military machinery, this

---

28. Patricia Politzer, *Altamirano* (Buenos Aires: Ediciones Melquiades, 1989), p. 62.

29. This is the point of view of the radical left, expressed both by Régis Debray in his *Critique des Armes*, and by Allende's nephew and leader of the MIR, Andrés Pascal Allende (interview with the author, Mexico City, June 25, 1991).

30. Altamirano claims this was Allende's decision (see Politzer, op. cit., p. 128); more important, Doña Tencha, the president's widow, has also made this point: "Salvador spoke little. . . . He was worried. Suddenly, he slapped the table and said: 'I have decided. Tomorrow, I will address the nation on radio and television and announce the plebiscite and let the people decide if I should leave, if I should withdraw from office, or if I should continue in power.' " This was September 10, the night before the coup. Atria, op. cit., p. 85.

would have probably only precipitated matters, without altering the final outcome. The Chilean military would have carried out a coup either because they possessed the "legal monopoly on the use of force" or because they were about to lose it.

The Chilean Communist Party's conundrum was not dissimilar to the Brazilian's, and to that of practically every other Communist Party in Latin America. On the one hand, no matter what it did or said, no matter how often or vigorously it stressed its moderation and pragmatism, it could not shake the image of Communist rule as it existed elsewhere. It was a victim of its own reputation and former policies—a credibility gap that made it nearly impossible for it to convince the forces of the center and center-right that it was a moderating force. Right-wing prejudice, nurtured by past Communist conspiracies and antidemocratic behavior in other parts of the world, made it psychologically difficult for the right to trust the party's avowal of conservative and moderate positions. This was, of course, reinforced by constant U.S. reminders of both real and invented Communist mischief and misdeeds across the globe. At the same time, the oldest, best-implanted Communist leaderships could not forsake their proverbial moderation and adopt the approach of the extreme left, given their conviction that the radical groups of this left could never succeed. The Communist parties of Latin America never overcame this contradiction, this powerful paradox that haunted them from their conception to their slow and silent passing toward the end of the 1980s.[31]

By the mid-eighties and the dawning of perestroika, Communist parties worldwide had become largely irrelevant. The reasons for their slow destruction in Latin America were substantially the same as those that brought about the gradual decline of the large, worker-based Marxist organizations in France, Italy, Spain, Greece, and Portugal. Social Democrats in office took their causes and constituencies away from them, as France's François Mitterrand had predicted all along. And changes in the industrialized nations' economic and social configura-

---

31. In Altamirano's words, again: "In my judgment, the central problem resided in the Communist Party's playing a key role in the government of another Latin American government besides Cuba. This was not a Chilean problem, but a global one. On the one hand, the United States did not tolerate another Cuba in Latin America, and on the other, the international communist movement had no democratic credibility. No matter how correct, sensible and realistic its stances, nobody believed them. They were even accused—derogatorily—of being reformists, but that would not give them democratic credentials. Whose fault was this? That of the anti-communists, who created a distorted and diabolical image of the Communists, as well as of the Communists themselves, who wherever they had been in power had established undemocratic regimes." Ibid., p. 65.

tion whittled away their traditional constituency—the old, heavy-industry, urban working class.

As the nineties began, they ceased to represent a significant force anywhere in Latin America, the exceptions being El Salvador and Uruguay.[32] Paradoxically, their greatest legacy to the left could well be their reformism and civility. In contrast with the Communists' internal behavior and their ideological roots, they had become, with time, electoralist, "establishment" institutions.[33] If the left in Latin America has a democratic ancestry today, it lies above all in the Communist parties' penchant for elections, nonviolence, and alliances: the right strategy, perhaps, though quite likely for the wrong reasons.

A long and troubled history had come to an end. The pain and sadness felt by those who had devoted their lives to the cause—often heroically—was real, but so was their defeat and failure.[34] In the words of Brazil's eighty-five-year-old Oscar Niemeyer, the continent's most renowned architect, the legendary builder of Brasilia, and one of the hemisphere's most talented and honest Communists:

> Today they want to change everything in the party. There are people who devoted everything, who gave an entire lifetime for their ideas, who sacrificed everything, who do not know how to do anything else, and now they tell them they were wrong from the very beginning. *Isto e una merda.*[35]

Until the Cuban Revolution, Communist parties had shared the Latin American left's political stage with another broad political cur-

---

32. Surprisingly, though, the Chilean Communist Party fared far better than expected in the June 1992 municipal elections, obtaining nearly 7 percent of the vote, though of a different texture than before: the urban, under- and unemployed poor.

33. In August 1991, Volodia Teitelboim, president of the Chilean Communist Party, announced that his organization had decided to abandon the reference to Marxism-Leninism in its statutes. *La Jornada* (Mexico City), August 6, 1991.

34. Jorge Amado, the great Brazilian novelist and one of the most long-lasting Communist intellectuals in Latin America and the world, put it more lyrically: "Fragments of what were the dream and the struggle, the hope and the certainty of millions of human beings are sold off around the world piece by piece by American salesmen to collectors of heirlooms, along with the fragments of the Berlin Wall. I know of men and women, magnificent people, who suddenly find themselves unprotected, empty, submerged by doubts, lonely, lost, and crazed. What inspired them and led them through life, the ideals of justice and beauty for which they fought, for which they suffered persecution and violence, exile, jail and torture, and for which so many others were murdered, turned into smoke, into nothing, into something worthless, into a lie and an illusion, a miserable and ignominious trick." Jorge Amado, "Sólo el futuro es nuestro," *La Jornada Semanal* (Mexico City), December 29, 1991.

35. Oscar Niemeyer, interview with the author, Rio de Janeiro, August 21, 1990.

rent that today partially retains its importance. The national-popular sectors that embody this movement trace their origins back to Latin America's so-called "populist" tradition that surfaced in the 1930s. Perón in Argentina, Cárdenas in Mexico, Vargas in Brazil, Jose María Velasco Ibarra in Ecuador, Haya de la Torre's APRA in Peru, and, up to a point, Victor Paz Estenssoro's Movimiento Nacional Revolucionario in Bolivia often continue to be central historical reference points for many contemporary political movements. These movements' original leaders, together with the historical periods of collective consciousness and popular enfranchisement, are symbols of an era and a certain idea of modernity in Latin America: the inclusion of the excluded.

The term "populism," while part of a long academic tradition in the region that applied to a period and a type of regime, has recently been attached to governments in Latin America that followed certain specific, superficially similar economic policies, regardless of the radically different historical, political and ideological contexts in which those policies were implemented.[36] The World Bank speaks of three "populist experiments in Latin America: Allende in Chile (1971–73), Perón in Argentina (1946–49), and Alán García in Peru (1985–88),"[37] thus lumping together examples that from other perspectives, notwithstanding their common macroeconomic traits, differed markedly.[38] The discussion is in the last analysis a political one: the adversaries of redistributive policies today in Latin America tend to emphasize the "economic" definition of "populism," and then associate widely varying attempts at social reform into a single paradigm. The more historical or social approach stresses the political facets of populism, focusing

36. Thus some economists, for example, define "populism" as "redistribution (or distribution) not disciplined by a budget constraint." John Willamson, ed., *Latin American Adjustment: How Much Has Happened* (Washington, D.C.: Institute of International Economics, 1990), p. 355.

37. According to the Bank, "Populist policies have emphasized growth and short-run distributional goals, brushing aside the risks of inflation and excessive deficits and ignoring external constraints and the responses of firms and households to their aggressive anti-market policies." The World Bank, *World Development Report, 1991* (New York: Oxford University Press, 1991), p. 133.

38. Suffice it to say that Perón, who remained president of Argentina until 1955, never had a socialist goal, which for Allende was central, and for García was as anathema as for Perón, even though his party was a member of the Socialist International. García got into trouble above all because of his unilateral curtailment of debt service, Allende partly because of an external constraint of a political nature—American hostility—and very rapidly both became exceedingly unpopular outside their core constituencies. Perón remained immensely popular among his followers and beyond, well after the 1955 coup that overthrew him and until his death in 1974, a year after he was reelected president by more than 60 percent of the vote.

on the contrasting historical or social contexts in which apparently similar economic policies are pursued.[39]

The sense of inclusion, of bringing millions of the disenfranchised and marginalized masses inside the political system—or simply into the city—explains one of the more striking characteristics of the national-populist sector of the left: its extraordinary staying power as a major force in each country's politics, despite the passage of time and the tremendous changes most Latin American societies have undergone in the interim. The change populism wrought is often best conveyed by literary narrative, as in the following description of the advent of Perón:

> A few days later, Jorge Luis Borges would have had to accept what he never did: the obvious. Peronism entered the city of Buenos Aires on the tops of the streetcars, in trucks, by foot and even on horseback, with drums and Argentine flags waving, later to be soiled and trampled on. The city was invaded by a mob that, manipulated or not by the Army, stimulated and aroused by Evita with the tacit complicity of the police, nonetheless existed, was there, loud and ragged, crying for its leader, in jail close by. These were people who had never breached the limits, people who, in doing so, had torn down a barrier. They occupied the center, the adjoining avenues, the Plaza de Mayo, and set themselves down there. They were the "small dark heads," people who should not appear, who should not exist in Argentina, but who did. They were dirty, brutal, irreverent, presented as cruel, exasperated animals. Argentina's new face, the real one, was reflected in Borges' mirror.[40]

Thirty years later, another novelist, Tomás Eloy Martínez, would describe how anywhere between 2 and 4 million Argentines—from a tenth

---

39. Thus one group claims that "For us 'economic populism' is an approach to economics that emphasizes growth and income redistribution and deemphasizes the risks of inflation and deficit finance, external constraints, and the reaction of economic agents to aggressive non-market policies. . . . A central thesis we advance is that the macroeconomics of various experiences is very much the same, even if the politics differed greatly." Rudiger Dornbusch and Sebastian Edwards, "The Macroeconomics of Populism" in Rudiger Dornbusch and Sebastian Edwards, eds., *The Macroeconomics of Populism in Latin America*, National Bureau of Economic Research project report (University of Chicago Press, 1991), p. 9. The response of the other viewpoint is categorical: "Latin American populism cannot be explained as an irrational set of self-destructive economic measures to redistribute income through deficit spending. Behind these policies is a political logic that propels the emergence and recurrence of populist programs despite the cautionary advice of orthodox economists." Paul W. Drake, comment in ibid., p. 35.

40. Estela Canto, *Borges a contraluz* (Buenos Aires: Espasa Calpe, 1989), pp. 179–180. Canto was the Argentine writer's fiancée from 1945 to 1952, and writes of him with corresponding affection and sensitivity.

to a fifth of the country's entire population—gathered on the grass around Eseiza Airport in 1973 to welcome their leader back from exile.[41]

Political longevity is a central feature of populism. Juan Perón's first appearance on the Argentine political scene took place in 1943; his second election to the presidency occurred in 1973, and as late as 1989, Carlos Saúl Menem was elected president on an ostensibly Peronist platform. Similarly, Haya de la Torre founded the Peruvian APRA in Mexico City in 1924; and in 1985 Alan García was elected to the presidency of that nation as the APRA candidate. Jose María Velasco Ibarra formed his first government in Ecuador in 1933; he was overthrown for the last time by a military coup in 1972. Getulio Vargas reached power through a coup d'état in 1930, was elected president in 1951, and committed suicide in 1954. His grand-niece Yvette Vargas disputed the legal right to use the name of his party in 1979 and won, conserving her great-uncle's letterhead more than half a century after he first assumed power.

In virtually all of the populist precedents, the other main category of society brought into the political process and governance were the intellectuals. Their role in the left reaches way beyond populism, of course, as we shall see in Chapter 6. For now it is enough to emphasize how under populism "The direct appeal to the people eliminates forms of political representation common to the West. And since the people do not organize themselves spontaneously, a key role is given to the intellectuals. . . ."[42] They participated in the process, conceptualized it, and tended to glorify it as time wore on and memories became thin. The perception many Latin American nations have of their recent past has been largely shaped by this confluence of working class, collective nostalgia, and intellectual reconstruction of events and people by participants wistfully regretting a time they helped create.

The era of populism and its dramatis personae awaken enduring nostalgic sentiments because of the basic tenets of the policies that emerged from the twin stimuli of Depression years and the Second World War: a redistribution of income through the incorporation of the popular masses—above all, the urban working classes—into the political system, a central role for the state in economic and social policy, and a constant invocation of the nation and its sovereignty in discourse.[43]

---

41. Tomás Eloy Martínez, *La Novela de Perón* (Buenos Aires: Legasa Literaria, 1985), the concluding pages.

42. Touraine, op. cit., p. 166.

43. "In this project, the State is the key institution, more than the president or the party when there is one. Popular nationalism is the common ideology to all of these different experiences." Alain Rouquié, *Amérique Latine. Introduction à l'Extrême-Occident* (Paris: Seuil, 1987), p. 292.

Despite an ever-present authoritarian streak, together with a constant tendency to conciliate with its adversaries and never carry reforms beyond a certain limit, the national-populist tendency undoubtedly belongs on the left of the political spectrum.[44] Although on occasion it tips over to the right (the case of Perón in his second regime and the problem of the threshold mentioned in Chapter 1), it can be included in the left because of the ideologies it evokes, the real changes it introduced when it was in power, and the stances it adopted when it was forced back into the opposition. The national-populist current reflects the unfulfilled Latin American dream of a painless modernity:

> Populism has always been the great Latin American temptation, representing a desire for change within continuity, without the violent rupture that both socialist and capitalist processes of industrialization experienced.[45]

The change was usually narrow in scope, and frequently reversed once the initial, heroic period came to a close in each country. But the legacy has outlived reality. It is this legacy that forms a part of the left, regardless of the exact nature of its authors.

In nearly every national-populist movement, urban labor movements were incorporated into politics and the state itself through corporatist union structures and labor legislation.[46] This meant union-

---

44. There is an abundance of literature on populism in Latin America. The following are among the most frequently quoted: Torcuato di Tella, *Populism and Reform in Latin America*, in Claudio Veliz, *Obstacles to Change in Latin America* (New York: Oxford University Press, 1965); Ghita Ionescu and Ernest Gellner, *Populism: Its Meaning and National Characteristics* (London: Weidenfeld and Nicolson, 1969); Francisco Weffort, *O Populismo na política brasileira* (Rio de Janeiro: Paz e Terra, 1978); Octavio Ianni, *La formación del estado populista en America Latina* (Mexico City: Ediciones Era, 1975); Paul Drake, *Socialism and Populism in Chile* (1978).

45. Touraine, op. cit., p. 12.

46. As with so many other terms in the literature on Latin America, "incorporation" means different things to different people. A recent, almost immediately classical work on the period in question and on "incorporation" defines it more specifically than it is used here. Here the term is used almost synonymously with inclusion or integration, in regard to the working class, the lower middle class, and other poorer sectors of society, and in relation to the economic, social, and political aspects of the process. Ruth and David Collier insist on the specific "incorporation" of the labor movement: "In the course of capitalist modernization, two broad new sectors produced by modernization, the working class and the middle sectors, began to be integrated into the polity. . . ." The authors then define labor incorporation as follows: "The period of initial incorporation of the labor movement is defined as the first sustained and at least partially successful attempt by the state to legitimate and shape an institutionalized labor movement. During this period, the state played an innovative role in constructing new institutions of state-labor and capital-labor relations." Ruth Berins Collier and David Collier, *Shaping the Political Arena* (Princeton, N.J.: Princeton University Press, 1991), pp. 7, 161.

izing workers, giving them the right to strike (even if this right was then curtailed or eliminated), enacting labor legislation, and establishing some form of welfare state. This period also signified a greater role for the state in economic and in social policy, taking over national resources and founding the large, state-owned monopolies that still characterize many Latin economies.

Finally, the populist epoch was a golden age of national self-assertion. It was a time when Latin American countries stood up to the rest of the world, gained attention and respect, and defended their pride, dignity, and many of their true interests. Often the issue of sovereignty accompanied acts of nationalization and the development of state-owned monopolies, as in Brazil in the early fifties with Vargas's creation of Petrobras, in Argentina through Perón's nationalization of the railways in 1949, and, above all, with Cárdenas's expropriation of Mexico's foreign-owned oil companies in 1938. In countries where the national consciousness and identity was newly formed or rekindled, recovering national wealth or patrimony from foreign control touched a deep chord in an otherwise apathetic, apolitical, and excluded population. Half a century later, Mexicans still recall how hundreds of thousands of their forefathers marched to the National Palace following the March 18 nationalization, contributing what they could to help "el Tata" compensate the oil companies. We shall note in Chapter 9 that the recapturing of a lost or confiscated national pride and identity was paramount in this populist process and explains a great part of the persistent longing for a return to those times.

There is wide debate among scholars of these trends regarding the aptness of including specific periods, parties, or policies in the overall category of the national-populist movement. There are also disagreements about the term's applicability to an historical period, state policy, government, party, or movement. Some populist parties or figures are included that, until very recently, had never governed, such as the Peruvian APRA and perhaps Gaitán in Colombia; certain regimes never transformed their policies into lasting political organizations. A few national-popular specimens derive directly from a revolution or limited reformist period: Cárdenas from the Mexican Revolution, the Bolivian MNR from the 1951 revolution, Velasco Alvarado and the Peruvian military from 1968 through 1975, and perhaps even the interval beginning with Omar Torrijos' accession to power in Panama in 1969 and concluding with his death in 1981. In certain cases, the same leader or party put in practice widely diverging policies at distinct stages in his or its long residence

in power: Perón in 1946–52 and then during his tragicomic return to power in 1973, the initial and later Velasco Ibarra regimes in
Ecuador, and the various reincarnations of Paz Estenssoro in Bolivia,
from 1951 to 1990. Similarly, the term "populism" can be applied to
a very brief period that was the culmination of a process which began
earlier and also left a singular sequel, even if the latter is not usually
labeled populist. This is the case of the Venezuelan Trienio, as the
period between 1945 and 1948 became known.[47]

There are, lastly, regional populisms. Possibly the best example is
Miguel Arraes, the quasi-mythical governor of the state of Pernambuco
in the Brazilian Northeast, who has been intimately involved with the
politics and power of his impoverished region for more than thirty
years. A French writer and companion-in-exile of Arraes who accompanied him on his return to Pernambuco in 1979, fifteen years after his
overthrow by the military, captured the reasons for the devotion he
commanded among the destitute inhabitants of his homeland:

> More than any other, one measure was engraved in the memories of the
> rural population: the 300% increase in the sugar-cane workers' wages.
> In a few days, the shelves of every store in Recife, the state's capital,
> were stripped of their products: shoes, radios, chairs, beds, clothing,
> meat. There was literally a rush by the agricultural laborers on goods
> heretofore inaccessible to them. This incredible and temporary opu-
> lence of the poorest is still described today as a sort of miracle.[48]

Until the Cuban Revolution, the relationship between the populist
movements and the Communist parties was the dominant issue in the
ranks of the Latin American left. In a realm of paradoxes, it was not
surprising that the populist current spent considerable time and energy
distancing itself from the Communists, while the latter tried everything to ingratiate themselves with the populists. Although a motive

---

47. "With the tremendous popular support that had been assiduously mobilized
during [a] decade, Acción Democrática joined a conspiracy by military officers. The coup
brought AD to power and ushered in a three-year period, known as the Trienio, characterized by party incorporation and radical populism. . . . The AD program was one of
modernization based on the opportunity to sow the seeds of petroleum. . . . The new
government adopted an oil policy in which the government would share the profits of
the oil industry . . . to pursue a broadly based pattern of economic development that
would diversify the economy . . . promote and stimulate agriculture and industry . . . and
state investment in infrastructure, power and steel. . . . This modernization policy also
meant a commitment to measures that would promote social welfare, particularly in
areas of health and education." Collier and Collier, op. cit., pp. 255–256.

48. Robert Linhart, *Le Sucre et la Faim: Enquête dans les Régions Sucrières du
Nord-Est Brésilien* (Paris: Editions de Minuit, 1980), p. 7.

for this relationship could be found in the Cold War mentality of many postwar regimes in Latin America, the principal explanation rests elsewhere. The reason why each party acted toward the other in exactly the opposite fashion lies in the basic features which characterized populism in the past, and which continue to define it today as an important, though fading, influence within the Latin American left.

The reforms actually put into practice by the national-popular regimes, while often pathbreaking and indisputably significant, were always restricted in scope. These were not revolutionary regimes willing to mobilize or be mobilized by mass popular movements. They were all, to one extent or another, governments that simply implemented innovative policies of social and economic change, from establishing the minimum wage to enacting labor legislation and expropriating foreign companies. Even the most revolutionary of them all—the Cárdenas episode in Mexico—went only so far in carrying out its reformist promises, and indeed, it was this moderation which insured that instead of continuing, the reformist process came to an end.

The fear inspired in Army officials by the undisciplined, often unmanageable introduction of millions of their poor countrymen into political life was decisive in fixing the boundaries on the breadth of reform. The links between the leaders and sitting elites were equally important: these were unquestionably not déclassé traitors who wanted a revolution. Whatever their original motives and actual social backgrounds, the leaders of the populist movements were ultimately enlightened representatives of an emerging class which sought to preserve its standing, but understood that, in order to do so, things had to change, sometimes radically. By the same token, the nature of Latin American societies a half century ago—still essentially rural, illiterate, poor, unorganized, devoid of many of the institutions of statehood—guaranteed that spontaneous mobilization from below, while spectacular on occasions, would rarely be able to force reform on recalcitrant regimes. The compromise between limited political will to impose reform from above, and limited capacity to fight for reform from below, was Latin American populism.

These limitations, in turn, imposed further constraints as equally enduring features of this typically hemispheric political fancy. The incorporation process was as restricted as the reforms it rested on. Only those who truly benefited from the latter could be brought into the political, institutional process. And only those who were incorporated could exert pressure to obtain the reforms they demanded. Above all, the entire integrating process was mostly applicable only to the urban, large-industry, more-or-less organized or organizable working class: stevedores and resource-industry laborers, transport and utility workers, and agricultural processing employees, from sugar mills to meat-packing plants. In some countries, such as Argentina and Uruguay, these sectors could represent a significant share of a small population. In other nations or regions, such as Chile, Rio and São Paulo in Brazil, they were not insignificant. But because these were essentially pre-industrial, still rural nations, by and large, throughout Latin America the vast majority of the population remained outside the incorporation process: the rural peasantry and the urban unemployed or informally underemployed poor were mostly, though not entirely, passed over. Many were indeed brought in; but a great many more were left out. Those instances of populist upheaval where land reform actually took place—as in Mexico and Bolivia—came to be known as revolutions or their equivalent. And it was large-scale land reform that made one of Latin America's most interesting reformist episodes—the Peruvian regime of the late sixties and early seventies led by General Juan Velasco Alvarado—exceptional. So much so that it does not fit any of the categories used here: too much grass-roots mobilization to be considered populist; too radical and confrontational with the United States to be labeled merely reformist; too moderate to dovetail with the Marxist-Leninist-Castroist creed.[49]

The narrow nature of the reforms and the socially enfranchised masses themselves inevitably leads to a further paradoxical characteristic: the oscillating but always underlying authoritarian nature of populist regimes. Their unwillingness to pursue reforms beyond a certain point, and the ensuing, circumscribed reach of the incorporation process, meant that those remaining outside politics could not be allowed to pressure peacefully to get in. There was always an ideological element to this: Perón's corporatist or Mussolinist penchant; the revolutionary tradition in Mexico together with the absence of any democratic history; the military mores in Brazil. If the purpose of the exercise is to conserve power, limits cannot be imposed on reforms and integration without establishing similar bounds on enfranchisement and democratic processes. The shifting emphasis the populists' present-day heirs or followers place on social justice and defense of the

---

49. In the Colliers' taxonomy, only Mexico and Venezuela are mentioned as peasantry-incorporating cases: "In Mexico and Venezuela . . . both the working class and the peasantry were mobilized electorally and organized into functional associations. . . . The inclusion of the peasantry . . . made the politics of incorporation appear like a more radical challenge, since . . . it necessitated a call for land reform . . . and seemed to constitute a more thorough-going attack on private property and capitalist (and precapitalist) relations of production." Collier and Collier, op. cit., p. 196.

nation, on democracy and human rights, reflects the founders' ambivalent stance. Perón reached power at the Ministry of Labor through a military coup, and was subsequently elected president; Vargas gained office through a military coup; Cárdenas won a sham election in 1934. Yet free elections returned the first two to power (Vargas in 1951 and Perón in 1973) after they had lost it through coups or palace revolts. Conversely, while Cárdenas shares the blame for one of the most blatant exercises in the long, sad history of Mexican voting fraud in 1940, he later became a symbol of the country's hope for electoral democracy and civil liberties.

All of which ushers in a final feature of the populist usage—one that only surfaced when the national-popular regimes began to lose power and spend more time in the opposition than in office. After the heady days of the thirties, forties, and early fifties (depending on the country), the populist movements were evicted from the central stage of most Latin American governance. Sometimes they were ousted through military coups executed by armies no longer acquiescing to the general disorder the populist regimes tended to generate in their later stages. On other occasions their policies were progressively abandoned by successors who broke softly with the "founding fathers." In the worst of cases they ended in tragedy, as with Getulio Vargas's suicide in 1954, when no other option seemed viable. Most of the old populist movements either faded away or mutated into political parties competing for power through different means. Others would hibernate, lying dormant in the collective psyche of millions whose memories they filled just enough to avoid being forgotten, yet not sufficiently to be fought for.

But to function as plausible opposition parties or movements, the populists had to comply with two requirements: they had to be more "popular" than their successors in power, and than they themselves had been during their tenure in office. Consequently, where only limited reforms had been implemented when the opportunity existed, now deeper and more radical reforms were called for. Where the populists failed to incorporate the masses whose demands they couldn't or wouldn't satisfy, they now aroused and agitated those same masses to, they hoped, their own benefit. And where they had never allowed—or at least rarely encouraged—democratic procedures for transferring power, they now became fervent advocates of free elections. They realized that the only way back to power was through the ballot box, and most importantly, that they held a singular advantage over anybody else in that peculiar sphere of competition: the memories they evoked, and their "touch" with the people.

Two other factors accentuated this relative radicalization. With time many of the policies that the populists had originally set in motion, and that seemed initially extreme or exceptional, entered the Latin American mainstream. The limited welfare state, a large state-owned sector of the economy, a certain degree of economic nationalism, labor legislation, and corporatist control, all became fixtures of societies. They were maintained even by regimes that acceded to power against the populists, or that appeared to break with them. In order to differentiate themselves from these new rulers, the national-popular current had to call for more populism, extended to more people.

The second factor was the Cuban Revolution and the shift to the left that it wrought in the continent's political constellation during the early years of the Castro experience. This also forced the national-popular current—in Brazil, Argentina, later in Peru, and even in Uruguay—to adopt more radical stances and to position itself further towards the extreme of the political spectrum. The conjunction of having to fight for a democratization of political competition to return to power and of the Cuban Revolution's pushing it to the left, set the stage for what would later become the populist current's final destiny: its gradual, sometimes traumatic, and frequently unconsummated transformation into an often radical Latin American social-democracy.

The proclamation of the end of populism in Latin America, as the economic and social policies of the last half century are forsaken for radical free-market policies, may appear accurate, to the extent that the current of thought and aspiration which brought populist programs to life has disappeared.[50] The parties, figures, and movements identified with it today either are discredited or no longer seek or accept the label. But if the national-popular current is as deeply rooted in the hemisphere's history and traditions as nearly all its students have concluded, then it may well be resurrected; either as a Luddite-like revolt

---

50. In an article entitled "The End of Populisms in Latin America," Alain Touraine formulated the region's options in the following way: "There are three ways out. The first is the most visible today: priority to outward-looking development and a growing duality that will not become dangerous because of the very effects of the social crisis, particularly the urban crisis, that greatly weakens the capability of collective action of the dominated sector. The second is that the new economic policies generate strong popular resistance and thus fail, leading to chaos. . . . Finally, the third option is based on the creation of left-of-center political alliances that combine export-led growth with improvements in services—education, housing, health—for the majority of the population. Many speak of social-democracy, but the litmus-test of a policy of this sort is the reduction in social inequalities through a tax policy that is diametrically opposed to the one presently being applied." Alain Touraine, "El fin de los populismos en Latinoamérica," *El País*, August 6, 1989, Madrid.

rooted in the despair of the dispossessed or as a mass-based Latin American social democracy that will finally combine traditional economic and national demands with the region's new democratic clamor. Efforts to achieve such a combination have heretofore fared poorly south of the Rio Grande, and present global conditions do not seem favorable to its prospects. Either way, a chapter in Latin American politics has come to a long-awaited conclusion.

3

The Cuban Crucible

■

In the Museum of the Ministry of the Interior in Havana, together with memorabilia glorifying Cuban intelligence and counterintelligence exploits, there is a letter in a glass case dated July 1960, addressed to "El jefe del G-2," or head of intelligence and security, identifying him as Manuel Piñeiro. From the very beginning of the Cuban Revolution, this man played a key role in building what became one of the most successful security agencies ever constructed. Over thirty years and despite innumerable attempts by Cuban exile groups, the Central Intelligence Agency, and disenchanted domestic opponents, not a single member of the Cuban leadership lost his life.[1] Piñeiro, as deputy minister of the interior from 1961 to 1974, helped put together an apparatus that infiltrated the opposition groups in Miami and penetrated the CIA itself. It achieved a degree of control over Cuban society that allowed the regime to maintain itself in power through the 1990s and under extraordinarily adverse conditions. This was done without resort to indiscriminate, bloody repression, but instead by the application of selective and mostly bloodless, though nonetheless brutal, security

---

1. Evaluating U.S. intelligence failures at the time of the Bay of Pigs and thereafter, the chairman of President Kennedy's Foreign Intelligence Advisory Board, Clark Clifford, offered the following comment: "We sent teams at one time after another into Cuba to try to get information. They were all 'rolled up,' is the expression, and never heard from again." Quoted in Morris H. Morley, *Imperial State: The United States and Revolution and Cuba, 1952–1986* (Cambridge, England: Cambridge University Press, 1987), pp. 147–148.

measures. Soviet involvement in this area was kept to a minimum.[2]

One of Fidel Castro's contemporaries, Piñeiro attended college at Columbia University in the United States, where he was sent to study business by his father, the Bacardi rum representative in the province of Matanzas. In New York, Piñeiro met and married his first wife, Lorna Burdsall, an American ballet dancer. He joined the revolution in 1958; rumor has it he began his revolutionary career by placing a bomb in the National Hotel in Havana. He then fled to Fidel Castro's refuge in the Sierra Maestra, where he was commissioned to work on intelligence matters, and soon dispatched to join Fidel's brother Raúl. Piñeiro began building the Cuban intelligence and security apparatus before the Revolution had even triumphed.

After the insurgents' victory on January 1, 1959, Piñeiro immediately began working in the G-2 security organization. When the traditional U.S.-armed-forces-style structure of the Cuban government was replaced by a Soviet configuration, Piñeiro set up shop there. By 1962 he was in charge of the Dirección General de Inteligencia (DGI) in the Ministry of the Interior, having relinquished part of his control over counterintelligence activities.[3] In exchange he obtained command over Liberación, a department in the Ministry responsible for "promoting the Latin American revolutionary movement." He would wear these twin hats—intelligence and hemispheric revolution—for more than a decade. His success in the first task brought him growing support in the second, which became the chief focus of his attention.

This was the period when Piñeiro acquired a reputation as a repressive hard-liner and one, moreover, with expensive tastes and an extravagant life-style. Many have blamed him for the harsh crackdown on the MR–26 de Julio organization, and for conspiring with Raúl Castro to prod Fidel toward a more leftward, pro-Soviet stance and

2. "At least as late as the 1968 crisis, the Interior Ministry was also a source of Cuban independence from the Soviets. Ministry staff undertook the surveillance of Soviet personnel in Cuba. . . . At the peak of that crisis, the chief of the ministry's Soviet advisers sought the arrest of Deputy Interior Minister Manuel Piñeiro. . . ." Jorge Domínguez, *To Make a World Safe for Revolution: Cuba's Foreign Policy* (Cambridge, Mass.: Harvard University Press, 1989), pp. 271–272.

3. Almost by definition, information concerning this period and the details regarding the construction of the Cuban security apparatus are sketchy. One of the reasons is the Cubans' obsession with secrecy and "compartmentalization": "The history of revolutionary Security is a secret history. The CIA would like to know how the Department of State Security [G-2] was built and what its present organization is. . . . Today the Cuban people can count on two silent armies to detect and destroy enemy intelligence: Military Counter-Intelligence and the Department of State Security. This, and only this, is what the Central Intelligence Agency can know, and knows already." Norberto Fuentes, *Nos impusieron la violencia* (Havana: Editorial Letras Cubanas, 1986), pp. 100–101.

toward a break with the moderate sectors of the revolutionary alliance and with the United States. Piñeiro probably was more to the left than others, and possibly more pro-Soviet, though this is uncertain. Cuban dissidents such as Carlos Franquí have stressed these views of him, as well as Piñeiro's apparent life-style:

> I walked past the . . . residence of Commander Manuel Piñeyro [sic], the famous and dangerous Red Beard: the deputy chief of Security and the man responsible for the Latin American revolution. Armed escorts were everywhere. This was one of those enormous residences that rich Cubans liked so much: gardens, many acres of land. A farm in the city. Piñeiro kept there, for all to see, his own farm: pigs, chickens, bananas, ducks. A little of everything, all cared for by military personnel. Army jeeps went in and out loaded with food. There was a sense of power, of arrogance, of indifference.[4]

However true this may have been in the initial years of the Revolution, it wasn't the case later on. In late 1987, Piñeiro's home was not located on the Quinta Avenida, nor did it house chickens, pigs, or any other animals. If anything, it was a plain and modest dwelling, similar to that of any mid-level Cuban professional. Piñeiro received his visitors there in shorts, while his daughter roamed through the living room and his wife wandered around with groceries. Piñeiro thus helped confirm the impression conveyed by many other high-ranking officials of the regime, i.e., that the corruption and grand life-styles which characterized the powerful in other Communist regimes were not the rule in Cuba.[5]

Whatever else he may be, Piñeiro (or Barbaroja—"Redbeard"—as he came to be known) is an extraordinarily charming man. Gabriel García Márquez has described his sense of humor as the best he had ever encountered. He is a marvelous yarn-teller, particularly about the old days in the Sierra. His stories resemble the Colombian Nobel Prize winner's tales of the absurd and incredible occurring in everyday life. With the years, his famous—and for some, dreaded—red beard has became salt-and-pepper, and his now-portly appearance belies the slender, purportedly womanizing Piñeiro of thirty years ago—perhaps because of the habits he picked up during the early years when he would meet at ungodly hours with Latin American revolutionaries at the

---

4. Carlos Franquí, *Retrato de familia con Fidel* (Barcelona: Editorial Seix Barral, 1981), p. 478.

5. Brazilian leader Lula put it this way: "I have been to Commander Piñeiro's house; it is a poorer home than mine. My house is larger than Piñeiro's." Interview with the author, Mexico City, June 6, 1991.

"Casas de protocolo" in the Laguito district of Havana, or in their suites in the better hotels of the capital, eating everything room service could deliver at a pace that hardly suggested an extravagant life-style.

Piñeiro has charmed countless interlocutors over the years: Mexican foreign ministers and young Chilean women; French intellectuals and gifted novelists from the Southern Cone. He has learned a great deal from his endless discussions: his survival in Cuba, and his presumed enlightened role in the twilight of the Revolution and his own career, are one possible consequence of this exposure. Reports and anecdotes of Piñeiro's cruelty and cynicism are common; they are balanced by far fewer, but equally reputable, accounts of his ability to listen, his intelligence, and his sense of loyalty to his men and his friends. His subordinates replicated most of Piñeiro's vices and virtues. Over the years his friends, as well as myriad Latin American revolutionaries, came to appreciate Piñeiro's—and his subordinates'—personal solidarity and kindness, whatever ferocity he displayed in regard to his enemies.

Piñeiro's *muchachos* were a faithful reflection of the strength and weakness of the Cuban "International." They knew the countries they "worked" on generally well, and were especially good listeners and open-minded with regard to the political situation in those countries. They also tended to be more independent-minded and liberal with respect to domestic Cuban issues than other members of the *nomenklatura*. But only up to a point: once the leadership had made a decision, or, in the jargon, once *la linea* (literally, "the line," but more accurately, the "politically correct" stance) was handed down, their sensitivity and broad-mindedness evaporated. Then they listened to no one, brooked no dissent, and rejected any alternate analysis or policy. They would stop at nothing to pursue their policies—scheming, manipulating, threatening, and going to any extreme to implement their boss's instructions.

Piñeiro's revolutionary recruits originated in the guerrilla movement and the urban front. They had belonged either to the 26 de Julio or to the PSP, but all came with some degree of experience in clandestine operations—a predilection they transmitted to two generations of Latin American revolutionaries, some of whom were predisposed to it anyway, others of whom would never have acquired it on their own. Piñeiro's *muchachos* were generally young, lower-middle-class or quite poor, uncouth but bright, resourceful, and daring, and totally devoted to him. As a Colombian oligarch who knew them from the outset would say years later: "Piñeiro taught these boys how to dress and use knives and forks at the table." He also gave them a splendid opportunity for social mobility: from the slums of Havana and the hardships of the mountains to embassy parties and the import-export business. Many left the Ministry in 1974 with Piñeiro, a few split off from his band earlier on, and others still never worked with him directly but had close affinities with his followers. All formed an elite that, along with the cultural apparatus, became the most important link between the Cuban Revolution and the Latin American left. The bond would endure through the nineties and the autumn and winter of the Caribbean experiment.

Piñeiro and the Revolution's attempts to fan the fires of revolt across Latin America began as the most heroic chapter in its history. From the earliest guerrilla landings in Venezuela and the Dominican Republic to Che's sacrifice in Bolivia, not to mention the countless Cubans who fought, or helped others fight, in guerrilla wars extending over three decades, Fidel's vision of a revolution that had to be exported included some of its finest hours: generous, idealistic, unselfish. In the brief moments of victory or success, and during the long years of defeat and retribution, the Cubans stood by their friends, cared for the widows, orphans, and maimed who survived the hemisphere's Thirty Years Wars. They opened their doors to many who had nowhere else to go and gave much of the best of themselves and their experience to bringing change in Latin America. One may disagree with the tactics, or even with the goals, but they pursued both with perseverance and dignity.

Their isolation explained this as much as their altruism. The island's aloneness was central in defining its attitude toward the rest of the region: it owed nothing to, and felt no liking or respect for, governments who had heeded Washington. The best way to end Cuba's isolation and also to settle scores with those who scorned Fidel and his cohorts, was to wreak havoc on them at home. When these attempts were carried out with the noblest of intentions and by the best and brightest of Latin America's youth and intelligentsia, few could have resisted the temptation to back or encourage them.

Cuba's activities abroad made the humiliated isle of the Platt Amendment and the whorehouses of Havana a player on the world stage. It was reviled by Washington, resented by Moscow, but respected, indeed admired and revered, throughout the Third World. The leader of the Cuban people became a world figure, someone they could be proud of in the *bohíos* and the beaches. At its high point—the Sixth Summit of the Non-Aligned, held in Havana in 1979 and presided over by Castro—Cuba's place in the sun was a source of dignity for its people, grudging respect for its leader, and endless irritation for its enemies.

The first directly confirmed instance of Piñeiro's involvement in a foreign revolutionary venture occurred in 1962: the Salta *foco* in Argentina led by Ricardo Massetti, who, together with Gabriel García Márquez, had founded the Prensa Latina news agency a couple of years earlier. It is not entirely clear whether all of the guerrilla *"focos"* created across the hemisphere during the 1960s were directly linked to Piñeiro, or if all areas of Cuban involvement remained under his authority. Thus there are reasons for believing that Che Guevara's effort to start a revolt in Bolivia was not handled by Piñeiro but by others, explaining why some considered Barbaroja to have mourned Che's death less than many: the tragedy of Nancahuazú did not occur on his watch. This would also explain why a series of obvious technical errors were committed in the course of the Bolivian mission, errors which Piñeiro would probably have avoided.

What seems undisputed is that the means soon became an end in itself, as the chief constituency in Cuba for supporting the armed struggle in Latin America emerged from within Piñeiro's own teams of agents, conspirators, and accomplices. In their endeavors they had both a strong suit and an intrinsic weakness. Piñeiro's strongest card was his exceptional personal relationship with Fidel and Raúl Castro, cemented by their time together in the mountains, but, perhaps more important, by the bonds established during the fiercest years of U.S. aggression and Piñeiro's success in protecting the lives of the Revolution's leaders. Despite a constant series of conflicts—beginning with the Soviets and the old PSP apparat, then with Carlos Rafael Rodríguez over control of foreign relations, and in the early 1990s with blossoming (then disgraced) heir apparent Carlos Aldana—Piñeiro escaped unscathed, consistently pursuing his own policies, with his own team and resources. He knew how to listen, how to learn, and how to change where change was required. Without the strong support of Fidel, however, he would never have made it: his bureaucratic clout was simply insufficient.[6] Although a member of the party's Central Committee since 1965, Piñeiro was never elected to the Politburo, never held

---

6. Even as extreme a group as the Cuban-American National Foundation accepts the fact—if not the conclusions derived from it—of Piñeiro's scant political weight in the Cuban apparatus. Speaking about the early seventies—before his eviction from the Ministry of the Interior—Rex Hudson, a Library of Congress researcher who has written the only known published account of Piñeiro's activities, points out that "the Soviets allowed Castro to keep Piñeiro, but the agency that he headed lacked bureaucratic status." Rex Hudson, *Castro's America Department: Coordinating Cuba's Support for Marxist-Leninist Violence in the Americas* (Miami: Cuban-American National Foundation, 1988), p. 12.

ministerial rank in the government or high-level standing in the military or Interior Ministry hierarchy. When he was finally removed from his post as head of the America Department in March 1992, it was largely because his business—the business of revolution—had come to an end.

Piñeiro's strength was also his weakness. As the regime's diplomatic and political needs became more evident and compelling, support for universal revolution dwindled. In 1974, after peace was made with the Soviet Union and became imminent with many of the region's Communist parties and centrist governments, Piñeiro and his comrades were banished from the Ministry of the Interior. Thus was born the (in)famous America Department of the Central Committee of the Cuban Communist Party, or, some might have called it, the Ministry of Revolution. This was, thereafter, where revolution was exported from; its agents were placed in embassies and press bureaus; its headquarters were just next to Fidel's office in the Palace of the Revolution; its links with the Latin American left were extensive, intimate, and decisive. Yet despite the legends that swirled around it during the seventies and eighties, both in Latin America and the United States, its creation and development were as much a sign of continuing island support for revolution in the hemisphere as of the constraints, contradictions, and declining enthusiasm for extracurricular revolutionary activities in Cuban politics as a whole.

The early seventies were dog years for the America Department. Revolution in Latin America seemed doomed, and the normalization of Cuba's diplomatic ties with many of the region's governments imposed a hands-off attitude toward local affairs. In addition, after the Chilean debacle, the prospects for spreading revolution further across the hemisphere became dim. But Piñeiro made good use of this time, marrying his second wife, Chilean journalist, author, and Marxist theoretician Marta Harnecker. He had met her in Chile during the Allende years. Harnecker would become the largest-selling Latin American author after Gabriel García Márquez, acquiring a distinctive niche of her own in the ranks of the Latin American left.

The Allende experience was important for Piñeiro. He spent many months in Chile during that time, and several of his closest aides worked there. However, Piñeiro did not control Cuban operations in Chile during that time. Instead, the Special Troops of the Ministry of the Interior were in charge: Antonio de la Guardia handled Allende's security, and his twin brother, Patricio, prepared Castro's month-long trip in 1972, subsequently remaining in Chile to manage the Cuban

presence there until the coup.[7] (Antonio de la Guardia was executed in
1989 for drug-smuggling; Patricio is now serving a thirty-year prison
sentence.)

There was little for Piñeiro to do during this period. The revolution
in Latin America was being rolled back nearly everywhere, while Cuba
was turning its insurgent enthusiasm to such places as Africa. Piñeiro
had virtually no connection with Operación Carlota, the dispatch and
active combat role of Cuban troops in Angola, from 1975 onward. This
was left in the hands of the other sector of the original Ministry of the
Interior, and then of the Army itself. Moreover, when relations between the Cubans and the Latin American Communist parties improved in 1974–75, Piñeiro's influence diminished still further: he was
never one to get along well with Stalinist bureaucrats. Until the end of
the decade, when the Sandinistas began to make a stronger showing in
Nicaragua, Piñeiro was out of fashion, if not out of favor.

But his sphere of action was not restricted to the armed or extreme
left. Despite his rivalries with other Cuban officials and his preference
for the revolutionary left, he was also in charge of relations with the
orthodox Communist parties, social democrats, and the intellectuals
and grass-roots groups that make up the constellation of the left in the
hemisphere. If on occasions his links with the armed groups seem
overemphasized in these pages, it is because these were the bonds to
which he himself attached the greatest importance, and which most
clearly exemplify his role over the past thirty years. It would be a
mistake, however, to suppose that Piñeiro dealt only with the *fierreros*,
as the fellows with the guns were familiarly known in the ranks of the
Latin American left. The America Department's ties with Chilean
Social Democrats, ranging from political activity to health care and
lipo-suction, summer camps for the children and conspiracy in the
Southern Cone, were well known in the Chilean exile community. But
Piñeiro's raison d'être was rooted in the guerrilla movements and the
armed struggle. That was what he knew and was best at. Therein lay
his comparative advantage over other contenders for Fidel's favor and
power in Havana:

> There was a subjective element in all of this (the armed struggle).
> Without guerrillas, Piñeiro was out of business. . . . To keep up a whole

---

7. Jorge Massetti, interview with the author, Paris, December 8–9, 1991. According
to Antonio de la Guardia's daughter, Iliana, her father was with Allende in the Moneda
presidential palace on the day of the coup and escaped the burning, bombed building
almost miraculously. "Entrevista con Iliana de la Guardia," *Proceso* (Mexico City),
January 25, 1992.

Department, with a secret structure, just to have relations with the PRD in Mexico or the Argentine Communist Party was absurd; he could do that with 10 men. . . . the America Department was a super-organization. Without the guerrillas we would have been oversized with a man per country, whereas in fact we had a specialist and five officials for each country.[8]

But by 1978 it suddenly seemed that the Nicaraguan rebels might actually beat Somoza, and the armed struggle in Latin America returned to the fore. So did Piñeiro, albeit under different circumstances. He and Cuba played a triple role in the Sandinista victory, a revolution that would probably have occurred regardless, but that undoubtedly owes an important share of its success to the support of its elders. Cuba served as a conduit between the Sandinistas and other revolutionary organizations. It supplied the Sandinistas with intelligence, communications, and personal security for many of the FSLN's leaders. Toward the end of the war, it even provided the "equipment" to launch a Sandinista air force, which played a minor but symbolic role.

Cuba sent arms, mainly old Belgian FAL automatic rifles, through Panama and the Costa Rican border town of Liberia. It supplied trained military professionals—exiled Chilean officers serving in the Cuban Armed Forces—and provided invaluable advice on how to unify the three Sandinista factions. It also advised the movement in relation to some military issues, the alliance with the moderate sector, the need for achieving and consolidating the support of other Latin American nations, and for avoiding American intervention. It is difficult to determine the specific weight of each of these types of assistance, and what role Piñeiro played in each of them. However, there is some available information which allows us to make an initial assessment.[9]

Some of Piñeiro's men, particularly Fernando Comás, "Salchicha" or "El cojo," played a key role in channeling arms and ammunition

---

8. Massetti, op. cit.

9. Hudson, probably on the basis of U.S. intelligence reports and official U.S. sources quoted in his text, gets some details wrong but the basic thrust of his reasoning is accurate: "Cuba became the FSLN's main supplier of military matériel and other essential support. . . . During the 1978–79 period there were at least 21 flights between Cuba and Costa Rica carrying war matériel for the FSLN; a minimum of 500 tons of arms destined for the Sandinistas were airlifted to Costa Rica from Cuba and elsewhere. . . . Piñeiro personally supervised the loading operations at Havana airport. Julián López Díaz, then chief of the America Department's Central American Section, directed the Cubans' main operations center based in San José for coordinating logistics and contacts with the FSLN and monitoring the airlift. When the FSLN launched its final offensive in mid-1979, Special Troops from the Ministry of the Interior's DOE were with the Sandinista columns and maintained direct radio communications with Havana." Rex Hudson, op. cit., p. 25.

through Costa Rica. Comás was the Cuban consul in San José; in his den he keeps a picture of himself in battle fatigues armed with an M-16 helping to cover the runway of Managua's airport the day the Sandinistas captured the capital. But the fact is that Piñeiro's America Department at this time was already far less operational than before. Indeed, in 1974, Piñeiro had lost control over three key facets of the export of revolution. He had no armed troops under his command—they remained in the Ministry of the Interior or Defense—he had no operational logistical capability for shipping ordnance and communications equipment, and documents were all handled now by the Departamento de Operaciones Especiales, or DOE. He may have retained the role of political training of the Latin America revolutionaries at the Ñico López Political School, but in all likelihood not military training.[10] Additionally, his organization received less and less money, obliging him to seek funds for his efforts elsewhere.

Piñeiro and his department were simply becoming the political wing of Cuban involvement abroad, and were increasingly obliged to rely on others to implement the decisions taken by Piñeiro and Castro himself. This implied two things: first, that Piñeiro would be constantly at odds with the DOE and others over their support (or lack thereof) for his activities; second, that he would consequently attempt to carry out many of the activities on his own, or have the Latin American guerrilla groups do it for him. Although Piñeiro's recommendations to Castro still carried a great deal of weight, and were decisive, the implementation of those decisions had left Piñeiro's hands. In the face of increasing DOE resistance, Piñeiro spent more of his time attending to documentation, logistics, and "fund-raising" to purchase arms.

Yet despite these limitations and obstacles, the Sandinistas' victory became Piñeiro's vindication. He remained in Managua during the first months following the revolution, and was able to ensure that an America Department member was named ambassador to Nicaragua. He took advantage of the ties he had established over the years with the Sandinista leadership, when few others had paid any attention to them. He

---

10. The ambiguity of the training situation can be seen in the way that task is generally believed to be shared by Piñeiro and the DOE: "The education of guerrillas in Cuba is overseen by the Department of Special Operations of the Cuban Army and the Department of the Americas, headed by Manuel Piñeiro. Piñeiro, a close friend of Fidel Castro, draws on two decades of guerrilla experience in the region and knows many of the area's leftist insurgent commanders personally." Peter Clement, W. Raymond Duncan, "The Soviet Union and Central America," in Eusebio Mujal-León, ed., The USSR and Latin America (Boston: Unwin Hyman, 1989), pp. 287–288.

also leveraged his newly recovered prestige as a revolutionary strategist into moral authority over the leadership of two other supposedly imminent revolutions: El Salvador and Guatemala.

Until the early 1990s, Piñeiro dedicated most of his time and men to the Central American and Grenadan revolutions (through late 1983). This meant building a new state and party structure in Nicaragua and (until 1983) Grenada, defending them against both internal and external hostilities, and supporting the campaign in El Salvador and Guatemala. Although the DOE and Sandinistas handled the operational aspects, Piñeiro, Ramiro Abreu, and "Ibrahim" made the key political and strategic decisions regarding Cuban support, transfer of arms, training and tactics for the Salvadoran FMLN. Their actual involvement, regardless of the Salvadoran revolutionaries' actual awareness of it, went well beyond what anyone at the time imagined. As long as victory remained possible in El Salvador, and there was something to defend in Nicaragua, Piñeiro's fortunes were intact. Defeats—Jamaica, 1980; Grenada, 1983; Guatemala, 1982; Nicaragua, 1990—were not directly attributed to his strategies. While the Cubans' dismal intelligence record in these countries can be blamed largely on Piñeiro, he did not suffer from the collapse of his pet projects.

His policies and activities followed simple, often unwritten rules. They can be summed up in three theoretical premises—*"las armas, la unidad, y las masas"* ("weapons, unity, and masses")—and one unspoken tenet: with Cuba's involvement. The first theoretical assumption meant that the armed struggle was central to the Latin American revolution: without it nothing was possible. In one of Piñeiro's few published texts, he states clearly that:

> Arms are indispensable for the triumph of any liberating revolution in the continent, and, more important, to preserve its continuity and full realization.[11]

As Piñeiro's power base and apparatus in Cuba shrank over the years, his only remaining source of strength and prestige were his links with the Latin American left. Deprived of arms, troops, money, intelligence, and counterintelligence activities other than those directly linked to backing the Latin American revolution, he conserved only his contacts and converts abroad.

---

11. Manuel Piñeiro, "La crisis actual del imperialismo y los procesos revolucionarios de la América Latina y el Caribe," in *Memorias de la Conferencia teórica internacional sobre Características generales y particulares de los procesos revolucionarios en América Latina y el Caribe*, Havana, April 26–28, 1982, p. 376.

The second theoretical premise involved unity: for Piñeiro and for Castro during these years, the need for close cooperation of all revolutionary forces, preferably under a single command, was more important than ever. Where there had been unity, revolution had triumphed; where unity had been absent—Chile, Grenada—it had been defeated. Moreover, Piñeiro's lease on life depended on the revolutionaries' unity: only if Communists and the different guerrilla factions remained together could he avoid having to take sides openly:

> This means that we should acknowledge that in most of our countries, together with experienced Communist parties, other organizations of the left have emerged that have through struggle gained the respect of their peoples and that often represent true examples of leadership. That's why the unity of these organizations among themselves, and of the latter with the Communist parties, is the first guarantee for the advance of democratic, popular and anti-imperialist revolutions.[12]

The third theoretical premise involved alliances—both domestic and foreign—and the terms of their engagement. Whatever he may have said, Castro understood full well both the true lessons of the Revolution itself and those of the years gone by. Without the support of broad sectors of the middle classes, part of the private sector, and the international community, revolution in Latin America was impossible. At the same time, if the revolutionary leadership did not control the alliance thus forged, the revolution rapidly became compromised, and the means used to achieve it soon overshadowed the ends originally sought. Inasmuch as it used the unwitting help of sectors who, if left to themselves, would act otherwise, this was a "stealth" theory of revolution. Nevertheless, it was also an accurate assessment of the situation in many Latin American societies, where such diverse groups as Catholics, students, businessmen, Indian groups, women, middle-class professionals, and other Latin American governments had authentic grievances against the status quo, and were willing to join forces with anyone opposed to what they saw as an intolerable situation.

With regard to the true Cuban stance on alliances and moderation, there is still much dispute throughout the academic and intelligence communities. Nevertheless, there is consensus that the Cubans generally preached moderation and strategic alliances when the revolutionary pole was in a position of strength. Conversely, Piñeiro tilted toward radicalism when the forces of revolution constituted the

---

12. Ibid., p. 370.

weaker element of an alliance, or when something else was at stake. This was the case in Nicaragua in 1990, when the Sandinistas' participation in the February elections under international supervision opened up two cans of worms for the Cubans: the possibility of losing power at the ballot box, a heresy for any true revolutionary, and the prospect of giving credence and moral authority to the principle of elections if they won, increasing the pressure on Cuba to do the same.[13]

Finally, there was the practical requirement of Cuban involvement in the entire affair of revolution in Latin America. Without it, Piñeiro and his men were redundant; with it, they were key players—and if their boys won now and then, they were heroes. A Salvadorean guerrilla cadre recalled how the America Department official assigned to his country repeatedly urged his colleagues to "take power" so that he could join the Central Committee. A successful protégé was a meal ticket for the America Department. A victorious revolution was simultaneously a source of sincere rejoicing and personal advancement.

The issue of Cuban interference was a delicate one, and Piñeiro addressed it obliquely and somewhat cryptically:

> Sometimes there are confusions or deviations with regard to the necessary and healthy independence that revolutionary parties and movements have a right to and a duty to defend. Their true sovereignty, however, instead of excluding others, implies uniting efforts to face common international problems and cooperation in support of the revolutionary movements that most need solidarity at a given time.[14]

The line between solidarity and cooperation on the one hand and heavy-handed pressure and interference on the other was a thin and fuzzy one. All the more so since three intrinsic characteristics of the parties involved pushed in the direction of meddling, and went against the grain of arm's-length nonintervention. First, the Cubans had the disposition to meddle: they honestly believed that they knew more about revolution, guerrilla warfare, international relations, and political alliances than the neophytes on the ground in Guatemala, Colombia, or El Salvador. When high-ranking Cuban officials deny vehemently ever having directly influenced Latin American revolutionaries other than through (sound) advice, they are not exactly lying, but they are being at the very least disingenuous. Castro indeed interfered rarely, and far less than Piñeiro, who in turn maintained greater

---

13. The conflicts and tensions between the Sandinistas and the Cubans over the former's participation in the 1990 elections have been most notably revealed in Andrés Oppenheimer, *Castro's Final Hour* (New York: Simon and Schuster, 1992), pp. 204–18.

14. Piñeiro, op. cit., p. 372.

distance than his deputies. And in turn these, needless to say, were more discreet than the agents in the field. All of them, however, were tireless in offering counsel, and their "advice" was often difficult to ignore. As one field agent put it:

> Often he [Piñeiro] didn't get involved himself; I personally witnessed cases where he found one of his people interfering in a revolutionary movement's decisions and reprimanded him for it. Piñeiro was not so clumsy. But many of his people, instead of being a link between the Cuban Communist Party and the revolutionary movement, wanted to become leaders of the movement from outside.[15]

Second, the Cubans also enjoyed wielding their power: no matter how sincere and devoted to the cause they may have been, they were all prey to the insidious effects of their years in power, of being constantly idolized, of their effective clout. They had a tremendous amount of leverage. The fact that they provided everything from rest and recreation in Havana to artillery and surface-to-air missiles put them in a position to mete out support judiciously, and play one faction off against another, depending on multiple factors. The Cubans did not create these factions or encourage their emergence; they simply used them to their advantage. There are endless accounts of Piñeiro choosing favorites among the different organizations making up the FMLN in El Salvador, the URNG in Guatemala, and the several guerrilla organizations in Colombia during the 1980s. Ideology played a role, but frequently the Cubans would open the arms spigot to one group—while closing it to another—simply because the former shared a tactical position with them, even if strategically great differences prevailed. Or, as has been rumored to be the case in El Salvador, the Cubans almost systematically favored the Ejército revolucionario del pueblo (ERP) largely because of Fidel's infatuation with Joaquín Villalobos. The ideological affinity between the Cubans and Villalobos was small, but the chemistry was right, and that was what counted.[16]

So did the third factor contributing to Cuban participation: the Latin American left's willingness to accept—even more: to invite—Cuban intervention by constantly seeking a privileged relationship

---

15. Massetti, interview with the author.

16. Salvador Samayoa of the FPL in the FMLN phrased this issue in more diplomatic but not dissimilar terms: "Cuba and Nicaragua at a certain point supported the ERP, a group that was less ideologically close to them than the FPL. Concrete, circumstantial factors contributed to this approach." Interview with the author, August 20, 1990, Mexico City.

with the island. Thus, many groups tended to tailor their stances on the major issues of the day to curry favor with Piñeiro; their intention was never to entice Cuban meddling, but, unavoidably, that was the result of their actions, as any Cuban operative in the field would immediately sense an opening and a possibility for greater influence. This would in turn earn him the approbation of Piñeiro in Havana. The chain of command and that of bureaucratic opportunism were often indistinguishable. Because Piñeiro wanted to affect the course of events and because he was able to do so, and finally because the Latin American left placed itself in a situation where such things could happen, the Cubans were frequently an integral part of many organizations, armed and civilian, moderate and extreme, directly political and "parapolitical": journals, the press, and student and academic groups.

In the critical years of the Revolution, after the fall of the socialist bloc, the disintegration of the Soviet Union, and Cuba's total isolation, along with the gradual disengagement of the armed struggle in Latin America, Piñeiro's role inevitably diminished. He was reduced to using his influence and agents to bolster support for Cuba within Latin America. He accompanied Castro to his meetings with Latin American chiefs of state, helping Fidel with his charm and experience in the intelligent but ultimately futile attempt to substitute his Soviet subsidy with a hemispheric economic relationship. His agents and sometimes even his wife lobbied intensely at every meeting of the Latin American left—the São Paulo Forum events, the Congress of Latin American and Caribbean Sociologists, Historians, etc.—with varying success. His Department was formally swallowed up by the International Secretariat of the Party, and his agents abroad lost their Foreign Ministry cover. He was finally eased out of the Department, retaining only his membership in the Central Committee. His passing from power was proof, if needed, that the contemporary age of revolution in Latin America had come to an end.

Piñeiro left intact a rogue organization that continued to act in Latin America: a tragic, unnerving legacy of a man and a team that more than any others personified the armed revolutionary struggle in the region. According to Jorge Massetti, and this has been confirmed by other sources, as Piñeiro lost the wherewithal to arm and support the revolutionary left, and thus to maintain his position in Cuba, he resorted to other measures and to the revolutionary organizations themselves. He called on them to prepare documents, take and send messages, and logically, to raise funds for arms purchases. America Department officials would seek out individuals of different revolutionary organizations—mainly Chileans, Uruguayans, and Argentines, but also Central Americans—and suggest that they carry out kidnappings, bank thefts, and other similar activities in countries "where the money was." Piñeiro's men would take aside the chief of logistics of a given Central American organization and ask him (or her) to contribute two or three individuals. Others would do the same with the Southern Cone people. Thus the leaderships were involved, but not entirely: only the logistics sector was aware of what was happening, and it was expectedly acquiescent since it knew that the money would be used for weapons. At the same time the rest of the leadership could plausibly—and honestly—deny any involvement. The Department planned the operations, transferred the necessary weapons into the country in question by diplomatic pouch, and expedited the money back to Cuba through the same channel.

Massetti, who was posted in Mexico City as a mid-level Department official from 1980 through 1983 when he was expelled by the Mexican government, is categorical about his own experiences. Weapons would be flown into Mexico, bank holdups, kidnappings, or other crimes would be carried out, and the proceeds would be handed over to the Department for safekeeping. It would then spread them around to revolutionary movements to purchase arms with. In this fashion, Piñeiro's staff achieved independence from the Cuban treasury, the DOE, and other areas of the state. Self-reliance, or self-management, it could be called: a number of bank robberies in Mexico City and Panama and several kidnappings in Mexico and Brazil of very wealthy businessmen that were later attributed to Southern Cone ex-revolutionaries acting on their own or in behalf of Central American groups (the kidnappings of Juan Diego Gutiérrez Cortina of the GUTSA construction firm and Abílio Diniz of the Pau de Azucar supermarket group in 1989 and 1990) can be presumed to have been Departmental activity, although they were officially blamed on Salvadorean and Chilean groups, respectively.

There has never been any insinuation that this was done for personal enrichment; in the minds of those who participated in these activities, there was always a categorical distinction between the means and the end. Neither Piñeiro nor any of his men got rich themselves or derived privileges from these unorthodox procedures beyond those they already enjoyed. Given the fanatical devotion to the cause and the sheer thrill of the struggle, the issue is a more complicated one: why should any tactic or instrument be illegitimate in view of the overriding virtue of the aspiration behind it? With time, the individual elements who continued these actions, even after Piñeiro's retirement, may have sought personal gain. Initially, they did not.

In a sense, the procedure was not dissimilar to that adopted by the Special Troops of the Ministry of the Interior and CIMEX, the Cuban import-export company set up by the de la Guardia brothers. They ended up dabbling, or even getting heavily involved, in drug traffic, but the original motivation is analogous. Nor is it entirely different from what Castro accused Arnaldo Ochoa,[17] the hero of Angola, of wanting the armed forces to engage in: fending for themselves, in order to fend for the revolution, raising funds in any way possible, from drugs to ivory traffic from Africa, but always keeping a safe distance between the illicit activities in question and the central leadership, between means and ends. Piñeiro played this game to the end, though the accusation that surfaced in the Manuel Noriega trial regarding his direct involvement in drug trafficking from Nicaragua was in all likelihood false.[18] Piñeiro was too smart for that, and too much of a survivor. The three decades of his life as conspirator, charmer, and cynic weigh heavily against such a possibility.[19]

∎

The Cuban Revolution impacted the left in Latin America as nothing had ever done before. It was truly a "Revolution within the Revolu-

---

17. Ochoa, executed on July 13, 1989, was described in Cuba as an arrogant, corrupt, high-flying traitor to the revolution. But the memories he left in Nicaragua at least, where he commanded the Cuban military mission in the mid-eighties, were different. "He always behaved like a true revolutionary in Nicaragua: honest, modest and unselfish." Humberto Ortega, conversation with the author, Guadalajara, December 5, 1992.

18. "Former Smuggler Ties Top Officials of Cuba and Nicaragua to Drug Ring," *New York Times*, November 21, 1991, p. 10. A recent, and generally excellent, book flatly disputes this: "Piñeiro is the only Cuban official to have used drug-trafficking methodically." However, no source or substantiation is provided, and without it I am inclined to believe Piñeiro kept his distance from the drug business. See Jean-François Fogel and Bertrand Rosenthal, *Fin de Siècle à l'Havana* (Paris: Seuil), 1992, p. 99.

19. According to some versions, his downfall was partially caused by the difficulties generated by this rogue organization. In particular a former Chilean MIR agent, René Valenzuela ("Gato"), arrested in Madrid on January 14, 1992, for participating in Basque ETA kidnappings and bombings, was closely associated with the Cubans, had been linked to Piñeiro for nearly twenty years, and ran "rogue" operations in Mexico. The right-wing Madrid daily *ABC* mentioned the Piñeiro-Valenzuela connection on its front page on January 23, 1992. Persons familiar with the case have speculated that when the Spanish government presented Castro with the evidence linking Piñeiro to the ETA it was the final straw, and that Castro reluctantly decided that "there couldn't continue to be two foreign policies in Cuba" and eased Piñeiro out.

tion." For the first time in the region's history, three processes occurred simultaneously. A radical revolutionary regime—pursuing profound social and economic reforms, from land distribution to the expropriation of national resources, from urban reform to mass education and health programs—took power, consolidated itself in office, and endured. Second, from 1961 onward, the new regime openly embraced "Marxism-Leninism," adhering geopolitically, if not ideologically, to the Soviet bloc, and designating itself the United States' principal enemy in the hemisphere. Washington, of course, reciprocated. The Revolution represented a threat to U.S. interests, not only in Cuba but, by virtue of its demonstration effect, throughout Latin America. Finally, and most important from this perspective, the Cuban Revolution was born with Latin American aspirations. It unabashedly proclaimed its intention of lighting the fires of revolution across the continent, seeing in the repetition of the Cuban experience elsewhere in the hemisphere one of its foremost duties and a major means of insuring its own survival.[20]

In 1959 the Cuban Revolution inaugurated a phase in the history of the Latin American left that lasted until the Sandinistas lost their elections, almost thirty years later to the day. The idea of revolution took center stage in the left's theater. In the words of a supporter who later broke with the Cubans:

> For the first time we thought that revolution was something possible in our countries. Until then the idea of revolution was romantic and remote to us, something we took more as an academic idea that could never become a reality in countries like ours.[21]

Before Fidel entered Havana, the left in Latin America was reformist, gradualist, or resignedly pessimistic about the prospects of revolution. For the three decades that followed, revolution was at the top of its agenda. The fact that it did not come about is a different issue, whose significance can only be appreciated with hindsight. After the fall of the Sandinistas and the Berlin Wall, revolution once again disappeared from the left's lexicon.

---

20. Even a scholar as opposed to traditional clichés about Cuban foreign policy as Pamela Falk is obliged to acknowledge that "Cuba provided military armed assistance to guerrilla insurgents in every nation of the Western hemisphere except Mexico during the first two decades of revolutionary rule." Pamela Falk, *Cuban Foreign Policy: Caribbean Tempest* (Lexington, Mass.: Lexington Books, 1986), p. 21.

21. Mario Vargas Llosa, "Transforming a Lie into Truth," in *A Writer's Reality* (Syracuse, N.Y.: Syracuse University Press, 1991), p. 145.

The importance of the Cuban Revolution for the Latin American left can be gauged by two facts which are often ignored today. First, as the French scholar and diplomat Alain Rouquié has pointed out, ever since the launching of the *Granma* expedition from Tuxpan, Veracruz, in 1956, the revolutionary armed struggle in Latin America has never ceased.[22] Second, at some moment or another throughout the 1960s and early 1970s, and practically everywhere in the hemisphere, a group adhering to the Cuban Revolution, its tactics, strategy, and theory, emerged and became an important actor on the domestic political scene. In virtually every Latin American nation the local left was permeated by Cuban influence. The left as a whole—Communist parties, intellectuals, union organizers, and erstwhile populist *caudillos*—was either converted to the Cuban line or split between pro-Cubans and everyone else—orthodox, pro-Soviet Communists, supporters of local governments, subscribers to the notion of an alliance with the "national bourgeoisie."

Fidel Castro and the Cubans did not invent the armed struggle in Latin America or the Caribbean. There was a long tradition of taking up arms in the region, dating back to the nineteenth century, and extending up to the eve of the Cuban victory. Those who did so were nationalists, radical liberals, and, every now and then, Marxists. Villa and Zapata in Mexico, of course; Martí, Mella, and Guiteras in Cuba itself; Sandino in Nicaragua; in a way, Farabundo Martí in El Salvador; the Colombian peasant uprisings examined below; José Figueres in Costa Rica; countless insurrectionary attempts in the Dominican Republic, Puerto Rico, and Haiti, dating back to Toussaint L'Ouverture: Fidel and his 26th of July had a rich ancestry. But they refined a tradition, and made it a policy of state and party. Had there been no tradition, the deliberate attempt to extend the armed struggle everywhere under the sun would have fallen totally flat (it wasn't exactly successful in any case). Had there been no state-sponsored policy, the tradition would have remained just that: a memory and a nuisance.

The similarities to the Russian Revolution are striking. Between 1917 and the mid-1920s Lenin and later Stalin broke the large Western European Social-Democratic parties into Communist and Socialist wings. They simultaneously created an International body that supported and controlled these new organizations. Like the Soviets, the

---

22. Alain Rouquié, *Amérique Latine, Introduction à l'Extreme-Occident* (Paris: Seuil, 1987), p. 303.

Cubans also generated divisions within the Latin American left. But unlike the Soviets, most of the time the Cubans did not intentionally create those divisions. In fact, they would rather have won over those who disagreed with them instead of destroying them.[23]

Another fundamental analogy with the Soviet Union can be made in relation to the Cubans' strategic mistakes, and the reasons they committed them. In what came to be perhaps the most perceptive criticism of "Revolution in the Revolution," Régis Debray's conceptualization of the Cuban strategy, his mentor, the French philosopher Louis Althusser, warned his student:

> It may be that your theses are correct, but your text doesn't really provide a positive demonstration of this; it simply gives what we could call a negative demonstration. . . . In your writings, the validity of guerrilla warfare is demonstrated less by its own merits than through the defects or drawbacks of past forms of struggle that you examine; it is supported less by its positive qualities than by the negative aspects of other forms of struggle.[24]

The Cuban Revolution's rift with the rest of the Latin American left was tantamount to a break with the past. The substance of the Cuban innovation can be summed up in six theses and one theoretical premise justifying the strategic and tactical considerations.[25] The theoretical premise was developed primarily by Cubans, but in an ad hoc fashion. Later in the decade and largely *ex post*, it came to be known as "dependency theory," a coherent, articulate corpus of historical, economic, social, and political assumptions about Latin

---

23. In 1967, without much success, the Cubans "inaugurated the OLAS (Organización Latinoamericana de Solidaridad) Conference in Havana, an International dominated by Cuba, created against the orthodox Communist parties that had chosen the reformist or peaceful and parliamentary road, and refused to make revolution according to Cuban dictums." Ibid., p. 298.

24. Louis Althusser, quoted in Régis Debray, *La Critique des Armes* (Paris: Seuil, 1974), pp. 262, 264.

25. The corpus of texts, proclamations, speeches and official documents in which these theses were formulated and divulged is far-reaching. It ranges from Fidel Castro's First and Second Declarations of Havana in 1961 and 1962, to Régis Debray's "authorized" theoretical translation of many of Castro's and Che Guevara's views in "Revolution in the Revolution," and includes the multiple pro-Cuban analyses in each country of Latin America. Given the diversity of the texts and the considerable number of treatises on the subject, and the ensuing difficulty of picking out the most useful or relevant ones, we have followed the most recent study of the Cuban ideological influence on the rest of the Latin American left, which also happens to be one of the most insightful. See José Rodríguez Elizondo, *La crisis de las izquierdas en América Latina* (Madrid and Caracas: Instituto de Cooperación Iberoamericana-Editorial Nueva Sociedad, 1990), pp. 94–98.

America.[26] In a nutshell, this perspective posited the virtual neocolonial status of the hemisphere, the dysfunctional nature of capitalism in the region and the consequent historical impotence of the local business classes, the complete lack of democratic channels of expression and reform, and the inviability of any form of nonsocialist development. While in its most radical elaboration dependency theory was formulated solely by non-Cubans like the Chilean-Dutch sociologist Andre Gunder Frank and the Brazilian Fernando Henrique Cardoso, it served as the theoretical underpinning for the Cuban condemnation of the Latin American version of Stalin's "construction of socialism in one country."[27]

The first defining statement proclaimed the *hemispheric* character of the Latin American revolution. In the Cuban view, whatever the specific features and peculiarities of individual countries, it was the common Latin American predicament they all shared that was decisive. The "objective conditions" of revolution were perceived as essentially identical throughout the hemisphere. The differences from nation to nation pertained to "subjective conditions," which had to be equalized through political will and revolutionary fervor.[28]

The second premise affirmed the *socialist* nature of this hemispheric revolution. Whereas the Latin American left had typically accepted—indeed, insisted upon—the need for an interregnum between the realization of democratic reforms—parliamentary democracy, nationalization of natural resources and land reform—and a truly socialist revolution, the Cuban approach placed the socialist revolution in a

---

26. "At the most general level of abstraction, dependency ideas attempt to marry Marxism and nationalism." Robert A. Packenham, *The Dependency Movement* (Cambridge, Mass.: Harvard University Press, 1992), p. 27.

27. The link between dependency theory and Cuba has been established on numerous occasions; some authors go beyond this and argue that "Third World ideology" in the industrialized Western nations was also linked to dependency theory: "Among Western intellectuals the ideology of the Third World (*tercer mundismo* in Spanish) experienced a qualitative leap with the triumph of the Cuban Revolution and the transformation of Che Guevara in the guerrilla's emblem. . . . Under the label of dependency theories André Gunder Frank, Theotonio Dos Santos, Ruy Mauro Marini, and Samir Amin through their works made it a commonplace conviction to believe that the only road to economic development passed through breaking the economic ties of dependency with the developed countries." Ludolfo Paramio, *Tras el diluvio: La izquierda ante el fin de siglo* (Madrid: Siglo XXI Editores, 1988), p. 152. For a radical critique from the left of dependency theory in Latin America, see Jorge G. Castañeda and Enrique Hett, *El Economismo Dependentista* (Mexico City: Siglo XXI Editores,1978). For a more recent and conservative approach, see Packenham, ibid.

28. Rodríguez Elizondo, op. cit., pp. 94–98.

position of priority.[29] Any pleading in favor of so-called "noncapitalist roads of development" was a reformist capitulation ignoring the fact that capitalism in the region was not a going concern.

The third thesis, which derived almost naturally from the first two, came to be the dominant underlying argument for Cuban strategy during most of the sixties. It stated that the continental, socialist revolution could come about and be victorious only through an *armed struggle*, as opposed to the traditional "peaceful paths" previously favored by the Latin American left, particularly the Communist parties. The classic *tactical* consideration of how to reach power became a central *strategic* precept. With time, in fact, it would become *the* strategic premise, allowing even those groups who never subscribed to the other founding propositions (the M-19 movement in Colombia or the Argentine Montoneros, for example) to conserve their revolutionary purity. This was the most contentious issue Cuba faced, not only with the Latin American Communist organizations but also with the Soviet Union.

The fourth assumption had to do with leadership. The responsibility for conducting this entire process was placed firmly on the purportedly strong shoulders of the region's urban, enlightened, middle classes—the so-called petty bourgeoisie. Through heroic and decisive exemplary acts, students, intellectuals, professionals, and teachers would ignite the consciousness of the disenfranchised, impoverished masses who needed only a vanguard to lead them into revolutionary action.

The fifth postulate held that revolution could allow only revolutionary alliances, and consequently that the Communist parties' existing conception whereby alliances were possible with the "national bourgeoisie," the existing governments, and the union bureaucracy, along with their political expression of populist leaders, parties, and movements, had to be forsaken. The local entrepreneurial classes were irrevocably deemed imperialist traitors, and incapable of taking a stand in favor of the revolution and against its enemies. It followed, by deduction, that the key alliance for the revolution had to be forged between groups that were as far apart as they could be: there was a great rift between the rural peasantry, often linguistically, geographically,

---

29. This not only displeased many Latin American Communists; it also made life difficult for the Soviet Union. It took more than a year "from April 16, 1961, through mid-April 1962 for Cuba to be definitively and regularly recognized as socialist in Soviet writings." Jacques Levesque, *L'URSS et la Révolution Cubaine* (Montréal: Presses de la Fondation Nationale des Sciences Politiques/Presses de l'Université de Montréal, 1976), p. 51.

and ethnically isolated by worlds and centuries, and the middle-class students and intellectuals of the cities. Che's expedition in Bolivia was an extreme example of this. The corollary of these hypotheses, and basic assumption of the "foco" theory was that the rural peasantry constituted the mass sector of society offering the greatest revolutionary-potential, not the small, co-opted, urban working classes. The bourgeoisie was a puppet of imperialism; the workers were stooges: these viewpoints amounted to a severe quandary for self-styled Marxists:

> The total negation of the two fundamental classes of society in the Marxist view—one, the bourgeoisie, because it wasn't national, the other, the proletariat, because it wasn't revolutionary—made existing political systems nothing more than devious but clever stratagems of domination.[30]

The sixth and final tenet was, inevitably, that the region's historical Communist parties had ceased to be valid revolutionary instruments. Corrupted and weakened by their allegiance not only to the Soviet Union but to its unconditional defense, accustomed to wheeling and dealing with governing elites, and supported by constituencies with a vested interest in the status quo, the hemisphere's orthodox Marxist-Leninist organizations were irremediably reformist and incapable of leading the revolution. The best proof of this central point lay in their rejection of the first five theses—they refused to accept the armed struggle, the socialist nature of the revolution, the need to abandon old alliances and adopt a truly hemispheric strategy.

It has been argued that the discontinuity between the Cuban revolution and the theory and practice of the traditional Communist parties of Latin America was tempered by an underlying, fundamental commonality of their one-party, Leninist, "dictatorship of the proletariat" conception of what socialism should be. In particular, the Chilean school of socialist renovation that surfaced in the mid-eighties has made this point eloquently; it is not entirely inaccurate. In terms of their intrinsic constitution, but not so much in their international relations nor in their conceptions of revolution, the Soviet Union and Eastern Europe *did* form the model the Cubans and their followers believed in. This was not true of all Cuban leadership—Che Guevara's criticisms of Soviet-style socialism were scathing—nor at all times. But one-party rule, a full expropriation of the means of production, and aspirations of social homogeneity did represent undisputed features of the model in question.

---

30. Rodríguez Elizondo, op. cit., p. 48.

Nonetheless, it is also true that in practice, and in the eyes of many Latin Americans and Cubans, at the outset the island revolution represented a major break with the Soviet model. It was freer, more democratic, disorderly, tropical, and spontaneous, as well as being intellectually more diverse and politically more liberal. With time, the resemblance between the models would grow, and Cuba would come to look much more like the Soviet Union. But in the early stages, at least, the discontinuities clearly outweighed the similarities.

Throughout the 1960s, starting with the Venezuelan and Dominican Republic guerrillas at the very beginning of the decade, the entire continent witnessed the emergence of armed "focos," or small groups of armed militants in the mountains or jungles. This was the logical, unavoidable consequence of the Cuban Revolution's adoption of the viewpoints outlined above. It was not so much a question of the Cubans exporting revolution or supporting these groups' activities in other countries. Rather, the Cubans' most important contribution to the emergence of the focos was one of ideology and example. If Fidel, Che and Raúl had overthrown the Batista dictatorship through the armed action of an initially tiny group of bold militants, the reproduction of the attempt was possible, if not inevitable. Castro's moral authority and prestige—together with the fascination he exerted over every young Latin American militant, intellectual, or political cadre to visit Havana in those early, heady years of the Cuban Revolution—were the island's principal revolutionary export. The arms, training, money, and other equipment were simply icing on the cake.

Armed groups in Latin America sprouted up in reaction to the Communist parties. One exception was Venezuela, where Douglas Bravo and Pompeyo Márquez led the Partido Comunista de Venezuela into a virtually suicidal attempt to wage an armed struggle against the recently established representative democracy headed by Social-Democrat Romulo Betancourt. Another exception was Colombia, which has lived through what French sociologist Pierre Gilhodes has called the longest peasant war of the century, together with that of the Philippines. The Marquetalia "armed resistance" guerrilla movement lasted for nearly twenty years.[31] For the entire decade of the fifties the Colombian Communist Party directed several different guerrilla forces—all of them descended from the Liberal insurgencies of "self-defense" actions of the previous decade, and the so-called "violencia":

---

31. Richard Gott, *Las guerrillas en América Latina* (Santiago: Editorial Universitaria, 1971), p. 222.

The Colombian guerrilla movement pre-dates the Cuban Revolution by at least a decade, with three stages:(1) the period dominated by the Liberal guerrillas (1949–1953); (2) the period marked by Communist guerrillas (1955–1958); and (3) the emergence of ideologically diverse groups in the wake of the Cuban Revolution (1962–1991).[32]

During the 1950s the Colombian Communist Party achieved what countless groups throughout the hemisphere would fail to do later: it created a mass base, with a significant peasant following. Its endurance rested on two pillars: "peasant self-defense groups, and the Communist guerrilla nuclei."[33] In 1965 the Marquetalia guerrilla movement was destroyed by the Colombian military, to a considerable extent because of hemispheric geopolitical considerations. A year later the Colombian Communist Party redefined its position on guerrilla warfare.[34] It proclaimed that all forms of struggle had to be combined, which often led to the devastating exposure of civilian urban movements to the bloody repression initially directed against the armed rural groups. This is clearly what occurred in the second half of the 1980s, when the CP founded the Patriotic Union mass movement and electoral front, which had thousands of its cadres, including its presidential candidate in 1990, Bernardo Jaramillo, assassinated in the cities, while the FARC pursued its armed struggle in the remote countryside. The Colombian CP continued to participate in the armed struggle in Colombia through the FARC, created in 1966 as a response to the destruction of Marquetalia and to the emergence of Cuban and Maoist armed groups on its left. The FARC was the last guerrilla movement dating back to the sixties to negotiate the laying down of its arms, in the early 1990s.[35]

In most cases the Latin American armed groups were led by former Communists; in others, as in Peru, they were headed by ex-

---

32. Eduardo Pizarro Leongómez, *Historia de la guerrilla*, vol. 1: *Las FARC: De la autodefensa a la combinación de todas las formas de lucha 1949–1966* (Bogotá: Instituto de Estudios Políticos y Relaciones Internacionales de la Universidad Nacional de Colombia/Tercer Mundo Editores, 1991), p. 20.

33. Ibid., p. 52.

34. "Our Party believes that there still isn't a revolutionary situation in Colombia. Today the guerrilla struggle is not the main form of combat." Gilberto Vieyra, secretary general of the Communist Party of Colombia, quoted by Gott, op. cit. p. 246. In fact, many analysts of this period maintain that the independent communist republics like Marquetalia were never really focos or guerrilla wars, but more accurately a peasant self-defense mechanism in the face of Colombian violence.

35. Its leader, Manuel Marulanda ("Tirofijo"), has spent nearly half a century in armed struggle.

members of the mainstream left-of-center populist parties like the APRA. In others still, former military officials led the armed struggle, be it in Guatemala in the early sixties, or in Brazil several years later. On occasions, the focos traced their historical origins back to earlier, abortive national liberation movements: the Sandinista Front in Nicaragua, created at least formally in 1961 by Carlos Fonseca Amador, proclaimed its fidelity to the guerrilla struggle of Augusto Cesar Sandino against American Marines in the twenties; the MR-13 in Guatemala, founded in 1962 by young army officers, was loyal to the memory of the Arbenz regime overthrown in 1954. Focos were created in Argentina, in Colombia—exemplified by Camilo Torres, the aristocratic guerrilla priest—in Peru—by Luis de la Puente's APRA Rebelde and by the MIR, Hugo Blanco's peasant rebellion—and in the Nancahuazú region of Bolivia, where Che Guevara would live out his final days in 1967.

The region's Communist parties were nearly unanimous in refusing to participate in armed adventures. They maintained their solidarity with the Cuban Revolution, traveled incessantly to Havana, on occasion even signed manifestoes and appeals for armed struggle, but never went beyond paying a peculiarly Latin American lip service to the idea. In nearly every case, either the local Communist organizations ignored the armed groups—collaborating with the regimes in place by denying the guerrillas supplies, money, weapons, or international contacts—or openly attacked them. Conversely, the Castroist spin-offs were often virulently opposed to the Communist Party, frequently formulating their extreme tactics and platforms, and establishing their chosen breeding grounds, in direct response to these parties' "treasons" and traditional stances. In the words of a leader of what would become one of the most successful guerrilla groups in the 1970s, the Salvadorean Popular Forces of Liberation (FPL): "The need to combat the deviations of the Communist Party led us to extreme and opposed positions, to an absolute negation of everything the Communist Party did. . . ."[36] Needless to say, the Communists did not take this lying down, and lashed back with their own viciousness and spite. Che Guevara's death would thus be attributed by many to the Bolivian Communist Party's boycott of his minuscule guerrilla war. Although "a compromise was reached between Cuba and the majority of the

36. Facundo Guardado, interview with Marta Harnecker, quoted in Marta Harnecker, *América Latina: Izquierda y crisis actual* (Mexico City: Siglo XXI Editores, 1990), p. 219.

[region's Communist] parties on the armed struggle in 1964,"[37] it proved short-lived.[38]

Later, urban guerrilla movements would surface.[39] These groups were also a reaction to the Communist parties' perceived inaction, and occurred mostly in countries where the very principle of a rural foco appeared senseless: Uruguay, half of whose population lived in the capital, Brazil, where the Communist Party's urban implantation in Rio de Janeiro and São Paulo gave the notion of urban guerrilla warfare a certain credibility; and Argentina, where the Peronist tradition and the overwhelming weight of the capital provided favorable circumstances.[40] The main urban guerrilla groups were Carlos Marighella's Army of National Liberation in Brazil, famous mostly for its drafting and distribution of Marighella's "Mini-Manual de la Guerrilla Urbana," the Montoneros in Argentina, and most notably the Uruguayan Movimiento de Liberación Nacional, or Tupamaros. Marighella, like so many other guerrilla leaders during those years, came from the Communist Party, where he was the head apparatchik for the São Paulo regional section, one of the most powerful in the country. As a result of the debate within the organization over the causes of and responsibilities for the 1964 military coup, Marighella began tilting toward armed struggle and encouraging dissident activities and acting on his own. He was gunned down in São Paulo in 1969; by 1970 virtually the entire Brazilian guerrilla movement had been destroyed. But, though it may have proved ephemeral, remarkably unsuccessful, and totally marginal to the country's political and social life, it was not so to its intellectual community. What's more, many of its chief traits, as studied years later thanks to documents made available during Bra-

---

37. Levesque, op. cit., p. 143.
38. "The Latin American Communist parties and particularly those that chose the 'peaceful road' were complaining to Moscow about Cuba's violation of the 1964 agreements." Ibid., p. 144.
39. Some students of this period consider the Venezuelan guerrillas to have been an urban movement predating other ones: "At the beginning of the sixties the urban guerrillas of Caracas, in contrast with their successors elsewhere in South America, assembled a powerful coalition including the Communist Party, the rebellious wing of Acción Democrática, students, and dissident sectors of the armed forces." Robert Moss, *La guerrilla urbana* (Madrid: Editorial Nacional, 1972), p. 212.
40. According to the British historian of the Montoneros, "In the following twelve months [from September 1974, soon after Perón died] the Montoneros would become the most powerful urban guerrilla force Latin America had ever known." Some estimates give them up to 7,000 well-trained men under arms at the height of their power. Richard Gillespie, *Soldiers of Perón: Argentina's Montoneros* (New York: Oxford University Press, 1982), p. 206.

zil's *abertura*, were common to the rest of the hemisphere's guerrilla movements:

> In their initial stage, guerrilla movements begin among the highly educated offspring of rural elites and the urban middle and upper classes. . . . In the subsequent stage of the movement, peasants come to dominate in numbers, while power remains in the hands of those with higher status and education.[41]

Of all those persons officially acknowledged to have died as a result of repression from 1964 to 1978—a sample more or less identifiable with the guerrilla movement—64 percent were so-called intellectual workers, of which half were students, and 33 percent were manual workers, of which 3 percent were trained technical personnel.[42] Already at this stage, the predominance of the educated, intellectualized middle class is obvious. In the larger universe of those "officially" tortured by the regime, intellectual workers represented 55 percent of the total, of which 12 percent were trained, technical manual workers: thus two-thirds of the tortured came from the same educated, urban middle class.[43] Students represented 25.9 percent of the total, and together with university professors made up 35.7 percent of those recognized as having been tortured during those years: more than a third thus being linked to the educational sector. In the larger universe of individuals "denounced to military authorities" or subject to prison terms for political activities, the ratios are similar: students and university professors made up 28 percent of the total, although intellectual and manual workers acquired almost equal weight: 45 percent and 44 percent, respectively.[44] These characteristics are largely applicable throughout Latin America during this period, with a few notable exceptions—Mexico, Peru in the early years, and Colombia in the 1950s—though not later. Herein lies one of the main differences separating the guerrilla movements of the sixties and early seventies from those of the second wave:

> The revolutionary organizations thus appeared not only as political elites, but as social elites. They were alternative elites, or counterelites, not mass-based movements.[45]

41. Timothy Wickham-Crowley, *Guerrillas and Revolution in Latin America* (Princeton, N.J.: Princeton University Press, 1992), p. 29.

42. Daniel Aarão Filho, *A Revolucão Falto ao Encontro: Os Comunistas no Brazil* (Rio de Janeiro: Editora Brasiliense, 1990), p. 153.

43. Ibid., p. 155.

44. Ibid., p. 157.

45. Ibid., p. 170.

Although the Tupamaros originally had a strong debate with the Cubans over the viability of an urban guerrilla movement, they encountered marked success for several years by acting almost exclusively in Montevideo. They also became the epitome of the armed Castroist groups. The single most important defining trait distinguishing them from the rest of the Uruguayan left would be precisely their recourse to armed struggle. In the words of one of their leaders at the time:

> We all proceeded from a mosaic of ideologies . . . but what united us positively was the will to create an apparatus for the armed struggle. . . . The armed struggle had to merge all other efforts; it had to become the main form of struggle.[46]

The Tupamaros were practically wiped out by the ferocious repression unleashed upon them—and on the entire Uruguayan left—by the *"golpe blanco,"* or civilian-led military coup of 1974. But for several years they seemed to represent the first successful guerrilla group to have surfaced in the hemisphere since Castro's triumph in 1959.[47] After the numerous defeats of the sixties, any organization that survived and remained active was noteworthy. This, undoubtedly, was what led the most informed observers of the continent's armed left, like Régis Debray, to declare the Tupamaros

> the only armed revolutionary movement in Latin America who knew how, or was able, to attack on all fronts (and not only at one point or one side) and to neutralize the bourgeois and anti-national dictatorship, questioning its very survival.[48]

The Chilean MIR, founded in 1967, probably came to be the most internationally appealing movement ("sexiest," some have said, in view of the attractive, charismatic nature of the young men and women from the "golden youth" of Santiago and Concepción who made up most of its leadership). It can also be considered an essentially urban movement, although it always contended that it included a peasant and urban marginal wing.

---

46. Entrevista con un Tupamaro, quoted in Maria Ester Gillio, *La Guerrilla Tupamara* (Buenos Aires: Ediciones de la Flor, 1970), pp. 185–186.
47. "For several years the most important and effective urban guerrilla organization in Latin America was the National Liberation Movement (MLN), the Tupamaros, in Uruguay." William E. Ratliff, *Castroism and Communism in Latin America, 1959–1976* (Washington, D.C.: American Enterprise Institute–Hoover Institution, 1976), p. 133.
48. Régis Debray, "Apprendre d'eux," in *Nous les Tupamaros* (Paris: François Maspéro, 1971), pp. 209–210.

The death of Che Guevara symbolized the end of an epoch, though it did not actually coincide with its conclusion.[49] As Debray puts it,

The physical disappearance of Che, brutal, precipitous, incredible, was like a cold shower for those living in the euphoria of this exceptional period. It is more than a symbol; his death represents a real shift in the struggle. In 1967 the rural guerrilla's curve turned downward, ineluctably, irreversibly.[50]

Guevara remains the icon of the armed Latin American left: its cross and its glory. He symbolizes an intellectualized middle class outraged by an intolerable estrangement from the society it lives in, and the abyss separating that class from the vast, undifferentiated universe of the poor. Che's travails in Africa evoke this gulf in its most extreme form: his wanderings across Tanzania and the Congo, leading a struggle of people "of another language in an unknown land" (as he wrote in his notes on the revolutionary war in the Congo) underline the absurdity of a white Argentine doctor trying to convince rebels in Kisoma to cross Lake Tanganyika for a meeting, something they were too terrified to do.[51]

But Guevara also represents the heroism and nobility of myriad middle-class Latin Americans who rose up in the best way they could find, against a status quo they eventually discovered to be unlivable. If ever there was an illustration of the anguish evoked in sensitive and reasonable, but far from exceptional, individuals at being affluent and comfortable islands in a sea of destitution, it was Guevara. He will endure as a symbol, not of revolution or guerrilla warfare, but of the extreme difficulty, if not the actual impossibility, of indifference.

One after another rural, and later urban, guerrilla movements were defeated. Some, emerging after Che's death, were destroyed by the mid-seventies, nearly ten years after his execution. Others, like the Tupamaros in Uruguay and the MIR in Chile, were just beginning to thrive when Che died, and passed from the scene much later, only to

---

49. Other students of this period establish a slightly different sequence, without altering the basic periodization: "The death of Guevara in Bolivia . . . is the first blow to 'foquismo,' though it also creates a heroic legend around the figure of the guerrilla fighter. Castro's support for the invasion of Czechoslovakia is the next blow: from then on it was clear that even in Cuba the only politics was *realpolitik*. But the decisive blow would be struck by the military coups in Chile and Uruguay and Argentina, where the groups that predicated or practiced the armed struggle were not only defeated but smashed in an indescribably ferocious fashion. Their defeat, and its cruelty, are accepted as the epitaph of the *foco*." Paramio, op. cit., p. 139.

50. Debray, *La Critique des Armes*, p. 245.

51. Tania Pajoni, "Che nel Africa" (Liberazione, Rome, August 21, 1992.)

reappear as civilian political organizations in the political thaw of the mid-eighties. The divisions between the Communists and the Castroists also outlived Che, although it became obvious with time that the infighting was partly to blame for many of these defeats:

> The division was deep and disastrous, because the *guerrilleros* needed the Communists—without them, where would they get their troops?— and the Communists needed the guerrillas—otherwise, how could they continue to be revolutionaries?[52]

Hopes for region-wide revolution faded. The Soviet Union demanded greater order and discipline as a condition for aid to Cuba, and, given its increasing reliance on Moscow, Havana was progressively forced to accommodate itself to Soviet wishes, both in economic policy and in international affairs. In reaction to this turn of events, it also began to develop relations with other Latin American governments.[53] Cuba established ties with the reformist Peruvian military regime in 1969, with Omar Torrijos in Panama around the same time, and later with new and more markedly social-democratic regimes in Venezuela and Jamaica, along with Barbados, Trinidad and Tobago, Argentina, and Colombia. The Cuban Revolution was mellowing; its support for revolution throughout the region was being subordinated to reasons of state:

> Cuba supported revolutionary movements in the Americas less often in the early 1970s than before because it bargained effectively to expand its state-to-state relations for the first time since 1960.[54]

It was high time. The view, sincere or disingenuous, of many American policymakers, that in the seventies and eighties Cuba dabbled more than ever in the export of revolution, arms, and ideology was largely false, at least as regards Latin America (although it was undeniably true in Africa).[55] Fidel Castro began supporting revolution

---

52. Gott, op. cit., p. 40.

53. "One crucial change that Havana made in its approach to international affairs was to become more ecumenical in defining its friends. Rather than relying on the strict criteria that in the past had tended to limit its political partners to like-minded radicals, Havana became more flexible. . . ." H. Michael Erisman, *Cuba's International Relations: The Anatomy of a Nationalistic Foreign Policy* (Boulder, Colo.: Westview Books, 1985), p. 33.

54. Domínguez, op. cit., p. 114.

55. For example two scholars state that "Latin American insurgents of the 1960s and 1970s had not yet developed a sense of unity and political organization, nor did they receive extensive support from external sources. . . . This third wave of insurgents . . . of the 1980s . . . (have heeded) the mistakes of the past . . . benefiting from strong coordination and support, especially internationally important support." Andrew Hoehn and Carlos Weiss, "Overview of Latin American Insurgencies," in Georges Fauriol, *Latin American Insurgencies* (Washington, D.C.: Georgetown University Center for Strategic and International Studies/National Defense University, 1985), pp. 10, 17.

abroad virtually weeks after he took power and never stopped. The difference between the early 1960s and the 1970s and 1980s in Latin America lay in the island's enhanced capability to provide such support in later years, and in the fact that on the receiving end, the capacity of Latin American insurgent groups to absorb aid was also far more developed. However, in relative terms, it is highly questionable that the Cubans delivered—or that their allies throughout Latin America obtained—more support in the seventies and eighties than during the first decade of the Revolution.

The process of rapprochement with the USSR was definitively inaugurated by Castro's famous speech in 1968, where despite all his twists and turns, the Cuban leader approved the Brezhnev invasion of Czechoslovakia: "We accept the bitter necessity that required sending those troops into Czechoslovakia."[56] It was accelerated by the Chilean experience, and by Castro's month-long sojourn in the southern nation. Salvador Allende's electoral victory in 1970 appeared to be a confirmation of the Communist parties' theses regarding "the peaceful road to socialism"; Castro's support for the Chilean experiment and thus for the CP could not but be perceived as a mellowing process.[57] Although Cuban sympathies perhaps lay equally with the Socialist Party and the MIR—and the training and arms MIR cadres received on the island as the Chilean drama unfolded were well known—Castro's "détente" with the Chilean Communists was undeniable.[58]

As the entire Southern Cone was submerged in the repressive bloodbath of national-security military dictatorships, starting with the Brazilian crackdown in 1968, including the Chilean coup in 1973, and extending to Uruguay in 1974 and the Argentine dirty war that started that same year with Perón's death, a double transformation was occurring within the ranks of the Cuban-inspired Latin American armed left. Something had to be done to solve the riddle in the aphorism that

---

56. Fidel Castro, "Discurso sobre Czechoslovakia," August 1968.

57. In one of his first speeches in Chile, Castro emphasized this point in his inimitable fashion: "There was never any contradiction between the conceptions of the Cuban Revolution and the roads followed . . . in Chile; we never questioned that path. . . . And we followed the events on Election Day with great interest, like you keeping track hour by hour of the tally and the predictions. But I must say that after a couple of hours I scribbled some calculations of my own and assured myself that we had won. And in our country this fact was received with great joy, it was received as a great popular victory." Fidel Castro, "En la reunión con la Directiva de la Central Unica de Trabajadores," Santiago, November 23, 1971, in Chile 1971: Habla Fidel Castro (Santiago: Editorial Universitaria Cormorán, 1971, pp. 18–21.

58. Andrés Pascal Allende, interview with the author, Mexico City, June 26, 1991.

so aptly described the fate of the Latin American revolution since Fidel's *barbudos* had come down from the Sierra Maestra in 1959. It was either *"las armas sin el pueblo"* ("weapons without the people") or *"el pueblo sin armas"* ("the people without weapons").

On the one hand, the old wounds between the Castroist guerrillas and the Communist bureaucracies began to heal. The Communists—encouraged by Moscow and now on good terms with Havana—increasingly acquiesced to Cuban leadership and the principle of the armed struggle.[59] For their part, the former "foquistas" and their advocates among the pro-Cuban political-military organizations accepted the need to work with the Communists as well as many of the latters' theoretical premises regarding the need for alliances, the nature of the coming revolution, and the character of *"el enemigo principal."* An initial convergence took place on the occasion of Leonid Brezhnev's first visit to Cuba, in 1974. The statement that emerged from this encounter included a reference to "party-to-party ties" that in the Communist liturgy could only be interpreted as a meeting of minds with regard to previous disagreements on the Latin American revolution.[60] But the true turning point was the meeting in Havana in June 1975 where the Communists, Cubans, and indirectly the political-military organizations associated with them finally made peace. Among the more striking formulations the Cubans accepted were resolutions stating, among other things, that:

> Without diminishing the struggle for democratic rights and the conquest of new structures within our countries, we Communists are willing to back and encourage the positions of those Latin American governments that imply the defense of our natural resources or the effort to set limits on multinational corporations. . . . There are sectors of the Latin American bourgeoisie that can adopt positions converging with the anti-imperialist struggle. . . . These bourgeois sectors can par-

59. The Communist parties that actually assimilated these changes proved more resilient to the passage of time than others. The best example is generally considered to be the Salvadorean Communist Party. With regard to the Castroist groups, its secretary general, Shafick Jorge Handal, in his own weighty jargon, has acknowledged that: "In many cases, some of these leftist organizations not only grew more rapidly than the respective Communist parties, but they matured before the Party, and led the workers and other classes to victory and transformed themselves into the Marxist-Leninist party leading the march to socialism." Quoted by Harnecker, op. cit., p. 94.

60. The joint communiqué stated that: "The most solid base for the unbreakable friendship between Cuba and the Soviet Union is the fraternal collaboration between the Communist Party of Cuba and the Communist Party of the Soviet Union, two Marxist-Leninist revolutionary parties. . . ." Quoted in *La política exterior de la Cuba socialista* (Moscow: Editorial Progreso, 1980), pp. 10–11.

ticipate in different forms of democratic and anti-imperialist unity with the popular forces.[61]

The governments actually mentioned in this connection were the Peruvian military regime headed by Juan Velasco Alvarado, Torrijos in Panama, and the military junta that took over in Ecuador in 1972.[62] The fact was that many Latin American governments had attained greater elbow room in their dealings with the United States, and were also tilting to the left, at least in international affairs. As they were able to defy Washington on Cuba, Cuba was able to break out of its regional isolation. This in turn diluted its interest in supporting revolutionary armed struggle, which made a rapprochement with the Communist parties possible. Soviet encouragement—and leverage—did not hurt, either.

For the Cubans, peace with other Latin American countries capped a major change in their policy toward revolution. The setbacks they suffered were real, as was the growing influence of the Soviet Union: the Cuban Revolution had grown tired; it would get its second wind years later, in Central America. The deal it cut with the Communist parties was advantageous for both sides. But in order to get what they wanted— i.e., the Communists' recognition of the validity of the armed struggle, and the beginning of their reconciliation with the Castroist organizations—the Cubans had to put their own revisions on paper. The Communists were obliged to make their concessions explicit too.[63]

The trade-off between the Cubans and the Communists could not have been more manifest.[64] Havana would henceforth desist from sup-

---

61. "La América Latina en la lucha contra el imperialismo, por la independencia nacional, la democracia, el bienestar popular, la paz y el socialismo," Encuentro de Partidos Comunistas de América Latina, La Habana, Junio 13, 1975, published in Boletín de información. Documentos de los Partidos Comunistas y Obreros. Artículos e intervenciones, 12/75, Editorial Paz y socialismo, Prague, December 1972, pp. 40, 43.

62. Ibid., p. 29.

63. "It is the right and the duty of all the popular and revolutionary forces to be ready to respond to counter-revolutionary violence with revolutionary violence, and to clear the road, through different forms of popular action, including the armed struggle, for the sovereign decision of the majority. . . . Outside our parties, there exists today a left with different nuances. . . . The Communist parties will take into account the fact that some of those movements are opposed to imperialist oppression and are advancing toward socialist positions." Ibid., pp. 49–50.

64. A distinguished student of Cuban foreign policy summed up the trade-off between the Cubans and the Communists the following way: "Cuba thus compromised on several points about the proper path to power for the sake of receiving the allegiance of the Communist parties. This was a necessary precondition for the unified Communist support that was given to Central American revolutionary movements in the years that followed. Cuba's newly recognized vanguard role helped it lead some of these cautious Communist parties toward the path of armed struggle in late 1977." Jorge I. Domínguez, op. cit., p. 126.

porting revolution in Latin America, unless and until multiple conditions were met: good chances of success, Soviet acquiescence, and unity among revolutionary groups. The foco era and its sequels had come to an end.

How much did Cuban intervention matter? For years conservatives, some in Latin America but mainly in the United States, reduced every revolutionary movement, whisper, or suspicion in the region to Cuban inspiration. The left, for its part, ranging from U.S. liberals to Latin American Marxist-Leninists, dismissed the idea of Cuban involvement, emphasizing always the home-grown roots of revolt and anger in a continent whose history amply justified both.

The left was correct in that the Cuban catalyst was no more than that: a factor contributing to the maturation and efflorescence of other, deeper processes already in motion. There had been revolutions, insurgencies, and subversion, Marxist- and Soviet-inspired or not, in Latin America long before the Cuban experience. There would continue to be such many years after its passing. But the right also had reasons for sticking to its guns, so to speak. Where conditions were ripe for insurgency, the absence of any overt Cuban connection did not necessarily imply the nonexistence of a Cuban factor, and where nothing else seemed to explain the outbreak of armed struggle and the emergence of guerrillas in town and country, the hypothesis of Cuban incitement was often a sound one. And finally, where a mysterious peace, perhaps sporadically punctuated by millenarist or peasant uprisings contrasted with the upheavals described in the preceding pages, the assumption of Cuban inaction enhanced its comprehension. Perhaps the best illustration of the impact of Cuban backing for revolution may well be provided by the dog that didn't bark: what happened when the Cubans truly stayed out of the way, as in Mexico.

Although the Mexican guerrilla movement never got off the ground, it acquired many of the features the Cubans would have wished guerrillas to possess throughout Latin America. The saga of the guerrillas of the late sixties and early seventies was long cloaked in silence— and then, as frequently occurs in Mexico, it inspired a rash of books, novels, articles, and essays nearly twenty years after the fact. Much remains to be revealed about those years, but several important aspects of this episode of Mexican history have been brought to light.

The postmortem assessment is not uniform, particularly with regard to one point: whether the armed movement included, like its counterparts in the hemisphere, a middle-class, counterelite, student component, or whether it was above all—and exceptionally—a truly peasant movement. In a novel that contributed significantly to renewing the debate in Mexico over those troubled years, Héctor Aguilar Camín sought to portray the guerrilla movement of the seventies as at least partly urban, middle-class, and student-based.[65] This it was: the 23rd of September League and the other small groups that carried out kidnappings, assassinations, and bank robberies during the turbulent times of President Luis Echeverría were chiefly composed of radicalized university graduates frustrated by the bloody defeat of the 1968 student movement and the unresponsiveness of an authoritarian political system.

Other writers have also stressed this point. Simply through the identities of the mothers of the disappeared and the way in which many of the guerrilla leaders who survived were reintegrated into society and peaceful political activity, it is clear that a significant number of middle-class youth helped fill the ranks of the urban armed movement in Mexico. They came from Monterrey and later from Sinaloa, from Guadalajara and the National Polytechnic Institute in Mexico City. And yet, while students joined the armed struggle, they did so only in the cities, not in the countryside, where another struggle was gathering steam. And they did so, in any case on a small scale, quite unlike—in relative terms—what occurred in Uruguay, Venezuela, Argentina, and perhaps even Brazil. No effective convergence of students and rural guerrillas ever took place. There were some attempts; all failed.

Two other features of the Mexican guerrilla wars, however, overshadowed this failure, so common to the entire hemisphere. First, there was a legacy of armed *peasant* uprisings in *rural* Central-Southern Mexico: in Morelos, from the days of Emiliano Zapata to the movement led by Rubén Jaramillo in the 1950s until his murder by the Mexican Army; and in Guerrero, where schoolteachers had kept alive a tradition of armed confrontation for the land. This became the real constituency for the rural guerrillas of the late sixties and early seventies: for Genaro Vázquez's ACNR in the Chilpancingo region, and for Lucio Cabañas's Party of the Poor in the Atoyac area. In another novel, less well written but perhaps more substantive and focused on the guerrilla movement than Aguilar Camín's, another Mexican author presents the fictional but strikingly realistic reflec-

---

65. Héctor Aguilar Camín, *La guerra de Galio* (Mexico City: Cal y Arena Editores, 1990), mainly parts 3 and 4.

tions of a high-ranking army officer on the subject of the armed movement:

> The main point is the concerted support of the villages in the sierra. We are not dealing with a fistful of men in arms going from one place to another independently and isolated, like other terrorist groups. This is a guerrilla movement that the people of the region support, maintain and hide. Our war is thus a war against everything and everyone that supports those armed men. The enemy is in the villages, not just in the fistful of men. . . . It may well be that we are combating a struggle of the Mexican people, not suppressing an uprising against the people. This century the entire region followed Zapata. Zapatismo never built a regular army; it was a guerrilla army, like Lucio Cabañas's.[66]

The movement Cabañas led was weak, localized, doomed to defeat, and largely devoid of any urban alliance or program. But it had one key attribute that most other Latin American armed focos direly lacked: a true peasant base or constituency, however territorially isolated it may have been.[67]

Cabañas and Genaro Vázquez were both rural schoolteachers, a product of the mass education drive in the countryside that was begun in the 1930s but foundered quickly as the Revolution of 1910 ran out of steam. Like tens of thousands of their colleagues, they were close to the communities where they lived and taught, and highly sensitive to the destitution and the aspirations of the peasantry, as well as to the permanent threat of violence by the authorities. Indeed, armed peasant movements in these areas arose largely out of the need for self-defense. In marginal, isolated communities like these, armed defense was usually the only safeguard against police and army brutality. This was the strength and weakness of the Guerrero movement.

In a nation of great, sprawling urban conglomerations like Mex-

---

66. Carlos Montemayor, *Guerra en el paraíso* (Mexico City: Editorial Diana, 1991), pp. 349–351.

67. "By late 1973, in a relatively small zone, the Party of the Poor had consolidated its hold. It never had territorial power, with a fully liberated zone. [But] the solidity attained by political-military organization and its consolidation among the rural population allowed it to solve the problem of traditional territorial control . . . The army had to concentrate many thousands of men to fight the guerrillas. By early 1971 it already had 24,000 men in the State of Guerrero. The movement . . . had no recruitment problems and had difficulty in absorbing the many peasants who wanted to join." Marco Bellingeri, *Del agrarismo armado a la revolución de los pobres. Ensayos de guerrilla rural en México contemporáneo* (University of Turin, Mimeo, 1991), pp. 100–101.

ico, no localized rural guerrilla movement had any chance of success, but the bonds that united the schoolteachers and the peasantry of Guerrero were undeniable. Had Cabañas and Vázquez received outside help, to break their isolation and increase their meager resources, and had the urban middle-class student movement been more developed and committed, history might have taken a different turn. The guerrillas could not have won, but they could have made contact with the students and forced the government to negotiate and accept a democratic politics or unleash the repression elsewhere that fell upon Guerrero.

History did not take a different turn partly because of the second key characteristic of the Mexican guerrilla wars, in contrast to the rest of Latin America. The Party of the Poor and the ACNR, not to mention the urban groups such as the 23rd of September League, never received a drop of aid from Cuba: no money, no training, nor arms. Cuba's policy toward the armed struggle in Mexico was similar to the one it would follow in relation to the legal Mexican left during the late seventies and early eighties, and toward the Cárdenas movement in the late eighties and early nineties: hands off. The game was well worth the candle for the Cubans: in exchange for their nonintervention in Mexican affairs, they were able to count on the maintenance of diplomatic relations during the worst years of their hemispheric quarantine, and on quite cordial ties later on. They gave up very little, obtaining much in return. This did not deter Havana from helping or inciting Central American guerrillas to operate in Mexico for different purposes, or to recruit Mexican leftists for "Central American" chores. But in the entire literature on Cuban involvement in the Latin American armed struggle, there is no evidence or claim that the Cubans ever supported guerrillas in Mexico.

This reluctance meant more than lack of arms or money for the peasants in Guerrero and the students in Monterrey and Sinaloa. It resulted in scant or no international resonance for their cause. If the Cubans didn't take them seriously—and the Cubans took everybody who was anybody seriously—then no one would. Only the North Koreans were ever known to have trained Mexican guerrillas: not exactly an international outpouring of mainstream support.

Conditions were ripe in Mexico for the emergence of a significant armed movement. There were angry students and peasants, a repressive government, and the beginnings of an economic downturn. Tradition, a culture of violence, and lack of alternatives seemed a perfect recipe for armed strife. Some have speculated that most students did not take up arms precisely because there had been a student movement: they were vaccinated.[68]

Cuba did not make revolution happen in Latin America. Where it tried to force things, it failed miserably. Similarly, where favorable circumstances prevailed, but Cuba was not around to help, little occurred. However, where a propitious environment and Cuban support coincided, revolution triumphed or made quite a go of it, as the next chapter will attempt to show.

---

68. "In the months following the end of the movement, thousands of us began searching for a road, inside the University and out. The worst of the wounded joined an urban guerrilla movement that bled to death for the next five years, in dirty war with no quarter. Most of the young went to the barrios, founding the neighborhood associations that for the next twenty years offered a hope of popular resistance." Paco Ignacio Taibo II, *68* (Mexico City: Ed. Joaquín Mortiz/Planeta, 1991), p. 113.

4

The Second Coming

■

One of the spin-offs from the mellowing of the Cuban Revolution was the emergence of new organizations from the ruins of those buried or defeated. Furthermore, the so-called "center of gravity" of the revolution in Latin America began to shift north. A "second wave" of guerrilla movements developed.[1] From the Southern Cone it moved to Central America and the Caribbean, and in particular to three small countries in the isthmus—Nicaragua, El Salvador, and Guatemala, and two small islands in the Caribbean—Jamaica and Grenada. The new policy of uniting forces within the "ranks of revolution" (between the Communist parties and what was left of the armed groups) and with domestic "democratic and national forces" (the middle classes, the Church, part of the business community) and finally, abroad, with the emerging Latin American social democrats, began to pay off.

In Central America the new political-military organizations gradually acquired the broad constituency their forerunners of the sixties had never achieved. Two new groups were established in Guatemala, launched from Mexico by distinguished participants in the battles of the past. The first was the Ejército Guerrillero de los Pobres (EGP), founded and led by Rolando Morán (alias Ricardo Ramírez) in Chiapas, Mexico, and the Ixcán region of Guatemala in 1973; the second-in-

---

1. This term is used extensively, and defined with precision in Timothy Wickham-Crowley, *Guerrillas and Revolution in Latin America* (Princeton, N.J.: Princeton University Press, 1992), pp. 209–230.

command of that expedition, and of the organization for many years, was Mario Payeras.

Luis Cardoza y Aragón was until his death in 1992 perhaps Latin America's foremost art critic. From the time he was forced to leave his native Guatemala for exile in Mexico in 1954, he served as mentor, foster parent, and source of consolation to two generations of Guatemalan dissidents and revolutionaries. One day in 1975, a left-wing militant came to visit. Cardoza's home in the Atrio de San Francisco in Coyoacán was somewhat different from others: the old colonial walls were covered with Picassos (including a portrait of Cardoza), Méridas, Mirós, and Diego Riveras and Orozcos, the creators of which had all been his friends. The visitor wanted advice about what he should be in life—a writer or a revolutionary. Cardoza, who knew a great deal about both fields of endeavor, as well as about his visitor's talent for and devotion to both, answered that, in the end, Mario Payeras should be both, if he could.[2] So it would be.

Mario Payeras, also known as Benedicto, is a captivating figure: his literary talent, military experience, and great gift for objective and incisive analysis of political events in his own Guatemala and Latin America in general make him stand out among his peers. Strikingly good-looking, with bright-blue eyes, a dark, not quite Indian face and graying hair, Payeras has been an important presence within the Latin American left for decades. Together with Rolando Morán, he headed a small group of Guatemalan revolutionaries who, after years of dabbling in guerrilla activities, participating in lengthy debates over the role of indigenous peoples in the Revolution, and trying to lure sectors of the local military into revolutionary politics, finally struck out on their own. They entered the Ixcán jungle of the Quiché from across the border in Chiapas, Mexico. In addition to the walking and fighting, Payeras wrote a fictionalized description of life in the jungle and the first weeks of guerrilla warfare. *Días de la selva* (*Days of the Jungle*), which won the Havana-based Casa de las Américas prize, remains one of the most impressive literary creations to emerge from the Latin American left.[3]

Payeras remained active in the EGP through the mid-eighties, surviving the internal splits and frustrations arising from the brutal defeat the Guatemalan guerrillas suffered at the hands of General Efraín Ríos Montt in 1982–83. Entire towns were destroyed or their populations

---

2. Luis Cardoza y Aragón, interview with the author, Mexico City, March 25, 1991.
3. Mario Payeras, *Days of the Jungle* (New York: Monthly Review Press, 1985).

forced into exile in Mexico, and the guerrilla forces, which numbered several thousand in 1981, were decimated, and forced to bury arms and ammunition for want of fighters to bear them. Payeras's description of the guerrillas' setbacks in the country's capital were painfully narrated in *El trueno en la ciudad*, earning him few friends among his colleagues or among the Israeli military, whom he directly blamed for the new counterinsurgency and interrogation tactics used—successfully—by the *kaibiles*, or Guatemalan Rangers.[4]

By 1985 his differences with Rolando Morán and other EGP leaders had become unmanageable, and he was expelled from the organization. He was in Mexico at the time, and Morán invited him to travel clandestinely to his jungle headquarters in the Quiché highlands to try and work out their disagreements. Rightly or wrongly, Payeras was convinced that the invitation was a trap, similar to those often set by other clandestine, militarized political organizations for dissident cadres. Whether he had become unjustifiably paranoid and cautious, or because too many years in the clandestine business had taught him that one is always at the mercy of the *aparato* that picks one up and leads one through the jungle, the army, and the borders, Payeras rejected Rolando Morán's invitation.

He subsequently broke with the organization and has spent his time since building a new one, exercising his talents as one of the best writers to emerge from the ranks of the Latin American revolutionary left, and becoming a path-breaking defender of the Guatemalan environment and jungle, which he knows better than most. His children's stories, published in Mexico in 1988, are a striking encounter of Indian folklore and children's fairy tales, reflecting the secular despair of the peoples of Guatemala.

Morán and Payeras's Ejército Guerrillero de los Pobres represented a break with the guerrilla organizations of the sixties in many ways.[5] The first and most important, perhaps, was the strong emphasis on the Indian factor in Guatemalan politics and society, and on bonding itself with the social struggles of the peasantry. In the words of its founder:

> One of our main differences with the past was something that would
> have unsuspected historical importance in the future, the indispensable
> relationship established by the EGP with the indigenous peoples of

---

4. Both failures, though more specifically the urban setbacks suffered by the EGP, are described in Mario Payeras, *El trueno en la ciudad* (Mexico City: Juan Pablos Editor, 1987), pp. 9–14 and throughout the book.

5. The differences in the sociological makeup of these groups are also important: "Claims that 'leadership arises directly out of the local peasant population' . . . probably apply to EGP and ORPA in Guatemala." Wickham-Crowley, op. cit., p. 214.

Guatemala from the outset. The EGP asserts for the first time that the revolution in Guatemala must have two facets: the class struggle and the ethnic-national struggle. It postulates that the two aspects are unseparately bound, that one cannot triumph without the other.[6]

This strategy, along with the emphasis on social movements and a secure rear guard in Mexico, allowed the EGP to quickly establish itself in the jungles of Ixcán and Huehuetenango, where it remains, though weakened, nearly twenty years after.[7] It also distinguished itself from the *foquista* legacy by refraining from public activities until it thought it was militarily capable of resisting the Army;[8] this contributed to its penchant for secrecy and introspection, which would hurt it greatly years later. In the late seventies and early eighties it became a political and military force to be reckoned with, controlling both a significant military apparatus and a large peasant and Indian following in the highlands. The fact that it organized its peasant following in the Central Unificada Campesina (CUC) was undoubtedly the most important contributing factor to its survival; a CUC leader and symbol, Rigoberta Menchú, would win the Nobel Peace Prize in 1992. But the link with mass organizations would also provoke serious divisions within its ranks, as many in the EGP came to believe that the Morán leadership had irresponsibly sent thousands of Indians to their deaths by unleashing an offensive in 1980–81 which it had no military capability to sustain in the face of Army repression. The EGP also tried unsuccessfully to establish itself in the capital. It survived its virtual eradication at the beginning of the 1980s, but just barely.

The other group, the Organización Revolucionaria del Pueblo Armado (ORPA), created in Mexico in 1972 by Rodrigo Asturias, the son of Guatemalan Nobel laureate and ambassador Miguel Angel Asturias, took hold further south and west in the regions of San Marcos and Sololá. It too stressed the importance of the Guatemalan indigenous

---

6. Rolando Morán, interview with the author, Mexico City, December 21, 1991.

7. Cesar Cereseres writes that "The leadership of the EGP began the highland-based insurgency with a revolutionary strategy distinct from that of the 1960s. . . . The second-generation guerrillas rejected the *foquista*-insurrectionist (*foco*) strategy of revolutionary warfare." According to Cereseres, the differences between the first wave and the second were threefold: "Reject *foquismo* and plan for a *guerra prolongada*. . . . Involve the Indian population; pursue a second, equally important front in the international community." Cesar Cereseres, "The Highlands War in Guatemala," in Georges Fauriol, *Latin American Insurgencies* (Washington, D.C.: Georgetown University Center for Strategic and International Studies/National Defense University, 1985), p. 110.

8. "It was a mark of the EGP's rejection of *foquismo* that it did not undertake any offensive operations for a further three years and held off from frequent combat until 1978, six years after its founding." James Dunkerley, *Power in the Isthmus* (New York: Verso Books, 1988), p. 456.

peoples. It tried to develop "a strategy of making broad alliances with progressive middle-class intellectuals and professionals."[9] From the outset, ORPA, along with the Colombian M-19, was perhaps the least ideological, the most pragmatic, and the most "un-Marxist" of Latin American political military organizations:

> It is possible that ORPA's more expansive platform reflected lessons drawn from the experience of the Nicaraguan FSLN in 1978–79 when the organization was preparing to launch its campaign. ORPA possessed some of the political pragmatism of the *Terceristas*, that lacked the depth of popular organization required by the strategy of prolonged popular war, and generally resisted the lure of insurrectionism.[10]

Later, as the socialist world disintegrated and revolution became anachronistic even among revolutionaries, many such groups would publicly renounce their previously flaunted Marxist faith; but ORPA, owing to its leadership and "indigenist" leanings, was one of the few whose Marxist convictions were weakly anchored from the outset.

The old Fuerzas Armadas Revolucionarias (FAR), left over from the early sixties movement in Guatemala, also reemerged from the defeats of the previous decade with an explicit notion of what had gone wrong before and what to do about it. Pablo Monsanto, who began his guerrilla career in 1960 and is still the leader of the FAR, phrased the break with the past the following way:

> When the guerrilla movement was defeated in the sixties, we began to think that guerrilla warfare was not an organizational form that could mobilize the masses, but that we needed a political organization. . . .[11]

Together with a faction of the old Communist Party (whose official name remained the Partido Guatemalteco del Trabajo), the four groups joined to form the Unidad Revolucionaria Nacional de Guatemala (URNG) in January of 1982. They were able to develop an armed capability and a mass base that in the early 1980s posed a serious threat to the military government's existence.[12]

The violence of the repression and the magnitude of the virtual genocide committed in the Guatemalan highlands is the best indica-

---

9. Suzanne Jonas, *The Battle for Guatemala: Rebels, Death Squads, and U.S. Power* (Boulder, Colo.: Westview Press, 1991), p. 138.

10. Dunkerley, op. cit., p. 483.

11. Pablo Monsanto, interview with Marta Harnecker, in Marta Harnecker, *Pueblos en armas* (Mexico City: Universidad Autónoma de Guerrero, 1983), p. 29.

12. "The movement was remarkable in having transformed itself from a *foco* into a force with broad popular support nationally, incorporating the indigenous population in massive numbers as members and middle-level leadership. . . ." Jonas, op. cit., p. 139.

tion of how much of a danger the guerrillas represented. It was also the confirmation of a basic fact of guerrilla warfare life: if there are no domestic, political, or international constraints on a sitting government's capability to wage war against an armed revolutionary group, it is almost impossible for the latter to withstand a major, unfettered, well-planned, and well-supplied onslaught.[13] EGP leader Morán, while refusing to acknowledge any major mistakes by the guerrilla organizations, perceived the underlying problem years later:

> The year 1981 catches us divided, and without the operational, political and military progress we needed. That is when in Guatemala, without any restraints and in all its strength, the doctrine of national security is applied. This is the time of the great massacres in Guatemala, that occurred without any international support for the victims, without any limits or obstacles for them to take place. The military simply realized that they had to direct their blows against the base, against the people, rather than against the revolutionary organizations themselves.[14]

The Guatemalan insurgents were unable to resist the scorched-earth policies implemented in 1982 and 1983 by General Efraín Ríos Montt, that drove entire peasant Indian villages into exile in Mexico and the United States, and left tens of thousands others dead in Guatemala. The guerrillas did not expect the Army's offensive and were totally unequipped to deal with it.[15] Despite that defeat, the political-military organizations built during the seventies survived. Regardless of their marginal military presence today, they continue to be a fundamental political actor in Guatemala. The issue of how to bring an end to the war against them and to the continued plague of human

---

13. Another factor in this equation is the absence of outside support: the Guatemalan guerrillas of the seventies and eighties received very little backing, if any at all, from the Cubans. They certainly received nothing compared to what the Nicaraguans, Salvadoreans, and Colombians obtained. The explanation given by the Cubans, despite its bureaucratic doublespeak, is clear: "The main difference was a different military prowess and yield. There was also a politically different presence of the FMLN in El Salvador from that of the UNRG in Guatemala. Of course, one could turn this around and say that the UNRG did not have a military yield as high as in El Salvador because we didn't give them as much support, but one shouldn't overestimate the role of our support in Nicaragua, for example. . . ." A senior official of the Cuban Communist Party with responsibilities in the area of foreign policy, interview with the author, Havana, November 6, 1991. The individual agreed to be interviewed on the condition that he be identified only as indicated.

14. Morán, op. cit.

15. "At the moment of the decisive army counter-offensive . . . the several hundred thousand highlands Indians who supported and even participated in (the guerrillas') efforts were left unprepared, unarmed and unprotected, with disastrous consequences." Jonas, op. cit., p. 140.

rights abuses remains the central short- and medium-term question facing that nation.

•

The break with the past began earlier in El Salvador, and differently. The 1968 split within the Communist Party gave birth to new groups that rapidly acquired a significant constituency. In 1969, Salvador Cayetano Carpio, the leader of the Salvadorean Communist Party, broke with the party and founded a political-military organization in whose ranks he would eventually die, the Fuerzas Populares de Liberación (FPL). Carpio, a bakery worker, had joined the Party in 1948. He quickly rose through the ranks, becoming the Party's secretary-general by the mid-sixties. His was the only schism in a Communist Party from the top: others had involved expulsions, splits from below, individual resignations or the dragging of the entire leadership along with them.

Carpio abandoned the party of his youth to channel what he perceived as a growing inclination of many young people in El Salvador to take up arms. He "was worried that a large part of our country's younger generation would join the armed struggle, and that the Party was going to be seen as an enemy."[16] His break with the Communist bureaucracy was the first "post-Che" rupture, or, more exactly, the first instance in which a split took place over the armed struggle after the defeats of the focos in the 1960s and the assimilation of those setbacks' lessons. Carpio was quite explicit about the differences between what he wanted to do and what his predecessors elsewhere had done:

> The new organization had to lead two struggles simultaneously: the mass struggle and the armed struggle. . . . The people had to be the direct authors of the armed struggle. . . . We understood that the people had to be the ones to make war and that the armed groups should not become an elite, a bunch of heroes unlinked to the masses, who were going to save the masses the trouble of making the revolution.[17]

By refusing to destroy his political alma mater, Carpio set the stage for his own death fifteen years later, and for the possibility of lasting unity among Salvadorean revolutionary groups, including the Communist Party.[18]

---

16. Salvador Cayetano Carpio, interview with Marta Harnecker, in Harnecker, op. cit., p. 144.
17. Ibid., p. 146.
18. "We did not want to create more sources of conflict with the party leadership, which was already highly upset over what we had done." Ibid., p. 147.

Through the 1970s, new organizations with a political-military disposition—the Ejército Revolucionario del Pueblo (ERP), the Fuerzas Armadas de la Resistencia Nacional (FARN), the Partido Revolucionario de Trabajadores Centroamericanos (PRTC)—would sprout up in the tiny nation, transforming the Salvadorean left into an alphabet soup of groups and subgroups, all of them with some sort of mass following.[19] A number of groups would eventually create an armed wing: the union- and Catholic-based Resistencia Nacional (led by Ernesto Jovel and Fermán Cienfuegos), the Ligas Populares 28 de Febrero (a group that in fact belonged to the ERP and was named after the date of a massacre in 1977), and even the Communist Party (now commanded by Shafick Jorge Handal). The continental quid pro quo was dutifully applied: the non-Communist groups accepted unity and alliances with whoever would have them, while the Communists accepted and participated in armed combat.[20]

These organizations did not actually achieve a serious military capability until 1980, when huge shipments of arms from abroad allowed them to retreat from the cities, where they had been violently repressed by the Army and the security forces, to the mountains.[21] This is where Cuba came in. When in late 1979 and mainly early 1980 the Salvadorean Army unleashed a no-holds-barred offensive against the mass movement in the country's cities, the organizations that had just formed the FMLN were faced with a choice: be decimated in the urban areas, or take to the mountains and prepare for armed resistance from the countryside. But that required guns, a lot of them, and quickly. In the course of 1980 and through 1982 several thousand, perhaps upward of 10,000 weapons with ammunition were brought into El Salvador. So much arrived that some fighters had two arms each, though they didn't necessarily know how to use even one. The revolutionary groups were already convinced that they could triumph only through armed con-

---

19. For an early map of the myriad groups and subgroups, see Tommy Sue Montgomery, *Revolution in El Salvador* (Boulder, Colo.: Westview, 1982), p. 124, and in general, pp. 119–140.

20. "Our decision to join the armed struggle was somewhat delayed, but it was on time. . . . We are convinced that the armed struggle is the only path to finding a real solution to the national crisis. . . . it is not a last minute, improvised act. . . ." Schafik Jorge Handal, interview with Mario Menéndez, in Mario Menéndez, *El Salvador: Pueblo contra oligarquía* (Culiacán: Universidad Autónoma de Sinaloa, 1981), p. 118.

21. The information supporting this analysis comes both from published American sources of the early 1980s and from a State Department white paper, which, while false in its major thrust—the Salvadorean insurgency existed only thanks to Cuban aid—and in much of its detail, had the gist of matters right, and from Salvadorean sources who wish to remain anonymous but whose reliability and knowledge of these operations is unquestionable.

flict; the Army's behavior confirmed their predisposition and left them no choice.

The first country that donated weapons was Ethiopia, after a visit by Shafick Jorge Handal in early 1980. The arms were shipped through Czechoslovakia, or directly from Addis Ababa, to Cuba. Several methods were used to smuggle in the weapons. Nicaraguan fishing ships would cross the Gulf of Fonseca, with up to 300 automatic rifles, or tens of boxes of ordnance. The boats off-loaded on the western coast of the Gulf, changing landfalls each time. Military maneuvers were implemented to cover the unloading; the weapons were then hidden in deposits nearby, though some were taken to strategic areas close to where FMLN forces were concentrated. Large-scale urban operations were often carried out to distract the Army away from the coasts precisely at the time when the arms arrived. Planes were used much less, and only at times of great need: they were vulnerable and incriminating. The most frequent passage was by land: the coastal routes were used later mainly to bring in and take out the FMLN's leadership.

The largest number of weapons came from Vietnam, abandoned by the United States in 1975. These were the best guns, because the Salvadorean Army also used M-16s and thus it was easier to obtain ammunition for them. Over the years, the amount of arms that entered the country was higher than the capacity to absorb them. Cuba was instrumental in organizing the operation: without Cuban logistical capability and approval, the other governments would not have provided the weapons, nor would a majority of them have arrived safely in the hills of Chalatenango and Morazán. Conversely, all the Cuban expertise and guns would have been useless if there were not several thousand guerrilla fighters willing and able to use them. Without Cuba and Nicaragua, it is doubtful that the mass movement of the cities could have been transformed into an army; without the movement, though, there would have been no one to arm.

As Joaquín Villalobos has acknowledged: "We had nothing then, we were a social movement that was unarmed, all our military personnel were a few guerrillas."[22] To a considerable extent, they became political-*military* organizations, or guerrilla movements, only after the failed January 1981 "final offensive." But during their entire formative years they flaunted their guerrilla vocation, while at the same time developing what many would later qualify as the most important mass movement in Latin America since the Popular Unity in Chile. Day

22. Joaquín Villalobos, interview with the author, Mexico City, September 5, 1991.

after day throughout the seventies, before elections or after, during strikes or protests over price increases, the Salvadorean extreme left finally put into practice what many Communist parties and Cuban-sponsored groups had recommended but never attained. They were able to combine the armed struggle with the peaceful one, the fight in the country with that in the city, spectacular armed acts with broad-based mass action. In a sense, and with the exception of the Sandinistas in Nicaragua, the Salvadorean political-military organizations achieved the highest degree of success in implementing the policy laid out after the defeats of the previous decade: the unity of "Cubans" and Communists, alliances with other forces, particularly the Church, and a combination of the armed struggle with traditional forms of mobilization.

The links with large sectors of the Church were perhaps the most notable feature in El Salvador.[23] From the outset, several groups that would later join in the FMLN forged close ties with the Jesuits of the Universidad Centroamericana. Many outstanding cadres or former militants, whether intellectuals like Salvador Samayoa and Luis de Sebastián or military leaders like the Nicaraguan Antonio Cardenal, had established connections with the Society of Jesus, ranging from simple friendship to full membership in the order. Another case was that of Father Rutilio Grande, whose death in 1977 awakened the long-conservative Archbishop Oscar Arnulfo Romero to his new radical vocation. Grande was murdered in Aguilares in 1977 after helping to merge the Federación de Campesinos Cristianos Salvadoreños and the Unión de Trabajadores del Campo into FECCAS–UTC.

It was no minor coincidence that where the Church, and specifically the Jesuits, became most involved with the left and politics in Latin America was also where it suffered the greatest casualties. The left in El Salvador, and its supporters elsewhere, including in the United States, have been understandably cautious in acknowledging the degree to which religious figures like Rutilio Grande, Romero, and Ignacio Ellacuría (the Jesuit rector of the UCA, murdered by the Army,

---

23. "This relationship was clearly established early on by students of all persuasions of the Salvadorean left: 'Christian base communities,' small Bible-study groups disseminating liberation theology's message of Christ's 'preferential option for the poor,' were formed in many parishes which later were to serve as rearguard zones for the guerrillas. The guerrilla-led mass 'popular' organizations formed in reaction to the electoral frauds of the early 1970s drew many of their activists and leaders from these Christian communities." Robert S. Leiken, "The Salvadorean Left," in Robert S. Leiken, *Central America: Anatomy of a Conflict* (New York: Pergamon Press/Carnegie Endowment for International Peace, 1984), p. 115.

along with five of his colleagues, in 1989) were engaged in the left's struggle.[24] The links varied over time, ranging from the role played by Rutilio Grande in the parish of Aguilares[25] to Archbishop Romero's gradual transformation from pastor to revolutionary.[26] They reached as far as the long-term effects of the Jesuits having trained a generation of Salvadorean intellectuals and bestowing respectability on many of the rebels' initiatives.[27]

For the deeply religious people of El Salvador—one of the few countries of the hemisphere where believers congregate in the streets and plazas outside the church—the political conversion of the parish

24. All the caution in the world cannot destroy the Salvadorean left's roots in the Church, and its support from the base communities and the Jesuit order. Needless to say, the right everywhere has emphasized this link, as if it excused the massacre of Church workers in Central America. Entire books have been written about this issue, as summarized in one of the more strident examples: "It was above all in Latin America that the strange alliance between Jesuits and Marxists gathered its first political momentum. It was there that this new Jesuit mission (began). . . . Quickly scores of Jesuits began to work with a passion and zeal that has always been so typical of them, for the success of the Sandinocommunists in Nicaragua; and when the Sandinistas took power, those same Jesuits entered crucial posts in the central government. In other Central American countries, meanwhile, Jesuits not only participated in guerrilla training of Marxist cadres, but became guerrilla fighters themselves." Malachi Martin, The Jesuits: The Society of Jesus and the Betrayal of the Roman Catholic Church (New York: Simon and Schuster, 1987), p. 17. In fact, the Jesuits' involvement in Nicaragua was less important than their participation in El Salvador.

25. "FECCAS was born inside the Church, and the latter gave it economic and social support. . . . As the repression increased, FECCAS sought and found support and cover in the Church, allowing it to survive and continue its consolidation. The birth of FECCAS within the Church was not arbitrary or accidental; given the conditions in the country, it could not have been otherwise. The attraction between the two was structural. . . . It was ideologically rooted, but could not be reduced to the historical fact of having been born in the parish of Aguilares with the help of a group of universitarians and Jesuits. . . ." Rodolfo Cardenal, Historia de una esperanza: Vida de Rutilio Grande (San Salvador: UCA Editores, Universidad Centroamericana José Siméon Cañas, 1987), pp. 457–458.

26. According to Romero's successor, Arturo Rivera y Damas, the best biography of the assassinated bishop is Jesús Delgado, Oscar A. Romero. Biografía (San Salvador: UCA Editores, 1990). Published by the Jesuit UCA University Press, it is also probably the most politicized. It traces Romero's transformation from a conservative, anti-Jesuit, anti-"liberation theology" establishment priest into the "bishop of the popular organizations" (Delgado, p. 165).

27. "The UCA never hesitated in the face of the challenge of confronting the reason of force with the force of reason and the search for the truth. . . . Estudios Centroamericanos or ECA, the UCA's main mouthpiece, launched one initiative after another in favor of dialogue and negotiations as a way to put an end to the armed conflict; its imagination—often utopic—led it to call on the Salvadorean Armed Forces in 1985 to transform themselves into a force at the service of the nation and the people and accept a professionalisation that would lead to the country's militarisation." Salvador Carranza, (ed.), Martires de la UCA: 16 de Noviembre de 1989 (San Salvador: UCA Editores, 1990), p. 76.

priests, bishops, and Jesuit thinkers became a decisive factor in their own commitment to social change. The Army and the Salvadorean death squads were in a sense quite logical in taking matters to the extreme: if it had not been for the deaths of Salvadorean religious leaders from 1977 to 1989—and their intimidating consequences —the outcome in that destitute and devout land would have surely been different. The conclusions of the so-called Commission on the Truth, made public in March 1993, confirmed what many had long suspected: the military and security forces of El Salvador, with the knowledge of many in positions of power in Washington, waged war not only on the guerrillas but also on the Church and on thousands of civilians.

Twenty years after their emergence on the Salvadorean scene, these new political-military organizations had fought a U.S.-backed, well-equipped army and air force, buttressed by over $6 billion of American aid, to a stalemate on the ground.[28] Of all the "second-wave" guerrilla groups across the Americas, only with the exception of the Sandinistas—because they won—the Salvadorean insurgents undoubtedly constitute the most successful. In comparison with their precursors, the Salvadoreans are in a league of their own, accomplishing what no armed group of the sixties had been capable of.

But the emphasis on unity and mass action would not endure; the diligence with which this was applied in the beginning dissipated in later years. Some of the most bloody internecine conflicts the Latin American left has experienced took place within the FMLN in the mid-eighties, and the increasingly military nature of the struggle eventually imposed its toll. As the concrete possibilities of developing urban, civil protests quickly diminished with the repression of 1980 and the actual outbreak of the country's civil war, the antimilitaristic warnings of the early years faded. Out of necessity the FMLN became essentially an army with a political wing, instead of remaining what it had set out to be—a broad-based political movement that also partici-

---

28. The most sanguine assessment of the war from a U.S. perspective was provided by a Rand Corporation analysis: "America has made an enormous investment in El Salvador. The conflict there has been the most expensive American effort to save an ally from insurgency since Vietnam. El Salvador has absorbed at least $4.5 billion, over $1 billion of which is in military aid. When combined with over $850 million in unsubsidized credits and an estimated CIA investment of over $500 million, the total expenditure approaches $6 billion. Only five countries receive more American aid each year than El Salvador, a nation of 5.3 million people. . . . If the FMLN has not gained victory, it has succeeded . . . in making the war, and itself felt everywhere in El Salvador." Benjamin C. Schwarz, *American Counterinsurgency Doctrine and El Salvador* (Santa Monica, Calif.: Rand Corporation–National Defense Research Institute, 1992), pp. 2–3.

pated in the armed struggle. This was the case for the FPL, which always strove to conserve its mass political base, and for the ERP, which regarded itself as the "army of the people" and had few difficulties with a militarization it often welcomed.

This militaristic drift was both a cause and a consequence of the most distinctive feature of the FMLN in the firmament of the Latin American armed left: the veritable construction of a lasting, viable standing army in opposition to a sitting government's constituted armed forces. Neither the Cubans in the Sierra Maestra nor the Sandinistas in 1979 fought more than relatively short, small-scale guerrilla wars, with less than a few thousand poorly armed combatants. This very accomplishment, along with the militarization it bred, contributed to the prolonged agony of the Salvadorean negotiations.

The FMLN proclaimed its desire to become once again a purely political force, competing for power through elections under stringent and enforceable guarantees. The eminently political, grass-roots origins of the FMLN encouraged the shift to an exclusively political, electoral vocation; the existence itself of an insurgent army and the dread associated with surrendering it strengthened the drive toward maintaining the armed stalemate the country had experienced since 1981. The FMLN's dilemma lay not so much in the transition from Marxist-Leninist theory and practice to representative democracy. It consisted mainly in finding a way to transform an army into a political party, when the opposing army after a decade of war is allowed to remain in place, albeit on a smaller scale.

The Peace Accords of January 1992 were a bet that this task could be fulfilled. But if the FMLN decided, at the end of the day, that the risk was worth taking, it did so largely for other reasons. The first was that the risk was a relative one: so much ammunition, arms, and even support weaponry had been smuggled into the country, or stowed away in warehouses and hideaways in Guatemala and Honduras, that the rebels were able to deliver the arms called for by the United Nations–brokered agreements and still have enough weapons left over and available to rearm, should the need arise. Secondly, the risk was almost unavoidable: regional and international circumstances, from the fall of the Sandinistas in Nicaragua to Cuba's isolation and Mexico's turning toward Washington, along with the resolution of other regional conflicts elsewhere in the world, had made the status quo untenable. Thirdly, the risk had an important "up side": it was not inconceivable that the FMLN's analysis of the historical process of the conflict would prove accurate.

If so, the powerful mass movement awakened in the late seventies would resurface.[29] Once the conditions for politics to displace military conflict were achieved, the same causes in El Salvador would produce the same effects: a popular mobilization unparalleled in Latin America. Only through deep reforms could the nation's problems be addressed; only with the FMLN's center-stage participation could those reforms be implemented, given most everyone else's reluctance to do so. In fact, this view was not so distant from the conclusions reached by the Rand Corporation as the war wound down in 1991:

> In El Salvador, as in Vietnam, our help has been welcome, but our advice spurned, and for very good reason. That advice—to reform radically—threatens to alter fundamentally the position and prerogatives of those in power. The United States, with its "revolutionary" means of combating insurgency, threatens those very things that its ally is fighting to defend. In El Salvador, as was the case in Vietnam, the inspiration for revolt arose in the first place from the resistance of those in power to political, social and economic reform. Those reforms that we have deemed essential—the absolute subordination of the military to civilian control, respect for human rights, a judicial system that applies to all members of Salvadorean society, radical land redistribution—are measures no government in El Salvador has been willing or able to achieve because they require fundamental changes in that country's authoritarian culture, economic structure and political practices.[30]

The most lucid insurgents continued to believe this would be the case even after the Peace Agreements went into effect: only time will tell if they were right. But from this perspective, and together with the other, above-mentioned factors, the negotiated accords looked like a good deal for the rebels.

The FMLN was perhaps the first sector of the Latin American left to face the central issue confronting the postrevolutionary left: whether to strive for consensus at the cost of considerable compro-

---

29. This was also the conclusion reached by the Cubans' most insightful academic international analysts, not always listened to by the operatives on the ground: "In fact, in relation to the FMLN's proposals of 1989, there is a substantial change. In 1990, they demanded the constitution of power-sharing arrangements; now they say that under certain conditions, they would be willing to enter the legal political struggle. This position rests on the conception that if elections are held under conditions of equality and guarantees, a majority of the people will vote for change." Julio Carranza Valdés, *El conflicto y la negociación en El Salvador, Cuadernos de Nuestra América*, vol. 7, no. 14, January–June 1990 (La Habana: Centro de estudios sobre América, 1991), p. 46.

30. Schwarz, op. cit., p. 61.

mises or to continue fighting—by different means—for major change with the support of only part of the population. The Peace Accords in principle opened both avenues: the FMLN could either latch on to the "civilized" sectors of the right and the United States and push for changes in Salvadorean society in the context of a broad-based coalition lasting through the 1994 presidential elections. Or it could raise its own banners of reform and attempt to coalesce "the people" around these demands, in a more polarizing mode, presenting a center-left candidate for the 1994 vote. The choice was not easy, since both options had advantages and drawbacks. The dilemma was excruciating; it would reappear throughout Latin America.

The FMLN made concessions it was forced to make anyway, obtaining significant government concessions in exchange, all in a Salvadorean context it honestly believed was favorable and in an international environment that had become increasingly hostile. They were not the first guerrillas to come in from the jungle, or, more precisely, down from the mountains;[31] they may ultimately prove the most successful.

•

But the big success story of the armed struggle's second stage in Latin America was the Sandinistas' 1979 victory in Nicaragua. Finally, almost twenty years to the day after the MR-26 de Julio entered Havana, another revolution had triumphed in the Americas. Together with its Cuban predecessor two decades back, it looked like a picture-perfect revolution: young, moderate, uniting an entire country in a cut-and-dried, morally irreproachable fight against the epitome of dictatorial rule. With broad-based international support and all the right intentions, it was also a blueprint revolution. It seemed to confirm most of the theses developed by the Latin American armed left's political-military organizations in the wake of the debacle of the late sixties and early seventies.

The Sandinista revolution typified the shift in the political-military organizations' Castroist line that had led so often to defeat and death in the years that had elapsed since the Sierra Maestra. The Sandinista Front learned its lesson well, albeit harrowingly. It was one of the first groups to take its cue from the Cuban Revolution

31. See James Lemoyne, "Out of the Jungle: El Salvador's Guerrillas," *New York Times Magazine*, February 9, 1992.

and suffered repeated setbacks, stagnation, and tragedies from its birth in 1961 to its resurrection in 1974.[32] But the Sandinistas' chief ideologues and strategists had pondered deeply on their own implicit break with the past, and on the militaristic deviations and absence of popular backing that characterized their own organization during its infancy.

The decisive discontinuity with the Cuban line—a leading vanguard role for the guerrilla force anchored in the countryside, etc.— occurred almost spontaneously and on the eve of victory. According to Humberto Ortega, who founded the Sandinista Army and remained its commander even after the Sandinistas' defeat in 1990:

> The truth is that we always thought of the masses, but in a supporting role for the guerrillas, so that the latter could destroy [Somoza's] National Guard, and not the way in which things actually occurred: the guerrillas acted in a supporting role for the masses, and these destroyed the enemy. Practice allowed us to see that we had to mobilize not only our guerrilla contingents but also succeed in having the masses participate actively in the armed struggle, because the guerrilla movement would never have the weapons to defeat the enemy militarily.[33]

Like Cuba before it, the Sandinista Revolution traveled both the armed and the peaceful roads to power. It was rooted in the cities, but also in the mountains of rural Nicaragua. The so-called vanguard, the Sandinista National Liberation Front, was truly revolutionary. Yet it was genuinely allied with important sectors of the national bourgeoisie, from Alfonso Robelo of the business community to Violeta

---

32. "The history of the Sandinista Front, had it stopped yesterday, would have constituted one of the longest litanies of failure that a revolutionary organisation could possibly offer." Régis Debray, "Mémoire Populaire et Lutte Révolutionnaire," Le Monde Diplomatique (Paris), September 1979, p. 7.

33. Humberto Ortega, interview with Marta Harnecker, December 1979, in Humberto Ortega, 50 años de lucha sandinista (Havana: Ediciones Especiales, 1980), p. 25. Tomás Borge had his own version of the same "rectification" as he reflected on the differences between what the Sandinistas did in the first years of their existence, and later, when they won: "The armed movement of this period [the sixties] had an 'invasionist' [a reference to Fidel Castro's "invasion" of Cuba in the Granma in 1956] character that underestimated organisational forms inside the country. The leaders of these groups, many of which we recall with respect, were dominated by subjective criteria and were particularly seeking personal prestige. . . . The guerrilla infant was born already contaminated by this 'invasionist' illness, and other than in our desires and imagination totally lacked an internal base of support, or even the minimum infrastructure in the 'invaded zone.' " Tomás Borge, La paciente impaciencia (Managua: Editorial Vanguardia, 1989), pp. 183, 186.

Chamorro of the traditional Nicaraguan political elite.[34] The alliance was the result both of deliberate policy and of particular Nicaraguan circumstances, which led much of the private sector to break with Somoza and join the opposition.[35] Needless to say, not everything was a product of Sandinista boldness or creative strategy; many authors, including several Sandinistas, understood that Somoza's own behavior—from the 1972 earthquake when he monopolized, then stole, much of the aid received from abroad, to the 1978 assassination of publisher Pedro Joaquín Chamorro—was the most powerful incentive for the private sector's alliance with the opposition.[36]

---

34. The author of what was until the late 1980s perhaps the best book in English on the Sandinistas grasped the Nicaraguan revolutionaries' break with the Cuban conception of the alliance with the national bourgeoisie, while at the same time indicating that there was a conceptual blind spot involved that would ultimately complicate matters for the Sandinistas: "The 1977 Platform also proposes the formation of a 'Broad Anti-Somoza Front,' including the bourgeois opposition to the dictatorship. This final enlargement of the movement, which proved to be a key element in Sandinista strategy, would seem to fully dissolve the class base of the revolution. But the anti-Somoza bourgeoisie was clearly not regarded as part of the inner-revolutionary 'bloc,' but as a partner in the Sandinista-dominated coalition. The Platform envisions the FSLN as 'hegemonic' within this coalition, which it describes as a 'temporary and tactical alliance.' . . . The ultimate role of the middle sectors and even of the bourgeoisie remains nebulous in Sandinista thinking." Dennis Gilbert, *Sandinistas* (Cambridge, England: Basil Blackwell, 1988), pp. 30–31.

35. Sergio Ramírez, the Sandinista architect of the alliance with the business elite, put it this way: "The Group of 12 was created in 1977 by the Sandinista Front to fulfill a political task that required drawing different sectors of society to the armed struggle. I already belonged to the FSLN, and I contributed to choosing the people we wanted: from business, the Church, intellectuals, industrialists, shopkeepers, people who because of their honesty and political position represented support for the FSLN in the eyes of the population at large. The Group of 12 initiative was part of the insurrectional strategy, and sought to give political support to the armed offensive." Sergio Ramírez, quoted in Claribel Alegría, *Nicaragua: La revolución sandinista* (Mexico City: Ediciones Era, 1982), pp. 267–268.

36. On this point nearly all analysts of the Nicaraguan revolution seem to agree. The Sandinistas saw it in this fashion: "There was a natural division in the country's economic development, whereby Somoza was in charge of agriculture and industry, and others took care of the financial side. With the earthquake, Somoza breaks the rules, provoking enmity, rivalries and creating a political faction against him." Henry Ruiz, quoted in Alegría, ibid., p. 223. Latin American students of the Nicaraguan Revolution read the process in a similar way: "The assassination of Pedro Joaquín Chamorro determined the break of the anti-Somoza bourgeoisie with the dictatorship." Lucrecia Lozano, *De Sandino al triunfo de la revolución* (Mexico City: Siglo XXI Editores, 1985), p. 16. And an American policymaker reached the same conclusion: "Thousands marched in [Pedro Joaquín Chamorro's] funeral procession, and the businessmen decided that the time had come to split decisively with Somoza. . . . If the earthquake was a watershed in the private sector's view of the venality of the Somoza dynasty, the killing of Chamorro was the catalyst that moved the private sector toward political action." Robert Pastor, *Condemned to Repetition: The United States and Nicaragua* (Princeton, N.J.: Princeton University Press, 1987), p. 59.

The Nicaraguan Revolution was initially pluralistic in Western, liberal terms, comprising within its ranks Marxists, Social Democrats, the equivalent of Christian Democrats, and probusiness conservatives. It was equally pluralistic in Latin American Marxist terms, that is, socially more than ideologically. It incorporated the Church, peasants, unions, bureaucrats, women, youth, English-speaking blacks from the Atlantic Coast, Misquito Indians, blue-blooded sons and daughters of the Nicaraguan aristocracy from León and Granada, Cuban-oriented Sandinistas devoted to the armed struggle as well as old-line, Stalinist Communists, who had cut every deal and stretched every imaginable principle with the Somoza dictatorship. In keeping with the Cubans' repeated suggestions, it sought and received wide international support, including social democrats in Venezuela and Western Europe, populists in Panama, nationalists in Mexico, and Christian Democrats in Costa Rica. It achieved even the tolerance, if not the enthusiastic welcome, of the Carter administration in the United States.

This idyllic postcard revolution was transformed along the way into a protracted, bloody international conflict and civil war that ended in the virtual disintegration of an entire country. Initially, however, it seemed to have solved all the problems confronting revolution in Latin America. The way in which the Sandinistas had united their three factions—the Prolonged Popular War group, the Proletarian Tendency, and the Third Road, or Tercerista insurrectionalists—seemed to close the cycle of defeat and tragedy for the Latin American left. The Sandinistas appeared to have assimilated all the lessons of the recent past and avoided the mistakes of their comrades in other hemispheric latitudes.

In fact, things were more complicated. With time, it would become apparent that the Sandinistas' victory was, like all revolutions, as much the product of exceptional circumstances converging fortuitously as of the adequate application of a correct line by a revolutionary vanguard. But the need to universalize, to present every victorious revolution as the ultimate example of how to make others equally triumphant— together with nostalgia for the Cuban years of glorious martyrs and ecstatic armed struggle—rapidly led to a mystification of the whys and wherefores of winning. The real reasons evaporated in the febrile enthusiasm of the new occupants of Managua's recently expropriated homes and gardens.

The national bourgeoisie was brought over to the revolutionary camp because serious concessions had been made in its direction, and because it had nowhere else to go. As soon as the concessions stopped coming, or were reversed, and Ronald Reagan's election seemed to provide an alternative for the future, the alliance fell apart. The leadership of the FSLN understood this and why it happened, but only much later:

> We began to govern in 1979 with a broad consensus and a great deal of legitimacy. This and other factors led to a certain authoritarian behavior, which made the alliances we forged in 1979 somewhat formal. We didn't really govern with the participation of our allies, who became very frustrated. This was a mistake that expressed itself most clearly by the 1984 election in which we ran alone and broke the alliance of 1979. We governed without giving our formal alliances any real political content.[37]

The Sandinistas' remarkable international backing was premised on their nonaligned—meaning non-Soviet, non-Cuban—stance and on an American policy based on the defense of human rights and a continuing rapprochement with the Soviet Union. When for internal reasons the Nicaraguan revolutionaries were forced to turn to their Cuban and Eastern bloc friends, the rest of the world's kindness quickly soured, with few exceptions—Sweden, for example.[38]

And as United States policy shifted during the Reagan administration, Latin American attitudes toward Nicaragua also changed considerably. Paralleling these trends, the support, money, and sympathy the Sandinistas had found and come to expect and depend upon from Western Europe and the rest of Latin America dried up.

Most of all, the longing for a successful, heroic outcome to the armed struggle that haunted the Latin American left drove many in Nicaragua to believe their own myths. They became convinced that they had militarily defeated Somoza's hated National Guard through a victorious guerrilla war, finally waged the right way and thus at long last triumphant. This was not quite true: at its peak, the Sandinista Front never had more than a few thousand men under arms. Moreover, the terms "arms" and "men" were both highly arguable: in many cases, particularly in the urban areas, the guerrilla warriors were teenagers with handguns taking potshots at the Guard, getting back at their tormentors the only way they could.

At a certain level of reflection and abstraction, the Sandinistas were fully aware of the fact that theirs had not been a military, but rather a popular, victory. They had not militarily vanquished Somoza:

---

37. Jaime Wheelock, interview with the author, Philadelphia, December 14, 1992.
38. The Sandinistas later acknowledged their mistakes in this realm: "We thought there was a great potential and vast resources in the socialist countries and the USSR. We underestimated the extent of the crisis of socialism." Wheelock, interview with the author.

As Commander Humberto Ortega states, for the FSLN the central axis of victory was not the military aspect, but rather the masses' participation in the insurrection. . . . it was the activity of the masses that allowed the armed movement to accumulate forces. . . . Our insurrectional strategy depended on the masses, not on the military front. . . . This must be clear.[39]

The passage—from a manual of Marxist theory used as a textbook for Sandinista cadres in the mid-eighties—betrays the same ambivalence discernible in nearly every other book, interview, or essay written by Sandinistas or their sympathizers. Time after time they show a clear tendency toward systematic overvaluation of the military, epic, heroic facets of their victory, and a corresponding sublimation of the political and international factors. Once the requisite lip service has been paid to the principle of not stressing the military side of things, torrents of poetry and analysis are devoted to the military side of things: the inevitable "return of the repressed." As always, there were powerful reasons for this quasi-psychoanalytical backlash. The Central American tradition of military legitimacy and empowerment is one obvious explanation: from time immemorial, the only source of power in Central American politics was the sword and gun. Another factor is undoubtedly the left's justifiable dread of military takeovers: the Sandinistas vowed that they would never suffer the fate of an Arbenz or an Allende, dutifully convincing themselves that the only way to neutralize a hostile conservative military was to build a sympathetic revolutionary one.[40] In the words of one British diplomat who followed this process closely, they built a Central American Sparta.

Whether through accounts such as Tomás Borge's memoirs or in ceremonies throughout Nicaragua during the initial years of the Revolution, or in schools for cadres and party propaganda, the Sandinistas gradually turned their political victory into a military one. They at least partly erased from their collective memory the real causes of their triumph. In a highly unconscious manner, they rewrote the history of their own revolution. With time, around campfires in the mountains during the war against the contras, in nostalgic conversations in the

---

39. Humberto Ortega, quoted in *Teoría y práctica revolucionarias en Nicaragua*, Equipo interdisciplinario latinoamericano (Managua: Ediciones contemporáneas, 1983), p. 145.

40. "Since 1979, the FSLN has maintained a special relationship with one sector of the revolutionary state, the security forces. The Sandinistas were determined to avoid the fatal mistake of left-wing governments from Guatemala (1954) to Chile (1973) that were overthrown by their own right-wing military. They were also unwilling to accept the military veto over national policy that has constrained the policies of many reformist governments in Latin America." Gilbert, op. cit., p. 62.

barrios of Managua, or at intellectual dinners given for visiting digni-
taries at beautiful homes above the capital, the tales told would all
come to center on military action, whether of genius or ineptitude.
The Revolution had become a war. When Ronald Reagan subsequently
transformed a diplomatic disagreement into armed confrontation,
there was no resistance left in Nicaragua to the normal, foreseeable,
military response to American hostility. Militarization in reaction to
the contra war came naturally, unavoidably. It also cost dearly.

The best way to understand the Sandinista Revolution's eventual
militarization,[41] as well as the enormous influence the Cubans attained in Nicaragua, is through the relationship between the Sandinista victory and everyone else's defeats of the sixties and seventies.
Everybody claimed the Sandinista triumph as their own: from Fidel to
Firmenich, from Rolando Morán to the Chilean MIR, from Régis Debray to Manuel Piñeiro. And everyone—perhaps less altruistically—
wanted to bask in the reflected glory, claiming a share of the credit as
precursor, mentor, or sponsor. Any qualification of that shared triumph, any doubts about its true origins and consequences, any reservations about how deep the support for the *muchachos* really extended,
was tantamount to betraying the memories of those fallen along the
way. The young combatants dressed in olive drab, waving red and
black flags, were Che Guevara's final vindication. They were giving
him a last chance to write his own epitaph.

Ultimately, the transformation of the idyllic rebellion of July 1979
into the devastating fratricidal conflict of the 1980s was probably an
inevitable outgrowth of the revolution's origins. Power was handed
over to the Sandinistas almost by chance, thanks to a remarkable coincidence of circumstances that the FSLN did not expect and had not
created. Faced with the choice between truly sharing a political hold
they were not forced to extend to others, or monopolizing a situation

---

41. This trend was clear to many observers from the beginning, even if they did not
see it as a worrisome one. "The Sandinista Front assumed from the beginning political
and military tasks, even though its general staff was subordinated to the national leadership. But it never existed independently from its combat structures. . . . It is thus not
surprising that the same men who led the war effort are leading the reconstruction
process; or that combatant be a synonym of 'militant,' and 'commander' of 'leader.' The
presence everywhere of olive-green uniforms shows that the same struggle goes on,
through other means. The total politicization of the military carried out by the Sandinista front should exclude any future militarization of politics." Régis Debray, op. cit.,
p. 10. Debray drew the wrong conclusions from the right analysis: the initial confusion
of political and military functions and consequences led to a militarization of politics,
not the other way around.

they were not prepared for but that opened wide its arms to them, they opted, understandably, for the second alternative.

Once they did, though, the die was cast. In particular, the role Cuba would play was all but predestined: To make a revolution, as opposed to a power-sharing scheme of deep reforms, meant building a new state, without the trusted cadres to do it with: those could only be borrowed, like the funds to reconstruct a nation torn apart by years of civil war. The Sandinistas could dabble with Panamanian policemen, Mexican debt negotiators, and United Nations economists. But in the crunch, the only people they could trust to create the army necessary to discourage an anticipated American invasion (which could well have occurred were it not for a Sandinista military buildup), the security apparatus indispensable for controlling an alienated opposition, and a police force to quell popular discontent, were the Cubans.[42]

It is the conclusion of many who followed the Sandinista Revolution during the early years that the real Cuban influence in Nicaragua came precisely at this juncture. Without the Cubans, the Sandinista army, police, and state security could not have been created. Without these institutions, the Sandinistas could not have survived the revolutionary decade, under extraordinarily adverse circumstances. The proof lies in the lasting power of the army and the police: well after the Sandinistas lost the presidency and encountered enormous difficulties in consolidating a party structure once out of power, the military remained the last bulwark of Sandinismo in Nicaragua.

The FSLN were master tacticians; but as strategists, they left much to be desired. In fact, they passed tactics off as strategy; from their improvised mass retreat from Managua to Masaya just before the final triumph, in 1979, to the so-called mixed-economy, democratic, and nonaligned program they stitched together with moderates in Costa Rica prior to victory, all the way to their negotiations with the contras from 1987 onward. This was their strength and weakness. Yet the strategic void it left had to be occupied somehow: the job was done by the Cubans and their militaristic ideology, which the Sandinistas received with open arms. It could not have been otherwise, and there are no adequate rejoinders to the Sandinistas' objection to such criticism: any alternative would have meant forsaking the revolution. If revolu-

---

42. "Without Cuban support, the Sandinistas would not have won in the same way, but they would have won anyway. The balance of forces in the victory of the Sandinistas perhaps would have been different." Senior official of the Cuban Communist Party, op. cit.

tion was the goal, theirs was probably, regrettably, the only way to go about it.

■

Apart from the Sandinistas, there were other groups which were representative of the second wave of political-military organizations in Latin America. With two exceptions, though, most of them never developed the strength or representation that justifies lengthy analysis. The two worth describing, because of their success and their break with the Castroist traditions of the sixties, are the Colombian M-19 and Sendero Luminoso (Shining Path) in Peru.

M-19 made its first appearance on the Colombian political scene in January 1974, when it stole the sword of the Latin American liberator Simón Bolívar from the museum where it rested, proclaiming: "Bolívar, your sword returns to the struggle." The spectacular, quixotic coup in a sense symbolized M-19's tactical and ideological break with the groups of the sixties and the Cubans. Nonetheless, over the years the Colombian organization maintained close relations with *la isla*, so close that it was often regarded by Colombian and American authorities as one of the Cubans' main partners in the export of revolution and—more sinisterly but less demonstrably—drugs.

The most suggestive evidence linking M-19, the Cubans, and drugs concerned a Colombian bon vivant by the name of Jaime Guillot Lara, who died in Havana of a heart attack in June 1991. With his death, most likely, was buried conclusive proof of the Cuban-Colombian link. Everything surrounding his case suggests complicity on the part of all parties involved, yet nothing has ever been established conclusively. M-19 did have drug connections of one sort or another; the Cubans were involved both in drugs and in shipping arms to M-19; but the three connections converged only upon Guillot.[43]

He was arrested on December 4, 1981, in Mexico City, where he was visiting a girlfriend. Careless—even reckless, some said—he trav-

---

43. "Moderates in the State Department, the CIA and the DEA did not doubt that some Cuban officials had seized the chance to arm the M-19 guerrillas and that they had raked off some drug money on the side, but they did not believe the case proved the Castro government had undertaken drug running as a matter of state policy. The ideological right wing of the administration, Congress and certain archconservative interest groups studied the Guillot Lara case with endless fascination, sure that it proved an international conspiracy of the extreme left and the drug cartels." Elaine Shannon, *Desperados: Drug Lords, U.S. Lawmen, and the War America Can't Win* (New York: Viking, 1990), pp. 142–143.

eled openly despite his well-known drug-related activities. Guillot had played go-between in 1979 in Colombia, bringing together a local lawyer by the name of Johnny Crump and Fernando Ravelo (the Cuban ambassador in Bogotá, who after the termination of diplomatic relations between the two countries was appointed Manuel Piñeiro's deputy in the Communist Party's Department of America). According to official U.S. sources, Guillot was responsible for setting up the drug connection between the Colombians and the Cubans, as well as safe passage and transshipment for drug loads through Cuba en route to the Florida keys.[44]

Once Guillot was apprehended in Mexico, both the Colombian and United States governments presented extradition requests. The Julio Cesar Turbay administration in Colombia was waging what it thought was the final battle against the M-19 guerrillas. Guillot Lara was a childhood friend of M-19 founder and *jefe máximo* Jaime Bateman—they had played soccer together barefoot on the beaches of Santa Marta—and one of the group's financiers and suspected arms smugglers. Assistant U.S. Attorney Richard Gregorie was preparing a Miami grand jury drug-trafficking indictment against several Cuban officials, including Ravelo. Guillot would have been a key witness in the trial.[45]

The Cubans showed what amounted to an extraordinary—one could almost say, suspicious—degree of interest in someone who was not a Cuban citizen, but rather a Colombian drug trafficker with guerrilla connections. They exerted enormous pressure on the Mexican authorities involved in resolving the issue of extradition. Ravelo practically settled in Mexico to take charge of the operation himself. Personal entreaties from Manual Piñeiro and Fidel Castro were sent through undercover agents—who burned coded messages in ashtrays after reading them aloud, and staked out the homes of their friends with clout in high places—to Mexicans in the decision-making process and exiled Chilean politicians close to Castro and to Mexican presi-

---

44. The entire U.S. version of Guillot's connections is taken from the transcript of "Frontline" Show no. 910, WGBH Educational Foundation, *Cuba and Cocaine*, February 5, 1991.

45. According to Miami *Herald* news reports, Guillot confessed to much of this, although under questionable circumstances: "Guillot Lara, undoubtedly under pressure, talked to CIA agents." According to a U.S. State Department document he talked a lot: "By his own admission, Guillot has been involved with arms trafficking operations to Colombia for the M-19 on behalf of the government of Cuba. The latter provided the funds for the purchase of arms." John Dorschner and Jim McGee, "The Case against Cuba," *Tropic Magazine*, Miami *Herald*, November 20, 1983.

dent José López Portillo. The Cubans argued a political case, as did Guillot's lawyers in the extradition hearings: that he was being politically persecuted for his relationship with M-19 and consequently extradition did not apply. The Mexican government, largely in deference to the Cubans, finally agreed and rejected both extradition briefs. On September 23, 1982, hours after the decision was made, security agents snatched Guillot from his cell, whisked him away to the airport, and put him on a midnight flight to Madrid, before anyone—the Cubans, the Americans, or the Colombians—could get their hands on him in Mexico.[46] Thereafter Jaime Guillot Lara wandered through Europe and Africa for a while, then settled in Havana, where he ended his days nearly a decade later. If Cuban interest in his case meant anything, it clearly indicated a degree of involvement far beyond what the island authorities ever confessed to before the Arnaldo Ochoa–Tony de la Guardia trials in 1989. The answers lie in the unopened Cuban archives, and in the unwritten memoirs of Fidel Castro and Manuel Piñeiro.[47]

But whatever else may have bound them, in the field of ideology there was a world of difference between the Cubans and M-19. The movement's name (Movimiento 19 de Abril) commemorates the date of April 19, 1970, when the Alianza Nacional Popular (ANAPO) presidential candidate, General Gustavo Rojas Pinilla, who ruled Colombia with an iron—but for some, popular—hand from 1953 to 1957, had a presidential election presumably stolen from him. It was founded by a group of former Castroist guerrilla fighters frustrated over the failure of previous organizations, mainly the Fuerzas Armadas Revolucionarias Colombianas (FARC) and the Ejército de Liberación Nacional (ELN). Its leader and founder, Jaime Bateman, had been a member of the Communist Youth and later of the FARC, the Communist Party's armed wing, in the sixties. It defined itself as nationalist, democratic, and revolutionary, and simultaneously devoted to the armed struggle. Its chief differences with the groups from the sixties were spelled out by Eduardo Pizarro, brother of M-19's assassinated presidential candi-

---

46. The State Department had the following comment on the release: "Obviously, it's a disappointment. We had hoped to have him tried." A DEA spokesman added that he "didn't know why Guillot was released." Fabiola Santiago, "Drug-Traffic Suspect Is Released from Jail," Miami *Herald*, October 24, 1982, front page.

47. In response to a direct question on the drug trade and Guillot, current M-19 leader Antonio Navarro said: "We have no connection to drugs whatsoever. We never produced or exported a gram of cocaine. About Guillot, our relationship was exclusively based on arms." Antonio Navarro Wolff, interview with the author, Cartagena de Indias, October 8, 1992.

date in 1990, and one of Colombia's leading authorities on the guerrilla movement:

First, the "second generation groups" have sought to establish their presence among the population (unions, neighborhoods, shantytowns) more effectively and broadly than their predecessors. Secondly, instead of the foco guerrillero tactics of the sixties, these new insurgent groups base their action on the prolonged war concept and on the formation of popular mass fronts that transcend the traditional Leninist vanguard. Thirdly, along with their broader domestic networks, they have developed extensive "diplomatic" relations abroad. Four, an important spectrum of international actors support them diversely. Five, these movements have undergone a process of "Latinamericanization" as they acquired a critical stance with regard to Communist centers (Moscow, Peking) and link their strategy much more to Central American conflicts. Finally, they have broken with orthodox Marxism and an "internationalism" that made them simple appendices on a global chess board, placing themselves squarely in the mainstream of Colombian history: Bolívar, patriotic symbols and cultural traditions were no longer seen as "bourgeois symbols," but as a revolutionary patrimony.[48]

M-19's success in navigating the passage from armed struggle to parliamentary representation was amply demonstrated by its impressive performance in the 1990 elections for the presidency and Constituent Assembly. Despite the fact that its original presidential candidate was shot dead just weeks before election day, it received 750,000 votes and 13 percent in the first vote, and 1,000,000 votes, more than 20 percent and the largest number of seats of any single list in the second. Polls taken in Colombia in early 1991 showed that a great number of Colombians (58.5 percent) believed M-19 would attain power, and its leader and former candidate Antonio Navarro Wolff was deemed the Colombian politician most likely to become president in the decade of the nineties.[49]

M-19 laid down its arms, descended from the mountains, and helped build a new political system in Colombia, with a new constitution and the potential end of the Liberal-Conservative grip on power that had dominated the country's politics for thirty years. One of the explanations for this remarkable transition lies in its origins: founded in anger and despair over electoral fraud, it took up arms in order to win the

---

48. Eduardo Pizarro Leongómez, "La guerrilla y el proceso de paz," in Gustavo Gallón Giraldo, ed., *Entre Movimientos y caudillos: 50 años de bipartidismo, izquierda y alternativas populares en Colombia* (Bogotá: CINEP-Cerec, 1989), p. 252.

49. *Semana*, January 8, 1991, quoted by *2010*, February 1991.

right to participate in elections, not to make a revolution, despite its self-definition as a "revolutionary" movement.[50]

Despite the Marxist origins of most of its founders, M-19 was able to follow Jaime Bateman's maxims: "We have to nationalize the revolution, place it beneath the feet of Colombia, make it a 'pachanga', do it with 'bambucos, vallenatos and cumbias' (Colombian rhythmic music), singing the national anthem."[51] It is a direct product both of the guerrilla experiences of the sixties and of a deeply rooted populist strain in Colombia's recent history. Thanks to this peculiar historical combination, M-19 resisted perhaps the worst demolition of a leadership to be experienced by any Latin American organization. Of its founding leaders, Jaime Bateman, Ivan Marino Ospina, Alvaro Fayad, and Carlos Pizarro all died "in the line of duty" between 1983 and 1989. If one adds Bernardo Jaramillo, the presidential candidate of the Unión Patriótica, a Communist Party–generated political coalition, also gunned down in 1989, the list is striking. The cost in leadership is a reflection of the far greater cost among the rank and file of the entire adventure: over 30,000 left-wing militants, activists, and sympathizers were killed, more than the organized left lost in El Salvador, and far more than in Argentina, Chile, or Uruguay during the Dirty Wars of the seventies. The repression of the Colombian left and the magnitude of its losses are unparalleled in modern Latin American history.

This was eloquent testimony to both the extraordinarily violent nature of Colombian politics and the enormous risks M-19 took when it began peace negotiations in the early eighties with the government of President Belisario Betancur. From purloining Bolivar's sword and kidnapping numerous ambassadors at the Dominican diplomatic mission in February 1980, all the way to the assault on the Palace of Justice on November 6, 1985, M-19 has shown a knack for the headline-

---

50. This central distinction separating the M-19 from other Colombian—and Latin American guerrilla groups—was made back in the mid-eighties: "Among the [left-wing] groups it is necessary to distinguish between those founded in the sixties in the wake of the Cuban Revolution or inspired by Marxist-Leninist theses and with foreign links, and those that emerged in the 1970s and particularly the Movement of April 19th or M-19. The former groups all have some degree of expectations of structural change in the social order. . . . The second group, on the contrary, was born in reaction against the fraudulent denial of the electoral victory of the populist, nationalist movement ANAPO . . . in 1970, and had repeatedly expressed its desires to participate in electoral contests." Fernando Rojas H., "El Estado colombiano desde la dictadura de Rojas Pinilla hasta el gobierno de Betancur (1948–1983)," in Pablo González Casonova, ed., El Estado en América Latina: Teoría y práctica (Mexico City: Siglo XXI Editores/United Nations University, 1990), pp. 461–462.

51. Patricia Lara, Siembra vientos y recogerás tempestades (Bogotá: Editorial Planeta, 1986), pp. 110–111.

grabbing, high-impact *coup de main*.[52] Its leaders acknowledge this openly:

> The difference between us and the Venezuelan guerrillas in the sixties is that they reached the bargaining table defeated. They never had the social and political influence that the Colombian guerrilla movement achieved. We were able to penetrate throughout society, whether people liked us or not. When we began to seek out public opinion, we already had a presence. Nobody defeated us. Afterwards, some said we had been defeated, but if we had negotiated from a position of weakness, we would not have obtained what we did, which was a tremendous penetration in public opinion. The people didn't perceive us as having been defeated, but simply as doing what had to be done for the country, opening the road to peace and tranquillity. The guerrilla war in Colombia was not a marginal thing in Colombia, it hit at the heart of the country.[53]

By the time of the October 1991 congressional and gubernatorial elections—the first under the new Constitution—M-19 was suffering from the typical problems of growth and transition. It fared poorly at the polls, but hardly knew why. Some of its members blamed the charismatic Navarro Wolff for allowing popularity to go to his head and making the party indistinguishable from others in its moderation, responsibility, and maturity (all code words for "nonrevolutionary"). Others believed that had M-19 stuck to a radical left-wing stance, it would have lost even more miserably, given the conservative mood sweeping Colombia and the entire hemisphere. Clearly there was an issue of losing touch with the popular movements that had provided the environment in which the M-19 had originally flourished after it laid down its weapons:

> Another demand [of the popular movements] concerned the need to define the economic and social content that democracy required in Colombia. Much of the distance that the popular movement established between itself and the M-19 and the outcome of the Constituent Assembly had to do with the weak commitment of the new center-left with economic democratization and with the interests and expectations of the poor majority of Colombia's people. . . .[54]

---

52. In the words of a guerrilla leader from another faction who joined M-19 and was elected to the Colombian Senate on its ticket in 1991: "With M-19 the left finally achieved an effective use of what had traditionally been called armed propaganda." Bernardo Gutiérrez, "La guerrilla del siglo XX," in *Partidos políticos en Colombia: Crisis y retos*, no. 15 (Bogotá: Revista Foro, September, 1991), p. 31.

53. Navarro Wolff, op. cit.

54. Fabio López de la Roche, *Crisis y renovación de la izquierda radical* (Bogotá: Revista Foro, 19), p. 62.

In either case, a very real problem of assimilation persisted. If M-19 attained the level of popularity it enjoyed during the Constituent period and at the time it laid down its arms, this was undoubtedly due to a combination of two factors: achieving peace and a degree of realism and moderation uncommon to guerrilla armies, and breaking with the stale, despised status quo. The Colombian people and electorate applauded M-19 for being both radical—in relation to the traditional two-party system—and moderate—in relation to its arms-bearing past. As long as the balance struck between these two qualities endured, so also did the spell cast by Antonio Navarro Wolff. As soon, however, as inertia, assimilation, and realism began to set in, the spell was bound to be broken. This is the classic contradiction of the Latin American left on those rare occasions when it is successful: too much success means assimilation and being tarred with the status quo's unpopularity. There are both ethical and practical costs for too much of a good thing: M-19 was abruptly made aware of this basic significance of civilian electoral politics for the left in Latin America.

Nonetheless, M-19 may be said to represent a successful (at least initially) passage from the Castroist armed struggle of the sixties to the quasi-social-democratic electoral competition of the nineties. If the traditional, narrow-based, and often purely formal Colombian democracy matures into a truly representative system, M-19 will almost certainly play an important role in this transformation.[55]

It is not, however, an example for everybody, and quite evidently not for Sendero Luminoso, the only other, yet very different, example of a successful post-Castroist, armed left-wing political organization in Latin America. "The Communist Party of Peru–Along the Shining Path of José Carlos Mariateguí," as the movement was originally and formally known, is not in the business of finding smooth, peaceful transitions from armed struggle to parliamentary discussion. It has become one of the most effective and thriving, terrifying and mysterious armed organizations ever encountered in Latin America. While it has certain similarities to highly secretive, hypernationalistic organizations in other nations and other eras—the Chinese Boxers at the turn of the century, the Mau-Mau in Kenya in the 1950s—Sendero is a

---

55. In the words of a late convert and perceptive observer: "In the circumstances of 1991, M-19 remains faithful to the gesture that truly constituted it as a movement: the recovery of Bolívar's sword, a symbol of the armed legislator and founder of the Republic. If in the course of this transition its aspirations are attained, it will have achieved what it sought: not a social revolution, but the passage from a closed and excluding oligarchical republic to an open and inclusive republic of citizens." Adolfo Gilly, "Colombia: la refundación de la República," La Jornada (Mexico City), June 7, 1991, p. 35.

unique phenomenon. Ultimately, it may prove merely a temporary aberration reflecting the peculiar qualities of the Peruvian *altiplano* and ethnic makeup, or else a harbinger of what awaits other nations in Latin America.

Sendero was founded in the 1960s as one of the myriad apparently insignificant pro-Chinese spin-offs that fractured many Latin American Communist parties. The new groups differentiated themselves from the "mother party" often by adding a hyphen and an adjective to the original party title and universally by their veneration of Chairman Mao. In Peru, the old pro-Soviet Communist Party was split in just this fashion. The regional Committee of the pro-Chinese faction, identified by the name of its newspaper—*Bandera Roja* ("Red Flag")—and located in the remote Andean city of Ayacucho, was headed by Abimael Guzmán, a young professor of philosophy at the recently reopened Universidad Nacional San Cristobal de Huamanga, who many years later would become "Presidente Gonzalo," undisputed leader of the Shining Path.

From the mid-sixties through the late seventies, Sendero Luminoso remained essentially a regional, student- and teacher-based, violent, but unarmed movement characterized by its radical rhetoric and uncompromising sectarian stances. It was never pro-Cuban or Castroist; if anything, it considered the Cuban Revolution "revisionist" and pro-Soviet. It preached the armed struggle but did very little about it. In practice, its Maoism was initially limited to recruiting a few Indian peasants around Ayacucho, paying scant attention, if any, to the ethnic facets of their poverty and aspirations. The Shining Path was not really a guerrilla movement, and certainly not a *foquista* Castroist political-military organization. Its Maoist ideology appeared to be above all that: an ideological tribute to China, rather than a guide for political action. The fact that as late as 1988, in the only interview he gave before his capture in September 1992, Abimael Guzmán referred to "Chairman Mao" in practically every response, only reinforces this impression.[56]

---

56. Guzmán defines Sendero's ideology as "Marxism-Leninism-Maoism-Gonzalo thought (*pensamiento Gonzalo*)"; the latter term is in turn defined the following way: "the application of Marxism-Leninism-Maoism to the Peruvian revolution has generated 'Gonzalo thought.' " Abimael Guzmán Reynoso, "Presidente Gonzalo rompe el silencio, entrevista con Luis Arce Borja and Janet Talavera Sánchez," *El diario* (Lima), August 1988, pp. 8, 13. In contrast to other Latin American revolutionary organizations—where what is said is often less important than what actually occurs, largely because the discursive tradition of the Latin American left has tended to make words frequently meaningless—Sendero's few public pronouncements actually shed significant light on its actions. The link between discourse and action is much tighter, because of ideological coherence, a mass base, and a quasi-religious obsession with laying down plans, often minutely and excruciatingly detailed ones, of what will happen. These plans, in contrast

The area in which it flourished, along with the students and teachers it recruited, would reflect its future prospects. Ayacucho was not just any part of Peru, and its inhabitants were not simply another cohort of the Peruvian poor and disenfranchised. Indeed, most students of the Sendero phenomenon have concluded that its appearance in Ayacucho and its subsequent survival in that region of the country for more than a decade, as well as its ultimate extension to other areas, are due precisely to the region's singular nature.[57] Together with the ant-like, patient work among the population that did derive from the Maoist dictum of "going to the people," the stage was set for what would become one of the strongest guerilla movements in the history of Latin America. Along with its fundamentalism and isolation it would also become the most violent, sectarian, and frightening group, as its regional and ethnic characteristics were overshadowed by its national presence and mestizo base.

Ayacucho is Peru's second-poorest province. Its per capita income is less than a third of the national average. Peru's per capita GNP, it might be recalled, is among the lowest in Latin America: at $1160 in 1990, it surpassed only that of Haiti, Bolivia, the Dominican Republic, El Salvador, Honduras, Guatemala, and Paraguay.[58] It is a predominantly agricultural area, with few salaried workers, little commerce and trade, and scarce resources. But what explains Sendero's emergence and growth is not just poverty but the conjunction of poverty with the spectacular growth of Huamanga University—one result of the enormous educational effort that successive Peruvian governments carried out during the sixties and seventies, taking the country from fourteenth place to fourth in Latin America. As Carlos Ivan Degregori, one of the most insightful Peruvian students of Sendero, has said, "The emergence of a highly modernizing university in the poorest region of the country, with one of the most archaic social structures of the nation was a veritable social earthquake."[59] Between 1959, when the

---

to those of much of the rest of the Latin American left, are actually carried out, or have been on many occasions.

57. "The southern highlands region that provided Sendero's original support has economic, political, and social characteristics that are *all* different from those of Peru's other regions and that would *all* be considered to make backing for guerilla groups more likely." Cynthia McClintock, "Peru's Sendero Luminoso Rebellion," in Susan Eckstein, ed., *Power and Popular Protest: Latin American Social Movements* (Berkeley: University of California Press, 1989), pp. 64–65.

58. World Bank, *World Development Report, 1992* (New York: Oxford University Press, 1992), pp. 218–219.

59. Carlos Ivan Degregori, *Ayacucho 1969–1979: El surgimiento de Sendero Luminoso* (Lima: Instituto de Estudioso Peruanos, 1990), p. 43.

university reopened, and 1966, registered students multiplied five-fold.[60] Between 1960 and 1977, the student body grew by 33 percent, in contrast to the national figure of 6.5 percent.[61] In 1961, university students represented 3.1 percent of the population over fifteen years of age; but by 1972 this figure had risen to 18 percent, and in 1977, including high school students, university faculty and staff, the total constituted more than a quarter of the overall population of Ayacucho.[62] This may also have something to do with one of the more unusual facets of Sendero: its relative appeal to, and glorification of, women militants. In its iconography, a schoolgirl martyr from Ayacucho, Edith Lagos, plays a key role. And countless visitors to the Sendero jails in the Lima area have been impressed with the numbers, devotion and discipline of the women prisoners.[63]

This, then, was the breeding ground for Sendero. Ayacucho and the neighboring provinces of Huancavelica and Apurímac were the greatest net generators of rural flight to Peruvian cities (essentially Lima), with Ayacucho's share of the national population shrinking from 4.1 percent in 1961 to below 3 percent by the mid-eighties; therein lies the explanation of how Sendero broke out of the Andean highlands. If in April 1980, when Abimael Guzmán began pursuing the armed struggle, his organization was still regionally based, within a very short time it would no longer be. Guzmán himself acknowledged that he did not build a "popular Guerrilla Army" until 1983.[64] And yet by the mid-eighties, despite various predictions to the contrary, it had acquired a national presence.[65]

---

60. Ibid., p. 42.
61. Ibid., p. 46.
62. Ibid., p. 47.
63. An initial explanation for this was provided by a journalist who visited these prisons and spoke at length with women Senderistas: "By joining Abimael Guzmán's movement, young people became better than whites; they went instantly from the bottom to the top of the social pyramid. For brown-skinned women, this meant achieving a double equality—to whites and to men. In Guzmán's world, class, not gender, is what matters. In the revolution, the sexes are equal. The power of this idea, in a Latin American context, can hardly be overemphasized." Robin Kirk, "The Deadly Women of the Shining Path," San Francisco *Examiner Image*, March 22, 1992. The same argument is made by Gabriela Tarazana-Secillano, "The Organization of Shining Path," in David Scott Palmer, *The Shining Path of Peru* (New York: St. Martin's Press, 1992), p. 180.
64. It is worth noting that even in reference to this latter period in his organization's history, Guzmán continues to stress the differences between Sendero and the Castroist "political-military organizations": "Our faction reconstituted . . . a Communist Party of a new type, a Marxist-Leninist-Maoist one, an organized political vanguard, and not a 'political-military organization' as is erroneously stated." Guzmán, op. cit., p. 22.
65. Thus, as late as the beginning of 1984, some American students of Sendero were insisting that "if anything Sendero's ability to effectively control territory has been

Sendero spread out to Lima and to other areas of the Peruvian hinterland, mainly the Upper Huallaga Valley and Amazonia. This meant, first, that, contrary to many analysts' expectations,[66] it was able to develop a constituency in urban areas, chiefly in Lima, which by 1990 contained more than a third of Peru's inhabitants. Second, its expansion to the Upper Huallaga Valley in the early months of 1987, and the organization's subsequent consolidation in the most important coca-leaf-growing region in the world, implied that it had finally solved the riddle of all Latin American guerrilla movements: how to finance an expensive, prolonged battle for power. Charging drug runners and coca growers for "protection" and levying the equivalent of taxes and customs duties was the solution: profitable, steady, and unlimited. Sendero's ideological justification for this drug link is self-evident and elegant in its extreme simplicity and logic:

> Coca cultivation responds to the economic needs of the immense majority of the peasants of the Upper Huallaga, who find in it a means of subsistence. We are not against coca growing because that would mean being against the peasantry. Who transforms the coca? Who consumes the coca? If we can avoid consumption in our country, for us, the coca problem is solved. Over there, the imperialists go crazy, but we have no reason to help them in their struggle, because they are our enemies.[67]

The amounts involved are also significant: ten to fifteen thousand dollars per shipment of paste to Colombia.[68] By early 1991, Sendero had expanded its drug-related presence to other regions (the Middle Huallaga Valley, the La Convención area of Cuzco, and the Ene River valley in Junín). According to newspaper reports from these areas, Sendero had begun to encourage farmers to cultivate coca, in contrast to its former policy in the Upper Huallaga of simply forging alliances with existing cultivators.[69] There is in fact a debate among *Senderólogos* about the exact nature of the Shining Path's links with the drug trade. On the one hand are the U.S. and Peruvian governments' asser-

---

reduced by the extensive military operations in the Ayacucho area. . . . even so a substantial reservoir of support or fear remains in the core areas of Sendero's historic activity." David Scott Palmer, "Rebellion in Rural Peru," in Fauriol, *Latin American Insurgencies*, op. cit., p. 71.

66. "Sendero's leaders have made little attempt to mobilize support in the sprawling capital of Lima. . . ." Palmer, ibid., p. 75.

67. Interview with Comandante Tomás, published in the Sendero daily *El diario*, quoted in Alain Hertoghe and Alain Labrousse, *Le Sentier Lumineux du Pérou: Un nouvel intégrisme dans le tiers monde* (Paris: Editions La Découverte, 1989), p. 12.

68. Ibid., p. 20.

69. For example, "Coca Cash Provides Aid for Rebels," San Francisco *Chronicle*, January 30, 1991.

tions that Sendero is a "narco-guerrilla" group and that drug-trafficking and subversion are one and the same thing.[70] The opposite view, best expressed by British journalist Simon Strong, is that while Sendero does protect the *cocaleros* from the traffickers and the Army, and gets money in return, its ascetic mystique, as well as the absence of modern arms, indicates that it is not involved in the drug trade itself:

> Shining Path views itself as the defender of the peasants' right to grow and trade coca at fair prices. . . . The party does not market coca: as an aspirant state, it taxes the trade by way of requesting collaboration money from it as well as other businesses. . . . Neither the amount of money which Shining Path has supposedly garnered from the coca trade nor its whereabouts can be ascertained. . . . They have apparently failed to purchase any sophisticated weaponry in Peru or abroad.[71]

Until the archives and interviews made available through the capture of Guzmán and part of the Sendero leadership in September 1992 are thoroughly reviewed, it will remain impossible to know which side is absolutely right. Nor is it entirely clear that the difference between the two assessments is terribly relevant. Strong and other skeptics agree that simply by taxing, Sendero has achieved a degree of financial independence that virtually no other Latin American guerrilla organization has ever attained. And clearly Washington and Lima have a self-serving purpose in linking the drugs and guerrillas: they can use the weapons and money destined to fight one to combat the other. If logic and history are any indication, it is probable that Sendero was originally what Strong and others have said: a group taking advantage of the savage repression waged against the peasants, and protecting them against their enemies, while at the same time encouraging them to grow coca and fetch better prices for it. But over time, it may well

---

70. A lengthy, well-argued case for this point of view was presented by Stephen G. Trujillo, former U.S. Army Ranger and Green Beret, in a two-part article on the *New York Times* op-ed page on April 8–9, 1992. Trujillo claimed: "The guerrillas are systematically involved in all levels of the drug trade in the Upper Huallaga Valley. . . . Shining Path's domination of the firmas or Colombian dominated drug mafias enables it to tax all levels of the cocaine industry: subsistence farmers, speculators, middlemen and lab owners, firmas and Colombian traffickers. It is clear that Shining Path is financing its revolution with cocaine." The same view, from a Peruvian perspective, has been cogently argued by José E. Gonzales, "Guerrillas and Coca in the Upper Huallaga Valley," in David Scott Palmer, op. cit. Gonzales quotes "estimates of Shining Path's annual revenue . . . from 20 to 100 million a year." Gonzales, p. 120.
71. Simon Strong, *Shining Path: The World's Deadliest Revolutionary Force* (London: Harper Collins, 1992), pp. 122, 125. Stephen Trujillo's pieces in the *New York Times* were apparently written in response to a short article by Strong summarizing the conclusions of the relevant chapter of his book.

have gotten hooked on the taxes, if not on the coke: it might have begun to promote the economic activity that generated the taxes.

If Sendero was originally an outgrowth of the dramatic encounter of a mestizo provincial intellectual elite and an equally mestizo provincial university youth,[72] its spilling over to Lima was due to a similar convergence:

> Sendero Luminoso's response is the most radical expression of those who have nothing to lose and everything to gain: thousands of marginalized people who have no jobs and will not find any. But it is not just a question of economic marginalisation. Through the radical and mystical gestures of Sendero the racially, culturally and socially disdained men and women of Peru are expressing themselves.[73]

The Shining Path is not an indigenous organization from a country where Indians are discriminated against. Although it clearly made inroads in many of the Indian communities of the *altiplano*, it is a mestizo organization in a nation where mestizos are a majority excluded from status, power, and society. Until 1982, Sendero had hardly touched Lima; by the beginning of 1984 it was constantly blowing up power lines, plunging the capital into darkness, and developing its political mission in the shantytowns around the city. When in 1985 the movement confronted difficulties in the highlands, it had already consolidated its urban hold. Its noose around Lima began to tighten.

The substantive issue behind this expansion was the question of its social base. Clearly Sendero has frequently committed acts of terrorism; its ideology is simplistic, it lacks any coherent alternative to the status quo, its brutal confrontational methods often leave its own supporters helpless in the face of the military's equally violent repression. But the brutality of the Shining Path hardly explains the constituency that neither the archaism nor the violence has alienated, or even disheartened. As a recent foreign analysis of Sendero Luminoso has phrased it:

> Sendero's shift, from 1987 onward, to emphasizing the revolution in the cities, is undoubtedly not the result of a theoretical process. Rather, it is the unexpected discovery that its message worked better than in the countryside, because of the mass presence of first and second gen-

---

72. Degregori, op. cit., p. 16.
73. Rodrigo Montoya, "Izquierda unida y Sendero, potencialidad y límite," *Sociedad y política* 13, August 1983, quoted in Hertoghe and Labrousse, op. cit, p. 204.

eration *cholos*. In a sense, Sendero belatedly followed the [geographical] movement of its original, Andean mass base.[74]

The key lies in understanding how Sendero became the first guerrilla organization to successfully recruit its social base among the urban disenfranchised and destitute. Abimael Guzmán stated the issue clearly:

> In the cities, there are immense *barriadas* [shantytowns], immense *barrial masses*. From 1976 onward we began our work in the cities . . . taking the *barrios* and *barriadas* as bases and the working class as the leader . . . the immense masses of the *barrios* and *barriadas* are like iron belts that will close in the enemy and hold in the reactionary forces.[75]

Whether by making a virtue out of necessity or through a deliberate strategy, Sendero Luminoso was certainly the first Latin American armed organization to massively incorporate the marginalized urban poor into its ranks.[76] The reason may have to do with the conditions created in Lima by what one of the country's foremost sociologists, José Matos Mar, has called *"el desborde popular."* By 1989, 65 percent of the country's inhabitants were urban dwellers; the city of Lima had grown from barely half a million inhabitants in 1940 to 6½ million in the mideighties. In 1956 there were fifty-six registered shantytowns around the capital; by 1989, there were 800, housing (so to speak) one of every two *limeños*.[77] This massive, incredibly swift migration has above all involved *cholos* from the Andean highlands, who reproduce their customs, neighborhoods, work, and self-help systems in the city. Sendero was a natural for these hundreds of thousands of young, impoverished, often desperate migrants, with no stake in existing institutions, no representation in existing organizations—not even the left-of-center Izquierda Unida, which held the mayoralty of Lima from 1985 to 1988—

---

74. Ibid., p. 206.

75. Guzmán, op. cit., p. 35.

76. The Chilean Movimiento de la Izquierda Revolucionaria (MIR) devoted great efforts in the late sixties and the early seventies to establishing itself among the *pobladores* that lived in the *callampas* around Santiago. In several such shantytowns—Nueva La Habana, La Victoria—it encountered some success and sympathy, but was quickly erased from the scene by the September 1973 military coup. The Chilean Communist Party also set down roots among the *pobladores*, but they were not exactly marginals but rather more regularly employed, poorly housed squatters. The Salvadorean FPL also enjoyed a degree of success in this regard, as did the Sandinista Front in shantytowns outside Managua before its 1979 victory (see Francis Pisani, *Los muchachos* [Managua: Editorial Vanguardia, 1989], pp. 92–93, for example). In theory, other groups also tried: the urban poor and slum dwellers, the Brazilian *favelados* were meant to be Carlos Marighela's most fertile recruiting ground. They never were.

77. José Matos Mar, *Desborde popular y crisis del Estado* (Lima: Instituto de Estudios Peruanos, 1984).

and little or no incentive for sticking with the system instead of attempting to destroy it. With some education, no jobs in Lima, and a vivid sense of exclusion from "*Lima la blanca*," they became logical candidates for Sendero's terrifying, forced recruitment. Strangely—and unknowingly in part at the time—Sendero was also recruiting among the capital's upper crust. Abimael Guzmán's capture on September 15 led to the arrest and identification of dozens of sons and daughters of the most distinguished members of Lima's intelligentsia: doctors, dancers, lawyers, composers. The surprise and secret of Sendero's penetration of the Peruvian cultured and professional establishment is shown, among other things, by the fact that an otherwise insightful and well researched book of essays on the Shining Path, published just before Presidente Gonzalo's downfall, did not touch on the issue.[78]

Even before the imprisonment of much of its leadership in 1992, most analysts of Sendero Luminoso maintained that despite its extension to new regions of the nation, well beyond its original bases, the movement was far from assuming power. As late as 1990, its inability to truly expand its mass base, as opposed to its regional implantation, particularly to any working-class constituency, was constantly underlined as an intrinsic, ongoing, and highly debilitating characteristic. But an equally plausible opposing argument was also heard: Sendero was not looking to gain power in the immediate future, under existing political conditions in Peru, but rather was bent on creating such a chaotic situation that a military takeover would become inevitable. This corresponds to Sendero's explicit plans and goals, and as Gustavo Gorriti, Peru's most noted historian of the Maoist organization, has stated, Abimael Guzmán has tended to be correct in his political forecasting.[79] Because of its existing organization, arms, and networks, Sendero would then become the leading and dominant force in any antimilitary coalition that would be constructed in response to a coup. The chaos in Peru after the 1990 election, the 1991 cholera epidemic, and the 1992 abro-

---

78. David Scott Palmer, *The Shining Path of Peru* (New York: St. Martin's Press, 1992).

79. "Guzmán's scenario and objectives were clear. . . . (1) During the eighties, the incapacity of the Peruvian State to govern the country would become evident; (2) within that process the insurrection led by Sendero would grow; (3) in this same decade, "the solution of the problem" would be defined, that is, the growth of the Senderista insurrection until it got ahead of the vulnerability curve, by achieving a strategic equilibrium. . . . On writing these lines in July of 1989, with the entire decade in perspective, it is impossible to avoid comparing the naïve and optimistic prophecies . . . of the leading elite and those of Guzmán expressed at the same time. They were diametrically opposed, and Guzmán was right, though not totally." Gustavo Gorriti Ellenbogen, *Sendero: Historia de la guerra milenaria en el Perú*, vol. 1. (Lima: Editorial Apoyo, 1990), p. 99.

gation of constitutional rule in a quasi-military coup headed by President Fujimori himself, all played into this plan. On the other hand, Guzmán's jailing may well have fatally weakened the organization.

It has long been surmised that "Shining Path is fundamentally the creation of one person, Professor Abimael Guzman Raynoso."[80] If so, his arrest, together with that of much of the leadership, may well signify the demise of Sendero. But there are at least some grounds for questioning the single-creator hypothesis: Sendero has sprung from deeper roots; it has built up a company of cadres; it has accumulated a significant amount of wealth. Much more time and information must become available to ascertain what Guzmán's capture implies for the prospects of the Shining Path.

But beyond the future possibilities that Sendero may, or may not, have to survive and prosper, it already represents a major component of the Latin American left, because of both its innovations and its archaisms. It is the first guerrilla movement to be truly and significantly involved with the drug trade; the Colombian precedents are not conclusive and were, according to available information, on a limited scale. With the possible exceptions of Genaro Vázquez's and Lucio Cabañas's Mexican guerrillas of the early seventies, it is the first Latin American armed group to be virtually 100 percent independent of foreign support, training, arms or money.[81] Although it has gradually built up an international network of support and solidarity—the Committee to Support the Revolution in Peru, the Revolutionary Communist Party in the U.S., and the Revolutionary International Movement and Sun Peru Committees in Europe—there is less behind all of this than meets the eye.[82] There is also a tendency to blame every terrorist act in Latin

---

80. Palmer, op. cit., p. 243.

81. Gorriti Ellenbogen gives the following appraisal of the Peruvian authorities' repeated attempts to link the Shining Path with Cuba: "If [Colombian president Julio César] Turbay's claim [of Cuban support for Colombian guerrillas] was half true—Cuba's support for some of the Colombian guerrilla movements was beyond doubt; but at the same time that support did not explain even a fraction of insurrectional violence in Colombia—in the case of [Peruvian president Fernando] Belaunde, the insinuation had no other explanation than his own indignant confusion." Gorriti Ellenbogen, op. cit., p. 176.

82. Simon Strong in particular has stressed Sendero's international connections: "Shining Path's potential to stimulate physical violence not only in the poorer countries of the world but also the rich should not be underestimated. . . . In the same way that the return of democracy in Peru converted the rest of the left into parliamentary revolutionaries, leaving the radical ground clear for Shining Path, so too has it been strengthened internationally by perestroika itself. Pro-Soviet Communist parties have been destroyed and moderates undermined, generating a political vacuum which Maoism, with Shining Path as its lead advocate, is on hand to fill." Strong, op. cit., pp. 252–253; also Simon Strong, *New York Times Magazine*, May 24, 1992.

America on an extension or outgrowth of Sendero: local governments need and enjoy easy scapegoats. Finally, it is for all practical intents the first military organization in the hemisphere to gain a mass base among the urban, marginalized poor on a relevant scale. If making the front page of the *New York Times* remains an indication of guerrilla prospects, Sendero was well on its way in late 1991.[83]

But Sendero Luminoso is, of course, also the last movement to openly proclaim its allegiance to "Marxism-Leninism-Maoism," to unabashedly put forward the goal of a Communist revolution, and to unhesitatingly reject any notion of electoral contention or dialogue with existing authorities or institutions. Sendero is in this sense a lingering remnant of an age gone by, of a time when revolution still seemed possible, both to the intellectuals who founded similar organizations in the sixties and seventies and to the masses who joined them. The degree of violence and sacrifice along with the existential asceticism, ideological certitudes, and ensuing cohesion that Sendero conserves to this day all seem obsolete in Latin America. The way in which more than 250 Senderista prisoners in the Lima penitentiaries went to their deaths on June 19, 1986, massacred in the wake of a prison riot that was doomed to end in bloodshed, is almost inconceivable elsewhere in Latin America today.[84] It wasn't exactly a collective suicide or mutually agreed-on supreme sacrifice, but it resembled one. At this stage it is yet unclear whether the Spartan fundamentalism inherent in the Shining Path belongs to the continent's past or to its future; it is certainly a determining feature of Peru's present.

---

83. "Defying the drift of recent world history, a Marxist rebel movement is rapidly expanding in Peru, carrying the fight from its Andean strongholds to this coastal capital's impoverished and politically crucial shantytowns. . . . The rebel strategy seems to be succeeding." James Brooke, *New York Times*, November 11, 1991, p. 1.

84. The heroism cannot be dissociated from the notion of *"la cuota,"* or the quota of blood, that in Guzmán's mind Sendero must pay to reach power, and from his conception of political cost and sacrifice. In Gorriti's words: "The way in which Guzmán understood the principle of the conservation of forces had nothing to do with the numeric calculation of a military technician, but rather with the evaluation of the political and military effect that a given sacrifice would have, in contrast with the advantage provided by survival." Gorriti Ellenbogen, op. cit., p. 282.

5

Squaring the Circle:
Reforming Revolution

■

For many years there has been both a reformist hope and resigned expectation in Latin America. For the enlightened right and center, the hope has focused on the possibility of change without risk, of justice without violence or social and international confrontation. For the defeated or disenchanted radical left, the resigned expectation is rooted in the relativity of the lesser of two evils: as the idea of revolution *hic et nunc* was discarded, a "sort of" justice, a sort of change, a sort of independence and equality became increasingly attractive. Not incidentally, it also allowed the radical left to keep despising the enemies it loved to hate while trimming its sails and expanding its traditional circle of friends. But perhaps most of all, everyone seemed to like reformists in Latin America because they had never really been in power, with the exceptions noted below, most of which could be explained away. Reformism in Latin America has been like a Spanish *posada*, or roadway inn: everyone brings along what he chooses, and finds what he or she wants on arrival.

The reformist quest finds its raison d'être in the recurrent Latin American—and almost universal—aspiration for squaring the circle: how to combine change with continuity, social justice with economic growth, representative democracy with effective governance. Reformism, in any one of its varieties, but chiefly in the social-democratic mode, seemed to be the answer: a moderate, left-of-center, intelligent, and sensitive response to the hemisphere's intractable problems. The hope also stems from relatively rational analysis, indicating that Latin America has finally "grown into" the social, economic, and political structures that allowed social-democratic reformism to flourish in Europe. It could well constitute the ultimate interface between two regions of the world tied together by centuries of missed opportunities.

It had been some time since social democracy in Europe reached as far to the left as during French president François Mitterrand's first two years in office. In the course of that brief period, when left and right continued to make a significant difference in a rich and modern nation, Régis Debray, Mitterrand's friend, erstwhile speech writer, and reluctant foreign affairs adviser, left his mark on France's last attempt at conserving its grandeur and presence in Latin America. That was where the friendships, debts, and loyalties built up over time permitted him to do so: in the ranks of the Latin American left, where he had spent the best years of his youth.

The renewed encounter between Debray and his former friends was bound to be tense: they would ask for the world, as leftists and Latin Americans are wont to do; he would have to spend most of his working day proving that he was not Che Guevara's posthumous mole buried deep in the entrails of the Elysée. The conflicts were formidable and predictable; so was the service Debray performed for the left in Latin America during that short span. If he failed to bring France and democratic socialism's influence to bear on Cuba and the armed left throughout the hemisphere, it was not for lack of trying.

Debray had a problem with the Salvadorean armed left. In contrast to his positive feelings about the Sandinistas, and how they had dealt with their internal conflicts over the years (without bloodshed and mostly without excommunication), in El Salvador, Debray had to face the issue and memory of his friend the revolutionary and poet Roque Dalton. A member of the National Resistance (FARN) before it split, he had been executed by a faction of the leadership in 1975, accused of being an agent of the Soviet Union and/or the CIA. Shortly after Debray began to buttress France's role in the Central American crisis, he met with FARN leader, and Dalton's comrade-in-arms, Fermán Cienfuegos in a hotel room in Mexico City, hoping to hear how Dalton had died, who had killed him, and whether the same sort of thing could happen again. Rumor had it that Joaquín Villalobos, then one of the leaders of Dalton's organization, had either directly carried out the poet's execution or given the order for it. None of this made Debray's relationship with the FMLN leadership, which Villalobos now belonged to, any easier. Cienfuegos answered well enough to confirm Debray's intentions of contributing strongly to a negotiated solution in El Salvador: the Franco-Mexican Declaration of 1981, bestowing legit-

imacy on the FMLN, was largely Debray's and a Mexican friend's doing. But he did not dispel the Frenchman's persisting doubts about the
FMLN's conversion to civilized norms of coexistence, if not with its
enemies, at least with its friends.

Thus in April 1983, when Debray learned of the murder in Managua
of Ana María, one of the FMLN's leading figures, followed by the
suicide of the legendary Cayetano Carpio, also in the Nicaraguan capital, he was furious at the Salvadoreans and at himself for trusting in
their capacity for peaceful resolution of internal conflicts. These feelings burst out during a strained and emotional dinner in Paris at his
overcrowded apartment on the Rue Notre Dame des Champs with
Salvador Samayoa, the Salvadorean guerrilla leader he probably knew
best and respected most. He also happened to be a member of the same
organization Carpio and Ana María had belonged to.

Fabricio, as the Cubans still called Debray (remembering the nom
de guerre he had lifted from Stendhal's *Charterhouse of Parma*),
wanted to know what happened. More insistently, he questioned
how it could be that nearly ten years after the death of Roque Dalton
and endless conversations with European Social Democrats and Latin
American reformists, some Salvadorean insurgents were still solving
their problems the old-fashioned way—like gangsters or hit men.
Worse still, the Nicaraguans' and Cubans' role in the matter was
frustratingly unclear. If anything, the Cubans made matters worse by
taking sides openly in the Salvadorean internecine dispute and awk-
wardly suggesting to Carpio that the only way out lay in his self-
inflicted demise.

Debray had no sympathy for the position Carpio, accused of Ana
María's assassination, had presumably espoused: against negotiations, in favor of a protracted armed struggle to the death. But he
could not understand how matters had deteriorated so much inside
the FMLN that the bloody outcome in Managua had become predictable and virtually inevitable. His Salvadorean interlocutor thus found
himself in an impossible situation. Having come prepared to answer
Debray's questions and doubts about the consequences of Carpio's
death for the FMLN's pronegotiations line, Samayoa was being forced
to address another, more complex and decisive matter. What did the
twin deaths say about the Salvadorean guerrillas and who they really
were? What role had the Cubans and Nicaraguans played in the entire affair and the revolution itself? Debray cared more about how
Carpio had died, and whether events truly occurred the way Samayoa
narrated them, than whether the net effect of both leaders' deaths

strengthened the negotiating stance. Samayoa stuck stubbornly to the official account—which actually coincided with his own sincere belief—and insisted on looking to the future. Debray resignedly acknowledged that his insurgent acquaintances from the Central American isthmus were not exactly social democrats. The trust and friendship between the two would last, just as would the conviction that they were worlds apart.

The irony of the high-strung conversation was that if the European–Latin American social-democratic convergence was ever to take place, the two participants were ideally suited. Debray, and through him Mitterrand and the left wing of the Socialist Party, were the most sympathetic, sensitive, and well-placed sector of the European left to link up with Latin America and the "Second Wave" of the armed left—mainly the Sandinistas, Guatemalans, and Salvadoreans. The Spanish Socialists, on paper a more natural option, had abdicated that role for many reasons, ranging from domestic necessity to infinite arrogance.

Samayoa, for his part, as everyone who met him over the years would concur, was the most lucid, open-minded, and honest representative of this second wave of the Latin American left. If anybody could become a radical social democrat under the conditions of Central American violence and poverty, it was he. The former schoolteacher and minister of education had become a political operative, but he was probably the best one the Central American left had unearthed in years. His personal loyalties and political straightforwardness would serve him well, but the meeting in Paris showed the distance still separating Europe and Latin America, reformism and armed struggle, Jesuit guerrillas and French intellectuals.

The contemporary history of left-of-center reformism in Latin America is brief but eventful. It includes social democrats—both those officially recognized as such and wanna-bes—and reformists of other persuasions: erstwhile populists, laborites, and ex-guerrillas. They will be examined in turn, with the understanding that the dividing lines between the various sectors are less precise and categorical than the concessions to descriptive expediency may indicate.

The reformist aspiration has often been identified with social democracy, European-style. As revolutionary groups changed their stripes, they eagerly sought to acquire social-democratic credentials. By 1990, organizations such as the Salvadorean ERP had drafted internal documents proclaiming their new stance, and in early 1991 were announcing their conversion in high-profile interviews with the *New*

York Times.[1] Along with the Sandinistas, the Colombian M-19, and the recently founded *cardenista* PRD in Mexico, the Salvadorean insurgents openly courted the Socialist International. Elements representing a large portion of the political spectrum now met under social democracy's banner, from the reluctantly reformist—the Alliance for Progress and its heirs among United States Latin Americanists—to the resignedly realistic—the revolutionary left as time caught up with it. As Michael Manley of Jamaica, one of its most eloquent hemispheric proponents, recalled:

> The People's National Party won a landslide victory in the general elections of February 1972. Before our eyes were these two models— Puerto Rico and Cuba. Surely there was another path, a third path. . . . we were to spend the next years in our periphery exploring that third path.[2]

But along with these largely illusory and consequently unfulfillable demands, an accompanying expectation has also emerged with regard to reformism and social democracy. In addition to believing that it represents the most *desirable* path for the hemisphere to follow, its advocates also consider that it is the most *viable* one. As Brazilian scholar Hélio Jaguaribe has phrased it,

> In these countries [of Latin America] the only *viable* democracy is a mass social democracy. The social democratic model . . . with a market economy, submitted to serious social programming or planning, that accelerates the incorporation of broad masses to higher living standards . . . obviously constitutes the *best* formula for dealing with the needs of these countries.[3]

Because of Latin America's demography, social structure, international position, and cultural and political traditions, social democracy looks like a perfect fit: the type of political and economic development strategy that takes into account aspirations and constraints, the past and the future, reform and revolution. Indeed, it has even become

---

1. Joaquín Villalobos, interview with Mark Uhlig, *New York Times*, March 10, 1991, p. 3.
2. Michael Manley, quoted in Clive Thomas, *The Poor and the Powerless: Economic Policy and Change in the Caribbean* (New York: Monthly Review Press, 1988), pp. 212–213.
3. Hélio Jaguaribe, "Introdução á social-democracia," in Hélio Jaguaribe, *A Proposta social-democrata* (Rio de Janeiro: José Olympio Editora, 1989), p. 11 (emphasis added).

perceived as an alternative to the brutal adjustment process the region has undergone in recent years.[4]

As the democratization process and the continent's economic and ideological transformations created a vortex in the political center that sucked everything into its heretofore empty space, a reformist, ersatz social-democratic left-of-center seemed heaven-sent to counter both the Christian Democratic right-of-center and the new probusiness, free-market, neoliberal modern right. But these excessive expectations thrust on social democracy may have rested on an implicit misunderstanding. Transition theorists have emphasized this point: while social democracy may dovetail neatly with Latin America's needs, it doesn't necessarily square with its structures, nor with today's international environment. The large, organized, homogeneous working class, which almost composed a sociological and electoral majority from the turn of the century to the late sixties in most Western European nations (with exceptions and nuances by country and period) and which came to constitute the mass base for social democracy, is simply not present in Latin America.

Perhaps the most damaging statement regarding the prospects for social democracy in Latin America is the fact that Argentina, the country where, since the beginning of the century, the social structure has seemed the most suited for its success, actually appears the furthest removed from giving birth to a typical social-democratic movement. Furthermore, the business community in most of Latin America has a choice today that its European counterparts of the Depression or postwar era did not enjoy when faced with the unpleasant prospect of reformist government and policies: pack up and go elsewhere, investing their money abroad thanks to worldwide capital flows.[5]

---

4. Some proponents of a "different" adjustment have straightforwardly labeled their aspirations as social democratic, and spelled them out in some detail: "Our 'social democratic' approach to market-oriented reforms calls for orienting reforms towards growth, for protecting, material welfare against the transitional costs of reforms and for making full use of democratic institutions. . . . Industrial policies, social policies and political compromises cost money and trade-offs are inevitable. . . . All we argue is that to be successful, reforms must explicitly aim at growth, income security and democracy." Luis Carlos Bresser Pereira, José María Maravall, and Adam Przeworski, "Economic Reforms in New Democracies: A Social-Democratic Approach," paper presented at the Conference on Democracy, Markets and Structural Reforms in Latin America, Buenos Aires, March 25–27, 1992, p. 24.

5. These points have been argued by, among others, Robert R. Kaufman, "Liberalization and Democratization in South America," in Guillermo O'Donnell, Philippe Schmitter, and Laurence Whitehead, *Transitions from Authoritarian Rule*, vol. 3 (Baltimore: Johns Hopkins University Press, 1986), p. 103.

In addition, the emergence of social democracy in much of Western Europe was a direct consequence of the rise of Marxism, either of a pre-Leninist breed before World War I, or of a Bolshevized version after the conflagration that began in 1914 and sundered many of Europe's socialist parties. But with the exception of a small number of immigrant intellectuals and labor organizers, Marxism in Latin America surfaced *after* the Russian Revolution and the founding of the Comintern,[6] and thus competed with social-democratic thought and practice for the same hearts and minds from the outset. In a sense, Marxism, as well as Communist Party–style Leninism, crowded out democratic socialism in Latin America from the left, while the national-popular currents that sprang up during the Depression competed with it later from the right. Between Leninism and populism, social democracy found little more than barren soil in which to take root. Only when the two currents began to truly lose sway within the Latin American working class did the democratic version of European socialism start to take hold. And it has still been forced to surmount important "structural" obstacles, ranging from the corporativist integration of unions from the populist era to the intrinsic weaknesses of the Latin American working class.[7] Even under ideal, laboratory-like conditions, such as those that prevailed in Brazil in 1979–1981, the creation of a reformist left-of-center party along Western European

---

6. This point was repeatedly made by the late José Aricó. In his words, "Until the breakdown of Communist hegemony in the culture of the left, the only Marxism in Latin America was 'Marxism-Leninism.'" José Aricó, "El Marxismo en América Latina," in Fernando Calderón, ed., *Socialismo, Autoritarismo y Democracia* (Lima: Instituto de Estudios Peruanos, CLACSO, 1989), p.116.

7. The virtually congenital contradiction that has plagued the continent's labor movement for decades has been summed up in the following fashion: "Sectoral employment in mining, utilities (gas, water, electric power), manufacturing and construction industries makes up half the total of the wage-earning population. These are the sectors where the rate of unionization and the tradition of struggle are generally greatest. Thus the union movement is potentially very strong in Latin America. But it is also weak because of:

"(a) insufficient control of the labor market because of 'urban marginality' accentuated by 'structural marginality,' that is, by the contradiction between high rates of population growth and rural-urban migration, and the introduction of capital-intensive technologies;

"(b) the persistence of 'sweetheart unions' and so-called parallel unions, that is, the organic weakness of the union movement (with the exception of Mexico, Brazil and Argentina) due to political divisions;

"(c) the ideological affiliation of the union movement to the populist models, seeking to rebuild national-popular coalitions that are unviable today." Julio Godio, *Historia del movimiento obrero latinoamericano/3 (1930–1980)* (San José, Costa Rica: Editorial Nueva Sociedad, 1985), p. 211.

social-democratic lines proved impossible. An unfettered, uncontaminated working-class constituency—the key ingredient—was there: a large new sector of the Brazilian working class just emerging from the spectacular, authoritarian industrialization of the previous fifteen years. It had a charismatic working-class leadership allied with nearly all of the intellectual left, and a budding process of democratization, as new political parties were suddenly tolerated. Yet all of this was to no avail. Ideological divisions, personal rivalries, and inexperience made the effort fruitless.[8]

But despite the obstacles, the hope endures. More important, the fact is that powerful reformist political parties have emerged in Latin America over the past two decades. There is a reformist left in the region today, which includes social-democratic parties of varying persuasions but extends beyond them. Their European origins or ties are sometimes evident, as witnessed by the fact that most of the Latin social-democratic parties belong to the European-based Socialist International (IS) born in Frankfurt in 1951 as a direct descendant of the Second International, founded, among others, by Karl Marx in 1884. Not all the Latin organizations that belong to the Socialist International are social-democratic, while other important reformist groups or movements are either not members or not fully social democratic: the Chilean Socialist Party before 1992, the Brazilian PSDB and PT, and the *cardenista* coalition in Mexico.

Interestingly enough, the oldest members of the social-democratic movement are also the most traditional and conservative today: Venezuela's Acción Democrática; Liberación Nacional of Costa Rica; the Peruvian Acción Popular Revolucionaria de América (APRA); and the People's National Party of Jamaica.[9] The Argentine Socialist Party (PSA), perhaps the oldest organization of its kind in Latin America, originally comprised most of the attributes of a classically social-democratic political party—a mass, working-class, union-organized constituency, in alliance with the intellectualized lower middle class,

---

8. "At that time [1979], a group of intellectuals tried to form a European-style socialist party. . . . They hoped to unite the new union movement emerging in Brasil around the Sao Paulo industrial suburbs [the so-called ABCD] with the political leadership of the opposition to the military regime. . . . The proposal to build a Socialist Party was unsuccessful, mainly because of political-ideological differences." Moacir Gadotti and Otaviano Pereira, *Pra que PT: Origen, Projeto e Consolidação do Partido dos Trabalhadores,* São Paulo; Cortez Editora, 1989), p. 26.

9. In fact until 1970 only the Argentine Socialist Party and the Jamaican PNP were full members of the IS; the other parties mentioned were so-called Consultative Members or, more simply, observers. Carlos Morales Abarzúa, *La Internacional Socialista en América Latina y el Caribe* (Mexico City: Editorial Patria Grande, 1981), pp. 56–57.

a reformist ideology, and a burgeoning bureaucracy. However, all this was lost when Perón repossessed the mass base and condemned the PSA to relative marginality. Similarly, APRA lacked the working-class base, and was forced by conditions in Peru into a more radical posture. The *trienio* in Venezuela, from 1945 to 1948, generally identified with Acción Democrática (AD), is another example. AD became social-democratic later; it was essentially a populist organization in its first incarnation. With the exception of the Jamaican People's National Party under Michael Manley's leadership, most of these parties were either born or resurrected under the influence of the Cold War and the fight against Communism and the USSR in Latin America, or subsequently as a response to the Cuban Revolution. They were strongly marked by this association, and can thus be included in any classification of the Latin American left only under the broadest of standards. Even later, when the entire center of gravity of Latin American membership in the Socialist International shifted to the left, these parties maintained their (relatively) conservative credentials. Juan Bosch's Partido de la Revolución Democrática from the Dominican Republic also maintained ties with the IS, and the Chilean Radical Party joined in 1972. Yet, by and large, these links were more formal than substantive, and even the International's most fervent backers in Latin America were forced to acknowledge that "Until 1970 the IS had only precarious ties with the Third World."[10] Former German chancellor Willy Brandt's election to the presidency of the International in 1976, however, changed its outlook considerably. By 1980 the strengthening of the social democratic current throughout the hemisphere was in full swing.[11]

By the end of the 1980s, left-of-center reformist movements, coalitions, or parties were either in office or seriously contending for it in countries like Brazil, Mexico, Chile, Peru, Ecuador, Venezuela, Costa Rica, Jamaica, and Uruguay. Some of these were traditionally conservative social democrats, a few found themselves quite to the left of the

---

10. Ibid., p. 56. The first significant meeting of Latin and European social democrats, including Mitterrand, González, Palme, and Mario Soares of Portugal, took place in Caracas in 1976. In 1980, leaders of more than thirty European parties met with a large number of Latin American organizations, personalities, and movements in Santo Domingo.

11. A Chilean socialist explained the flourishing of social democracy in Latin America in the following manner: "The social-democratic tendency acquired singular vigor as a result of three different phenomena: the organized action toward Latin America of European social-democracy; the 'social-democratic' role that many important 'populist' and national-conservative parties assumed; and the central importance the concept of 'democracy' acquired in the Latin American political and ideological debate." Jorge Arrate, "El socialismo autonómo sudamericano: Sus antagonismos y convergencias con Europa," *Nueva Sociedad* (Caracas), no. 72, May-June 1984.

local political spectrum, and others, like PNP leader Michael Manley in Jamaica, oscillated—perhaps inevitably—from one extreme to another.[12] All of these parties shared a number of characteristics, as well as many of the same obstacles. Their origins are diverse, ranging partly from the Cuban legacy of armed struggle—the M-19 in Colombia, factions of the Frente Amplio in Uruguay, and parts of the Partido dos Trabalhadores in Brazil—to the populist roots of Cárdenas in Mexico, Brizola in Brazil, and Torrijos in Panama, and finally including the anti-Communist baggage as yet unjettisoned by Oscar Arias in Costa Rica. They all belong to what, *faute de mieux*, can be called the reformist left, and may be described as follows.

To begin with, all of these movements are as of now exclusively electoralist: none of them even remotely refers to any other road to power, nor to any alternative mechanism for transferring power. Although many features distinguish the reformist left from *the right and center* of the hemispheric political spectrum, its basic defining difference with other sectors of *the left* lies here. In addition, it has rejected any association with the Leninist, single-party, vertical conception of governance or political organization. While some reformist parties maintained their references to Marxism until quite recently, these were more analytical than programmatic, a distinction often lost on Washington, but not on Latin America. Finally, though some Latin American reformists forged close personal and political ties with Moscow, their organizations were never pro-Soviet, neither in fact nor in most of their constituencies' perceptions. This was true even for those with close bonds to Cuba.

Whereas the Communist parties in the past advocated other "possible" means of accession to power, and as the armed left unabashedly proclaimed its rejection of the electoral road, the reformist, quasi-social-democratic component of the left distinguishes itself by its radical fidelity to electoral mechanisms. In a continent where the left has repeatedly witnessed how elections do not always function as a viable means of acceding to power, this is a major point of convergence and an important change in Latin American politics. Similarly, and largely because of this electoral single-mindedness, these parties also share a commitment to the democratic process, human rights, free expression, and freedom of association. Only under across-the-board democratization can movements advocating reform

---

12. In 1972, Manley won 70 percent of the vote in Jamaica; in 1976, after four years of social-democratic policies, the PNP obtained 78 percent; but by 1980, having accepted IMF economic austerity and major confrontation with the United States, it fell to 15 percent.

and opposition to entrenched interests even hope to reach power peacefully and implement the changes they favor. Whether their zeal for facets of democratic life is absolutely sincere and deeply rooted or springs directly and recently from an involuntary decision to follow only the electoral path is of diminishing importance, though not irrelevant. As one author has characterized the alteration of Latin American political culture of the seventies and eighties, they end up "attributing a high intrinsic value to the achievement and consolidation of political democracy."[13]

For the same reasons, these movements tend to act in favor of enfranchisement, mass-based politics, and, in general, of transforming what Hélio Jaguaribe has called "restricted, liberal middle-class democracies" into broad-based, inclusive political systems.[14] Even in countries such as Venezuela, where the actual options presented to the electorate by social-democratic reformists are meager and the apparent participation of a significant majority of the population in the political process is often meaningless, high turnouts are both a feature and an aspiration of the reformist parties. Again, the original motivation for this desire to broaden political participation is less important than the links and logical necessities that bind it to the electoral choice these parties have made. No political organization in Latin America can realistically expect to contend for power electorally from the center-left without pinning most of its hopes on greater voter representation. In particular, the reformist left must inevitably seek the involvement of the impoverished urban masses and the rural poor, despite the risks of manipulation.

The second broad characteristic of Latin American reformism is a significant dedication, in word and generally in deed, to the "social question": social justice, reducing inequities, enacting distributive economic and social policies, promoting equality, social development, etc. While no political grouping in Latin America can eschew the reference

---

13. Guillermo O'Donnell, "Introduction to the Latin American Cases," in O'Donnell, Schmitter, and Whitehead, op. cit., p. 14.

14. Jaguaribe, op. cit., p. 10. In the case of Brazil, Jaguaribe substantiates his claim that mass-based democracies are the only solution, at least for a social-democratic party, the following way: "From the middle of the forties through the mid-sixties it was possible to administer a middle-class democracy in Brazil. But in the face of growing pressures from the masses, the middle classes, through their military vanguard, interrupted the democratic process to save their interests. But industrialization, urbanization, and the generalized access to the mass media made the survival of the military dictatorship inviable by the mid-seventies. But they also made evident the impossibility of restoring the restricted middle-class democracy of the preceding period. The country demanded democracy, and this could only be a mass social democracy [*democracia social de masas*]. Ibid., p.15.

to the "social question," clearly the main redeeming virtue of the reformist movement with regard to the traditional Latin right and center lies in its social commitment. The affinity between the latter and the reformist left's democratic, electoral posture is obvious: it makes sense for a political organization to compete for power exclusively through electoral means only if it believes that it stands a reasonable chance of achieving its aims. This necessarily entails seeking the uncaptured votes of the urban and rural poor, together with the lower middle and working class in Latin America.

These votes are only available, and conquerable, through a social platform centered on promising these sectors at least part of what they have always lacked: land, jobs, education, health care, public services and housing, pride, and dignity. The fact that nearly all of the new reformist parties in Latin America arrived relatively late on the scene, when most of the right and center had already acquired its constituency, implied that they could find votes only beyond that constituency: the unincorporated, disenfranchised, not-yet-manipulated poor.

But in addition to reasons of political expediency, the social vocation of Latin reformism is also rooted in ideological considerations, in the narrow but not unimportant working- or middle-class origins of many of its members, in its ties to social democracy abroad, and to the progressive intellectual community. Finally, it derives both from the populist heritage and its long-standing rivalries: most Latin American reformist parties are either populist offspring or rivals of the populist holdouts or traditional Communist parties. If they had to be "socially oriented" to conquer votes and constituencies on their right, they also had to be socially conscious in order to cover their flank on the left. Given the social one-upmanship that both the national popular opposition currents and the Communists traditionally resorted to, this implied building and hanging on to a mass base through radical social policies and programs.

Reformism in Latin America has been "incorporative" or "inclusionary": invariably, when it is in the opposition; moderately, when it attains power. The region has constantly been conceptualized through the inclusion-exclusion mode, and its main social challenge has repeatedly been defined as the inclusion or incorporation of millions of "excluded" into the formal economy, the job market, the political system, the social welfare net, and the social services system (education, health, housing, drinking water, sewage). But if social democrats are "inclusionary," they are consequently, and incorrigibly, redistributive. The injustices in Latin America are so blatant, the disparities in wealth and income so striking, that any effort to incorporate the poor into "modern" society has necessarily presupposed a redistribution of wealth and power, not just the generation of new riches.

The reformist insistence on social and political reform stems from this premise: without reforms (fiscal, agrarian, labor, welfare state, etc.) any new wealth created would be as inequitably distributed as before. It is simply not sufficient to generate wealth; the conditions under which it is distributed must also change. The importance of redistribution leads directly to the principle of strong state intervention in the economy. It has been thought that only through such intervention can new wealth—or old wealth for that matter—be distributed in a manner that will in turn bring about the inclusion of the excluded masses. Regulation, subsidies, state ownership of economically or socially strategic sectors of the economy, an incomes policy are all features of this overall conception. Although many other sectors of the Latin American left—the old populists, even the military have actually implemented policies of this sort, often unwittingly— share these points of view, the reformist left is the most explicit in its views. The reason probably lies in the above-cited truism: there is a strong bond between the democratic, electoral constraint and a strong social vocation.

There is a similar connection between these two characteristics and the third distinguishing trait Latin social democracy has acquired over the years. This third characteristic is the strong nationalist dictum that virtually all the hemisphere's reformist left subscribes to, and that generally translates into opposition platforms or—with some watering down—government policy. In contrast to movements ranging from the center to the right, which have tended to attach less importance to issues of national sovereignty, in recent years Latin American reformism has shared with the rest of the region's left a forceful, often visceral insistence on strengthening nationalism and the nation's standing in the world. This is analogous with many of the populist regimes and with some of their military or civilian successors—Brazilian generals or the PRI in Mexico.

This disposition of the social democrats and other reformists led to both the adoption for analytical purposes of an overall nationalistic approach to understanding the region's problems, and a stance on specific issues reflecting that perspective. In fact, a Socialist International meeting in Mexico City in 1979 went so far as to espouse as radical a view as the following:

> Historically, the countries of Latin America and the Caribbean have suffered from a system of exploitation and dependency, from which they have not liberated themselves even today despite their achieve-

ment of political independence as nations. The savage capitalism that
they are subject to has kept their peoples subject to neo-colonialism.
Through numerous forms of intervention, imperialism has blocked
their full social, economic and cultural emancipation.[15]

A more detailed expression of this perspective was formulated with
regard to then presidential candidate Ronald Reagan's positions on
Central American issues a few months later by the Socialist International at its Fifteenth Congress, held in Madrid in 1980: "We are particularly worried about some comments with regard to Latin America
made by the Republican candidate for the presidency of the United
States, mainly his signs of support for the dictatorships of Guatemala
and El Salvador, and his attacks on Grenada and Nicaragua."[16] On
foreign policy matters, the Latin American reformist left, with counted
exceptions, has systematically embraced the more nationalistic stance
available to it, avoiding confrontation with the United States when
possible, but not dodging confrontation when it became unavoidable.
As with so many other characteristics of this current, this type of
stance was considerably more resolute when adopted from the less
dangerous vantage point of opposition than when it involved governmental responsibility. But overall, on the main foreign policy issues of
the day over the last fifteen years, Latin American reformists—in
power or not—have tended to sustain nationalistic, antiinterventionist
stances, which often translate into positions contrary to those of the
United States. (Venezuelan president Carlos Andrés Perez's second
term in office is an exception.)

This left-of-center, reformist nationalism is not limited to foreign
policy. Its most important manifestations have in fact lain elsewhere:
in economic policy and domestic considerations. Social democrats in
particular—ranging from the most moderate, like Carlos Andrés Pérez,
to the more radical, like Michael Manley in the 1970s or the Peruvian
APRA in the 1980s—have all implemented policies of natural resource
nationalization or regulation (oil, bauxite, copper) and/or unilateral
stances on foreign debt renegotiations over the past decades. They have
also maintained or strengthened the inward-looking development policies of the populist past, usually reinforcing the protectionist barriers
around local industry, tightening restrictions on foreign investment,
and advocating reforms of the international economic order and finan-

---

15. "Final Statement," Conference of Vice-Presidents for Latin America and the
Caribbean, Socialist International, Mexico City, April 1979, quoted by Morales Abarzúa,
op. cit., p. 156.
16. Ibid., p. 245.

cial system. While in recent years the wave of free-market radicalism has driven many Latin American social democrats to alter their policies on these matters, within the revised paradigms they remain more nationalistic than others.

As other currents of the Latin American left fade away or transform themselves, the hemisphere's reformist organizations are becoming a melting pot. Communists turn reformist, guerrillas come down from the mountains, and populists fight for free elections, as their legacy becomes a memory and ever less a lingering commitment. Four such transformations are worth examining, largely because their success or failure will determine the long-term viability of a Latin American reformism that combines a mass constituency with a coherent program and idealistic motivation: each displays a characteristic that previous parts of the left has possessed but that have rarely come together in one. The four are Brazil and Mexico, at a certain length, Chile and Venezuela, much more briefly. These transformations will also determine whether a more stable, virtually social-democratic left channels the energy and strength of Latin American reformism, or whether the unique social traits of the region will generate a peculiar, lasting form of left-of-center reformism, social-democratic in many of its aspects, but quite different from European social democracy in many more.

Although formally the Brazilian left is divided into several parties and factions, many would agree with Fernando Henrique Cardoso that "In Brazil social democracy is divided into three: the Brazilian Social Democratic Party (PSDB), Leonel Brizola's Partido Democrático Trabalhista (PDT), and Luis Ignacio de Silva's ("Lula's") Partido dos Trabalhadores (PT)."[17] In fact, it might be more precise to say that Brazilian reformism is made up of the above-mentioned three currents, that coalesced in the so-called *palanque da segunda volta*, or "second-round front," that supported Lula in the 1989 presidential election. This was a broad, typically reformist coalition, even if formally it was far from united. Indeed, its divisions sharpened since the 1989 presidential election, and many of its members would feel squeamish about the social-democratic label.

Geographically, how the three factions complement each other is obvious: The PT is strong just outside São Paulo, and sometimes in the city itself (where the PSDB is also strongest), and in the Center-North and Northeast, in states like Bahia and Pernambuco (where Lula fin-

---

17. Interview with the author, São Paulo, August 11, 1990. Cardoso is both a leading Brazilian social scientist and a leader of the PSDB. (In 1992, he became foreign minister of Brazil.) Sometimes he is quoted as one, sometimes as the other.

ished a strong second in the first round of the 1989 presidential election) and Brazilia, where Lula came in first. Conversely, the PDT's strength is limited to Rio de Janeiro, Rio Grande do Sul, and Santa Catarina, the three states where Brizola came out ahead. But beyond geography, they complement each other in other ways: the PSDB has a program and "respectable" leaders; the Workers Party has an organization, a working-class constituency, and thanks to the Catholic Church, a rural following. Finally, the PDT, because of its historical roots, has both an urban, shantytown (favelado) base and international standing.

Largely as a result of the talents and experience of many of its leaders, such as Mario Covas, economist José Serra, social scientist Hélio Jaguaribe, and former governors like Tasso Jereissati, the PSDB has an articulate typical social-democratic program.[18] It sometimes looks and sounds like a "kinder, gentler" version of the neoliberalism sweeping the hemisphere, but a series of uniquely Brazilian restraints on this trend make the PSDB less neoliberal than it might otherwise be. Cardoso outlined the differences between his party and Brizola's the following way:

> They do not have a modern way of thinking. They are influential because Brazil is stuck; Brizola always saw us as "Paulista snobs," without a constituency, without the people, and always mistrusted us because we were too modern and not tough enough. He made an alliance with us because alone he cannot win. He wants a Brazilian-style social-democracy, whereas we say that because here the levels of inequality are too great, you can't have tax policies or redistributive policies without growth and vice versa: you can't have one without the other. You have to worry about development. We are not populists and Statists like Brizola, but we will not accept the privatization of efficient parastatal firms. In some cases the private sector has failed.[19]

Those restraints have to do with the overall, apparently paradoxical consensus that has traditionally prevailed in Brazil with regard to a

---

18. Jereissati was elected governor of the state of Ceara in the impoverished Nordeste in 1986, and is reputed to have been one of the most effective and popular governors the state ever had. He went on to become secretary-general of the PSDB. See "Working for the People: A reformist state government in Brazil," *Newsweek International*, June 15, 1992. His policies in Ceara were highly praised by UNICEF in its *1992 State of the World's Children Report:* "This impoverished state has shown the world that the child health goals set for the year 2000 can be achieved." United Nations Children's Fund, *1992 State of the World's Children Report* (New York: Oxford University Press, 1992), p. 28.

19. Fernando Henrique Cardoso, interview with the author, São Paulo, August 11, 1990.

series of key items on the neoliberal agenda. It is often thought and said that Brazil is paralyzed by its political system's gridlock and its seeming inability to reach agreement on anything. But behind the bickering and division lurks a consensus on certain issues which are not the object of convergence elsewhere.

Three typically Brazilian characteristics explain this exception. The first is the existence of a truly competitive manufacturing and agricultural export sector in the economy: Brazil is the only nation in Latin America to have a sustained trade surplus—on occasions the third largest in the world—based significantly on manufactured exports.[20] Brazil does not have to open its economy indiscriminately and overnight to become competitive abroad. It followed a more Korean or Japanese model, of forcing certain parts of the manufacturing sector to export and adapt to international competition without exposing the rest of the economy to the often unsustainable rigors of that competition. Growth rates of Brazilian exports slowed in the 1990s (they had risen by almost 10 percent per year from 1965 to 1980, but then grew at only 5.6 percent from 1980 to 1989),[21] and there is an undeniable problem in maintaining previously acquired competitiveness. Nonetheless, of all the countries in the region, there still seems to be more underlying agreement in Brazil with regard to the merits of a degree of state-led industrial policy, protection, and subsidies for an export sector. Consequently there is less receptivity to external pressure for across-the-board trade liberalization and more room for domestic consensus.

Second, because of its extraordinary diversity and ensuing disparities of all types—geographical, ethnic, economic, social, topographic, and even climatological—there can only be so much of a reduction in the role of the state in the economy. Only the state can redistribute money from the wealthy South and Center—the quadrangle of relative prosperity composed of Porto Alegre, São Paulo, Rio de Janeiro, and Belo Horizonte—to the appallingly poor regions of the Northeast. Only the state can hope to integrate the ethnic diversity that characterizes Brazil and eliminate the discrimination against and exclusion of important parts of the black community. And only the state can try to achieve some attenuation of the abysmal inequities that Brazil's society has built up over the years. So although there are differing opinions among Brazilians with regard to state intervention, the spectrum of

---

20. In 1989, Brazil's trade surplus amounted to $16.1 billion, the third largest in the world, after Germany ($72 billion) and Japan ($68 billion). World Bank, *World Development Report 1991* (New York: Oxford University Press, 1991), p. 232.
21. Ibid., p. 231.

opinions is narrower than elsewhere. The reason lies in a third factor: the existence of an industrial, entrepreneurial class.

Brazil possesses, if any country in Latin America does, the long-sought, oft-regretted "national bourgeoisie," despite all its shortcomings, shortsightedness and provincialism. Every nation tends to believe that its "business elite" is the most mediocre in the world, and Brazilians are no different. But in comparison to the rest of Latin America, the Brazilian private sector looks more like a typical capitalist entrepreneurial class than any other, including the Chilean. It reinvests most of its money in Brazil; it is competitive and outward-looking (there are a number of Brazilian multinational firms operating throughout the world); it has established a type of relationship with the state that, while often incestuous and even outrageously advantageous for the private sector, is more similar to the Japanese or Korean model than to those of other nations in Latin America. It even partly opposed authoritarian rule in the 1970s, though not too vigorously, too quickly, nor unanimously. None of this should be idealized: the Brazilian private sector is no paragon of strategic vision or sensitivity to social or political issues. It has looted the state, rejected the most basic social demands, and supported a repressive, antidemocratic regime for years.

All of this allows groups like the PSDB to be "modern" and coherent in their economic program without going overboard and renouncing any social policy or industrial strategy. To appear moderate and reasonable, the PSDB does not have to go as far to the right as other groups in Latin America often feel the need to do today. And it can maintain its links to the rest of the left without excessive difficulty, although obviously this is not an easy task. The PSDB leadership was far more supportive of Lula in the 1989 presidential runoff than the rank and file or the electorate, and his defeat in São Paulo, the PSDB's stronghold, was largely due to the social-democratic voters' defection. Unity with the rest of the Brazilian left is all the more arduous a task in view of the specific features of its other two components.

A fine portrait of the leader of the only Brazilian group actually affiliated with the Socialist International can be found in Thomas Skidmore's description of Leonel Brizola's political behavior in the early sixties:

> His career was a history of electoral triumphs culminating in his election as federal deputy from Guanabara . . . with a record-breaking total of 260,000 votes. Brizola had . . . an electrifying campaign presence. He could translate the rhetoric of radical nationalism into the language of the street. Overbearing and vulgar, he was given to brawling with his political enemies on the floor of the Congress or in airport waiting

rooms, his courage reinforced by several armed bodyguards. This crudely virile side of Brizola increased his lower-class following at the same time it outraged the middle class and the "respectable" political elite. In short, Brizola was the most dynamic left-wing populist.[22]

After being elected governor of Rio de Janeiro in 1982 by an overwhelming majority, one of his most "popular" accomplishments was the construction in 1984 by Oscar Niemeyer of a "Sambadrome," where the traditional Carnival parade of the *escolas de samba* could take place in a more orderly fashion and be viewed from permanent stands. Though criticized for its expense ($20 million) and "populist" connotations, Brizola stuck by the idea. According to his deputy governor: "In previous years it cost half as much to build the temporary stands, so the Sambadrome will be paid for in two years. During the rest of the year, the part under the bleachers will accommodate 200 classrooms for 16,000 students. The area will be used for dances and concerts every weekend."[23]

On the occasion of his second inauguration, in February 1991, he went further, calling on the *favelados* to forcibly enter and take over the many unfinished and more or less abandoned high-rise apartment buildings in the swankier neighborhoods of the city, provoking the outrage and panic of thousands of next-door upper-middle-class residents, and of most of Rio's affluent political elite. Nearly thirty years after Skidmore's description and Brizola's initial antics, he keeps getting reelected by a constituency he has endeared himself to through policies, gestures, and charm. In the 1989 presidential elections, he obtained 61 percent of the vote on the first round in his home state of Rio Grande do Sul, and 51 percent in Rio de Janeiro, his "adoptive" entity. Brizola and his PDT enjoy the devotion of the mass urban-poor constituency that any social-democratic party in Latin America must have. And in the policies Brizola actually implemented during his years as Rio de Janeiro governor, the PDT possesses some of the facets of a typically reformist program in action, as opposed to only on paper. Moreover, Brizola and his party are not quite traditional populists simply nostalgic about the past. Their view of the past and the future of Brazil is more complex:

> In a country like ours, modernity must mean putting an end to poverty. We must integrate our economy with the rest of the world, but a moral

---

22. Thomas Skidmore, *Politics in Brazil, 1930–1964: An Experiment in Democracy* (New York: Oxford University Press, 1967), p. 281.
23. Alan Riding, "Rio Carnival: Hard Times Crowd the Good Times," *New York Times*, March 3, 1984.

precept of eradicating poverty is essential. For this the presence of the national State is very important. It cannot substitute itself for the market, but must orient the distribution process and establish priorities. We cannot simply let the market decide everything. We are living at the end of the previous model of development. We have strangled the consumption capacity of our import-substitution industry; the only possibility we have of continuing to grow is to dismantle the archaic structure of Brazilian society and integrate the rest of the population into the market.[24]

Brizola did many things in Rio, from balancing the state's budget to establishing bus routes from the *favelas* to the sea, thus "desegregating" many of Rio's fancier beaches, to the great disappointment of many of the more affluent bathers, and to the enormous joy of tens of thousands of *favelados*. He also, and perhaps more importantly, created the CIEPs, or Centros Integrados de Educaçao Popular, where the children of the poor would be cared for and educated during the entire day, in a combination day-care/school facility. This truly changed the lives of countless Carioca families. No wonder the *favelados* revere Brizola, and his street-fighting, macho urban politics; no wonder he was reelected governor in 1990 and will probably run for the presidency again; no wonder his political career has spanned more than four decades.

The PSDB and Brizola's PDT have the center-left well occupied; but they largely lack the working-class constituency and rural following that any social-democratic movement must have to thrive in Latin America. The Workers' Party (PT) is much further removed from the center of the ideological spectrum, but has what the others don't: the organization and constituency of a classical reformist grouping. It is the newest and certainly most leftward member of this sometime coalition. It is even considered "modern," an indispensable attribute in today's Latin politics. As José Aricó has said: "The debate in Brazil within the left is a modern one, because it does not carry the ballast of an old left. The PT is an organization of the new left, even with its radicalism, bringing together nationalism and Catholicism. It has a vision more consonant with the modern world; it is more aware of the difficulty of change."[25]

The Workers' Party is also the faction of the Brazilian left which most forcefully rejects the reformist and particularly the social-democratic label and has the greatest difficulty associating with a front it doesn't control. In the 1990 gubernatorial elections, it refused to

24. Waldir Pires, interview with the author, Salvador de Bahia, August 16, 1990.
25. José Aricó, interview with the author, Buenos Aires, December 9, 1989.

back any PSDB or PDT candidates in the first round, and the leadership provokes great resistance among the rank and file when it suggests joining other factions of the Brazilian left.

Yet the Workers' Party is also one of the most original experiments to take place on the left, not only in Brazil, but in Latin America as a whole. The PT is a combination of things: "radical unionists, landless peasants, shantytown activists and the progressive wing of the country's powerful Roman Catholic Church."[26] It was born directly out of the new Brazilian labor movement in the region of São Paulo in the late seventies and early eighties. The rapid industrialization of the country under military rule created a new working class, which sprang up chiefly in the multinational factories of the automobile and metal industry around São Paulo.[27] Before the 1964 coup, the industrial proletariat of Brazil had been relatively small and highly domesticated by the corporativist-populist system set up during the 1930s, with some Communist influence.

In 1980, thanks to the strike led by Lula and the newly founded Metallurgical Workers Union in the so-called ABCD (the towns of Santo Andre, São Bernardo, São Caetano, and Diadema) outside São Paulo, labor militancy became a fixture of the country's politics. And after a more than monthlong strike actively supported by the Paulista Church, the need, desirability, and viability of creating a political party surfaced rapidly. The hope was that it would unite the three components of what had become the most important movement against the military dictatorship since 1964: the intellectuals, journalists, and university professors who had already achieved prominence in protests against the regime; the Church activists; and the new unions. The expectations were not fulfilled: many of the intellectuals, particularly in the moderate opposition, did not join; part of the unions, reluctant

---

26. Emir Sader and Ken Silverstein, *Without Fear of Being Happy: Lula, the Workers' Party and Brazil* (New York: Verso Books, 1991), p. 3. As could be expected with regard to a relatively young and strongly ideological organization, most of the literature concerning it is partisan: mainly from within, or close to, the ranks of the PT, partly virulently anti-PT. This book as well as the various biographies of Lula (Frei Betto's being perhaps the best) are highly sympathetic to the PT. None of this detracts from their analytical validity, but these facts must be mentioned in order to impart a clearer notion of the sources quoted on these pages.

27. "The number of people employed in the manufacturing, mining, construction, and transportation sector—i.e., the industrial working class—increased from 4.4 million in 1960 in Brazil, to 12.5 million in 1980, reaching 29 percent of the economically active population, a share similar to that which existed in Europe at the end of the last century, when the large social-democratic parties were founded." Margaret E. Keck, *The Workers' Party and Democratization in Brazil* (New Haven, Conn.: Yale University Press, 1992), p. 13.

to become politicized—and in the eyes of the military, delegitimized—
did not go along. But nonetheless, the party was founded on February
10, 1980, with a working-class and intellectual membership.[28]

Over the next eight years the PT underwent several transformations. Its most important advances related to its penetration of rural
areas, mostly thanks to Church activists and the struggle for land in
the Brazilian countryside. The PT was the only left-wing party to truly
put the question of land reform high on its agenda. With the help of the
Church and Christian base communities, it sent activists and leaders
into the most contentious regions of rural Brazil to participate in land
seizures and defense of peasant organizations, such as the Movimento
dos Sem Terra ("Movement of the Landless").

Secondly, after 1988, the Workers' Party achieved important gains
in municipal elections throughout Brazil by establishing close links to
the urban movement that exploded throughout the country from the
mid-eighties onward. Its first electoral participation, in the 1982 congressional and state gubernatorial votes, was disastrous. But by 1985
the PT began to reap the fruits of its patient grass-roots organizing. It
was active in squatter movements; urban mobilizations over housing,
transportation, and urban services in general; and in protests over price
rises. The party extended its involvement in this area from São Paulo
to other cities throughout the country; after the movements subsided
and electoral politics took over, it won municipal elections in many of
the cities where it had been engaged in urban protests. Its first victory
came in the Northeastern, poverty-stricken city of Fortaleza in 1985.
Two years later, that unexpected win became a national sweep as
Workers' Party candidates were elected in São Paulo (a woman teacher
and militant) and its industrial belt, as well as in Porto Alegre, Vitoria,
and Santos. The PT elected more than 1,000 city council members
across the nation. In the 1992 elections, in the wake of President
Fernando Collor de Mello's impeachment, the party expanded its influence to dozens of mid-sized cities. Although it lost the mayoralty of
São Paulo, it retained Porto Alegre, won Belo Horizonte (the nation's
third largest city) and almost conquered Rio de Janeiro, where its candidate, a black, female evangelical *favelada*, nearly carried the day.

Largely as a result of this participation in electoral politics at a local
level, but also from its involvement in parliamentary politics and the
drafting of the new Brazilian Constitution, the PT achieved its third

---

28. According to Sader and Silverstein, "60% of the members of the first Provisional
Regional Commission in São Paulo (the only existing organization) were tied to unions;
the other 40% were mostly politicians, journalists and representatives from extreme left
groups." Op. cit., p. 50.

important mutation: a much more solid, widely based commitment to democratic politics, and to the spirit of compromise and responsible governance. This was not an easy transition, provoking tensions and surprises, as Lula testified in the following conversation during the 1989 presidential campaign:

> That woman [PT mayor of São Paulo Luiza Erundina de Souza] gives me a pain in the ass [*só me fode*]; now she has decided, of all things, to put City Hall's finances in order and suspend all public works. She's worse than the former governor [PMDB member] Franco Montoro, who said he was against big works but didn't even do small ones. But he had his entire term of four years to recover; I have only the five months left of the campaign.[29]

From the radical, dogmatic ambiance of the Roman Catholic Church, the previously armed left, and union activism, to parliamentary debate and municipal coalition building, the jump was long and complex, but was mostly accomplished in less than a decade. Undoubtedly, the PT is still often a dogmatic, uncompromising organization, but it has come a long way and even its most radical factions have been forced to deal with the logical conclusions of their original choice: making the fight for democracy a cornerstone of their program, excluding any road to power that was not electoral.[30]

It was true that the specific impact of its municipal victories and participation in Parliament were different: in the cities, the PT invariably rode a wave of protest-vote and popular movements that did not necessarily moderate the party's policies. Indeed, on occasion, it was radicalized by the grass roots. But its participation in Congress made it more sensitive to the spirit of compromise, partial solutions, and gradual improvements, and more willing to take half a *cafezinho*, so to speak, as even the more left-wing congressmen acknowledged.[31] Even at a municipal level, after the protest vote, and despite overblown expectations and ensuing disenchantments, the drift toward the center was inevitable. In Lula's words:

> We lost a great deal of popularity, mainly at the beginning, because the PT generated great expectations. Everybody thought that when the PT

29. José Nêumanne, *Atrás do Palanque: Bastidores da Eleição 1989* (São Paulo: Edições Siciliano, 1989), p. 78.

30. As radical a Partido dos Trabalhadores leader as Eduardo Suplicy—elected president of the São Paulo City Council in 1988 and senator from the state of São Paulo in 1990, and head of the left-wing faction of the party—acknowledged that by participating in city politics, his organization was inevitably learning and consolidating democratic practices. Interview with the author, São Paulo, August 8, 1990.

31. Jose Genoino, interview with the author, São Paulo, August 14, 1990.

won the elections for mayor, we would solve problems of housing, unemployment, etc. But the PT did not solve those problems, nor could it. And so people became disappointed with the PT; even I was hurt by this in the 1989 presidential campaign. Today we are recovering our prestige. . . . It is difficult to say if our municipal policy is right or left. The PT follows an administrative policy within the framework that is allowed. Our municipal governments are subject to the municipal organic law. The Mayor has duties and cannot do what he or she wants. They have rules to work by. And our people are working correctly.[32]

The PT did not betray itself by administering its cities prudently, as many of its mayors, and particularly Luiza Erundina of São Paulo, were often accused of doing.[33] But clearly, there is a huge difference between presiding over an honest and competent, even efficient and humane, municipal administration and changing people's lives and living up to their hopes. It is not at all evident that the PT, or anybody, can do both, which is after all what it wants to accomplish, and what its supporters expect of it.

The PT also failed to achieve some of its original goals. It was unable to conserve all of the original labor constituency that predated its founding, and proved incapable of "hegemonizing" the Brazilian intellectual left. After the labor mobilization of the early eighties and the obvious obsolescence of the old unions, the radical unions from the São Paulo region decided to form their own national brotherhood, the Central Única dos Trabalhadores, or CUT. This inevitably led to the development of other national confederations. Their leaders came to be known later as proponents of a *"sindicalismo dos resultados"* (a results-based union policy) and became the archenemies of the PT in the labor movement.[34]

---

32. Lula, interview with the author, Mexico City, June 6, 1991.

33. "São Paulo was the largest and most visible of the municipalities that PT mayors were to administer after 1988, and the Luiza Erundina administration generated a correspondingly large volume of internal controversy in the party. . . . During its first year, Erundina was primarily occupied in putting the city's financial house in order—a process that bore fruit over the long run but which brought little or no short-term political accolades to the party. . . . Although few of its early accomplishments were highly visible, the Erundina administration achieved a great deal rather quickly. . . . Benefits for workers and the poor were longer in coming, with a few exceptions. For PT members who had hoped to see São Paulo revolutionized, the pragmatic approach of the administration was both frustrating and unexpected. . . . Leftist factions in the PT accused Erundina of betraying her mandate and led marches on city hall demanding more public housing and social services." Keck, op. cit., pp. 230–232.

34. As early as 1985, "The CUT began to be recognized as the predominant organization in the labor movement. It included about 1,250 unions, representing about 15 million members." Ibid., p. 197. According to a survey published in the newsweekly

Still, as the neoliberal policies of the Collor administration began to bite and privatization, as well as strikebreaking and antiunion salary freezes, was implemented, it became evident that even the organized, large-industry Brazilian working class was deeply divided. The PT was the party of part of that working class, and the union closest to it was that which represented a majority of the country's industrial proletariat, but this was not a British- or German-style, all-encompassing situation. The PT was not able to become *the* party of *the* Brazilian working class. It fell prey to the dilemma other, more radical, working-class parties had found themselves in: consensus was in the center, and any deviation from it, however justified or even politically expedient, divided the union movement and weakened the working class.

A similar process occurred within intellectual circles. The idea of founding something like a workers' party had originally enjoyed the wide support of many intellectuals and professionals. The PT was able to conserve a good deal of the loyalty of artists, university professors, and white-collar yuppies that surfaced in the 1989 presidential campaign. But the fall of socialism in the East, the wave of neoliberal policies and ideas flooding the hemisphere, and the difficulties the PT experienced in crafting unified, marketable, and fully developed stances on a number of issues hurt it. Its ideological dispersion, an inevitable feature of a party essentially defined by its social composition—working class—rather than by its program or ideology, diminished its intellectual scope. While a good number of Brazil's outstanding intellectuals were PT members, many more were not.

Every now and then, the Brazilian Workers' Party claims that it does not wish to become a reformist, social-democratic organization.[35] But if one looks at what it does and not so much at what it says, it is in fact becoming just that. The difference between social-democratic reformism and revolutionary socialism consists above all in renouncing the idea of revolution and socialism as a distinct stage of world history, and accepting that the so-called minimum program, or the sum of tactical objectives, and the maximum program, or the sum of strategic aims, become indistinguishable. Once that difference is

---

Veja, quoted by Sader and Silverstein (op. cit., p. 153), in late 1989 the CUT represented 65 percent of the workers, while the CGT was dominant among only 16 percent. The CUT controlled 89 percent of the unions in the state sector, 51 percent in national industries, and 56 percent among multinationals.

35. "Its leaders have expressed deep concerns over the dangers of becoming a social-democratic organisation." Keck, op. cit., p. 279. "At the same time the party's innate anti-capitalist stance led to a critical approach to social-democratic experiments. . . . Although a party faction supports social-democracy, their position is a minority one and firmly opposed by the union-led directorate." Sader and Silverstein, op. cit., p. 107.

bridged, the rest are nuances: how much transformation of a democratic, market-based society inserted in the world economy does one want? The span of possibilities is broad, ranging from the deep reforms of French capitalism that the Socialist Party subscribed to from 1971 to 1983, or those the British Labour Party implemented during the fifties and sixties, all the way to the almost complete acceptance of the status quo that the Italian Socialist Party, or its Spanish counterpart, adhered to in the late 1980s.

The PT was never a "Marxist" or "Marxist-Leninist" party, though many of its leaders and ideologues were clearly holders of Marxist beliefs. But it is a formally "socialist" party in that it considers its ultimate aim as socialism, although that socialism is subsequently defined as substantively different from existing socialism anywhere, including Cuba. And although in everyday political life it has clearly deprived the term "socialism" of much of its content, the weaning process is far from consummated. This process can involve discarding the term "socialism," as the German Social-Democratic Party did in 1959, or conserving the words but eliminating the meaning, as the French Socialist Party did from 1983 onward. If one listens to some of Lula's statements, like the following declaration, or sees what the PT does both on the campaign trail and in city halls throughout Brazil, one concludes it is an undeniably reformist organization:

> If you feed millions of starving Brazilians, food is the revolution. You give a dentist to children with no teeth, a pair of shoes for the children, that is a true revolution. That they do not have these things is one of the evils of capitalism, but it is also one of the most important things in life, because you do not need real socialism to be able to eat, to have a job. Capitalism can go very far: it is sufficient for the capitalist to have the decency to reduce his profit margin, to increase labor's share. In other words, simply to distribute: That is my thesis, and I have been accused of being a communist for stating it. If capitalism guarantees the possibility of every human being to have a standard of living like the Swedish people, or the Danes or the Belgians, then I am a pro-capitalist. I want somebody to guarantee that the wealth of the world be adequately distributed.[36]

And as the idea of socialism itself ceases to be viable in the contemporary social imagination in most nations, even if the content of that definition continues to be current as an aspiration, it will be increasingly difficult for those groups inside the PT that wish to retain the reference to socialism to succeed in doing so. On the other hand, it

---

36. Lula, interview with the author, Mexico City, June 6, 1991.

is also quite likely that a simple de facto shift may not be enough: the ideological demands of Brazilian and international politics may force the PT into holding its own Bad Godesberg Congress and putting its statements and convictions in tune with its practice and the world at large. This would not be as easy an aggiornamento as might be imagined. Important sectors of the Worker's Party remain devoted to the idea of revolution and socialism and would experience great difficulties in remaining within—or at least devoting their time and frequently tireless efforts to—an organization that no longer subscribes to the assault on the Winter Palace. But if the PT wants to continue winning elections at a municipal level, and electing more members of the Federal Congress, it will have to mellow. If it does so successfully, such a meeting could well be as historic an occasion as the German precedent, and help transform the PT and the entire Brazilian left from a radical working-class party with a rural and shantytown constituency into a truly Latin American exponent of modern reformism. Its leading role in the fight against the scandalous corruption of the Collor government, and in impeaching the President, positioned it ideally for the 1994 race for the presidency. Lula quickly became the front-runner, and whatever the actual outcome, was bound to achieve a respectable tally.

A similar reformist option has emerged in Mexico, and Cuauhtémoc Cárdenas and the Party of the Democratic Revolution (Partido de la Revolución Democrática, or PRD) have already requested admission to the Socialist International.[37] Paradoxically, their entry was initially blocked by the Spanish Socialist Party, ostensibly because of critical remarks Cárdenas had made regarding its leadership, but in fact at the behest of the PRI and the regime of Salinas. While not wanting to join the International themselves, the PRI did not wish to relinquish to its archenemy the mantle of legitimacy that such membership would have bestowed on it. Years before, the PRI had toyed with the idea of SI membership, and acquired observer status. And many current members of the PRI or the Salinas team still flirted with the idea, as at least some of the packaging of the neoliberal policies applied in

---

37. Cárdenas's own stance on the question of his party's social-democratic vocation was ambivalent: "If anyone can tell me what a social democrat is today, I would like to know. If Carlos Andrés Pérez and Olof Palme can both be identified as social democrats, where does everyone else stand? They are oil and water, black and white, and so I prefer to define the PRD on the basis of its national reference than an international one. I personally identify myself politically more with our historical references in Mexico than with social democracy, particularly since in Mexico we have not had much of a relationship with social democracy in the past." Cuauhtémoc Cárdenas, interview with the author, Mexico City, January 15, 1992.

Mexico could be construed as "new age" social-democratic. But through the first two-thirds of Salinas's term, in any case, the PRI regime resembled more a Reagan-Bush conservative experiment than a European social-democratic one.

The tensions arising from transforming a complex mass movement into a reformist party were obvious in the PRD from the outset. The organization was created by Cárdenas and Porfirio Muñoz Ledo, the other PRI leader to break with the ruling party in the wake of the 1988 presidential elections. The importance of that vote cannot be overestimated. For the first time in the country's postrevolutionary phase, a split-off from the PRI had captured a huge chunk of the ruling party's electorate (30 percent according to official figures, much more according to most observers).

Until 1988, the Mexican left had been badly split into two currents, mostly devoid of followers: small groups of activists outside the PRI who were sporadically heroic and every now and then supported by mass movements (workers in 1958, students in 1968, urban dwellers in 1985); and those inside the PRI, the latter's number and influence being by definition unfathomable. The Cárdenas schism merged the two groupings. The mass constituency became electoral, and the identity was established as the left from the PRI joined the one from the streets and ideological ghettos. The split was a watershed: it broke the back of Mexico's famous elite consensus and mass acquiescence, which had provided stability and continuity since the late 1920s.

Everybody was inside the tent pissing out—in Lyndon Johnson's colorful metaphor—instead of outside pissing in. The institutional left in Mexico had, since 1940, received just enough to keep it inside the tent, yet not enough to run it. But by 1982 it had begun to lose even the meager crumbs previously thrown its way: foreign policy; a strong state sector of the economy; agrarian reform. By the mid-1980s there was nothing remaining for the left inside the tent, and it finally went its own way, helped/pushed by the new tent-dwellers: the young, U.S.-educated technocrats from the Finance Ministry and the Central Bank who in 1982 extended their domain to the entire government.

But if the reasons that had made it worth the establishment's while to keep the left inside the tent persisted—and they did persist—then the left now set adrift outside the PRI would pick up whatever constituency or support it had acquired when it was inside. The 1988 presidential election, with all its confusion regarding voter motivation and the candidates' true colors, nonetheless showed that the potential PRD constituency was real and large.

The second reason why the Cárdenas break was important revolved around the type of electorate he took with him. Reliable data was particularly difficult to come by, since the publicly announced precinct-by-precinct results were far from complete, and consequently could not be satisfactorily analyzed; the ballots were incinerated in January 1992, as a permanent defense against the curiosity of concerned citizens or historians. The broader characteristics of Cárdenas's electorate in 1988 were largely urban, young, and lower-middle-class. He obtained more than 50 percent of the vote in Mexico City and the surrounding state of Mexico.

But Cárdenas also received large percentages of the vote in some rural states, for regional, personal, or historical reasons: Michoacán (his native state), Morelos, and Guerrero. A majority of the country's university students voted for Cárdenas, judging at least by the impressive rallies he presided over at the National University and at the University of Guadalajara (the nation's two largest schools) just before the election. His electoral coalition, then, was not simply a reservoir of the poor: it was a broad-based, multiregional, socially and ideologically plural front. Herein lay both its strength and its weakness. One of its chief ideologues, Adolfo Gilly, thus characterized the sources of the PRD:

> The party has emerged from the confluence of four currents of ideas: (a) *cardenismo*, coming from the National Liberation Movement of the 1960s, the nationalism of Rafael Galván in the 1970s and Lázaro Cárdenas' political legacy; (b) state nationalism, coming from those sectors of the PRI thrust aside for good from 1982 onward; (c) independent socialism, whose origins go back to the twenties and thirties and were revived in 1968, in the 1970s and the first half of the 1980s; and (d) Mexican Communism, whose paradigm and reference point were the regimes of the Soviet Union, Eastern Europe and Cuba, basically united in the old Mexican Communist Party. The political mass movement that surfaced in 1988 made possible the convergence of these four currents in a single party, which is why it is a pluralistic party.[38]

There has been endless debate in Mexico since 1988 about whether the vote for Cárdenas was a lasting phenomenon or a flash in the pan; whether it was primarily for Cárdenas or in reaction against the PRI; whether it indicated a preference for the nationalist, socially oriented left, or was simply a vote for "secure change"; and whether, finally, it

---

38. Adolfo Gilly, "El perfil del PRD: cuestión abierta," *Nexos*, May 1991.

represented a vote for Cuauhtémoc Cárdenas or one in memory of his revered father.[39] Either way, from the perspective of the Mexican left, the 1988 election was a sea change. The problem was how to consolidate it, and that was where the heterogeneity of the Cárdenas coalition—both sociologically and ideologically—became a serious weakness.

After the election, Cárdenas and Muñoz Ledo, together with a small group of ex–left-wing activists and a handful of intellectuals that made up the leadership of the coalition, confronted a deceptively simple choice. They could refrain from creating their own political party and continue to lead a coalition of existing splinter groups and small, legally registered parties. Or they could form their own party, either by complying with the government's draconian requirements which give the regime discretion in legalizing or banning new parties, or by taking over the legal registry of one of the existing groups.

The respective advantages and drawbacks of given options were not totally apparent and were never fully discussed. There is nothing more difficult anywhere than transforming a leader's personal following into a political party with its own candidates, banners, slogans, and programs. Charles de Gaulle's failures during the Fourth Republic and Gamal Abdel Nasser's similar setback in Egypt between 1953 and 1970 are perhaps the two outstanding examples. There existed a serious risk that if the *cardenista* forces chose to build a new organization, they would expend their best efforts and most of their time over the next six years in trying—ultimately, unsuccessfully—to mold the often contradictory currents that supported Cárdenas in 1988 into a single unified, coherent construct. Moreover, this would have to be accomplished at a time when such organizations were on the decline, in a country where they had never really flourished; against the wishes and strenuous efforts of the government; and with the need to craft a broader coalition for the 1994 presidential elections.

The downside of the other option was also self-evident. It meant putting the movement's electoral fate in the hands of small parties that had been traditionally corrupt and coopted, and submitting to their

---

39. Perhaps the most serious study of voting behavior in the 1988 and 1991 elections concluded that: "Mexican citizens approach elections as if they were plebiscites. First and foremost they ask themselves: am I for or against the party of state and its leader. . . Consistent with plebiscitary behavior, attitudes on issues hardly matter, nor do social cleavages matter in a consistent fashion." Jorge I. Domínguez and James A. McCann, "Shaping Mexico's Electoral Arena: The Construction of Partisan Cleavages in the 1988 and 1991 National Elections," American Political Science Association, September 1992, p. 16.

will. It signified refraining from participation in many state elections, or making endless compromises with local groups and national leaderships that would systematically bargain their legal credentials against Cárdenas's coattails.

Cárdenas chose the first, and naturally easier, option; hindsight suggests that it was probably an unfortunate choice. His reasons were more negative than affirmative:

> The same problems of coordination, unified action that we had during the presidential campaign of 1988 and during the post-election phase continued. This led a group of us to think about—then to proceed with—calling for the creation of a political party that would allow us to act differently. We reached the conclusion that it would be convenient to create such a party as soon as possible, as broadly as possible, a pluralistic party, and we called for the formation of the PRD in October of 1988.[40]

This immediately generated greater, more intractable contradictions. Perhaps the single most important enticement to take over an existing party was time: this more expeditious procedure allowed the new organization to participate immediately in a number of elections, build a territorial base, and start up a bureaucratic machine. But Cárdenas underestimated how far the Salinas administration was willing to go to make him lose his momentum; he also overestimated his own capacity to transfer his personal popularity to unknown candidates. The Michoacán vote in July of 1989 was the first fiasco for the new party: the election was undoubtedly stolen from the PRD, but it proved unable to prevent the theft in its own backyard.

This initial setback and the problems it reflected would plague Cárdenas and the PRD throughout the Salinas years. On the one hand, the *cardenistas* were an electoral organization: their raison d'être was to win elections. They had no nonelectoral option: their struggle was for the democratization of Mexico, respect for the vote, and an end to the country's one-party system. But the system was indeed rigged, the deck was indisputably stacked: any participation in a fraudulent electoral system—totally controlled by the government, with one party enjoying all the privileges, funds, and advantages, and the others making do with goodwill and devotion—was doomed to failure, unless overwhelming force could be brought to bear. After 1988, this overwhelming force was not generally available, except regionally, or on occasions. Thus the PRD participated in elections it knew beforehand were going to be stolen.

---

40. Cuauhtémoc Cárdenas, interview.

The PRD was a reformist, quasi-social-democratic party in some ways, and wasn't in others. Programmatically, it was clearly reformist: it placed the democratization of Mexican politics at the top of its agenda; social justice and an economic policy ostensibly subordinated to that goal were also clearly its objective; and the nationalist defense of Mexican sovereignty and revolutionary heritage—the oil monopoly, an independent foreign policy, a degree of autonomy of the Mexican state in economic policy—were all part of its ideological baggage.

Electorally it also looked quite reformist, although here matters were more complicated. As Salinas's six-year term wore on, the new government achieved its greatest political success in regaining a significant part of Cárdenas's 1988 middle-class electorate. The PRD voters were increasingly hard-core and extremely poor, urban or rural. At the same time the party attracted fewer young, lower-middle-class, and ideologically diverse supporters. In the cities, Cárdenas or the PRD, or both, were losing ground, and only gaining relative strength in states like Tabasco, Veracruz, Oaxaca and Tlaxcala: there a semirural, small-town electorate protested against corruption, violence, and continually sinking standards of living by voting for the PRD.

This last problem was central: the PRD got caught in a dynamic of confrontation and intransigence. In a country where every so-called "opposition" politician had sold out to the establishment over the past half century, where corruption is rampant and the total mistrust of the people for every political leader is widespread, Cárdenas could not afford to be seen by his backers as caving in to Salinas on the one issue Salinas really cared about: his legitimacy as president. But as long as Cárdenas did not make this concession of recognizing Salinas as president, his party would continue to bring down on itself the fury of the Mexican machinery on every possible occasion. This then radicalized the shrinking rank and file. From a moderate, responsible image of "change with security" in 1988, Cárdenas and his party were later portrayed, sometimes successfully, as a dogmatic, extremist party seeking violence. This in turn drove them toward the fringe, making it easier for the government to continue to ostracize them.

Most important perhaps, the type of constraints that democratic politics and a working-class constituency have generally placed on more radical, eventually social-democratic parties elsewhere, were not yet truly affecting the PRD. It was not allowed to win any major electoral victories—no state governorships and only a handful of small cities and congressional seats. It was consequently not being driven to the center by the force of its electoral participation. The government's iron control over Mexican labor unions—a sine qua non condition for the implementation of the radical free-market policies pursued by the Salinas team—made attempts to capture union votes a question of political activism, not of electoral campaigning and vote gathering. The PRD could hardly become social-democratic without working-class membership.

Similarly, as presidentialism in Mexico became even more accentuated under Carlos Salinas, parliamentary debate, deliberation, and compromise were even rarer occurrences, depriving the PRD of the much needed vehicle for another moderating factor. All the centrifugal forces at work from its founding were compounded by others that emerged, but were not compensated for by some sort of success at the polls. Likewise, Cárdenas's own role remained contradictory. Because the party did not really prosper on its own, he continued to be its only political asset, thus reinforcing the personalized, caudillo-type characteristics everyone, including Cárdenas, deplored from the beginning. All these problems and contradictions were highlighted by the 1991 midterm elections, undoubtedly the low point of the party's fortunes. The PRD officially received only 9 percent of the tally and proved unable to defend the vote or contest electoral fraud, even in its former bastions.

Nonetheless, from a broader, more long-term historical perspective, the PRD had made considerable headway. Despite its losses, it was able to generate the impression, throughout Mexico and abroad, that the 1991 elections had been massively tampered with, or as the *New York Times* put it, that along with Cuba, Guyana, and Surinam, Mexico remained the only country in the hemisphere where free and fair elections still did not take place.[41] The PRD mobilized local forces against electoral fraud and broadened the breadth of its alliances to include sectors from the center and center-right. Regional leaders emerged, as local conflicts blossomed all over the country and were transformed by government policies into national problems. The party finally began to build a halfway coherent organization: a national leadership, a congressional caucus, an ongoing press. It became a meeting ground for many of the grass-roots groups that resurfaced in Mexico. Human rights activists, civic groups, unions, and peasant organizations began once again to congregate around Cárdenas. What remained unresolved was how large this zone of the political spectrum really was: did it still represent a plurality of the citizenry, as in all likelihood it had in 1988, or had it shrunk over time, as Salinas's policies brought prosperity to Mexico, and/or as Cárdenas and the PRD became more easily identifiable as an extreme left-wing organization and were no longer a center-left, democratic, nationalistic, and socially conscious alternative.

41. "The Missing Reform in Mexico," *New York Times*, August 26, 1991, p. 18.

On paper, then, Cárdenas and the PRD were ideal candidates for modern reformist status, if they could become credible electoral contenders for power. The *cardenistas* were clearly "democracy oriented": by conviction (Cárdenas had accommodated right-of-center PAN electoral victories in various cities when he was governor of Michoacán), by convenience (the only way the former PRI figures could reach power, or even consolidate their status as a "real" opposition, was to insist on the practice of democracy), and by sheer inertia (once embarked on the democracy roller coaster, it was difficult to get off). On economic and social policy, Cárdenas had on his side the Mexican tradition of economic pragmatism and the coexistence of a strong state-owned sector with foreign investment and a fair-to-middling private sector. He confronted, of course, the same ideological problems facing every left-of-center, liberal, or radical dissenter in the world in devising a credible, viable alternative to the current neoliberal craze. This problem was substantively central, but electorally it was not the chief obstacle to the PRD's progress.

Cárdenas's nationalist credentials were impeccable—not a minor political asset in a country where the ruling party had successfully rebuffed every opposition challenge since 1940, partly thanks to its stranglehold on the sovereignty issue and its repeated accusations of national treason directed at anyone questioning the status quo. But at the same time, Cárdenas was able to avoid a corollary stigma, that of being associated with Cuba and/or the Soviet Union, as much of the Mexican left had been since the fifties and sixties. Because of Lázaro Cárdenas's status as a national hero, Cuauhtémoc Cárdenas's independence from Cuba and the Soviet Union was never really in question.

Yet Cárdenas was sensitive to changing moods regarding nationalism in Mexico and the need to be seen as a valid, if not welcome, interlocutor in the United States. His constant travels north, his willingness to take his case to U.S. audiences, and the memory in Mexico of the way his father had dealt with the United States over the oil expropriation of 1938, defusing tensions without backing down, all contributed to the perception that while Washington much preferred Salinas, it would not go to extremes over Cárdenas.[42] Moreover, Cár-

---

42. As one American observer sympathetic to the Salinas regime but balanced in his views of Cárdenas remarked: "U.S. relations with [Cárdenas] would be similar to those in the pre-Salinas era, distant and more difficult, with minor problems becoming major crises or tests of sovereignty." Robert Pastor, *Whirlpool: U.S. Foreign Policy toward Latin America and the Caribbean* (Princeton, N.J.: Princeton University Press, 1992), p. 263.

denas realized that other sectors in the United States, for their own reasons, could sympathize with him and his quest for clean elections in Mexico.

The problem lay in two apparently insurmountable obstacles that Cárdenas and the PRD faced in their efforts to emerge as a credible electoral option for Mexico's potentially huge reformist constituency. The first had to do with the viability of any electoral option: the lack of international pressure to implement authentic political reform in Mexico, severing the ties between state and party and permitting the accession to power of whoever obtained more votes, made the Salinas administration particularly resistant to change. The relative national weakness of the movement for democracy also made change less likely.

Secondly, there persisted in Mexico an enormous fear of change on the part of the governing and business elites. Many of the probusiness policies pursued by the Salinas administration were not enthusiastically supported by parts of the political elite; many of the dirty political tricks resorted to by Salinas and the PRI were not well viewed by the business elite. But both sectors had developed such a degree of panic over an end to the "old way of doing things" that they preferred the status quo to any change that entailed the risk of Cárdenas's coming to power.

On the business side, the greatest fear was how an opposition victory would destabilize the nation's economy, disrupt exchange and financial markets, and put an end to the economic restructuring that had taken place. But the fear was largely a self-feeding one. The more Cárdenas was ostracized by the business elite, and the more any economists or administrators from the government or the private sector were harassed or fired for approaching the opposition, the greater the latter's reluctance to commit itself to continuity on economic and social policy. And the fewer signs of compromise it demonstrated, the greater the private sector's panic over an opposition victory.

On the part of the political elite, the problem was more complex. Although Cárdenas, Muñoz Ledo, and many of their advisers, activists, and friends were as much a part of the political establishment as those remaining in the PRI, the question of corruption, revenge, and a "night of long knives" after a hypothetical Cárdenas victory inevitably surfaced every time the subject of the opposition and the sitting government alternating in office was broached seriously. Very few Mexican politicians were completely free of skeletons in the closet; their fortunes, incomes, and life-styles are secret, for the same reason their

declarations of assets and income tax returns are state secrets. If subjected to a new government that would "rock the boat," few would
emerge unscathed from scrutiny or popular wrath over the perception
and often the reality of a political elite that has enriched itself fabulously over the past half century, in a country where more than half the
population makes less than $250 a month. Mexico was not unlike
other Latin American nations, where "democratic transitions from
authoritarian rule" had required compromises, whitewashing, and protection from persecution for past misdeeds. But as long as it seemed
unlikely that the opposition would take over, none of these issues was
addressed forthrightly either by the government or by the opposition.
On this front also, Cárdenas's reformism lacked one basic ingredient:
the acceptance by the other side of his party's competing for power on
a level playing field.

After a fashion, Cárdenas and the PRD's ultimate fate were inextricably bound to the prospects for the democratization of Mexican
politics, understood as free and fair elections, a free press, free labor
unions, a business sector weaned from the government, and a northern
neighbor who would finally tolerate the relative turbulence that any
doses of democracy would inevitably entail. If such an opening took
place, some reformist, left-of-center organization or leader was almost
condemned to success, given Mexico's sociological and ethnic composition and its glaring disparities of wealth and opportunity. Whether or
not Cárdenas would be that leader depended on many things, ranging
from his age and health to the ideological climate in the U.S. and the
state of the Mexican economy. But mainly, it depended on time and
the Mexican people.

•

Time has also changed the Chilean Socialist Party, transforming a
classically Marxist revolutionary organization into an increasingly
typical social-democratic one. It had not only been the party of Salvador Allende; it was his own left wing. For several years before his
electoral victory in 1973, and for some time after his violent overthrow, the Socialist Party represented the radical fringe of the coalition that supported Allende, and paid the price for doing so after his
downfall. Through the mid-1980s it espoused a "Marxist-Leninist"
line and even the idea of the armed struggle, though it never actually
had the capability to carry it out. It was perhaps less radical than its
reputation suggested, but it was certainly no gang of Scandinavian
moderates.

During the years of the Pinochet dictatorship the Socialist Party oscillated between hard-line, left-right confrontation—not only with the regime, but also with the Christian Democrats—and movement beyond the polarization of the Allende era toward more negotiated stances. It was badly divided between the two strategies, but as Chilean politics edged toward the center and the issue of bringing down the dictatorship became paramount, the moderate faction carried the day. In 1985 the Socialist Party signed the National Accord for the Transition to Full Democracy with the Christian Democrats and other more conservative groups. The accord called for a democratic transition but also committed its signatories to respecting private property, a major change for the Socialists. They formed a legal group to participate in the 1988 referendum on Pinochet's proposed transition, the Party for Democracy, which would eventually group together the Socialists and many other left-of-center politicians who were not party members. In the words of one of its leading founders, Ricardo Lagos:

> In a dictatorship, the alternatives are to reestablish democracy or to continue with the dictatorship. With this new party we are trying to recover the diversity of Chile, of the Chile we were and of the Chile we want. With different parts of the political spectrum, a center, a right and a left, like in the past, but with a common denominator, a democratic mechanism to solve our conflicts, and to restore democracy.[43]

After the "No Coalition" defeated Pinochet in the 1988 referendum on presidential elections, the Socialist Party was forced to assume the logical consequences of its rapprochement with the center. The only way to beat the Pinochet candidate in the presidential elections scheduled for December of 1990 was with a united coalition, which logically would be led by a Christian Democrat. And given the perceived balance of political forces, the Socialist Party's participation in the coalition, in the future Cabinet, and in the soon-to-be elected Congress was not going to be overwhelming. The party decided to go along with the seemingly inevitable tide of history and joined the Concertación para la Democracia and accepted its tacit trade-off:

> The Concertación adopted a program that basically stressed tasks of political democratization combined with redistribution tasks in the framework of a firm decision to conserve economic growth. In its program there are no references to structural changes in the Chilean economy, no major allusions to the issue of property or the degree of State

43. Ricardo Lagos, "De cara al país," as transcribed in *Fortín Mapocho* (Santiago), May 8, 1988.

intervention in the economy, but in exchange there are long paragraphs devoted to specifying in detail the democratizing thrust of the document.[44]

The Chilean Socialist Party thus acquiesced to the implicit quid pro quo behind the agreed-upon transition. This was the pursuit of many of the Pinochet regime's economic policies, the acceptance by civilians of the military's role and protection from prosecution, as well as the former dictator's permanence as Army commander, all in exchange for elections, the legalization of political parties and unions, and the reestablishment of Chilean democracy. It wasn't a bad deal for the country; the Chilean socialists probably had no alternative but to go along. One of their members, Carlos Ominami, a former MIR guerrilla, was named minister of economics; another, an architect of the shift toward the center, Ricardo Lagos, was appointed minister of education; and yet another party member, Enrique Correa, became minister of the presidency and one of President Patricio Alwyn's chief aides.

By early 1991 it was obvious that the Socialists were not infiltrated radicals bent on using their meager influence in the government, the Congress, and the country to push them all to the left but, if anything, had a more moderate stand on many issues than important factions of the Christian Democrats themselves. They were certainly reformist, then, if moderation was to be the determining criterion. But they were not alone in being moderate, and the issue then was how to distinguish themselves from the rest of the political spectrum.

Perhaps the most adequate way of viewing the Socialist Party–PPD role in the Chilean transition and after was to look beyond the narrow confines of the party itself. The Alwyn government, with all its limitations—its inability or refusal to deal with the past and human rights, to remove Pinochet as the commander in chief of the armed forces, to pursue regional integration with the rest of South America instead of free trade with the United States—was perhaps an archetypal, left-of-center, reformist government in the prevailing conditions in Latin America. It was as social-democratic as possible, its separate components each contributing something to the sum. In fact, the reformist experiment in Chile was not limited to the PS–PPD, but extended to the Alwyn administration in its entirety. Under these circumstances, if the coalition survived the end of its honeymoon, and the inevitable beginning of economic difficulties by strengthening its "social" orientation, it would consolidate itself as a reformist example. The exact

---

44. Gabriel Gaspar, *La transición en América Latina: Los casos de Chile y El Salvador* (Mexico City: Universidad Autónoma Metropolitana, 1991), p. 61.

role the party would play in that model was perhaps less important than the existence of the alliance as a whole and its lasting power. This was bound to be all the more true as the traditionally combative Chilean social movement began to pick up after a long hibernation under Pinochet.

The new Socialist Party was in fact the logical culmination of a long, painful process. It had its theoretical side: the *"renovación socialista"* school that posited the need for a reformulation of traditional "Leninist" dogmas regarding state power, democracy, and civil society. It had its sense of expediency: the left was shattered in Chile, demoralized and defeated everywhere else in the world; the best that could be done was to avoid ideological confrontation and maintain the alliance with the Christian Democrats, at least until an independent stance would not be immediately and automatically condemned to failure. It had its political and ideological thrust: if macroeconomic stability and a fiscally responsible policy were now the essence of desirable governance, the Socialists had every reason in the world to remain in a governing coalition that was conserving the economic accomplishments of the Pinochet regime, while doing its best to repay the "social debt" run up by the very economic policies responsible for those accomplishments. The crunch would come when these two objectives started becoming less compatible.

As on so many other occasions, Chile—and now the Chilean Socialist Party—constituted a weathervane and laboratory of prevailing winds and trends in Latin America, and on the Latin American left. If a broad consensus, going well beyond an electoral plurality or even a majority was the only path to reform and development in the hemisphere, in Chile this consensus had been achieved. More importantly, it was surviving the supreme test: everyday public administration. If a "responsible" economic policy, devoted to the principles of the free market and consonant with international trends, was an unmovable fixture of any regime, in Chile, more than anywhere, the left, right, and center subscribed to it. And if a democratic transition in post–Cold War times meant a convergence of ideologies and policies in the center of the political spectrum, in nowhere more than in Chile had this process taken hold.

But this transformation of the Socialist Party begged two questions. The first was, again, one of expediency: could the left all together keep its 20–25 percent by sticking closely to the Christian Democrats and the Alwyn government, let alone increase its share and reconquer the entire left's 35–40 percent of the electorate of the sixties and early seventies? Only time would tell, but for the first years of the Concertación experiment, it seemed that the shift to the center was serving more to conserve what remained of the left's shrinking electorate than to rebuild a new, left-of-center force. The Socialist Party was undoubtedly receiving some traditional Communist votes, as the old Communist Party succumbed to the twin blows of the fall of socialism and its continuing support for armed struggle through the Manuel Rodriguez Patriotic Front.[45]

Indeed, one of the key issues facing the new Socialist Party consisted precisely in determining whether it could expand its base to the left—to the former Communist electorate in industry and to the new potential electorate among Chile's officially certified 5 million poor—and not only toward the center. In a way, the Socialist party was lacking the constituency of its ideology: the voters and union and shantytown organizers who would ensure that the ideologically moderate discourse would fall upon receptive ears. It was far easier to craft that discourse than to find its respondents.

In fact, the divisions that erupted between the PS and the PPD after the 1992 municipal elections and with a view toward the next presidential vote stemmed from this dilemma. The left-of-center coalition had two options. The first was to hug the Christian Democrats and support their candidate—centrist Eduardo Frei—in the first round of balloting, and relinquish the chance of comparing forces in exchange for an honorable share of posts and power in the next government. The second was to try to rebuild the left coalition with a Socialist candidate on the first ballot, and then support Frei in the runoff, using the voters garnered in the first round as leverage for the composition of the new government. The actual numbers hinted that this latter alternative was less farfetched than it sounded: an attractive candidate, Ricardo Lagos, could shoot for 25–30 percent of the vote.[46] The choice was a tough one for the PS and for the left as a whole: join a consensus in a subordinate though not insignificant role or strike out on its own, risking the resurrection of past polarization.

The second question, though, was more complicated still: had the Socialist Party solved the riddle of what a left-wing organization meant

---

45. Initial indications were inconclusive. In the July, 1992 municipal elections, the Socialist coalition obtained 18 percent of the vote, about what it expected and what this area of the political spectrum traditionally received. The Communist Party did better than forecast, getting nearly 7 percent, showing that the Socialists' shift toward the center was leaving some voters behind.

46. According to Enrique Correa, one of the leaders of the Socialist Party: "The ideal would be to have a single candidate for the first round. But what is important is that it is now as legitimate for that single candidate to be a socialist or a Christian Democrat." Enrique Correa, interview with Raquel Correa, El Mercurio (Santiago), February 2, 1992.

in the post–Cold War world, or did its solution simply signify eliminating the problem? For many, the Chilean Socialist Party had ceased to be a party of the left: it was nothing more than a junior member of a right-of-center coalition that had forsaken most of the economic and social goals that the Chilean left had traditionally set. For others, it was going through an excruciating process unavoidably entailing erratic behavior, mistakes, and a break with the past, but that with time would lead to a truly renovated, reformist left. The Socialist Party was not yet that renovated left, and it has a way to go before attaining that goal; but the movement had been set in motion.

•

Another movement that embarked on a similar venture more than two decades ago is the Venezuelan Movimiento al Socialismo (MAS). It was born in 1971 when a group of young Communists who had participated actively in the guerrilla wars of the sixties broke with their leadership and founded a splinter group that generated enormous expectations in Venezuela and elsewhere (Gabriel García Márquez donated the $25,000 Rómulo Gallegos prize to the MAS in 1972, and Greek composer Mikis Theodorakis wrote its anthem). MAS never delivered in electoral terms and its failure at the polls could be blamed at least in part on the very ambiguity and elitism that made it initially so attractive in certain quarters. But its evolution is not conclusive, and the outcome for the "modern" reformism MAS has come to stand for is still uncertain.

When it requested membership to the Socialist International in 1980, its entry was vetoed by Acción Democrática, already a member. Nonetheless the movement and its leaders were never comfortable with the social-democratic label:

> Masistas see themselves as occupying a political space between the traditional left and social democracy. Thus MAS has made great efforts to distinguish itself from the far left at the same time that most party leaders rule out evolutionary socialism in the absence of class struggle, as put forward by social democrats.[47]

---

47. Steve Ellner, *Venezuela's Movimiento al Socialismo: From Guerrilla Defeat to Innovative Politics* (Durham, N.C.: Duke University Press, 1988), p. 216. Manuel Caballero, the historian of the Comintern in Latin America and MAS member puts the difference between MAS and social democrats as follows: "In opposition to the social-democratic Acción Democrática of today, socialist forces should adopt a new policy based on . . . the deepening of their socialist character, message, and content." Quoted in Ellner, ibid., p. 115.

Erratically and often unconsciously, it fluctuated between hard-line, quasi-revolutionary positions—as when it stressed the immediate possibility of socialism in Venezuela in the 1973 presidential cam-paign—and moderate, even brazenly conciliatory positions, as when it supported many of President Carlos Andrés Pérez's policies between 1974 and 1979. While MAS possessed some of the ideological accou-trements of a social-democratic party—its insistent, almost obsessive attachment to democracy, including within its own ranks; an important degree of nationalism, even with regard to the Soviet Union and Cuba; and an obvious social commitment—it lacked a working-class base.[48]

Indeed MAS faced a central problem from its birth through 1989, but was never able to deal with it effectively. In the words of its chief leader and spokesman over the past twenty years, Teodoro Petkoff, MAS initially fared poorly in electoral competition for three reasons:

> The oil boom and middle-class shopping frenzy that Venezuela experi-enced during the seventies . . . the entrenchment of the two-party sys-tem from 1973 onward, by which 90 percent of the population voted for one of the two parties and destroyed everything else; and the "Com-munist handicap": we emerged at a time when the Communist move-ment began to succumb to its most severe crisis ever, and this affected us, even though we had taken our distances from them from the very beginning.[49]

The problem began to solve itself when the oil boom came to an end in the early eighties and the two-party system started to crumble as a result of a decade of economic stagnation due to low oil prices and the foreign debt crisis. Most importantly, because of these trends, MAS's main contradiction from the outset—wanting to become a left-of-center reformist party in a country where a social-democratic party already existed and where it had (oil) money to spend—began to wither away. Acción Democrática appeared increasingly corrupt and out of touch, thus opening up the political slot that MAS had always wanted to occupy. Other Venezuelan forces on the left, mainly Causa Radical (Causa R), profited from this situation, particularly at a municipal or state level. But MAS, which had been around for years waiting for the opportunity, benefited as well.

---

48. "MAS ever since its founding has lacked a base of support in the labor move-ment. . . . MAS's membership has always been predominantly middle class, as demon-strated by its electoral success in professional and student organizations. . . . In spite of MAS's success in drawing votes from the low-income sectors in the 1978 elections, the party continued to be based on well-educated, urban youth." Ibid., pp. 72, 139.

49. Teodoro Petkoff, interview with the author, Mexico City, February 14, 1992.

By 1988, MAS made its first qualitative electoral leap forward, passing from its previous "historical 6 percent" of the electorate to 10 percent in that year's presidential elections. The following year, in municipal and state votes, it jumped to 18 percent, coming in second in a number of important regions, attracting 25 percent of the electorate in Caracas, and winning one "*gobernación*," or state governorship. Again in Petkoff's words: "MAS has been a modestly successful effort. Our growth has not been spectacular, like the M-19 in Colombia [whose ensuing drop was equally spectacular], but it has been steady, upward, and broadly based, and against heavy odds. Our progress will continue to be slow, but steady."[50]

The process whereby MAS reached this broader base was not an easy one, nor is it necessarily lasting. The organization has changed lines and discourse a number of times over the past twenty years, and its frequent ideological U-turns have contributed to the overall decline of its credibility along with that of the entire Venezuelan political system. To the extent that MAS consolidated the social and electoral base to go along with its ideology, it did so only because it radicalized its stance, and because the economic and social situation in Venezuela deteriorated so rapidly. But that new constituency—partly made up of tens of thousands of shantytown dwellers outside Caracas, who in February of 1989 rioted against the neoliberal policies implemented by the just reelected Carlos Andrés Peréz—is not easy to conciliate with the type of "new-look" socialism that MAS had espoused in its early years. The election of Aristóbulo Isturiz of Causa Radical as mayor of Caracas in December 1992, and the accompanying defeat of Teodoro Petkoff, showed that other groups on the left were benefiting much from the decomposition of the country's two-party system. Causa R (as it is legally labeled) is a PT-like group that was born in the metal industry union movement. After winning union elections in the steel, iron ore and aluminum industries, Causa Radical captured the mayoralty in several mid-sized cities in 1989, along with the governorship of Bolívar, Venezuela's largest state. Causa Radical distinguishes itself from MAS with social and political arguments:

> The powerful social movement [of the seventies and eighties] was used by MAS to gain positions from which it subsequently negotiated and acted in a political fashion totally contrary to the expectations it generated.[51]

---

50. Ibid.
51. Farruco: Pablo Medina en Entrevista, Ediciones del Agua Mansa, Caracas, 1988, p. 21.

The example of Causa Radical highlights the weaknesses of "modern" reformism in nations with growing poverty and unrest. It also shows the potential of socially based, more radical groups that nonetheless eschew the armed struggle and espouse democratic, electoral politics.

MAS reflects the contradictions and expectations of the four reformist movements we have examined. They all tend to possess a reformist constituency, but not an equivalent ideology and electoral behavior; or else to have the discourse, but not the electorate. In some cases, particularly Mexico, the two factors coincided, but just for a fleeting moment, only to come apart afterward and become exceedingly difficult to reassemble. Merging a constituency with a label or ideology is the central challenge they all face, and in the midst of an ideological, social, and economic crisis, it is not a simple one.

The ideology cannot be a carbon copy of what European social democracy was in the past, largely because one of the central constitutive elements of this ideology—the presence on its left of a powerful Communist movement—has disintegrated. The constituency cannot be purely working-class, because this sector is simply not large enough in Latin American societies, and not sufficiently excluded anymore, to be the bulwark of any party or movement that aspires to govern an entire nation. But the other sectors of society that logically could make up the rest—the urban poor, the rural dispossessed, and the impoverished lower middle class—have demands and often emotional stances that can lead well beyond the ideological prudence that political action dictates. Worst and most importantly of all, perhaps, the economic and social evolution of Latin America since 1982—the lost decade followed by radical conservatism—has undermined and partially destroyed part of the constituency for reformism, while feeding the typical social base of a more extreme stance: the urban poor.

The emerging organizations or coalitions described above are coming to terms with their new identity, as "reformists have been forced by circumstances to become revolutionary, and revolutionary groups have come to understand that socialism cannot be built in a single country without establishing new forms of dependency."[52] In Western Europe, social democrats like François Mitterrand and Felipe González trimmed their socialist sails and partially adopted many of the free-market policies made popular by Ronald Reagan and Margaret Thatcher, and partly renounced Keynesian traditions. There is a ten-

---

52. Pierre Schori, *El desafío europeo en Centroamérica* (San José, Costa Rica: Editorial Universitaria Centroamericana, 1982), p. 261.

dency in Latin America among analogous parties or groups to follow a similar path, often without taking into account numerous differences and departures from the conventional wisdom regarding the end of the welfare state. The shift away from traditional socialist policies in Spain and France, while undeniable, has been nowhere near as draconian as the Thatcher transformation in Britain, or as Reaganomics in the United States. The welfare state in France, West Germany, and elsewhere is very much intact.

Secondly, in Spain and France, socialist governments changed their course after having carried out deep economic and social reforms—in France—or a lasting democratization of its country—in Spain. Mitterrand espoused the semiconservative policies of the latter part of his decade in office after the bold social reforms of his first three years at the Elysée. Felipe González spearheaded a business-driven, somewhat short-lived, economic boom in many parts of Spain after having fought the Franco dictatorship for years, and largely thanks to his country's joining the European Community. Finally, throughout Western Europe, transformation of the welfare state comes after its resounding success and the virtual elimination of dramatic poverty for the majority of Western Europe's nationals—though not for immigrants from Asia, Africa, and the Caribbean.[53]

None of these conditions has been met in Latin America. The deep, socialist-inspired reforms have not yet been achieved, or are now almost half a century old and getting stale, having only affected a minority of the population anyway. Poverty has not only been a continuing problem, but if anything, has become more widespread.[54] Thus the Latin American attempt to shift away from traditional reformism occurs in an entirely different context. It has logically generated dra-

---

53. It is also true that in many social-democratic parties in Europe the working class and wage earners in general are overrepresented today, as a result of the changes in the social structure of these nations. But the weakening of their labor roots does not necessarily imply only a drift to the right: "A sociological 'bourgeoisification' or weakening of the working class presence in these parties strengthens both their 'technocratic' tendencies and the left-wing ones." Therein lies the explanation for the rivalry and problems many of these parties have had with the Green Parties of Western Europe. Alain Bergounioux and Bernard Manin, *Le Régime Social-Démocrate* (Paris: Presses Universitaires de France, 1989), p. 175.

54. Even the most fervent admirers of the Mitterrand and González brand of socialism among Latin American social democrats acknowledge that the reformist inspiration cannot be abandoned: "In addition to a consolidated democracy, social democracy demands an ongoing mechanism of social reform, undoubtedly limited by internal and external economic constraints and by class structure, but which must, at any given moment, be as bold as possible." Torcuato di Tella, *Hacia una estrategia de la social-democracia en la Argentina* (Buenos Aires: Editorial Puntosur, 1989), p. 144.

matically different effects. The bloody, widespread riots that erupted in Caracas when just-inaugurated President Carlos Andrés Pérez announced his free-market conversion were a telltale sign of this basic difference between the European reformist left and its Latin counterpart. The socialist policies of yesteryear may after all turn out to be as obsolete in the region as elsewhere, but the middle-class European constituency for their rollback is absent in Latin America.

As left-of-center reformism in Latin America is pushed to the fore and transformed into the meeting point for many of the other, historical currents of the Latin American left, it is also being driven to the center. Over time, as Latin America's demographic, social, and economic structures have been significantly modified, the environment for the emergence and consolidation of reformist parties and governments of the left has become more propitious. But simultaneously, these regimes and movements have been led to temper the very traits that attracted new constituencies and old warriors to their ranks. On the main issues and debates of the day in Latin America, the reformist left has a better chance of providing answers than other sectors of the left; but it also runs the risk of drifting to the right and losing its roots, and consequently, its way.

6

Changing of the Guard: From Intellectuals to the Grass Roots

■

In 1918 Arnaldo Orfila was a young chemistry student at the Universidad de la Plata, barely fifty miles south of Buenos Aires. He had just been elected one of his school's five representatives to the upcoming Córdoba Latin American Student Congress, the venue of what would become known as "La reforma universitaria." From this congress would spring a move toward increased university autonomy, student and faculty participation in the designation of administrators, academic freedom, and hemispheric student and faculty contacts: all mainstays of Latin American universities since that time.

In 1991, in his Mexico City home above the offices and warehouse of his publishing firm, Orfila could look back on almost a century of an exemplary intellectual life. It was fitting that he lived just a block from Mexico's National University, the region's oldest, largest, and, through the 1960s, most respected center of higher education. In the interim, Orfila had become the archetypical Latin American *intelectual de izquierda*. Through a publishing career spanning most of the twentieth century, he remained faithful to his Argentine socialist roots: never a Communist and mostly anti-Soviet. To the very end, though, he would refuse to publish books critical of the Cuban Revolution or Nicaragua—"self-censorship" he called it.[1] Yet he became a symbol in Mexico and Argentina of freedom of expression, and, during the dark hours of the 1970s when books were burned in Santiago and Buenos

---

1. Arnaldo Orfila, interview with the author, Mexico City, March 25, 1991.

Aires, the only refuge or solace myriad authors found in many countries of the hemisphere.

Orfila published one edition of Adam Smith's *The Wealth of Nations* and three translations of Marx's *Capital*. An unrepentant anti-Peronist, he left Buenos Aires for his adoptive Mexico in 1944, where for thirty-five years he reigned supreme over the publishing world of social science and fiction. Initially, he worked at the government-owned Fondo de Cultura Económica. But in 1965 he was fired by President Gustavo Díaz Ordaz, who became incensed over the publication of Oscar Lewis's *Children of Sánchez*, an anthropological first-person narrative of life in a Mexican tenement. It was no small irony that twenty years later Orfila turned down—sight unseen—the Spanish translation of Alan Riding's *Distant Neighbors*, a work that many in Mexico considered a worse affront to the country's dignity than Lewis's saga of the Casa Blanca *"vecindad."*

After Orfila left the Fondo, he founded his own publishing concern, Siglo XXI, in association with much of the Mexican intelligentsia. At Siglo XXI Orfila left his strongest and most lasting impression on the Latin American mind and literature. In the sixties he published Octavio Paz and Carlos Fuentes as well as Jorge Luis Borges, Régis Debray's *Revolution in the Revolution*, and Che Guevara's diary, which he still recalls as the high point of his life in the publishing business.[2] During the next decade, as Mexico welcomed many of the hemisphere's exiled academics, poets, revolutionaries, and aspiring novelists, they shaped their thinking and spread their gospel largely through Siglo XXI. The firm dominated Mexican highbrow, nonfiction publishing, branching out to Madrid and to Buenos Aires and Bogotá. Orfila brought contemporary French thought to Latin America, through the best-selling translations of Althusser and Poulantzas, Barthes, Foucault, Lévi-Strauss, and Jacques Lacan. He published most of the French epistemological school of philosophy, as well as the entire psychoanalytic current associated with the École Psychanalytique de Paris. Through the more than 700,000 copies sold of Chilean Marta Harnecker's *Conceptos fundamentales del materialismo histórico*, Orfila probably contributed more to the diffusion of elementary Marxism in Latin America than anyone else.[3] Yet one was hard pressed to find a single Soviet author in Siglo XXI's catalogue. Perhaps it was in deference to his wife, French anthropologist Lorette Sejourneé. Before Orfila, she had been married to exiled Russian revolutionary and writer

---

2. Ibid.
3. Ibid.

Victor Serge, who spent his childhood in Lenin's and Trotsky's laps, and part of his later years in Stalin's work camps in Siberia. In this, Orfila was like much of the Latin American left of the sixties and seventies: rabidly pro-Cuba, sharply critical of and disenchanted with the Soviet Union.

As much as writers like García Márquez, Carlos Fuentes, or Julio Cortazar, Pablo Neruda or dependency theory social scientists, Uruguayan historian Eduardo Galeano and liberation theologists, Diego Rivera and Brazilian songwriter Chico Buarque, it is countless individuals like Orfila who make the Latin American intellectual left an entity unto itself. Newspaper editors like Julio Scherer in Mexico or Jacobo Timerman in Argentina—the latter proclaiming himself a man of the left, which he probably isn't; the former rejecting the same label he certainly merits—publishers and translators, composers and muralists, all make up a separate estate.

In Latin America, where societies are polarized, and knowledge and social recognition are rare, almost anyone who writes, paints, acts, teaches, and speaks out, or even sings, becomes "an intellectual." The meaning of the word is more analogous to the French tradition than the American one. The scope of the term is very broad, because the activities of those it is associated with are equally diverse. It applies to much more than academics or journalists, though not absolutely every singer, muralist, or actor is "an intellectual."

Intellectuals have always fulfilled a central function—and perhaps played a disproportionate role—in Latin American societies and politics. Since independence and during the nineteenth century, partly through the importance of European traditions, and partly as a result of the weakness of representative institutions, key intellectuals occupied a decisive space in many Latin societies. Domingo Faustino Sarmiento participated in the founding of Argentina's Army, educational system, and immigration policy (and also in rationalizing the massacre of the remaining native population) and Rui Barbosa in the abolition of slavery and the establishment of the republic in Brazil. Myriad Mexican journalists-historians-politicians, from Valentín Gomez Farías to Ricardo Flores Magón, helped form their country's national identity, as poet José Martí fought for Cuban independence: a thin line between intellectual activity and political activism made for a tenuous distinction as much then as now. Political parties were frequently nonexistent or unrepresentative, and electoral systems were almost always purely formal. Nation building was incomplete, and in the vacuum created by these absences, the intellectual stood out.

Keepers of the national consciousness, critics and constant demanders of accountability, bulwarks of principle and honesty: for nearly five centuries, intellectuals, dating back to Fray Bartolomé de las Casas's fruitless attempts to protect the Indians in New Spain, have through their writings, teachings, speeches, and other activities systematically substituted for innumerable institutions and social actors. These were either unable or unwilling to assume these responsibilities, transferring them to those who for one reason or another could shoulder them. Needless to say, not all Latin American intellectuals, or even a significant majority of them, filled this function. Yet enough of them did over the years that they came to occupy in many Latin American nations a place no other society really granted them.

As the twentieth century wore on, the native intelligentsia continued to play this role, in revolutions and reforms, opposition to coups and dictatorships, education, culture, and the media. Where structured, enduring political parties emerged, intellectuals participated in their leadership or drafted their platforms. When the mass media finally surfaced in some Latin American nations, they occupied its editorial pages and newsrooms. When modern systems of higher education were built, they contributed to their creation or reform, giving university movements scope and lasting influence far beyond their initial intrinsic merits. And when the opportunity to govern presented itself, they embraced it. As the following quotes from distinguished Brazilian intellectuals of the 1930s demonstrate, in their view an intellectual and a ruler were often one and the same thing:

> According to Martins de Almeida, "the capacity to govern of modern man depends on specialized knowledge, on sociological culture, on intellectual conceptions." According to Cândido Mota Filho, "every statesman, in modern society, is more or less a sociologist." And according to Mario de Andrade, speaking jokingly, "sociology is the art of rapidly saving Brazil." These are several ways of proclaiming that between the trade of the intellectual and that of the governant, there is a deep resemblance. It is also . . . a way of presenting their candidacy to posts of political leadership.[4]

In the much more recent past, as Latin America underwent the traumatic events of the seventies and eighties—coups, dirty wars, revolutions and counterrevolutions, torture and book burnings—intellectuals remained stars on the political stage. Through the long night of

---

4. Daniel Pécaut, *Entre le Peuple et la Nation: Les Intellectuels et la politique au Brésil* (Paris: Editions de la Maison des Sciences de L'Homme, 1989), pp. 21–22.

the South American military dictatorships and dirty wars, intellectuals denounced human rights abuses, resisted attempts at censorship, often becoming, at great personal risk, the core of the resistance against authoritarian rule.

In Brazil, during the toughest years of *a ditadura*, lawyers and journalists, bishops and musicians and social scientists and singers were all central figures in, first, leading the struggle against repression and, second, ensuring a peaceful and inexorable—albeit lengthy—transition. It was at this time that the center-stage role traditionally occupied by intellectuals in Brazil reemerged, and was bestowed upon the country's sociologists and economists, along with its singers and songwriters. Social scientists like Helio Jaguaribe, Francisco Weffort, Florestán Fernandes, Fernando Henrique Cardoso, Candido Mendes, Bolivar Lamounier, and economists like Celso Furtado all were decisive in criticizing the military dictatorship and in sketching out an alternative. When democracy surfaced, they founded political parties, wrote weekly columns in the mass-circulation press, and helped guide a country from the problems of the past to the challenges of the future.

In Argentina, psychoanalysts and journalists, together with novelists and human rights advocates, were all victims of and activists in the fight against the dirty war. It was no accident that the Alfonsín government that presided over the end of the nightmare handed the task of reviewing the past and coming to terms with it to a commission headed by Ernesto Sabato, one of the country's leading, and relatively apolitical, writers. And in Peru, where a substantial segment of society turned against spreading chaos, Mario Vargas Llosa, the country's most distinguished author, was virtually drafted to run for office against the perceived origins of the country's debacle.

An important explanation can be found in the nature of the gaps intellectuals have always attempted—more or less successfully—to bridge. To a large extent, they have served as mediators between two sets of separate actors that often proved incapable of communicating directly with each other. Intellectuals are frequently situated right at the seam between Latin America and the rest of the world, and between a strong state and a weak civil society.

Since the formation of its independent nations, the hemisphere has been a major importer of ideas, ideology, social theory, and doctrine. Even as early as colonial times the importing of ideas and theories created the intellectual climate for independence. Constitutional liberalism was imported from Europe and the United States at the onset of the nineteenth century, frequently in flagrant disregard of the complete local inoperativeness of the ideology's components. While constitutions with splendidly liberal credentials were drafted, adopted, and promulgated with astonishing regularity, simultaneously civil wars, foreign intervention, bondage, disenfranchisement, and even slavery prevailed as the true characteristics of national life.

In the early twentieth century, and more markedly from the second decade onward, Marxism and Leninism were also imported. However, they were equally unadapted and possibly unadaptable to the conditions of the time. Marxists sought to build orthodox working-class parties where there were no workers, to distribute wealth that did not exist, and to lead revolution on behalf of a sector of society that constituted the smallest of minorities. And today, as if nothing had been learned from the past, free-market radicalism is being brought in by shiploads and faxes, establishing a remarkable uniformity of economic and social policies over a region whose diversity is matched only by its resistance to such force-fed imports. Suddenly the entire continent, by magic, has been converted to economic doctrines whose native rooting is questionable.

But societies do not import ideologies; rather their intellectuals do. Latin American intellectuals have served as the local agents of the continent's ongoing ideological importing frenzy, like Socony and Speed operatives in the British colonies of yesteryear. They have bridged the multiple chasms opening wide between the rest of the world and Latin American political and economic elites. Traveling the globe, seeking out ideologies on the market, they assimilated them and packaged them for shipment and local consumption. Hordes of contemporary Latin American intellectuals have lived overseas, from Mexican writer-diplomats José Gorostiza, Alfonso Reyes, Carlos Fuentes, Octavio Paz, and Fernando del Paso, to the muralists who painted in Paris, Detroit, New York, Dartmouth, and Pomona as much as they did in Mexico, to Colombian novelist Gabriel García Márquez, Argentine writer and naturalized French citizen Julio Cortazar, Guatemalan ambassador Miguel Angel Asturias, and Chilean poet-diplomats Gabriela Mistral and Pablo Neruda, ranging back to José Martí and many others in the nineteenth century.

Herein lies an initial explanation for intellectuals' prominent function in Latin society. It stems partly from their role as a conduit between a region avid for ideas, experiences, and doctrines from abroad, and an outside world where these commodities were produced and generated. They are like the honored poets and minstrels of Homeric times, who traveled through the Aegean world with news, gossip, and songs, except that the modern intellectuals mainly brought back notions, whereas the Greeks would also spread them.[5]

Nonetheless, the effect of this privileged situation is not exclusively positive. Many participants and observers of the Latin American intellectual scene have recently criticized the penchant of thinkers and analysts in the hemisphere to tailor their research and tastes to the international public, funding agencies, or even employers. From the right of the political spectrum, Mario Vargas Llosa has denounced the way in which the anti-U.S. Latin intellectual panders to the "cultural establishment of the United States, doing and saying what it expects of him, and confirming its every stereotype of the Latin American worldview."[6] And from the left, this trend was roundly rebuked by two American authors who asserted that:

> In Latin America twenty years ago it was virtually impossible to find a leftist intellectual willing to accept financing from externally funded foundations. Today it is rare to find a researcher connected with any established institute who is not financed by one of the major or minor European or North American foundations. And for most of those who are not funded, it is not because they object, but because they have not yet established the proper contacts or connections.[7]

The comment was not totally false, or entirely new. The internationalization of Latin American intellectuals and their subsequent subordination to the whims, dictums, or simply perceived inclinations of friends and funders abroad has been a constant in debates about the role of the intelligentsia in the continent's politics. It is true that the period of exile in the seventies and eighties bred closer ties internationally, and that the specific nature of the work involved was changing.[8] But Latin America as a whole was undergoing a dra-

---

5. Alan Riding has noted that Latin America ended up exporting its own way of thinking about itself to the United States and the rest of the world, either through liberation theology, its views on the Sandinista Front in Nicaragua, the FMLN in El Salvador, or Cuba. Indeed, some of the last *Fidelistas* in the world were to be found not in Cuba, but in Ecuador, Mexico, and Brazil.

6. Mario Vargas Llosa, "El odio y el amor," *Unomásuno* (Mexico City), December 30, 1991. Without saying so in so many words, Vargas Llosa singles out Chilean author and Duke University professor Ariel Dorfman as an example of this syndrome.

7. James Petras and Morris Morley, *U.S. Hegemony Under Siege* (London and New York: Verso Books), 1991, p. 147.

8. Petras and Morley went as far as to suggest a much stronger link: "The transformation of Latin American intellectuals centers on their incorporation as research functionaries into institutes dependent on external funding. Their work requires them to provide information that their benefactors would not otherwise possess, and even more important, to circulate and implant the ideas and concepts acceptable to their benefactors as the dominant ideology within the political class." Ibid., p. 150.

matic transformation in relation to its affinity for foreign influences. Perhaps its intellectuals were simply doing what its governments, businesses, and migrant workers were, at roughly the same time. The mood shifted from "Yankee go home" to "Yankee go home, but take me with you."

But this only explains part of the phenomenon. The role of intellectuals also originated in the enormous gap that existed, and that endures today on a lesser scale, between the state and civil society in Latin America, between traditionally strong states and chronically weak civil societies:

> In a continent like Latin America, with countries characterized by weak civil society, the intellectual finds exaggerated responsibilities foisted upon him. He is transformed into a tribune, a member of parliament, a labor leader, journalist, a redeemer of his society in the absence of the functions that civil society should fulfill. As the latter becomes stronger, the intellectual's role diminishes. But in the meantime, the intellectual is important because he represents the other elite. Latin America has been a continent governed by elites, by a power elite and a critical elite, with a sort of dialogue between the two.[9]

A close look at the type of function intellectuals have frequently fulfilled in Latin America reveals they are nearly always substituting for someone or something. They write, speak, advocate, or do what is accomplished elsewhere by more specialized institutions or groups. They fight for labor rights in lieu of unions and denounce human rights abuses in the place of judges or the courts. They decry injustice, oppression, and electoral fraud on behalf of weak or nonexistent political parties, and write pamphlets revealing and condemning corruption, substituting for a fettered, often marginal press. They call for the protection of the environment, in the place of embryonic or yet-to-be-created ecological groups or associations. Indeed, the fundamental role cast on intellectuals' often slight shoulders springs more from the absence of others able to fulfill this role than from their own desires, capabilities, or merits.

The reason for this recurrent substitution is evident, and has been stressed in innumerable histories and studies of Latin American politics and societies. The latter evolved without developing most of the strong sectors of civil society that emerged in other countries together

---

9. Carlos Fuentes, interview with the author, Mexico City, September 10, 1991.

with at least formally representative institutions. This is partially because almost throughout the hemisphere the state emerged before the nation was truly constituted as such. This led to an overpowerful state in relation to civil society once national consolidation effectively began. Even when, as during much of the last century, the state itself was not particularly strong in absolute terms, in relative terms it consistently towered over civil society. Labor unions, political parties, the mass media, peasant cooperatives, are all institutions that, while not absent in Latin America in the past, lacked the strength they attained in Europe or North America.

A direct product of the role intellectuals of all stripes have played in the hemisphere's politics for scores of years is the Latin American intellectual left. Obviously not all, or even a majority, of the continent's distinguished, well-known intellectuals have been men or women of the left; and by no means have all left-wing intellectuals been especially distinguished. But by and large, from the early twentieth century until recently, most of the better-known intellectuals in Latin America placed themselves on the left of the political spectrum. Not that they dominated the region's thinking or politics. As Carlos Fuentes counterintuitively but accurately puts it:

> I think since Lucas Alamán [in Mexico's nineteenth century] we have had a series of distinguished thinkers of the right in Latin America, some simply more out in the open than others. They are the ones that have had real influence in Latin America, even if they don't make as much noise as a novelist of the so-called literary boom of the sixties and seventies. There has been a current of thought of the right that has informed and influenced life in Latin America much more than the left. The left-wing intellectual has always been an exception.[10]

The Latin American intellectual left constituted a tightly organized and coherent current of political action and ideological orientation, which the intellectual right-of-center began to resemble only recently, as several former members (Mario Vargas Llosa, Octavio Paz) of the

---

10. Ibid. Among the other examples Fuentes could point to are: the positivists and *"científicos"* in Brazil and Mexico toward the end of the nineteenth century, the "Chicago-Boys" economic school of thought in Chile under Pinochet, economic commentator Luis Pazos in Mexico today, whose books sell tens of thousands of copies more than those of any novelist, poet, or Marxist theoretician. Other examples could be Leopoldo Solís in Mexico, Roberto Campos in Brazil, and Jaime Guzmán in Chile. In a broader definition of the term, newscasters like Jacobo Zabludovsky and Mario Grondona, in Mexico and Argentina, could be included. José Ortega y Gasset and Milton Friedman also qualify by their influence, if not by their nationality.

left abandoned it.[11] Latin American left-wing intellectuals have been traditionally powerful because they have constituencies (albeit until twenty years ago reduced ones), because they have channels of expression, though they may often be shut down, and because governments and the rest of the world chose them as interlocutors. The substitution of the structures of civil society by intellectuals is an arrangement that has generally suited everyone—except for the substituted, who were never consulted. The surrogates were functional to their interlocutors: attitudinally and linguistically, foreigners understood them, and they understood foreigners. Governments dealt with them smoothly, as family and school ties, together with other complicities, facilitated matters. The issue of representativity was papered over, as it was in no one's interest to question credentials that were taken at face value: the intellectuals refused to endanger their own legitimacy, and governments or the international community preferred not to risk losing spokesmen—real or not—for sectors of society or opinion usually unspoken for.

The Latin American intellectual left served a primary function in the conceptualization and socialization of the populist regimes of the thirties and forties. While it never dictated policies actually executed, it wielded great influence in preserving their accomplishments and legacy in the minds of citizens. In the 1960s, as the Cuban Revolution found itself totally isolated from hemispheric officialdom, intellectuals came largely to substitute for governments and embassies. Every Latin American intellectual worth his pen, canvas, or songbook made the journey to Havana at one point or another. As Gabriel García Márquez has put it:

> The definition of a Latin American *intelectual de izquierda* became the unconditional defense of Cuba. And the Cubans, through their own mechanisms, determined who complied with this solidarity, and who did not, taking advantage of the situation that prevailed for many intellectuals in their countries. The second-tier intellectuals, without opportunities in their own lands, found a way of acquiring power: by becoming the paladins of solidarity. Entire pilgrimages of

---

11. Paz was never a great enthusiast, for example, of the Cuban Revolution, but Vargas Llosa was, and has never denied it: "During the late fifties and early sixties I was politically committed to extreme leftist causes and ideals. Like many Latin Americans, my enthusiasm for the triumph of the Cuban revolution was very strong. When Fidel Castro entered Havana, that was something extremely important for the Left in Latin America. . . . I had been very close to leftist ideals; the idea of socialism was extremely appealing to me." Mario Vargas Llosa, "Transforming a Lie into Truth," in *A Writer's Reality* (Syracuse, N.Y.: Syracuse University Press, 1991), p. 145.

second-rate intellectuals wended their way to Havana with the purpose of displacing the front-line intellectuals from their position of
leadership.[12]

The number of meetings, congresses, symposia and assemblies
held on the island from the outset through the late eighties was astounding.

As early as 1968, however, the near-unanimity of support for Cuba
among Latin American intellectuals began to break down. According
to one of the Cuban writers who had crafted that consensus, this was
due to a number of outside factors:

> There was a line of ascension from 1959 onward, which reaches its
> high point in 1967–68, at the Cultural Congress of Havana and the
> Salón de Mayo, which nearly everybody in the Latin American intel-
> ligentsia came to. From there on, it was all downhill . . . for two rea-
> sons: the first was the invasion of Czechoslovakia, and Fidel's support
> of it, and the second was the Padilla case, which was used against
> Cuba in a very interesting way. Then after 1970 and particularly in
> the 1980s, the line continues downward as we adopt traditional mod-
> els. In the Revolution there was a whole aspect of freshness, spon-
> taneity, and originality that faded as we began to adopt more and
> more Soviet patterns of behavior, from the red kerchiefs to centralized
> planning. . . .[13]

Cuba would not be a matter of consensus again. The breaks varied
in intensity: Vargas Llosa became a strident critic of everything that
happened in Cuba; Fuentes never went back but refused to criticize the
Revolution directly, whatever his doubts and reservations. Nicaragua
gave many another chance, although the Sandinistas did not develop
the romance with the Latin American intelligentsia that Havana did in
the sixties. Several great writers of that time worked for Cuba in one
capacity or another; virtually none of their successors twenty years
later did so for the comandantes in Managua.[14]

---

12. Gabriel García Márquez, interview with the author, Mexico City, July 10, 1992.
13. Lisandro Otero, interview with the author, Havana, November 7, 1991. Heberto
Padilla is a Cuban poet who received the Casa de las Américas prize in 1967, then had
it stripped from him and was expelled from the Union of Writers because of his views
regarding the Revolution. The incident sparked an uproar on the part of many former
friends of Cuba, from Jean-Paul Sartre to Mario Vargas Llosa.
14. With hindsight, the intellectuals' support for Cuba was immensely important, as
was their devotion to the cause. As García Márquez looked back on those years, he
acknowledged: "Only now can we see how organic we really were, and how useful this
whole intellectual support for the Cuban Revolution actually was." García Márquez,
interview.

In the seventies, the region's intellectuals retained their prominent roles, often participating in leadership positions in the burgeoning revolutionary movements in Central America, and in the resistance to the authoritarian regimes of the Southern Cone. It was no coincidence that many of the leaders of the Nicaraguan and Salvadorean insurrections had taken their revolutionary tutorials in the universities of the isthmus, where left-wing lay or Jesuit intellectuals held sway. It was almost as important—and revolutionary character-building—an experience to have attended one of the continent's public universities—preferably Santiago or Mexico City—as it was to have been enrolled at the Ñico López school for cadres in Havana, or at the Punto Cero shooting range outside the Cuban capital.

As the transition from authoritarian regimes inched forward, the Latin American intellectual left heightened its involvement in the region's politics. Intellectuals conceptualized, negotiated, narrated, and frequently led the often tortuously slow process toward civilian rule, respect for human rights, and the construction of democratic institutions. During the eighties, they were also in the forefront of two debates and struggles common to the entire hemisphere: the issue of United States intervention in Central America, and the economic debacle that devastated the region as a result of the debt crisis. With a few exceptions, the intelligentsia overwhelmingly opposed Ronald Reagan's support for the Contras, as well as his "drawing the line in the sand" over El Salvador, and the 1989 invasion of Panama by the U.S. Instead, the region's leading writers, poets, artists, priests, journalists, and publishers adopted stances directly countering Washington's policy. By a huge majority, they supported successive, but unsuccessful, Latin American negotiating initiatives, frequently backing the foreign policies of governments they bitterly disagreed with otherwise.

On the debt issue, they attended mammoth and interminable conclaves across the continent and repeatedly urged governments to cease placing their commitments to the international financial community above those to their own people. It was perhaps to be expected that this last, quasi-consensual nationalistic hurrah would be quickly succeeded by disenchantment and division. For the first time in decades, Latin America's intellectual community was sundered by truly important disputes: some from overseas, some closer to home, and some in the very heart of the region's soul.

In the same fashion that the Cuban Revolution came to symbolize the intellectual left's unity, strength, and high-water mark, with time it also became a central dividing line and catalyst for other, more domestic and arcane disagreements. If the sixties and seventies were authentically the heyday of this sector of the left, this was due to the fact that on the region's main issues of the day it articulated a coherent, quasi-unanimous vision, with heroes and villains, models, martyrs and acolytes, and because it acquired, precisely during those heady times, a mass constituency. Every left-wing intellectual in Latin America had his or her own private Cuba, which fitted his or her own preferences and priorities. As the Cuban Revolution "defined itself," and matters became more hard and fast on the island, this became increasingly difficult.[15]

Even before its prime, but certainly as the driving influence of the Cuban Revolution got under way, the intellectual left generally spoke to three clusters of issues, all of which predated the Cuban experience but were clearly brought to the fore by the reverberations of the adventure on the island. First, the region's intellectuals systematically raised the theme of nationalism and national integrity, often directly linking it to United States policy toward a country or the entire region, and usually under the heading of intervention. The record of American involvement in the region's affairs reinforced many intellectuals' convictions: the countries of the region had been long deprived of their national pride and integrity by the United States. Worse still, the war in Vietnam gave this sentiment a universal connotation, simultaneously confirming it. The facts—both local and overseas—together with the explanation and the emotional charge, meshed nicely. The intellectual left had a case, made it well, and convinced a jury of millions of students growing up out of the region's baby boom and acceding for the first time to public, mass higher education—that leaned naturally to the left.

In what could be labeled the populist baby boom, the sons and daughters of the workers and urban dwellers who make up the iconography of Latin American populism, from Perón to Cárdenas, were going off to college. They would also take to the streets of their cities,

---

15. There is a paradox in the bureaucratic evolution of the Cubans' links with the intellectuals. Through most of the seventies, the key institution was Casa de las Américas, which, while it was directed by Haydée Santamaría, was viewed by many the way Lisandro Otero described it: "If there was an agency that even during the most gray years refused to follow the official roads it was Casa, thanks to Haydée Santamaría. It maintained a kind of marginality, which caused many problems and put many obstacles in the official machinery's path. Some said it was a bunch of liberals, a group of marginals. But it kept its freshness." Otero, interview. When Carlos Fuentes was invited to Cuba in the late years of the Revolution, he replied only half jokingly: "Only after Roberto Fernández Retamar [Haydée Santamaría's successor] has been put up against a wall and shot."

from Tlatelolco in 1968 to Ayacucho a dozen years later. Extremely sensitive to issues of national dignity and U.S. arrogance, they were in search of an explanation and an alternative. Left-wing intellectuals ranging from pop singers to Cambridge- or Sorbonne-trained economists were willing and able to provide it.

The intellectual left also showed great receptiveness to traditional Latin American preoccupations: social justice, income distribution, inequality, and poverty. Not only had the intellectual left always been haunted by the images and traumas of the region's ancestral, abject poverty, but several additional reasons prompted its growing interest. The sixties and mainly the seventies witnessed the prolongation and, subsequently, the unforeseen conclusion of a long period of economic expansion. Nonetheless, this growth did not produce the expected and hoped-for improvement in the distribution of wealth and income. Since intellectuals of the urban, upwardly mobile, foreign-educated middle class have the necessarily skewed vision of society that their upbringing and vantage point affords them, they were far more impressed with the maintenance of the contrasts and injustices of Latin American life than with the very real gains achieved in "absolute" living standards. Many rapidly confused one with the other, mistakenly concluding that the persistence of outrageous inequalities was tantamount to the radical absence of progress.

In the role they played, left-wing intellectuals were conditioned by their ubiquity and the diverse nature of their involvement in issues and debates. They were by no means specialists or experts providing scientific assessments or well-thought-out, authorized opinions on technical matters; nonetheless they spoke out and wrote about nearly everything. Painters and composers were thankfully and completely ignorant of matters economic: if they knew anything, it was about the deeper wishes, loves, and hatreds of the peoples they drew and sang of. As the reception and sales (though not the actual text or the intention of the author) of Eduardo Galeano's *Open Veins of Latin America* showed in the late sixties,[16] the hemispheric intellectual left was proverbially *miserabiliste*. It was revolted by the poverty and inequities that stared it in the face, and occasionally described the destitution in terms whose beauty and power were surpassed only by the number of consciences they touched. The Brazilian songwriters combined lyricism with a mass audience better than anybody else, and the plight

---

16. Galeano's book sold more than 400,000 copies in Latin America, an enormous amount for a region not used to best-selling books, or to mass reading audiences. Arnaldo Orfila, interview.

of the construction worker sung by Chico Buarque in the late sixties
is as illustrative of the intellectual left's role as dozens of dependency
theory drafts:

> He loved then as if it were the last time.
> He kissed his wife as if she were the last one
> and every son as if he were the only one
> and crossed the street with his timid step.
> He climbed to the top of the construction site as if he were a machine
> and erected four solid walls
> brick by brick in a magical design,
> his eyes watery with cement and tears.
> He sat down to rest as if it were Saturday.
> He ate his measly rice as if he were a prince.
> He drank and sobbed as if he were shipwrecked.
> He danced and laughed as if he were hearing music
> and stumbled in the sky with his drunken step.
> And he floated through the air as if he were a bird
> and ended up on the ground like a limp bundle
> and lived his agony in the middle of the public passage.
> And died in the wrong direction blocking traffic.[17]

But the intellectual left also fawned over its victims, often not
seeing that their lot was no longer what it had once been. In this
condescension lay the weakness of its theoretical, political, and even
humanistic approach: the misery described was real, but the chasm
between the intellectuals' analysis of it and the actual experience of
poverty was wider than ever. While correct in most of their criticisms
of the drawbacks and insufficiencies of the development process, and
of the persisting lags in education, health, nutrition, and overall standard of living, they often did not realize that the economic growth that
was taking place made a difference to many people. They did not always grasp that while the inequalities continued or even got worse, the
absolute improvements were significant to millions of poor who previously had nothing and little by little were acquiring something. The
poor were right, in their way: their lot was improving. The intellectuals had a point, too: the improvements were exceedingly small and
slow in coming, and did so at the cost of the rich getting much richer.
But the revolution many intellectuals expected because the poor were
not getting a better deal more quickly did not come.

---

17. Chico Buarque de Holanda, "Construção," 1969. (Translation by the author.)
This song became one of the most explicit indications of the role Brazilian songwriters
and musicians played in denouncing the effects of military rule between 1964 and the
late seventies, when other sectors of society could not speak out but they could.

A further reason for the intellectual obsession with social justice was the apparent existence of another way: through the sixties and seventies, the Cuban model seemed sexier and more effective than it had or would ever seem again. The impact of intangibles like those reflected in the García Márquez shoe-and-photo anecdote was unquestionable. When his elder son was fifteen and asked his father for a trip to Cuba as a present, the Colombian writer agreed. He gave his son a camera and some spare change and asked the young man to travel the island, find a barefoot child, and bring back a snapshot of that archetypal image of the region's poverty. The story has it that Rodrigo crisscrossed Cuba and found no shoeless child, much to his father's and his own pride and delight. If it wasn't true, it could have been, and most intellectuals familiar with the anecdote thought it should have been. Cuba *did* eradicate what is now called extreme poverty. It did provide education for everyone, and did deliver free, universal, quality health care for the immense majority of its inhabitants. No price seemed too high to pay for these achievements. Moreover, Cuba, in the eyes of its intellectual supporters, avoided one great cost: the abdication of national sovereignty. Long before it became evident that sugar and the Bay of Pigs had forced the island to forge sovereignty-limiting ties with the Soviet Union, Cuba symbolized Latin American independence from the United States.[18] Cuba had defied the United States, and got away with it. There was a great deal of real and sometimes feigned ignorance in Latin America about the nature of the Soviet system, and certainly a total lack of familiarity or direct experience with Soviet domination of other countries. Exchanging American imperialism for dependency on the Soviet Union, even when the trade-off was acknowledged, seemed a good bargain: American imperialism was real while the instances of Soviet impositions were few and far between, and very distant. Thus, for a typical intellectual of the left in those times, poverty and injustice at home had a solution and a paradigm abroad: the land and revolution of Fidel.

Third, in the late sixties and early seventies the intellectual left acquired something the area's intellectuals had never possessed before: a mass base.[19] Universities had always occupied a fundamental place

---

18. "More than anything else, when I finally got to know Fidel in 1972, for me he was a barrier to the United States in Latin America, a true Latin Americanist barrier." García Márquez, op. cit.

19. Carlos Monsiváis gives this aspect of the advent of the intellectual left in Latin America the highest priority. The argument that follows is largely inspired by his comments. Interview with the author, Berkeley, California, April 7, 1991.

in Latin American politics and society; and many of the left's leaders in the past had emerged from university politics, starting with Fidel Castro and the University of Havana Law School. But by the mid-1960s a major transformation was under way. For various reasons in different nations, these decades were marked by the access of millions of lower-middle-class youths to a public higher education that decisively shaped their lives and their countries.

The importance of the increase in the student population between 1960 and 1980 cannot be overestimated. While in Argentina the student population simply doubled—higher education had been extended to the middle class earlier in the century—it increased fifteen-fold in Mexico (from 76,000 students in 1960 to 247,000 in 1970 and 1.3 million in 1987) and Brazil (from 95,000 in 1960 to 430,000 in 1970 and 1.4 million in 1980). During the same period, Peru's student population also grew more than fifteenfold: from 16,000 in 1950 to 246,000 in 1980. In Chile the progression was similar: 9,000 in 1950, 120,000 two decades later.[20] Increments in faculty and administrative staff were by definition analogous: in most of Latin America during this period, higher education entered the mainstream of development. Regional universities, in areas where they had vegetated for years or had simply not existed, became centers of political and cultural ferment, as well as power bases and budgetary items. From Puebla and Sinaloa in Mexico, to Ayacucho and Concepción in Peru and Chile, they rapidly became hotbeds of radical political activism.[21]

In Mexico the student riots of 1968 so severely shook what Mario Vargas Llosa later aptly called the "perfect dictatorship," that it proceeded to spend billions of dollars in the following years co-opting the same students it had fired on at the Plaza de las Tres Culturas. In Peru

---

20. UNESCO Statistical Yearbooks 1970, 1982, 1989. It is worth noting that the exact definition of "university" or higher education enrollment varies from country to country. Some, like Mexico, include certain high schools as part of the latter; others do not.

21. Some scholars have taken the correlation between university expansion and the emergence of a constituency for the intellectual left a bit further. "Increasing social density in the university should be associated with generalized student radicalism, one particular form of which might be guerrilla warfare, in extreme cases. . . . The four nations with the closest and strongest guerrilla-student connections in the 1960s—Venezuela, Guatemala, Colombia and Peru—are concentrated at the top of Latin America in the relative increase of their university populations (between 1955 and 1965). Hence there was a correlation, even a striking one, between collective student susceptibility to the call of the armed struggle, and conditions within the university itself." Timothy P. Wickham-Crowley, *Guerrillas and Revolution in Latin America* (Princeton, N.J.: Princeton University Press, 1992), pp. 47–48.

the educational effort of the fifties and early sixties examined in the previous chapter was developed and intensified under the reformist military rulers who took power in 1968. In Brazil an anything-but-reformist military regime also spectacularly expanded enrollment in higher education: at the same time it was torturing and jailing students, it was also incorporating them into social mobility and cultural enlightenment. In Chile an analogous trend led to the social effervescence of the 1960s which generated the popular movement that took Salvador Allende to the presidency in 1970. The Uruguayan Tupamaros were also a typical outgrowth of the "new" university.

These countries were more often than not unready for the extraordinary expansion that occurred. Teachers were ill prepared or unavailable; secondary and even elementary education remained deficient at best; jobs did not exist and would not be accessible if and when the exploding student bodies graduated. The ensuing politicization that shook many universities was unavoidable as centers of higher education became stakes in political games. These accorded scant priority to training but constituted inevitable by-products of the rapid extension of higher education to new sectors of society.

Over a span of nearly twenty years, millions of Latin American students entered a university system seeking answers to the questions their parents had never known well enough to ask. They found most of the satisfactory responses in the teachings, writings, and preachings of the social scientists, in the novels and poems of the writers of the "literary boom," in the lyrics of Violeta Parra and Victor Jara and the rhythms of Caetano Veloso and the Nueva Trova Cubana. The novelists created a Latin American literary and imaginary specificity; the singers and musicians found words and rhythms that were both recognizable and authentically Latin American, finally reversing the import syndrome of the past.[22] The Latin American social scientist, for his part, provided a coherent, all-encompassing explanation for the status quo—what later came to be known as dependency theory—and

---

22. The importance of the arts in the intellectual *kulturkampf* in Latin America was well known in the past; it continues today. Witness the battle in the 1989 Brazilian presidential elections over who had the most singers, actors, and musicians on their side. The left (all told: Brizola, Covas, and Lula) put together quite a battery, including: Jorge Amado, Beth Carvalho, Martinho da Viola, Paulinho da Viola, João Bosco, Regina Duarte, Chico Buarque, Ruy Guerra, Lucelia Santos, Caetano Veloso, Gilberto Gil, Fernando Morais, Milton Nascimento, Gal Costa, Maria Bethania, Djavan, Antonio Callado. While these may not be household names outside Brazil, they include many of the country's most important composers, movie directors, singers, and writers.

a blueprint for a better world.[23] It featured continental heroes—Che Guevara first among them—and national second-stringers—Luciano Cruz in Chile, Camilo Torres in Colombia, the Tupamaros in Uruguay, and Marighela in Brazil. The students purchased books on an unprecedented scale, while the authors discarded any doubts or insecurities since their wisdom was ratified by the truest of measuring rods: a mass following in an ancestrally elitist environment.

After nationalism and social justice, a third cluster of issues of interest to the intellectual left, of more recent vintage than the previous two, concerned democratization, human rights, elections, and resistance against authoritarian rule. The Marxist tradition many intellectuals of the left were imbued with, as well as the effectively formal character—at best—of representative democracy in Latin America, made this issue less of a burning one. Indeed, much of the intellectual left probably did not subscribe to the intrinsic merits of democratic accountability and elections until it directly suffered the consequences of their elimination. While the Latin American left and its intellectual mentors had always found themselves in the forefront of the struggle against repression, torture, human rights violations, and the suppression or weakening of labor rights, these combats had tended to be subsumed under other demands: national independence and social justice. The links many intellectuals of the left (from Siqueiros to Neruda) had forged and maintained with local Communist parties, and consequently with the Soviet Union, did not facilitate the evolution toward a more aggressive stance on this issue. There was a very strong belief that issues such as elections were less important than furnishing social justice, jobs, and better living conditions; and that the best way to achieve this aim was to establish the kind of system that would provide it, whether the people wanted it or not, and regardless of whether such governments had been successful elsewhere.

But by the 1980s the effects of the authoritarian wave that swept through the continent in the late sixties and the seventies started having a direct bearing on freedom of expression in the media and journals where the intellectuals published, and in the universities

---

23. "A Chilean economist wrote that 'in one way or another the dependency perspective has so dominated work in the social sciences in Latin America . . . that it would be literally impossible to review the overwhelming mass of writing . . .' A Spanish sociologist and Latin Americanist wrote that. . . . 'dependency theory has been the predominant sociological theory of recent decades in Latin America.' " Robert A. Packenham, *The Dependency Movement* (Cambridge, Mass.: Harvard University Press, 1992), p. 188.

where they taught. The intellectual left awakened to the virtues and significance of these values. And for many of the same reasons that led it to concern for national sovereignty and social justice, it quickly acquired notoriety for its advocacy of democracy.

The additional explanations for the intellectual left's impact on the struggle for democratization, and for its participation in the transitions from dictatorships, lay largely in its role in the media and in the region's interface with the rest of the world. In nearly every country where the military took over during this period, outside pressure to contain repression and torture and then to force the dictatorships to withdraw constituted a decisive factor in bringing transitions to fruition. In Argentina, Brazil, Uruguay, and of course Chile, as well as in Nicaragua in the last years of the Somoza dynasty and later in El Salvador and Guatemala, worldwide condemnation of human rights abuses and the suspension of democratic procedures, along with accompanying tacit or explicit economic sanctions—suspension of credits, arms sales, trade privileges—were of the utmost importance. And since intellectuals tended to be the only nongovernmental Latin Americans known abroad and the most vocal in publicizing and denouncing atrocities, together with exiled political leaders they became standard-bearers and effective lobbyists in the struggle for democracy. In the United Nations and on the op-ed pages of U.S. and European dailies, in conferences and symposia held in the region where it was still possible to do so, left-wing intellectuals occupied a central position in bringing international pressure and outrage to bear on the authoritarian regimes that darkened that long Latin American night. In doing so, whatever doubts those intellectuals may have harbored in the past about the importance or intrinsic desirability of representative democracy began to be dispelled. The disparagement of "bourgeois democracy" as a front for imperialist domination had in fact been widespread. Suddenly, intellectuals who had previously considered such issues secondary or even counterproductive, were confronted with them through their own experience. They were gradually obliged to attribute far greater importance to these matters and could be drawn to criticize human rights violations and the lack of democracy in the socialist countries, though not so often in Cuba.

But the intellectuals' privileged position was not limited to situating themselves at the seam of Latin America's relations with the rest of the world. The media also played a singularly significant role in the opposition to hard-line regimes. Censorship, the closing down of dailies like Jacobo Timerman's La Opinión in Buenos Aires or the assassination of Pedro Joaquín Chamorro, and attacks against La Prensa in Nicaragua, along with the general harassment and intimidation of reporters, editorialists, writers, and publishers, was a distinctive feature of the antidemocratic drift in the hemisphere. The right-wing rulers controlled the media because the media counted and was the conduit through which many of each country's most respected and well-known citizens were able to express their dismay or repulsion at events taking place. But by attempting to silence them locally, dictators made these respected individuals even more influential abroad. This in turn enhanced their prestige at home.

Intellectuals were directly affected by the crackdown on the media, but were also, insofar as their most distinguished elements were concerned, among those most capable of resisting. Because they could publish abroad, because it was more costly politically and culturally for censors to shut them out from existing publications, because their signatures carried moral authority and weight almost independently of what they said, left-wing intellectuals during this period were more directly involved in the fight for freedom of information and opening up of the mass media than perhaps at any other time. When the transitions culminated, and the formerly oppressed, heavily censored media opened up even slightly, these same intellectuals could hardly return to their previous relegation of such issues to a lowly rung on the political ladder.

A final motivation that drove the intellectual left into the newly discovered arms of the democratic muse was the link the intelligentsia developed during the dirty wars and *dictaduras* with the popular movements blossoming in the region. The intellectuals thus hooked up with another sector of the Latin American left, its newest and perhaps most attractive addition, the grass roots cohort commonly identified with what came to be known as the "explosion of civil society." Not everyone believed that their bonds with this sector, or with the rest of society as a whole, were as tight as before, or tight at all. The social polarization of Latin American society had taken its toll and placed a distance between groups that, even in the best of times, lived in different worlds.[24] As new trends developed in the hemisphere, perhaps it was best that intellectuals take a few steps back and allow a partial changing of the guard. Not that they easily countenanced any restraints—voluntary or otherwise—on their influence and status: this is the other, regrettable, side of the coin.

---

24. "In the past the organic intellectuals struggled with a self-sustaining, self-financing intellectual existence. They lived and suffered the economic cycles of their countries. Today the institutional intellectuals live and work in an externally dependent world, sheltered by payments in hard currency and income derived independently of local economic circumstances." Petras and Morley, op. cit., p. 151.

The immense power of Latin American intellectuals of the left—and of all persuasions—inevitably had a corollary: their becoming power brokers, power players, and ultimately power sources. García Márquez stretches things perhaps, but he says out loud what many think:

> There is a curious relationship between intellectuals and political power in Latin America. The State and the powers-that-be both need us and fear us. They need us because we give them prestige they lack; they fear us because our sentiments and views can damage them. In the history of power in Latin America, there are only military dictatorships or intellectuals. No wonder then—and it is a fascinating thing—that there was so much coddling of the intellectuals by the State. Under these circumstances, one cannot be always completely independent.[25]

Because intellectuals were so sought out and pandered to by the politicians and the officials, they inevitably tried to exercise the enormous power that was thrust upon them. Herein lie the origins of Latin American intellectuals' fascination with power: they get so close they are caught up by it, precisely because they are so alien to it. Those who come from the tradition of the left—the major non-left exception being Jorge Luis Borges—have practically all engaged in a process of seduction-alignment-disenchantment with political power. The temptation to wield the immense force that the state acknowledges and that society apparently also recognizes, by entering government or getting intimately involved with it, is generally irresistible. Octavio Paz was a member of the Mexican foreign service for many years before he requested a leave of absence in 1968 to protest the Tlatelolco massacre. By his seventieth birthday, in 1986, he was allowing the De la Madrid administration to hold an official celebration; later as Carlos Salinas astutely courted him, he became as adamant a defender of the new PRI authoritarian regime as he had been a critic of the old one.

Carlos Fuentes not only became President Luis Echeverría's friend and ambassador to France for several years; he also articulated the most eloquent justification for intellectual support of Echeverría's administration. He broke violently with José López Portillo but became a staunch defender of the Sandinistas in Nicaragua, always subsuming their mistakes and excesses to the overwhelming reality of American aggression. García Márquez himself was the only well-known confidant Fidel Castro retained in the autumn of his patriarchy, and the Colombian writer knew full well that his closeness made it virtually

25. García Márquez, interview.

impossible for him to truly exercise his influence and ease Fidel toward change and history. Mario Vargas Llosa, finally, took the bond between the intellectual and the Prince to its ultimate conclusion: he tried to *become* the Prince, running for president of Peru in 1990. The too-close-for-comfort ties all of these intellectuals, and so many others less renowned and affluent, established with power stem from the fact of their own power. The chumminess and, in the last analysis, the erosion of critical distance are a logical consequence of the intellectuals' strength: one cannot exist without the other.

This same clout and willingness to use it explain why intellectual debates in Latin America are often a contact sport: much is at stake, and the struggle is waged with no quarter. Debates over funding, protégés, jobs, and perks are savage, frequent, and consuming; their ferocity has earned them the label "cannibalistic." They seem puerile, even absurd to outsiders convinced that no one really cares whether the Cubans refused to publish Heberto Padilla's poems or insulted Pablo Neruda at a Pen Club Congress; or if Octavio Paz really got that upset with Mario Vargas Llosa for having criticized the Mexican government at a colloquium largely financed by the government's main ally, Televisa, the private television monopoly; or finally, whether Carlos Fuentes should have invited Paz on time to his own colloquium two years later. Through these internecine squabbles, the region's intellectuals do battle for what really counts: the region's soul and direction. Because the rest of society is so weak, whatever the intellectuals do or say, write or denounce, is decisive—or was, until the so-called "explosion of civil society" in the 1980s.

Intellectuals played a key role in this "explosion" too: conceptualizing it (the Chilean FLASCO school), narrating and socializing it (Carlos Monsiváis in Mexico), leading it in its demands for justice and human rights (Nobel Peace Prize winner Adolfo Pérez Esquivel in Argentina), or symbolizing it and channeling it into political expression and structured political parties, as the Brazilian singers and social scientists did. Thus while many of the original circumstances that had led intellectuals to assume such a high profile for centuries were now beginning to shift, these same intellectuals kept contributing to that transformation. They remained important actors in the development of civil society as it started to take over where they left off. They were central in encouraging and attempting to define the social protest that began to awaken from the hibernation of the initial years of authoritarian rule. Together with the movements themselves, they confronted many of the problems that accompanied the greening of the grass roots in Latin America.

The first problem involved the degree of terminological haziness that needed to be dispelled: terms such as "civil society," "popular movements," "grass roots organizations," and even "nongovernmental organizations" (NGOs) are used interchangeably. In addition, the object generally designated by these haphazardly used, high-sounding terms is diversely a source of expectations and despair, of disappointment and rectification.

Because in Latin America most forms of organization of society have traditionally taken place at the behest of the state, sponsored by the state, or directly within the state, for many years the idea of social organization outside the state was innovative or anathema. It is worth recalling that among the myriad legacies of the populist era in Brazil, Argentina, and Mexico, as well as other nations that share this heritage, the corporativist integration of unions, associations, business councils, and peasant organizations figured prominently. Even during the most arduous times for labor organizers, students, and other sectors of society, everything seemed to occur within the realm of the state, or "political society" in Hegelian terms. At the same time, the Latin American left's Leninist heritage meshed neatly with this statist preeminence: the only power worth fighting for and conquering seemed to be state power.

But the authoritarian regimes of the sixties and seventies in most Latin American countries closed down even the scant space previously reserved within the state for many elements of society. Parliaments and political parties were abolished, while previously existing labor or employee unions, peasant leagues, and student or university groupings disappeared, or were rendered impotent or illegal. The only other available forms of organization seemed by definition to be "outside the state."

Countless institutions and grass roots groups flowered in the course of the struggle against the authoritarian dictatorships. One of their chief new characteristics lay in their dissociation from the state. The repressive regimes left little room for traditional organizations. And since the resistance to the oppressive, often brutal action of the state had to come from outside rather than from within, the "new movements" that emerged were largely exterior to the state. Human rights groups in Chile, Argentina, and Brazil; grass roots labor unions in the São Paulo industrial suburbs and in Peru; squatter associations in Lima and Santiago; Church base communities in Brazil, Chile, El Salvador, and elsewhere; higher education associations and women's groups; new media initiatives: all flourished in the struggle against the dictatorships.

As importantly, the emergence of these movements coincided with, and sometimes overlapped, an "existential transformation" among the region's middle classes. The year 1968 set the process in motion, but it became socialized through the seventies and early eighties. Changes in life-styles, customs, forms of political engagement, and attitudes toward the "other," and a major upheaval of cultural mores and production took place across the continent. The young attempted to incorporate political opinions into their everyday life; the cultural realm became politicized and transformed by the alterations around it. In literature, the arts, the theater and music, in sexuality and dress codes, through growing up and giving birth, the urban, intellectualized middle classes were undergoing a major transformation. In highly conservative societies, this represented a monumental shake-up. It reinforced the impact of the popular movements, often merged with it, and seemed to indicate a different path: through the grass roots, everyday life, and the cultural sphere.

The traditional division of the state and civil society, proper to both classical political philosophy and early, Hegelian Marxism, reappeared in Latin America with a vengeance. Marxists (re)discovered Antonio Gramsci and the Italian school of Marxism; organizers were fascinated by the awakenings of old sectors or the blossoming of new sectors organizing themselves in unprecedented ways. But behind this ideological and political bewitchment lay a theoretical misunderstanding and a facile solution to real problems.

The theoretical confusion stemmed from the fuzziness of the state/ civil society dichotomy: how separate from the state was civil society, and how autonomous could it truly be? The Gramscian reinterpretation of Marx and Hegel was an extraordinarily positive philosophical development. It broke with the dictum attributed to orthodox Marxism-Leninism according to which all politics was reduced to the realm of the state, and the only politics worth engaging in was that involving the state itself. But by resurrecting the old state/civil society duality, this rectification ran the risk of creating new misunderstandings and contributing to new confusion. The fact was that most of the movements that burgeoned throughout Latin America during the sixties and seventies only appeared to be "exterior" to the state because the states they faced were typically authoritarian ones, in contrast to previous movements that had been totally incorporated by the state.[26]

---

26. A typical example of this confusion, all the more illuminating in view of the good faith of its exponents, can be found in the following passage written by a Nicaraguan intellectual (interviewed below) and his radical American coauthor: "By civil society we mean all the groups and organizations that are not part of the dominant order or the ruling class." (Roll over, Hegel and Feuerbach.) Roger Burbach and Orlando Nuñez, *Fire in the Americas: Forging a Revolutionary Agenda* (London: Verso Books, 1987), p. 12.

This view of the world, based on the state/civil society split, contradicted most of the work of the more innovative and perhaps advanced philosophical writings of the time.[27] While Latin Americans were reinventing "civil society," many bolder Europeans were arguing that, as a separate entity from the state, it had never really existed. But there were political reasons for the region's theoretical untimeliness. An initial one has already been emphasized: the struggle against the dictatorships took place, by definition, outside previously existing "state" structures, and multiple new forms of grass roots organizations and movements were sweeping Latin America. Second, the defeat of the Chilean experience in particular, and, more broadly, the setbacks suffered in the struggle for "state power" led several Latin American analysts on the left to hypostatize the importance of the grass roots. They were suddenly seen as a substitute for political parties, traditional unions, armed groups, etc. Both the armed left, since Che Guevara's death, and the peaceful, reformist left—since Allende's—had been defeated in their respective quests for power; perhaps a new left, it was thought, emanating from the plural, proliferating popular movements could succeed where others had failed.

This mechanism of substitutive wishful thinking outlasted the introspective times that gave it birth, resurfacing more recently in Nicaragua and El Salvador. In the wake of the Sandinistas' electoral defeat, many of their more imaginative thinkers sought a way out of their dilemma as well as an explanation for their setback, in their relationship with popular movements in Nicaragua.

> Although revolutionary parties traditionally monopolized opposition to the status quo, in Nicaragua there always existed social movements that questioned the prevailing order. The crisis of the Leninist conception and exercise of power coincides with the emergence and rediscovery of social movements that have a different nature, organization, objectives, and motivations. A transition takes place within our party [the Sandinista National Liberation Front]: a revolution fundamentally led by a vanguard party takes power and becomes a state. There is a transition because during the revolution, both before and after the con-

---

27. This was particularly the case with the French school of philosophers, historians, psychoanalysts, and linguists: Foucault, Lacan, Lévi-Strauss, Barthes, Poulantzas, and Althusser. In one form or another—and the nuances were not insignificant—they all posited transcending the state/civil society dichotomy. They stressed the fact that the "State was everywhere," and that thanks to "micro-powers," linguistic, ideological, and anthropological structures, there was no area of society actually "exterior to the state." Distinctions such as those between "public" and "private," political and civil society, structure and superstructure, were deemed more philosophical and historical than ontological.

quest of power, a series of social movements exert a great deal of influence on Sandinism. They force the Sandinista Front to function
differently from a vanguard party in Eastern Europe and the Third
World.[28]

And in El Salvador, military commanders like Joaquín Villalobos
were touting the importance of "civil society" in the guerrillas' blueprint of a peaceful solution to the civil war in that country: "The
classical concept of a vanguard that hegemonizes power is history.
What we are pursuing in El Salvador is a revolution of civil society."[29]

The theoretical confusion and the undue expectations—two different caveats—kindled by the force and originality of the grass roots
explosion clouded what should have been evident. On the one hand,
the new movements, far from being foreign to the state, were intimately related to issues of public policy: land, housing, water, wages,
universities, human rights. They were not state organs, but neither
were they radically exterior to the state. Most of the solutions to their
demands inevitably involved the state. This need not have detracted
from their importance, but should have served as a warning.

On the other hand, as the fight to overthrow the dictatorships triumphed, these movements inevitably lost some of their revolutionary
appeal and vigor, while at the same time settling into more traditional
roles. They could not maintain in a democracy the drive and symbol-
ism they had generated under authoritarian conditions. The democratic advance for the entire continent was nonetheless enormous, and
the strengthening of the left implied by the mere existence and survival of these movements was indisputable. But perhaps too great an
emphasis was placed upon them.

The way in which many of these movements eventually banded
together with entities of "political society"—parties, unions, local governments, etc.—in the wave of left-wing, grass roots municipal authorities elected in many Latin American cities in the second half of the
1980s underscores the importance of the trend, as well as its limits.
Without the electoral connection and the association with parties, the
movements were often condemned to fester and vanish, as the reasons
that brought about their emergence disappeared.

Among the contradictions so generated is what Salvador Samayoa

---

28. Orlando Nuñez, interview with the author, Berkeley, Calif., February 18, 1991.
Nuñez was one of the Sandinistas' main theoreticians during their years in power and
one of their leading strategists of agrarian reform, and director of the Center for the Study
of Agrarian Reform in Managua.

29. Joaquín Villalobos, interview with the author, Mexico City, September 5, 1991.

has called the difference between the "party left" and the "movement left."[30] For many years, the left has flirted with a Cartesian-like dictum: "I create a political party, thus I exist." The party has been the privileged, if not exclusive expression of political will, action, and reflection. In keeping with this tradition, much of the left remains party-wedded and continues to perceive itself as building a party, consolidating it, or about to give birth to one.

This in turn has various implications: a party entails a structure, a coherent program, rules and regulations governing its internal life and debates, alliances, and a certain notion of its place in society. Does it represent a class or an ill-defined sector of society ("the people")? Would it like to rule supremely and alone, only resignedly accepting the existence of other, competing parties, or does it acknowledge that a diverse society, and polymorphous classes within it, cannot be represented, ever, by a single party? More important, the "party line" implies that all grass roots trends, civil society impulses, and other expressions of popular demands should be subordinate to the party, or eventually incorporated into it. The relationship between political parties of this left and these movements has been a recurrently strained one, as the "party left" longs for when it will become all-encompassing and complete unto itself.

Many point out, though, that the trend in Latin America is away from this "party"-based left to a more movement-inspired one. Indeed, from this perspective, the left's most important successes of recent years are all of the "movement" variety. Lula's coalition in Brazil in 1989, Cárdenas's broad front in Mexico in 1988, the Coalición del NO in Chile in 1988 constitute examples of this. All of these electoral fronts were broad, often unwieldy, but richly diverse coalitions not only of many political organizations but, most important, of various popular movements springing from civil society. Church groups and unions, intellectuals, peasant organizations, human rights associations, and student groups, all participated in the pursuit of an electoral objective, but their activity was by no means restricted to those narrow considerations. This left, which many are reluctant to call "new" because the term is so worn-out, not only is different in conception from the old, party-based one but, above all, is distinct in real life. Its strength lies in its links to the grass roots movements.

---

30. Salvador Samayoa, interview with the author, Mexico City, May 20, 1990.

7

The Grass Roots Explosion

∎

If there is ever a Mexican version of Sendero Luminoso, Leobardo Ordaz would be a prime candidate for founding-membership. He was born in 1964 in the Portales neighborhood of Mexico City when it was still one of the meanest, darkest areas of the capital. His father, an unskilled mason, died a year after his birth, and like so many of Mexico's urban poor, Leobardo was brought up by his mother. She worked for years in the home of a Mexican intellectual, doing domestic work by day and raising a family by evening and night. Her employer's help, her own fortitude, and Mexico's boom and mobility of the 1970s laid out the path Leobardo would follow as a child and teenager: elementary school, junior high, then a job in a cardboard-box factory.

By the mid-1980s, when jobs weren't paying much anymore and his own ambition and curiosity led him on, Ordaz returned to school, aided again by his mother, and by his older brothers. First he enrolled in a government training school, then at the Prepa Popular Tacuba, a notoriously radical public high school that achieved fame and scandal during those years. It was a hotbed of student activism, so-called self-management—there were no grades at Tacuba—and violence. Its students burned buses, painted walls, and, on occasion, threw bombs, most notably at the 1984 May Day parade in front of the National Palace. Although Ordaz was not particularly politicized, or extreme in his few and simple political opinions, he quickly became known as an *acelerado* (a radical). By default, he was soon associated—falsely—with the "Sorianos," a pseudoguerrilla group whose official name—the Party of the Poor (PROCUP)—dated back to the rural armed struggle in the state of Guerrero in the early seventies. As late as 1991, it would still be planting bombs in Mexico City.

Whatever the rumors and insinuations, Ordaz never actually became a Soriano, and shied away from the bomb throwers. By 1986 he left the Prepa Popular and enrolled at the National University's College of Science and Humanities in the eastern part of the city, one of the roughest high schools in the capital. He continued dabbling in student politics, was suspected once again of frequenting the violent groups, yet still stayed out of trouble. But if the law of averages, historical precedent, and personal proclivities meant anything, he should have been on the verge of taking up arms in a shantytown outside Mexico City.

He came from the right background: urban and poor. He had ample justification for the kind of class and ethnic resentment that breeds violence. He was dark-skinned, streetwise, and marked deeply by his mother's efforts to bring him up decently. Most important, perhaps, he experienced firsthand the growing contradiction between the expectations raised by education and the economic crisis that indefinitely postponed their fulfillment. Everything pointed in the direction of armed struggle: this was the same urban base that Sendero achieved in Lima, after Ayacucho.

But other things were not the same. In late 1986, Mexico City was rocked by a broad-based student mobilization unseen since 1968. Hundreds of thousands of high school and university youths marched down to the Zócalo, this time protesting the government's attempt to impose fees and entrance exams at the National University. The students once again captured the imagination of the capital. Their debates with the academic authorities were transmitted live on radio. The students organized, marched, fought back, and won. Upper-middle-class activists mingled with poorer ones, united by a common foe and a sense of fleeting solidarity that only the heady days of demonstrations and strikes can instill. Ordaz was one of them: instead of an urban guerrilla he became a student leader—dogmatic and extreme, radical and charismatic, as they are wont to be.

He met and befriended the other, more famous chieftains of the movement, part of a group known as the CEU: Carlos Imaz and Immanol Ordorika, who moved on to Ph.D. studies at Stanford University, and Antonio Santos, who joined the leadership of Cuauhtémoc Cárdenas's PRD in 1990. After the movement receded, Ordaz became involved in the 1988 presidential campaign, helping to bring Cárdenas to the university a month before the elections, and contributed, along with the other student leaders, to his showing among the urban, younger lower middle class. By 1992, Ordaz had almost completed his university studies in political science, working part-time with an electoral watchdog group. He remained a member of the PRD, had renounced much of his earlier radicalism, but retained the passion and the rage that got him through his youth on the streets of the world's largest city. As with so many of the students of 1968, a social movement had saved Ordaz from the ravages of guerrilla warfare. For a while still, there would be no Mexican Sendero, partly because there was a Mexican *movimiento estudiantil*.

Grass roots movements like the CEU-led mobilization in Mexico in 1987 have become a fixture of Latin American politics in recent years. Reaching well beyond students and labor, their proliferation awakened great expectations as well as the theoretical confusion previously outlined. What were these movements that everybody expected so much of and saw so much in? They vary from country to country and in time, but clearly constitute a new component of the Latin American left, whatever their exact relationship with the established parties and the state. Perhaps their most important common trait was how they transcended traditional class cleavages in Latin America. Practically every one of these movements aspired to be or was "nonclass" in nature. Church groups, urban dwellers, women, students, and human rights activists all organized and mobilized along lines of issue, not class.

In a continent where class divisions (in a Marxist sense) had always created conceptual problems for the left, the appearance of movements that did not have to be categorized, analyzed, or led on a class basis was a welcome development. It was also a dangerous one, because while it was undoubtedly true that the new popular movements did not follow class lines, they tended in many cases to reproduce a rich/poor cleavage of society. The new movements were partly the product of the new poverty in Latin America.

The most important movement, because it is so firmly anchored in the region's history and psyche, is the grass roots Catholic movement generally known as ecclesial base communities (CEBs, from the Spanish and Portuguese *comunidades eclesiales*—or *eclesiais*—*de base*) that has dramatically transformed the role of the Church in several important nations of the hemisphere.[1] While linked to liberation theology, this grass roots process cannot be reduced to it, nor should it be mistaken for it. There are virtually no CEBs untouched by liberation theology, but by no means has every advocate of liberation theology

---

1. The terms Christian, Catholic, ecclesial, or ecclesiastic base communities, or base communities period, are used interchangeably in the literature, and will be utilized similarly here.

acquired the mass constituency that the CEBs represent in various key countries. These countries are Brazil, El Salvador, Peru, and, to a lesser extent, Nicaragua, Colombia, Chile, and Mexico.

Ecclesial base communities are "small local religious groups . . . almost always created by pastoral agents—bishops, priests, nuns and lay people trained and commissioned by the Church . . . of fifteen to twenty-five people [who] spend most of their time praying and reading the Bible."[2]

In urban areas they are based in a neighborhood; in rural areas, in the countryside, in a region, or a farm. They were a product of a number of trends, beginning with a practical one: the perception by the Church of a shortage of priests in Latin America.[3] But the CEBs also and more substantively emerged from other, deeper trends in Latin American society and Church. They were a response, first, to the Vatican II Council in 1962–65 and the 1968 Latin American Bishops Conference held in Medellín, Colombia, in 1968.[4] As a result of the significant shifts these gatherings entailed on many issues, the Church in Latin America began to bridge the traditional gap separating it from the poor. It started to shed its centuries-old stance of defender of the status quo and the ruling establishment. The "preferential option for the poor" and the social commitment by the Church strengthened previous trends encouraging the creation of CEBs, and gave birth to what became known as liberation theology. The CEBs did not constitute a political party within the Church, much less a radicalization of the Church. They were part of its evolution toward a different pastoral leaning.[5]

---

2. Scott Mainwaring and Alexander Wilde, "The Progressive Church in Latin America: An Interpretation," in Mainwaring and Wilde, *The Progressive Church in Latin America* (South Bend, Ind.: University of Notre Dame Press, 1989), pp. 5–6.

3. In Brazil, "The first base communities were created around 1963. . . . Progressive priests working in rural areas realized that they could not come close to covering their entire geographical region on a given Sunday, so they began to encourage the peasants to hold a religious ceremony without them." Scott Mainwaring, "Grass Roots Catholic Groups and Politics in Brazil," in ibid., p. 158.

4. "The Second Vatican Council thus moved international Catholicism from a generally conservative and even authoritarian position to one that supported democracy, human rights and social justice. . . . The most important single influence to modernize and galvanize the Latin American church was the Second Vatican Council." Paul Sigmund, *Liberation Theology at the Crossroads: Democracy or Revolution?* (New York: Oxford University Press, 1990), pp. 19, 23.

5. Many authors have stressed the importance of not overemphasizing the political nature of CEBs. "Most CEBs are not necessarily, or even usually, interested in revolution. CEB members generally have more urgent needs and more modest goals. To see them primarily as tools for political change (as the left often does with praise, and the right with condemnation) is to overstate their political involvement and to misread their religious nature." Daniel H. Levine and Scott Mainwaring, "Religion and Popular Protest in Latin

The political and social context in Latin America also had a great deal to do with the flowering of grass roots Church groups. Above all, the military dictatorship in Brazil and the electoral fraud and repression derived from the 1972 elections in El Salvador created an environment where one of the very few, if not the only, channel for political and social discontent was precisely the Church. As unions, peasant leagues, and universities were banned, shut down, or violently repressed, it became the only outlet for protest and social organization. In Brazil the progressive tradition of the episcopate, as well as the size and strength of the Brazilian Church, made it ideally suited to play this role after the military intensified its repressive policies in 1968:

> Through some 80,000 CEBs organized along the length and breadth of the country, the Brazilian hierarchy has emerged from this decade [the 1980s] as perhaps the single most important voice for the nation's lower classes. Moreover, from the Church's point of view, the CEBs have become as much an "alternative" form of cultic organization as they are schools for educating the exploited in their inalienable human rights.[6]

Through the seventies and eighties, the CEBs and the episcopate became more than simply important actors in the democratization process in Brazil. In the case of the former, they also constituted a breeding ground and source of support for countless popular movements that sprouted up in response to the military's accelerated industrialization drive and the authoritarian political structures that made it possible. Among these groups the most innovative and decisive was logically the "new" labor movement that flourished in the industrial suburbs of São Paulo from 1978 and the wildcat strikes of 1980 onward. Through institutions such as the Workers Pastoral Commission, created by the Church in the 1970s, and the convergence of religious work by the CEBs and labor organizing in industrial neighborhoods,[7] the CEBs established virtually organic ties with the new Brazilian union movement that acquired such a high profile in the 1980s. Grass roots movements for housing, public transportation, and

America: Contrasting Experiences," in Susan Eckstein, *Power and Popular Protest: Latin American Social Movements* (Berkeley: University of California Press, 1989), p. 209.

6. Ralph Della Cava, "The 'People's Church,' the Vatican and *Abertura*," in Alfred Steppan, ed., *Democratizing Brazil: Problems of Transition and Consolidation* (New York: Oxford University Press, 1989), p.143.

7. "Political exclusion seemed to make the neighborhoods [barrios] the only possible space for workers' action. . . . The emergence of the neighborhoods as a space for labor action also enhanced, at the same time, the importance of the Church." Vera Silva Telles, "Anos 70: Experiencias e Praticas Cotidianas," in *A igreja das bases no tempo de transição* (São Paulo: L&PM Editores/Cedec, 1986), pp. 56, 59.

other urban services, as well as for land in the rural areas, were influenced by the CEBs.

Squatters, women's groups, landless peasants, and Indian peoples in the Amazon all began, pursued, or consolidated movements of one sort or another in conjunction with the CEBs. Yet without the acquiescence, or in many cases the open support, of the Brazilian hierarchy, the grass roots Catholic organizations would never have thrived as they did.[8] The reverse influence is also true: the powerful impulses emanating from the base had a direct bearing on the positions adopted by the upper echelons of the Brazilian Church. This partly explains its defense of human rights during the worst years of the dictatorship and its contribution to the protracted process of democratizing Brazilian politics.

As this process pressed on, the issue of the CEBs' function—as well as that of all grass roots movements in Brazil—in a democratic society came to the fore. As politics stopped focusing on the moral, inevitably Manichaean acceptance or rejection of a dictatorship and moved on to choosing among contending parties, or movements, a cluster of options sprang up. Should the CEBs become involved in electoral politics, or should they restrict themselves to the social sphere? If they chose to enter the electoral arena, should they support certain parties, or should they adopt a more distant stance?

The CEBs' intrinsic contradictions came home to roost as Brazilian society worked its way through the transition to democratic rule. One of the base communities' most eloquent advocates—and also one of the senior Catholic members of the PT, the party picked by a majority of CEB members who did make a political choice[9]—formulated the dilemma the following way:

The Church cannot attempt to substitute for political parties, unions, neighborhood associations, . . . which are the mechanisms specific to

---

8. "In Brazil about 80 bishops [out of 350] have actively promoted CEBs, and most of these bishops have also encouraged CEB people to participate in institutional politics. Arguably the most distinctive feature of the Brazilian Church has been the harmony between progressive–grass roots experiences and the hierarchy, a harmony made possible only because of the the progressive character of many Brazilian bishops." Levine and Mainwaring, op. cit., p. 215.

9. "A survey done in 1982 by Antonio Falvio de Oliveira Pierrucci among parish priests in the São Paulo area confirmed the widespread sympathy among priests and church activists for the PT. In the sample of parish priests surveyed, 49 percent expressed a preference for the PT. . . . This preference was particularly marked among younger priests, with 83 percent of those thirty-five and under in favor of the PT. . . . It was evident in the 1982 elections that the support of a high percentage of priests and lay activists was not general enough to guarantee that an equally high percentage of the Catholic vote went to the PT." Margaret Keck, "Change from Below: The Workers' Party in Brazil's Transition to Democracy," dissertation, Columbia University, 1988, p. 163.

the political struggle . . . Asking the base communities to also become the union movement, a grass-roots party organization, or a social center, is a mistake. The specificity of the base communities lies in their religious character. Participants are not motivated by professional, educational or political interests. They are there because of their faith.[10]

As could be expected, intentions such as these did not always materialize. The inclusion of many grass roots movements in political parties in Brazil politicized the base communities. Similarly, the generalized offensive launched by Pope John Paul II against the popular Church generated nuances in the Brazilian hierarchy's attitudes, further complicating matters. By the end of the eighties the CEBs were no longer what they used to be. Nonetheless, the base communities' lasting influence was evident.

That influence was most obvious in electoral terms. Since 1982 large sectors of the Brazilian poor ceased being electoral cannon fodder for traditional local bosses and began voting in consonance with other regions or sectors of society. In areas where the CEBs thrived and had established close ties with powerful popular movements, and where a political commitment was possible—i.e., sought by the CEBs, allowed by the hierarchy, accepted by the faithful—the base communities contributed decisively to the election of state or municipal authorities related to the grass roots.

By the 1989 presidential election, the CEBs' work among the poorer segments of Brazilian society modified the country's electoral map. For the first time, a significant sector of the poorest, most excluded part of Brazilian life voted with the most organized sectors. They cast their ballots for the PT in the first round, and every study of Lula's surprising defeat of Leonel Brizola and Mario Covas emphasized the unsuspected strength of the Workers' Party in the rural areas, attributing it largely to the CEBs. And they voted for Lula again in the second round, showing remarkable rural strength for a candidate of the left in a country where boss politics in the backlands had traditionally elected corrupt politicians with rural constituencies to run the country.

The Church's influence in the countryside was not devoid of contradictions. It had organized patiently for years and had succeeded in placing the issue of land reform at the top of the country's social agenda.[11] And the Brazilian Bishops' Conference was central in pro-

---

10. Frei Betto, "Da Pratica da Pastoral Popular," quoted in Mainwaring, "Grass Roots Catholic Groups," op. cit., p. 171.

11. On his second visit to Brazil, in 1991, even Pope John Paul II was forced to speak to the land issue. "Much remains to be done before it is possible to speak of an equal

tecting squatters and peasant organizers against wanton killings in the countryside. But often the Church was far ahead of the peasantry, particularly when activists encouraged land seizures. The frustration was real, as seen in the difficulties encountered in the Movimento dos Sem Terra, or Movement of the Landless.

On a much smaller scale, a similar broad process took place in Nicaragua. The Church's contribution to the Sandinistas' 1979 victory, however, lay less in the grass roots and more in the role of the hierarchy. Cardinal Obando y Bravo of Managua, along with the rest of the Nicaraguan Episcopal Conference, adopted an increasingly firm stance in condemning the atrocities of the Somoza dictatorship. In addition, various members of the local Church, from Maryknoll priests to poets, acquired a singular presence in the formation of a mainstream group of Nicaraguan citizens allied with the Sandinistas.

The situation was different from that in Brazil. The CEBs did prosper in the poor neighborhoods of Managua, Zelaya, Estelí and Nueva Segovia, but events moved perhaps too quickly in Nicaragua, and at the time of the Sandinista takeover, these base communities were weaker than many believed. When the conflict within the Church burst into the open over the issue of priests' participation in the revolutionary government, the so-called "popular Church" was unable to resist the overwhelming offensive unleashed by the Vatican, the Latin American Episcopal Conference, and the bishops of Nicaragua. As a political factor, the role of the progressive Church was important before and during the revolutionary period; as a grass roots movement, it never attained the breadth and potential it did in other countries.

A somewhat distinct situation arose in Peru from the 1960s onward. Peruvian theologian Gustavo Gutiérrez is perhaps the best-known theoretician of liberation theology, and his writings have possibly had the greatest impact. And clearly, base communities emerged in Peru at the same time as elsewhere, or even before. Some lay apostolic movements surfaced in Peru in the 1940s and, during the initial years of the military regime, between 1968 and 1974, when various social movements of the poor sprang up and organized base communities enhanced their influence. Then in the course of repressive military rule, the Church hierarchy was central in denouncing

distribution of land in this country. . . . It is impossible not to see in this disparity the existence of factors of genuine injustice," said the pope, urging "a just agrarian reform." Alan Cowell, "Pope Challenges Brazil's Authorities," *New York Times*, October 15, 1991, p. A7.

human rights abuses and supporting the transition to civilian governance.

In 1968 a group of priests headed by Gutiérrez created an agency named ONIS (National Social Information Office) that over the years, and largely with the approval of the hierarchy, constituted a meeting point and center of activism for the radical Church.[12] Until its dismantling in 1978, ONIS fulfilled a central function in developing a grass roots Church in Peru, though on a relatively limited scale. Although the hierarchy remained favorable to changes within the Church, to the Medellín-sponsored "option for the poor," and to base communities, the scope of the grass roots movement was narrower than in Brazil. One reason was the strong influence of the highly conservative Opus Dei in the Peruvian Bishops' Conference.

From the end of the Velasco Alvarado episode—which the Church originally supported, particularly on land reform—through the broader democratization that began in 1982 and the unification of the Peruvian left under the banner of Izquierda Unida, radical Catholics dabbled in leftist politics and pursued their grass roots activities. But the former activity overshadowed the latter, with the exception of the base communities directly linked to the *pueblos jóvenes*, or new shantytowns, that were mushrooming around Lima. These quickly became showcases of urban, grass roots organization in conjunction with Catholic base community activity: Villa El Salvador, San Martín de Porres, El Agostino. Some priests ran for office on the Izquierda Unida (IU) slates in 1985, and without a doubt the strong showing made by IU that year, as well as Alfonso Barrantes's election as mayor of Lima, was partly attributable to the dynamism and extension of Catholic base communities.

In Mexico the Church has been much more conservative and impervious to trends sweeping through the region. Its ambiguous status in relation to the state—separate, unequal, but acknowledged—and its history as an elitist defender of the establishment have made its transformation problematic. The Mexican hierarchy remains one of the most orthodox in Latin America. Nevertheless, from the early seventies onward, changes did begin to seep into the Church. In August 1976 three Mexican bishops participated in the Riobamba, Ecuador, meeting of Latin American clergy, in which the seventeen bishops attending

---

12. As elsewhere, many of these priests were foreign: "The majority was made up of foreigners, as is the clergy as a whole in Peru, but an overwhelming number of these were from the U.S., Canada, and France." Luis Pásara, "The Leftist Angels," in Mainwaring and Wilde, op. cit., p. 281.

were arrested and deported by the military regime.[13] Bishops like Sergio Méndez Arceo of Cuernavaca (beginning much earlier), Samuel Ruiz of San Cristobal de las Casas, José Pablo Rovalo of Zacatecas, and later Arturo Lona of Tehuantepec and Bartolomé Carrasco of Oaxaca embraced "the option for the poor."

Base communities surfaced in Mexico in the mid-seventies. During the eighties they progressed and grew as the country's economic and social situation deteriorated, and the seeds sown earlier by the Society of Jesus in particular began to ripen. Since the early 1970s the Jesuits had modified the order's conception of their role in society, and instead of channeling all their efforts toward the education of the elite through their high school—the Instituto Patria—and the Iberoamerican University, they tilted toward the "option of the poor." Other Christian groups, especially in the context of what became known as the "labor insurgency" from 1973 to 1975, achieved short-lived influence in several powerful unions, mainly in large automobile plants outside Mexico City and in the textile and clothing industry in the Bajío.

By 1988 there were more than 5,000 CEBs in Mexico, concentrated in the states of Oaxaca, Chihuahua, Veracruz, Jalisco, Chiapas, and Mexico. Up to 80 percent of the country's dioceses had CEBs, mostly tolerated by the hierarchy, sometimes encouraged, and on other occasions strongly opposed by the local archbishop. During the 1988 election campaign and postvote antifraud movement, the CEBs played an important role in support of the *cardenista* coalition. They were subsequently exposed to the onslaught of the hierarchy, which waged a major campaign against them with the Vatican's support—the pope visited Mexico for a second occasion in 1990—and also suffered from the generalized demoralization of much of the Mexican opposition as a whole. But in innumerable towns, local priests or lay groups have organized base communities. They are active in local elections, denouncing fraud and human rights violations. Perhaps the best proof of their importance lies in the statements John Paul II felt forced to make against liberation theology and base communities during his May 1990 visit to Mexico, and in the growth of Protestant sects in many areas of the country.

Colombia, another nation with a conservative Church that often led the fight against liberation theology, has also undergone changes. The grass roots Church has grown, building on the heritage of Camilo

---

13. Rafael Roncagliolo and Fernando Reyes Matta, *Iglesia, prensa y militares: El caso Riobamba y los obispos latinoamericanos* (Mexico City: ILET, 1978), p. 33.

Torres, the martyred guerrilla priest of the 1960s, and the work of the Society of Jesus:

> From the United Front [Torrés's umbrella group], which was a movement where the priest played the role of a *caudillo* in popular culture, we went on to Golconda and SAL [Sacerdotes para América Latina, or Priests for Latin America] Church movements . . . where priests centered their struggle inside the hierarchy; today the process follows a different road: that of the Christian base communities. These are communities of the people, especially of popular sectors [peasants, shantytown dwellers, workers] . . .[14]

While the Church hierarchy in Colombia remains remarkably conservative and monolithic, at a local level "there is an active participation by priests, nuns, and ecclesial base communities in civic strikes and regional movements, occasionally with the approval or support of the local bishops."[15] The Jesuits in Colombia are key players in the Church's commitment to the poor, particularly through a nongovernmental organization known as CINEP (Centro de Investigación y Educación Popular, or Center for Popular Education and Research). CINEP carries out a wealth of activities, ranging from publications, weekly supplements in the Sunday newspapers, and symposia to popular education projects on drugs and human rights. It receives funding from all over the world and is generally considered to be one of the most important, financially well-sustained, and multifaceted NGOs in Latin America. CINEP provided advice and technical expertise to the M-19 and other left-wing members of the 1990 Constituent Assembly. In 1981 it was the object of a solemn condemnation by the Colombian episcopal conference, because its publications and activities were "imbued with ideologies and purposes that gravely opposed the doctrines and the discipline of the Church."[16]

CINEP and its controversies reflect the impressive and potentially revolutionary role the Society of Jesus has played in Latin America since

---

14. Luis Alberto Restrepo, "Alternativas populares en Colombia," in Gustavo Gallón Giraldo, ed., *Entre movimientos y caudillos: 50 años de bipartidismo, izquierda y alternativas populares en Colombia* (Bogota: CINEP/CEREC, 1989), p. 392. The Golconda group was founded in 1968 by Monseñor Gerardo Valencia Cano with the purpose of building the heritage left by Camilo Torres and the Medellín Celam Conference. SAL was founded in 1972, proclaiming itself the follower of Torres and Golconda from a theological point of view.

15. Fernán González, "La iglesia jerárquica: actor ausente," in Francisco Leal Buitrago and León Zamosc, eds., *Al filo del caos: Crisis política en la Colombia de los años 80* (Bogotá: Instituto de Estudios Políticos y Relaciones Internacionales/Tercer Mundo Editores, 1991), p. 231.

16. Ibid., p. 242.

the sixteenth century. In modern times it has done so in El Salvador perhaps more than anywhere else, though other cases are equally striking: from Fidel Castro—who studied with the Jesuits—to Abimael Guzmán in Peru, who according to many accounts attended a Jesuit high school, and countless left-wing activists in Mexico, Guatemala, and Nicaragua. One does not have to believe in conspiracy theories to acknowledge that the role of the Jesuits in bringing change to the hemisphere has been permanent and decisive, from the sixteenth-century missions in the Paraná to the UCA in Central America today.

As we saw in Chapter 4, the links between the Salvadorean armed left and the Church have been one of the chief features of that country's insurgency since the early 1970s. The anonymous priests and religious personalities murdered along the way by the Salvadorean security machinery bear tragic but eloquent testimony to the closeness of the ties between sectors of the Church and the left. A strong, widely based, and radical grass roots religious movement set the stage for the virtual symbiosis that appeared later.

From the Medellín conclave onward, the Jesuits in El Salvador "went to the people." The first pastoral missions began their work in 1969 among the returning migrants from Honduras, in the wake of the so-called soccer war between the two nations. But broader evangelical work began in 1972 in parishes located in the country's most populated departments: Chalatenango, Morazán, San Vicente, San Salvador, Cuscatlán, and La Libertad. Nearly two decades later, several of these regions remained guerrilla strongholds, particularly the first two. Literacy campaigns, Bible-reading groups, and, increasingly, labor and peasant organizing were among the activities pursued by the Christian base communities, largely led by the Jesuits:

> The conscientization work carried out by the "liberation" priests soon had its effects on the practice of the poorer peasants and agricultural workers . . . and in the change of orientation of FECCAS [the Salvadorean Christian Peasants Federation] brought about by the changes in the peasants' behavior.[17]

The other strong peasant organization, the Union of Rural Workers (UTC), also had pastoral origins and eventually merged with FECCAS.[18] The work of Father Rutilio Grande and other Jesuits among the

17. Sara Gordon, *Crisis política y guerra en El Salvador* (Mexico City: Siglo XXI Editores, 1989), p. 176.

18. Carlos Rafael Cabarrus, *Génesis de una revolución: análisis del surgimiento y desarrollo de la organización campesina en El Salvador* (Mexico City: Ediciones de la Casa Chata, 1983), p. 142.

peasants of Aguilares served as a catalyst for the radicalization and rapid expansion of organizations such as FECCAS and drove them to greater militancy. The absence of other channels of expression of social and political discontent enhanced the importance of the Church. After the electoral fraud of 1972 and the growing repression during the rest of the decade, religious groups became one of the few voices of El Salvador that could be heard, even if they were certainly not invulnerable to the repression around them.

The Jesuits did not have the support of the entire Salvadorean Church, nor did the hierarchy back the existence and development of the Christian base communities from the outset. Monseñor Romero, the martyred archbishop of San Salvador, was originally no friend of the Jesuits. According to the Church's more or less official biography of Romero:

> Some bishops, and specifically Romero, thought that FECCAS and UTC, while disguised as Christian movements, were nothing more than leftist organizations created by university youths led by the Jesuit brains of the UCA (the Society of Jesus' University of Central America).[19]

Romero would change his views with time, and end up being the Jesuits' leading ally, his own radicalization perhaps leading him even beyond them.[20] As the Jesuits became more active, drawing greater support for their views, the opposition to them grew stronger. When they changed the curriculum and opened up the secondary school they

---

19. Jesus Delgado, *Oscar A. Romero: Biografía* (San Salvador: UCA Editores, 1986), p. 74.

20. "Monseñor Romero also underwent a process in five stages: before he was appointed archbishop he could be characterized as an intelligent and simple man, but with a view of the world removed from the people. The assassination of Father Grande of Aguilares led him to an indirect opposition stance against the regime, which at that time—March 1977—prohibited any public demonstration. . . . A second stage was crossed with the sermon he gave on the occasion of the assassination of Father Navarro, where he clearly confronted and blamed the government for not solving the murder of the two priests. A third and longer stage was his steadily growing awareness of the national suffering. Through the agencies of the archdiocese he was in direct contact with the suffering and oppression of the people: mothers of the disappeared and political prisoners, widows and orphans paraded through his offices. All of this led him to a fourth stage, to begin to be *the voice of the voiceless*. His Sunday homilies were clearly a denunciation of the country's prevailing injustice. . . . One notices how his political positions become more clear-cut, more *politicized*. The fifth and final stage clarified everything: he not only approves the right of the people to organize but speaks of how the popular organizations can come to be the only political alternative; he rejects any type of intervention and speaks of the possibility of insurrection, since other roads have been blocked." Cabarrús, op. cit., p. 158.

ran—the Colegio Externado del Seminario Jesuita de San José de la Montaña, attended by many of the golden youth of the Salvadorean oligarchy—they provoked the ire of a great many wealthy parents. And as they became increasingly involved in popular organizations and political parties at the end of the seventies, the polarization of Salvadorean society in relation to the Church's role was severely accentuated. The expression that began circulating in wealthier neighborhoods in 1977 was chilling: "Be a patriot. Kill a priest" ("*Haga patria: mate a un cura*").[21] As in Brazil, this involvement of the Church in peasant and urban struggles sometimes created difficult choices, evoking issues of conscience among its participants. The Jesuits were on occasion accused of sending the peasants and workers to the slaughter: radicalizing their struggles against a repressive machinery they could not protect them from. Once the guerrilla movement became the only option, these doubts faded, but the question remained: was this an appropriate role for the Church, whatever the justice of the cause and tactics?

The death of Romero—and, eight years later, of the six Jesuit priests of the UCA University—simply confirmed what was evident in El Salvador from the beginning. If and when the Church ceases to be a defender of the status quo and becomes a force for social change, the consequences are momentous. While the role of the Church itself diminished during the eighties as the movement for change in El Salvador shifted from political to military, the presence of those who came from the CEBs and joined left-wing guerrilla groups grew significantly. Likewise, the grass roots' importance in the slowly reemerging Salvadorean labor and peasant movement toward the end of the 1980s was a result of the previous experiences.

At stake in El Salvador were not so much the direct links between the Jesuits and the FMLN, or between the hierarchy and the left in general, nor even the support given by the hierarchy to the idea of a negotiated solution to the civil war. The issue was the fusion of three trends always present in Latin American society and politics, but that had rarely come together: the Church, with its moral authority, history, and the devotion it inspires; the left, ever active but often lacking a mass base; and finally, popular movements, ever present but frequently leaderless and defenseless in the face of repression.[22]

---

21. Robert Armstrong, Janet Shenk, *El Salvador: The Face of Revolution* (Boston: South End Press, 1982), p. 94.

22. The key to this symbiosis lies in the politicization of the Church and the evangelization of politics. Romero's biographer intuitively grasps this: "The immense ma-

The importance of the grass roots religious movements in Latin America has been both idealized and exaggerated. The drawbacks and consequences of the Church, and of religion itself, as a factor of political motivation are the same in Brazil as in Beirut, in Chalatenango as in Teheran. The religions are different; the implications are uncannily similar. Likewise, too much has been asked of the idea of a "popular Church" in Latin America, and the weight of the Vatican's history, tradition, and hierarchical structures have often been underestimated. Rome and the conservative local hierarchies, even in Brazil, have reconquered much of the ground they lost earlier. Moreover, not all base communities or Catholic grass roots movements are left-wing, and not all religious grass roots movements in Latin America are Catholic.

The rise of the Protestant Church, or Evangelicals, as they are known in Latin America, is a contradictory trend.[23] It is divided into three currents. The first is made up of the historic denominations: Presbyterians, Methodists, Baptists, and Lutherans. These first appeared at the turn of the century, and many were originally affiliated with Progressive Protestant movements in the U.S. After World War I, many denominations split, and the second current arose: the fundamentalist sects. They rejected social orientations, concentrating initially on pastoral activities. They included groups such as the Assemblies of God, the Church of God, and various interdenominational missionary groups, known as faith missionaries.

Through the forties and fifties the liberal denominations' efforts to proselytize fell apart but the fundamentalists persisted, leading to the emergence of a third group: charismatic groups, mainly Pentecostals.[24]

---

jority of the members of the popular organizations were Christians. . . . A huge number of them had learned to discover their own situation as one of sin and injustice in the ecclesial base communities. There they became motivated by the word of God and there they discovered the need, as lay citizens, for a political commitment that would allow them to realize their aspirations for liberation. This is how the popular organizations were born." The line between politics and religion, faith and political ideology, fighting for justice and for God, is a fine one indeed. Delgado, op. cit., p. 143.

23. There is broad agreement that the Protestant trend is important; there are wide disagreements as to its scope. The highest estimates claim up to 18 percent of the population in Brazil, up to a half in Guatemala, and a majority in El Salvador. David Stoll, *Is Latin America Turning Protestant? The Politics of Evangelical Growth* (Berkeley: University of California Press, 1990), pp. 8–9. There are grounds for doubting these figures, not so much in their accuracy as in their longevity: it is quite probable that while a significant number of people have become Protestant in recent years, not all those who said they converted at any one time have remained so.

24. This typology has been developed by José Valderrey and Jean Pierre Bastian, quoted in Luis E. Sarmandú, ed., *Protestantismos y procesos sociales en Centroamérica* (San José: Editorial Universitaria Centroamericana, 1990), p. 15.

Today the fundamentalists still believe in hierarchies and church structures but have become very conservative and far more politicized, seeking to win control of the state. The charismatic groups are also conservative, but in practice apolitical. The historical sects remain divided, but many are progressive and assimilable politically to the Catholic base communities. In El Salvador the Lutherans have been characterized by their progressive stance; in Guatemala certain sectors of the Presbyterian Church have played this role.

As the Catholic CEBs became more progressive and politicized, the expansion of their influence began to stagnate. Their politicization strengthened the left, but partly weakened themselves. The rise of Protestant sects in the region is not a direct consequence of this political drift, but it cannot be ignored as a contributing factor.[25] What remains indisputable is that as the economic and social situation in the region continues to stagnate or regress, while forms of political expression open up, the role of the Church in grass roots social movements will continue. It will also be ideologically important as the void generated by the disappearance of socialism and the decline of Marxism, coupled with the persistence of the "objective conditions" that gave rise to both, creates a demand for answers increasingly difficult to satisfy. The Church continues to search for answers, and to criticize an economic and social status quo it finds increasingly unacceptable. The October 1992 Latin American Episcopal Conference in Santo Domingo emitted one of the most scathing criticisms to date of the so-called "neo-liberal" paradigm in the region, despite the Vatican's strenuous efforts to avert the adoption of such a stance.

Beyond their own significance, the Church grass roots communities extended their reach to other "new" social movements, beginning with of the most typical and at the same time innovative one among them—the urban movement:

> A good part of these new experiences arise from simple living situations, many times in the poor and ragtag neighborhoods that have

---

25. Some students of the emergence of the Protestant Church stress the links between the radicalization of the Catholic Church and the growth of the Evangelical movement: "In Guatemala . . . certain Catholic clergy practicing liberation theology were partly responsible for the military's identification of church organizations as subversive, which led to a wave of terror from which the Catholic Church may never recover its former stature. . . . In Central America, as revolutionary conflict turned into a war of attrition with no end in sight, conservative evangelicals appealed to the traditional resignation of the poor in ways liberation theology could not. . . . In contrast to liberation theology, evangelicals offered to improve one's life through a simple personal decision, to surrender to Christ. That sounded easier than overturning the social order." Stoll, op. cit., p. 314.

become a habitat for millions of working families across the continent. These struggles—largely ignored by the press—take place in all the great cities of Latin America. In many cases the struggles for housing, water, light, and basic urban services no longer occur in isolation, but begin to build a network of "neighborhood movements." New forms of self-help and political education emerge, in groups of neighbors, ecclesial base communities, women's and worker groups, or food cooperatives, or even in their more negative expressions, as collective delinquency on the part of gangs of unemployed youth.[26]

Everywhere in Latin America, the rural exodus and exploding demographic growth rates transformed already overcrowded capitals into urban planners' and mayors' nightmares. Grass roots struggles for land, deeds, housing, drinking water, sewage, public transportation, health, education, and sometimes simply food dotted the landscape of the continent's cities. Huge, unmanageable, nearly apocalyptic urban areas became the scene of squatter riots, self-help programs, and heroic responses to natural catastrophes and their man-inflicted consequences. Classical patronage and corruption—a mainstay of Latin American city politics for decades—gave way to more democratic, more politicized networks. The extraordinary ballooning of the region's cities and the concomitant prodigious growth of the informal, often marginal, and invariably destitute sectors of urban societies had a political and leftward effect. In one metropolis after another—São Paulo and Rio de Janeiro, Asunción, Lima and Montevideo, Mexico City and Rosario, Caracas and Santo Domingo—urban grass roots movements blossomed, voted to the left, and then encountered the disappointments and contradictions of electoral politics at any scale, let alone at a local level.

Lima was perhaps the best example, partly because its transformation could be perceived as an extreme case of what the entire region was experiencing, and partly because many tendencies surfaced first in the Peruvian capital. The spectacular expansion of urban sprawl in Lima coincided with two other trends. The first was the political mobilization and relative opening-up that took place in regard to urban dwellers—squatters, street vendors, etc.—during the first years of reformist military rule. Second, as the rural exodus was burgeoning and more people were moving to the cities, the government's attitude toward the ensuing problems was also changing.

---

26. Tilman Evers, Clarita Muller-Plantenberg and Stefannie Spessart, "Movimentos de Bairro e Estado: Lutas na esfera da Reprodução na América Latina," in Cidade, Povo e Poder, (São Paulo: CEDEC/Ed. Paz e Terra, 1981), p. 111.

Repression, while not eliminated, receded. Self-managed, self-help political associations were encouraged.[27] But by the second half of the decade, and chiefly by the end of the 1970s, resources available to satisfy the growing demands for housing, water, sewage, paved streets, education, and health began to contract. Falling export earnings, austerity policies adopted at the instigation of multilateral funding agencies, more people to house, feed, educate and care for, and—after 1982—the virtual disappearance of private lending, all made an already dire situation dramatic. While this state of affairs was true everywhere in Latin America, it was particularly acute in Lima.

Together with a powerful organizational process involving the Peruvian labor movement and including the creation of the Peruvian General Labor Confederation (CGTP) between 1968 and 1982, an enormous number of so-called *pueblos jóvenes* sprang up. In Peru overall, more than 900 *pueblos jóvenes* joined one of the two large federations of urban dwellers, with some 2.4 million members; in Lima from 1978 to 1980 some 350 *pueblos jóvenes* signed up, affiliating over 1.5 million members.[28] It is possible, however, that many of the memberships and organizational structures have been inflated, and the true grass roots movement is much more localized in a few "model cases": Villa El Salvador and San Martín de Porres, both established in the 1970s and thriving nearly twenty years later.

Villa El Salvador was founded in 1971. In April of that year, a former guerrilla leader, Antonio Aragón, led the "invasion" by 7,000 families of a large plot of land in the city. The government panicked and ordered the Army to clear the property: several wounded, one dead, and a huge commotion were the result. The Church got involved and encouraged the squatters to stay put; the government backed down, and a new, huge tract of desert twenty-five kilometers outside the city was expropriated and transferred to the families, partly led by priests who had joined their fight.

They moved, occupied the new premises, and began one of the better-known, most politically appealing urban experiments in Latin

---

27. "The years of the political dictatorship of General Velasco were ones during which the masses had access to many areas that before were marginal or limited, and in which they could participate politically in the strongest sense of the word." Eduardo Ballón, "Proceso de constitución del movimiento popular peruano," in Daniel Camacho and Rafael Menjívar, eds., *Los movimientos populares en América Latina* (Mexico City: Siglo XXI Editores/United Nations University, 1989), p. 318.

28. Ibid., pp. 334–335.

America. With the hyperbole often used in these cases, its founders declared that "Villa El Salvador was a synthesis of Yugoslavian self-management, Cuban neighborhood committees, and Andean peasant communities."[29] Housing was built by the inhabitants themselves, with credits and technical assistance provided by the government. Teachers came to set up schools; they participated in strikes with the support of the squatters, and then supported the townspeople in their struggles for hospitals, jobs, food, etc. One of them, Miguel Arcueta, a Basque-born elementary schoolteacher, organized the town's legal conversion into a city with duly elected municipal authorities and was subsequently voted in as mayor in 1982 on the Izquierda Unida list, with 70 percent of the vote.[30] The combination of urban movements, grass roots Church groups, and the political left made the city of by then 300,000 inhabitants a showcase in Peru and Latin America. It also made it an example of the limits of such models:

> Forty-seven percent of its inhabitants had attended elementary school and almost as many, junior high school. Villa El Salvador can proudly point to the fact that it sends 9 percent of its children to college, and only 4 percent of its people do not know how to read and write . . . but by February 1989, two adults out of every three had no stable jobs, and the monthly salary of the head of a family of four barely reached twenty dollars. . . . Alone Villa El Salvador had no chance to resist the country's crisis.[31]

The same phenomenon was sweeping through the rest of Latin America. Democratization processes were allowing new forms of urban organization to develop, more people than ever were rushing in from the countryside, and the economic crisis that hit the continent harshly in 1982 made less money available than ever to satisfy exponentially increasing demands. Either services were simply unavailable or their cost and the difficulty involved in securing them skyrocketed. An excellent example can be found in the cost of housing in relation to

---

29. Jean-Michel Rodrigo, *Le Sentier de l'Audace: Les Organisations Populaires à la Conquête du Pérou* (Paris: Editions L'Harmattan, 1990), p. 50.

30. The town's commitment to self-organization and the democratic left cost it dearly and, over time, may have signed its death warrant. On February 15, 1992, its new deputy mayor, Maria Elena Moyano, was shot, then blown to bits by five pounds of dynamite tied to her body, by Sendero Luminoso. Villa El Salvador had been a bulwark against the Shining Path's attempts to penetrate into Lima's shantytowns; it might not continue to be so.

31. Rodrigo, op. cit., pp. 63–64. That 9 percent of the children of a shantytown go to college may not seem impressive; it is in fact an astounding statistic in a region where generally none of the children of the shantytowns go much beyond elementary school.

the minimum wage. In São Paulo in 1959, it took 65 hours of work at minimum wage levels to purchase a square meter of housing. By 1972 the time had doubled, and in 1986, 233 hours of labor were needed.[32] Similarly, in Lima, obtaining legal building permits, land titles, and final approval of construction required six years and eleven months of patience, and cost $2,500, or four years and eight months of working for the minimum wage.[33]

In Colombia throughout the 1970s and most of the following decade, the so-called Movimiento Cívico (Civic Movement) became one of the most important grass roots processes and organizational experiences in that country's modern history. Urban dwellers banded together to demand services, municipal democracy, more resources, housing, land, and security. The movement's high point was the Paro Cívico Nacional in 1977, which nearly brought down the government, and paralyzed most of the nation. These urban strikes continued throughout the early eighties, and together with the breakdown of the traditional two-party, elite system, contributed to two important political reforms just previous to the drafting of a new Constitution. These were Constitutional Act No. 1 of 1986, providing for the direct and popular election of mayors and municipal authorities, and the Code of the Municipal Regime, which transferred revenues—and expenditures—to towns or municipios. The civic movement was made up of:

> Social sectors such as peasants displaced by rural violence, inhabitants of marginal neighborhoods or slums, participants in the informal economy peddling their wares on streets and highways, peasants in their home regions, shantytown dwellers, Catholic priests committed to the "option for the poor," nuns, etc. . . . Initially, neither the political parties nor the intellectuals of the left had anything to do with the civic movement. . . . Nor did the unionized labor movement have any participation.[34]

The Colombian urban movement is of recent origin. The greatest number of paros cívicos (urban strikes) occurred during the 1980s, two and a half times more than in the previous decade, and much more

---

32. Lúcio Kowarick and Milton A. Campanário, "São Paulo: metrópole do subdesenvolvimento industrializado," in Lucio Kowarick, ed., As Lutas Socias e a Cidade (São Paulo: Ed. Paz e Terra/CEDEC, 1988), p. 38.

33. Hernando de Soto, El otro sendero (Mexico City: Editorial Diana, 1987), pp. 175, 179.

34. Ramón Emilio Arcila, "Reflexiones sobre el conjunto de los movimientos cívicos," in Gallón Giraldo, op. cit., p. 289.

than in the sixties, when none took place.[35] It has often been considered the most powerful in Latin America, thanks to several characteristic traits.[36] It derived almost directly from three causes that are particularly important in Colombia. The first was the intensity of the rural-urban exodus as a result of the civil wars of the 1950s. At the beginning of the 1950s, 30 percent of Colombia's population was urban, the rest rural. By 1980 the ratio was exactly the opposite. Secondly, the Colombian state, in contrast to other Latin American nations, ran a chronic deficit but at a much lower level of operation. As President Cesar Luis Gaviria once phrased it, Colombia has a small state, where there is not much to dismantle.[37] One of the reasons, of course, was the lack of natural resource rents in the hands of the public sector. Coffee, the Colombian equivalent of Mexican oil or Chilean copper, belonged to the private sector, which abhorred taxation or anything that approached it. The Colombian state was thus more poorly equipped than others to deal with far greater urban pressures. Third, the general crisis of the traditional parties and the left in the 1980s allowed what one student of the *movimientos cívicos* has labeled the "incipient emancipation of the social movement in regard to the partisan tutelage it suffered from since 1936."[38]

Urban movements have blossomed throughout Latin America because the same causes tend to produce the same effects. The percentage of large-city inhabitants living in shantytowns varied from 30 percent in Bogota to 70 percent in Caracas.[39] But specific circumstances led to the actual emergence of urban movements, their extension to other areas of society, and their translation into electoral consequences. The best example of this occurred in the hemisphere's largest capital, as a result of the devastating earthquake of September 19, 1985.

Mexico City already had an urban movement.[40] It had been active

---

35. Ibid., p. 382.

36. It is these features that explain Colombia's specificity with regard to the rest of the region: "In fact, in many countries in Latin America, there exist economic conditions that are similar or even worse than those that exist in Colombia, yet in none of them has a comparable urban movement emerged." Ibid., p. 396.

37. Conversation with the author, and other members of the *Time Magazine* Conference on Latin America in the Year 2000, Cartagena, October 7, 1991.

38. Luis Alberto Restrepo, "Movimientos cívicos en la decada de los ochentas," in Francisco Leal Buitrago and León Zamosc, op. cit., p. 402.

39. Evers, Muller-Plantenberg, Spessart, op. cit., p. 117.

40. "From the seventies onward, organizations sprang up in every popular neighborhood. Before, there was not even a democratic whisper in the cardboard, brick, and human shacks where scared families hid in fear of photographers hunting for them. And

in the seventies, in countless struggles for housing, land and urban services, in a city where all of the above were painfully scarce, but where independent efforts to obtain them were not always the shortest road to success. Corruption, patronage, repression, and co-optation/cooperation with the authorities seemed to be the true features of an urban movement that existed in a democratic vacuum: the relatively benign, but by no means kind or gentle, authoritarian Mexican political system. The earthquake unleashed a combination of anger, organizational drive, and desire to act independently of the overpowering Mexican state that shook Mexico City almost as much as the earthquake. As Carlos Monsiváis, the foremost chronicler of Mexican social trends, put it:

> At the center, the lessons of the quakes of 1985. Thanks to this great common, existential experience an unknown (and unexpected) force unveiled the enormous rewards that collective effort can bring. The omnipresence of the state quickly and peacefully deactivated most of the initiatives taken, trusting only the magnitude of resources available and the dilution of the masses' efforts. But not even the power of the state could erase the common accomplishments, nor eliminate the cultural, political, and psychological consequences of those four or five days during which brigades and rescue teams, among the rubble and the desolation, felt responsible for their behavior, placed at the head of the city that was emerging in front of them. Although in the strictest sense only the movement of the homeless emerged at first, among hundreds of thousands of others it strengthened the will to act, to contemplate the small and immense consequences of individual action within collective action. The experience of the earthquake gave the term "civil society" an unexpected credibility.[41]

For days students, housewives, bureaucrats, and workers helped pull babies and bodies out of the rubble. The rescue operations lasted for up to a month, and their sequel took over where they left off: organizing the homeless, the jobless, the maimed and sick. These efforts continued for nearly two years, and the urban groups survived into the 1990s. They were personified by "Superbarrio," a paunchy masked man with a gold lamé cape and red leotards, who from Los Angeles to Nezahualcoyotl became the symbol of the struggle for change of Mexico City's poor and homeless.

---

then after a time of lethargy barely shaken by the antics of a few anthropologists, the student movement of 1968 sparked an awakening of consciousness." Carlos Monsiváis, *Entrada libre: crónicas de una sociedad que se organiza* (Mexico City: Ediciones Era, 1988), p. 239.

41. Ibid., pp. 12–13.

This same aspiration, coupled with a corresponding resentment against an increasingly unpopular regime and continuing deterioration in living standards, sent Leobardo Ordaz and the students into the streets by the thousands just a year later, as the government tried to impose a necessary, but insensitive and unjust, university reform on a generation that either went to college or went nowhere: no jobs, no technical training, no hope. In 1968, students continued to be a privileged minority; twenty years later they were part of a lower middle class that was rapidly becoming impoverished in a city without resources or democratic rule to share the burden.

The narrator of all this became its participant. Monsiváis himself came to personify the grass roots organization of Mexico City's social movements. He also symbolized, through his writings and insistence, the confluence of social movements and cultural renewal. More than anyone, Monsiváis stressed the changes that had taken place—and those that hadn't yet—in the young Mexican lower middle class. He emphasized the relevance of cultural change, of transformations in everyday life, and the importance of linking the need for a revolution in this sphere to political reform and social change.

In late 1987, at the Coyoacán presentation of his book describing and singing the praises of these movements, more than 1,000 people showed up out of nowhere: students, women's groups, squatter representatives, and gay activists. The gathering was a harbinger of a new earthquake beginning to shake Mexico City: the political effervescence coalescing around left-wing presidential candidate Cuauhtémoc Cárdenas that would culminate in the July 8, 1988, election, which Cárdenas won overwhelmingly—two to one—in Mexico City. Three quarters of the inhabitants of Mexico City voted against the ruling PRI. The *chilangos*, as the natives of Mexico City are referred to elsewhere in the country, went from mass movements to a single-issue organization, to cultural diversity, and finally to electoral expression. This could not last, and it didn't: three years later the PRI reconquered an apparently apathetic and resigned city.

•

A final variety of grass roots, popular movements that surfaced in Latin America in recent times, and that inevitably must be viewed as a trend with a future, is the women's movement. It is perhaps the most difficult to define and grasp, both because of its simultaneity and similarities with gender-related organizations and activism in other latitudes, and as a result of its own specificity. Like the environmental movement and some of the human rights groups, it differs from the other grass roots movements by its political orientation. If in most of the cases mentioned here, it was relatively safe to speak of the social "left," with regard to the women's movement one treads somewhat shakier ground. Although most of the more important women's organizations do belong on the left—in Brazil, in Chile, in Peru—this is by no means universally true.

The women's movement emerged from an unfavorable background: societies characterized by centuries of male domination, Church influence, and gender exclusion. While none of these dismal features of Latin American societies has disappeared, the women's movement has left a mark, and, above all, has been founded. It existed, to a point, before democratic transitions took hold and grass roots organizations developed in Latin America, but within strict limits. The struggle for universal suffrage was important in some nations in the hemisphere, and in certain countries women had already played a role in given areas of political and cultural life. In the initial decades of the century, women activists were engaged in social protest in many nations— Argentina, Brazil, Chile—above all through teachers' movements.[42] As processes of modernization took hold in the middle decades of this century, more women began to shed some of their traditional functions and participate in activities heretofore forbidden to them. They also began to question their status and the nature of a society that excluded them from so many of its realms.

But it was clearly the coincidence of the rise of feminism in the industrialized countries and the onslaught of the authoritarian regimes in the 1970s that awoke the women's movement in Latin America. Throughout the Southern Cone and in Brazil, a number of factors converged to create a grass roots trend that maintained its multifaceted characteristics and united only with time and to a quite modest degree. Most students of the women's movement in Latin America identify three intersecting streams, and two stages in its development: first dur-

---

42. "It was female schoolteachers drawn from different classes who formed the nucleus of the women's group. . . . They were the first to protest against the pervasive inequality of the sexes in legal status, access to education, and political and economic power. Two factors are of great importance. First, the teachers represented a new group in Latin American society—the educated middle sector—which included skilled workers, clerks, and government employees as well as educators, who were well aware of their precarious social, economic and legal status. Second, these women were in touch with one another through their institutions of learning and through professional associations, forums in which they could share their common experience. *Seminar on Feminism and Culture in Latin America. Women, Culture and Politics in Latin America* (Berkeley: University of California Press, 1990), p. 3.

ing the democratic transition, and then in the period of institutionalization, with the movement alternating between consolidation and
letdown, depending on the country and the time. In one scholar's words:

> The women's movement was in fact a collection of diverse groups with
> different patterns of organization and different goals. Women's hu-
> man rights groups were organized by women who were mothers or
> grandmothers of the disappeared; feminist groups formed to com-
> bine consciousness-raising with political and social action; and
> neighborhood-based organizations of poor women banded together to
> ensure the survival of their families under increasingly harsh economic
> circumstances. Despite differences in goals and styles, these three
> strands of the women's movement worked together during the transi-
> tion and continued to cooperate, though less successfully, once demo-
> cratic institutions were restored.[43]

The three currents varied in importance and differed country by
country. The military dictatorships reproduced the gender bias of the
social and political systems they inherited: much of the repression was
directed against men, because most of the leaders of the left, the
unions, and civil society before the onslaught of authoritarian rule
were male. Women often remained free and alive, searching for or
trying to protect disappeared, tortured, or imprisoned husbands, sons,
or fathers. In many cases this new form of political activism simply
prolonged previous militancies; but in many others, this incursion into
political, and often dangerous, life was a novel experience. It was limited to women and became identified with them.

The best-known example was of course the Madres de la Plaza de
Mayo in Argentina. The mothers of the disappeared who rallied for
years in downtown Buenos Aires became a symbol not only of the
"need to know" but of the necessity for Argentine society to come
to terms with the dirty war. The fact that many of the more deeply
felt narratives of this dark page in the country's history were written by women—as, for example, the script of the film *The Official
Story*—was no coincidence. Another example of this trend was Doña
Rosario Ibarra de Piedra's obsessive insistence on finding the disappeared in Mexico, including her own son, and forcing society and
government to publicly recognize the reality of the human rights
violations of the 1970s. The Confederation of Widows of Guatemala
(or Conavigua) is a more recent and perhaps more broadly based group
that reflects the characteristics of repression in Guatemala, extending

---

43. Jane S. Jaquette, "Conclusion," in Jane S. Jaquette, ed., *The Women's Movement
in Latin America* (Boston: Unwin Hyman, 1989), p. 186.

to the indigenous peoples in the highlands, labor leaders, and peasant activists as well as middle-class intellectuals. It was founded in 1988, and in 1992 included more than 10,000 widows in its ranks.

The defense of human rights rapidly became a centerpiece of the emergence of a women's movement in Latin America. However, where the Church was strong and conservative, as in Argentina or Colombia, the movement remained marginal, limited to spectacular but isolated human rights initiatives. But in countries where the Church was strong but progressive, as in Brazil and to a certain extent Chile, it went beyond human rights issues, extending into the cost of living, housing, urban services, and even more private areas, such as sexual violence. This was also the case in Peru, for example, where activism emerged in a wider context of burgeoning grass roots activism but at the same time reproduced the country's classic political and social polarization.[44] But in these cases its involvement with matters such as contraception and abortion was complicated by the links with the Church and the Christian base communities. In Brazil, as was the case of so many other areas of grass roots affairs, the movement probably merged the currents that made it up more effectively than elsewhere. Several factors contributed to the Brazilian expansion:

Four political developments . . . fueled nascent feminist consciousness and gave rise to popular women's movement organizations. First the Church urged women to participate in community struggles and fostered the creation of mothers' clubs and housewives associations among the poor. Second, in the aftermath of military defeats, the Brazilian Left took up intensive organizing among the urban popular classes, leading some women militants to work with neighborhood women's groups. . . . Third, the regime's protracted process of political liberalization increased the political space available to women's organizations. And fourth, the regime allowed women to organize while still actively repressing other sectors of civil society.[45]

The connections between the different components of the women's movement were sometimes obvious, but on occasion convoluted. In

---

44. "Catholic women, Communist women, radical feminists, government workers, the splits and splinters in the new women's movement accurately reflect the ethnic and racial divisions and class struggles in Peruvian politics and society. While the Catholic and Communist groups in particular sought to organize among women and families of the *barrios* and *pueblos jóvenes* . . . nearly all of the women initially involved in the new movement were ethnically Hispanic, urban and middle class." Francesca Miller, *Latin American Women and the Search for Social Justice* (Hanover: University Press of New England, 1991), p. 197.

45. Sonia E. Alavarez, *Engendering Democracy in Brazil* (Princeton, N.J.: Princeton University Press, 1990), p. 262.

countries where economic policies or circumstances seriously threatened many people's standards of living, bringing hardship and destitution, women began to organize in response to adversity. First they tried to find work, or in any case develop some sort of income, mostly through the informal economy. Then they concentrated on managing their household income more efficiently, joining with other families in the fight against hunger and deprivation. Groups, committees, workshops, or teams joining to cook and make common kitchens or dining rooms, *vaso de leche* groups in Peru for day-care centers, or *creches* in Brazil: grass roots organizations along these lines brought the movement to life.

The process of creation, transformation, and development of Popular Economic Organizations (Organizaciones Económicas Populares, or OEPs) described—in somewhat idealistic terms, perhaps—in Chile, for example, is typical of many countries, and symptomatic:

> The OEPs shifted from self-employment schemes to consumption. . . . At the beginning, they responded basically to the demands of survival. . . . "We began one year and four months ago. Life was tough; we had to pay light, water, and mortgage bills, and couldn't meet them. Then we set up this common kitchen." . . . The organization begins to be, for many women, a place where their problems can be understood, where they can find support. Thus, if many of the women's organizations emerged to solve economic problems, soon the group acquires its own intrinsic value. . . . As one shantytown dweller who attended a common kitchen put it: "I liked it a lot; I felt very lonely at home. . . . I went to listen to a common kitchen leader, and she was like any other housewife, very poor, and her words meant something to every woman." Within women's shantytown dwellers' organizations, sexuality and couple work groups, self-knowledge and health encounters sprang up. Through them, the shantytown dwellers discover their own gender and its problems. Feminism emerges in the popular world.[46]

The incorporation of females into the formal work force has not played the role in the creation of a women's movement in Latin America that it did in Western Europe and the United States, mainly because the Latin American work force has incorporated very few laborers of either sex in recent years. In northern Mexico the mass hiring of young women by the *maquiladoras* (in-bond assembly plants) has partly filled this function, and something of a women's movement has begun

---

46. Maria de la Luz Silva Donoso, *La Participación política de la mujer en Chile: las organizaciones de mujeres* (Buenos Aires: Fundación Friedrich Neumann, 1987), pp. 110, 116, 119, 120.

to develop along the U.S.-Mexican border. But by and large the economic component of the emergence of women's movements has been the necessity families have felt of organizing to face hardship and scarcities, and simply to survive the difficulties derived from ten years of economic crisis and social spending cutbacks.[47] Women entering the informal economy, socializing their poverty and difficulties, joining to cook, build, care for children, improve living conditions, or struggle against exorbitant rises in the cost of living (*movimento contra a carestia* in Brazil): this is certainly one of the key components of women's activism in Latin America. In some countries this process remains a marginal one; in others, it has become more broadly based.[48]

Nations with large and long-standing exile populations, for example, were more affected by the feminist explosion that took place in Europe and the United States during the seventies and eighties: this was clearly the case in Chile, Uruguay, and Argentina. More generally, the influence of feminism as such, in contrast to the other facets of the women's movement, had a stronger foreign tint to it, and evidently a more clear-cut, middle-class connotation. Some students of women's struggles in Latin America have concluded that the stronger the feminist emphasis, the narrower the constituency, and that only women's organizations or movements that reach beyond a strict feminist agenda can actually become mass-based. Others are inclined to view the movement less as simply filling an empty space opened up by the weakness and blindness of the political left, and more as a transformative organization, cutting across ideological and class lines.[49] The fact that the left often did not know what to do with the women's movement strengthened this impression. Nearly every emerging movement tries to occupy the vacuum unfilled by the left and labor until they discover that the obstacles others confronted are not easily overcome.

The conflict between feminist and nonfeminist women's groups is

---

47. "But new groups arose in the 1980s; women domestic workers have organized on an unprecedented scale. Female domestic workers compose the single largest category of women workers in several Latin American countries. In Uruguay . . . there were an estimated 90,000 female domestics in 1984, many of whom had previously held factory jobs but had been laid off." Miller, op. cit., p. 228.

48. "The beginning of the 1980s in Peru witnessed a great growth and diversification of women's popular organizations. By 1986 in metropolitan Lima there were 800 dining rooms; 7,500 'glass of milk' committees bringing together 100,000 women; production shops; and by 1988 more than 300 health groups." Alicia Grandón G., "Organizaciones populares de mujeres: Movilización y prácticas," in *Crisis y organizaciones populares de mujeres* (Lima: Pontificia Universidad Católica del Perú, 1987), p. 7.

49. Gwen Kirkpatrick, letter to the author, Berkeley, April 16, 1992.

real, and not simple to solve or manage.[50] As with other grass roots movements, the transition to democratic rule has proved more convoluted than expected. The secret of many of these movements' success lay precisely in their role in the struggle against authoritarian rule, and the fruits of their success often made the aftermath less agreeable than desired. Still, these issues have been institutionalized in many nations: Women Vice-Ministries have been created, funding has been provided, and congressional committees were formed.

Under electoral, democratic regimes, women's groups have had to decide how to relate to political parties, elections, parliamentary and government posts, international organizations, and lobbying. The Brazilian song that in many quarters came to symbolize the Latin American women's movement tells the story of women's ambivalence and aspirations, of the heroism and suffering of women who, like women everywhere, have much to live for, and much more to fight against:

> Maria Maria is the magic of the day,
> The power and the force that alerts us,
> A woman who deserves to live and love
> like any woman on earth.
> Maria Maria is the sun, the sweat and the heat,
> The strongest and slowest dose,
> Someone who knows how to laugh
> when she must cry,
> And can't live and can't stand it.
> One needs a lot of strength.
> One needs a lot of ancestry.
> One needs to really want to.
> Maria Maria melds joy and pain.[51]

There are other important, emerging grass roots movements in Latin America that must be mentioned. They include environmental associations, Indian groups, and human rights organizations that have survived the passing of authoritarian rule in most countries. The fight for a more protected environment is just beginning in Latin America, and it will be some time before it truly gets under way. Brazil is probably the leader in this field and will be more so in the future, thanks to the impulse given to its "green" movement by the 1992 Earth Summit in Rio. Its most well-known figures are Fernando Gabeira, Chico

---

50. "It became increasingly clear that the so-called women's movement in fact was made up of feminist, non-feminist and anti-feminist groups." Alvarez, op. cit., p. 123.
51. *Maria Maria*, lyrics and music by Milton Nascimento and Fernando Brant, 1983.

Mendes, and Davi Kopenawa, a leader of the Yanomami Indians.[52] Gabeira, a former urban guerrilla, author of a best-selling memoir,[53] is currently president of the Green Party, a group that has obtained up to 10 percent of the vote in Rio de Janeiro and has created a space for itself in Brazilian politics. Mendés, a PT member and leader of the *seringueiros*, or rubber workers, was assassinated in the northwestern Amazonian state of Rondonia by landowners in 1988. He has become a symbol of the fight of the workers and Indian peoples of the Amazon for the land and the defense of their homes and way of life. Finally, the Yanomami Indians have been highly successful in publicizing their struggle, thanks partly to Milton Nascimento's songs and the Indians' presence at the parallel meetings of the Earth Summit. Davi Kopenawa received the United Nations Global 5000 prize in 1989 for his work in defense of his people.

Other Brazilian singer-composers, notably Gilberto Gil, who founded the Ondazul, or Blue Wave, Foundation in 1989, have also contributed to this trend. The environmental movement in Brazil also includes several strict conservationist groups like SOS Mata Atlantica and Funatura. Though often the existence of real people behind the letterheads is arguable, the fact is that numerous ecological groups have sprung up across Brazil, making it the first Third World country to have an authentic environmental movement. Certainly some of its members would reject inclusion within the ranks of the left, while many others would welcome it and in fact have close ties with the left.

The indigenous grass roots associations are perhaps the most recent group to surface in the realm of popular protest in Latin America. Although the best known may be the Brazilians, for the reasons just mentioned, the Indian peoples have in fact been practically exterminated in Brazil.[54] But the 500th Anniversary celebrations in 1992 across the hemisphere gave Indian movements in other nations a major impetus, as one might have expected: the constituency for an indigenous protest in Latin America is enormous, from Peru to Guatemala, from Bolivia to Mexico. The first international meeting of indigenous peoples was held in October of 1991 in Quetzaltenango, Guatemala, and

---

52. One author has labeled this coalition the "grouping of ecologists, or greens, *seringueiros*, and Indians, the last two being the peoples of the forest, or *os povos da foresta*." André Corten, *Les Peuples de Dieu et de la Forêt* (Paris: Vld Éditeur/L'Harmattan, 1990), p. 123.

53. The book, *Que e Isso, Companheiro?*, had enormous success in Brazil, because of both the author's talent and his self-critical reflections on what the armed left represented in the late 1960s.

54. There are only 220,000 members of indigenous tribes living in their communities, according to most estimates. Corten, op. cit., p. 144.

drew far greater crowds and attracted many more delegations from around the hemisphere than expected. Although the exact definition of what is Indian and what is not is the subject of endless debate in Latin America, the broadening of the movement to the mestizo culture bodes well for its prospects. It is also a symptom of the awakening of the region to the incomplete nature of its nationhood, and of the growing awareness of racial and ethnic exclusion or discrimination in the hemisphere. A young Guatemalan woman became a symbol of this movement: Rigoberta Menchú.[55] She was awarded the Nobel Peace Prize in 1992 partly in recognition of her own struggle, partly to acknowledge the emerging indigenous consciousness as the rest of the Americas commemorated 1492.

There are finally the myriad human rights groups and refugee organizations that blossomed across Latin America from the mid-seventies onward and that continue their work today. These include, but are not limited to, the many groups advocating nonviolence in the "liberation struggle." Their principal spokesman in Latin America has been Argentine Adolfo Pérez Esquivel, who received the Nobel Peace Prize in 1980.[56] Movement organizations include Servicio Paz y Justicia en América Latina, Asamblea Permanente por los Derechos Humanos, the Vicaría de Solidaridad in Santiago, Servicio de Desarrollo para la Comunidad, the Permanent Commissions of Guatemalan Refugees, and local Human Rights Commissions in El Salvador, Mexico, and Cuba. These overlap with the Christian base communities.[57] The best example of the new problems they confront is the defense of children from wanton execution in Brazil's larger cities.[58]

In Mexico, human rights organizations of all stripes and colors have sprung up across the country since 1988, as the human rights situation

---

55. Her book, written with Elizabeth Burgos and originally published in Paris in 1983, *Me llamo Rigoberta Menchú y así me nació la conciencia,* was eventually translated into many languages and became a cult text in many nations.

56. For a description of these groups, see Philip McManus and Gerald Schlabach, *Relentless Persistence: Non-violent Action in Latin America* (Philadelphia: New Society Publishers 1991).

57. For a dated, but detailed, description of the Catholic Church's role in the struggle for human rights in Latin America, see Penny Lernoux, *Cry of the People* (New York: Penguin Books, 1982).

58. "At last count there were more than 600 groups in greater Rio alone tending to street kids' needs. Of the dozens of street children interviewed for this story [on the slaying of street children in Brazil], every one had been in touch with at least one nongovernmental organization, whether a church shelter, a community soup kitchen or a human rights group." *Newsweek International,* May 25, 1992, p. 19. The most active and heroic group of these is perhaps the Centro Luiz Freire, originally founded by Waldermar de Oliveira Neto in Olinda, to defend the children of Recife, Brazil's poorest large city.

deteriorated and various Church groups, from Dominicans to Jesuits, and regional associations, from Chihuahua to Chiapas, devoted part of their energy to this issue. At last count there were twelve national human rights groups in Mexico. All are part of the universe of non-governmental organizations (NGOs), that extends beyond human rights groups, including religious, urban, women's, and environmental associations, but not identical to them. They are a new strain of Latin American left, though they do not all belong to it. They are an increasingly important component of the left and of the expression of popular movements.

The NGO milieu has several common characteristics everywhere in Latin America and indeed, in Europe, Canada, and the United States. In the region, NGO activists, in a far greater proportion than the rest of the left, have Catholic origins: ex-Jesuits, ex-Dominicans, or ex-Marists. They either left the Church or never completed their religious education. They consequently tend to be extraordinarily generous and hardworking, but also dogmatic and sectarian. NGO militants are also frequently of more popular extraction than other sectors of the left: they actually live, or lived, in the urban neighborhoods they are trying to organize and help. Their closer ties to "the people" make them sometimes more radical than the rest of the left, but also, on occasion, more reluctant to engage in activities or movements that imply confrontation with the authorities.

NGOs all have an international link. Many of them, in fact, exist thanks to the foreign financing they received, either from government-funded NGOs (an oxymoron exemplified by the Interamerican Foundation in Washington or the EEC funding agencies in Brussels) in Europe and the United States or from private American foundations (chiefly Ford, Kellogg, and MacArthur). While the great majority of NGOs are scrupulously honest in managing the money they are given, their members often quibble or fight over resources, and they have an inevitable tendency to tailor their projects to the possibilities of obtaining funds.

In the last analysis, NGOs faithfully reflect both the enormous potential and the very real limits of popular, grass roots movements in Latin America. They are now a reality, and an integral, important part of the regional left. As the traditional sectors of the left fade or disappear, these social or popular movements will undoubtedly enhance their presence. And as the democratization process in the hemisphere takes hold, the empowerment of what continues to be called civil society will also contribute to the growing clout of these forms of organization and struggle.

Their conversion to, or occasional expression in, electoral bodies has become both a fixture of these movements and a problem for them. Without participating in ongoing, electoral competitions at all levels, they run the risk of being rendered marginal, forsaking significant opportunities to advance the aspirations of their members. But by participating, they are immediately subject to the contradictions of any electoral process: whom to vote for, whom to run, what to do if elected, how to govern.[59] There is no solution to this dilemma, other than to acknowledge its existence and deal with it case by case. Even this is not easy.

Beyond this problem lies a conceptual one. The left has always been troubled by a central theoretical paradox: its Marxist origins and inclinations have led it to accentuate *class*, while the incipient configuration of a class structure in Latin America, and the numerical weakness of the working class in particular, have led it to place a great emphasis on the *people*: "*El pueblo unido jamás será vencido.*" The proliferation of grass roots movements compounded this difficulty: the "new" social protest was not class-based, and with the exception of the new unions in Brazil, formal and open class conflicts remained subdued or nonexistent. So where did class go?

The Marxian dilemma for years, in Latin America, Asia, and Africa, but also in Western Europe, had been that the working class in fact rebelled and won—if just partial victories—only when it acted "as if it were the people."[60] Even in nations where and at times when the industrial working class constituted a majority of the population, the proletariat made revolutions or in any case tried to by transcending itself (in a non-Hegelian sense) and identifying with other causes or sectors: the nation, the poor, the peasantry. This was the case in France in 1871, in Germany in 1918 and 1923, again in France in 1936, and in France and Italy during World War II and the Liberation. This was more true in the Third World or its equivalent: Russia in 1917, China in 1927 and from 1935 through 1949, Vietnam, and perhaps Cuba. While class cleavages and conflicts determined how every sector of society acted, these did not act as classes, but "as a people."

---

59. The wariness of the social left with regard to the political left mirrors the latter's suspicions of the former: "As the social movements become more 'political' . . . they will have the responsibility to guarantee that the popular alternative is not converted into an electoral one . . . being viable within the neoliberal framework translates into being unable to modify the structures of power . . ." *Envío*, Universidad Centroamericana, Managua, vol. 11, no. 128, March 1992, p. 9.

60. Immanuel Wallerstein has formulated this paradox the following way: "A very important part of political activity based on the notion of class has taken the form of a political activity based on the notion of 'people.' " Etienne Balibar and Immanuel Wallerstein, *Race, Nation, Classe: Les Identités Ambiguës* (Paris: La Découverte, 1990), p. 115.

The grass roots movement in Latin America is an expression of the same paradox. Social classes exist, of course, and most of what goes on in each one of the region's societies is ultimately determined by its class structure and conflict. But the effects are different from the causes, and they tend to be of the "popular" kind: squatters, students, peasants, Church groups, women. The emergence of the popular movements should thus not lead the left away from class; it should simply force it to pay more attention to the way in which class conflicts actually take place. In particular the movements should lead it to focus more on how the rural and working-class sectors become a smaller relative part of the overall population and how the urban poor become a majority.

The existence of the grass roots movements, along with the democratization process and the widening belief that more can be accomplished at a local level, generated a shock wave of left-wing municipal electoral victories in Latin America through the 1980s. Simultaneously, each nation was electing conservative national governments or regimes that ran on the left and governed on the right. This paradox carried the left into the last decade of the century—which saw the fall of socialism and the end of the Cold War—and left it out of touch, out of power, and out of tune at a national level yet locally strong, popular, and increasingly mainstream. This trend represented the only apparent consolation for the left: it was being abandoned by world events. The fall of socialism hit the left hard. At the same time, though, events in the region and beyond opened up new prospects for it.

8

La Guerre Est Finie:
The Latin American Left and
the Fall of Socialism

■

His father died in the French Resistance, just before he was born, in
1945. Victor Romeo (or Victor Joffrey, also known as "El Guajiro")
began his revolutionary journey very young, in the early sixties, in the
Cuban Air Force. It ended years later in Managua, on the night the
Sandinistas lost the 1990 presidential elections. His career in revolution reads like a thirty-year history of the Latin American left: its
tragedy and vitality, the dedication it evoked and the frustration it
wrought, and finally, the sense of loss that permeates it today.

Fed up with Cuban bureaucracy, authoritarianism, and conformity,
he left the island in the mid-sixties. With his French passport and
Chilean mother, Romeo went to live in Santiago, where the armed
revolutionary left was gaining ground. He knew how to handle arms
and how to give military instruction. He joined the Movimiento de
Izquierda Revolucionaria (MIR) and began to teach the young, radical-
chic leftists of Chile how to shoot straight and avoid being shot. Over
the years he would become one of the best political-military instructors in the Latin American armed left.

Although he never got along well with Miguel Enríquez and the rest
of the MIR leadership, Victor Romeo stayed with the organization
through the Allende years. When the coup d'état came in September of
1973, Romeo did what virtually no one else was able to: he led a pocket
of armed resistance against Augusto Pinochet's military takeover in an
industrial suburb of Santiago. The shooting lasted less than a day, and
by September 12 Romeo had several rounds of Mauser ammunition in
his body and was given up for dead. Instead, he was captured by the

Chilean military, tortured, and treated in a military hospital, and then sentenced to death. Months of formal protests by the French government brought about a suspension of his sentence, and after nearly eighteen months in a military prison, Romeo was expelled from Chile. He carries two feet of scars down his back as a souvenir.

For the next four years Romeo wandered across Latin America and Europe, living intermittently in Ecuador and the Parisian *banlieue* and traveling for the MIR on delicate missions facilitated by his French passport. During this time, he escaped Chilean, Uruguayan, and Argentine repression, as well as traps and frame-ups occasionally set for him by revolutionary colleagues who disagreed with his views. He smuggled money, people, and arms back and forth but nevertheless became listless and bored with his work. But then came the Nicaraguan Revolution.

The Chilean MIR, the Montoneros from Argentina, and others— through agreements with the Sandinista National Liberation Front— sent specialized cadres to fight in Nicaragua against Anastasio Somoza. The Salvadorean guerrillas gave money; the Cubans provided Chilean nationals from their own armed forces; others sent whomever they could. The MIR dispatched a group of former combatants, including Victor Romeo, their artillery specialist. He never got the opportunity to fight, but his skills in guerrilla warfare instruction were put to use among Chileans and Nicaraguans in the small northern Costa Rican town of Liberia, just south of the border with Nicaragua. His comrades in the MIR tried to set him up for arrest by Costa Rican authorities; he survived. By the time Romeo's pupils were ready for combat, Somoza had fallen. Romeo arrived in Managua in August 1979, a few weeks after the Sandinistas' triumphal entry, and settled there permanently.

Romeo began his residence in Managua by fighting with the local MIR leadership and breaking with the organization: by September he was on his own. He quickly connected himself with the Sandinista Police and soon was the commanding officer of its main barracks in Managua. Romeo continued to teach the Nicaraguans how to shoot, but now also how to direct traffic, arrest delinquents, and treat criminals according to the law. He tried to bring French and Chilean customs, civility, and efficiency to the newly founded Sandinista police machinery, sometimes successfully, but more often than not, in vain. This evoked admiration and respect from the rank and file, but also— predictably—insecurity, envy, and resentment from the Sandinista hierarchy.

As a result, by 1985 he was out of the police force, retaining his rank of lieutenant in the Ministry of the Interior but relegated to over-

seeing a small airline running cargo flights to the Nicaraguan Caribbean. His friends in the leadership of El Salvador's Forces of Popular
Liberation asked him to join them to fight and train cadres in the
mountains of Chalatenango. He turned down the offer, knowing he
was getting tired and intolerant, and would end up battling the guerrilla commanders as often as the Salvadorean Army. Instead, he dabbled in various activities: from making television videos for the
Ministry of the Interior to ensuring diplomats' security in the Las
Colinas section of Managua. But his character—rebellious, arrogant,
and independent—his nationality—French, with a Chilean accent—
and his politics—anti-Cuban, increasingly reformist—divided him
from his Nicaraguan colleagues.

By the time Nicaragua's elections occurred, in February 1990,
Romeo was still in Managua, managing an export-import firm for the
Sandinista Front and making a decent living as, in essence, a businessman. And a prosperous one, at that: he traveled frequently to Miami,
Mexico, and Panama to shop for wares, peddling them to his best
customers—the ex-Soviets in Managua. In the ultimate of ironies, the
U.S. invasion of Panama caught him spending Christmas on the Canal;
he was marooned there for several days, certain that his new profession
and old French passport guaranteed him eventual safe passage out of
the way of Operation Just Cause.

Over the years he never stopped supporting the Revolution, but
neither did he ever refrain from criticizing its mistakes, abuses, injustices, and corruption. His criticisms were sporadically published in
Barricada, the Sandinista party daily, and were well known to most
Sandinista insiders. When changes began to occur in Eastern Europe,
Romeo was both elated and depressed: happy because, along with most
of the new generation of revolutionaries that emerged from the 1960s
in Latin America, he had always opposed the authoritarian bureaucratic socialism that had prevailed in those nations; sad because he
sensed that an entire historical era was coming to a close and that his
own life was too closely identified with it not to suffer from its conclusion. The demise of the socialism he detested did not give birth to
the rise of the socialism he had dreamt of. His life had been a full and
splendid adventure, punctuated by heroism and abnegation, loyalties
and an unending sense of generosity. A happy and rewarding life; as he
boasted: *"Lo bailado no me lo quita nadie"*[1] ("They can't take that
away from me," as the Johnny Mercer song says), and neither he nor
those who had the privilege of knowing him would have traded his

---

1. Interview with the author, Berkeley, California, January 30, 1992.

years in the ranks of revolution for anything else. He had just run out of time.

Until the night of the February 25 elections, Romeo remained convinced that Daniel Ortega would win and that the Revolution would stay in power indefinitely. When the Sandinistas' defeat became apparent, he was despondent, though respectful of Violeta Chamorro's victory. He understood that the Sandinistas had lost the vote but that their defeat, in the long run, would probably help them. Romeo also knew, however, that he had lost far more than an election: the cause he had dedicated his life to for the past thirty years had vanished. He had ceased to be a guerrilla fighter, or even a fully dedicated revolutionary, years before. But the fall of the socialist bloc and the end of the Nicaraguan adventure transformed Romeo into the ultimate castoff: a man with no country, no job, no money or roots, but most of all, a man without a meaning to his life. His life exemplified the history of the Latin American left over the last three decades. He was a tragic example of the best of the left, of its disillusionment and helplessness in confronting a bleak future and a seemingly futile past.

The years brought Romeo mixed blessings: the end of an era and an ideal, but also prosperity and security. He owned two homes and a healthy and growing bank account. He was able for the first time to help his twenty-year-old daughter, bringing her from Ecuador to work in Managua. The thought of trading one thing for the other was terrifying, and true. The conclusion of the Cold War and the falling of the curtain on socialism and revolution had changed him as much as they had transformed the world around him.

The fall of socialism is a watershed for the left in Latin America. On the surface of things, the debacle in the East and the end of the Cold War constitute a terrifying blow to the left; in fact, matters are far more complicated. On the one hand, the disappearance and discredit of socialism cannot but damage the left in Latin America and elsewhere. On the other, the conditions in Latin America that gave birth and recognition to the left in the past are as pervasive as ever, and in fact have become more severe with recent trends. Therefore, in order to determine the current status and future prospects of the Latin American left, both sides of the ledger must be perused: first, those aspects of the present state of affairs that affect the left negatively; then those that might strengthen its prospects, whether directly linked to the end of the Cold War or not.

To a considerable degree, the most damaging effect of the Cold War's conclusion on the Latin American left lies in the generalized perception of defeat, that Victor Romeo—an archetype, not a typical member of the rank and file—personifies. This sense of defeat is derived from the left's perceived or real connection with existing socialism. For the left, the fall of socialism in the Soviet Union and Eastern Europe represents the end of a stirring, effective, nearly century-old utopia. Indeed, the very notion of an overall alternative to the status quo has been severely questioned. It is now practically impossible for the left to think outside the existing parameters of present-day Latin American reality. Moreover, the idea of revolution itself, central to Latin American radical thought for decades, has lost its meaning. In the words of José Aricó, "The transfer of the paradigm from old thinking to new situations is necessary because the idea of revolution has been shaken from top to bottom by the collapse of the East."[2]

The crisis of revolution does not stem from fundamental changes in the causes thought to be the foundation of its inevitability and desirability. If anything, those causes are more present and relevant today than ever before. But the idea of revolution has withered and virtually died because its outcome has become either unwanted or unimaginable. Equally important, after the Nicaraguan elections of 1990, revolution has also become reversible.

The reversibility or defeat of previous, decisive, historical experiences for the left could be explained away by military treason (Chile in 1973, Brazil in 1964), American duplicity (Guatemala in 1954, Grenada in 1983), or errors and naïveté on the part of the left. But the Sandinista Liberation Front's loss in the 1990 elections was a rejection by the people themselves, albeit under duress or even blackmail. The Bush administration made it perfectly clear that only by unseating the Sandinistas could the Nicaraguan people achieve an end to the war. Whatever its roots, the electoral setback demonstrated that the revolutionary process was no longer exclusively reversible by force, but that it could be peacefully rolled back with the consent or even enthusiastic support of those for whom it had been ostensibly conceived. It is true that the dissolution of the notion of irreversibility affects mainly what Salvador Samayoa of the Salvadorean FMLN has called "revolutionary elites"—students, intellectuals, professional cadres:

> I believe that the people have different motivations for fighting than those acquired by a more sophisticated leadership. Politically, people have more rudimentary motivations: often they simply have no choice, like in the case of the peasantry, such an important component of the struggle in El Salvador, which joined the guerrillas because it couldn't be on the other side, because their families were simply murdered.

2. José Aricó, interview with the author, Buenos Aires, December 10, 1989.

They know since they were born that the Army is evil and that the guerrillas are against the Army. That's about it; the rank and file have a great deal of political vision, but as far as elaborating much more with regard to socialism or Marxism, this has never been its strong suit. That is more a problem for the elite.[3]

The poor peasants of Chalatenango are far less affected by the idea of a reversible historical process and by the collapse of the philosophical underpinnings of the idea of revolution than the former Jesuit student radicals of the Universidad Centroamericana. But time and communications inevitably make themselves felt, and the dismal prospect of fighting for partial, ephemeral gains trickles down to everyone.

Under these new conditions, revolutionaries can hardly survive. But without revolutionaries, the vision of revolution vanishes or is condemned to endure only under extreme circumstances like those of the Peruvian highlands. People do not die, go to prison, resist torture, or devote years of their lives to fighting for something that cannot be visualized or thought of in concrete terms, something that is not definitive. This hypothetical end of revolution does not imply an end to history, but what could be called the end of a certain idea of history, of the future. Revolution has become dystopian; but revolutionaries without utopia are inconceivable.

Since the nineteenth century and the beginning of socialist and subsequently Marxist thought, the idea of a qualitatively different— and implicitly better—future has been a constant of progressive, antiestablishment political movements. This future was to be a substantively distinct, ontologically superior state of being. The notion of progress was of course central to this strain of thought, but the progress it involved was never linear in nature. This view of the world meshed perfectly with the Catholic roots or origins of much of the Latin American left, and also dovetailed neatly with the particularly repugnant, unacceptable characteristics of the hemisphere's endless present. The worse the present looked, the more important the idea of a qualitatively better future became. Catholic influence, the Marxist notion of progress, and the intellectual's despair over an always dramatic status quo formed the stream of contemporary, left-wing thought: the future included redemption, revenge, and a final reckoning where good would triumph over evil, the poor over the rich, the autochthonous over the alien. The disappearance of the left's paradigm has left it, so to speak, without a future. For now, this vision of a better state of things to come is no longer credible and, consequently, no longer functional. The only

3. Salvador Samayoa, interview with the author, Mexico City, August 31, 1990.

thing left to fight for is a future that is simply the present, plus more of the same.

The left in Latin America hardly knew how to respond to the collapse of socialism in Europe. The traditional Communist parties initially reacted in a simplistic, formal way, insisting that the changes in the East were nothing more than additional proof of socialism's vitality and its capacity to renovate and transform itself. Once this argument became unsustainable, more complex reactions began to surface. Predictably, Fidel Castro adopted the most direct and critical stance, because his own revolution was to suffer far more severely the effects of change in Europe and the Soviet Union. In his first major speech dedicated to the transformations in the ex-socialist bloc, Castro distinguished two types of effects on Latin America and Cuba. The speech was notable because of its reflective tone and timing, December 7, 1989, only days after the destruction of the Berlin Wall and immediately before the U.S. invasion of Panama. Castro's first point was strictly economic: "From the crisis in the socialist camp, we can expect only negative consequences in economic matters for our country."[4] The Cuban leader then specified the particularly pernicious possibilities opened up by the broader, geopolitical consequences of the collapse of the socialist world:

> The acceptance of the principle of universal intervention by one great power is the end of independence and sovereignty in the world. . . . If events continue along their present course, if the United States is not forced to abandon these notions, the bipolar world we knew in the postwar era will inevitably be transformed into a unipolar world under American hegemony.[5]

Some Communist parties responded differently. Despite the persisting resort to tired rhetoric, their overall position was more nuanced. In a joint declaration made public in early 1990, the Communist parties of Costa Rica, Honduras, the Dominican Republic, El Salvador, and Argentina, while acknowledging that "perestroika emerged as a necessity for facing the crisis of socialism and renovating it," also criticized the turn of events in the Soviet Union. Most important, these five Communist parties recognized the effect of events in Europe with unusual frankness:

> These problems have had a contradictory effect on the revolutionary and progressive forces in Latin America: in some cases they have

---

4. Fidel Castro, *"Discurso ante los restos de los caídos en Angola,"* December 7, 1989, published in *Proceso* (Mexico City) 684, December 11, 1989, p. 39.

5. Ibid., p. 40.

brought demoralization and stimulated conceptions far removed from our needs and transplanted from European processes; in other sectors, they have served to reaffirm socialist, revolutionary, and antiimperialist convictions, together with a clear determination of creative independence.[6]

Other Communist parties or leaders initially adopted a much more "pro-perestroika" or "pro-Gorbachev" stance. The best example was perhaps the Brazilian party, one of whose current leaders, Roberto Freire, has gone so far as to say that "the fall of the Eastern Bloc is one of the best things to happen to socialism in many years."[7]

Luis Carlos Prestes, the legendary founder of the Brazilian Communist Party, was also highly optimistic about Gorbachev, despite having been expelled from the party for being too Stalinist. Its leaders speculated that Prestes was pro-Gorbachev not so much out of sympathy with perestroika and glasnost, but, more simply, out of a primal devotion to the Soviet Union.[8] In one of the last interviews Prestes gave before his death, at the age of ninety-two, he seemed quite aware of events in the Soviet Union, hardly regretting the fall of socialism.[9]

For all of these political movements and ideological currents in Latin America, the collapse of socialism meant the loss of a paradigm. It signified the erasure of the reference point with which the left had lived for more than half a century. Even China seemed implicitly to be making a drastic rejection of the past, a shattering disavowal of socialism as it had always existed. Cuba, finally, because of its own crisis and acute isolation, was rapidly becoming obsolete and/or irrelevant.

Whatever criticisms—and they were often deeply substantive and sincere—many parties or individuals of the hemispheric left had made of "truly existing socialism" over the past thirty years, they were almost always kept within the fold. Cuba itself became part of the paradigm, even though originally its revolution represented a break with the type of socialism constructed in the Soviet Union and Eastern Europe. Each Latin American party, movement, government, or progressive intellectual supplemented, deleted, or modified those aspects of Soviet and, later, Cuban reality that required changes. Yet the underlying reference to the Soviet Union, and then Cuba, was always present. The blueprint just had to be adjusted to local peculiarities, once the features that any given sector of the left deemed unacceptable

---

6. Ibid.
7. Interview with the author, Recife, Brazil, August 14, 1990.
8. Ibid.
9. Interview with the author, Rio de Janeiro, December 22, 1989.

had been factored out. Thus the self-destruction of the basic model signified the disappearance of the left's framework for conceiving of an alternative to Latin America's current state of affairs. Even the Cuban Revolution's impressive achievements in education, health, and the eradication of absolute poverty came to be perceived as nonviable: too costly, too statist, too dependent on foreign subsidies to be sustainable or applicable elsewhere.

The effects of the passing of the paradigm extended beyond those sectors of the left directly identified with the socialist experience. They helped discredit a central concept that was equally dear to every segment of the Latin American left: the role of the state in economic and social policy. If the Soviet Union, Europe, and Cuba were a failure, then it followed for many that the policies applied there, especially in economic matters, were clearly responsible for that failure. Among those policies, a major role for the state in the economy was especially relevant to Latin America. Protected, import-substitution industrialization, a large state-owned sector of the economy, across-the-board subsidies, and the pretense of a social safety net were all salient features of postwar economic development. Because of its own contradictions, but also by association, this model of development was seen as particularly deleterious. And, logically, the abandonment of centrally planned economies in Europe and the Soviet Union came to be viewed as an additional reason for reducing the role of the state in the Latin American economy.

The moderate left had already abdicated many of its convictions in favor of the conservative economic policies implemented in various Latin American nations since the mid-1980s. The debt crisis and its endless renegotiations, together with the stepped-up conditionality that each new agreement brought had dramatically weakened the so-called welfare state. Ronald Reagan's "conservative revolution" possibly achieved a greater following outside the United States than domestically. Free-market policies, wide-open trade and investment approaches, and total reliance on the private sector came to be seen as a foolproof recipe for economic success in Latin America. This belief was buttressed by the perception that these policies had worked in countries like the United States and Britain, and that they were also responsible for the Asian success stories.

Therefore, the shift from state-sponsored, protected, inward-looking, and subsidized economic development to the "free-market" model was already under way in Latin America before the collapse of socialism. However, the collapse accelerated it and enhanced the attractiveness of the alternative, which owed its popularity much more to a worldwide trend and the exhaustion of previous approaches than to a careful analysis of whether the policies involved would actually work in Latin America.

The fact that in countries like Brazil and Mexico, for example, the previously existing state-led model of development was not put in practice by the left, but rather by the military, in one case, and by the one-party PRI establishment, in the other, was simply ignored. Nor was it noted that the "Asian tigers" and Japan had not followed radical "free-market" policies at all, and that the success of Ronald Reagan's and Margaret Thatcher's model was both relative and arguable. The cost and consequences of the Reagan administration's policies became apparent by 1990, and the extent of privatization in Great Britain and the true dismantling of the British welfare state turned out to be less significant than originally thought.[10] The cutback in state intervention was far more ideological and forward-looking than economic and retrospective. Nonetheless, its reality became common wisdom.

Moreover, the so-called "statist, populist, closed-economy" policies of Latin America were unjustifiably identified with the socialist, command economies of the East. In fact, even the most "state-led" Latin American economies were characterized by market pricing mechanisms, large private sectors and important areas dominated, sometimes overwhelmingly, by foreign investment. The only fully socialist economy in the hemisphere was Cuba. In many cases the state-owned sector of the Latin economies was bloated, but nowhere was it like the dominant behemoth of the centrally planned economies of Europe. The distinction between a command economy, centrally planned and almost totally state-owned, and a regulated, protected social market economy was lost in the ideological fervor of the early 1990s.

The left in Latin America became identified with the failed, discarded economic policies of the socialist world, while the right came to

---

10. The following table illustrates the true evolution of government spending in the industrialized nations during the period in question:

GOVERNMENT SPENDING AS PERCENTAGE OF GDP

	U.S.	UK	FRANCE	GERMANY	CANADA	ITALY	JAPAN
Ave. 1961 – 1973	29.5	31.1	33.4	32.3	28.8	29.4	14.1
Ave. 1974 – 1980	32.6	38.6	39.8	42.3	36.1	34.9	22.1
Ave. 1981 – 1990	34.9	40.1	47.3	43.5	42.7	45.4	26.4

If anything, the 1980s were an argument for a "conservative revolution" still to come, not palpable proof of its having occurred. The statistics are all taken from Institute Français des Relations Internationales, *Ramses 92: Rapport Annuel Mondial sur le Système Economique et les Stratégies* (Paris: Dunod, 1991), pp. 401–407.

stand for the changes under way in the formerly socialist nations. The left found itself in a no-win situation. Either it stuck to its guns—which were not really its own, but were foisted on it—and defended the undefendable: a state-run, closed, subsidized economy in a world in which such a notion seemed totally obsolete; or it turned around and supported the opposite, apparently modern, competitive, free-market course. In that case, it ended up imitating—or being assimilated by—the right and losing its raison d'être.

The moderate left had in this way been forced, as Régis Debray said of European socialism, to succeed only when it put in practice the policies of its adversaries, and was condemned to failure when it applied its own program.[11] The entire process contributed to the impression that the left was devoid of any theoretical or policy alternative at all. The dismembering of the socialist bloc represented the ultimate confirmation of this sentiment, which in turn reflected an undisputable reality. As political competition in the world seemed to hinge increasingly on economic policy, and the latter's viability depended essentially on foreign financing, the left in Latin America was unable to come up with a marketable, coherent, and adequately funded alternative to the "free-market" consensus.[12]

Not that the free-market alternative was even theoretically applicable to every country at the same time. Almost by definition, it required abundant resources from abroad—like the preceding model—which under no conceivable scenario were available to all Latin American economies simultaneously. Moreover, as the years went by, it became readily apparent that even those countries most likely to receive foreign funding were only doing so in magnitudes and at the pace they expected because of exceptional, "one-time-only" situations. But the consensus regarding the need and desirability of "free-market" policies owed nothing to actual success; it was an entirely ideological

---

11. "The Left has lost its sense of mission. Ever since it learned that a political platform cannot in itself alter exchange rates or the rate of inflation, the Left has become reluctant to raise expectations or to speak of social projects, fearing that it may be branded an irresponsible dreamer by its adversaries. Socialists in Europe have had shining successes, but I'm not certain what they had to do with 'socialism.' It is as if socialism can serve all other ends except its own." Régis Debray, "Identity Crisis for the Socialist Left," San Francisco *Chronicle*, March 7, 1990. Others, like Ralf Dahrendof, simply state the obvious: "The domesticated left . . . is barely distinguishable from the right." (El País, Madrid, quoted in *Courrier International*, Paris, April 23, 1992.) And others still, such as *The Economist*, suggested that the left was taking up ideas "that have a Thatcherite ring to them, or resemble an editorial from The Economist." Ibid.

12. In regard to this consensus—the so-called Washington consensus—see Note 19, Chapter 10.

phenomenon, backed up by the failure of the past—in Latin America as well as in Eastern Europe and the Soviet Union.

The left's only imaginable, immediately formulable alternative course was particularly difficult—if not impossible—to sell politically. With time the left might come up with something else, and truly different. For the moment, its options were limited. Its response was inevitably made up of nuances, shades of pale colors, instead of catchy one-liners and attractive, easy solutions. At best, the left's alternative seemed to be nothing more—though nothing less—than an adjusted, middle-of-the-road economic policy. Different intrinsically from the free-market extremes, it would also distinguish itself by the context it was applied in, by the varying political and economic circumstances under which it was implemented.

This alternative involved more debt relief and less debt service—a difference of degree, although with qualitatively distinct effects. It included more social spending—education, health, housing, sewage, drinking water, etc.—and a far greater sense of social justice—but again, within limits imposed by the scarcity of resources. It advocated less privatization and more honest, accountable administration by a necessary state-owned sector of the economy—again, a significant nuance but a nuance nonetheless. It implied less trade opening and of a more selective nature, but certainly did not mean a return to full protectionism, which had never really existed in the first place. It signified a larger and more important role for the state in the economy, but of a different state—democratic, accountable, honest—and less dependence on the private sector, local or foreign. It required a new relationship with the business community, as removed from the baiting and hostility of the traditional left as it was from the pandering of the right. It also demanded a new understanding with the United States, distant from the tensions of the old left and the subordination of the new right.

But a platform of this type seemed condemned to failure because of the meagerness of disposable funds from abroad. It lacked the ideological sex appeal that was deemed indispensable for obtaining foreign funding. The left's program as described above was thus too radical and out of ideological touch to be funded, but too watered down in many cases to mobilize mass constituencies on its own and win elections or lead insurrections. It amounted to not much more than an updated, adjusted version of the traditional Latin American development model, but applied now in societies that were urban, largely literate, politically democratic, and embedded in a multipolar world and scarcity of foreign resources. In theory, this modernization might be sufficient to guarantee both election and success. In practice, given the ideological floodtide submerging Latin America in the late 1980s and early 1990s, it hardly was. Paradoxically the left, always known for its extremism and improvisation in Latin America, was for the moment proposing a moderate, long-term, unspectacular course that would improve the living standards of a majority of the population slowly and modestly, but surely. The right, traditionally prudent, had become the advocate of "revolution," albeit of a conservative nature, and of dramatic gestures and quick, radical solutions.

The guilt by association syndrome mentioned above affected more than just economic policy. In particular, events in Eastern Europe had a direct bearing on the perception that important sectors of the population in Latin America had of the left, and of its connection with Cuba, the Soviet Union, and Eastern Europe. In many sectors of Latin American societies the final failure of the East was also perceived as the definitive downfall of the left at home. In every Latin nation, even the most moderate left-of-center was identified with the bankrupt socialist regimes, while even the most repressive right-wing group associated itself with the struggle for the democratization of Eastern Europe.

The relation between the left and the despotic Eastern and Soviet blocs was never as direct as the right and the United States had made it out to be, but it nevertheless did exist. The incidents of complicity by the left with antidemocratic practices or human rights violations were real, though few and far between: Cuba after the early honeymoon, and Nicaragua sporadically and arguably. Regardless of suspicions concerning what the left would do to democracy throughout the region if it ever reached power, or whatever could be deduced from its support of antidemocratic practices in other countries, the left consistently opposed authoritarian rule. The antidemocratic atrocities most often identified with Latin American politics were carried out by conservative authoritarian governments of the right, not of the left: the closing of parliaments, the disappearances and torture of dissidents, the shutting-down of newspapers, and the persecution of labor leaders, peasant organizers, and intellectuals took place in Brazil, Argentina, Mexico, Chile, Uruguay, and most of Central America. The reason was obvious: the right was in power, the left was not.

But the closeness of the left's ties with the Soviet Union and above all with Cuba—and later with Nicaragua and the FMLN guerrillas in El Salvador—made its democratic credentials suspect in the eyes of the right and the United States. And the lack of a clean break with the undemocratic practices actually taking place in Cuba and Nicaragua made the originally tenuous link much stronger in the eyes of many.

This in turn facilitated the identification of the Latin American left with the collapsing regimes in Europe: the road to Prague, Bucharest, and Moscow ran through Havana and Managua. It also cleared the way for the accusation of irrelevancy: the Latin left had become obsolete now that democracy and free-market economics had won the Cold War. Intellectuals, parties, or governments of the left were on the losing side; their adversaries, on the winning one.

The left received an additional blow resulting from the end of the Cold War. It was perhaps of a more intangible nature, but with greater immediate consequences: the elimination of a counterweight in international affairs that had proved useful in the past to many nations, particularly those governed by center-left regimes. It was much more difficult to be truly nonaligned in a one-superpower world. Granted, few of the continent's governments had ever truly dared to play one superpower off against another, as regimes in different latitudes had often done. The Indian, Chinese, Egyptian, or even French tactic of flirting with one superpower in order to win the graces of the other was never entirely credible in Latin America and was executed only in exceptional or extreme cases, and even more rarely by left-wing regimes. The purchase of Soviet MIGs in the 1970s by the Peruvian military was one instance of this diplomatic gamesmanship.[13] Another was the long-standing economic relationship between Argentina and the Soviet Union, dating back to 1953 and Juan Domingo Perón's overtures, which antedated the sale of Argentine grain to the Soviet Union during the 1980 U.S.-imposed embargo.[14]

But the broader idea of a functioning deterrent to U.S. ambitions and free rein was ever present in the minds of many members of the left and, indeed, in those of Latin American statesmen of all persuasions. It seemed self-evident that the existence of another superpower, militarily and perhaps even politically the equal of the United States, acted as a brake on U.S. policy. The United States could not do anything it wanted in Latin America, despite the tacit Soviet acceptance of a U.S. sphere of influence. The rule of worldwide symmetries, precedents, implicit understandings and reactions to every action was in

---

13. "During the 1970s the Soviet Union achieved a broader and closer relationship with Peru than with any other Latin American country except Cuba." Ruben Berríos, "The USSR and the Andean Countries," in Eusebio Mujal-León, ed., *The USSR and Latin America* (London: Unwin Hyman, 1989), p. 352.

14. "The Soviet Union became Argentina's most important commercial partner, absorbing 80 percent of its grain exports and 33 percent of its total exports in 1981." Aldo C. Vacs, "Pragmatism and Rapprochement: Soviet Relations with Argentina and Brazil," in ibid., p. 326.

play. Whatever the United States did in the hemisphere could produce similar Soviet behavior in its own "backyard." Ronald Reagan's policies in Central America showed this view of superpower rivalry to be naïve. But U.S. actions in Panama at the end of the 1980s demonstrated that the end of the Cold War had changed matters. There was no longer any reason for the United States to fear reprisals elsewhere for breaking the rules in Latin America.

It was no small paradox that the most recent instance of U.S. intervention in Latin America coincided almost to the day with the disappearance of the last vestiges of the Soviet bloc. The invasion of Panama was, on the surface of things, a repeat performance of previous instances of U.S. interference. In fact, appearances notwithstanding, the 1989 intervention contrasted sharply with former examples of U.S. involvement. Panama was the first instance of overt, direct U.S. action in Latin America since the Second World War that did not possess a geopolitical, East-West cause or connotation.

The Panama invasion marked the end of the traditional anti-Soviet packaging, or ideological justification, for United States interference. It also signaled the resumption, on a different footing, of a long-standing debate on the nature, origins, and consequences of United States involvement in Latin American affairs. If the sole motivation for U.S. intervention had always been purely geopolitical—i.e., countering a Soviet threat—then the era of American intromission was clearly coming to an end. Conversely, if the hypothetical level of United States interference in the hemisphere's politics was a historical given, then the elimination of the Soviet "alibi" could not significantly alter matters. The United States continued to be a great power—indeed, the only remaining one. If intervention could be reasonably defined as the overwhelmingly asymmetrical exercise of U.S. power and influence in myriad fashions throughout the continent to defend and further its national interests, the epoch of interference was far from over. Invasions, covert operations, aid and boycotts, destabilization for the hostile and unwavering support for the cooperative, military action when necessary, political measures when sufficient, were all to remain fixtures of hemispheric relations.

The most moderate sectors of the political spectrum were more sensitive to the elimination of the counterweight than others. But the left was also affected: thanks to superpower rivalry, submission to the United States had not been an unshakable fact of Latin American life. Many on the left, but also some of the Sandinistas' fiercest critics, like Mexican poet Octavio Paz, were persuaded that the Nicaraguan revolutionaries' acceptance of elections, and subsequent electoral defeat, was directly linked to the termination of Soviet support.[15] This in turn was seen as a consequence of the Soviet Union's elimination as a superpower with worldwide interests and strategies. Cuba's dramatic difficulties and the isolation of the Salvadorean and Guatemalan insurgents reinforced this perception: a one-superpower world was not a friendly one for the Latin American left.

To the extent that the end of the Cold War had brought about the disappearance of a Soviet danger to the United States, and that the persistence of the latter for nearly half a century had determined the types of U.S. intervention, its reasons, and timing, nothing remained the same. Those instances of American involvement in Latin American affairs that stemmed from geopolitical considerations were relegated to the past; those that possessed different motivations—drugs, immigration—were now cast in a different light. The coincidence in time of the Cold War's conclusion and the advent of more-rigid international economic constraints made certain types of U.S. intervention in Latin America redundant. By eliminating the reality and perception of a Soviet threat to U.S. security in the hemisphere, the end of the Cold War redefined United States policy in Latin America.[16] For nearly half a century, anti-Sovietism was an indispensable ingredient of U.S. policy toward Latin America. Without it, the Bay of Pigs and the Alliance for Progress, U.S. support for the dictatorships in Brazil, Uruguay, Bolivia, Argentina, and Chile during the sixties and early seventies, as well as the successive multibillion-dollar Mexican debt rescues and the contra adventure in Nicaragua in the eighties, are incomprehensible.

•

With all this said, there is nevertheless a silver lining for the Latin American left in the vanishing socialist cloud. It first expresses itself

---

15. "Although the U.S.-backed contras contributed to the pressure on the Sandinistas to accept free elections, they were not the decisive factor. The transformation of the Sandinistas was primarily a consequence of the momentous changes in the Soviet Union and Eastern Europe." Octavio Paz, San Francisco *Chronicle*, March 7, 1990.

16. In a speech presented at the Mexican Foreign Ministry's Lincoln-Juárez Lectures on March 7, 1990, Henry Kissinger formulated this point in the following manner: "When I began to deal with the hemisphere and to establish contacts in the region, there was an important ideological element on both sides of the divide: in the United States a crusade against Communist penetration in the hemisphere, and in Latin America a fear of U.S. intervention. . . . Changes in the continent will have profound consequences, mainly on the United States, because as the perception of the Soviet threat in the hemisphere has virtually evaporated, fear as a unifying principle of hemispheric relations has also faded." Henry A. Kissinger, "Un mundo en transformación," *Revista Mexicana de Política Exterior* (Mexico City), no. 27, summer 1990.

through the elimination of three "handicaps" or burdens the left has suffered for over thirty years: the Soviet-Cuban, democratic, and anti-American handicaps. Second, the fact that the economic and social injustices which brought about the left's existence in Latin America are still present, if not worse than ever, implies a continued role for the left in the future.

The left no longer has to demonstrate that it is not pro-Soviet. Nor does it have to prove that its accession to power in any country would not turn the unfortunate nation in question into a Soviet satellite. In addition, it no longer must demonstrate that it is not a mortal enemy of the United States, and that its rule would not entail ostracism and embargoes, with credits drying up and contras blooming in every field and jungle. A U.S. administration may not like a left-wing regime for whatever reasons; it will experience growing difficulty in mobilizing public opinion against it without the specter of a threat. Finally, the left has been freed from having to prove, a priori, that it will not transform every nation it rules into a tropical authoritarian wasteland: the Soviet model of one-party rule can no longer be waved as a bogeyman now that it has ceased to exist.

In a nutshell, the Latin American left has suddenly been offered the opportunity of shedding the Communist stigma. This is partly true for the region's few remaining Communist parties, as well as in those cases where the left was essentially non-Communist. But it is above all valid for the socialist, or semisocialist left and center-left without close ties to Cuba, Marxism-Leninism, or armed struggle. This triple absolution is, in most cases, scarcely of the left's own doing. It is a direct effect of the end of the Cold War and the collapse of the Soviet Union as a superpower. In the words of a Guatemalan guerrilla: "The future is no longer dark, but simply complex. We are now in a better situation to fight fascist governments, as long as we clearly break with the left's militaristic and authoritarian tradition."[17]

The lifting of the "geopolitical" handicap for the Latin American left, however, simultaneously entails the emergence of a new challenge: showing it can live without the United States as its principal enemy. The end of the Cold War has deprived the left of what was often an excuse for not coming to power, or for failure when it did. The United States can no longer justifiably antagonize the left for geopolitical reasons; but if it ceases to do so, then the left cannot continue to blame the U.S. for its weakness or mistakes. The situation that rapidly emerged from the Salvadorean Peace Agreements of January

---

17. Mario Payeras, interview with the author, Mexico City, February 15, 1990.

1992 bore eloquent witness to this quid pro quo: the sort of honey-moon lived by the FMLN insurgents and the Bush administration forced each side to reassess its view of the other. The United States was obliged to stop anathemizing the guerrillas as Soviet surrogates, and the former rebels could no longer use Washington as a whipping boy. They needed American aid and protection. Only time would tell whether these changes were deep-rooted and lasting, or ephemeral.

Likewise, time alone will also indicate whether the lifting of the left's handicaps will eventually lead it to power, or, in any event, enhance its capacity to influence the course of history and policy in Latin America. For the moment, however, notwithstanding the diffi-culties it encounters in what Marxists have traditionally referred to as "subjective" conditions, the "objective" ones seem particularly propi-tious for the left, perhaps more so than at any other time in recent memory. It is important, then, to qualify the conceptual, emotional amputation suffered by the left. And Paco Ignacio Taibo II, Mexico's most distinguished and successful detective novelist and, together with Carlos Monsiváis, the Mexican writer most in touch with the country's urban youth, has done so as follows:

> The fact that the revolution is impossible does not make it morally less necessary, nor the reasons for revolt less urgent, even without an al-ternative. The PRI [in Mexico] are still scum, and the country they propose is still a mixture of economic misery for many, social misery for the majority, and moral misery for all.[18]

The rationale for revolution, from seventeenth-century England to Romania at the close of the second millennium, has always lain as much in the moral indignation aroused by an unacceptable status quo as in the attraction exercised by an existing blueprint for the future. The most powerful argument in the hands of the left in Latin Amer-ica—or anywhere else—has never been, and in all likelihood will never be, exclusively the intrinsic merit or viability of the alternative it proposes. Its strong suit is the morally unacceptable character of life as the overwhelming majority of the region's inhabitants live it. If the Latin American left were to forsake its sense of outrage and surrender the moral high ground to the cold, viable imperatives of realpolitik, it might win kudos in scholarly journals and the international media, but lose votes and sympathies.

The region's poor, like the poor everywhere, are not spontaneously revolutionary or consciously aware of their tragic fate. Immigrant mo-

---

18. Paco Ignacio Taibo II, interview with the author, New York, October 10, 1990.

bility, the rural exodus, religion, violence, the myriad shapes and forms of ideological acceptance of the status quo, ensure that revolts are few and far between. But this opaque relationship to reality works both ways: the decision to accept life as it is cannot be more rational than the choice to rebel against a situation that suddenly appears as unbearable, whereas in fact it is only marginally worse than before. To the extent that the inevitability of the present is central in the acceptance of it, events in Europe and the left's predicament in devising a new utopia for the end of the twentieth century constitute a serious obstacle to attaining mass support and accession to power. But insofar as the moral offense in the face of massive poverty, injustice, squalor, and oppression are the factors that move men to revolt, the disappearance of the socialist world is a secondary factor in determining the fortunes of the left. It would become decisive only if it were to abandon its moral vocation and role as a voice for the dispossessed, transforming itself into a well-behaved and realistic option, distinct only through tradition and style.

This is why it is important to unveil the hidden meaning of the historical transformation Latin America has undergone since 1982. During the 1980s and through the beginning of the 1990s, it suffered its worst economic and social crisis since the Depression. As a result, and as a consequence of multiple world trends, the conservative wave that swamped the region produced Latin America's own brand of so-called neoliberalism: Reaganomics in the tropics, as Muhammad Ali would have phrased it. At the same time, despite serious shortcomings, the hemisphere enjoyed its most widespread, substantive, and lasting process of democratization in the century. The conjunction of these developments enhanced the relevance of social change and political alternation more than at any other time since the 1930s.

In aggregate terms, the region's per capita gross domestic product dropped 8.1 percent between 1981 and 1991.[19] It fell in every single Latin American country except Colombia, Chile, Cuba, Belize, and Barbados, and even these cases were arguable: Colombia due to "unreported transactions," Chile because of statistical contrast with the economic disaster of the previous decade, Cuba due to accounting discrepancies. In some countries the drop was astonishing: 28 percent

---

19. Comisión Económica para América Latina y el Caribe (CEPAL), *Balance preliminar de la economía de América Latina y el Caribe*, December 1991, Santiago, p. 40. It is worth noting that even these dramatic figures make the situation look somewhat brighter, as they include one very good year—1981—and two so-so years—1990 and 1991—particularly for Mexico, Venezuela, and Argentina. If the series were to start in 1982 and stop in 1989, the drop would be sharper.

in Peru, 20 percent in Argentina, 17 percent in Venezuela; in others it was simply tragic: 6.5 percent in Brazil, 5.4 percent in Mexico.[20]

The social implications of this economic catastrophe were equally traumatic. While the argument can be made that there is often a "disjunction between economic and social indicators, with the latter doing far better [than the former] during temporary economic downturns,"[21] the length of the economic slowdown, along with its intensity and breadth, produced serious social involution. Employment declined sharply in relative—and often in absolute—terms, as even the open unemployment rate rose, and, more importantly, as significant shifts occured from full employment to underemployment, from the formal sector of the economy to the informal sector, and in a reduction in the working period for the underemployed. In 1980, 136 million Latin Americans, or 41 percent of the continent's population, lived in poverty; by 1986 the figure had grown to 170 million individuals, or 43 percent;[22] toward the end of the decade it was estimated at the horrifying figure of anywhere between 203 and 270 million.[23] Unemployment and underemployment had reached 80 million, representing 44 percent of the labor force.[24] The real minimum wage for the entire

---

20. Ibid., p. 40. Economic statistics in Latin America are often imprecise, and there may be minor discrepancies between these figures and those provided by other sources. By and large, though, the CEPAL–ECLA figures, the Interamerican Development Bank numbers, those put together by the World Bank, and statistics published by individual governments all coincide.

21. Albert O. Hirschman, "The Political Economy of Latin American Development: Seven Exercises in Retrospection," *Latin American Research Review*, vol. 22, no. 3, 1987, p. 12.

22. Comisión Económica para América Latina, "Nota sobre el desarrollo social en América Latina," presented at the First Summit Meeting of Iberoamerican Heads of State and Government, Guadalajara, Mexico, July 18–19, 1991, p. 5.

23. There is, of course, a great deal of debate about the best way to measure poverty. The figures for 1990 come from United Nations Development Program, Proyecto Regional para la superación de la pobreza, in Desarrollo sin probreza, Bogotá 1990, quoted in "Magnitud y evolución de la pobreza en América Latina" (Mexico City) *Comercio Exterior*, vol. 42, April 1992, p. 380. According to this study, in 1990 there were 270 million poor in Latin America, or 61.8 percent of the population. Other estimates show a range of 203 to 209 million. The World Bank estimated a lower figure of approximately 70 million in Latin America, defining poor as those below a poverty line of $370 per capita per year (in 1980 dollars). This line may be adequate for Africa and parts of Asia; it seems low for Latin America, since it implies that anyone making above $30 per month—$150 for a family of five—is not poor: a dubious proposition in most Latin American cities during most of the decade of the 1980s. World Bank, *World Development Report* (New York: Oxford University Press, 1991), p. 29.

24. Ibid. In Mexico, although the total population grew from 66 million in 1980 to about 78 million in 1988, total employment remained virtually stagnant for the same period, going from 20.3 million to 21.8 million. Banamex, *Mexico Social 1990–91* (Mexico City: 1991).

region fell 13 percent between 1980 and 1987, but this aggregate figure masks profound differences among countries. In Mexico, Brazil, and Chile, the drop was 43 percent. The decline in median real wages was almost as drastic: 23 percent in Mexico, in Uruguay nearly 30 percent, Peru 62 percent by 1991.[25]

Country by country, impoverishment was rampant. In Brazil, advances in the reduction of poverty during the previous twenty years were largely erased. Between 1960 and 1981 the number of poor in Brazil dropped from 36 million to 24 million, and, more strikingly, from 50 percent of the population to 19 percent. But by 1987 the figure for individuals living beneath the official—and overly optimistic—poverty line rose to 33 million, or 25 percent of the country's inhabitants.[26] In Mexico, even according to official figures renowned for their cosmetic treatment, the number of poor grew from 32.1 million and 45 percent of the population in 1981 to 41.3 million and 51 percent in 1987,[27] and nutrition levels plummeted.[28] In Venezuela, the percentage of the poor increased from 12 percent in 1982 to 16 percent in 1987, in Colombia from 6 to 7.5 million between 1978 and 1988.[29] The deterioration in the Buenos Aires metropolitan area during the 1980s was equally dramatic. In 1980 approximately one in five households was poor; by 1987, one in three was.[30] At the same time real spending on education, health, housing, and extreme poverty dropped sharply:

> In the last decade, spending on education as a share of total central government expenditure diminished in most of the countries. . . . In terms of gross domestic product, the education sector suffered cuts in most of the twenty-five countries.[31]

World Bank figures for the period between 1980 and 1985—not the worst of the crisis—show a decline in real per capita social expendi-

25. CEPAL, *Balance Preliminar*, op. cit., p. 44.

26. World Bank, op. cit., pp. 41, 43.

27. Consejo Consultivo del Programa Nacional de Solidaridad, "El combate a la pobreza," *El Nacional Ediciones* (Mexico City), 1990, p. 20.

28. Mexico's per capita consumption of rice, black beans, corn and wheat—the poor's basic staples—was halved between 1981 and 1988, and not because they all preferred to "eat cake," or anything else. The actual figures were: rice, from 7.3 kilos per capita in 1981 to 3; black beans, from 25.5 kilos to 14.2; corn, from 245 kilos to 142.4, wheat, from 60.5 to 49.3. Consejo Consultivo, op. cit., p. 38

29. World Bank, op. cit., p. 43

30. Alberto Minujin and Pablo Vinocur, "¿Quienes son los pobres del Gran Buenos Aires?" *Comercio Exterior*, op. cit., p. 397.

31. *Economic and Social Progress in Latin America*, 1989 Report (Washington, D.C.: Interamerican Development Bank [IDB], 1990), p. 60.

tures of 18 percent for the entire region.[32] It was no surprise then that exit polls from the 1989 Brazilian elections showed that approximately 70 percent of the voters had no more than an elementary education, and most had less.[33] Nor was it unexpected that as late as March of 1991—well into Mexico's presumed economic recovery—about 60 percent of the income-earning population received a maximum of two minimum wages per month, about $250, or less.[34] As far as the consequences of sharp reductions in health expenditures were concerned, the Pan American Health Organization summed them up neatly in mid-1991:

> The increasing deterioration of socioeconomic conditions in Latin America, as well as the decrease in social investment and basic infrastructure, has resulted in an increase in the marginalization of the population and in levels of poverty, which in turn have created conditions of high risk conducive to violent outbreaks of epidemics such as cholera, the magnitude of which has placed several countries in a state of emergency.[35]

This trend remained intact through the early nineties. Although the adjustment process came to an end in some nations (i.e., Mexico and Chile) public spending on education in real terms had not regained anywhere near its predebt crisis levels. The underdevelopment spiral was intact: as less was spent on education than elsewhere, the labor force was less educated and productive, the local economy was less competitive, making less money available for education. In the eighties the growth of real international interest rates, together with the deterioration in the hemisphere's terms of trade, imposed a negative resource transfer to the rest of the world, and a virtually identical domestic adjustment process for every country, regardless of political, social, or even economic policy distinctions. The only significant dif-

---

32. World Bank, op. cit., p. 116.

33. Instituto Brasileiro de Geografia e Estadistica (IBGE), quoted in José Nêumanne, *Atrás do Palanque* (São Paulo: Edições Siciliano, 1989), p. 14.

34. Banamex, op. cit., p. 190. The precise figures provided by the 1990 Census showed a total working population of 23,403,413; of this, 14,796,715, or 63.2 percent, received a maximum of or less than the equivalent of two minimum wages. Instituto Nacional de Estadística, Geografía e Informática (INEGI), *XI Censo General de Población y Vivienda, Perfil Sociodemográfico*, Mexico City, 1992, p. 63.

35. Pan American Health Organization/World Health Organization, *La salud como pilar fundamental del desarrollo social de Iberoamérica*, presented at the First Summit Meeting of Iberoamerican Heads of State and Government, Guadalajara, Mexico, July 18–19, 1991, p. 27. The cholera epidemic had affected 250,000 individuals by mid-1991, with 90 percent of them in Peru and the rest scattered through Ecuador, Colombia, Mexico, and parts of Central America.

ferences between nations lay in the time period over which the cost of adjustment was paid, and in the availability of foreign resources to stabilize a chronic nongrowth environment.

But perhaps the worst consequence of this drama was that it made terribly inequitable societies even more unjust. Income distribution throughout the hemisphere worsened. The ancestral injustice of Mexican society attained appalling proportions. When in 1992 the Mexican government published the first income distribution statistics in fifteen years, those numbers proved shocking. In 1984—already two full years into the crisis—the poorest 40 percent of the population received 14.4 percent of total income. By 1989 the same 40 percent got only 12.8 percent, but the richest 10 percent saw their share jump from 32.4 percent to 37.9 percent.[36]

The most damning reflection on the 1980s was perhaps what occurred in the showcase of structural reform: Chile. Although the methods used were acknowledged as repugnant, Chile emerged during the 1980s as a double paradigm: of what not to do—the Allende experience—and of the course sensible governments should follow—the Pinochet economic model. A quick examination of the Chilean experience is thus useful to underline how bad things have gotten for the following case to become a model.

It was true that with the exception of Colombia, the only nation in Latin America where per capita income grew during the 1980s was in the land of Augusto Pinochet's free-market experiment.[37] And certainly the country had followed most stabilization and adjustment policies to the letter: trade liberalization, privatization, reducing subsidies, welcoming foreign investment, letting the market pick winners and losers. But not until 1988, that is, after fifteen years of a totally unconstrained application of free-market policies, did Chilean per capita income reach its 1970 or even 1973 level.[38] And in constant 1977 pesos, per capita *consumption* was identical in 1973 and in 1989 and remained below that of the first two Allende years.[39] Setting aside the political price of a decade and a half of brutal dictatorship, the social

36. INEGI, *Encuesta Nacional de Ingresos y Gastos de los Hogares, 1989* (Mexico City: 1992), p. 39. It was unclear whether the situation improved later, but census figures showed that in 1990 only 7.6 percent of the entire income-earning population made more than $500 per month.

37. Comisión Económica para América Latina (CEPAL), *Balance Preliminar de la Economía de América Latina y el Caribe, 1991*, Santiago, p. 19.

38. Manuel Delano and Hugo Traslavina, *La Herencia de los Chicago Boys* (Santiago: Ediciones Ornitorrinco, 1989), p. 16

39. Barbara Stallings and Philip Brock, *The Political Economy of Economic Adjustment: Chile. 1973–1990*, Draft, Table 3, p. 67.

costs were also staggering. Between 1978 and 1988, the richest decile of the population increased its share of national income from 36.2 percent to 46.8 percent, whereas the lowest 50 percent saw its share drop from 20.4 percent to 16.8 percent.[40] Chile, formerly one of Latin America's very few quasi-middle-class societies, became a "classic" Latin American nation:

> Chile was a country with a typically "mesocratic" distribution of income [in which the greater share of income is bunched together in the middle sectors], like Argentina and Uruguay; the recent modernization, however, has brought it close to the "elitist" distribution [with larger shares of income concentrated at the top], characteristic of the Andean countries like Peru, Bolivia, Ecuador, and Colombia.[41]

Supporters of the Pinochet regime pointed to its apparent success in combatting extreme poverty: a government survey as early as 1982 indicated that only 14.2 percent of Chileans belonged to that category. By the late 1980s improvements in public services had made it possible to deliver clean drinking water to most homes, and sewage systems to three-quarters of them.[42] By 1988, unemployment fell below 10 percent for the first time since 1975.[43] But half the work force in the city of Santiago made less than $66 per month, and, as two distant but insightful observers concluded:

> By the end of the decade Pinochet's Chile had become a widely touted model of economic reforms for the rest of the continent. Viewed from Conchalí or La Pintana, however, the new Chile remained a dual society of winners and losers. . . . The income gap between rich and poor was wider than at any other time in half a century.[44]

---

40. Delano and Traslavina, op. cit., pp. 168–170. Chile has become "a country with only two social classes: one very rich and numerically small class, and a very poor and very large one: according to the National Statistics Institute, in December of 1988, 70 percent of the population had an income below the cost of the basic food basket, whereas the other 30 percent lived very comfortably." It is true that certain important social indicators, such as infant mortality, did decrease constantly throughout the Pinochet years; others, though, worsened shamefully. In 1973 each Chilean received an average of 71.3 grams of protein daily; by 1987 the amount had dropped to 57.7; in 1973 each inhabitant of the country received an average of 2,692 calories daily, in 1987 the figure was 2,227; at no time during Pinochet's rule did either statistic reach its 1973 level. Ibid., p. 202.
41. Eugenio Tironi, Los silencios de la revolución (Santiago: Editorial Puerta Abierta, 1988), p. 92.
42. Pamela Constable and Arturo Valenzuela, A Nation of Enemies: Chile under Pinochet (New York: Norton, 1991), p. 231.
43. Ibid., p. 245.
44. Ibid., p. 245.

Chile's imports were largely manufactured products; its vaunted "export drive" included—up to 90 percent—sales of copper, pure and processed; fruit, mainly table grapes;[45] wood; and fish.[46] While nothing to sneer at, these exports were all linked to Chile's natural comparative advantages: the type of economic development that had been tried before—until the Great Depression—and discarded in modern Latin America because it eventually ran into insurmountable problems.[47] Furthermore, the fruit export boom had its roots back in the late sixties and early seventies, in the land reform and state-sponsored agricultural promotion schemes of Eduardo Frei and Salvador Allende. Extension of fruit production to other temperate zones, falling copper prices, and protection for fishermen of the industrialized nations could drag the Chilean model into a trade deficit and a dead end.

But the deterioration of equality in the region's largest country was undoubtedly the worst. From 1981 to 1990, the top decile of the Brazilian population increased its proportion of total income from 46.6 percent to 53.2 percent; the poorest half of the population had its cut sliced from 13.4 percent to 10.4 percent.[48] In Argentina a similar trend took hold: in 1974 the 40 percent of the population with the lowest income obtained 16 percent of the total; by 1989 its share had fallen to 12 percent. Conversely, the highest two deciles saw their share rise from 39 percent in 1974 to 57.7 percent in 1989.[49] If countries like Mexico, Brazil, Peru, and Venezuela had among the most inequitable social structures in the world before the crisis, the magnitude of their injustice was staggering by the early 1990s. It was illustrated by the appalling increase of violence and tragedy, the extreme instance of which was child murder in Brazil and Guatemala. In Rio, urchins were

45. In the 1989–1990 export season, of 57,905 boxes of fruit exported from Chile to the United States, 73 percent were grapes, the rest, in small shares, nectarines, plums, peaches, pears, and apples. Sergio Gómez, "La uva chilena en el mercado de los Estados Unidos," paper presented at the Workshop on the Globalization of the Fresh Fruit and Vegetable System, University of California, Santa Cruz, December 1991, p. 8.

46. As the *New York Times* put it: "The United States has a widening trade surplus with Chile. In 1991 the U.S. sent Chile 1.84 billion dollars worth of aircraft, computers, cars and other mostly manufactured goods, while importing from Chile only 1.3 billion dollars worth of fruit, copper, fish and other raw materials." *New York Times*, May 2, 1991, p. 23.

47. Among these problems, wildly oscillating and falling prices of these exports after an initial period. For Chilean Flame grapes, prices ranged from an index of 100 in 1984–85 to 53 in 1986–87, to 85 again in 1990–91, all the while showing a tendency to drop over time. Gómez, op. cit., p. 17.

48. *Veja*, November 21, 1990, quoted in Margaret E. Keck, *The Workers' Party and Democratization in Brazil* (New Haven, Conn.: Yale University Press, 1992), p. 238.

49. FIDE (Fundación para el Desarrollo), Buenos Aires, April 1986, p. 26, and October 1991, p. 33.

being literally massacred; in Brazil over 1,000 children were slain every year between 1989 and 1991,[50] and the number was nearly doubling annually by 1992:[51]

Who kills them? Three out of ten killers are policemen or death squad members who pronounce them to be unrecoverable. . . . In the Rio slum of Baixada Fluminenese alone, there are more than 400 professional child-murderers.[52]

Half a century had elapsed since the continent had lived through such a sustained period of economic and social deprivation. Were it not for drug exports, emigration, and an income-reducing but shock-absorbing informal economy, the outcome could have been even more tragic than it was. Indeed, had it not been for the considerable, though often silenced, progress of the previous thirty-five years, the effects of the downturn of the eighties could have been more ghastly than they were.[53]

One reason for this dramatic economic regression was the hemisphere's massive decapitalization. In the 1980s, Latin America became a net capital-exporting region. Debt service payments for the entire continent's $415 billion foreign debt reached nearly $40 billion per year, or more than $400 billion for the decade.[54] The net negative transfer of resources—i.e., the difference between total capital inflows and outflows—also reached alarming proportions. But debt was not the entire story: as a result of shrinking domestic markets, lack of confidence, and worldwide trends, foreign investment also stagnated.

Capital flight further devastated the region's finances. By 1989, total Latin American capital abroad was estimated at $243 billion. Even countries previously unaffected by massive capital flight, such as Brazil, were suffering its consequences.[55] While some of the interest on

---

50. "Dead End Kids," *Newsweek International*, May 25, 1992, p. 13.
51. Gilberto Dimenstein, *Brésil: La Guerre des Enfants* (Paris: Fayard, 1991), pp. 25–26.
52. Ibid., p. 22.
53. Albert Hirschman's use of the term *les trente glorieuses* (coined by Jean Fourastié to describe the thirty years following World War II in Europe) for the period stretching from 1945 to 1980 regarding Latin America's huge strides in standard of living and incomes, health and education, productivity, urbanization, and the rise of a middle class is partially warranted: "It should have come as a major revelation to most regular readers of current reports about Latin America that that continent may have had its *trente glorieuses*—and perhaps a few more." Hirschman, op. cit., p. 8.
54. CEPAL, op. cit., p. 25.
55. "*América Economía*," Capitales Fugados, September 1989, p. 11. The numbers are all taken from the *Journal of Commerce*. There is obviously a great deal of debate in Latin America regarding the exact figures for capital flight from the region, and all

assets held abroad began to return after 1990, particularly in Mexico, Argentina, and Venezuela, the damage was done. In addition, there was no guarantee that new speculative waves would not shake the hemisphere's finances once again.

Largely because the development policies of the past stopped working—owing to politically originated mismanagement, their own intrinsic weaknesses and the combination of high real interest rates and low commodity prices—and partly because of the ideological drift in the world toward conservative, free-market attitudes, this economic and social crisis led to the adoption of a sharply different economic policy mixture from the late 1980s onward. Trade liberalization, enticing foreign investment, privatization, "leave-it-to-the-market," and the "end of the state" became the rage in Latin America, as they had been in the United States during the Reagan era, and in Britain under Thatcher. While the objective of these policies' implementation was ostensibly an end to the economic stagnation of the eighties and the ensuing social regression, neither goal was easily attained. Rollercoaster patterns of economic growth appeared. The difficulty of building up sustained growth, even under almost ideal circumstances, was patent. But above all, free-market radicalism, whatever its other merits and long-run fruits, was sure to aggravate income inequality and lower standards of living of much of the population in the short and medium term.[56]

The numbers were not readily available; in most cases, the policies began to bite only in the early 1990s, and their social effects did not mature overnight. But judging by the Chilean experience and the consequences of analogous programs in the United States and Britain, it seemed safe to expect a growing gap between rich and poor. The debate in the United States during the 1992 election campaign brought to the fore some of the consequences of the Reagan-Bush policies on the specific issue of inequality. In particular, a Congressional Budget Office report issued in early 1992 showed that the top 1 percent of American families saw its share of total income rise from 7 percent to 12 percent, whereas the lowest 20 percent saw their share drop from 6

numbers in this regard should be seen as ballpark figures, not precise statistics.

56. Indeed, the question of whether the new policies were generating long-term growth is the paramount issue: "If the ostensible purpose of market oriented reforms is to increase material welfare, then these reforms must be evaluated by their success in generating economic growth. Anything short of this is just a restatement of the neoliberal hypothesis, not its test." Luis Carlos Bresser Pereira, José Mará Maravall, Adam Przeworski, "Economic Reforms in New Democracies: A Social-Democratic Approach," paper presented at the Conference on Democracy, Markets and Structural Reforms in Latin America, Buenos Aires, March 25–27, 1992, p. 5.

percent to 4 percent, and the lowest 40 percent drop from 18 percent to 14 percent, all between 1977 and 1989. Most dramatically, the 1 percent of American families with the highest incomes concentrated 70 percent of the average gains in income.[57] While different calculations produced varying results, the basic thrust of these data was the same.[58]

The comparison was especially depressing, since the aggravation of social disparities and tensions in the United States during the eighties occurred in a largely middle-class nation with an extensive safety net and often unmovable entitlements. The situation was quite different in Latin America: the middle classes rarely represented more than 30 percent of the population; when it existed, the safety net was full of holes. Constituencies for entitlements were weak and fragmented. The logical reaction against programs such as these—coming in the wake of ten years of economic and social involution and to a large extent independently of what was put forth in their place—constituted a huge reservoir of hypothetical support for the left everywhere in Latin America. Whether it translated into votes and backing for a coherent alternative platform was a different matter.

Why didn't this tragedy lead to a hemispheric explosion of incalculable social and political consequences? The striking process of democratization that most of the continent experienced during the "lost decade" figured prominently among the many reasons. For the worst economic contraction in recent Latin American history coincided with the broadest and most meaningful process of democratization in half a century. (Exceptions or actual regression, of course, persisted in some nations in Central America where elections were barely short of meaningless; in Cuba and Haiti, for very different reasons; in Mexico, where one-party rule, modernized to some degree, endured; and in countries like Peru, where ominous steps backward were taken.) Moreover, this broad movement often went well beyond the simple celebration of elections. It included a newfound respect for human rights in the former dictatorships (Argentina, Chile, Uruguay, Paraguay) and an

---

57. Sylvia Nasar, "However You Slice the Data, The Richest Did Get Richer," *New York Times*, May 11, 1992, p. C1. The economist generally credited for having highlighted this aspect of the Congressional Budget Office figures is Paul Krugman of MIT.

58. By assets instead of income, the trend was the same. According to the Federal Reserve, in 1983 the richest 1 percent of American families concentrated 31 percent of total net worth; by 1989 their share rose to 37 percent. The lowest 90 percent saw their part diminish slightly, from 33 percent to 32 percent, with the outrageous result that the richest 1 percent of American families had more wealth than the bottom 90 percent. *New York Times*, April 21, 1992, p. 1. The percentage of full-time workers earning less than $12,000 per year climbed from 12 percent to 18 percent. *New York Times*, May 12, 1992.

opening up of the press, unions, and civil society in Brazil and other nations. There were of course constraints: more often than not, political democratization and a return to civilian rule were achieved at the expense of maintaining the social and economic status quo, and the democratization process itself was frequently restricted to the trappings of elections. By and large, though, Latin America was a far more democratic part of the world toward the end of the 1980s than at any other time in recent memory, and the legitimacy extended to many regimes under terribly adverse circumstances could be largely attributed to this fact. But it also meant that discontent, debt and austerity fatigue, and demands for a "different course" could all be expressed at the polls in support for the left, rather than only in the streets, the mountains, and the universities.

If historical precedent means anything, this situation, rendered more acute by the persisting neoliberal shock, should benefit the Latin American left. True, it has not always been successful in its efforts to improve living conditions for a majority of the people on the scarce occasions when it has had a chance to do so. Nonetheless, Latin America has tended to turn to the left in times of prolonged economic and social crisis presided over by regimes of the center or the right. At least, that was the case in the 1930s and 1940s, with the emergence of the populist governments of Cárdenas in Mexico, Vargas in Brazil, Perón in Argentina, and the Popular Front in Chile in the midst or aftermath of the Great Depression. The current antiincumbency bias sweeping Latin America points in the same direction.

Needless to say, there is no automatic, mechanical link between impoverishment and rebellion, between economic and social deprivation and radical politics. The revolutions that have actually taken place in Latin America during the course of this century responded to multiple factors that could not be simply reduced to immiseration. But a significant, long-lasting downturn in economic conditions, coincident with a broad process of democratization, has given birth before, and could well give birth again, to "center-left" or "populist" regimes. Whether these regimes would be of a military, Nasserite type—as suggested by the aborted military coups in Venezuela in 1992—fundamentalist—as demonstrated by Sendero Luminoso in Peru and the Bolivarian lieutenants in Venezuela—or democratically elected, renovated left-of-center regimes was a central choice facing Latin America at the end of the twentieth century.

True, there have been occasions in the past when democratization and economic regression have not brought the left to power; today, there are countries in Latin America where the same causes have not produced the same effects. Initially, appearances indicated that the opposite was occurring—i.e., the election or accession to power of regimes espousing conservative policies in Mexico, Brazil, Peru, and the defeat of clearly identified left-wing forces in Nicaragua. In other elections across the hemisphere, it often seemed that the more leftward-leaning contenders were in fact the winners, although they then proceeded to implement their conservative rivals' platforms, as in Argentina, Peru, and Venezuela.

But for the first time since World War II and the beginning of the Cold War, the left faced the possibility of contending for power on a level playing field, freed from the handicaps that have infinitely weakened it over the past half century. In a continent where nearly three quarters of the population are poor and have gotten poorer during the elapsed decade, the left can finally compete on its own terms, and with its own platform: democracy, sovereignty, economic growth and social justice all at the service of improving the lot of millions excluded from the benefits of previous booms and current experiments. The left may win and receive a chance to prove its worth in office. Or it may be exposed as irretrievably incompetent and obsolete. But at least it will be judged on its own merits, and not through the distorted anti-Communist, anti-Soviet shadows projected from afar. The end of the Cold War could thus achieve what nothing and no one else has: the "Latin Americanization" of the left and its definitive rooting in the hemisphere's still barren native land.

9

Nation-building and the Origins of the Left's Nationalism

■

No one is likely to build a monument honoring Enrique Haroldo Gorriarán Merlo. But he himself is a monument, a vivid example of the meanders, riddles, and mysteries that came to characterize a key portion of the left and its paradoxes. He was the ultimate internationalist, but with an essentially nationalist motivation.

Gorriarán was born in San Nicolás, a small town of the province of Buenos Aires in 1942. He studied economics at the University of Rosario and joined the semi-Trotskyist, semi-Castroist Partido Revolucionario de los Trabajadores (PRT) in the late 1960s at the age of twenty six.[1] Arrested in 1970, he participated in the legendary escape from Rawson penitentiary in August of 1972, together with the leader and founder of the PRT, Mario Roberto Santucho, and several Montonero leaders. He first fled to Chile, then to Cuba, and from there launched a long career as a truly internationalist revolutionary. His links with the Cubans date back to the early 1970s, but predictably—for a Trotskyist with Catholic roots—he never got along well with them.[2]

---

1. According to a biographer of his leader in the PRT, Mario Roberto Santucho, Gorriarán came from a typical Radical Party, upper-middle-class provincial family from the provinces. María Seoane, *Todo o nada: La Historia secreta y la historia pública del jefe guerrillero Mario Roberto Santucho* (Buenos Aires: Planeta-Espejo de la Argentina, 1992), p.105.
2. The PRT itself recognized its differences with "official communism," and on occasion flaunted them. "The leadership always tried to guarantee the democratic functioning of the party's organs. We recognized the positive influence of Trotskyism in this regard. These concerns came largely from our criticism of the Soviet bureaucracy and of Stalinist totalitarianism." Julio Santucho, *Los ultimos guevaristas: Surgimiento y*

During the first half of the seventies, he played a leading and brutal role in the PRT's war against the Argentine military.[3] Most of the leadership of the PRT's armed wing, the Ejército Revolucionario del Pueblo (ERP), died in a firefight with the Argentine Army in July of 1976 at Villa Martelli, on the outskirts of Buenos Aires. But Gorriarán emerged unscathed. He was already leading the charmed life of one of the region's most resourceful, resilient members of the armed revolutionary left.[4] And in 1979, having resigned himself—without acquiescing—to the PRT's dissolution, he traveled to Nicaragua and joined the Sandinista National Liberation Front.[5]

After Somoza's fall and his subsequent flight to Paraguay, "El pelado" Gorriarán continued his international revolutionary activities. In 1980 he planned and organized "Operación Reptíl," the commando raid in the capital of Paraguay that blew away Somoza and his Mercedes Benz with a single bazooka shell. Although he personally did not participate in the execution, the entire operation was set up and carried out by guerrillas under Gorriarán's command. Instead, he remained in Nicaragua for most of this period, working with Tomás Borge at the Ministry of the Interior. Gorriarán was directly involved in the conception, training, and deployment of the Sandinista Army's "Batallones de lucha irregular" or "BLIs," the relatively effective, irregular counterinsurgency troops that eventually neutralized the contras. At the same time he developed his contacts with the Salvadoreans and Guatemalans.

---

eclipse del Ejército revolucionario del pueblo (Buenos Aires: Ediciones Puntosur, 1988), p. 221. The author is the late Mario Roberto Santucho's brother. Gorriarán's relations were not tense with all Cubans. For years he was close to Antonio de la Guardia, the Ministry of the Interior official executed in 1989 on charges of drug trafficking. De la Guardia was apparently godfather to one of Gorriarán's daughters.

3. His reputation for brutality and cold-bloodedness stems from this period. He was temporarily suspended from the leadership in 1975 for "abuse of power. Gorriarán Merlo had killed a presumed spy in the organization without complying with the strict norms that the guerrilla fighters themselves had drawn up for such a decision." Seoane, op. cit., pp. 258–259.

4. The data concerning Gorriarán's life and exploits come from a number of sources. One is his own book of quasi-memoirs, published in the form of interviews with an Uruguayan journalist. Unfortunately most of Gorriarán's extra-Argentinian activities are barely touched upon. Other sources are interviews with Central American revolutionaries who knew him well but cannot be named, and finally, articles published in the aftermath of the Tablada barracks attack.

5. Gorriarán claimed that his involvement in Nicaragua was directly inspired by his two illustrious Argentine predecessors: "I am part of a generation that was influenced by the thinking of the hero of our nation, General José de San Martín, who was guided by a Latin Americanist conception that viewed our continent as a whole. Our generation was also influenced by the example of Che Guevara, who put in practice those Latin American ideals." Samuel Blixen, *Conversaciones con Gorriarán Merlo: Treinta años de lucha popular* (Buenos Aires: Editorial Contrapunto, 1988), p. 250.

Gorriarán's relationships were based partially on money—the Argentine ERP donated a significant sum to the Chilean MIR in the seventies[6] and approximately $110,000 to the FMLN in 1980—but mainly on his military and commando-organizing expertise.[7] He is said to have planned and organized two of the FMLN's most spectacular and successful commando operations during the early 1980s: the blowing up of El Salvador's principal bridge, and the destruction of nearly 70 percent of the Salvadorean Air Force in April of 1981.

In 1983, Gorriarán was indicted in Argentina for homicide, illegal association, public instigation to commit crimes, and attempts against public order, together with other Argentine revolutionaries, essentially the same crowd dating back to the early seventies and the Rawson prison escape. As the Argentine democratization process moved forward, time began to run out for all of the guerrillas of the seventies. They were either arrested, gave themselves up hoping for amnesty and a new life, or were led to more and more extreme acts. Gorriarán organized the most extreme act of all: the assault on the La Tablada military garrison, on January 23, 1989.[8]

The Tablada barracks, housing the Third Infantry Regiment of the Argentine Army, were attacked by a group of young and inexperienced guerrillas. The military installation went up in flames, and the guerrillas were defeated, losing between fifteen and twenty of their combatants in the actual fighting; another twenty or thirty were executed by the police and the Army after combat had ceased and the assailants had surrendered. All told, thirty-four people died, another forty-four were injured, and the fragile texture of Argentina's civilian rule was severely strained. For the first time since the mid-seventies, armed struggle had returned to Argentina, if only for a few brief minutes of combat at La Tablada.[9]

---

6. According to Santucho's biographer, Seoane, the ERP gave the MIR a million dollars in 1973. Op. cit., p. 225. Former MIR secretary-general Andrés Pascal Allende confirmed that the ERP delivered more than a million dollars but noted that some Uruguayan Tupamaro operatives in charge of transferring the money ran off with it. Andrés Pascal Allende, interview with the author, Mexico City, May 10, 1991.

7. Not everyone concurred on the issue of Gorriarán's mastery of commando tactics. For example, one of his feats of greatest prowess, the ERP's attack on the Azul Armored Cavalry Division of the Argentine Army, in January 1974, was considered in fact to have been a "military defeat" by the colleague with whom Gorriarán would later take over the leadership of the organization after Santucho's death at Villa Marteli. Luis Mattini, *Hombres y mujeres del PRT–ERP* (Buenos Aires: Editorial Contrapunto, 1990), p. 276.

8. The ERP's assault on the Monte Chingolo barracks in December 1975 was a clear precedent for this action.

9. The hyperbole and hysteria surrounding the events at La Tablada have left what actually occurred far from clear. Suffice it to say that not everyone in Argentina shared

Gorriarán Merlo was behind the operation, although once again he did not participate directly. He planned it, recruited most of the young Argentines involved, including many sons and daughters of former exiles who had remained abroad or returned only recently to their country. Sources in the Argentine military claimed that Gorriarán's wife, Sonia, as well as his two daughters, Cecilia and Adriana, took part in the attack and escaped safely.[10] This was never confirmed, but there can be little doubt that both the political decision to carry out the operation and the logistical planning and organization were Gorriarán's. The arms were said to have been supplied from Panama by Manuel Antonio Noriega, whose contacts with Gorriarán Merlo dated back to 1979 when, as Omar Torrijos's chief of intelligence, Noriega helped many Latin American internationalists, including the Simón Bolivar Column comprising Argentine and Chilean ex-guerrillas, to enter Nicaragua's "Southern Front."

Gorriarán was subsequently reported active in Europe, participating in several nongovernmental organizations intent on strengthening Argentine and Latin American civil society. In mid-1991, as President Carlos Saúl Menem began to encounter some political turbulence, he whipped out the old Gorriarán menace, accusing him of plotting new, dastardly subversive deeds.

Enrique Haroldo Gorriarán Merlo is a Latin American classic. His life itinerary reflects the internationalist traditions of the hemisphere's progressive, dissident, and nationalist thinking and political action, as they date back to the nineteenth century. On his better days he is a modern-day Baltasar Bustos, Carlos Fuentes's wandering, lovelorn veteran of the continent's wars of independence.[11] His total devotion to the causes he espoused, the constant fanaticism rooted in the Catholic origins of his militant career, are recurrent features of the Latin American left. The militaristic vision of life, revolution, and politics is also ar-

---

the conventional wisdom regarding the actual facts, and that many of the Army and government's claims were exaggerated: "It was said that the participants were foreigners, Central Americans and Cubans, which turned out to be false. It was said that they had Cuban and Soviet arms, and now the official report states that 'Brazilian, Belgian, English, and American arms were found.' It was said that the attackers were 'suicidal' and 'bloodthirsty,' and now the army recruits declare that those who occupied the barracks treated them well." Jorge Altamira, *La estrategia de la izquierda en Argentina* (Buenos Aires: Ediciones Prensa Obrera, 1989), p. 236.

10. "At this stage we know that several of those who participated in La Tablada have direct connections with Managua; nobody doubts the almost certain participation of Gorriarán Merlo, and even of his wife, Sonia, and his two daughters, or Martín, who together with Gorriarán fought in the Sandinista southern front under the command of Eden Pastora." *Gente* (Buenos Aires) no. 1228, February 2, 1989, p. 73.

11. Carlos Fuentes, *The Campaign* (New York: Farrar Straus Giroux, 1991.)

chetypical: an entire wing of the left has been nothing but militaristic for at least thirty years. His authoritarian streak, the fascination with arms and violence, the scant attention paid to what he was fighting for, and the obsession with how to fight, all paint him in somber colors. Gorriarán's total disregard for the human costs of political decisions, including the selfless exposure of his own life and the lives of those closest to him, are inescapable characteristics of this largely dominant chapter of the military left during the last three decades. The sinister cult of guns, clandestinity, and conspiracy are common to many of his colleagues, even if the delusions and compulsion are peculiar to him.

But what makes Gorriarán and his peers remarkable figures of the continent's recent history is not only the dark, sordid side of their lives and political endeavors. In response to the criticism of Gorriarán and others like him, some of the more insightful and sensitive members of the armed left point to many redeeming virtues in the errant Argentine's adventures. He is respected because he knows and acknowledges the true origins of the Argentine left's defeat. He is admired for having forsaken everything in Argentina and Cuba, plunging into the Nicaraguan experience wholeheartedly: actually fighting and living there with his family and making his home in Managua, always remembering his status as a guest, not a prophet.[12] His views of Nicaragua and Cuba and of the type of relationship he should establish with the Salvadoreans were, according to his defenders, different from what one would expect: critical and conflictive with the revolutionaries in power, nonsectarian and loyal to those who were not.[13]

He is a symbol of a generation, with its immense commitment to revolution and the destitute, and its infinite capacity to delude itself, act at cross purposes to its own ends, and eventually destroy its best and brightest. Gorriarán is the extreme example of the lives that so

---

12. Needless to say, not everyone familiar with Gorriarán's career shares these views; some of his former colleagues reject them categorically: "What really deserves profound reflection is to observe how the myth of Gorriarán Merlo was constructed during the eighties, and did not emerge from the work of the scant number of members of the PRT–ERP who were still with him, but rather as a consequence of the exacerbated cult of 'courage' and 'direct action,' the cult of the 'hero' which permeates a part of our culture. . . . In this case the mystification was fed by the distortion of the past: Gorriarán's military activities in Nicaragua gave him his 'political-military credentials,' and only on that basis could he be construed as the main, if not the only, heir to the PRT–ERP's tradition." Mattini, op. cit., pp. 12–13.

13. Many of these views were formulated by Salvador Samayoa, a member of the FMLN's leadership and friend of Gorriarán's, in an interview with the author in Mexico City in November of 1990. Another source was Andrés Pascal Allende, of the Chilean MIR, and a comrade of Gorriarán's in the mid-seventies. Interview with the author, Mexico City, June 25, 1991.

many lived during the thirty-five years running from the Sierra Maestra and the birth of the armed struggle in its contemporary form, through the signing of the Salvadorean peace agreements in January 1992. Like the Montoneros, he was, perhaps most of all, an Argentine middle-class nationalist, hoping for a better place in the sun for his country, his class, and himself, and resentful over his difficulties in achieving it.

He constitutes a splendid example of the power of the nationalist ideal and of the ravages it can wreak. Gorriarán also illustrates the versatility and ambivalence of this ideal in Latin America: it could drive men and women to risk their lives, and those of their spouses and children, for another country, another class, another group. Nationalism in Latin America is so potent a potion that it can transform itself into its apparent opposite: an internationalist wanderlust, so common and so notable in the region's history. Only the Church moves Latin America this way, which is why the inclusion of the nationalist ideal in any paradigm, past or present, the left can construct is absolutely indispensable. Abandoned to itself, or to the way it was, nationalism of this species is monumentally self-destructive; yet it still mobilizes men and women in Latin America like nothing else has.

Consequently, the matter of the region's place in the world, its relationship with the United States, and the central issue of nationalism in an area of the globe where nation-building is an unfinished business, remains the best starting point for the left's aggiornamento. To understand this phenomenon, as well as to reformulate it pragmatically, entails answering three questions: why has the left been nationalist, should it continue to be so, and if so, what type of nationalism should it espouse in the post–Cold War world?

These questions lead to others. Placing the tasks of nation-building, and subsequently of defending that nation above all else, was part of the nationalist tradition in Latin America; should it continue to be so? Stressing the imperative of preserving and expanding national autonomy—meaning the leeway to be different; sovereignty—implying control over resources, land, and destiny; and dignity—signifying an intangible sense of pride in standing up to the rest of the world on any issue that allowed it, are the chief components of this nationalism. Should they be maintained? The close identification of national independence with social change has been a mainstay of the left's ideology for nearly a century; is it time to unlink the two? Are the nationalism and antiimperialism or anti-Americanism of the traditional left and the Cuban Revolution common to the entire Latin American left, and if so, should they be? Why has this broad, ill-defined but ever present sentiment and political stance occupied such a decisive place in the left's thinking and practice? The issue is simple: whether the nationalism of the past was necessary and desirable, and if the nationalism of the future should be the same or different from that of an age gone by.

For the left, its homeland is a marvelous and beloved but forsaken region. As one of Carlos Fuentes's crazy old generals tells Baltasar Bustos:

> Every time he told more unknown stories, of wars against the French and the Yankees, military coups, of torture and exile, an endless history of failure and unfulfilled dreams, with everything postponed and frustrated, of nothing more than hope where nothing ever ends, but maybe it was better that way, because, here, when anything ends, it ends badly.[14]

To a significant, perhaps decisive extent, the left has been nationalistic because of a key ingredient in the continent's "social imaginary," a powerful reason for despairing over the region's destiny. Over the past 150 years, and undoubtedly during the twentieth century, in this "social imaginary" the left has proceeded in two-step fashion. It has first normatively identified the "people" and the "nation": the nation *should* belong to the people; there is no true nation that is not of the people. It has then, rightfully and analytically, bemoaned the fact that the "nation" *has not* belonged to the people. The first term reflects a certain notion of the "poor," misbegotten and banned, dark-skinned and ethnic. The destitute and excluded from society make up the people, and thus the "real nation," or its soul. The rich, white, educated elite do not; they are the "other," the defining feature of a different nation. The key difference between nationalism in an area like Latin America and Europe or the United States lies herein. The social divisions and heterogeneity of highly segregated, polarized societies, are reflected in attitudes, sentiments, traditions and stereotypes—the social imaginary, once again—in regard to the nation and society itself.

A series of identities and differences run through this theme. The "real" country—the true Mexico, Brazil, Peru, or Argentina—is perceived to be the nation of the marginalized poor, illiterate, ethnically distinct. The elite is exterior to the nation: it is foreign in so many ways that any individual feature of its "foreignness" is lost in the generality. The elite is white and rich, associates itself with the foreign community, speaks foreign languages, sends its children to foreign schools, travels abroad, lives in different parts of town and country,

---

14. Fuentes, op. cit., p. 184.

and, most important, is a minority. The poor are dark, know only Spanish or an Indian tongue, speak it deficiently and sometimes not at all, live in the slums and villages, and above all, are a poor majority.[15]

The variations from country to country are undeniable, but they confirm this commonality. In some nations, the social/national split is so obvious, it requires no demonstration: Peru, to a lesser extent Bolivia and Guatemala. In other cases, the contrasts appear more stark in given regions: the Brazilian Northeast, or indeed from Salvador de Bahia up, and even in individual Brazilian cities.[16] The old Colombian colonial city of Cartagena de Indias is a perfect dramatic example of "otherness" on a tiny scale: one side is modern or beautifully restored, prosperous, white and open to the world—cruise ships from the Caribbean, businessmen from the international drug market. The other side is poor, black and marginal, closed off from the sea and the world, deprived of services or any of the trappings of modernity: as the inhabitants themselves say, Africa. Recife, in northern Brazil, has its Avenida Bôa Viagem, with its beaches and high-rises; the old town is indescribable: teeming with people and animals during the day, crisscrossed by dark, abandoned streets at night.[17] The separations are multifold and universal: even in largely African-populated nations like the islands of the Caribbean, the exclusion is far-reaching: "Why has Ja-

15. In Brazil, after years of glorifying the racial democracy invented by Gilberto Freyre (*The Mansions and the Shanties*), the reality of racism and exclusion is increasingly acknowledged; slightly more than half the population is black or Afro-Brazilian. According to the "new definition" of race adopted as of 1980 by the Brazilian Institute of Geography and Statistics (IBGE), "of Brazil's 119 million people, 53 percent were Afro-Brazilian: 7.1 million pretos (blacks) and 46.2 million pardos (browns; IBGE determined that people of both pure and mixed African ancestry are seen as a single racial group)." George Reid Andrews, *Blacks and Whites in São Paulo Brazil 1888–1988* (Madison: University of Wisconsin Press, 1991), pp. 265, 250.

16. An example of this is São Paulo, Brazil's most prosperous urban area. According to a recent study of race relations in the city from 1888 to 1988: "In the years and decades immediately following emancipation [in 1888], black and brown workers in São Paulo were denied admission both to urban industrial employment and to the more desirable jobs in the agricultural sector. These color bars began to break down during the 1920s and 1930s, and by the 1940s were mostly defunct. . . . As racial barriers weakened and eroded in blue-collar employment, they asserted themselves very strongly indeed at the middle-class level, producing a severe under-representation of black employees in these sectors of the economy, and high levels of salary inequality. . . . Of the more than half-million abandoned children cared for in São Paulo's state-supported orphanages, 90 percent are black." Ibid., pp. 234–235, 239.

17. How much of an "independent variable" race is in determining "life outcomes" in Brazil is shown by a 1976 National Household Survey that revealed that "browns" and blacks in Brazil earned between 40 and 80 percent of whites' earnings in the same job, across the professional spectrum. Thomas Skidmore, *Fact and Myth; Discovering a Racial Problem in Brazil*, Kellogg Institute Working Paper no. 173, April 1992, p. 13.

maica, 80 percent of pure African descent, continually elected light-skinned leaders?"[18] Another illustration is Santiago, as described by one of President Patricio Alwyn's advisers:

> The inhabitants of the other Santiago, those who live poorly in the "marginal belt" of the city, are generally known as "pobladores" [shantytown dwellers]. . . . Hit hard by unemployment, falling incomes and the deterioration of public services, and forced to live in poorer and less well-serviced urban areas, the "pobladores" have been clearly left on the *other side* of the frontier that divides Santiago into two cities. . . . The emergence of two cities in Santiago—a "cultured" one and a "barbarian" one, as Vicuña Mackenna would have said in the 1870s—the latter on the urban periphery, has made it possible for poverty to become invisible for the affluent. It no longer is part of their daily environment nor of their personal responsibility, and they only perceive it as a diffuse threat to public order and tranquillity.[19]

To different situations, different segregations. Mexico, with its truly mestizo past and its firmly rooted syncretism, seems on the surface to be one of the least heterogeneous societies. Yet as anyone who has lived or traveled extensively through the country knows, the impression is misleading:

> A thousand "criollos" govern from the highest offices in the land. Rare are those mestizos today who can become under secretaries or cabinet ministers, governors and high-level advisers to the president. The country's 500 most important businessmen are almost unanimously criollo. This is equally the case of the 500 most important intellectuals, who all live in the capital. . . . With a maddening slowness we are beginning to acquire a consciousness of this phenomenon. But the denial of it is still severe, and we will probably need another generation before we awaken to it fully.[20]

---

18. Mark Kurlansky, *A Continent of Islands; Searching for the Caribbean Destiny* (Reading, Mass.: Addison-Wesley, 1992), p, 44. The author gives countless other examples, from Dominican dictator Trujillo using pancake makeup to whiten his own skin, to the splits and tensions between Indians and blacks in Trinidad and Guyana.

19. Eugenio Tironi, *Los silencios de la revolución: Chile la otra cara de la modernización* (Santiago: Editorial Puerta Abierta, 1989), pp. 22–23.

20. Jose Agustin Ortiz Pinchetti, "El festin de los criollos," *La jornada* (Mexico City), March 29, 1992. Part of the Mexican school of anthropology has been insisting on this type of issue for some years now, particularly through the work of scholars like Rodolfo Stavenhagen, Guillermo Bonfil, and others. Edmundo Flores, a wry academic-politician, whose skin color betrayed his social origins, summed up the question with what became a celebrated aphorism: "The only *moreno* [person with a dark skin] we see in Cabinet photographs anymore is the soldier standing behind the president." Even the American press, during the time of its most uncritical view of Mexico (during the initial Salinas years), could not help but noticing something strange: "Is Mexico Blond? You

Alan Riding, who covered Mexico for the *New York Times* for nearly ten years and wrote one of the more sensitive books on the country, picked up the meaning of the "popular nationalism" deeply imbedded in the Mexican psyche at a ragtag demonstration in March 1988. Riding commented:

> The people out there think that Salinas [the PRI candidate at the time] is a foreigner; they think Cárdenas is one of them. They may be wrong on both counts, but that is unquestionably what they believe.[21]

Even in Argentina, Chile, and Uruguay, which together with Costa Rica constitute the continent's most socially (and ethnically) homogeneous societies, the sense of belonging to a national community that has been confiscated or sequestered by the "foreigners" and the elite amalgamated into one is undeniable. The real nation in these lands is perceived by the poor as theirs, while the rich—the landowning aristocracy in Argentina and Uruguay, with their continental or English upper-class vocation, their resorts in Punta del Este and Mar del Plata, their country clubs and thoroughbreds—belong elsewhere. Even if ethnically the differences in these countries are much less important than in the rest of Latin America, the social, cultural—including linguistic—and even psychological distances separating social classes become quasi-ethnic, and create a national/foreign split. In Chile, where ethnic distinctions were not extensive, and where the local aristocracy was less well established than in the rest of the Southern Cone—perhaps because Chile was less prosperous than its neighbors—the sense of inclusion/exclusion was already well rooted even before the social transformation of the Pinochet years.

The relevance for the left of this worldview—which is seemingly confirmed by myriad incidents, anecdotes, experiences, and patterns, from everyday life to political activity—can be found in its effect on the left. In order to be with the "people," it has to be with the nation and against the "antination" (*el anti-patria*). Anyone who is socially minded must be nationalistic, since focusing on the "social" inevitably implies emphasizing the recapture of the confiscated nationality, of the nation sequestered. The opposite can sometimes—not often—be true:

---

might think so, watching television there." *Newsweek International*, February 17, 1992, p. 27.
 21. Conversation with the author, Mexico City, March 18, 1988. Other Mexicans have detected this paradox: foreigners are more sensitive to Mexico's racial segregation than Mexicans: "The foreigners are aware of the caste divisions in Mexico. They see an upper criollo class, the heir to the Spanish and alienated by its desire to copy whatever is foreign." Ortiz Pinqueti, op. cit.

there are Latin American rightists, from Brazilian generals and Augusto Pinochet to Salvadorean fascists like Roberto D'Aubuisson, who can be nationalistic while also totally impervious to the social situation of their nations, and who may even contribute actively through their policies to its deterioration. But the reverse is never true: up to now, there are no social leftists who are not convinced radical nationalists.

When Mexican, Cuban, Chilean, or Nicaraguan revolutionaries waxed eloquent over the past half century over how the greatest achievement of their respective upheavals consisted in the restoration of their people's sense of dignity, this is what they meant. The reason Lázaro Cárdenas, Castro, Allende, and the Sandinistas all touched a chord of their followers' collective psyches was precisely to be found in this bequeathing or devolution of a country and a social identity. If only briefly, the revolutions—or their reformist equivalent—gave back their country to the poor, taking it away from the rich. Better still, they made the poor feel at home in their own country and transferred the impression of "foreignness" to the elite. The poor felt at home, the rich felt excluded: for a few scant moments, the tables were turned.

The difference between the prevailing sentiments in other areas of the world can be highlighted by the contrast between the labels attached to the left and right of the political spectrum in Latin America and elsewhere. In the United States and in much of Western Europe, it is the left that has been mainly branded as "traitorous" to the mother- or fatherland. Red scares in the United States at least since the 1920s to the McCarthy years identified the left (from Italian anarchists to Jewish Communists) as agents of a "foreign power." In France and Italy, not to mention Britain and Germany before World War II, Communists were labeled *"le parti de l'étranger."* French-Jewish Socialists like Léon Blum fared scarcely better. The left was seen by a significant sector of society at different moments in time as a foreign blemish on the homogeneous national skin. The right did the seeing; the left suffered the consequences.

In Latin America, with few exceptions, Red-baiting with a national tint has not truly worked. Of course nationalistic Communists were accused of being *"agentes de Moscú,"* and after 1959 many leftists of different persuasions were often attacked for being servants of the bearded fellow in Havana. And at certain critical junctures—Brazil in 1964, Chile in 1973, perhaps Nicaragua in the late 1980s—important segments of the middle class did come to resent real or perceived Soviet or Cuban influence. But by and large, it is the right that associates itself—and is identified—with the external world, while the left identifies with "the nation." It is far more common for the left to attack elites, the business community, the military, and certain ideo-logical circles, as being appendices of the United States ("La em-bajada"). This difference is partly attributable, of course, to the disparate weights associated with the powers in question: American influence in Latin America was incommensurate with Soviet or Cuban influence, whereas a lesser distance existed between U.S. and Soviet pressure in Europe. But a more important explanation can be found in the factors mentioned above: it is the elite in Latin America that has been identified as foreign, i.e., American, for nearly a century now.

The nationalism that emerged from this identification was rooted in a perception of reality: the elite was perceived as "foreign" and part of its "foreignness" stemmed from its association with "real" foreign-ers: the strong, omnipresent, multifaceted, and remarkably recogniz-able reality of an external factor in virtually every Latin American nation from colonial times through the end of the twentieth century. This was a conquered continent, where independence took the shape of a transfer of authority from a distant and detached foreign power to the local elite it created and then confronted. It was a continent where domination and the exploitation of local wealth originated with the conquest but continued long after under a formally distinct guise and with different beneficiaries: during the nineteenth century, the Eng-lish, the French, and as it came to a close, the Americans.

The type of foreign economic presence—in resource-based en-claves—and its visual effects—the existence of a social strata that was "different" or "other"—could not fail to strengthen the impression of continuity: the single most important theoretical premise of every Latin American abstract reflection on the region's history and identity. Everything looked the same: foreigners all seemed alike, their economic and cultural impact was identical, and the more time passed, the more things remained unchanged. The notion of neocolonialism, and, later, dependency theory, were rooted in this sense of continuity, which con-tained its grain of truth though it was factually false. Indeed the impact of changing external influences transformed Latin America: the mines and plantations of the colonial period were radically different from those of the nineteenth century, which in turn contrasted sharply with the oil fields and railroads of 1900, and subsequently with the import substitution industries of the second half of the twentieth century.

This impression of a motionless, lasting foreign link, with its do-mestic relay perceived as an "internal exteriority," has instilled a sense of impotence in those segments of Latin American elites sensitive to the need for change. From independence wars onward, certain sectors of Latin elites have traditionally thought that the principal causes of their nations' dramatic fate lay abroad, and—more important—that the decisions regarding their destiny were invariably made elsewhere. Evidence of this perception lay in the search, prior to independence, by criollo elites for ideas and support for emancipation from Spain in Europe and from the United States. Moreover, they believed that the ultimate outcome of the struggle for independence would be settled in Europe, if not on the playing fields of Eton, then certainly by Napoleon's fate in Spain, and Fernando VII's at the Cortes in Cadiz.

Throughout the nineteenth century, elites in Latin America fought each other over countless issues, but almost always with some sort of recourse abroad. The sensation that the main decisions regarding life, death, economic progress, and political development were made beyond the frontiers of their own nations was often accurate. The caricature of this state of affairs can be found doubtlessly in the Mexican civil wars of the 1850s–60s, when the conservative faction of the elite established a sort of search committee to recruit a European prince—eventually a confused and decent Austrian intellectual from the Adriatic—and French support to put him on a nonexistent throne. Not to be left behind, the liberal elite sought United States backing to the point—in 1856, before the French intervention—of selling a significant part of the national territory in exchange for arms and money through the disgraceful McLane-Ocampo Treaty, thankfully voted down by the United States Senate.

Today, as in the past, a significant sector of most Latin American elites continues to be persuaded that the principal decisions on key issues at home are made abroad. This perception is not limited to the left, even though right and left approach the situation differently. The more conservative sectors—sometimes the military and nearly always the business community—see compliance and accommodation with the United States today and with prevailing international trends as categorical imperatives: nothing can be done outside the bounds of orthodoxy and alignment, deviation being exorbitantly expensive. Credit, investment, technology, know-how, culture, and, in the more extreme versions, "civilization," all come from abroad. During the 1980s—not for the first time—numerous Latin American regimes pursued economic reforms they felt had to be "imposed" on their nations, thanks to pressure from abroad. The "short leash" theory, whereby the regions' governments had to be coerced into implementing economic transformations, was broadly subscribed to by conservative elites: without the external factor, reform was impossible.

The left largely agrees with this assessment of the state of affairs, but with a negative spin: everything is decided abroad, but that is not the way matters were meant to be. From time immemorial that part of the elite positioned on the left and desirous of changing the status quo in favor of a more just, democratic, and autonomous society, located the main obstacle to such a transformation abroad. In the thirties and forties the impediment to change lay in the foreign ownership of natural resources and existing wealth; in the fifties and sixties, in the CIA and American multinationals; later, with the International Monetary Fund and the World Bank—all making decisions and imposing choices contrary to the national interest.

The point is not which side is right or wrong, but rather that both sides share a common matrix for conceptualizing the region's position in the world. This estrangement places the issue of national autonomy and local decision-making at the center of the entire political spectrum's obsession with the national question. For those who favor social, economic, and political change, and detect the original cause of the status quo and the main obstacle to change abroad, the struggles for change and autonomy are one and the same. Conversely, for those defending the status quo (through self-interest or sincere conviction) and for whom its best defense in the face of varying, domestic dangerous mutations lies abroad, the struggle for permanence at home and consonance with the rest of the world (mostly, since the Second World War, in Latin America, a euphemism for the United States) is also identical.

The exclusion-inclusion syndrome and the matrix of foreign influence are not the product of spontaneous combustion in Latin America. Their persistence, as well as the part they play in shaping perceptions of the region's role in the world, can be explained only by deep-rooted origins and historical considerations. Hence a previously explored theme: how the state appeared before the nation and how the process of nation-building in Latin America, artificially begun in the early nineteenth century through partly European-induced independence wars, is still a largely unfinished business.[22]

There have been innumerable scholarly studies concerning the formation of a national consciousness in Latin America. The more modern works have placed a greater emphasis on anthropological origins, and a number of authors have found important religious factors, for

---

22. Not everyone who has recently returned to the issue of state and nation sequence shares the view that much of the time in most areas of the "old world" the nation preceded the state. "A systematic examination of the history of the modern world will show, I believe, that in almost every case, the state preceded the nation, and not the other way around, contrary to a widely believed myth." Immanuel Wallerstein, in Immanuel Wallerstein and Etienne Balibar, *Race Nation Classes: Les Identités Ambiques* (Paris: Editions La découverte, 1990), p. 110.

example Jacques Lafaye's work on the role of the Virgin of Guadalupe[23] in the emergence of a national consciousness in Mexico.[24] But two broad trends stand out in most of the literature and are practically accepted as conventional wisdom: (1) the state was created before the nation and consequently before the national consciousness was truly developed or existent; and (2) the emergence of a national consciousness or identity was first an elite affair, long before it became—when it did—a mass, popular characteristic. In the meantime, in the best of cases, it was an urban, generally professional, middle-class concern. In French anthropologist Roger Bastide's words, regarding Mexico, Argentina and Brazil:

> Since the state generally existed before the nation in Latin America, nationalism was originally psychological in nature, a dream of living individuals, before becoming a structural matter, that is, the expression of a society. In Brazil, the national consciousness was born around 1900, not from within as in Europe, but as a mythical reality, crafted by intellectuals.[25]

These twin features marked the left from its very birth in Latin America.[26] There was a task of nation-building still pending, and the burden descended disproportionately on the shoulders of an intellec-

---

23. It would be unfair to summarize a book like Lafaye's in a sentence, but in his own words: "Guadalupe was first the 'mother of the Indians.' The Mexican criollos [then] demanded their part of the grace bestowed upon the 'Indian nation.' . . . [An] olive-skinned Virgin that appeared before an Indian, Guadalupe made of the criollos, the mestizos, and the Indians a single people . . . united by the same charismatic faith." Jacques Lafaye, *Quetzalcóatl y Guadalupe: La formación de la conciencia nacional en México* (Mexico City: Fondo de Cultura Económica, 1977), p. 392.

24. Other scholars insist upon the same point: "To rally the Criollos, castas and Indians against Spain, [Fray Servando Teresa de] Mier and [Carlos María de] Bustamante [two intellectuals in New Spain and early Mexico] proclaimed what was essentially a fiction, the myth of a Mexican nation, which was the lineal heir of the Aztecs. In practice, however, the insurgents fought under the banner of the Virgin of Guadalupe." D.A. Brading, *The Origins of Mexican Nationalism* (Cambridge, England: Cambridge University Press, 1985), p. 110.

25. Roger Bastide, *Le Prochain et le Lointain*, quoted by François Chevalier, *L'Amérique Latine de l'Indépendance a nos jours* (Paris: Presses Universitaires de France, 1977), pp. 401–402.

26. The issue of the state's predating the nation and the elite origins of Brazilian nationalism is a recurring theme in Brazilian intellectual history. Thus another French student of these questions states: "Brazil is perhaps in the nineteenth and at the beginning of the twentieth century a nation still being formed. But at least it has a state. Rare are the moments when Brazilian intellectuals can doubt this, and when they do, they feel responsible for the consolidation of the state." Daniel Pécaut, *Entre le Peuple et la Nation: Les Intellectuels et la politique au Brésil* (Paris: Editions de la Maison des Sciences de l'Homme, 1989), p. ix.

tual faction of the elite[27] upon which also fell other, equally daunting responsibilities: building democratic political institutions and combating levels of poverty and social exclusion that were simply overpowering.[28] Who could accomplish the duty of nation-building? Not the broad masses: national consciousness, when not incipiently blended with religious myth, syncretism, and tribal or regional loyalties, was nonexistent in their midst. Not the Church: a strong and centralized institution, it had on occasion participated, or even led the struggle for independence, but was unsuited for the chore. And not the landed, commercial elite: attached either to the former metropolis or to later substitutes, its interests were too entwined with those of the outside world, and too estranged from the disenfranchised masses. The task fell to the intellectual elite, or so it thought:

> Thirty years apart, two generations of Brazilian intellectuals [the generation of 1925–40 and that of 1954–64] expressed their conviction that they had an essential responsibility in the building of the nation. By influencing both opinions and governants, they acceded in both cases to a level of exceptional social visibility and effectively contributed to imposing new representations of the political sphere.[29]

But nation-building, and national consciousness-raising, was not an easy thing. Four impediments became readily apparent, and rapidly pushed anyone who ventured into this field toward other concerns, superficially unrelated but in fact tightly bound to it. First, no national construction could be achieved without a popular constituency, and building the latter meant getting involved in its social demands: land, labor rights, protection or support for national industry or commerce. Again, the Mexican mid-nineteenth-century civil wars and responses

---

27. This was not only the case in Latin America. According to Swedish Nobel Prize–winning economist Gunnar Myrdal, author of the 1940s classic *The American Dilemma*, in the United States: "The craving for 'historical identity' is not in any sense a people's movement. These cravings have been raised by a few well-established intellectuals, professors, writers. . . ." Quoted by Arthur M. Schlesinger Jr., *The Disuniting of America* (New York: Norton, 1992), p. 42. Schlesinger himself puts it this way: "Nationalism was invented by the intellectuals in the interest of aspiring elites and thereafter propagated to receptive masses." Ibid., p. 47.

28. The fact that these same nationalist intellectuals devoted to building a national identity were also the most cosmopolitan of the region's citizens then and still today is a paradox that escapes no one, but that shouldn't be surprising or much less detract from the enormity of the task or the sincerity with which it was—and continues to be—undertaken: "Nationalism and cosmopolitanism have always mixed well, as paradoxical as it may seem; and since Fichte, numerous examples attest to it." Jacques Derrida, *L'Autre Cap* (Paris: Editions de Minuit, 1991), p. 49.

29. Pécaut, op. cit., p. 3.

to foreign intervention are illustrative: Benito Juárez rallied the country around his horse-drawn carriage and against Maximilian, the French, and the Conservatives largely because he took up many of the demands raised by other sectors.

Balmaceda in Chile, the Mexican Revolution, Martí and Macedo in Cuba, Yrigoyen in Argentina to a point and Batlle in Uruguay are all examples of this simple dilemma: without an economic and social agenda, there was no "mass" constituency (even in relative terms); without a mass constituency, the national consciousness in question was stillborn. But even the most minimal social and economic agenda implied some form of confrontation with defenders of the status quo, with the landed, commercial, and foreign-based elite. The line between national aspirations and social demands was an extraordinarily difficult one to draw. There was no lasting, solid nation-building without the homogenization or "nationalization" of society: that the inhabitants "inside" a territory perceive they have more in common with each other than with those "outside."[30] But this meant reducing social, regional, and ethnic disparities, instilling a common language, and developing a notion of citizenship and equality before the law not too flagrantly at odds with inequality before society and power. Latin America was so far behind on all of these counts that its nation-building was bound to lag. The fact that all "modern" societies are characterized by what Etienne Balibar has called "the contradiction between the pretension of the modern state to constitute a 'community' and the reality of different forms of exclusion"[31] does not dilute the Latin American exception. In Latin America, as in many other areas of the developing world, the gap between "formal belonging" and "real exclusion" is abysmal: the first term of the contradiction—formal belonging to a community of equals—has been in most cases and certainly until the middle of this century mostly meaningless.

Second, the most successful and effective recipe—whether deliberate or not—for nation-building was not much different in Latin America during the hundred years following independence than the one that forged nationalities in Europe centuries before. This was some form

---

30. This was no recent matter; according to Carlos Monsiváis (and many students of Mexican nationalism): "[By the time of the revolution] Mexico was formally a nation but didn't believe it: what unified it, divided it; and people belonged to regions, ethnic groups, political causes, trades, social classes, armed bands. One was Maya Tarahumara, a peasant, an anarchosyndicalist, from Sonora or Veracruz, a petty bourgeois, a lawyer, a cobbler, poor or rich, much more than a Mexican." Carlos Monsiváis, "Muerte y resurrección del nacionalismo mexicano," *Nexos* (Mexico City), no. 109, January 1987, p. 13.

31. Etienne Balibar, in Wallerstein and Balibar, op. cit., p. 242.

of confrontation with the "outside world," from Joan of Arc and la Reconquista against the Moors in Spain to Clausewitz, Fichte, and Schiller in the German struggle against Napoleonic invasions. Nationality and nationalism go together, albeit in an uncomfortable, complex partnership, generally defined by the contradiction, or open conflict, with the "other" and with itself. Belonging is intimately linked with nonbelonging; there is no national consciousness without the identification of "another" that is characterized by its alien qualities or exclusion. And any attempt, as the French philosopher Jacques Derrida has stated, to find the identity of a culture in itself, to develop a culture in relation to itself, is doomed to failure. Thus:

> *The characteristic of a culture is that it is never identical to itself.* Not that it does not have an identity, but that it cannot identify itself, say "me" or "we," that it cannot take the form of a subject other than through a nonidentity with itself, or, if you prefer, the difference *with itself.*[32]

There is no culture or cultural identity without this "difference with itself." Thus, it has been repeatedly demonstrated that the first true inklings of Mexican national identity surfaced with the successive confrontations the country engaged in through the first two-thirds of the nineteenth century: the Texan Secession of 1836, the American invasion of 1847, and, more significantly, the war against the French and Maximilian in the 1860s. Even as late as the 1960s, Brazilian national consciousness was still portrayed as emerging from confrontation with other nations: "Nationalism sets the stage for political life. No one doubts anymore that the Brazilian nation exists, [but] it now experiences life as a nation by affirming itself, every day, against the dominant nations. The sentiment of identity is relayed by that of confrontation."[33]

Third, nation-building and the crafting of national consciousness through resistance to external threats brought to the fore the issue of whether the rest of the world appreciated the types of demands, policies, and movements that such a process inevitably entailed. True, intellectuals and politicians conjured up images of foreign opposition to the emergence of a national character and identity throughout Latin America that were farfetched or blatantly untrue. But this did not alter the fact that an authentic reluctance frequently did exist, and often translated into political opposition. Whether Balmaceda was driven to

---

32. Derrida, op. cit., p. 16.
33. Pécaut, op. cit., p. 87.

suicide by the loss of Chile's just appropriated nitrate wealth in 1891 or by his own demons; whether the Spanish-American War was waged by the United States to take over what was left of the Spanish colonial empire and derail Cuban independence, as Martí basically believed, or by domestic American considerations devoid of any great imperial ambition; whether Britain actively conspired against the Mexican Revolution and tried to trick or coax Woodrow Wilson into accompanying His Majesty's counterrevolutionary activities in Mexico, or whether all foreign power involvement in Mexico during those years was merely the product of ambitious local diplomats engaged in free-lance meddling—all of these, and many more questions, are less important than the one basic issue lurking behind them. Most attempts to implement policies furthering the formation of a national identity tended to encounter some type of resistance from the outside world. Thus for different reasons, the only way to succeed in forging a nation was to pick fights with a number of adversaries that otherwise would not be enemies, but indifferent partners or even allies. To build a nation was to enter into conflict with many of the powers that were.

Fourth, the situation varied enormously throughout Latin America. If continuity is a constant in Latin American thought, homogeneity is also. It looked like every country was the same. A common origin, geography, religion and language (partly) pointed to a common present and future, and thus what worked in one nation would certainly work in another. But in fact the shaping of a national consciousness differed from region to region, depending on preexisting situations and on what occurred after independence.

There were pending, long-overdue liberations in various regions of the continent, where an undeniably colonial situation existed, or where it persisted—in one form or another—well past its disappearance elsewhere in the region. In these cases, where barely a modicum of independence would be achieved as late as 1900, or that remained in a virtually neocolonial state until the second half of this century, the identification between attaining nationhood and satisfying popular demands of inclusion and dignity was complete. This is where, years later, revolution would take place: Cuba and Nicaragua.[34]

But in most of the rest of the region, for a majority of the remainder of the time, a conjunction of factors and circumstances *had* generated a national consciousness, albeit a precarious and unfinished one, while

---

34. Without taking this argument too far, it can be suggested that the Cuban Revolution encountered the most favorable reception for its support for revolution or reform where a colonial or neocolonial situation prevailed: Angola and Ethiopia in Africa; Nicaragua, Jamaica, Grenada, and Panama in Latin America.

nation-building *did* occur, however slow the pace and limited the scope. The great populist movements and caudillos of the thirties and forties, with the inclusionary waves they activated and rode, contributed to this process. Recurring conflicts, large and small, substantive or anecdotal, with the United States, Britain, and France all played a role, while urbanization, literacy, and great power rivalries all helped.

The hemisphere's left, born and raised under the notion that fragmentary nation-building and a brittle national consciousness created a political and cultural status quo analogous to colonial rule, was missing something: the all-important, though apparently semantic difference between colonial domination and partial national consolidation. When Luis Carlos Prestes on the eve of his death looked back over nearly a century of left-wing militancy and singled out this question as the most important self-criticism he would address at the Brazilian Communist Party, and as his greatest disagreement in the last years of his life, this is what he meant:

> The greatest difference, the biggest problem, the most serious mistake, lay in our identification of the United States as the principal enemy, in placing all our emphasis on the external factor.[35]

From the outset the left thus found itself forced to be nationalistic: it could not be otherwise. If it wanted to be on the side of the poor, oppressed, and excluded, it had to be nationalistic. If it wanted to help build a national identity in countries where only centuries of religious imposition, ineffective colonial rule, and fragile linguistic unity held together extraordinarily powerful centrifugal forces—ethnic, religious, tribal, geographic and climatic, political and cultural—it had to be nationalistic. But if it sought to be nationalistic with a following, and sustain a given level of confrontation with the rest of the world in order to build that missing nation, this implied the adoption of a series of social demands that strengthened its "left" character.

This nationalism, while anchored in a fundamentally correct assessment of Latin American reality, was plagued by two misconceptions and one intrinsic weakness. The misconceptions were a typical by-product of a nineteenth century, progress-imbued view of history. If nation-building was incomplete or insufficient, it was nonetheless under way, and would be achieved at some point if a certain number of fortunate factors or circumstances fortuitously converged. This begged a central question: whether those nations that did not finish up the

---

35. Interview with the author, Rio de Janeiro, December 22, 1989.

business of their construction "in time," would actually be able to conclude it, or whether, as some asked:

> *For whom is it too late, already, today?* In other words, which are those societies that, despite the constraint of the world economy and the system of nation-states it generated, can *no longer* fully carry out their transformation into nations—or can do so only in a purely legal fashion, and at the cost of interminable conflicts without a definitive outcome?[36]

The left has traditionally prejudged that nation-building is a viable task in the modern world, and that it can be consummated under the right set of junctures, policies, and structures. But it could well be—indeed, everything today suggests—that for many, if not all, of the developing countries, time has run out to construct nations like others: with their own national language, administration, market, and currency, and with a truly autochthonous local ruling elite. The fact that national institutions are withering away in the "old world" or "center" and the only nations that apparently are reproducing themselves can be found in the "periphery" does not mean that the new emerging nations will all look like those shaped in centuries gone by. Nation-building in Latin America proceeded so slowly, is so unfinished and ill defined, that it probably will not take place the way the left—and nearly everyone else—has supposed.

The left's nationalism has tended to ignore this basic fact of "modern" life: historical time is not eternally open, not everyone (every society or nation) has the possibility of treading the same path others have ambled down previously. Moreover—and herein lies the second misconception—the path is usually less well explored and oft trodden than is frequently thought by the left in Latin America. Nation-forming in the "old world" was a much slower, more painful, reversible, and never-ending process than might appear in school history books about *"nos ancêtres les Gaulois"* in France, or the Pilgrims and Puritans in the United States. The process was much more time-consuming and partial than hindsight and rewritten history have reconstructed it. For example, if language is a fundamental attribute of nationhood, and France is as well-formed and longstanding a nation as any other, it is surprising that as late as the 1860s, before universal elementary public education was established, a third of the French people did not speak the French language.[37]

---

36. Balibar, in Wallerstein and Balibar, op. cit., p. 124.
37. "In 1863, according to official figures, 8,381 of France's 37,510 communes spoke no French: about a quarter of the country's population. The Ministry of Public Instruc-

Furthermore, the "modern" nations seem obliged to constantly commence their nation-forming process anew, as immigration, renewed racial tensions, regional integration, and the (re)emergence of local and regional aspirations take place. It is no accident that so many of the racial or ethnic tensions in the most affluent nations are being viewed from a "national" perspective, as their excluded minorities are increasingly seen as deprived not only of rights or dignity but of "full nationality," in Andrew Hacker's felicitous re-coining of a famous phrase.[38] Even where it began centuries ago, nation-building is by definition a perpetual chore, never laid to rest, never fully, finally achieved.

Lastly, the socially rooted nationalism of the left suffers from an internal contradiction that remains unsolved and probably has no short-term solution. It is a nationalism of the intellectual elite whose chief reason for being consists in doing away with social cleavages and exclusions characteristic of Latin American societies. It correctly identifies those social traits as the main obstacle to nation-building, and also acknowledges that only by "giving the nation back to the people" can the social indignities and disparities so typical of the hemisphere be significantly reduced. But the intellectual elite is by definition on the wrong side of the divide: it does not belong to the excluded, but to those doing the excluding.[39] It is part of the "foreign" growth on the social, impoverished national body, as foreign to the poor and "denationalized" as the business community, the governing elite, or the "legally foreign" estate.[40] Because the chasm sep-

---

tion found that 448,328 of the 4,018,427 schoolchildren (ages seven to thirteen) spoke no French at all, and that another 1,190,269 spoke or understood it but could not write it, suggesting an indifferent grasp of the tongue. . . . In short, French was a foreign language for a substantial number of Frenchmen, including almost half the children who would reach adulthood in the last quarter of the century. . . ." Eugene Weber, *Peasants into Frenchmen: The Modernization of Rural France 1870–1914* (Stanford, Calif.: Stanford University Press, 1976), p. 67.

38. Andrew Hacker, *Two Nations* (New York: Scribner, 1992). Or in Schlesinger's words: "The American identity will never be fixed and final; it will always be in the making." Op. cit., p. 138.

39. It is fascinating to observe how a similar mission—the construction of a European "identity"—is also being assigned to intellectuals, and how a similar contradiction is bedeviling them: they have to build an identity for sectors of society far removed from their life and times, their customs and habits: "I see at this table mainly men and citizens from Western Europe, writers or philosophers, following the traditional model of the European intellectual: a guardian held responsible for the memory and the culture, a citizen charged with a sort of spiritual mission for Europe." Derrida, op. cit., p. 27.

40. A longtime student of Afro-Asian nationalist guerrillas has underlined a well-known, even more accentuated contradiction in Africa and Asia: "The backbone of the national movement is provided by the urban petty bourgeoisie, or at least a fraction of it. This does not prevent its elders from belonging to the more affluent social strata. Their

arating it from the people is so great, the intellectual elite never truly understands its own people, as Mexican historian Lorenzo Meyer has repeatedly emphasized. This gap has become even greater in recent years, as strident but not inaccurate critics of the "metamorphosis of Latin American intellectuals" have pointed to the transition from organic to institutional intellectuals living off foreign grants and funding, accentuating their separation from the mainstream of their societies.

The great nationalist leaders of modern Latin America did not belong to the intellectual elite. But they were rapidly obliged to take over its nationalist mantle and the ideology, although what made it possible for them to extend their support beyond the narrow, generally middle-class nationalist constituency was precisely the social and economic content of their broader political discourse and practice. The intellectual elite, by contrast, was boxed in by the middle-class constituency to which its nationalist rhetoric was directed. This explains some of the more paradoxical, sometimes suicidal behavior by the left on nationalism, particularly its anti-American variety.

Two such examples are often cited: the invitation extended by Salvador Allende to Puerto Rican independence movement leader Juan Mari Brás to attend his November 1970 inauguration as president of Chile, and the Sandinistas' insistence, from 1979 through the 1980s, on conserving the lyrics of their party anthem that proudly proclaimed their struggle against *"el yanquí, enemigo de la humanidad."* Both acts were perceived by many Americans as immature, irresponsible, and totally unnecessary shows of nationalist bravado that needlessly complicated already strained relations with the United States.[41] They were also seized upon by American conservatives such as Henry Kissinger and Jeane Kirkpatrick as proof of the irredeemable anti-American bent

---

characteristic has almost always been (the most famous exception being Mao Ze Dong) to have studied in the West or to have been marked by it." Gérard Chaliand, *Terrorismes et Guérillas* (Paris: Flammarion, 1985), pp. 37–38.

41. Another, previous episode is also worth recalling: "On March 12, 1953, thirty deputies of the Guatemalan Congress introduced a resolution asking for a minute of silence "to honor the memory of the great statesman and leader of the Soviet Union, Joseph Vissarionovich Stalin, whose passing is mourned by all progressive men." Following a violent three-hour debate with the handful of opposition deputies, all but two members of the majority voted in favor of the resolution and the Guatemalan Congress rose in silent homage to the late leader. It was, as a U.S. official pointed out, "the only government body in the Western hemisphere to do so. The desire to give a slap to the Yankees explains the overwhelming vote." Piero Gleijeses, *Shattered Hope: The Guatemalan Revolution and the United States, 1944–54* (Princeton, N.J.: Princeton University Press, 1991), pp. 181–182.

of the regimes in question.[42] Their true colors showed more transparently in these defiant frenzies, it was argued, than in their constant breast-beating declarations of willingness to improve ties with the United States.

Both assessments were valid: the acts were unnecessary, and they revealed a great deal of the Chilean left's and the Sandinistas' deeper feelings. But they also reflected a greater problem: the left-wing intellectual elite's middle-class constituency in Chile and Nicaragua was certainly in tune with acts of that sort. Its nationalism—as expressed in anti-American machismo—did not allow Allende or Daniel Ortega the latitude to step away from provocations of that nature and get on with the business of effectively managing diplomatic relations with the United States. There is little doubt that the broad majority of the Nicaraguan and Chilean peoples had no tremendous sympathy for Puerto Rican independence, and did not consider Americans the enemies of humanity, whatever their feelings with regard to U.S. policy toward their country during the previous half century.

But much of the intellectual elite did harbor those sentiments, and the distance separating it from the people made it impervious to the self-evident imperatives of political compromise. On the positive side of the balance sheet, of course, there is the usefulness of the nationalist discourse: what begins as a concession to the intellectual elite, and by the latter to its middle-class constituency, rapidly becomes an extremely efficacious way of mobilizing and controlling wider segments of the population. During the years of the contra war in Nicaragua, as in Cuba at the beginning of the Revolution and in the most recent stage of isolation and suffering, the nationalist button was the easiest and most effective one to push. In the words of one Sandinista intellectual: "The conflict with the Americans was what galvanized all the enthusiasm and discipline; without it, who knows what would have happened?"[43]

But if the left had to be nationalistic, why did it have to be anti-American? The reply is as obvious as the question is naïve: from the turn of the century onward, there was virtually no one else to be

---

42. The question of Allende and Puerto Rico is raised in Henry Kissinger's memoirs: "As a foretaste of Allende's anti-U.S. bias, the leaders of the Puerto Rican independence party were also invited to the inauguration." *White House Years* (Boston: Little, Brown, 1979), p. 680. Jeane Kirkpatrick's complaint about the Sandinista national anthem appeared in her well-known essay "U.S. Security and Latin America," *Commentary*, January 1981.

43. Orlando Nuñez, interview with the author, Berkeley, California, February 1991.

nationalistic against. If the principle of confrontation with the "other" is acknowledged as a constitutive element of any national identity or consciousness, it is also true that the choice of the "other" is limited by myriad considerations: relevance and the relative frequency and intensity of conflicts. When other opportunities existed in Latin America, they were, to be sure, seized upon: consider, for example, the nationalist fervor against Britain (though also against Washington) in Argentina under Perón, and in Mexico in 1938 at the time of the nationalization of Mexican oil (owned largely by British and Dutch firms). But other than these rare exceptions, conflict invariably flourished with the United States, because of economic, geographic, and later military and security factors. The left had virtually no choice but to be anti-American. It had to target the United States, not because it was the United States, but because it was the "other," and it was the main adversary of both social change and national maturity in the continent. In addition, when the United States lived up to Latin America's worst expectations, taking up the gauntlet of virtually every challenge thrown at it by the left and engaging Latin America in most of the "national" confrontations that surfaced, the fate of the left's anti-Americanism was largely sealed.

Again, the importance of the intellectual elite in this configuration is central. In his own way, Peruvian author Mario Vargas Llosa, while lamenting the Latin American intellectual's anti-Americanism, emphasizes its historical persistence, importance, and breadth:

> The influence of the intellectual in all of this has been enormous; no one has contributed more than he to feeding the hatred and spreading the stereotype against the United States. Denouncing the "colossus of the North," the attack on the "empire" is an old tradition that has been fed equally by left-wing and right-wing intellectuals. . . . Until the First World War, more or less, the Latin American intellectual elite was almost always of the right, Francophile or "Hispanist" and violently and condescendingly anti-American. . . . Since the Mexican revolution [1910], intellectuals in Latin America became "progressive" . . . They took up anti-Americanism, coloring it with economic and political hues.[44]

The main bone of contention between the Latin American left and the United States over the past half century has nonetheless not focused on the former's anti-Americanism, or on the latter's opposition

---

44. Mario Vargas Llosa, "Piedra de toque: El odio y el amor," *Unomásuno* (Mexico City), December 30, 1991.

to national affirmation and social change. Both were real, yet often denied by each side. The main point of friction has resided in the geopolitical, ideological effects of this central contradiction: in the left's pro-Soviet inclinations, and in the United States insistence on detecting not so much a Red under every bed, but a Russian behind every Red. While a number of caveats are in order at this point, the issue was indisputably real. First of all: "As the Soviets have discovered elsewhere in Latin America, the latent anti-Americanism found in much of the region does not automatically translate into support for the Soviet Union or affinity with its style."[45] Secondly, it was equally undeniable that American policy toward the Soviet Union in Latin America, and toward successive, more or less enthusiastic Latin American rapprochements with Moscow, was singularly one-sided:

> The list of cases in which the United States has established double standards for third world superpower behavior is a long one indeed. It is simply asserted that sovereign Nicaragua—1,000 miles from U.S. shores—cannot be allowed to accept Soviet MiG-21s, while the United States must be able to send the equivalent of much more advanced MiG-29s to Pakistan, which virtually borders on the Soviet Union. America's use of France as a proxy in African activities is taken for granted . . . but the Soviet Union has no right to use Cuba as its proxy in Africa. The United States has every right to send armed forces to rescue hostages in Iran, but imagine the reaction if the Soviet Union would send a naval armada to the Caribbean and then send helicopters to rescue Soviet hostages in Mexico City.[46]

Finally, it was also quite clear that Soviet policy toward Latin American revolution and reform over the last fifty years was far more varied and complex than many simplistic analyses in Washington made it out to be. From Stalin's profound mistrust and skepticism regarding any possibility of independence for Third World countries, and Khrushchev's gamble on Cuba, all the way to the initially unwilling, then reluctantly cooperative attitude toward Nicaragua, the Soviet Union did not actually push revolution, Marxism, and anti-American subversion at every arising opportunity.[47]

---

45. Peter Clement and W. Raymond Duncan, *The Soviet Union and Central America,* in Eusebio Mujal-León, *The USSR and Latin America* (London: Unwin Hyman, 1989), p. 277.

46. Jerry F. Hough, *The Struggle for the Third World: Soviet Debates and American Options* (Washington, D.C.: Brookings Institution, 1986), pp. 3–4.

47. Ibid., pp. 227–257.

The traditional debate over which came first, the left's pro-Soviet penchant, or United States harassment and alienation of the left—driving it into Moscow's embrace—plagued relations between the U.S. and the Latin American left for years. In fact, the endless and often superficial discussions over the true motives for American intervention—strategic and anti-Soviet (the mainstream American point of view), or essentially linked to U.S. economic interests (generally the Latin American nationalistic and left-leaning stance)—had no answer in the confines of the Cold War. Did Castro become a pro-Soviet, convinced Communist as a result of American hostility and ostracism? Or was he always a fervent Marxist who knew from the very moment he quartered his guerrilla army in the Sierra Maestra that his ultimate goal lay in bringing socialism to Cuba and incorporating it into the socialist bloc? Did Salvador Allende incur U.S. wrath because he expropriated Chilean copper owned by American companies, as well as other U.S. holdings in his country? Or was the United States bent on his overthrow even before he took office, because of his left-leaning, Cuban-sympathizing alliance with the Chilean Communist Party? Were the Nicaraguan Sandinistas hard-core Marxist-Leninists from the outset of their revolution? Or did they end up being pro-Soviet hard-liners because the United States, particularly during the Reagan years, ostracized and antagonized them, eventually transforming them into exactly what Washington stated it did not want them to become? And finally, in what was perhaps the least important case but the most succinct formulation of the stubbornly immutable and ever present problem:

> Which was it? Was Grenada pushed into the waiting arms of the Soviet Union and Cuba by insensitive and counterproductive U.S. policies? Did Grenada become dependent on the Soviet Union and Cuba because U.S. hostility left it no other choice? Or did the Grenadian government leap onto the unsuspecting shoulders of the Russian bear because of the ideological predisposition of its leadership? Did the People's Revolutionary Government (PRG) try to provoke the United States in order to disguise and justify its international preference to ally with the Soviet Union and Cuba?[48]

The debate in the 1980s over U.S. policy toward the Sandinista Revolution probably framed this issue in the sharpest, most starkly

---

48. Robert Pastor, "The United States and the Grenada Revolution: Who Pushed First and Why?" in Jorge Heine, *A Revolution Aborted: The Lessons of Grenada* (Pittsburgh: University of Pittsburgh Press, 1990), p. 182.

defined terms.[49] The left in Nicaragua, and more broadly, throughout Latin America, emphasized the explanation centering on Washington's hostility toward economic and social change as well as the impact of Ronald Reagan's obsessive, primeval enmity toward the Central American left wing. Reagan himself, and more articulately and conceptually his advisers and supporters, tried repeatedly to establish a distinction between American hostility toward the Sandinistas as Soviet and Cuban surrogates, and American neutrality with regard to change in Nicaragua or anywhere else. This dichotomy was most explicitly—and perhaps most eloquently—formulated by the Henry Kissinger–chaired Presidential Commission on Central America:

> There is room in the hemisphere for differing forms of governance and different political economies. Authentically indigenous changes, and even indigenous revolutions are not incompatible with international harmony in the Americas. They are not incompatible even with the mutual security of the members of the inter-American system—if they are truly indigenous. . . . The Soviet-Cuban thrust to make Central America part of their geopolitical challenge is what has turned the struggle in Central America into a security and political problem for the United States. . . . Indigenous reform movements, even indigenous revolutions, are not themselves a security concern of the United States. History holds examples of genuinely popular revolutions, springing wholly from native roots. In this hemisphere Mexico is a clear example.[50]

But no matter how precise the formulation, the dichotomy remained abstract and partial. To begin with, there is an assimilation of origin and consequence in the reasoning: in many cases, initially homegrown revolutions or reforms *acquired* Soviet or Cuban support, on

---

49. The extent of the Reagan administration's efforts to overthrow the Sandinistas did not become fully public until the early 1990s. For example, the Robert Gates confirmation hearings in 1991 revealed a 1984 memorandum from Gates to then CIA chief William Casey calling for: "Withdrawing U.S. recognition from the Nicaraguan government in favor of a government in exile; overt provision of military assistance to that government, economic sanctions that could include a quarantine combined with internal measures by the resistance to maximize the economic dislocation to the regime [an apparent reference to sabotage]; the use of air strikes to destroy a considerable portion of Nicaragua's military buildup." "The Gates Hearings," *New York Times*, September 20, 1991, p. 14. If the difference between what American governments would *like* to do and what they actually carry out is an important one as seen from Washington or history, it is sometimes lost upon the victims.

50. *The Report of the President's National Bipartisan Commission on Central America* (New York: Macmillan, 1984), pp. 14, 100.

occasion as a consequence of American ostracism. In other cases, the Soviets and, more likely, the Cubans ignited a revolutionary movement that went nowhere, and that consequently was not a threat to the United States. The Kissinger report emphasized the question of origins: did revolution or reform *start out* as Soviet- or Cuban-inspired? The historical process itself, though, stressed the question of evolution and transformation: why did some "authentically indigenous" changes *become* "part of the Soviet-Cuban thrust"?[51]

Because of its rivalry with the Soviet Union, the United States had no choice but to be hostile to anti-U.S. nationalism in Latin America. This in turn led it to nearly always constitute a force in favor of the political, economic, and social status quo. The fact that this "tilt" also corresponded on many occasions to other interests in the U.S. just made it easier.

Yet if the United States was not free to act as it wanted—supposing it would have wanted to act otherwise—the Latin American left also suffered from severe restriction on its freedom of action. The Sandinistas were ideologically prone to pro-Sovietism, and their Cuban links as well as their anti-Americanism drove them in Moscow's direction. But the actual leeway the revolutionaries in Managua enjoyed in terms of stepping away from confrontation with Washington was not enormous. The number of times the *comandantes* seemed to be foolishly thumbing their nose at the U.S. on readily avoidable points of friction was deceiving: it was not that easy from them to retreat from contention and compromise with *el imperialismo yanqui*.

Specifically, on the issue of accepting American security concerns regarding the Soviet Union in hypothetical exchange for United States acquiescence to their revolutionary domestic program, the Sandinistas could not separate one from the other. They could not countenance the (relative) abdication of sovereignty that accepting limits on their "foreign policy" implied, even if the acceptance of those bounds had signified a quasi–blank check for revolution at home (which was not necessarily the case). One of the reasons for revolution—not necessar-

---

51. This line of reasoning also begs the following question: "Probably the most effective argument in favor of U.S. interference is that failure to counter Soviet interference yields the field to Communism. Thus, this argument requires U.S. leaders to counter Soviet involvement in Latin America where they find it. Among the difficulties of applying this strategy is that it has often been difficult in particular cases to determine whether or how the USSR has been interfering." Cole Blasier, *The Giant's Rival: The USSR and Latin America* (Pittsburgh: University of Pittsburgh Press, 1987), p. 185.

ily for the tens of thousands of Nicaraguan peasants, workers, and students who made the revolution, but rather for the far fewer Nicaraguans who led it—was precisely to win the right to thumb their nose at the United States after decades of domination, humiliation, and intervention: to do what they wanted, especially if Washington did not like it.[52]

In a bipolar world characterized by geopolitical confrontation with deep ideological connotations, anti-American nationalism inevitably favored the United States' enemy. If the United States opposed the Sandinistas because they became friends of its geopolitical enemy, the Sandinistas came to be allies and clients of the Soviet Union, Libya, and the PLO because they wanted to befriend the enemies of their enemy. Or, as a Mexican revolutionary from the twenties put it:

> Hostility to Washington easily translated into verbal support for the Soviet Union, according to the formula enunciated by a Mexican general in the early 1920s: "We are all Bolsheviks! I don't know what socialism is; but I am a Bolshevik, like all patriotic Mexicans. . . . The Yankees do not like the Bolsheviks; the Yankees are our enemies; therefore the Bolsheviks must be our friends, and we must be their friends. We are all Bolsheviks![53]

This was the inescapable, infernal logic of the Cold War. What made nationalist revolutions or reform movements in Latin America threatening or dangerous to the United States was, from the Kissinger perspective, the Cold War and the Soviet Union. In order for this to

---

52. One of the most frustrating and at the same time enlightening experiences the author has encountered over the years consisted in a few weeks spent helping the just installed Sandinista government to prepare for the Sixth Summit of Non-Aligned Heads of State in Havana in September 1979. The team of consultants assembled by the Nicaraguan Foreign Ministry emphasized the need—indeed the absolute imperative—for the Sandinista delegation to get as little involved as possible in the internecine struggles within the nonaligned movement, particularly in the conflict between the Cubans and the Yugoslavians over the direction and soul of the movement. The team also insisted—more strongly—on the importance of Nicaragua not supporting positions that would needlessly antagonize the United States, for example, regarding the Middle East. Similar advice was given to the Sandinista delegation at the Havana summit by other friendly governments—chiefly Mexico—to no avail. The comandantes seized every occasion to incur American wrath and systematically supported the most strident option at every juncture. While their debts to the Cubans and to Yasser Arafat were not foreign to this penchant, much of this was of their own volition. The author, the Mexicans, and many other friends and sympathizers of the Sandinistas missed the point: the revolutionaries wanted to defy the Americans, not worry about or accommodate them. With time this would pass, but the initial effects were disconcerting.

53. Gleijeses, op. cit., p. 178, quoting M. N. Roy's Memoirs (Bombay: Allied Publishers, 1964), p. 154.

change, one of three conditions had to be met: either revolutions or left-of-center reformist movements in Latin America desisted from their nationalism, or they redirected it against someone else, or the Soviet Union disappeared. The first two options were impractical: the left could not avoid being nationalistic, and there was no other power to direct this sentiment against. The last option, the most unreal, unthinkable, and unlikely to occur, did occur. The disappearance of the Soviet Union has eliminated the problem, erasing the Kissinger dilemma and granting the Latin American left an opportunity to re-define its nationalism.

10

Reformulating Nationalism: Longitudinally and Regionally

■

Because nation-building in Latin America is incomplete, and the cause of social change inseparable from redeeming the nation for the "people," the left in Latin America has no choice but to remain nationalistic. The goal of constructing nations to which millions of excluded Latin Americans (the overwhelming majority of the population, in contrast to Western Europe and North America, where the excluded exist but represent a minority) can belong is as valid and urgent as ever. And much of the left's nationalism will continue to be directed towards the United States, as it lingers awhile as the sole great power in the region or the world and new shapes of and reasons for American involvement in the hemisphere replace old ones. But as the parameters and definition of the nation under construction change, the way in which that nationalism must also evolve has yet to be determined. Before proposing a new nationalism for the left, it is worth examining how the traditional trappings of U.S. intervention, which underpinned much of the region's nationalism and many of the conflicts of the past fifty years, are replaced by other, newer forms.

In the immediate aftermath of the Cold War's conclusion, a substitute for anti-Sovietism in the United States' policy toward Latin America rapidly emerged: drug enforcement and, to a lesser but growing extent, immigration. After the evil (Soviet-Communist) empire to the east, the evil (drug-producing, migrant-generating) slum to the south.[1]

---

1. The other, better though perhaps excessively European metaphor that has been used appears in the title of one of the more insightful books written on the North-South

As American national security is redefined in the post–Cold War era, new links are established between instability, change, and certain policies in Latin America, and their effects on U.S. welfare. While the causal relationship between revolution (or reform) and drugs or immigration is not evident or simple, it can be theoretically, albeit convolutedly, posited, as in the cases of Peru and Colombia.

The emergence of drugs as an important facet of U.S. policy in the region did not start with the thaw in East-West relations. Drug enforcement had played a significant role in U.S. policy toward Mexico, the Andean countries, Colombia, and Cuba for a number of years. And that role had already been sharply "interventionist," providing pretexts and motivations for United States involvement in the domestic affairs of many Latin American nations. This was the rationale for the longstanding presence of Drug Enforcement Administration agents in Mexico, and also for new forms of highly intrusive cooperation (including counterinsurgency).

The most disquieting trend in this respect may well have been the argument whereby Washington affirmed the unilateral right to prosecute individuals beyond U.S. national jurisdiction. There was a precedent in American purported counterterrorist actions in the Middle East, and the extension of U.S. law beyond American borders. The United States would use whatever means were necessary to bring to justice whomever it considered a criminal, no matter where the suspect was found or his or her political or diplomatic status. It followed that international conventions, principles of common law, and foreign legislation and judicial systems were all superseded by U.S. authority.

The February 28, 1990, decision by the Supreme Court in *United States* v. *Urquídez Verdugo* established a legal precedent in this regard. Chief Justice William H. Rehnquist and five other justices ruled that search and seizure operations conducted abroad by U.S. law enforcement agents, military personnel, or other government agencies against foreigners should not be restricted by the provisions of the Fourth Amendment of the Constitution. Thus the Court determined that con-

---

question in the aftermath of the Cold War: Jean-Christophe Rufin's *L'Empire et les Nouveaux Barbares* (Paris: Editions JC Lattès, 1991). The metaphor states: "The ideological revolution occurring in Rome after the fall of Carthage is comparable to that which today has substituted the East-West confrontation with a world dominated by a North-South opposition. . . . Yes, a new unification of the North is possible, by defining its values by their opposites, by that which runs contrary to them or threatens them. The emergence of the South in the role of the new barbarians achieves this goal. . . . This is the pact: on one side, security for the North, a form of eternity, and on the other, the simple abandonment of justice." Pp. 13, 18, 208.

stitutional rights meant to protect Americans from the abuses of power of their government were not applicable to foreigners abroad.

Simultaneously, the Justice Department issued an internal legal opinion authorizing its agents acting abroad to abduct foreigners in order to bring them to trial in the U.S.[2] The document, drafted by Attorney General William Barr, stated that the President and the attorney general had the "inherent constitutional power" to order the capture of fugitives abroad. It affirmed that "the extraterritorial enforcement of United States laws is becoming increasingly important in order to protect vital national interests."[3]

This policy was first applied in two nearly simultaneous cases: the 1989 invasion of Panama and subsequent arrest of Manuel Antonio Noriega, and the kidnapping of Dr. Humberto Alvarez Machain in Mexico in February of that same year. Alvarez Machain was abducted from his home in Guadalajara by bounty hunters contracted by the Drug Enforcement Administration, which wanted him brought to trial for his presumed involvement in the 1985 torture and murder of DEA agent Enrique Camarena in Mexico. Although Washington's explicit participation in the Alvarez Machain case was initially less evident than in Noriega's, Attorney General Richard Thornburgh's statements and actions clarified the Justice Department's stand on the issue. When a federal judge in Los Angeles ruled that Alvarez Machain's kidnapping violated the U.S.-Mexican Extradition Treaty and ordered him set free, the department took the case to the Supreme Court. In June 1992 the Court ruled in the Bush administration's favor, and against Alvarez Machain, Urquídez Verdugo, and the Mexican government, legalizing their abduction and just about anyone's, in the opinion of many legal scholars. Alvarez Machain was freed and returned to Mexico in December 1992 after the judge presiding over his case ruled there was insufficient evidence to present to the jury for deliberation. But the issue was not laid to rest; behind the Noriega affair and the Alvarez Machain case lay the same reasoning: limitations on other nations' sovereignty and the extraterritorial extension of U.S. law enforcement capability and justice were deemed valid practices in the war against drugs.[4]

---

2. The Mexican Foreign Ministry requested a clarification from the United States regarding the Supreme Court ruling and the Executive's interpretation. No reply was ever made public; there may well have never been a reply at all. For the effects of the *Urquídez Verdugo* ruling for Mexico and Latin America, see Adolfo Aguilar Zinser, *Siempre!*, March 29, 1990.

3. Washington *Post*, August 14, 1991.

4. One analyst linked the principle of extraterritoriality to the Noriega affair from the very beginning. "The administration also moved to make 'hardball' legal. At the

Many believed that American insistence on drug enforcement was simply a disguise for further U.S. domination. A Washington *Post/* ABC News poll taken in February 1990 in Colombia showed that 65 percent of those interviewed "suspect the drug war is a U.S. attempt to control their government."[5] But only with the coming of the drug age in American domestic politics and the elimination of other ideological justifications for U.S. policy in Latin America did drugs acquire their full importance in hemispheric relations. Although the Bush administration paid lip service to the principle of parity between supply and demand as the drug crisis's root cause, supply-directed policies were easier, cheaper, and more popular, though undeniably less effective.

It was no accident that the Panama invasion was at least subliminally presented as a drug-motivated action and that its popularity in the United States—in addition to Noriega's own villainous image—was due largely to the perception of Noriega as a drug dealer. The first U.S. intervention in Latin America without Cold War packaging was also the first attempt by the United States to justify the use of force abroad on the grounds of drug enforcement. There were sufficient other examples to prove conclusively that drugs had become far more than simply another item on the inter-American agenda. These instances ranged from sending U.S. military detachments to Bolivia in 1987 to the escalation of the DEA presence in the Upper Huallaga Valley in Peru.[6] They included the construction of a second base and the signing of U.S.-Peruvian military agreements with a joint drug enforcement,

---

Justice Department, Assistant Attorney General William P. Barr asserted that U.S. law enforcement officers could make an arrest in a foreign country even if the foreign government did not grant permission. Barr and other officials explained that such powers were necessary to combat narco-traffickers and terrorists. . . . To some legislators, Barr's claim represented a dramatic and dangerous change in policy and was nothing less than a license to kidnap. . . . Representative Don Edwards (D-California) said: 'I can think of no law passed by the Congress or any provision of the Constitution that licenses the United States to be an international outlaw.' " Kevin Buckley, *Panama: The Whole Story* (New York: Simon and Schuster, 1991), p. 221.

5. *Newsweek* (Latin American edition), February 19, 1990.

6. According to one critical source: "[Given the limits established by the Pentagon on U.S. troop involvement] the U.S. military involvement in the drug war in the Andes is expanding sharply. The administration has approved plans . . . for a host of new drug-related activities in the Andes. In recognition of the increasingly diffuse and flexible cocaine trade, the plans foresee expanded U.S. military operational support for security forces in Central America and the rest of South America. . . . The military component of the Andean strategy is historically, doctrinally and operationally linked to U.S. counterinsurgency strategy." Washington Office on Latin America, "Clear and Present Dangers: The U.S. Military and the War on Drugs in the Andes," Washington, D.C., October 1991, pp. 21, 43.

counterinsurgency focus, the growing militarization of the Southwest U.S.–Mexican border and the enhanced role of U.S. armed forces in patrolling the Caribbean drug routes.[7]

Immigration has not yet achieved the same urgency or implications, and the absence of a domestic consensus in the United States leaves open the possibility that it might not ever attain such levels of import. In addition, its emotional impact is not yet in the same league as drugs. Nevertheless, as the effects of two significant trends of the 1980s began to bite, immigration was likely to acquire significant foreign policy implications. The unintended effects of the 1986 U.S. Immigration Reform and Control Act and the fully foreseeable consequences of ten years of Latin American economic stagnation—extensive unemployment, falling wages, and the ensuing mass exodus to the north—began to make themselves felt in the 1990s.

Widespread and continuing documentation of undocumented aliens rapidly emerged as one of the most important and immediate impacts of the Simpson-Rodino Immigration Bill. As a result of the law's amnesty and family reunification provisions, together with other mechanisms and the special agricultural worker clauses that permitted the legal entry of individuals previously employed in the harvest of perishable agricultural produce, nearly 3 million formerly undocumented Mexicans regularized their migratory status.

Similarly, ten years of economic stagnation in Latin America, coupled with the "new," fashionable free-market policies that included low real wages as a major competitive advantage, contributed to maintaining or increasing the magnitude of the flow north, not only from Mexico but from many other countries. For years, Mexican and American researchers had been compiling data showing that the single most important contributing factor to immigration—illegal or not—was the wage differential.[8] The unemployed do not emigrate: they lack the

---

7. The extent to which this process evoked memories of previous forms of American intervention was highlighted in a *Newsweek International* investigative report published at the outset of 1992, "The Newest War": "A two-month *Newsweek* inquiry has documented a Pentagon drug war, parts of it secret, that has quietly escalated to dimensions greater than most Americans yet realize. It involves thousands of U.S. and Latin troops, at a cost of more than a billion dollars per year." *Newsweek International*, January 13, 1992, pp. 6–11.

8. According to an oft-quoted American study of Mexican migration, in Los Altos de Jalisco (a strong emigration-generating area for nearly 100 years) in 1976, 77 percent of interviewed migrants stated that the main reason for leaving Mexico was to improve their income; only 9 percent gave unemployment as a reason. Wayne Cornelius, "Mexican Migration to the United States: Causes, Consequences, and U.S. Responses," Center for International Studies, Massachusetts Institute of Technology, Cambridge, Mass.,

money to pay the cost of doing so. Those who leave tend to be individuals who already have jobs, either in rural areas, or, more frequently today, in large cities, and who choose to leave them in search of higher wages elsewhere. As long as the wage differential between the United States and Mexico, for example, averaged roughly eight to one, enterprising young Mexicans of all social strata were going to continue their trek north. In 1990 the Mexican minimum wage was 55 cents an hour, whereas its counterpart in California, where fully half of all undocumented Mexican immigrants make their home, was $4.75 an hour. Similarly, a tenured university professor in Mexico, Brazil, or Argentina, with a Ph.D. and recognized publications, took home at most $1,000 per month in the early nineties (and often much less), yet could often make between $5,000 and $6,000 or more per month, after taxes, in a major American university.

As the consequences of these trends took hold, reasons became stronger for fearing that immigration would occupy a growing role in U.S. foreign policy toward migration-generating countries, as opposed to being a domestic issue with sporadic, secondary foreign implications. If immigration began to be perceived as a significant threat to U.S. welfare, national security (defined, inevitably, in a new sense), and even national identity, the same causes could well produce analogous effects. The problem's roots would again be found abroad and hypothetical solutions would increasingly be localized in countries of origin. The United States had already pressured Mexico with regard to so-called third-country immigration, that is, the transit of undocumented emigrants from Central America, South America, and Asia through Mexico to the United States. It also demanded that several Central American nations be more forthcoming in deterring migratory flows north by controlling highways, airports, train stations, and bus terminals, to hold the line as far south as possible, with each country limiting migration from its neighbor to the south, whatever the domestic costs. If Latin authorities prove unwilling or unable to comply, intrusive U.S. cooperation could follow.

For these reasons, and for all of the deeper, more historical ones outlined above, the left's updating cannot involve discarding the nationalist agenda or forsaking the nation-building tasks that are still pending. More than ever today, the social situation in Latin America resembles the type of "social apartheid" pattern that constitutes the

---

1978 (mimeo). According to a Mexican and an American expert, "The determining factor [in migration] is the difference between the wages that Mexican workers receive in the two countries." Manuel García y Griego and Mónica Verea, *México y Estados Unidos frente a la migración de los indocumentados* (Mexico City: UNAM, 1988), p. 56.

very antithesis of nation-building: the gap between rich and poor, whites and others, included and excluded, is greater than at any time in the past twenty years, and getting worse. At the same time the temptations and pressures from abroad on Latin authorities to step away from the nationalist stances of the past are also more intense than before. The need to secure scarce funding, to appear responsible and "mature," and to conform to post-Marxist, postsocialist globalization fads are all powerful constraints, forcing sensible politicians from the center and right-of-center into antinationalist stances they would not otherwise adhere to.[9] Both motives—the yawning domestic chasms in Latin American society, and the "denationalization" of elites—are powerful incentives for the left to retain a nationalism so unfashionable in these times, yet so necessary.

The conclusion of the Cold War means the cloture of a certain form of United States anti-Communism in Latin America. This in turn implies that the nationalist stances and policies that Latin America may devise and sustain will not propagate the type of excessive reaction in the United States that tended to occur in the past. In particular, such developments open the way for an affirmation of sovereignty in areas that are fundamental to Latin America (and to any country), while at the same time not infringing upon the type of economic relationships that the transformation of the world economy is undoubtedly provoking. Thus the first chapter of the left's new nationalism must be the restatement and assertion of sovereignty on issues involving domestic noneconomic affairs. The left should strive to oppose the new forms of intervention that run contrary to its principles, while accepting new commitments to abide by international standards on issues that are consonant with those principles. It should continue to reject any foreign involvement in drug enforcement, immigration control, and extraterritorial law enforcement of any sort. But conversely, the left should embrace the notion that on matters such as human rights, the

---

9. An interesting example of how this paradoxical process unfolded in the early nineties emerges from a *New York Times* account of a visit to Capitol Hill by Peruvian president Alberto Fujimori in September 1991. House of Representatives Western Hemisphere Sub-Committee chairman Robert Torricelli was quoted as saying: "Peru is a nation facing an almost complete security, economic and health collapse. . . . Fujimori represents a real balance between the legitimate interests of the United States and his own people." In the midst of collapse, for an elected leader to be qualified as striking a "balance" between the interests of his people and those of another power is a remarkable situation, particularly since those who elected him did not do so for him to represent, even only partly, the interests of that other power. Governments have fallen for less reason than this in Latin America; in the post–Cold War days, times had obviously changed. *New York Times*, September 24, 1991, p. A3.

environment, labor rights and consumer protection, and the monitoring of clean elections, international obligations and cooperation enhance nation-building, not the other way around. This mixed, more principled, and at the same time more pragmatic stance becomes possible.

Yet changes such as these solve neither the question of unfinished national construction in Latin America, the issue of continuing forms of U.S. intervention in the hemisphere, nor the problem of greater constraints placed on Latin American sovereignty and autonomy by international economic factors. These can range from actual stringent requirements to obtain substantial if costly and ephemeral funding, to the ideological constraint of having to conform to fashionable ideologies or policies in order to qualify for always disappointing volumes of resources.[10]

Likewise, the ongoing relevance of nationalism to the left's agenda does not address the question of the type of nationalism or the translation into policy of a broader nationalist aspiration in the post–Cold War, post-Marxist world. Crafting a new nationalist response is one of the chief challenges the left must face today. Needless to say, that challenge can only be met over time and across the hemisphere. But certain ideas or general trends can be sketched out here. The left's "new nationalism" has to be reformed in two directions: with regard to whom it is targeted against, and in the institutional level or tier from which it emanates.

The first point, that different sectors of the left have discovered often intuitively in recent years, is that directing nationalist passions or policies toward the United States is a contradictory affair. There is almost always someone, or a given political sector in the United States, opposed to his or her government's policy and far more supportive of a Latin American aspiration than of a U.S. one. This unconscious, superficial sensation has rarely led to a more conceptual approach. It is high time it did, as conditions for it seem uncommonly favorable at the end of the Cold War.[11] Although this overhaul of Latin American nationalism must by no means be limited to

---

10. Less than a month after an attempted coup that nearly toppled him, Venezuelan president Carlos Andrés Perez made the following confession: "The economic reforms [I have implemented] were done partly as a result of pressure from international lending agencies." He made this statement to a group of external advisers (headed by Henry Kissinger) who strongly urged him to persevere in his free-market policies. *La Jornada* (Mexico City), March 22, 1992, front page.

11. An initial attempt to devise such an approach, not for the left in particular but for Mexican policy in general, can be found in Jorge G. Castañeda, "La larga marcha de la politica exterior de México," *Nexos* (Mexico City), no. 101, April 1986, reprinted in Castañeda, *México: El futuro en juego* (Mexico City: Joaquín Mortiz Editores, 1987).

the United States and should extend to Western Europe and elsewhere, particularly in view of the older ties between the Latin American left and European socialists, it is inevitably centered on the U.S. What follows must be read as an indication of what the left must accomplish in relation to the world as a whole, but the emphasis here is placed on the United States.

It has been a long time since U.S. politics stopped at the water's edge. At least from the Vietnam War onward, various segments of American public opinion have adopted differing or opposing viewpoints with respect to those of their government on various foreign policy issues. Once a distinct stance has been adopted, the next step, i.e., fighting to convert it into government policy, or at least attempting to change the prevailing, contrary course, has been only a matter of time. Since Jane Fonda's trip to Hanoi, but undoubtedly more often and significantly since then, other countries and slices of the political spectrum outside the United States have enjoyed access to American support and sympathy of diverse sincerity and conviction, expediency and opportunism.

In the case of the Latin American left, although Fidel Castro unearthed several American politicians and intellectuals critical of U.S. policy toward Cuba and its revolution during the sixties and seventies, the convergence of sensibilities stopped there. While the Cuban Interest Section in the U.S. capital was on occasion adept at "working Washington," it was selling such "unwanted goods" that it rarely made much headway. The Cuban interface with Washington never transcended itself, failing to become a true alliance with specific goals, tactics to achieve them, and a strategy to frame them. No change of U.S. policy on Cuba was perceived as likely or realistic as late as 1992—and in consequence there was scant margin for an alliance. The Chilean left and center-left also underwent a similar experience, although greater skill and sensitivity on the part of the Chileans, and the existence of at least minimal stakes in the United States, justified the effort.

But the advent of Ronald Reagan and the antipathy he evoked in many liberal American quarters, together with the sympathy the Sandinista Revolution initially awakened in many grass roots, semi-left-wing circles, laid the ground for a much clearer convergence and the beginnings of an alliance, if only of convenience. During the 1980s it was clear to the Sandinistas that "Washington," the "United States," "*el imperialismo americano,*" and even "*el yanqui, enemigo de la humanidad*" was a far more heterogeneous and double-edged notion than originally suspected. The most important opposition to Reagan's

support for the contras originated in the United States itself. It included liberals and church groups, left-wing *"sandalistas"* (the name
given to American and Western European radicals who traveled to
Central America in search of the perfect revolution), and middle-of-
the-roaders mobilized by their respect for the rule of law and outraged
by Reagan's neglect of it, whatever their opinion of the Sandinistas.
The Sandinistas learned to "work Washington," and though they were
never as skilled at it, or as conspiratorial in forging alliances with such
strange bedfellows as former House Speaker Jim Wright or Connecti-
cut senator Christopher Dodd as the Reagan administration charged,
they achieved a great deal.[12] Mainly, they understood that the most
effective ally, if not the most reliable friend, that practically anyone in
Latin America with a U.S. agenda could seek was to be found within
the United States.

A similar convergence, and much more rewarding alliance, was
slowly established by the Salvadorean left—all shapes and sizes mixed
together. Again, the ties in question were much less intimate and
collusive than many conservatives in Washington imagined. CISPES,
or the Committee in Solidarity with the People of El Salvador, was
undoubtedly linked closely to the FMLN, and its positions were much
more sympathetic a priori to the Salvadorean insurgents than independently arrived at. But CISPES itself was only a small part of a much
broader coalition, or more accurately, of a wider area of encounter,
convergence, and occasional common effort. The radius of this circle
stretched from influencing the U.S. Congress's votes on aid to El Salvador to prosecuting Salvadorean death squad members for the mur-
ders, diversely, of American nuns, local Jesuits, or human rights
activists.

Other activities included fund-raising, securing access to the U.S.
media, and building bridges between the Salvadorean left and that part
of the U.S. establishment that would have any truck with it. They also
extended to organizing encounters between guerrilla leaders and American members of the foreign policy elite, the most important of which
was perhaps the one organized by former American ambassador to El
Salvador Robert White and his International Center for Development
Policy, in Cocoyoc, Mexico, in July of 1989. They paved the way for the
exchanges that began to take place between the Bush administration
and the FMLN in 1992.

---

12. Alan Fiers, a former CIA official and a key witness in the Iran-Contra trials was
quoted by the *New York Times* on September 20, 1991 as testifying that conversations
between Sandinista leaders and Democratic members of the U.S. Congress were tapped
by the CIA. *A tout seigneur, tout honneur.*

The Salvadorean left—like the Sandinistas before it, and like, somewhat later, Cuauhtémoc Cárdenas's involvement in the Free Trade debate in the United States and Canada—thus began, in practice, to redefine the profiles and contours of the left's new nationalism. On a higher plane of abstraction, this nationalism had to be premised on one fundamental assumption. While there undeniably did exist an American central government and all the fragmentation of power in the world could not water down its existence and its capacity to greatly affect the destinies of most Latin American countries and people, the U.S. political system did provide a large margin of action to those who wanted to take their case to the American public.

Sometimes the "natural" ally of the Latin American left would be the "liberal" faction of the establishment and its friends in the media, academia, Hollywood, and Washington. These interlocutors were more powerful and entrenched in American society and politics than others, but they were generally less involved in the substance of issues and more fickle in their friendship. On other occasions only the grass roots groups in the U.S. would prove willing to establish close ties with certain sectors of the left in Latin America: church activists, human rights groups, radical environmentalists, progressive faculty—in sum, the solidarity network. This faction was usually more devoted and loyal but less influential, although at the margin it could wield considerable power. At other stages still, U.S. labor, mainstream environmental organizations, and consumer associations would become the logical interlocutors for the Latin American left in the United States: this was the case of the "fair-trade" type of coalition that developed between Canadian, American, and Mexican groups in the course of the early 1990s free-trade negotiations.

What this all meant was that the fault line for left-wing nationalism in Latin America should not run between the United States and the nations of the hemisphere, but rather across them. The new, "longitudinal" nationalism of the left should not be directed against the United States, but against specific policies put in practice by the U.S. government and deemed pernicious to the national interests of a given country in the region. The goal of the new nationalism, then, lay not in opposing the United States but in building coalitions in the United States, as well as domestically, in favor of certain policies and against others. It is less "attitudinal," and more policy-oriented.

As the effects of the end of the Cold War continue to make themselves felt, there will undoubtedly be fewer Americans willing to tolerate many of the traditional tenets of their country's policies toward

Latin America.[13] As the left engages in debate, confrontation, and the search for convergences with diverse interlocutors in the United States, it will find that people in a growing number of walks of American life will be willing to listen, sometimes agree, and on occasion, put a shoulder to the wheel. And, as the fall of socialism and the disappearance of a Communist or Soviet threat to American (in)security has its effect and the costs of winning the Cold War come to the fore, the political center of gravity in the United States will in all likelihood shift. It will surely bring more and, most importantly, different sectors in contact with the policies and attitudes that affect Latin America. Regardless of whether time brings greater involvement or growing indifference on the part of the United States as a whole in relation to Latin America, it is safe to say that there will always be sufficient room to move in and interest to work upon. Granted, the margin of maneuver will always be contradictory and subject to severe constraints that could easily shatter inordinate expectations. Americans will always have their own priorities, which is as it should be as long as politics in the world remain essentially national in nature. Whoever has attempted to forge a lasting bond with a U.S. member of Congress or the editor of an American news organization cannot be too cynical or enthusiastic about their loyalty and attention span. The Latin American left should head for Washington and the heartland with its eyes wide open and scant illusions. But that is the landfall it should seek.

Since, as most of the left and a good portion of the right have traditionally thought, many of the most important decisions affecting Latin America are made in Washington, then that is where the left should leave its mark. It should lobby, speak, write, and study in the United States, as it has already begun to do. The number of visits by leftists of all persuasions to U.S. campuses, editorial boards, Committees on Foreign Relations, radio talk shows, and ethnic neighborhoods is rising exponentially. It is both fitting and expected that two of the smallest nations in the hemisphere, Nicaragua and El Salvador, because they were among the most affected, and the two largest, Brazil

13. Some scholars link the end of the Cold War with the development of an "internationalized politics . . . i.e., the involvement of international organizations, foreign states and internationally based nongovernmental groups in the so-called domestic politics of a country. . . . There has been a significant broadening of the types and number of groups penetrating Latin American societies. . . . Classic types have been joined by a wide range of advocacy groups, non-governmental organizations and international agencies. These . . . organizations have formed what has been called an 'issue network.' " Douglas Chalmers, "The Internationalized Politics of Institution Building in Latin America," paper presented at a Joint Conference of the Institute of Latin American Studies (Columbia University) and the Centro de Estudios sobre América, Havana, July 4, 1992.

and Mexico, because of their very size, were where the left first and most vigorously began to forge this new nationalism. For example, Lula took his 1989 Brazilian presidential campaign to New York and Washington in the spring of that year: a blue-collar worker from Pernambuco and the suburbs of São Paulo discussed economic policy with the notables of the U.S. Council of Foreign Relations.

Later, the poorest nation in the hemisphere also got involved: when overthrown Haitian president Jean-Bertrand Aristide saw his attempts to return to office endangered by American indifference, he "took his case directly to the American people,"[14] benefiting from two specific strong suits the Haitian left had going for it in the United States: the large Haitian immigrant community and Aristide's Church connections, both of which allowed him to organize meetings, speeches, and travel across the United States. Other leaders of the left enjoyed these same connections, or others: Cárdenas relied on a powerful Michoacán community in California and Washington State; the FMLN, on the large Salvadorean community in Washington, D.C., Los Angeles, and San Francisco, together with its Jesuit contacts between the Universidad Centroamericana and the Society of Jesus in the United States. Even Sendero Luminoso had its supporters among some Peruvian émigrés. And the Sandinistas benefited from similar associations with other religious orders.

The left must sustain and intensify its efforts to build American constituencies for change in the hemisphere. They are decisive when the left is out of power and seeking to equalize the conditions whereby it competes—respect for human rights, election monitoring, a free press, union and labor rights, etc. These American alliances are equally or more significant when the left is in power, becoming bulwarks for the type of social and economic change it wishes to accomplish, and that cannot be carried out without support *in* Washington, if not support *from* Washington. These constituencies are not necessarily identical to each other, and on occasion they run at cross-purposes. The best way to lobby the International Monetary Fund or the World Bank is not necessarily through solidarity groups, grass roots Church activists, and American left-wing academic faculty. However, these pillars of support are indispensable if the left in Latin America is to succeed in governing. Not only must it not blame Washington for failing, but it must ensure that political and cultural forces in the United States contribute emphatically to its success.

Latin American networking with the United States is not new, of

---

14. Barbara Crossette, *New York Times*, March 10, 1992.

course. The military, the business community, academics, and the new, business-school and economics-educated technocracies of the hemisphere have been pursuing it for some time. The left lagged behind largely because it was a prisoner of its traditional outlook: if the enemy was the United States as country and monolith, its citizens, while not all enemies, could hardly become allies other than at a purely personal level. Thus networking of this sort is new for the left, because in practice it implies a totally different mind-set. The United States as an all-encompassing, uniformly and universally evil entity becomes unthinkable once parts of it become valuable allies in any given endeavor.

The entire nationalist issue becomes vertical, following a North-South axis, rather than horizontal, dividing entire nations. On many clear-cut issues regarding the defense of national sovereignty—American intervention, drugs, immigration—groups, governments, or organizations of the left will discover that they have more in common with many sectors of the United States than with groups or elements in their own countries. And on many social, economic, environmental, and human rights issues, they will find that their interlocutors in the United States, from the grass roots to Capitol Hill, can be more firm and loyal backers than domestic interests that, more often than not, will in fact be their enemies. Evidently this means opening up to the rest of the world: the Latin American cannot seek to influence Washington politics, in alliance with myriad American groups, without accepting that this gives many foreign entities a lever and a right to sway Latin politics. Likewise, the left will have to understand that this different type of nationalist politics entails outside oversight and accountability, sometimes against a government's will. But the left cannot have its enchilada and eat it too.

A refashioning of Latin American nationalism can find encouragement in a trend that resembles what has been described above, but is nonetheless a distinct process. This is what has been called the birth of global civil society, which acquired considerable relevance at the 1992 Rio de Janeiro Earth Summit. The proliferation of nongovernmental organizations that took place in Latin America in recent years has been matched and outpaced in fact by a similar phenomenon throughout the world. NGOs in Europe, North America, and, to a lesser extent, in Asia have become increasingly active and have begun to network across the globe. In this way, on issues such as the environment and human rights, but also in broader economic policy matters, a emerging web of groups and relationships has been woven across borders and traditional, state-to-state international relations.

As one advocate and scholar of these trends has noted, the process involves:

> exertions of influence on state and market forces that will produce a degree of voluntary restructuring of international relations and the existence, in rudimentary but evolving form, of an ensemble of norms, actors, tactics, identities that underpins international relations with a reality that can be called international civil society.[15]

Groups such as Greenpeace, Amnesty International, and the Brandt, Palme, Brundtlandt, and Nyeyere-South commissions are all examples of this emerging process. While it should not be overstated or idealized in terms of its strength or representativity, something along the lines of an international civil society is beginning to come forth, and the Latin American left, which has been part of this process, should support it and find encouragement in it, even if on occasion it involves sovereignty loss or implies forging alliances with groups from the North whose motivations are impeccably honest but who do not necessarily control the effects of their intentions. If the South is coming North in so many ways, and if—as many authors, politicians, and poets believe—the key to change in the South, and specifically in Latin America, lies in change in the U.S., the left from the South should look and, whenever possible, head North.

•

This cross-cutting, longitudinal nationalism, emphasizing causes and their natural allies more than permanent enmities and immutable goals, dovetails neatly with the second facet of what the left's new nationalism should consist of. Economists can argue endlessly—and they do—about whether the post–Cold War world is breaking up into trade blocs (probably not), and whether regionalism and economic integration is the wave of the present and future.[16] But in Latin America,

---

15. Richard Falk, "New Dimensions in International Relations and the Birth of Global Civil Society," paper presented at the Nobel Jubilee Symposia, Oslo, December 8–9, 1992, p. 2.

16. "The recent discussion of regionalism ['The world is fragmenting into rival trading blocs'] has serious flaws. First . . . it has rested on a view of underlying trade patterns that is highly misleading. Under several different definitions of the relevant regions, interregional trade is growing as fast or faster than intra-regional trade. . . . A second point is that the discussion of regionalization has tended to overlook the status of the United States as, in effect, a member of several regions at the same time. . . . A third weakness is that the discussion has been focused on trade issues, ignoring the growing internationalization of investment flows. . . . Finally, a number of studies have placed

after years of failures, disappointments and formalism, certain serious efforts at regional integration are finally under way.[17]

The left, while mostly opposing attempts to develop forms of economic integration with richer, industrialized nations, should take up the banner of regional economic integration in general, and of a certain type in particular. It should do so because regional integration represents an intermediate solution between a largely unsustainable status quo and a highly harmful progression toward the dissolution of sovereignties and economic and social options for the developing nations. This maiming of the latter's national autonomy is occurring through their subordinate inclusion in wealthy nations' economic spheres of influence, at a juncture when the rivalries and conflicts between the great powers have not yet acquired a paradigmatic, ideological connotation. Conserving the nation-state as the prime area of economic activity appears impossible; joining one of the three large economic spheres of influence at a time of great flux and under conditions of gaping disparities and overwhelming weakness cannot be a desirable option, even if some resignedly accept it. Regional economic integration is a halfway house that possesses intrinsic merits and is preferable to existing alternatives. It can be either a lasting solution or a stepping-stone to a better world, when it arrives.

Mercosur in the Southern Cone (uniting Brazil, Argentina, Uruguay, and Paraguay, and soon Bolivia), the reborn Central American Common Market, and the Colombian-Venezuelan economic integration process are all regional initiatives that the left should not only support, but take the lead in promoting and strengthening, as long as they meet a number of conditions and are steered in a certain direction. There are various reasons for doing so. To begin with, the left should encourage these processes because in many cases—with the possible exceptions of Brazil, Mexico, and Argentina—there is a problem of economic viability among many Latin American nations. Even regarding the "big three," it is unclear whether under conditions of economic globalization, single nations with one currency, one market, a national business community, and an autonomous economic policy are viable propositions. Continental integration could be such a slow and ardu-

---

too much weight on the role of political decisions in structuring trade flows." Albert Fishlow and Stephen Haggard, "The United States and the Regionalization of the World Economy," Research Programme on Globalization and Regionalization, OECD, Paris, January 1992 (mimeo), p. 13.

17. The first Latin American trade grouping, the Latin American Free Trade Association (or ALALC) was founded in 1960. It died a silent death in 1982, never having amounted to much.

ous process that it would implicitly postpone any real enlargement of economic space almost indefinitely. On the contrary, regional economic integration broadens markets, provides economies of scale, enhances regional autonomy, and concentrates trade and investment among equals, diverting it from other, far more economically powerful partners.

There is a trade-off involved: more economic relationships among equals slows the pace of technological advancement and could deter foreign investment and curtail competition and modernization induced from abroad. But as worldwide competition increases with or without trading pacts, and now that the transfer of technology is possible from many sources, it would seem that the benefits of greater economic exchange among equals outweigh the disadvantages of restricting flows with unequals.

Moreover, the trade-off today is not between integration and economic stagnation but rather between integration among (relative) equals and the integration of small fish with bigger ones. The three groups mentioned, even in the case of a refurbished Central American Common Market with the hypothetical inclusion of Mexico and the Caribbean, are economic integration strategies among essentially equal partners. That is their strength and their weakness: because they are relatively equal, their economies are not terribly complementary; but because of their similarities, few nations can truly impose their will on others. Brazil is the exception. Even Mexico would have found itself in a stronger negotiating stand when it decided to seek a free-trade agreement with the United States had it pursued a policy of regional economic integration previously; it didn't, partly because of the wars of Central America and political divergence, partly because the country's powers-that-be were unconvinced.

At the same time, the formation of these regional groupings protects nations from the more intrusive, potentially damaging integration processes being proposed by the United States, which essentially boil down to opening local markets to American exports and concentrating trade with the least competitive of the world's trading zones. This does not mean that Latin American integration should be based exclusively on import substitution industrialization (ISI), as it was in the past. As we shall see, the question of trade liberalization versus protectionism has been framed incorrectly. Regional economic integration in Latin America today can be different both from ISI integration of the distant past and from Reagan-Bush free-trade dogma of the recent past and lingering present.

President Bush's Enterprise for the Americas Initiative rested on three singularly slender pillars: investment promotion (without tax subsidies), aid via debt reduction (along Brady Plan lines), and the elimination of trade barriers (essentially already low tariffs). It demanded in return large-scale trade liberalization in Latin America, foreign investment regime reform, and privatization. According to two American economists, "The underlying bargain in the Bush initiative appears to exchange relatively small amounts of new money for quite substantial policy reforms."[18] The reciprocity on the part of the United States with regard to trade and the static gains arising from free trade between many Latin American nations and the United States are both small. Most Latin American exports to the United States enter under low or nonexistent tariffs,[19] and most nontariff barriers are not really included in free-trade agreements, as the Mexican and Canadian precedents tend to prove. Moreover, with regard to dynamic gains—i.e., investment and credit from the United States and third countries, as well as ensuing increases in exports—the outlook is also mixed. As for policy reform, this is a synonym for policy convergence with what has been called the "Washington consensus":[20] a list of instructions derived from the perceived workings of the American economy that has not proved in recent years to be the best suited to dictate recipes to the rest of the world.

There are sound reasons for most of Latin America to be wary of economic integration with the United States. The first is that with the exception of Mexico and Venezuela most of the larger Latin economies have quite diversified trade ties with the rest of the world: the average of their trade concentration with the United States is in the 20–25 percent range. Free-trade agreements with the United States, either individually or collectively, would divert their trade from other coun-

18. Ibid., p. 30.

19. "In 1989 a quarter of U.S. imports from Brazil entered the U.S. duty-free under the Most Favored Nation clause (MFN), an additional 16 percent received the benefits of the Generalized System of Preferences (GSP), and the remaining 59 percent paid generally low tariffs." Roberto Bouzas, *A U.S.-Mercosur Free Trade Area: A Preliminary Assessment*, FLACSO, Documentos e Informes de Investigación no. 143, Buenos Aires, November 1991, p. 11.

20. The term was coined by John Williamson and includes "agreements" by what the distinguished economist refers to as "the political Washington of Congress and senior members of the administration, and the technocratic Washington of the international financial institutions, the economic agencies of the U.S. government, the Federal Reserve Board, and the think tanks." The "consensus" refers to ten areas: fiscal discipline, public expenditure priorities, tax reform, financial liberalization, exchange rates, trade liberalization, foreign direct investment, privatization, deregulation, and property rights. Cf. John Williamson, "The Progress of Policy Reform in Latin America," in Williamson, ed., *Latin American Adjustment: How Much Has Happened* (Washington, D.C.: Institute for International Economics, 1990), pp. 358–378.

tries, exactly the opposite of what they have been attempting for years. But most importantly, as even a study carried out by two World Bank experts was forced to acknowledge,

> Overall, full Free-Trade Agreement preferences would raise Latin American exports only 8 or 9 percent. . . . U.S. trade gains, particularly for highly protected transport and machinery products, are likely to be considerably greater than those for Latin America in the U.S. market.[21]

But if the left takes up the banner of regional economic integration and a new regional nationalism emphasizing cooperation within the new areas and competition with those outside, how would it differentiate itself from other zones of the political spectrum? To begin with, it need not distinguish itself from everybody: the left's nationalism today, as on occasions in the past, should unite countries, not further divide them. Secondly, the banner of regional economic integration is inevitably contrary, even in the case of Mexico, to the cause of hemispheric economic integration or the creation of a free-trade zone "from Alaska to the Antarctic," both euphemisms for the creation of a United States zone of economic influence where the battered U.S. economy could curtail competition with its European and Japanese rivals.

Most importantly, though, regional economic integration is not a blank sheet upon which nuances and details, as well as broader philosophical currents, leave no lasting imprint. The left should not only favor regional economic integration, but should push mainly for a certain *type* of regional economic integration. As we shall underline later, there are substantive differences between the types of "capitalisms" prevailing in the modern world—i.e., between the American, radical free-market type, the Rhineland social market economy, and the Japanese, hyper-*dirigiste* cultural model. Consequently, there are also terribly important distinctions between a "leave-it-to-the-market," laissez-faire notion of integration, along the lines of the U.S.-Canadian Free Trade Agreement of 1988, and similar to the North American Free Trade Agreement, or NAFTA, as the conservative Bush, Mulroney, and Salinas governments negotiated it, on the one hand, and the European Community model, on the other. Likewise, there are various, contending options within the EC: more or less "social," more or less regulated, slower or more rapid, more or less political. The EC, whose

---

21. Refik Erzan and Alexander Yeats, "Free Trade Agreements with the United States: What's in It for Latin America," World Bank Policy Research Working Paper, WPS 827, January 1992, inside cover summary.

underlying philosophy dates back to the late 1940s and the first European institutions—the Steel and Coal Community, the Euratom, the Benelux—was first conceptualized in the 1958 Treaty of Rome and in myriad subsequent enlargements and is a highly regulated, planned, socially centered form of integration with a strong role for the state.

It implies an important—indeed, decisive—common external tariff, common subsidies—in the case of the Common Agricultural Policy—and a regulating mechanism for channeling public funds—often on a massive scale—from the wealthier regions to the poorer ones: the Italian Mezzogiorno in the sixties, Ireland in the late seventies, and Spain, Portugal, and Greece in the eighties and nineties. It includes labor mobility, a central bureaucracy—"Brusselles," as it came to be known, and reviled but respected, throughout Europe—common environmental norms, consumer protection standards, and occupational safety and health considerations. The social charter, which was not laid down as such until late in the game, encountered multiple obstacles to its application. But this was less important than elsewhere because of the relatively high degree of harmonization that already existed in Western Europe regarding social issues. The principle of a social charter and harmonization was ever present, as the need to harmonize was acutely felt in order to stop firms from one country "running away" to another to circumvent regulations or lower costs by cutting wages. Most of the harmonization was mid-level: not up to the most stringent standards, but not down towards the most lax.

All of these features must be part and parcel of the regional economic integration the Latin American left should be proposing when it is in opposition, and implementing when it is in office. The left's blueprint for regional economic integration should not only exclude the United States, Europe, or Japan, but should be accomplished in a manner that is, in particular, diametrically opposed to the American free-market "old-fashioned way." Instead, the strategy should include: compensatory financing funded by windfall profit taxes and duties, labor mobility, a common external tariff to protect sectors of industry and agriculture that are jointly considered strategic and worthy of support, subsidies and credit facilities in order to make them competitive, in a business-government alliance and industrial policy along East Asian lines, a social charter or its equivalent and an environmental charter that harmonize up, not down, and include financing provisions for the adoption of superior norms in one area or another, common subsidies and expenditures for research and development, and dispute settlement mechanisms open to all interested parties and relevant issues. These characteristics are all the more desirable and necessary given the far greater regional, economic, and social, as well as ethnic, disparities that exist within and among most of the hemisphere's nations. Leaving these imbalances and historical differences to the market will simply accentuate them, not gradually wear them down.

This said, the European example should not be idealized or stripped of the infinite problems it has encountered. The Economic Community has been roundly criticized, from the left and from the right, for countless deficiencies, inadequacies, failed commitments, and unfulfilled promises. Some regret its bureaucratic excess: the Brussels Commission having transformed itself into a regulatory nightmare. Many more accuse it of not being sufficiently regulated or socially and environmentally aware, or fair, no matter how great the contrast between its institutions and inspiration on the one hand, and those of the United States on the other.[22] It has also been faulted from both the left and the right for the total absence of a political chapter and lack of definition on supranationality.[23]

Despite its marked contrasts with the Anglo-Saxon, conservative free-market paradigm—amply demonstrated by Margaret Thatcher's constant, lost battles over restricting the community's encroachment into social, political, and legal realms—the EC is certainly not a perfect model of social, regulated, planned, environmentally sound, and politically democratic and accountable integration. But it is a space in constant flux: it can be more or less social and regulated, more or less accountable, more or less democratic. The farther developed the political institutions, the more rigid the regulatory framework; the more stringent the social clauses, the greater the possibilities of transforming Europe into a more humane, democratic, fair, and historically meaningful enterprise. This, and not so much in its specific aspects or presently functioning mechanisms, is why it. is an example for Latin America.

The items on the above regional agenda are not farfetched; they

22. In the words of a none-too-left-wing critic (a businessman and economics journalist): "In the last analysis, it is the American philosophy that is carrying the day, but taken to the extreme. . . . The risk is that the great new market will function in a permanent state of imbalance, without regulation or counterweights." Alain Minc, *La Grande Illusion* (Paris: Grasset, 1989), pp. 115, 119.

23. "The state in Europe today is neither national nor supranational, and this ambiguity instead of fading with time is getting worse. In practice, this means that on the economic and financial side, as well as on the legal and social one, in the distribution of power between the level of "national states" and that of the community institutions, there is a constant redundancy, a constant competition among institutions." Etienne Balibar, *Les Frontières de la Démocratie* (Paris: La Découverte, 1992), p. 186. Balibar does come from the left: he was a member of the French Communist Party until 1981 and has continued to sustain markedly left-of-center stances.

have been included either in some legal instruments or in proposals made by mainstream economists in the United States. Thus the June 1986 Argentine-Brazilian Economic Cooperation and Integration Programme (the antecedent of the Mercosur agreement) foresaw the signing of numerous protocols, many of which were concluded during the first three years of the accord, on matters including capital goods, wheat, agroindustries, binational firms, and those creating an Investment Fund and a common currency. While these did not all proceed at the same pace, they indicated the type of integration these countries were seeking. In March 1991, Paraguay and Uruguay joined Argentina and Brazil to create a South American Common Market by December 31, 1994. The four countries agreed to remove all nontariff barriers, promote gradual tariff reductions, and progressively eliminate exemptions for intraregional trade. This acceleration of the initiative responded to two factors: the rapid rise in intra-Mercosur trade (from $2.2 billion in 1987 to $4.9 billion in 1991)[24] and to the political necessity of both Brazil and Argentina to move forward quickly. They also decided to negotiate a common external tariff.[25]

It is true, of course, that many of these noble intentions will remain just that: wishful thinking in a continent where it has been a rampant feature of economic and social, regional and international theory and practice. But this type of integration, involving industrial policy coordination, sectoral planning, investment funds, and external tariffs, as opposed to the laissez-faire model, is firmly rooted in Latin America. If the left is able to transcend its traditional resistance to any supranational scheme and position itself firmly in favor of this approach, it will both place itself squarely in the mainstream of traditional hemispheric doctrine and simultaneously differentiate itself from much of the right, the United States, and the international financial community's agenda.

Moreover, thanks to this kind of economic integration, the regional-federalist impulse that Latin America needs can become a reality: as the level of decision-making rises supranationally, it also makes state or local decision-making more plausible and effective. This view also converges with a broader trend, formulated elsewhere and for other areas, perhaps still far off for Latin America, yet already relevant for its future:

> a confederal union of semi-autonomous communities smaller than nation-states, tied together into regional economic associations and

24. "The New World's Newest Trade Bloc," *Business Week*, May 4, 1992, p. 50.
25. Bouzas, op. cit., p. 5.

markets larger than nation-states—participatory and self-determining in local matters at the bottom, representative and accountable at the top.[26]

But only through considerable resource transferring mechanisms can the risk that greater local autonomy inevitably entails be reduced. Otherwise, it reproduces and aggravates existing disparities. The poorer regions of each country, and of the entire hemisphere, require funding from the richer ones if they are ever to escape from their prostration. Without regional integration, this will never come about.

If the left should favor those facets of regional economic integration that make it "kinder and gentler," it should also favor ratcheting up the noneconomic domains in which integration takes place. Grass roots regional integration and the creation of regional political, social, and legal institutions should gradually fill the intermediate void created by economic globalization. If Europe failed in any one way, it may well have been by proving incapable of keeping the political, economic, and social levels of integration reasonably abreast of each other. Instead, it let the economic agenda jump far ahead, leaving the political and social ones lagging behind. The European left was partly to blame for this failure, as it convinced itself of the inevitability of a united Europe only late in the game.[27]

In Latin America, the time may have come for building regional political institutions and legal mechanisms of a supranational appellate nature, above and beyond national jurisdictions. Little has been actually accomplished in this direction, and new steps taken along this road are not progressing speedily, to say the least. But the left now has a tradition of understanding how most of the time, in most places, certain supranational initiatives—on human rights, election monitoring, judicial review and due process, labor rights and environmental protection—favor its causes, not those of its opponents. If deeper, more participatory and broader democracy favors the left, as many believe it does, then the greater its supranational facets, the better. With one condition, though: that it remain among equals and be sufficiently regional and close enough to home to make a difference. Otherwise,

---

26. Benjamin R. Barber, "Jihad vs. McWorld, *Atlantic Monthly*, March 1992, p. 63.

27. "Economic citizenship has led to the emergence of a bizarre 'homo europeanus' that represents the most Marxist of beings: only his economic rights make him a European, and not his culture, his roots and his right to vote. What a paradox: a Greek doctor can settle in Lyons and compete freely for patients with his French colleagues, but he cannot elect the local mayor, much less his congressman." Minc, op. cit., p. 108. The Maastricht Treaty of 1991 in fact provides for electoral rights for all European nationals across the community.

the new supranational institutions would simply become another distant, detached bureaucracy and authority in a continent that has suffered through too many such estrangements.

This new nationalist program must be presented to the left's supporters through an original political discourse that starts by telling the truth. The truth in this respect means, to begin with, that there can be no elevation of sovereignty, no regional integration, economic or otherwise, without a certain reduction in national autonomy. Regional institutions cannot be created without the abdication of a given amount of sovereignty by each member; moreover, those abdications, even if the process is only economic at the outset, will not remain exclusively economic in nature. Economic integration leads to political and cultural convergence, and generates indisputable constraints on national policy-making. It makes no sense for the Latin American left to strive for regional integration and then to state that the political and cultural costs will be nil or that there are no trade-offs involved. On the contrary, the more political the process, the better for the left, if it is a democratic politicization that takes place. As a French philosopher wrote recently about Europe: "Not every state is democratic; but a nonstate, by definition, cannot be democratized."[28]

Similarly, it would be meaningless for the left to maintain that a socially progressive, environmentally harmonized, regulated, planned, and fair model of integration is totally devoid of internal contradictions and unintended consequences. In fact, the entire process is intrinsically ambivalent, and many of the social clauses, economic protection, or sovereignty-saving provisions not only fail to function adequately but occasionally produce results that are the exact opposite of those pursued. Harmonization does not always lead up the ladder; sometimes it entails a lowering of standards. Compensatory financing can help but often does not achieve the desired aims: the Italian Mezzogiorno has improved its desperate situation of the 1950s largely because it has been emptied of its inhabitants, and the sums funneled into it over the past three decades are disproportionate to the difference they made. The left in Latin America, here too, has to go forward with its eyes wide open, and with a healthy dose of skepticism and dampened expectations.

Lastly, there is, of course, a Mexican question in this respect, or more accurately, a Mexican exception. Although President Bush's Enterprise of the Americas initiative addressed the entire hemisphere, and smaller Latin American nations have negotiated trade agreements

---

28. Balibar, op. cit., p. 190.

of one sort or another with the United States, only Mexico has truly embarked on a full-fledged process of economic integration with a "nonequal": the United States. Thus for the Mexican left, the issue was couched in different terms: to be initially in favor or against economic integration not with the rest of the region, or even with the United States together with other nations previously integrated in a Meso-American, Caribbean Basin Common Market, but alone with Washington. As the debate was framed in Mexico at the time, it was difficult, if not impossible, for the Mexican left not be against the Free Trade Agreement as signed.[29]

Then, once it became clear that this course was irrevocably chosen or imposed, the left was faced with the option of struggling to overturn it, or redirecting it in a fashion more conducive to its principles and ethics, and to its perception of the national interest. Thus, up to a point, the platform suggested above for the rest of the left was not totally applicable to Mexico. In fact, however, the Mexican left's new nationalist banner should also be based on regional economic integration, precisely of the type outlined previously, and even more so. If any country should strive to make its integration more regulated, more noneconomic, more planned and subsidized, encompassing more areas such as labor mobility, compensatory financing, industrial policy, environmental soundness, it is Mexico in its integration with the United States. But this should be conditional on its accomplishment within a regional framework—i.e., with Central America and the Caribbean—and in a strong, lasting alliance with those sectors in the United States and Canada that for different but equally valid reasons want to transform the existing NAFTA.

An example of the novelty, difference, and viability of this approach is provided by the proposal for a North American Development Bank and Adjustment Fund, presented by three American economists in

---

29. Not that this process was unforeseen or that a nuanced position on the issue of integration was not staked out by center-left academics years before: "Opposition to formal economic integration with the United States is widespread in Mexico, yet it rings increasingly hollow. Many Mexicans favor the changes the economy is undergoing, but fear their consequences; many support the premises of economic integration, but oppose the political and cultural changes they may lead to. A substantial part of the nation's political, intellectual and even entrepreneurial establishment is against greater economic ties with the United States, but believes the growth of such ties may be inevitable. The question for Mexico is thus changing from 'Is integration desirable?' to 'Is it reversible, and if not, what are its consequences for Mexico; can it be successfully administered and can Mexico get the most out of it?' " Jorge G. Castañeda, "Sliding Toward Economic Integration," in Robert Pastor and Jorge G. Castañeda, *Limits to Friendship: The United States and Mexico* (New York: Knopf, 1988), p. 241.

1991.[30] The bank would be an intergovernmental institution, capitalized by paid-in shares of its three member governments and would raise funds by selling bonds on the international market. The proposal borrowed explicitly from the European Regional Development Fund and the European Social Fund set up to deal with adjustment costs incurred by the inclusion in the Common Market of less developed areas such as Ireland, Portugal, Greece, and Spain. It is a typical *dirigiste*, interventionist idea. Its purpose would be as follows:

> The investment bank would focus on long-term development projects in: physical infrastructure that would facilitate improved trade, such as roads, bridges, ports, railroads, border facilities, and integrated border development; social infrastructure aimed at improving trade performance, such as technical assistance, worker training, collaborative research, educational exchanges, research and development. . . .; investment projects aimed at promoting sustainable rural development, given increased trade and the need to manage labor market integration; investment projects for environmental improvements, including establishing institutions for monitoring, enforcement, cleanup and adoption of new technologies; institutional development aimed at improving the operation of capital and labor markets to facilitate efficient, equitable and environmentally sound integration across the three countries. The assistance fund would focus on short-to-medium term financing to help affected communities adjust to changes emanating from the establishment of a North American FTA . . . including plant closures, labor retraining and conversion investment.[31]

Needless to say, none of the three governments negotiating the Free Trade Agreement paid the proposal any heed, initially the Mexican government least of all.[32] Its inclusion in the negotiations, like that of labor mobility, might have slowed down the entire process, but the rush was much more the Salinas administration's than that of the nations involved. Moreover, Mexican opposition leader Cuauhtémoc Cárdenas had previously presented a similar, though less technically elaborated idea in a speech at the Americas Society in New York.[33]

30. Albert Fishlow, Sherman Robinson, and Raúl Hinojosa-Ojeda, "Proposal for a Regional Development Bank and North American Adjustment Fund," *Mexico Policy News*, Consortium for Research on Mexico, San Diego State University Institute for Regional Studies of the Californias, no. 7, winter 1992, pp. 16–18.

31. Ibid., p. 17.

32. In the course of his adjusting to the new situation arising from Bill Clinton's election, President Salinas de Gortari flirted with the idea of compensatory financing and a regional bank. See the *Wall Street Journal*, December 7, 1992.

33. Cárdenas stated that: "In an economic integration process such as the one currently under way, the more disadvantaged economy inevitably has to make more and

Again, the issue was less whether any of these schemes were actually put in practice than whether they were mainstream ideas that stemmed from concrete precedents elsewhere and specific needs in the cases in question.[34] They also ran counter to the way things were being pursued by the conservative, right-of-center regimes in power in the three countries as the NAFTA negotiations went forward.

The left as a whole has already begun to move in this direction. For, example, virtually all the Salvadorean ex-guerrilla groups favor a process of Central American economic integration: "In the same way a regional war was fought, we can now proceed to implement democratic transformations on a regional scale, combining them with a process of regional economic integration, and remove the remaining dictatorships."[35] A Latin American left-of-center coordinating group known as the São Paulo Forum comprising virtually all of the organizations examined in the previous chapters, held a meeting in Lima in February of 1992 devoted to economic integration. The conference agreed that:

> A long-term alternative for Latin America has, as a fundamental premise, the strengthening of processes of integration among the countries of the region. . . . This implies restructuring, in favor of the peoples of the region, the existing mechanisms of regional integration such as the Andean Pact, Mercosur, and the Central American Common Market. Items such as the regulation and control of foreign capital, the establishment of norms governing investment, taxation, the environment, and transfers of technology should be included.[36]

---

costlier adjustments. It also suffers more dislocations in the short-term. . . . The disparities between the three economies [Canada, the United States, and Mexico] mean that, over and above the market-induced funds that could come as a consequence of the FTA, Mexico will require substantial funding to finance, first, the adjustment process, including needed investments in infrastructure and education in order to absorb additional new investments; second, the harmonization of norms, and third, the provisions of a social charter. We know that financing is not easy, but making the fundamental disparity of the three economies the cornerstone of the agreement means making compensatory financing its centerpiece." Cuauhtémoc Cárdenas, "A Continental Development and Trade Initiative," Council of the Americas/Americas Society, New York, February 8, 1991.

34. Similarly, in a speech at the Institute for International Economics in Washington on July 27, 1991, House Democratic Majority Leader Richard Gephardt proposed an environmental tax for inclusion in the NAFTA, to finance environmental harmonization.

35. Joaquin Villalobos, interview with the author, Mexico City, September 5, 1991.

36. Documento Final, Seminario/Taller sobre Integración y Desarrollo Alternativo, organizado por los Movimiento y Partidos del Foro de São Paulo, Lima, February 26–29, 1992. More than twenty papers were presented specifically on the three regional integration initiatives, mostly critical of their current status, and proposing alternatives within the existing mechanisms.

While the rhetoric remains largely unchanged, the content is different. A few years ago, the very notion that the Latin American left could subscribe to the idea of restructuring existing mechanisms of integration would have been virtually inconceivable.

In the end, the Latin American left's nationalism, new or old, must be above all a function of its hope and struggle to "give back the nation to the people," or more accurately, to give the millions of excluded citizens of the hemisphere the nation they never had. This nationalism is at least as much part of a domestic agenda as it is of an international one. It means extending the democratization process begun throughout Latin America in the 1980s far beyond its present limits in every country. Without bringing a majority of the people into the nation, the nationalism of the few—the intellectual elite, the urban, professional middle class, the impoverished lower middle class of urban schoolteachers, students, and part-time workers—will never attain a true constituency. Nationalism in Latin America today has to become once again, as it was in a distorted and often authoritarian, but nonetheless inclusive, way in the 1930s and 1940s, a force for incorporating the excluded into the nation. But this time it has to do so democratically.

11

The Democratic Imperative

•

Democracy has never been a simple matter for the Latin American left. More than the rest of the political spectrum, it has suffered gravely from the absence of democratic rule in the hemisphere; yet it only recently placed the issue near the top of its agenda. It has often emphasized its commitment to representative democracy, respect for human rights and the exclusivity of the electoral road to power, but has at the same time, occasionally but flagrantly, violated all of these maxims within its own ranks. It has rightly (though for the wrong reasons) believed that representative democracy in Latin America has nearly always been woefully devoid of content but has frequently acquiesced to democratic transitions based on purely formal, bureaucratic arrangements. More recently, the left has (re)discovered social movements and civil society, glorifying them to the heavens, while simultaneously and stubbornly seeking to dominate them whenever and wherever feasible.

Any analysis of the left's stance on democracy must take all of these contradictions and oscillations into account. Any attempt to craft a democratic platform for—and program of democratization of— the left, has to start by recalling its historical relationship with the issue. Has the left been truly, lastingly, and convincingly committed to democratic rule in the past? If not, or only partly, why? What has it understood and meant by "democracy," and how has its thinking and practice evolved? And given this, what type of democratic agenda should it adopt for the future?

For the purposes of this exercise, the basic requirements of democracy are: electoral competition for power, with free choice, fairness, and at least a moderately level playing field. In addition, representative democracy involves the prevalence of the rule of law and relatively independent judiciary and legislative branches of government; respect for human rights by at least Latin American standards (i.e., that the central government not wantonly torture people or permit others to do so); and the upholding of basic freedoms of the press, association, demonstration, and organization, including free labor unions, collective bargaining, and the right to strike. Since a great many of these simple traits—all of which admittedly subsume several contradictions, perverse paradoxes, and unwanted consequences—are absent in many Latin American countries, this type of denotation is adequate. With a few exceptions, most people in Latin America and within the ranks of the left agree on the definition of the notion, even if interminable discussions continue on qualifying adjectives.

Much of the left wrongly dismissed representative democracy for many years as a sham: a bureaucratic, corrupt device invented by local elites and foreign agents to trick the Latin masses into tolerating forms of government and domination contrary to their interests.[1] This vision was simplistic, inherently authoritarian, and, more succinctly, false. Moreover, for years, the majority of the left's behavior and beliefs were not especially democratic. Part of the left claimed that the armed struggle was the only road to power; another sector revindicated the dictatorship of the proletariat and the Soviet Union against wind and high water; another faction still argued that democracy was a secondary goal subordinated to economic and social development and justice, along with national sovereignty. In the name of these postulates large portions of the left ignored the growing democratic clamor. Only when authoritarian rule of a particularly odious variety spread across the continent and directly affected the left did much of it begin to rectify these stances.

But its skepticism about democracy, rooted as it may have been in false assumptions and distorted visions of the past and the rest of the world, pointed to a real problem. Even in the best of cases there was a lack of content in the scarce, ephemeral instances of democratic rule in Latin America. The stage show of elections, separation of powers, a free press, and competing political parties and labor unions masked an entrenched elite, the exclusion of millions, and the marked narrowing

---

1. The few notable exceptions to this trend were the old-school social democrats, Chile's Salvador Allende, and a smattering of intellectuals. On occasions, the Communist parties, more out of habit than conviction, also subscribed to the tenets of representative democracy.

of meaningful options in a continent where existing choices did not seem to work.

The overriding difference with Western Europe, Canada, and the United States lay not only in the degree of representativeness of their democratic institutions. The more important contrast lay in the fact that in the North and West, these systems could wear success as their best argument. They had contributed to hauling up the living standards of the majority of these nations' inhabitants, homogenized their societies insofar as that was possible and desirable, and erased many of the flaws and horrors of their own history. It was one thing to be faced with "not much of a choice" in Gaullist France or Tory Britain in the early sixties; it was quite another to accept a similar foreclosing of options in the slums of Caracas or the *callampas* of Santiago.

The so-called "instrumentalist" approach to democracy often attributed to the left in Latin America was neither inaccurate nor totally unjustified. "Instrumentalist" meant that the left's different factions—the armed left, the Communist "peaceful road to socialism" left, the intellectual left, and later the grass roots left—neglected the intrinsic merits of democratic rule and tended to support democracy only when it supported them. The left placed representative democracy in a lowly slot on its list of priorities, because other priorities were far weightier: economic development, social equality, national emancipation. The political realm was limited to the debate about access to power. Thanks to the strength of the Leninist creed and the lack of a democratic tradition, how power was wielded was rarely touched upon. Nonetheless, not too much should be read into this last point: the Jacobin, antidemocratic streak was present in Latin American political culture long before anyone had ever heard of Lenin or read *The State and Revolution*. The story of Andrés Pascal Allende's old-boy Chile, and oil-fed, deceivingly civil Venezuela were harrowing illustrations of the congenital defects the left perceived in "bourgeois democracy," and partly explains why it so mistrusted it.

Andrés Pascal Allende was a splendid example of the vices and virtues of the *jeunesse dorée* of Santiago and other South American capitals. In the 1960s he was one of the many sons and daughters of the continent's political, artistic, intellectual, and, on occasion, even business elite who took up arms against a seemingly inflexible, repulsive establishment. Pascal Allende was Salvador Allende's favorite nephew. Good-looking, originally married to another member of the Chilean political and intellectual "oligarchy," the soft-spoken, tall, phlegmatic sociologist became a founding member of the Movement of the Revolutionary Left (MIR). He remained its secretary-general through the

1980s, until he had his fill of the whole affair and returned to academia in Mexico in 1991.

Pascal Allende, along with many of his Chilean friends and admirers, was not supposed to feel the way he did about his country's political system. After all, his society, together with Costa Rica and Uruguay, was the most democratic, middle-class, corruption-free, and unrepressive in Latin America. Che Guevara, the dean of the armed struggle in Latin America, had been quite categorical about this: resorting to weapons and insurrection made sense only when there was absolutely no alternative:

> It must always be kept in mind that there is a necessary minimum without which the establishment and consolidation of the first [guerrilla] center is not practicable. . . . Where a government has come into power through some form of popular vote, fraudulent or not, and maintains at least an appearance of constitutional legality, the guerrilla outbreak cannot be promoted, since the possibilities of peaceful struggle have not yet been exhausted.[2]

But Pascal Allende and his colleagues intuitively grasped how abstract Guevara's commandment was. Or, in any case, how inapplicable it seemed to Chile, the continent's longest-standing, best-rooted representative democracy, where apparently Communists, Socialists, Christian Democrats, and conservatives openly and freely contended for power at the ballot box, respectfully acknowledging each other's victories, defeats, perspectives, and aspirations. Behind all this, in Pascal Allende's words, lay a "big lie":

> For my group of friends the liberal-democratic political system we lived in was increasingly discredited. We saw it as an efficient but empty instrument, without any real participation, because that is how it really was. A lot of us came from political families (myself, Miguel and Edgardo Enríquez, etc.), my uncle was a senator, many of the others' parents came from the Radical Party. I was shocked to read the paper and listen to the news on the radio about violent debates in Parliament, or heated election campaigns reflecting apparently insurmountable, gaping disagreements, pitting one faction against another, and then to see all the participants wining and dining together at my uncle's home or other houses in the better neighborhoods of Santiago, as if nothing

---

2. Ernesto Guevara, *Guerrilla Warfare* (Lincoln: University of Nebraska Press, 1985; orig. ed., New York: Monthly Review Press, 1961), p. 48. It is worth noting that on various occasions and in several countries, the Cubans and Latin guerrillas themselves disregarded Guevara's law: in Venezuela in the early 1960s, in Chile later on, in Argentina after 1973.

had happened. This was how I met President Eduardo Frei, for example: they were all political enemies, but in the end, they all belonged to the same political elite from which the popular sectors were all excluded. We quickly discovered that the marginal sectors, the people, had no participation in this democratic life, even if they voted.[3]

With time, Andrés Pascal Allende would learn that, warts and all, the traditional Chilean political system was a far sight better than what came after: fifteen years of dictatorship under General Pinochet. But he had a point, as did his comrades-in-arms: there was a high degree of old-boy networking, of a closed-circle, tightly knit elite nature to this model of democracy. The best proof lay precisely in what occurred under his uncle's presidency. When put to the test of breaking the tacit understandings and unwritten rules instead of protecting them, that democracy did not survive. When the excluded ones began clamoring at the gates and knocking down the doors of the smoke-filled rooms of Lo Curro and the "*barrio alto*," the right went calling at the military's barracks. The system disintegrated, confirming that its ultimate purpose was the conservation of the status quo, not to allow change if so decided by a majority or a plurality of the country's inhabitants.

This same problem was illustrated years later by one of the most disconcerting and telling events in recent Latin American history. On February 4, 1992, after months of rumors, a large group of Venezuelan mid-level army officers came within a hair's-breadth of overthrowing and executing President Carlos Andrés Pérez and installing a military junta. The broad cross section of *golpistas* who had conspired for at least two years prior to the aborted coup identified themselves as the Revolutionary Bolivarian Movement. They claimed to represent a proto-Nasserite tendency within the Venezuelan military with a strong nationalist, anticorruption, and social agenda. Their leader, Lieutenant Hugo Chávez, quickly became a national hero. They attempted a second coup in November of 1992; everything hinted at a third one in the future.

That a reformist, somewhat fundamentalist, demagogic, and resentful faction of the Venezuelan armed forces tried to intervene in politics was not altogether out of keeping. There was a populist, anticorruption strain in the country's military that had surfaced on several occasions in the past. That there was widespread discontent among the Venezuelan population fueling the ambitions of the erstwhile junta leaders was equally self-evident. The policies implemented by President Pérez were generating yawning disparities, accentuated by the

---

3. Andrés Pascal Allende, interview with the author, Mexico City, 1991.

perception of outrageous corruption in the government. But there was a deeper, far more serious problem underlying the failed coup that would entail grave consequences for Venezuela and Latin America.

The Venezuelan democratic transition of the late 1950s had been viewed for some time as an example of what was both right and wrong with democratization processes in Latin America. On the positive side of the ledger, it was a fortunate transition. After decades of coups, military rule, and populist experiments, a functioning, stable, two-party system was established and consolidated whereby political power was contended for at the ballot box, alternation in office was assured, and civil liberties were guaranteed.[4] There was a guerrilla problem during the first half of the decade, but it was successfully contained. Venezuela was a showcase of the Alliance for Progress's riposte to the Cuban export of revolution: social democracy, blended with U.S. aid and support for reforms, carried the day. Oil, of course, did not hurt, as petrodollars were available to finance all this reformism, particularly after 1973. Even civil society flourished: unions, political parties, and the press, along with student organizations and squatter associations, were among the most vibrant in the continent. Venezuela had become a best-case scenario.[5]

It was thus not so much the coup attempt itself that astonished observers, but the fact that it provoked such a meek response in defense of democratic rule. Indeed, the "pronunciamento" tapped into a deep well of sympathy for a break with the institutional framework.

---

4. A typically enthusiastic view of the 1960s can be found in this passage from an article in 1966: "At a time when many Latin American countries find themselves involved in crises induced by economic collapse or military golpes de estado, Venezuela in 1966 is moving at an extraordinary pace toward material growth and political stability. . . . The Venezuela that today overflows with optimism is the same country of which, three decades ago, a foreign observer could say 'Venezuelans feel inferior, and they should.' . . . The bases now seem firmly laid for continued democratic action regardless of which party wins the general election of 1968." Philip B. Taylor, Jr., "Democracy for Venezuela," Current History 51, no. 303 (November 1966), p. 284.

5. As one analysis put it: "At this stage, Venezuela was fortunate that determined and capable political leaders, dedicated to successful fulfillment of an experiment based on these very norms (institutionalization of political rules based on self-restraint and limited cooperation), came to power. . . . In the face of authoritarian tradition and severe violence on the part of leftists and rightists, they insisted upon respect for the electoral process, minority rights and the rule of law. [Rómulo] Betancourt, long a champion of peasants, workers, small-town merchants and even leftist intellectuals, consciously adopted centrist policies. He thereby signaled the historic elites that while their former monopoly of class, status, and power hierarchies was at an end, they could retain substantial privileges by accepting democratic reformist rules of the game." John D. Martz and David Myers, "Venezuelan Democracy and the Future," in Martz and Myers, eds., Venezuela: The Democratic Experience (New York: Praeger, 1977), p. 359.

There was something very wrong with the Venezuelan model. It was obviously not a best-case scenario for everybody, and it sadly lacked the defenders it supposedly deserved: the people of the country, those who voted with exceptionally high turnout ratios at every election, and who in principle were the chief beneficiaries of the democratic system. This was the negative side of the Venezuelan ledger, also stressed by numerous students of the process.[6] For a transition to work it seemed that power had to be shared in a way that made alternation and competition far less meaningful than appearances indicated:

> Venezuelan democracy was specifically set up to accommodate the demands and desires of new politically organized actors without significantly threatening the interests of those who were strong enough to reverse the process of change—the military, foreign and local capital and the United States. . . . Regardless of who won the elections, each party was promised concrete participation in the political and economic pie through access to state jobs and contracts, a partitioning of the ministries, and a complicated spoils system which would ensure the political survival of all signatories. . . . The essential compromise was captured in the classic exchange of the "right to rule for the right to make money." . . . Fundamental issues concerning policies toward industry, the petroleum companies, labor and the peasantry, were decided before the elections.[7]

"Democracy" in Venezuela meant excluding millions from the real process, or limiting their participation to voting alternatively for one party or another, with the understanding that which party governed at any one time did not really matter. This arrangement, or "pacted tran-

---

6. Five constraints or limits have been identified as weakening Venezuelan democracy: "1. The adoption of the rule of consultation of actors deemed fundamental, granting them even veto rights over decisions that affect their vital interests . . . 2. The creation of a system of participation and representation of a semi-corporativist nature, separate and parallel to the strictly democratic system . . . 3. The encouragement and establishment of a hyper-organized and elitist democracy . . . 4. The development of a conservative and tutelar conception of democracy, where the possibilities of the electorate controlling and holding the elected accountable for its actions are strongly restricted . . . 5. An additional factor that limits democratic accountability is constituted by the development and consolidation of a two-party monopoly on power." Juan Carlos Rey, "Pasado, presente y futuro de la democracia en Venezuela," paper presented at XV Latin American Studies Association (LASA) Meeting, September 21–23, 1989, pp. 17–20.

7. Terry Karl, "Petroleum and Political Pacts, The Transition to Democracy in Venezuela," paper presented at conference, Transitions from Authoritarianism and Prospect for Democracy in Latin America and Europe, 1981, pp.27–33, subsequently published in shorter version in *Latin American Research Review*, January 1987, pp. 630–694. The original pact that gave birth to this scheme came to be known as the Pacto de Punto Fijo, for the name of the home of COPEI politician and subsequent Venezuelan president Rafael Caldera.

sition," became a condition for the passage to democratic rule in various republics, from Colombia and Venezuela in the fifties and sixties to Chile after Pinochet in the nineties. The hope lay in evolution. Once democratic institutions plunged their roots deeper into the authoritarian soil, the limitations on their reach and breadth would gradually crumble. With time, representative democracy in these nations would become indistinguishable from its equivalent elsewhere.

But in Venezuela, this course never really materialized. By 1990 the Venezuelan situation had been stretched to the breaking point. Voters elected a known quantity, Social Democrat Carlos Andrés Pérez, because of his promises to drag the nation out of its economic and social backslide. They discovered abruptly after his inauguration that he proceeded to apply International Monetary Fund recipes for austerity, price hikes, wage freezes, and subsidy cuts. The inhabitants of Caracas rioted, looted supermarkets, and burned buses, drawing upon them the wrath of a disoriented police force that killed anywhere from 400 to 1,000 *caraqueños*—depending on whose numbers one trusts[8]—and setting the stage for the attempted coup two years later. The *"caracazo"* was a damning comment on the state of things past:

> The riots began as a result of exasperation in the face of continuing, frustrated demands of the poorer sectors towards political actors and successive governments. The inability to fulfill promises of distribution and limiting extreme poverty in the richest country in Latin America seemed to be an insoluble problem that the political system had created for itself.[9]

In Chile and Venezuela, for different reasons and with sharply varying consequences, even the best of the region's democratic systems showed surprising fragility. The left could not fail to take note of this fact. If democracy was a desirable ingredient of national life only when it was useful—i.e., when its enforcement allowed the left to reach power, and it nearly never did—it was rarely going to seem very endearing to the left. In the best of cases, it became a goal worth fighting

---

8. "The government claimed that 300 died, but other estimates placed the number of fatalities between 800 and 1,000 after a week of violence in nineteen cities. Ten thousand troops were needed to suppress the revolt in Caracas, where one third of all supermarkets had been looted. An estimated 2,900 businesses were damaged or destroyed nationwide, resulting in an estimated $1.5 billion in losses for insured and uninsured businesses." Daniel C. Hellinger, *Venezuela: Tarnished Democracy* (Boulder, Colo.: Westview Press, 1991), p. 3.

9. Luis Gómez Calcaño, "La vitrina rota: interrogantes sobre la democracia venezolana," paper presented at XV Latin American Studies Association (LASA) Meeting, September 21–23, 1989, p. 16.

for only when it ceased to exist and its absence rendered the left illegal and persecuted, unleashing ferocious repression on it.

Latin-style democracy usually did not permit the left to reach power. Yet, although the left's democratic credentials had not always been impeccable, it suffered far more than other political sectors from the extension of authoritarian rule: Chile after 1973, Uruguay after 1974, Brazil after 1964, and Central America from 1932 to the present. Conversely and logically, the left has also benefited the most from the spread of democratic institutions. The great majority of the hemisphere's ruptures of institutional order have been directed against the left. Coups d'état with enduring consequences were all carried out largely because of the military's perception that the persistence of democratic practices favored the left and led to its accession or consolidation in power.

One of the explanations for the succession of military takeovers in Latin America over the past half century lies precisely in the fact that representative democracy in the region has generally led to the political expression of sociological majorities. Not always, of course: in disintegrating societies, elections can bring forth lottery-like, postideological populism, through the outright manipulation of the poor's fears and hopes. Alberto Fujimori's apparent popularity after his 1992 semicoup is an example. But generally, in the words of Peru's Julio Cotler, representative democracy means the open expression of the formerly disenfranchised masses' economic and social demands, which implies a shift to the left, which in turn scares money away, creating economic chaos and a virtual invitation for the military to take matters into their hands.[10] Thus when the left won an election and proceeded to govern in consonance with its program, its victory was rapidly nullified or neutralized. Left-wing governments brought to power through the democratic system were soon overthrown by the military, the United States, the business elite, or a combination of the three: Guatemala in 1954, Brazil in 1964, and Chile in 1973. Or as in the Dominican Republic in 1964 and Mexico as recently as 1988, the election was simply stolen or overturned. In other cases, such as Uruguay in 1974, preemptive coups against a left-wing victory foretold (not always accurately) were undertaken. As John F. Kennedy put it in relation to American policy toward the Trujillo dictatorship in the Dominican Republic:

> There are three possibilities, in descending order of preference: a decent democratic regime, a continuation of the Trujillo regime or a Castro

---

10. Julio Cotler, interview with the author, Lima, June 11, 1990.

regime. We ought to aim at the first, but we can't really renounce the second until we are sure we can avoid the third.[11]

No wonder the left felt alienated from institutions and procedures that worked for others but never, apparently, to its own benefit. The syllogism was flawless: any left-wing government was unacceptable to the United States, the military, and the business elite, since by definition it was imposed against the consent of the people, regardless of whether it was elected or not. As they viewed it, no informed consenting people would ever tolerate a Communist or revolutionary regime. Under these conditions the lure of democracy for the left was quite minor. It did not make much of a difference if power was obtained through the ballot box or an insurrection in jungles or mountains: either way, there was the devil to pay. In fact, it seemed the only power worth winning was the one that sprang from the barrel of a gun: at least it lasted.

While so-called democratic regimes only fleetingly granted the left access to power, they frequently reduced its sphere of action. Elected governments in many nations banned Communist parties during the worst years of the Cold War, imprisoned union, student, and radical leaders, muzzled the critical press, and countenanced, or engaged in, widespread harassment and occasionally torture of the opposition. What then was the purpose of defending, much less promoting a "democracy" that provided few benefits for the left and "the people," and undeniable disadvantages?

This was the other rub. For the left, the drawbacks of democracy resided not only in what it did not do, but equally in the perverse effects it did beget among "the people." It neutralized discontent, engendered illusions of reform and participation, and reversed hard-fought gains of consciousness and commitment to "real change." If all of this sounded like traditional Leninist conceptions of "bourgeois democracy," there was an excellent reason for the association. That is exactly what it was. Except that in nations where representative democracy had neither proved its worth nor delivered the goods, the validity of the Leninist left's cynical skepticism was enhanced by everyday life and endless experience.

But why did the persistence of democratic rule seem unceasingly to

---

11. John F. Kennedy, quoted in Arthur Schlesinger, Jr., *A Thousand Days: John F. Kennedy in the White House* (Boston: Houghton Mifflin, 1965), p. 769, quoted by Abraham Lowenthal, "Learning from History," in Lowenthal, ed., *Exporting Democracy: The United States and Latin America, Themes and Issues* (Baltimore: Johns Hopkins University Press, 1991), p. 248.

bring about either the emptying of its significance—the Scylla of Venezuela—or the advent of left-wing majorities and right-wing coups—the Charybdis of Chile? Over the years countless scholars have offered myriad, generally accurate explanations, but one perhaps deserves greater emphasis in light of the most recent experiences. Again the comparison with Western Europe is enlightening.

The struggle for enfranchisement in Europe (and the United States, for that matter) was a painful and protracted one. Its gradualism was regulated by other, concomitant processes: employment, destruction of previous forms of economic and social life, generalization of public education, "incorporation into society," the forming of a nation, the diffusion of middle-class values and behavior patterns, and the stabilization of living standards. The process was mutually reinforcing. As industrial workers, their families, and the poor in general were incorporated into society, they were granted the right of suffrage; as greater numbers conquered the right to vote, they strengthened the impulse toward incorporation through social legislation, public spending, and a stricter regulatory framework. The formation and enfranchisement of the working classes were simultaneous, parallel and gradual processes. In the words of historian Karl Polanyi in relation to the Chartist movement in Britain in 1848:

> In England it became the unwritten law of the Constitution that the working class must be denied the right to vote. The Chartist leaders were jailed; their adherents, numbered in millions, were derided by a legislature representing a bare fraction of the population, and the mere demand of the ballot was often treated as a criminal act. Not before the working class had passed through the Hungry Forties and a docile generation had emerged to reap the benefits of the Golden Age of capitalism; not before an upper layer of skilled workers had developed their unions and parted company with the dark mass of poverty-stricken laborers; not before the workers had acquiesced in the system which the New Poor Law was meant to enforce upon them was their better-paid stratum allowed to participate in the nation's councils.[12]

Without the gradual extension of the franchise, proceeding more or less at the same rate as the incorporation into capitalist society and the extension of market devices, the gears of the whole machinery would have gripped. Voters would have turned against the economic mechanisms that gave birth to universal suffrage; the initial—and many of the later—effects of those mechanisms would have alienated the vot-

---

12. Karl Polanyi, *The Great Transformation* (Boston: Beacon Press, 1957), p. 226.

ers. Which is what enfranchisement in Latin America has implied for several decades.

Because of the internationalization of economic exchange, political ideas and practices, information and customs, and even of health services and industrial and agricultural technology since the beginning of this century, but at a much more accelerated pace after World War II, many of the features of "First World" life were transmitted to the "Third World" long before it was "ready." This term is of delicate usage: it signifies simply that natural, historical processes are being "rushed" by the extension of the products of modernity to societies that have not generated them. The most illustrative example is demographic.

As late as the 1940s, most of Latin America had a typically preindustrial demography: high birth rates, high death rates, high infant mortality. Logically, over time, as societies became more urban, literate, and "modernized," trends similar to those that had taken hold elsewhere would also emerge in Latin America: a lowering of morbidity, and a gradual but continuous and significant decline in fertility. Population growth rates would rise, but not inordinately. However, the introduction of advanced health techniques from the industrialized nations—hygiene, vaccination, epidemic controls, minimal health care—led to a quite different evolution. Mortality rates dropped dramatically, yet since the processes that bring about lower fertility are far slower, the combination of low death rates and continuing high birth rates engendered a population explosion: growth rates of over 3 percent annually for more than thirty years.

On the political front, a similar pattern developed. While it took time for universal suffrage to be truly implanted throughout Latin America, by mid-century most nations had extended the franchise to the majority of their citizens. The miniwave of democratization in the early 1960s confirmed this. But in contrast to the industrialized nations, the extension of voting rights was not accompanied by a parallel process of incorporation. Although the urban working classes and a growing but still minuscule middle class were brought into society in the 1930s, the right to vote was granted to large, excluded, dispossessed masses who, more often than not, lived in conditions of extreme poverty and marginalization. In Brazilian sociologist Francisco Weffort's words:

> The classic electoral maxim—one man, one vote—presupposes the individual's autonomy in expressing his opinion. Still today, in Brazil . . . only 7.5 million pay taxes, while 75 million are registered to vote. This means that electoral citizenship has "anticipated" or outpaced political

citizenship in a broader sense. To say it differently: There are millions of citizens electorally speaking who, in reality, are nothing more than second-class citizens.[13]

The introduction of "modern," First World political procedures devoid of the restrictions (restricted suffrage) or tricks (electoral fraud, one-party systems, massive manipulation of a large rural vote, etc.) of the past—but without First World social characteristics—to a "Third World" society where the majority of the population lives under the poverty line, sets the stage for an explosion. Until a majority of the population is economically and socially incorporated into the modern, urban, employed, and literate network, something has to be done to defuse its explosiveness. One way is to make the vote relatively meaningless—the Venezuelan solution. Otherwise, suffrage contributes to the alignment of political majorities with social ones—the first stage of the Chilean outcome. This in turn leads to the second stage or solution: the suspension of democratic rule.[14] Another option has consisted in traditional manipulation of the poor: buying their votes, deceiving them, and betraying their trust. This solution is widespread, but increasing literacy, urbanization, modern communications, and politicization make it more difficult, though still feasible.

The above does not imply that "the poor are not ready for democracy" or that democracy cannot coexist with poverty, as some have argued. It means only that giving the poor the vote, and allowing their votes to be counted when they represent the majority of a society's inhabitants, leads to demands, policies, and ruptures that in Latin America have historically tended to provoke military coups and the end of representative democracy. Herein lies the cause of the obsession of so many Latin American democrats who read well the writing on the walls of their slums and villages. Poverty and democracy don't mix easily; since the postponement or abrogation of democracy is not an acceptable option for them, only the elimination of poverty will do. Failing to bring this about is tantamount to democratic suicide: in the midst of destitution and exclusion, and absent any trend toward their

---

13. Francisco Weffort, *Qual Democracia?* (São Paulo: Companhia das Letras, 1992), p. 24.

14. Raúl Prebisch, founder of the United Nations Economic Commission for Latin America and father of modern Latin American development economics, phrased this problem the following way: "The advance of structural change in peripheral capitalism brings forth a contradiction between the process of democratization and the process of appropriation of the surplus and redistribution. There are only two options to solve this contradiction: one is to transform the system and the other is to resort to force in order to suppress democratic institutions." Raúl Prebisch, "Capitalism: The Second Crisis," *Third World Quarterly*, July 1981, vol. 3, no. 3.

eradication, democracy will not survive. When politicians with impeccable democratic convictions, who have suffered directly the consequences of military intervention, insist on the incompatibility of massive, unalleviated poverty and representative democracy, that is what they generally mean. The Brazilian old guard—who experienced in government the country's unmitigated deprivation, its fragile democratic construction before 1964 and after 1982, along with the 1964 military coup and the ensuing two decades of authoritarian rule—is more sensitive to this than most. This is why figures like Waldir Pires, whose progressive, democratic career speaks for itself, harp on a view which elsewhere, or at other times, could be considered highly reactionary: "If we do not do something about poverty in this country, our new, fragile democracy will not last."[15] That this same argument can be twisted around—and often is, most recently by the authoritarian Mexican political system—and made to mean that democracy should wait for economic prosperity, does not subtract from its truth and relevance.[16]

This explains partly why the region's democratization drives in the recent past have not been unconditional or unrestricted. As innumerable scholars of the period and the process have pointed out, in many cases the military's acquiescence was achieved only in exchange for promises not to punish it for past crimes, thus weakening from the outset the restoration or creation of an independent, trustworthy, and respected judicial system. In other instances, the business, landed, or

---

15. Waldir Pires was governor of the incredibly segregated northern state of Bahia from 1982 to 1986. But he was also Brazil's attorney general in the administration of João Goulart, ousted by the military in 1964, and was exiled for many years. Interview with the author, Salvador de Bahia, August 17, 1990.

16. In a recent reflection on his own evolution, Albert O. Hirschman quoted an Argentine official justifying the postponement of democratic rule: "First we must straighten out the economic problems, that is, restore economic stability and stimulate growth; thereafter we will look out for greater equity; and only then will the country be ready for a restoration of civil liberties and for other political advances." Hirschman argued back: "I was appalled by this suggestion. . . . There is no general reason why these various good things should necessarily go together except for the fact that we wish it were so. . . . Once economic progress is being achieved by an authoritarian regime, the government could very well find itself more popular and more strongly entrenched and therefore under less pressure than before to evolve in the directions of pluralism and human rights. Accordingly, one might suspect the good faith of such a government when it 'says the time is not ripe' for moving in those directions while proclaiming its determination to do so eventually." Albert O. Hirschman, "The Case against 'One Thing at a Time,' " in Simón Teitel, *Towards a New Development Strategy for Latin America: Pathways from Hirschman's Thought* (Washington D.C.: The Inter-American Development Bank/John Hopkins University Press, 1992), pp. 13–14.

political elite's conditions for the democratic opening entailed the maintenance of the prevailing social and economic order. Political change was bought at the expense of social and economic evolution. The absence of economic and social reforms quickly emerges as a condition for political change.[17] Where, as sometimes occurs, the left is praised for having learned the lessons of the past, the statement is generally a euphemism for the acceptance of this regrettable, though often inevitable, quid pro quo.

The left had sound reasons for being wary of all the hyperbole surrounding representative democracy, respect for human rights, and a thriving civil society. Its suspicion and disdain for "formal" democratic rule emanated at least as much from the region's historical familiarity with the very real limits of democracy as from the Leninist critique of "bourgeois democracy." This latter source of mistrust was dogmatic and abstract; the former was quite the opposite. Overcoming both has been an arduous task, still incomplete and fraught with complications. Because of the presence of both explanations, one was either frequently mistaken for the other or subsumed by it. It is important, nevertheless, to distinguish between the left's attitudes toward democracy and the effects of democracy on the left. The left may not have attributed the highest values to democratic rule; it still benefited enormously from it while it lasted. Conversely, as has already been stated, when democratic rule vanished, the most negatively affected sector of the political spectrum was the left.

In consequence, democrats outside the left were on solid ground in sheltering doubts about the left's democratic convictions. In addition to democracy's secondary rank on its agenda, there were two further motives for questioning its credentials in this regard. One was its stance in relation to concrete, specific cases. This involved the left's behavior in power in Cuba and Nicaragua and its attitude elsewhere in the region toward the socialist bloc and Nicaragua. Secondly, there was well-founded incredulity concerning the left's democratic deportment—or more accurately, its lack thereof—within its own ranks.

Simply put, how could the left's protestations of democratic faith be taken at face value when one part of it implemented authoritarian rule in Cuba while the rest either applauded or, in the best of cases, remained silent. As late as April of 1992, Octavio Paz, whose own democratic credentials were far from impeccable, given his silence

---

17. See mainly Philippe Schmitter, Lawrence Whitheead, and Guillermo O'Donnell, *The Transition from Authoritarian Rule* (Baltimore: John Hopkins University Press, 1986), particularly O'Donnell's chapter.

regarding recurrent electoral fraud and egregious human rights violations in Salinas's Mexico, nonetheless had a strong case when he charged that:

> A leitmotiv of the Colloquium [a left-of-center gathering of intellectuals from Europe, the United States, Latin America, and Mexico held in early 1992 at the National University in Mexico City] was the obstinate defense of the Cuban regime, precisely at the time when the Castro government was executing its opponents and jailing free union organizers and university professors. . . . As the intellectuals in Mexico spoke incessantly, poet Maria Elena Cruz Varela was thrown in prison and humiliated by the Cuban police. The Colloquium's silence in the light of the indignities Maria Elena Cruz Varela suffered is a spot that will not easily wash off or be forgotten.[18]

The thrust of this reasoning, whether stated in good faith or simply as a by-product of the rough-and-tumble world of Latin politics, was not unlike the arguments brandished previously in Europe. From the end of World War II through the early 1980s, the most effective logic dispensed against the large European Communist parties was exactly the same: How could their democratic vows be trusted if they never readily condemned the authoritarian nature of the socialism prevailing in the USSR? How could their word be taken that they would respect democratic rule if propelled into power, given their acceptance of its destruction in Eastern Europe?

The argument in Latin America was analogous: how could Cuauhtémoc Cárdenas's commitment to the electoral process and Lula's adhesion to democratic institutions acquire credibility if they did not criticize the lack of both in Cuba?[19] The two leaders' statements were ambiguous at best. Cárdenas's public comments in the course of visits to Cuba in 1990 and 1991, as well as in press conferences and statements during that period, show an unquestionable internal tension. As he summed up his stance:

> As long as Cuba is subject to the attempts to suffocate it through economic strangulation, as the United States is doing, many of the

---

18. Octavio Paz, "La conjura de los letrados," *Vuelta* (Mexico City), April 1992, pp. 11–12. The Colloquium was in fact none of the things Paz charged it with being; Paz himself was just as silent regarding the imprisonment or harassment of Mexican intellectuals or political activists by the Salinas regime. But on the Cuban issue, he had a point, one he had been making for many years.

19. These were not new questions. They were asked—formally, in writing—and received a written reply by Chile's Christian Democrats (PDC) in September 1970, of Salvador Allende. The PDC demanded a formal Statute of Guarantees and Freedoms from Allende as a condition for making him President through their votes in the National Congress. Allende acquiesced to the request.

possibilities of transformation that the Cuban system may have are closed down. One cannot demand of a country in a state of war, as Cuba has found itself in in recent years, that it carry out measures that in normal times some—not all—could view as reasonable. I put self-determination first.[20]

On the one hand he found himself justifying Cuba against the United States' unrelenting hostility, and refraining from hitting the Cubans when they were down. Yet at the same time he was forced to admit that what he was defending was inherently and substantively different from what he was struggling for in Mexico.

Lula, for his part, stated time and again that:

In the first place the PT defends the right of self-determination of the Cuban people and is for the end of the U.S. embargo of Cuba. We cannot accept the idea of an embargo because it is contrary to the right of self-determination. What we disagree on with the Cubans, what we always discuss with our Cuban comrades, is that they have to permit union autonomy, that they have to allow arguments, open up political debate, allow opposing ideas. The PT has tired of saying that we do not agree with the idea of one-party rule. . . . From the strategic perspective of a presidential campaign, we had to act in solidarity with Cuba.[21]

Similarly, in the 1960s and early 1970s, before the coup in Chile, how could the Chilean Communist Party's statements of democratic faith and dedication to the "electoral road to socialism" be swallowed if it also vaunted the "armed path" elsewhere? And what about the Salvadorean guerrillas' response to the Cuban imbroglio, particularly in a context where a newly sought and yet unsure democratic credibility was of the utmost importance. Joaquín Villalobos, the FMLN leader personally most attached and psychologically most similar to the Cubans, provided an answer much like Lula's and Cárdenas's— loyal and honest, but awkward:

Cuba represents a Stalinist form of socialism and the Army-Party-State triad, and a whole one-party conception that in our opinion is not applicable or possible in El Salvador. But I take into account the differences in historical context and historical moment, because we cannot

---

20. Cuauhtémoc Cárdenas, interview with the author, Mexico City, January 15, 1992.

21. Lula, interview with the author, Mexico City, June 6, 1991. On Eastern Europe and the Soviet Union, Lula clearly feels more comfortable, as his statement on these matters indicates: "The PT criticized Eastern Europe from its birth. We criticized the Berlin Wall, state bureaucracy, the absence of union freedom; we defended Walesa from the moment we were founded." Ibid.

separate things from the time when they took place. If we had achieved a victorious revolution in El Salvador in 1959, maybe we would have done exactly the same thing. And perhaps without doing the same thing it would have been extraordinarily difficult to resist the United States for more than thirty years. It would be ungrateful on our part to become critics of a system's origins, of its historical projection, when this is what has permitted Cuba to resist, to maintain a firm position in the face of the United States. How did Cuba do it? She did it with what she has now. If she wants to change, that is a decision for the Cuban people. We have our disagreements with regard to what they are doing today, and those disagreements might make us seem critical of the Cubans, but we do not need their methods.[22]

This dubious stance couched the left's conversion to the principle of democratic rule in a highly relative light and cast doubt on the depth of its redemption. As many of the transition commentators had initially surmised, the left had begun to apprehend the importance of the electoral process, the rule of law, and the strength of civil society as a result of its more recent encounters with dictatorships and repression. But it was far from certain that the instrumentalist conception of democracy had entirely faded.

It was one thing for the left to persuade itself that an independent judiciary was crucial when it was fighting for the liberation of its political prisoners; a separate matter involved grasping that this was an intrinsically, perennially important question regardless of its immediate relevance to a given person or organization. In fact, the left started to acquire a democratic consciousness and assume the democratic imperative only when it began to see how it could benefit from the democratic process under normal circumstances. It was through actual participation in recurrent elections, municipal administration, Parliament, and popular movements that the left undertook its gradual and often tortuous transformation into a more democratic political current. But serious problems persisted.

Most dramatic among them was Cuba's own demeanor. No matter how much "participatory democracy" may have blossomed initially on the island, or how stark the contrast between the isolated, sporadic, and selective human rights violations under Fidel Castro and the widespread, constant, and generalized repression in Eastern Europe, Cuba

---

22. Joaquín Villalobos, interview with the author, Mexico City, September 5, 1991. Or take the Sandinista view, for instance: "It is difficult to express an opinion until many of the factors that are weighing down on Cuba disappear. Any categorical judgment would be out of place." Jaime Wheelock, interview with the author, Philadelphia, December 14, 1992.

was under no meaningful definition of the term a "democracy." U.S. aggression, an economic embargo, and a three-decade-old virtual state of siege, however real, could not explain many of the repressive measures taken. Either democratic rule was a paramount issue, or it wasn't. Cuba was the left's beacon and its penitence. If it didn't criticize Cuba on this score, it was identified with the island; if it expressed its disagreements frankly, it felt guilty and unworthy. The left's incapacity to respond to the guilt-by-association syndrome was a symptom of the contradictions enveloping it on the issue of democracy. The proof that the left had not yet fully internalized the higher priority it was bestowing upon the political side of the reformist equation could be found in this ambivalence with regard to Cuba. What occurred in Nicaragua in 1990 was an additional bellwether of how far the left had come on the issue of democracy, and of how long a road it still had to travel.

The Nicaraguan Sandinistas passed through several stages in their conception of elections and civil society. At the outset of the revolution, they indisputably believed that they did not want, and were not obliged, to hold elections to legitimize their power. They had led a revolution, overthrown a universally despised dictatorship, and needed no mantle of representation to sanction what in their eyes was as obvious as night and day: the people of Nicaragua supported them and had bequeathed to them the title of vanguard.[23] In the worst of cases and for purely tactical considerations, elections would be held in five years' time, largely in deference to foreign entreaties and pressure by the Sandinistas' friends and enemies, respectively. Except that on this, as on so many other accounts, tactics in a strategic void quickly became a strategy, and the logic of accepting the electoral straitjacket started wreaking havoc with their plans. In passing, it is worth recalling that practically no important member of the Latin American left prodded the Sandinistas into scheduling a vote right after their revolutionary victory. They would have won by a landslide—they had no

---

23. A good example of how even critical Sandinistas had a totally different perception of their democratic faith than their critics did, or how difficult it was to break with the past on this score and in the context of incessant American aggression is the following passage: "The revolutionary leadership in Nicaragua was comprised of Marxists, Marxist-Leninists, liberation theologists and radicalized social democrats. Few other successful revolutions have had such a pluralistic ideological leadership. . . . The positions of the Sandinista Front on national liberation, anti-imperialism, the mixed economy, political pluralism, and non-alignment all reveal a broad ideological orientation. The revolutionary movement is multi-class, multi-ethnic, multi-doctrinal and politically pluralistic. A National Directorate . . . discuss the issues with broad input from the base before reaching agreements by consensus." Roger Burbach and Orlando Nuñez, *Fire in the Americas: Forging a Revolutionary Agenda* (London: Verso Books, 1987), p. 52.

opponents—and the absence of advice to this effect underlines how recent the left's electoral devotion truly is.

The first strategic chicken came home to roost in 1984. The Sandinistas finally held a presidential election, but nobody came. Their main potential adversary was compelled by the United States to withdraw from the race months before the vote. The Sandinistas had staked a great deal—mainly, the international goodwill they felt slipping away—on holding a clean, competitive, and meaningful contest. Suddenly, they were faced with an insurmountable obstacle: the lack of someone to run against, and the self-evident conclusion that whatever actually happened, Washington would not bestow its seal of approval on the vote, or call off the contra war, the trade embargo, and other expressions of hostility.

The 1984 election was certainly not a paragon of cleanliness, but by Latin American and certainly by Nicaraguan standards it was a shining example. Various delegations of international observers were present; most of them attested to the validity of the vote. The fact that they were there at all signaled a change. If the same tough standards the Sandinistas were being obliged to abide by had been applied to Mexican elections, for example, the PRI would been removed from power years ago. Nevertheless, the tactical move was backfiring: the costs of holding an election and accepting the principle of the electoral source of legitimacy were rising, whereas the benefits—international acceptance, U.S. tolerance—were nowhere to be seen.

But this was nothing compared to what occurred in 1990. Again for tactical reasons a presidential election was scheduled. But the vote had to be sufficiently free and fair for a hefty share of the Sandinistas' enemies to participate, believing that they had a decent shot at a victory. Moreover, the cleanliness of the process had to be visible enough in the United States to force American pressure and aggression against Managua to cease. That meant letting foreigners, and particularly Americans, monitor the vote, which in turn implied inviting them to observe the preparation and evolution of the entire electoral process. This signified the acceptance of a series of modifications that would otherwise not have been incorporated: enhanced access to the media by the opposition; a more equitable sharing of state resources among all contending parties; tighter inspection of voter rolls and registration; closer monitoring and more safeguards against tampering on election day. Most of all, it meant transmitting a far greater sense of trust to the disgruntled, cynical Nicaraguan electorate. Voters had to be convinced that their vote counted, because it would be counted partly by foreigners impervious to Sandinista intimidation. This in turn bestowed a deeper relevance to the election itself: because it would be fair, the vote was actually going to signify something. As a mere tactical election, matters were straying out of control.

The Sandinistas eventually accepted a defeat they had no way of avoiding, but did so unwillingly and in a virtual state of shock. With hindsight, the Sandinista leadership acknowledge the inevitability of defeat:

> The elections were not winnable, whatever we would have done. Our own attrition, the perception that the war would continue, and the economic situation contributed largely to this. But also there was the question of our whole model: it was too expensive. We wanted to give out land, increase spending on health and education, improve the people's living standards, industrialize our natural resources and defend the revolution, all at the same time. This was not possible.[24]

Prior to the results, they had repeatedly stated that they would not relinquish at the ballot box the power that had been conquered through the revolution; they did just that. Their leaders had made such foolhardy statements because they had no intention of losing: they announced their unwillingness to be removed from office by the vote because they were utterly convinced that they would win.

Tactical considerations had led the revolutionaries first to accept the principle of electoral legitimacy, then to hold another presidential election under more intense scrutiny than before.[25] It subsequently obliged them to acquiesce in procedures that were truly democratic, finally forcing them to lose the election and accept their defeat. But all these shifts from tactics to strategy could not alter attitudes and age-old traditions. To their immense credit, the Sandinistas left power democratically, something no other revolutionary group in Latin America had done, and that many governments, military or otherwise—from Mexico to Bolivia—had repeatedly failed to do. The Sandinistas' holding of clean elections and their ensuing acknowledgment of defeat not only helped establish their commitment to the democratic process, but also demonstrated that at least parts of the left in Latin America had finally understood that the way power is achieved is not unrelated to what is done with it. But the way in which the Sandinistas relinquished power also showed how skin-deep their

---

24. Jaime Wheelock, op. cit.

25. The supreme commander of the Sandinista army put it this way: "We wanted as many observers as possible to monitor our elections because we were sure we were going to win." Humberto Ortega, conversation with the author, Guadalajara, December 5, 1992.

attachment to democratic rule remained, and how far they still had to go. That is the story of *la piñata*.

It broke in the press of Managua, mainly in *La Prensa*, the formerly opposition and later government-friendly paper owned by the Chamorro family, in the months following Violeta Chamorro's swearing in as president of Nicaragua. The term was used to generically describe the way in which the Sandinista leadership, but also the mid-level cadres and even the rank and file, had discovered that they could "take it with them" using the two-month transition period between election and inauguration days to transfer to their keeping a substantial part of the state's wealth. In *La Prensa*'s strident tone:

> What occurred between February 25 and April 25 of this year and even after the new government took office, is unprecedented in the history of the Nicaraguan Booty-State. More than 700,000 *manzanas* of land were handed out during this period, creating a new class of landowners that took over the best agricultural and grazing lands of the country. In just two months half of the year's entire budget was spent. Thousands of vehicles of all types, from motorcycles to tractors, ceased belonging to the state and passed into private hands. Radio stations, stores, industries, hotels, restaurants, agricultural and cattle units that were public patrimony, became private property overnight.[26]

It was undoubtedly the largest and most expedited privatization program anywhere in Latin America. The Sandinista directorate offered multiple explanations for it, some coherent and convincing, others absurd.[27] Beyond the gossip and the gory details, and behind the looting that took place, lurked a patrimonial conception of the state, as well as an ill-disguised disregard for its fortunes after the Sandinistas' departure.

---

26. "La Transición del FSLN," *La Prensa* (Managua), September 21, 1990. A week earlier *La Prensa* had published revelations about huge transfers of money from the Central Bank to President Ortega's office, as well as payments to Panama, the Air Force, etc., just before the Sandinistas left office. See *La Prensa*, "Frenética piñata en los últimos días de Ortega," September 14, 1990.

27. Daniel Ortega's exasperation with the commotion led him to emphasize singularly unpersuasive points on some occasions: "Why should only the rich, the *somocistas*, the capitalists, the proimperialists have dish antennas. . . . We did not fight to have people live in misery. We fought so they could live better. It would be absurd to play a fool's game and ask people who are for the revolution to starve while others get rich. . . . The homes that existed belonged to the *somocistas*. It was better to place Sandinista Army officers there than to build new homes. In Spain, Franco's army was not done away with; here we did away with Somoza's army. Here they went to hell ["*se fueron al carajo*"] and their homes remained. And the *compañeros* took them over." Joaquín Ibarz, "Entrevista con Daniel Ortega," originally published in *La Vanguardia*, *La jornada semanal* (Mexico City), May 12, 1991, p. 37.

Needless to say, corruption in Latin America was not limited to the Sandinistas. Indeed, in the last analysis they constituted the most honest and responsive government Nicaragua ever had. Furthermore, hemispheric history and political developments show no perfect correlation between democratic rule and the absence of corruption: the latter thrives nearly everywhere, almost always. The fact that over time there has been less of it in Chile, Uruguay, and Costa Rica, the three nations with the longest-standing tradition of representative democracy establishes a tenuous link, but not more. Yet the case can be made that without some form of accountability there is no restraint on corruption: democratic rule is a necessary, though far from sufficient condition for its eradication. Since corruption has become a habit and natural course, it will endure unless institutions and mechanisms are built to deter it.

With the Sandinistas, the bond between a lack of democratic commitment and the corruption that erupted on the eve of their departure appears undeniable. Of course there had been corruption in Nicaragua since time immemorial. And from the beginning, it was apparent that the comandantes enjoyed many of the traditional perks of Nicaraguan power: Cherokee trucks, fine houses, an extravagant life-style. The austerity of personal demeanor that marked the Cuban Revolution, during the early years at least, was scarce in Managua along with many other goods and services.[28]

When they found themselves rejected by the voters, their true colors—undemocratic, not congenitally or intrinsically corrupt—peered through the olive drab revolutionary uniform. If they had to leave, they might as well take with them what they could; if that complicated life for those who followed, too bad. That a certain degree of similar comportment occurs in all transfers of power did not excuse the grand scale on which it took place on this occasion. Nor did it dissipate the impression that alternating in office was indeed a notion quite foreign to the Sandinistas. The thought that all of this would come back to haunt them seemingly did not cross their minds. In fact, it probably became the single most important discrediting factor in their "crossing of the desert" after the defeat of 1990. According to all accounts it contributed decisively to destroying "*la mística*," or revolutionary mystique,

---

28. Some *comandantes* were reputed to be worse than others, however. Tomás Borge, for example, was said to have taken the traditional Latin American practice to new heights, by enriching himself at the expense of both the Mexican and Nicaraguan treasuries. His mansion hidden behind a modest dwelling in Managua, and his homes in Mexico City and Cuernavaca (some purportedly bequeathed by Mexican government officials) became part of the accepted (though never proven) truths about *la piñata*.

that many of the mid-level militants and rank and file were still imbued with. If the Revolution had become a way to get rich, only fools could remain poor out of romantic idealism or abstract visions of statesmanship.

The FSLN argued, not unreasonably, that much of what happened in those fateful weeks between February 25 and April 25—when they lost the election, and left office, respectively—was just the logical consequence of what had occurred before. With regard to the question of land giveaways to officials during that two-month period, for instance, a Sandinista white paper stated:

> In fact 85 percent of the land titled during the period in·question corresponded to areas already in the possession of the beneficiaries of the land reform program and that had been given to them years before. . . .
> The land was not given out to large landowners: 87 percent of the individual beneficiaries received titles for lots, or lots ranging between 0 and 50 *manzanas*. . . . The great majority of the land given away during the transition period corresponded to institutions that requested land with proper credentials and justifications. The land was transferred to their legal representatives or individuals authorized by them. . . . There was no "piñata." There was simply a transfer of property to beneficiaries of the agrarian reform and responses to individual cases related to the war, the economic crisis, and negotiations with producers.[29]

Regarding the land distributed to Sandinista sympathizers, the white paper provides another logical explanation: "Many Sandinistas who had properties before the Revolution or during the ten-year period actually donated them to the Revolution, and in some cases, the government, after the electoral defeat, decided to return them to their previous owners."[30] On the question of houses, cars, and other personal possessions, Sandinista vice-presidential candidate and writer Sergio Ramírez offered an explanation that rang true. It would be repeated frequently in the course of the debate on *la piñata*, mainly when part of the ruling coalition that succeeded the Sandinistas in power sought to overturn the decrees signed into law just before the transfer of power. Those decrees froze the status quo and extended virtual blanket amnesty to all former officials who could be accused of having appropriated official property from the state. The former vice-president pointed to the central issue:

---

29. Jaime Wheelock Román, *La verdad sobre la piñata* (Managua: IPADE, 1991), pp. 67–68.
30. Ibid., p.4.

When we lost the last elections, *without thinking that we could lose*, we suddenly faced the fact that no Sandinista militant, be he a minister or a rank and file activist, had anything, was even the owner of the house he lived in. Many had turned over to the state their inherited properties; others had survived any old way, poorly paid. In March [1990] we passed a law that granted in property the houses of the state to those who lived in them, thus benefiting thousands of families in the country, and obviously, the Sandinistas. . . . This measure, which we debated at length, awakened a pharisaic scandal for those always avid for riches at any cost, for the avenging right, ready to expel us not only from our homes but from our country: we Sandinistas, who never had a house of our own, were accused of looting the state.[31]

What Ramírez and Wheelock claimed—i.e., that the whole scandal was a politically motivated ploy to discredit the Sandinistas and overturn the agrarian reform—was not far off the mark.[32] But the key was in the first sentence: the Sandinistas never thought they would lose the election, never expected to leave office, never believed that the status quo would change. Many of the things they did during the transition period were justified and provided effective solutions to real problems. Moreover, their bottom line, that the entire matter should be laid to rest, was not erroneous. In Ortega's words:

What is fair is that those properties stay in the hands of those who paid for them, or who rented them for long years. Ethically, it is better for the businesses to stay in the hands of the workers than in those of a guy who went to Miami and who now wants his property back. It would not be ethical to return the property of a *latifundio* owner, a capitalist or a *somocista*. Who can show how they obtained that property before the revolution? We would have to investigate, there would be no end to it. . . . Stability will not come by giving back the properties of the capitalists.[33]

But these views, taken together, also reflected the state of mind of an undemocratic group: until the electoral defeat, the state was theirs to do with as they pleased, and there was no need to foresee or plan for a purely hypothetical departure. The discredit the Sandinistas brought upon themselves through *la piñata* was undeniable. It was a reflection of the strength, limitations, and contradictions of their democratic

---

31. Sergio Ramírez, "Nicaragua: Confesión de amor," *Nexos* (Mexico City), 152, August 1990, p. 44. Emphasis added.

32. "It is obvious now that the great enterprise of the cave-dwelling right is to sabotage the Revolution's only capital, its moral integrity." Ibid., p. 44.

33. Ortega, op. cit., p. 37.

faith. They behaved much better than most ousted Latin American rulers, but much worse than they should have. They showed that there was much more to winning an election than simply holding one, and much more to having an election than just losing it.

There is a positive evolution within the left in power in Latin America. The Sandinistas were a far more democratic regime than the Cubans, even if all the origins of this improvement cannot be claimed by the Nicaraguan revolutionaries themselves. But on the other serious doubts concerning the left's commitment to democratic rule, the amelioration is more difficult to gauge. It involves the way in which the left settles its own differences and manages its disagreements, internal squabbles, and violent divergences.

For many years, left and left-of-center organizations in Europe and Latin America have argued that the way they run their internal affairs is nobody's business but their own, and in any case, is no reflection on how they would govern their respective countries. This contention has rarely held water: the link between domestic life and external outlook is too tight to be dismissed on request. In Europe, many of the Communist parties' difficulties in expanding their influence and electorate resided in their inability to sustain this dichotomy between inside and outside. If democratic centralism, as Lenin labeled the organizational mechanism he constructed, was practiced among Communists, it was hardly believable that they would not apply something roughly analogous to society as a whole if ever given the chance.

In Latin America this argument was never as widely brandished, partly because it wasn't necessary, since the examples of internecine divisions and schisms among left-wing organizations, while common, remained largely ignored. Center and right-wing groups in the hemisphere were not very democratic themselves, for that matter. An additional factor that explained the greater indifference lay in the fact that there was a certain rationale for maintaining strict internal discipline in organizations struggling against the status quo: the constant threat or reality of repression and infiltration under which most groups of the left lived and acted enhanced the relevance of unity and centralism. Thus the question of the democratic practices and principles *within*, even when the left was not in power, while not insignificant, did not surface as a burning issue. But it inevitably came to the fore as the importance of democracy grew on the continent's political agenda.

This became all the more evident as a novel trend emerged among political-military, and even civilian, unarmed organizations from the latter part of the 1970s onward. Partly because of Cuban influence, partly as a reflection of everyday political imperatives, the question of unity among groups of different persuasions—armed or unarmed, radical or moderate, urban or rural—became increasingly crucial. Unity meant alliances among equal and different partners and new procedures for dealing with disagreements, forming joint leaderships, merging forces, and sharing resources. It implied allowing social democrats, reformists of distinct stripes, Catholics, and grass roots movements to peer into previously hermetic mechanisms of control and discipline.

Meeting all of these new demands was not easy, especially for individuals and structures accustomed to deep clandestinity and constant secrecy, for reasons of both survival and command. Its handling of these matters was no longer deemed irrelevant to the manner in which the left aspired to govern if it won wars or elections. As the popular movements or "explosion of civil society" burst forth across the region, the issue of the type of relationship they sought to forge with the "political left" became paramount.

The grass roots groups were often wary of the political left. They frequently asserted their autonomy with vigor and obstinacy, and the political left on many occasions sought to conquer, influence, or burrow into the popular movements to use them to its advantage. The question of internal democracy and the democratic procedures for building alliances and broad coalitions suddenly acquired urgency and relevance. In this context, the following tragedy revealed much about the state of mind that still prevailed in many organizations.

In April of 1984 a vicious internal struggle rocked the Salvadorean insurgency to its foundations. At the highest levels, it involved Salvadoreans, Nicaraguans, and Cubans, and it threatened to destroy the credibility and cohesion of what had become the strongest military grouping in the history of the Latin American armed left. The leader of the Fuerzas Populares de Liberación (FPL), Salvador Cayetano Carpio ("Marcial") was found dead in Managua with a bullet hole through his heart or his head (depending on whose version one believes), a suicide note on his desk, and myriad unanswered questions. All of this occurred just days after he had attended the funeral of his deputy, Mélida Anaya Montes ("Ana María"), also found dead in Managua, in her case with eighty-three icepick-inflicted stab wounds in her body and a bloodied bedroom as the only clues to her murder. The Sandinistas blamed the CIA, then threw a veil of silence on the affair, finally providing a harrowing explanation.

The official story went as follows. As the Salvadorean war got bogged down and the Christian Democratic government headed by José Napoleón Duarte stabilized—thanks largely to American backing—disagreements over strategy within rebel ranks widened. Although in principle all factions subscribed to the idea of a "negotiated solution" to the war, some subscribed more than others. The FPL in particular showed greater reluctance, as the strategy meant renouncing the idea of winning the war and watering down the entire struggle's aims. The rest of the armed organizations, mainly the ERP and the civilian groups, supported by the Sandinistas and Manuel Piñeiro's America Department, were far more enthusiastic about the prospect of a political settlement.

Soon though, divisions mirroring those among the other components of the FMLN began to surface within the FPL. Marcial had built the organization around several ideological and social pillars: Salvadorean labor and the Bloque Popular Revolucionario emanating from the mobilizations at the end of the seventies; the peasant movement that spread from Aguilares earlier in that decade; the teachers' union and its activists; and Jesuits from the UCA. The strength of the FPL lay in this mixture, and in the devotion to the cause that its militants espoused. Its weakness consisted of the way in which the organization gradually outgrew Marcial. His charismatic, romantic, and at the same time extraordinarily dogmatic and authoritarian leadership, invaluable at the group's birth, became a serious obstacle to its further development. This division dovetailed with the split on substance: Marcial distrusted the negotiating posture; his partners favored it.[34] The latter patiently isolated Marcial and were about to impose their call for a more accommodating stance on negotiations and relations with the other groups or evict him from the organization's ruling councils. According to one authoritative account:

> Cayetano Carpio's line was finally and decisively overthrown at a meeting of the FPL's central command in January 1983. The document was approved overwhelmingly by the Central Command, signifying that Ana María was now the de facto leader of the organization.[35]

Marcial, no neophyte at the conspiracy game, discovered the ploy and fought back. He spun his own web of cadres, lines of command, resources, and loyalties and began plotting against Ana María, the Je-

---

34. Marcial's last statement of his stance was formulated in a speech he gave to his cadres on April 1, 1983, five days before Ana María's death. This speech was subsequently published in Mexico City under the title "¡Revolución o muerte! ¡El pueblo armado vencera!" All of the documents involving these incidents were consulted at the Hoover Institution on War, Revolution and Peace archive, in the Latin American subjects collection, boxes 7 and 8.

35. Robert Leiken, "The Salvadorean Left," in Leiken, ed., *Central America: Anatomy of a Conflict* (Washington, D.C.: Pergamon Press, 1984), p. 122.

suits, and the social movement leaders. In that context, Rogelio Baz-zaglia, one of his faithful co-conspirators, decided to take advantage of Marcial's absence in Libya and assassinate Ana María, seeking to make the crime as gruesome as possible so it could then be attributed to either the CIA, another organization of the FMLN, a lover, a maniac, or all four together.

Marcial returned from Libya as soon as he was apprised of the situation. When the Sandinistas confronted him with the evidence of his backers' guilt, and of his own at least tacit responsibility, the aging revolutionary took his own life rather than face the prospect of a trial, prison, and disgrace.[36] The FPL initially processed the matter at the highest echelons, then ventilated it semipublicly for most of its mid-level cadres through a series of meetings and a formal communiqué dated several months after the fact. That was the ostensible end of the story.

There was, however, more to Marcial's end than met the eye. While the overall explanation was fundamentally accurate, a number of discrepancies, omissions, and misrepresentations marred its credibility. To begin with, Marcial's differences with the rest of the FMLN coman-dantes, with the moderate allies, the Cubans and the Nicaraguans, were somewhat more complex. He did indeed oppose a political solution rather than a tactical gesture, but the Cubans and Nicaraguans were pressuring the Salvadoreans into more concessions than they would have agreed to otherwise. The contra war was heating up in Nicaragua, Ronald Reagan was at the peak of his radicalism and pop-ularity, and the invasion of Grenada was only months away.

The Sandinistas tended to believe that a U.S. invasion of Nicaragua was imminent. So did the Cubans. The war in El Salvador was the easiest meaningful concession the Cubans and Nicaraguans thought they could make to placate Ronald Reagan's wrath. They meant busi-ness when they pushed the FMLN and its allies along that road. But the fact was that a U.S. invasion was not about to happen and the Salva-dorean revolution was not theirs to barter away. A negotiated settle-ment in the tiny country, like anywhere else, required the acquiescence of the government, the army, and the right—and these were nowhere to be seen.

Marcial refused to go along. He had been fighting the Cubans and

---

36. According to one published version of the incident, "Rather than comply [with demands that he divulge information on his independent support network and go to Cuba to take an extended rest], Carpio went home and shot himself through the heart." James LeMoyne, "The Guerrilla Network," *New York Times Magazine*, April 6, 1986, p. 75.

Nicaraguans precisely over this for months. The other organizations tended to be more forthcoming with their "older brothers," largely because of their greater reliance on Cuban and Nicaraguan support: arms, logistics, an international network. The FPL's superior share in the five groups' aggregate force—demonstrated nearly ten years later, when they were formally acknowledged by the United Nations and the rest of the FMLN as representing half the insurgents' military strength—made them less compliant. The Cubans, for their part, played skillfully on the differences and suspicions among the organizations, doling out support and perks after their own sympathies.

The internecine strife was thus not limited to the question of negotiations. It involved the "independence" of the Salvadorean movement from the Cubans and the Nicaraguans as well as diverging analyses of events in Central America and U.S. policy toward the region. It was also intensified by the Cubans' insistence that the FMLN become a single organization with a unified command, resources, and troops. The FPL had the most publicly known leader and was the most powerful of the groups. It was logically most skeptical about the virtues of single-party unity. Marcial believed that in a unified leadership he would be systematically outvoted, partly because of the others' convictions, partly through greater Cuban and Nicaraguan influence.

Cayetano Carpio probably did kill himself. He may even have done so with the oft-commented-on four-barreled pistol presented to him by Manuel Antonio Noriega (some say by Panamanian National Guard commander Rubén Paredes; others say Kim Il Sung was the generous soul in question). But the actual conditions of the suicide, as well as the role the Cubans and Sandinistas played, are far more difficult to ascertain. Many of Marcial's sympathizers, within the FPL and without, later claimed that while he may have pulled the trigger, the gun was placed in his hand and the decision to proceed imposed upon him by his close friend Tomás Borge, the Nicaraguan minister of the interior, and by his not-so-close friend, Manuel Piñeiro.[37] Numerous journalistic inquiries during that pe-

---

37. Leiken mentions Borge's presumed role, though not Piñeiro's: "Borge is reported to have told Carpio that he had to choose between suicide and public disclosure of his own and his comrades' involvement in Ana María's murder. Suicide would ensure that the murder would remain an internal FPL affair." Op. cit., p. 122. Leiken makes no reference to the question of Cuban interference and attributes virtually no significance to Carpio's anti-Cubanism. Perhaps this springs from the affair's counterintuitive na-

riod, as well as several conversations held by observers of the whole affair with people close to Marcial, including his wife, Tulita, point in that direction.[38] This author recalls how he first heard of Marcial's death in the company of a senior guerrilla commander from another country, whose ties with Carpio and his wife dated back thirty years: the *comandante's* first reaction was: "Marcial would never commit suicide and would never have Ana María murdered. He might try her and then have her executed, but would not do so surreptitiously." The Cubans and Nicaraguans certainly had a motive for pushing him to suicide: alive, he posed a serious, ongoing problem; dead, the issue could be laid to rest, so to speak.

In any event, the air was never truly cleared. The incident remained shrouded in a cloud of rumor, mystery and suspicion, mudslinging and endless recriminations. Many FPL members, including the nucleus in San Salvador and much of the international network, left the organization, disgusted over their leader's death, the defeat of his positions, and the impossibility of carrying out an open discussion. The story confirmed many analysts' fears that the same vices and attitudes that drove Joaquín Villalobos of the ERP to execute his colleague and adversary, the poet Roque Dalton, less than a decade before, or Hebert Anaya, an ERP-linked human rights activist several years later, had contributed to the death of the "Ho Chi Minh" of Central America, as the megalomaniacal Marcial was wont to label himself.[39] The constant meddling by Piñeiro and the Sandinistas in the internal affairs of the region's revolutionary organizations, as well as the obvious inability of these groups and their leadership to solve disagreements peacefully and coexist with one another, cast a serious

ture: the most hard-line organization was in fact the most anti-Cuban; the Cubans were pressing for a negotiated solution, not a continuation of the armed struggle.

38. LeMoyne's account is the best informed. The former *New York Times* correspondent was the most knowledgeable of all the American journalists to write on the Salvadorean left. He did detect the broader issues: independence from the Cubans, the formation of a single party. LeMoyne substantiated Carpio's anti-Cuban sentiments by quoting him as having told Fidel Castro "to go to hell" months before the incidents. Yet even he acknowledged years later to the author that he did not fully grasp the extent of Cuban involvement in the Carpio incident, nor how much of Carpio's dislike for the negotiated solution and the creation of a single organization stemmed from his resistance to Cuban influence. See LeMoyne, op. cit., pp. 71–78.

39. The most articulate formulation of these doubts, as well as the best in-depth analysis of the entire affair, is Adolfo Gilly's "El suicidio de Marcial," originally published in *Nexos* (Mexico City) no. 76, April 1984, and reprinted in Gilly, *La senda de la guerrilla* (Mexico City: Editorial Nueva Imágen, 1986), pp. 225–262. Gilly made public Marcial's suicide note, as given to him by one of Marcial's closest intellectual friends, Salvadorean economist Rafael Menjívar.

shadow on the revolutionaries' capacity to achieve the goals they were ostensibly fighting for.[40] When eight years later the FMLN signed the New York peace agreements that put an end to the civil war and committed themselves, under adequate protection and conditions, to compete for power exclusively through electoral means, apprehensions lingered about their sudden democratic conversion. Would it apply also within their organizations and among themselves? Would subsequent disagreements breed renewed distrust, generating solutions the old-fashioned way?

On democracy, the left has a point and a past. The point is well taken: representative democracy in Latin America has functioned poorly at best, and mostly when reduced to a meaningless exercise. The past is turbulent and sometimes sordid: the left has demonstrated undemocratic patterns of behavior both in power and in opposition, and serious doubts have floated over its commitment to democratic rule. With this baggage and the Cold War behind it, the left must fashion a new democratic agenda: how can it reconcile its conviction that the democratic cause is in its interests with the evidence of the historical record? The answer lies in democratizing democracy.

---

40. From the author's perspective, the last act of this drama occurred in a small apartment in downtown Mexico City early in 1984. One of Marcial's closest non-Salvadorean friends, a shady journalist, activist, agent, and adventurer by the name of Mario Menéndez, who had dabbled in revolutionary activities for years, had initially taken Marcial's side in the "debate." On July 28, 1983, his magazine *Por Esto* published Marcial's suicide note and the letters he addressed to his organization and to the rest of the FMLN, with an adulatory foreword by Menéndez. This was a strange attitude for Menéndez to take, given the fact that he often had been associated with the Cubans, that his magazine ran large Cuban advertisements, and that he was known to be friends with Fidel Castro and Manuel Piñeiro. In the course of a long conversation, Menéndez, no longer as *"Marcialista"* as before, placed the incident in perspective and tried to convince the author to let it lie. In particular, he repeatedly exonerated the Cubans. Rightly so: after a major crisis in his lengthy, turbulent links with Havana, he had reached an accommodation with the Cubans once again. The version he was giving of the affair had obvious Cuban blessing, as was amply demonstrated by the presence of another guest at the dinner: Edna Castro de Lomelín, Fidel's younger sister. She had been living for years in Mexico, had married a Mexican engineer, and retained affectionate and excellent political ties with her brother. She attended every official event involving the Cubans in Mexico, and while she did not participate in the conversation between Menéndez and the author, she evidently was aware of its gist. In a sense, the point the Cubans and Menéndez were making was: let everyone believe what he or she wants, and let bygones be bygones. The conversation took place in the presence of Joel Ortega, today an editorial writer for *La Jornada*.

12

Democratizing Democracy

■

Before the left draws up its new, postsocialist agenda, it must settle scores with the past. Beyond self-flagellation and self-imposed emasculation, this means three rectifications that together constitute an indispensable first step toward the new democratic imperative. First, the Latin American left must adopt an uncompromising position on the absence of representative democracy and the existence of human rights violations wherever they occur, whenever they take place, and for whatever reason. Second, the left must be absolutely above suspicion and steadfast on the issue of combating corruption—the scourge of Latin American governance and politics, and generally a strong suit for the left. Third, the left must confront the question of internal democracy and implement democratic decision-making and dispute-solving procedures not only within its own ranks, but at the intersection of the political and the social grass roots left.

The first correction of course does not entail ignoring the conditions under which some problems exist, or dismissing everything the Cuban Revolution, for example, has achieved. Nor does it force the left to systematically align itself with every article of propaganda and disinformation spread by its enemies. Not everything that is said, proved, or stated in these matters is as straightforward and incontrovertible as it often appears. But it does mean placing the issue of democracy at the top of the agenda, as well as unequivocally criticizing those who do not conform to these standards. Reasons of conviction and convenience encourage this orientation.

This rectification implies being adamant in relation to the past, the present, and the future; it obliges the left to refrain from excusing any suspension of democratic practices and any violation of human rights, regardless of its motivations. Nonetheless, personal histories should not be a litmus test, as many Latin American right-wingers frequently demand. Outside of direct, immediate complicity, what one did in the past cannot be a reason for exclusion or rejection today, on the condition that a clear stance be taken on whatever may have occurred before. Without such a radical, obstinate stand, it will be difficult for the left to be taken seriously in its protestations of democratic faith. Moreover, it will forsake the banner of democratization to a right and center who have far more skeletons in the closet. Simple arithmetic proves this: because there have been so many more right and right-of-center regimes in the region's recent history, their balance sheet registers a far greater number of violations of democracy and human rights than the left's. There are far more politicians, businessmen, soldiers, and intellectuals on the right who countenanced such acts than there are peers of theirs on the left.

The second deck to clear involves the acceptance of the principle of competing groups alternating in power, and of the conditions and constraints in which they do so. It makes no sense for the left to accept the idea of attaining power and subsequently losing it, only to spend its time in office building so-called irreversible momentum, and then destroying everything in its wake when forced from power unexpectedly or prematurely. Salvador Allende and most of the Chilean left played an exemplary role in this respect: Allende always accepted the principle and the reality of his election for one term only and never aspired to remain in office longer than that term, or otherwise than through an electoral mandate. But the Popular Unity did have a penchant for irreversibility, and this may well have contributed to its undoing.

Accepting alternation at any level—federal, regional, municipal— entails renouncing and combating any form of corruption. The left has generally not been corrupt: the military, the center, the business elite, and most governments have. The Chilean left was spick-and-span honest in office; the Cuban Revolution, while it undoubtedly bred varieties of corruption in later years, did so on an incomparably more modest scale than virtually any other government in the Caribbean or in the island's history. Jacobo Arbenz left Guatemala penniless and died a poor man in exile.

But there are worrisome trends in Central America, not only concerning the Nicaraguan *piñata*. The best way to deal with them is through principles and convictions, not coercion or personal virtue. It is only through the apprenticeship of democratic rule in unions, municipal or regional administrations, and the freewheeling world of parliamentary debate and an open press that the revolutionaries who come down from the mountains in El Salvador, for instance, will learn the secret of honesty: only ideas can stop corruption, even if laws are necessary to give the ideas force.

The example of the Partido dos Trabalhadors in São Paulo is noteworthy in this respect: their former head of the city council, Eduardo Suplicy, was elected senator from the state of São Paulo in 1990 with over 30 percent of the vote while at the same time the PT candidate for governor of the state received under 10 percent. One of the reasons: Suplicy had become well known in São Paulo for combating corruption in city hall and municipal services. The PT's strong showing in the 1992 municipal elections across the country was partly the result of its leading role in the drive to unseat the corruption-ridden government of ultimately dethroned President Fernando Collor de Mello.[1] A similar situation affects the PRD in Mexico. Where Cárdenas has followers known locally for their honesty and perceived to be extensions of his own reputation for personal probity and denunciations of the Mexican political system's turpitude, his party performs well electorally. On the contrary, where his regional representatives are PRI clones or renegades who split off from the ruling party and took with them its traditional vices and not quite saintly customs, the PRD fares poorly.

In a continent devastated by corruption, rooted as it is in centuries of political culture, economic realities, and social inequities, the banner of honesty in government is one to raise as high as can be. If only because it has governed more seldom, the left is less guilty of corruption than others. Probity must be a cornerstone of its democratic agenda; it is an indispensable prerequisite for the erection and viability of a democratic platform for the left or for anyone. As democratization has spread through the region, tolerance for corruption in high office has plummeted. Scandals involving presidential families, less-than-kosher privatization schemes, insider trading on booming stock exchanges and astonishing insensitivity to widespread poverty have erupted in Brazil, Venezuela, Argentina and Mexico.

A similar situation prevails regarding internal democracy, the establishment of democratic bylaws within the left's organizations, and governing relations with other popular movements. As we have seen, this is both a paramount issue and a delicate one. The left's scorecard on this matter is not impressive. There is a publicly perceived trade-off

---

1. For an eye-raising account of corruption in high places under and including Collor, see James Brooke, "Looting Brazil," *New York Times Magazine*. November 8, 1992.

involved here, as well as a truly substantive problem. "Democratism," a synonym for endless meetings, and divisive votes, conveys a distinct and negative impression of everything but efficiency, modernity, decisiveness, and leadership.

There are two different issues involved. One is internal procedure: the new Latin American left has to leave behind decades of democratic centralism, authoritarian, vertical decision-making processes, and ideological conformity and move on to freer and more diversified intraorganizational mechanisms. None of the rules that can be adopted are flawless or risk-free. Holding primaries to select candidates for elective office, for example, can be a terribly fratricidal affair, pitting factions, regions, and personalities against each other without the healing, postprimary reconciliation of other latitudes. Where cohesiveness, common goals, and a sense of political community is incipient, such practices seem too dangerous and counterproductive. In fact, they are not.

Likewise, the penchant for grass roots democracy, where leadership structures have to consult on every single decision and seek a mandate for every initiative, can be a paralyzing, frustrating process. It impedes the formation of alliances and dilutes the leadership's legitimacy and capacity for presenting itself as a valid interlocutor with other organizations, the government, or international partners. It engenders interminable meetings and debates, allowing adversaries to sow discord. Worst of all, it sends a signal of indecisiveness and chaos to the outside world. Yet despite all these very real drawbacks, the ravages of the Leninist tradition are so pervasive and the distrust regarding the left's democratic convictions so widespread and justified that there can be no excess in this direction for now. The inconveniences of too much democracy are preferable to the scourge of its absence or insufficiency. The left will have to make do, accommodating more intensive and frequent democratic practices, managing the perverse by-products as best it can.

This type of contradiction has plagued two of the newer and most promising members of the left: the PRD in Mexico and the PT in Brazil. Both were born from the convergence of several political and ideological currents, rendering some form of democratic coexistence imperative in the first place. Furthermore, given the importance played in their gestation by the struggle against authoritarian rule, a cult of internal democracy quickly sprang up. Everything had to be voted on, debated openly, and questioned anew. In addition, the electoral expectations they awakened, though only sporadically fulfilled, made a place on their slates of candidates a much sought-after prize. Finally, their "basist" character made life miserable for a leadership besieged by myriad other problems. Alliances, deals, and negotiations were subject to virtual vetos by the most radical elements among the rank and file. The emotional strength of the call for political purity, together with the rejection of compromise and the recurrent demand for all-encompassing debate, shackled Cárdenas and Lula along with the rest of the core leadership, transforming them into prisoners of the very forces they unleashed.

Thus the PT was unable to fortify, or even maintain, the alliances in the 1990 and 1992 elections that it forged during the 1989 presidential campaign. Lula and his colleagues were unable to convince the party to support other parties on the first round even in the case of former ally and *carioca* native son Leonel Brizola, who sought election as governor of the state of Rio de Janeiro, once again, in October of 1990.[2]

Similarly, every time a PRI-dissident would split off from the ruling party in Mexico, Cárdenas found himself hamstrung by internal strife and was often unable to provide a safe and dignified haven for the few Mexican politicians brave enough to break with the "system." He was frequently unsuccessful in persuading his followers to accept them, much less respect them. He also encountered stubborn resistance to postprimary reconciliation. Whenever one faction lost to another in a runoff vote for the PRD candidacy for the governorship of a state or the mayoralty of a city, or top of the ticket slots in congressional elections, it pouted and withdrew from the fray or even sabotaged the winning faction, preferring its defeat to that of the PRD's nominal adversary, the ruling party. The fact that the PRD was largely Cárdenas's party compounded the dilemma: he had often to refrain from intervening, lest he find himself criticized as no more than another caudillo with a mass following.

Worst of all, like all new organizations whose very creation was inextricably bound up with the demands of the poor and disenfranchised, the Partido dos Trabalhadores and Cárdenas faced a problem of credibility in governance from the outset. They were portrayed, sometimes accurately but often in bad faith, as unfit to manage an admin-

---

2. "Last year the problem was that the PT proved incapable of forging political alliances. The national leadership showed up in every state and stated that it would be important for us to recuperate the alliances made in the second round of the presidential election. But a lot of people in the PT thought that since Lula got 48 percent of the vote, those votes belonged to the PT and would be transferred to local candidates. And we lost those votes, because we didn't make alliances in places like Rio, Bahia, Pernambuco." Lula, interview with the author, Mexico City, June 5, 1991.

istration at any level, let alone to run the country and solve its problems. What better proof of this inadequacy than their failure to put their own house in order, as demonstrated amply by the chaos and divisions besetting their parties?

And yet there was no solution but to persevere in the democratic effort, hoping that time, success, and growing familiarity with both the benefits and complexities of this course would tone down the divisions and negative side effects. Likewise, there was indeed no choice but to keep hoping that the electorate would eventually appreciate the guarantees that internal democracy extended to everyone who supported these parties—and to those who did not—and not just for left-wing activists with hours to spend on never-ending deliberation. What's more, this behavior was unavoidable, as it had become an essential condition for molding lasting ties of trust with the grass roots movements that formed the political left's bedrock, and the only real hope for social change and electoral success.

One of the foremost components of the left's new democratic agenda has to be its encouragement and strengthening of popular movements. Consequently, the relationship between the political and social left is key: only if democratic, respectful bonds among equals can be tied between these two varieties of Latin American activism will the left play the role it aspires to. In view of the inherent disorder and spontaneity of most popular movements, and their heterogeneous and almost seasonal nature, the responsibility for building a democratic relationship between the grass roots and the political machinery and party bureaucracy—an inevitable, however undesirable ingredient of political life anywhere—falls chiefly to the political left.

The challenge is immense. How to provide political expression to social movements without betraying them, altering their nature, or destroying their originality is an ancient quandary that surfaced as early as the middle of the last century. The link between labor unions and political parties in nineteenth-century Europe was a central theme of practical discussion and theoretical reflection for the founders of many of England's, Germany's and France's powerful social-democratic organizations. It remains so today, as exemplified by the ongoing vicissitudes of the relationship between the Trade Union Congress and the Labor Party in Britain, or the relationship between the environmental movement in Germany and the Green and Social Democratic parties. Yet these tensions pale in comparison to the difficulties confronting the Latin American left, as the homogeneity and discipline of the labor movement contrast sharply with the diversity and exuberance of students, base communities, peasant groups, intellectuals, and squatters.

The left cannot abdicate the responsibility of empowering grass roots groups, no matter how narrow-based, ephemeral, or conflictive they may appear. Despite its frequently well-founded wariness of politicians and understandable frustration over the formality and paralysis of many Latin American institutions, popular protest must transcend its purely social origins and forms of struggle, reaching into the political arena. Imposition and manipulation of the social left by the political one will no longer function in Latin America. Small groups of hard-core left-wing militants can still take over a movement, but they soon find themselves with nothing more than the carcass of a once thriving hotbed of organization and solidarity. Conversely, the grass roots groups cannot expect that by keeping their distance from electoral politics and the give-and-take of the political process they can preserve their virginity and achieve results. This attitude just contributes to their transcience and decline once the conjunctures that gave them birth come to an end.

The political left has to empower the social left by making available to it the devices and rights it has conquered, starting with slates of candidates for municipal, regional, and national office at both the executive and legislative level. It means furnishing access to the media, be it the left's own, or that opened to political parties by law. It involves granting international legitimacy to and establishing contacts for the grass roots organizations, through political parties' foreign associations; and finally, placing the social left's demands and aspirations in a broader, programmatic perspective that includes economic viability, compatibility with other demands, and long-term sustainability.[3]

That agenda has two chapters. The first one concerns giving content to representative democracy through the reinforcement of civil society, without which it is an empty shell. But it also entails building the bridge between the former and the latter, through municipal or state-level democracy, in a context of decentralization presided over by a strong state. Second, it means extending the reach of democratic

---

3. As one student of the attempts to do so in the city of São Paulo has put it: "Deepening democracy entails devising political-institutional information about, access to, and influence in the governmental arenas in which collectively binding policy decisions are made. Social movements, specifically urban popular movements [in São Paulo], have contributed to deepen Brazilian democracy in [several] ways." Sonia Alvarez, "Deepening Democracy: Social Movement Networks, Constitutional Reform and Radical Urban Regimes in Contemporary Brazil," mimeo, 1992, pp. 2, 33.

institutions far beyond the limits of electoral processes. There can be no strong civil society without representative democracy; nor can the democratization of other institutions and procedures—from economic policy to an independent judiciary, including labor unions and the media—be achieved without elections. But elections alone are not enough.

The intersection of Latin America's recent institutional democratization and the nearly simultaneous blossoming of popular movements has been municipal democracy. The hemisphere has become urban, and its most lacerating, depressing problems are increasingly city- and town-based, as the villages of the *sertão* and Juan Rulfo vanish into dust and nostalgia. Rubem Fonseca and his descriptions of organized beggars and the Art of Walking through the streets of Rio take over where Pedro Páramo stayed behind:

> We are not the Union of Beggars: that's an opposition fabrication. Our name is the Union of Homeless and Shirtless. . . . We don't beg, we don't want to beg, we just demand what people throw away. We don't hide under the bridges and the freeways, or in cardboard boxes, and we don't sell gum and lemons at the crossings. We want to be seen, we want everyone to smell our filth, our sweat, to feel our stench everywhere; we want the others to see us cooking, sleeping, fucking and shitting in the nice places where the rich go by or where they live. I gave orders for our men not to shave, for our men and women and children not to bathe. . . . And no one begs. It's better to steal than to beg. . . .[4]

History, identity, and abject poverty persist in the countryside, but an overwhelming demography and social conflict are increasingly the attributes of urban life. The importance then, of transforming the politics of city-dwelling is growing, as is the Latin America left's awakening to this reality.[5] As was noted earlier, grass roots movements in dozens of the hemisphere's large cities were able to successfully negotiate the transition from resistance to authoritarian rule to electoral participation and municipal administration. The passage was not de-

4. Rubem Fonseca, *Romance Negro* (São Paulo: Companhia Das Letras, 1992), pp. 45–46.

5. "Under present circumstances, in which the totality of the nations of Latin America have as their goal the consolidation of democracy, the municipal issue occupies a central place on the agenda, appearing as the locus of interaction between the state and society. This can lead to the concrete possibility of municipalities becoming useful instruments to solve citizens' problems." Pedro Jacobi, "Descentralização municipal e particpação dos cidadãos: apontamentos para o debate," *Lua Nova, Cultura e Modernidade* (São Paulo), May 1990, p. 128

void of contradictions and setbacks, but both in theory and in practice municipal democracy became the seam uniting the political and social left of the continent's sprawling metropolises. Without the advent of representative democracy, this would have been impossible and, of course, exceptions endure. At this writing, Mexico City and Buenos Aires still do not elect their municipal authorities; Colombia did so only in 1986, and Chile held its first municipal election since 1971 in 1992.

The Mexican exception stretched beyond the capital and underscored the necessity of a democratic transition. Outside an overall process of democratization, even the strong grass roots urban movement that burgeoned in many Mexican cities, as well as various experiments and reforms in municipal activism and decentralization, was doomed. Isolated experiences did exist, the most important one of which was probably the Juchitán process in the state of Oaxaca dating back to 1980 and the first left-wing municipal council elected in Mexico. But as elsewhere in the country, lack of resources and constant hostility from the central government destroyed these attempts, breeding corruption, abuses, and ultimately failure. The conditions for success are simply nonexistent: of the country's 2,378 *municipios* in 1983 only 1.7 percent were led by an opposition mayor; in 1986 the figure rose to 2.4 percent. By 1990 it had risen to barely 5 percent: the one-party system was alive and well at the municipal level.[6] At the same time, the need for decentralization was more urgent than ever. Despite the De la Madrid government's ostensible efforts to undertake reforms between 1982 and 1988, Mexico's centralism persisted:

> Municipal autonomy, which was declared with the reform of 1983, has remained a dead letter, since 80 percent of municipal revenues originate in federal or state governments. Many rural *municipios* lacking resources cannot even hire an administrative employee. Of almost 3 million public servants in Mexico, only 150,000 are municipal employees.[7]

Municipal democracy should be the centerpiece of the left's democratic agenda, not so much because the region's problems can be solved at this level but because it typifies the kind of change that is viable, significant, and constitutes a stepping-stone for the future. While it is a relatively new phenomenon in the region, it traces its

---

6. Dieter Paas, "Municipio y organización no gubernamental en México: Una relación difícil," in *Municipio y democracia* (Mexico City: Friedrich Nauman-Stiftung/ Praxis, 1991), p. 28.
7. Ibid.

distant origins back to the Ibero-American tradition of the *cabildo abierto* of sixteenth-century Spain and colonial times and the *municipio libre* of the nineteenth century. Municipal democracy has also been inspired by the reflection in Western Europe regarding decentralization and local self-rule that stems both from the Italian Communist Party's experience in Emilia-Romagna since World War II, and the Spanish Socialist and French decentralization and municipal reforms of the 1980s.

Municipal democracy means encouraging social movements and autonomous institutions outside the state. The left's antistatism, to the extent it exists, must direct its energies in this direction; where it doesn't exist, given the left's statist tradition, it must be sown and nurtured.[8] By so doing, the left can tap into the deep well of antistatist sentiment in Latin America and redirect it into the political arena, instead of standing by and watching the right monopolize it in the economic domain. Municipal democracy allows the left to do so and at the same time supplies an antidote for social movements' tendencies toward rapid exhaustion. It is close enough to the ground—even in the monster cities of Mexico, São Paulo, Caracas, Buenos Aires—to be approachable by popular organizations. But it involves a sufficiently elevated level of administration to make a difference: a growing number of tasks of everyday life and social development can be tackled only at a municipal scale. Latin America's classic macrocephalia implies that the political stakes of running a capital are high. Excepting Brazil and to a lesser extent Colombia, capital cities are also financial, commercial, and cultural nerve centers: whoever holds office controls countless strings, including those of important purses.

The apparent schizophrenia recently affecting Latin American electorates has already been mentioned. Right-of-center, probusiness regimes are voted in at a national level, while left-of-center, socially oriented administrations are elected at a municipal one. Starting in

---

8. There remains a great deal of skepticism within the left on the virtues of decentralization: "The decentralization proposal can respond to very different interests and situations: counterinsurgency in Colombia, a more strict control of popular sectors in Chile, privatization of the state in the U.S., some of the latter but also the broadening of rights and liberties in Argentina, state abdication of responsibility in the face of growing social demands in Mexico, etc. . . . The term 'state decentralization' maintains a high degree of ambiguity, both because of its multiple meanings and because of the diversity of the actors that subscribe to it. Suffice it to say that two authors as opposed in their ideology as Hernando de Soto—a representative of the Latin American new right—and Jordi Borja—whom we could label as a member of the post-Marxist new left—both appear as unconditional defenders of the decentralization of the state." José Luis Coraggio, *Ciudades sin rumbo* (Quito: Ciudad-SIAP, 1991), pp. 151, 155.

Lima and Rio de Janeiro in 1982, the trend then went on to the Brazilian elections of 1988, when PT or other left-of-center mayors were elected in numerous cities, including São Paulo, Santos (the nation's most important port), Porto Alegre, the largest southern city, Vitoria, among others. It then shifted to Montevideo, where Tabaré Vazquez was elected at the head of a Frente Amplio (Communists, Socialists, grass roots groups) coalition; to Rosario, Argentina's second-largest city, where a socialist ran and won in 1988 and was subsequently reelected in 1991; to Asunción in post-Stroessner Paraguay, where a socialist doctor was elected mayor in May 1991 on a grass roots ticket; and finally to Caracas and Belo Horizonte in late 1992.

The democratization process that allowed this proliferation of left-wing city halls was obviously insufficient in itself. If unaccompanied by a transfer of fiscal resources and responsibility, the reforms made matters worse: they spared federal authorities the wrath of electorates provoked by cutbacks in education, health, housing, sewage, drinking water, urban transportation, and everything else under the sun, without granting municipal authorities the wherewithal to cope with mounting demands and shrinking budgets. In some cases, such as Colombia, a loudly praised municipal reform shifted resources and tax-collecting authorities to the towns and cities. In other countries the federalist tradition was well rooted but the opposite dilemma besieged the poorer cities: without funding from the wealthier areas of the nation, raising living standards and providing basic services was virtually impossible.

The left's banner on this issue cannot be limited to fostering grass roots democracy and involving social movements in municipal administration. Nor can it simply be content with holding free and fair, frequent and meaningful local elections. The cause of municipal democracy requires money and ways to raise it and spend it locally, while at the same time ensuring that the often abysmal regional disparities that beset many of the region's countries are not locked in place. Part of the solution lies in establishing minimum, uniform property tax rates and policies everywhere in the nation, and transferring responsibilities to cities and states only together with the money and revenue-raising mechanisms to shoulder them.[9] The regional revenue-sharing mechanism of course must remain national: otherwise the multiple Belindias of Latin America (the name given wryly to Brazil because its south-central region resembles Belgium and the rest of the nation looks

---

9. This is exactly the opposite of what is occurring. For example, in June 1992, the Mexican state of Oaxaca, one of the poorest in the nation, drastically lowered its urban property tax in order to "attract investment and be more competitive."

like India) will never change. This is why regional leaders of the poorer regions of Brazil clamor for a strong state and denounce attempts to weaken it:

> Brazil's great problem is the high mobility of the population. The intervention of the state is necessary to ensure that the poorer regions, with fewer resources, less investment and infrastructure can compete with the richer regions. Without state intervention, the poorer regions would be left with nothing.[10]

Accountability, fairness, and citizens' involvement are only possible at a low administrative threshold. The region's Jacobin centralism has contributed greatly to stifling local initiative and discouraging local searches for solutions to age-old problems. But many of the obstacles confronting most of the hemisphere's large and mid-sized cities can be overcome locally, on the condition that resources be available: transportation, land regularization, sewage and drinking water, housing, public safety and security, and certain spheres of education and health.[11] The conservative antistate trend in Latin America and the world must be reoriented. It is now generally accepted that the private sector will not meet these challenges, but that the federal and distant state can do so only with exorbitant costs and a frequently corrupt, inefficient bureaucracy. Municipal responsibility with local oversight and accountability through urban social movements and city institutions—elected authorities, councils composed of providers and recipients of services, the Church, teachers' associations, labor unions—can square the circle. They can do so all the more when they are flexible and able to learn from experience, as has partially occurred with the PT in Brazil, both practically and ideologically:

> The confrontation with the neoliberal project has forced the left to revise many of its views. . . . for example, the PT had a very ingrained, strategic vision of state ownership of mass transport. And yet, the experience of our administrations shows that state ownership is not a necessary con-

---

10. Miguel Arraes, interview with the author, Recife, August 12, 1990.

11. The temptation to transfer all responsibilities to municipal governments is perhaps stronger among those who have held both federal and state office, like Waldir Pires in Brazil: "My experience is that we need strong local powers. Democracy can be consolidated only if we include the participation of the local community in government, and have stronger municipal governments. Even if a municipal and a state government can join forces, they shouldn't. Education, for example, should be municipally administered, though the curriculum should be set by the federal union." Waldir Pires, interview with the author, Salvador de Bahia, August 16, 1990. There is a risk here, detected by observers of current education decentralization efforts in Latin America: sacrificing the poorer regions in favor of the richer ones.

dition for making transportation cheap and efficient. The establishment by the authorities of control over the provision of service—by controlling prices, frequency, and quality—proved to be a fundamental element for improving mass transport. . . . This experience shows that making things public does not necessarily mean turning them over to state ownership and that state ownership is not an end in itself.[12]

Although there are no guarantees of success, this is the only hypothetical remedy to the traditional Latin American bane of patronage and clientelism: a vice not unknown in other areas of the globe, but one that achieved true fame and fortune south of the Rio Grande. Only through municipal democracy, accountability, and organization can basic services become a citizens' right and cease being favors doled out by the powerful to their meek and disadvantaged friends, supporters, or captive electorates. The history of patronage and clientelism in the region is a rich and folkloric one, from the land distributed to squatters by urban caciques of the thirties and forties, to Mexican President Carlos Salinas's modernized pork-barrel program known as Solidaridad, and even including Evita Perón's love affair with the *descamisados* of Buenos Aires in the late 1940s. Transforming favors into rights is not a simple task, and the cultural, social, and economic obstacles are daunting. Obviously, these scourges are not limited to the urban realm, and can certainly not be eradicated exclusively at a municipal level. Public-sector featherbedding, import licensing, doling out good jobs in government to cronies and allies is certainly not going to disappear thanks to municipal democracy.

But without accountability or social movements organizing and pressuring responsive municipal authorities to provide fair and adequate services without an immediate, direct payback, reform is unthinkable. What cannot be accomplished municipally can scarcely be achieved elsewhere. Through municipal participation, the left can begin to do away with this historical parasitism.[13]

---

12. Jorge Bittar, *O Modo petista de governar, Caderno Especial de Teoria y Debate* (São Paulo: Publicação do Partido dos Trabalhadores, 1992), pp. 18–19.

13. Not that this is easily accomplished, as "popular participation" is no simple thing to achieve: "[In São Paulo] the PT municipal administration of Luiza Erundina proposed to create its own version of 'Popular Councils' which would genuinely be representative of popular sectors. . . . According to the mayor's early pronouncements, the precise shape of the Popular Councils would emerge 'from the people themselves.' . . . But during the first year of the PT administration, 'the people themselves' did not organize spontaneously to form Popular Councils. In a few neighborhoods . . . embryonic Popular Councils were formed, but soon ceased to function. . . . By its second year, the Erundina administration began to acknowledge the need for local government to institutionalize and regularize the Popular Councils." Alvarez, op. cit., pp. 21, 25, 26, 27.

It is on safe ground here. Although there have long been important centrifugal forces at work in the business community in São Paulo, Medellín, and Monterrey, for example, the region's traditional right and center are often centrally or nationally oriented. By and large the right's power base and constituency is made up of nationwide institutions or interlocutors: the Army, the Church hierarchy, the United States, and the business community as a whole.[14] The left, while not alone in taking up the banner of decentralization and municipal democracy, can be confident that it will not find itself competing for the same turf with other sectors of the political spectrum. What's more, it might attract to its cause social strata or political factions that would normally favor such transformations but cannot take the lead.

Though the centralist, Jacobin, statist tradition of the left is not easy to undo or overcome, a growing number of organizations and thinkers on the left throughout the continent are grasping the importance of this agenda. Even—or perhaps, most of all—former guerrilla fighters are convinced of the priority of municipal democracy:

> The hardest thing is to build local democracy. And that is the most important effort and the central effort: to develop local democracies and citizens' administration at the level of municipal government, and in that way lay the foundations for a democratic country.[15]

As the left wins mayoralties, it becomes more convinced of the virtues of decentralization and municipal democracy. As it bestows greater priority upon these issues, it will in all likelihood win more towns and cities. Similarly, to the extent that people become better organized and more involved with their local authorities, the services provided will improve. The Brazilian left is beginning to understand this dynamic:

> The new progressive municipal administrations have the opportunity of fostering a change in public policies, by stimulating the expansion of

---

14. Perhaps the most notable exception to this trend was the 1983 municipal and decentralization reform in Colombia. In the words of the first mayor of Bogotá, certainly no left-winger: "The election of mayors, which constitutes the support and encouragement of the decentralization process, is above all a political step, and its main consequences are also political . . . That process, because of its content and scope, constitutes an authentic municipal revolution, because it is the equivalent of a peaceful, gradual and slow change, but no less substantive and deep, in everything that has do with administrative organization of the state, and the opening of political spaces for the expression of all democratic positions. Its consequences, though mainly visible at a local level, will also involve many aspects of national life." Jaime Castro, *La reforma municipal: perestroika colombiana* (Bogotá: La oveja negra, 1989), pp. 62–63.

15. Bernardo Gutiérrez, interview with the author, Cartagena de Indias, October 6, 1991.

decentralizing practices. In the meantime, it is important to stress that participation will work only if users are organized, and if they meet the greatest challenge, which is to guarantee their autonomy from the authorities.[16]

The banner of local democracy and decentralization meshes with the already suggested nationalist demand for regional integration. Funding for flattening regional disparities and transferring local responsibilities can come from the type of institutions described in Chapter 11 and which would result from the right type of regional economic integration. By providing resources for the poorer regions, regional integration and funding agencies permit wealthier cities and states to manage a greater part of their own money. The double movement—downward, bringing administrative responsibilities, services and expenditures closer to each community—and upward, elevating sources of funding to a regional scale through international agreements—can contribute strongly to solving the problem of municipal fiscal policy. There is at least a measure of truth in the argument that decentralization, municipal democracy, and the emphasis on social movements do not in themselves necessarily represent a step forward, that it all depends on the specific content of each and all of these developments. There is a neoliberal decentralization trend; the left's program of democratization must be different, but not naïvely optimistic or fraught with idealizations:

> As far as the administrative and economic aspects are concerned, the democratizing project bets on a territorial decentralization of the state, trusting that the multiplication of areas of local administration will open up areas favorable to cultural struggles. But they must combat their tendency to idealize a certain space—the local one—or level—the municipal one—or "daily life" as false answers to the wrong questions. In any case the democratizing project has emerged in the shadows of the neoliberal one, and must win credibility as an alternative.[17]

Here, then, is the first democratic order of battle for the left: to encourage every conceivable expression of civil society, every social movement, every form of self-management that Latin American reality generates. It must make its contribution toward this goal at the municipal level, where it can count and not betray itself: municipal democracy is the meeting point of an increasingly proliferating and

---

16. Jacobi, op. cit., p. 142.
17. Corraggio, op. cit., pp. 203, 205.

vibrant grass roots organization and a real, though limited, process of electoral democratization. Finally, the left must ensure that this municipal renaissance will not be stillborn, by coupling it with a drive for decentralization of responsibilities and resources, but without forever freezing existing regional, ethnic, and social and economic disparities.

∎

But this can only be part of the Latin American left's democratic agenda. Making the region's democracy more responsive and less formal is an endeavor that cannot be limited to the strengthening of civil society and developing new forms of political expression. It also entails a profound reform of existing democratic institutions, making them more accountable, meaningful, and representative. The reform of politics, the state, and democracy is the second chapter of the left's democratic agenda.

The Latin American debate over the breadth of democracy has been distorted by two false alternatives. The first one juxtaposes in turn two definitions of the term: elections, the prevalence of the rule of law and civil liberties, versus its extension well beyond the political sphere and into the economic and social realm of society. The left has sustained the second approach; the right and often the United States, the first. The left has often dismissed democracy as a sham because it did not alleviate poverty, reduce inequalities, and protect national sovereignty. The right and the United States have on countless occasions declared that "x" percentage of the nations, peoples, or regions of Latin America "live under democracy" simply because they held an election, regardless of the conditions under which it took place or whether the country was at war, its people tortured and in prisons, or there was a higher voter turnout of the dead than of the living. Perhaps the best summary of this situation can be found in a most unlikely source: a report by a group of U.S.-led observers to the Guatemalan presidential elections in November 1990:

> The most difficult problem underlying the formal success of the electoral process is the exclusion of large sectors from effective participation in Guatemalan society. The climate of violence and the assassination of political leaders has discouraged the discussion and debate of many issues such as land reform and human rights. Our delegation wishes to state that, as successful as the electoral process was, it occurred within an excessively narrow frame of reference. Most of those who did not register or vote are indigenous peoples [who make

up half the population]. Elections do not automatically translate into successful, even viable democracies.[18]

This conceptual polarization has precluded the possibility of a third stance representing a synthesis of the two aforementioned viewpoints: that democracy, while admittedly limited to the political sphere, should not be restricted to elections and the formal existence of the rule of law and the bureaucratic preservation of civil liberties. This conception holds that even without broadening its definition to economic and social matters, democracy in Latin America can become far more representative and significant through profound reforms within the political sphere.

The second false alternative concerns the status of the state. One party to this false dilemma posits that the central problem of the Latin American state and of its necessary reform lies in its size and illegitimate penetration into the economic and social sphere. The solution resides in its reduction, although the results may prove contradictory.[19] The other side stresses the opposite view, that the state should not shrink and must intervene in economic and social life. Both sides attribute the utmost importance to the state's size and reach.

In fact, the real problem of the state in Latin America can be found in its lack of accountability, its undemocratic nature, and its inability to do much that is required of it. It can and must be radically overhauled, without necessarily shrinking. Indeed, in order to perform adequately, it might even have to grow. The crux of the matter is the nature of the state, not its dimensions or even the type of relationship bonding it to the economic and social spheres. The issue is principally political; the chore of reform is decidedly democratic.

The two false alternatives have their origins and explanation. But they can mainly be retraced back to a couple of characteristics of modern democratic political systems and to an intrinsic tension that has beleaguered them from their conception onward, following them like a shadow. As the French philosopher Louis Althusser concluded after a lifetime studying Marx as well as Montesquieu and Machiavelli, contemporary ideology and representative democracy is wrenched by two internal contradictions. First, for it to function, everyone—the masses

---

18. Statement by the National Democratic Institute International Delegation to the [Guatemalan] Presidential Elections, Guatemala City, November 12, 1990.

19. Indeed, as Brazilian sociologist Fernando Henrique Cardoso has remarked, and any halfway perceptive inhabitant of Mexico City, for example, can confirm, laying off public employees is no solution: they simply reappear on sidewalks and on street corners, or, if they are policemen, on the other side of the counter, so to speak: carrying out holdups and kidnappings through their previously acquired expertise.

and elites, the dominated and their dominators—has to "believe" (in) the tenets of democratic rule: equality before the law, the power of the vote, the fairness of the judicial system, the consent of the governed, and the accountability of those who govern.[20]

For everyone to "believe" (in) these canons, they have to "work," more or less. There cannot be a flagrant, constant discrepancy between principles and their daily application. But if everyone "believes," and the mechanisms "work," the fundamental division of the existing order between masses and elites, dominated and dominators, poor and rich, leads eventually to the revolt of the majority against the existing order. So modern democracy is forever torn between the need to make its tenets believable and functional and at the same time to ensure that their too perfect performance not lead to an overthrow of the order that installed them in the first place. The mechanisms have to "work" just well enough to be "believable" and just ineffectively enough to ensure the survival of the system.

The second contradiction concerns the status of the downtrodden. To paraphrase a worn-out proverb, "*Si el pueblo estuviera unido, jamás sería vencido*" (if the people were united, they would never be defeated). The point is that the "people" *are* mostly divided and generally defeated. Maintaining their divisions and accentuating them if need be is thus a fundamental requirement for preservation of the status quo. But although modern democratic, liberal, and individualistic ideology engenders a divisive, fragmenting dynamic by addressing people as "individuals" or "subjects," at the same time it possesses powerful collective connotations through its symbolic references: God, the Law, the Nation, and the Revolution. Modern ideology needs to divide the "people" addressing them as individuals, different from each other (different nationalities, races, religions, languages, color, gender, work qualifications, wealth, political preference, and ideological affinity) because their unity would undermine the stability of the existing order. But it unites "the people" by addressing them through collective entities: citizenship, the nation, culture, electorates, unions, political

---

20. These remarks about the conclusions Althusser reached in the years before his death are taken from Etienne Balibar, *Ecrits pour Althusser* (Paris: Editions La Découverte, 1991), mainly pp. 111–118. Althusser, as well as most of the European thinkers and historians of ideology, from Foucault to Coletti, would perhaps be shocked by the use of the terms "believe," "believable" to describe an extraordinarily complex process whereby a set of ideas, customs, representations, rituals, and traditions becomes an ideology. The simplification is extreme, and possibly pernicious, but for the purposes of this discussion it is permissible. The point is not to mistake belief for a conscious, deliberate, and immediate process; or to imply through its use that behind it lurks a (mis)belief, or illusion, false consciousness, or any idea of manipulation.

parties. If the division goes too far, the "collective imaginary" disintegrates and the gears of society grip. If the unifying effect is too successful, the "*pueblo*" becomes "*unido*" and then is "*jamás vencido.*"

The whole trick of contemporary, representative, political democracy lies in its constantly being refashioned to deal with these two contradictions. Ideology, institutions, class, race, gender, and income divisions have to be continuously remodeled. When things go too far in one direction, a rectification becomes necessary. Whatever works too well must be toned down; whatever functions inadequately must be perfected. This explains perhaps the pendular movement of the welfare state and economic and social policy, together with the seemingly ongoing, repetitive and never-ending debate about institutional fine-tuning. As democratic (or social and economic) conquests of the oppressed are achieved, they are almost simultaneously whittled away, overturned or distorted to reduce their impact. As democracy becomes more representative, equal and fair, responsive and accountable, it is rolled back; if it strays too far from the norm and the principle, it is improved.

Each modification is self-contradictory. It can imply greater representativity, accountability, or honesty and complicate governance; or produce the opposite effect. No step forward is every totally erased: something always lingers. Debates about proportional representation versus majority rule; presidentialism versus parliamentarism; term limits versus re-election; campaign financing versus privatization of political funding; state-owned but democratically administered media versus a privately owned, market-oriented press; a strong civil service assuring continuity and permanence versus a spoils system that makes everyone accountable; the jury system of justice versus the Napoleonic Code's judicial instruction and decision by judges; the election of everyone, including the fire chief and the justice of the peace, versus the centralized "prefect" system with top-down lines of authority and effectiveness: all of these dichotomies, and myriad more, are symptoms of this quasi-tidal, self-regulatory mechanism of modern political systems generally labeled "democracy."

Where the social and economic bedrock upon which this edifice is built encloses even greater disparities or gaps between masses and elites, the swing of the pendulum is much more abrupt and perturbing. The system performs far less effectively. Fewer people "believe" and the mechanisms "work" far less adequately. The dividing function is more active; the unifying trend, less pronounced. Democratic rule is less democratic, and revolutions, or preemptive coups to forestall them, are far more frequent.

Such is the case of Latin American democracy. There is still a great deal to accomplish in terms of the perfection or implementation of changes that have not yet been even institutionalized. The left's political agenda is thus obvious: pushing democratization as far as possible, knowing full well that no reform will ever bring about a truly and definitively level playing field, and that it will undoubtedly generate unintended consequences and perverse effects. The left's greatest challenge in the political sphere is the enormous chore of "democratizing democracy" in Latin America.[21] The fact that today every sector of the left, from old-hat social democrats to the most recently disarmed commandantes, adheres to the democratic creed is an illustration of the power of the message:

> We had begun to lay out a series of criticisms firstly of the Colombian left's overvaluation of the armed struggle, and its underestimation of the political struggle. There was a true militarization of left-wing politics, there was real cult of the guerrilla fighter. We began to say that we had to erase the dichotomy between socialism and democracy, that the two were not opposed, that on the contrary, any socialism had to be deeply democratic. We also concluded that part of the responsibility for the right-wing drift in our country fell on the left and the guerrillas, and that we had to stop that drift by disarming the guerrilla movement and throwing all its weight into democratic politics.[22]

The abstract nature of that adhesion underscores the seriousness of the conundrum the left faces in fleshing it out. Another ex-guerrilla, Joaquín Villalobos of El Salvador, reveals the depth of the change and how far the left still has to go:

> I began to grasp what Guillermo Ungo used to say about how there cannot be a revolution without democracy, nor can there be a democracy without a revolution. Without making this link we seem to be divorced from a key concept in the current modernization of political thought. We would be abandoning this concept totally to our adversaries. In Latin America any gorilla dictatorship that held fraudulent elections or was friendly to the United States was labeled a democracy. So

---

21. To the best of this author's knowledge, the phrase was coined (in a Latin American context) by Argentine Nobel Peace Prize winner Adolfo Pérez Esquivel. See Adolfo Pérez Esquivel, "Democratiser la Démocratie," in Anne Remiche-Martynow and Graciela Schneider-Madanes, *Notre Amérique Métisse* (Paris: La Découverte, 1992), p. 313. The term is also used as a chapter heading in Arturo Escobar and Sonia E. Alvarez, *The Making of Social Movements in Latin America* (Boulder: Westview Press, 1992), p. 206.

22. Bernardo Gutiérrez, interview with the author, Cartagena de Indias, October 8, 1992.

we believe that the left in Latin America must fully appropriate the notion of democracy and take it to its ultimate consequences.[23]

Democratizing democracy in Latin America today implies introducing processes, mechanisms, and institutions that either do not exist, or do so only on paper. Nowhere in Latin America today—Costa Rica may be an arguable exception—do all of the attributes of democratic rule function properly, even if this means only as they do in the industrialized nations. Parts of the system have performed acceptably in different countries at different times. But by and large, if Mexico is the perfect dictatorship, as Mario Vargas Llosa has lamented, the rest of Latin America's regimes are certainly imperfect democracies, as Carlos Fuentes has pointed out in response. Placing the relevant reforms on its agenda and articulating their desirability, coherence, and urgency is a viable option for the left.

The left can be confident that the reforms are possible, that they do make a difference, and that the right will never strive for them if not obliged to, although it may accept or pay lip service to them. The beneficiaries of the existing order rarely encourage change. Most of these reforms are generally not on governments' agendas, or on those of the right, the business community, the United States, or even the Church. At the same time, there are numerous segments of the right and center that for varying reasons could well support many of them, and consequently forge temporary or issue-based alliances with the left. This type of agenda is a no-lose proposition for the left: it takes up banners that are both beneficial to the left and truly advocated by large sectors of society—but not of the political spectrum.

First, democratizing democracy in Latin America means improving the hemisphere's electoral systems. Nothing can be done without this initial step, though taken alone it is evidently insufficient. All electoral systems are partially defective: from persistent tampering in Cook County, Corsica, and Sicily to skewed representation in Britain's first-past-the-post procedure; the French philosopher Condorcet's paradoxes of voter preferences provide yet another example. But in Latin America, electoral goods are more damaged than elsewhere, reflecting the region's traditional halfway status. The hemisphere holds better and more frequent elections than other Third World continents do, but does so more sloppily and unfairly than the First World.

Electoral reform in Latin America must start with combating outright electoral fraud, which is still endemic in many countries, not just the best-known ones. Truly independent electoral authorities; government neutrality as far as is feasible; international monitoring whenever necessary; closely watched rolls; voter identification with photographs; quick tally and result publication procedures; and exit polls and parallel "quick-counts"—all these can significantly enhance the "cleanness" of votes in the hemisphere. None alone will transform Latin America elections into Swiss or Swedish ones, but they certainly can make a difference. So can the eradication of marred voting customs: quasi-public voting in rural areas or specifically for women (thus in Chile, men and women cast their votes in different polling booths, reducing the possibility of intimidation), and collective voting in indigenous communities.

Improving electoral legislation and practice must also include a further push for enfranchisement. Many of the region's citizens do not yet quite enjoy the right to vote. Some legislative chambers are still or once again not fully elected. Inhabitants of capitals like Mexico City and Buenos Aires cannot elect their municipal authorities. Finally, there is the question of voting abroad: millions of Mexicans, and hundreds of thousands of Nicaraguans, Salvadoreans, Guatemalans, Haitians, Dominicans, Jamaicans, and Ecuadoreans who live permanently or temporarily outside their countries of origin (mainly in the United States) are deprived of a right that most citizens of industrialized democracies do enjoy: absentee voting. The left should support their struggle to gain the right to vote—as it does in the case of Mexico and El Salvador—as a matter of principle. No one else will.

Finally, electoral reform probably means introducing doses of proportional representation where it does not exist, or increasing its weight where it is already in place. Given the novelty of democratic rule in many nations, as well as the constant flux in which their political systems find themselves, stable two- or three-party regimes tend not to be the norm. Under these circumstances proportional representation allows for a better, more democratic expression of the plurality of political discourse. It can, of course, fragment legislative houses and atomize political currents, often contributing to an overabundance of parties lacking authentic roots or following. But in fluid ideological situations, it is probably preferable to the two-party straitjacket created by majority district seating.

Making elections more meaningful and fair, however, implies going well beyond the elimination of traditional tampering. It also involves laying the proverbial level playing field in three specific spheres: party and campaign financing, access to the media, and freedom from political, professional, or fiscal intimidation, harassment, or overt repression. The question of money in politics is evidently a complex one. The modern, older middle-class democracies have gone back and forth on it for decades, and a final, perfect solution has yet to be found. Once again, however, in Latin America, the problems are more acute than elsewhere. Resources from abroad or from the state are simpler to come by and can skew the competition far more dramatically than in order countries. Business community financing as well as drug money is also a problem, particularly when it is opaque or under the table. In a poor country, with scant electoral traditions and an inexperienced opposition, a little money from a large firm or group of businesses, from a ministry, or from the United States can be decisive.

It is thus of the essence that electoral laws both provide the same volume of public resources to everybody and limit financing from illicit sources. Public, transparent financing of campaigns and parties, together with meticulous oversight by independent electoral agencies on the lookout for illicit transfers of funds can largely—though imperfectly—accomplish this purpose. Indeed, in certain nations adequate provisions had been established at different points in time: Chile before 1973 and partly again today; Uruguay until 1973; and Brazil since 1986 to a certain extent.

Although these are nebulous reaches of electoral regulation where nothing is ever picture-perfect, precedents and acceptable stipulations also exist in some nations regarding access to the media. Two recent incidents serve as eloquent examples of this twilight zone of democratic reform. On December 14, 1989, the two candidates in the Brazilian presidential election squared off in a final three-hour debate. Lula had won his previous encounter with Fernando Collor de Mello hands down: so polls showed, as did the fact that from the debate onward, he had risen in the public's preference, while Collor was slipping. Brazil, like practically every nation in Latin America today, has become television-friendly. More than 80 percent of the nation's homes have TVs, which are watched assiduously. Politics has reached the media age, even in the Amazon and among the *favelados*. Not all the contenders commanded comparable resources to produce their ads—this requires regulation everywhere—but free, official airtime was equitably distributed.

News coverage was another story. Rede Globo, a privately owned, immensely prosperous network—controlling nearly 75 percent of the audience and considered the fourth-largest television company in the world—bet on Collor from the beginning. Roberto Marinho, the eighty-year-old founder and owner of the Globo empire, devoted his resources and airtime to backing the young candidate. The nightly news was strongly slanted in his favor, and, more important, heavily weighted against Lula and Leonel Brizola, initially deemed the more likely left-wing runoff candidate. Brizola took Globo to court, in vain, for so distorting the electoral process as to have rendered it meaningless.

Immediately after the second debate—which Collor probably won, in view of Lula's utter exhaustion and psychologically impaired state—Globo went for the jugular. The news shows immediately aired highlights from the confrontation showing Collor at his best and Lula at his worst. They reported polls declaring Collor the winner, failing to mention that the surveys were carried out by Collor's pollsters. In sum, Globo used the debate to throw the election to Collor, something that a network with a 75 percent rating can achieve, but should not be permitted to do. Through overt news manipulation and blatant favoritism, Rede Globo played a crucial role in anointing Brazil's first elected president since 1959. The 1986 constituent assembly, as well as all the nation's political parties, underestimated the power of television and the insidious ways in which a quasi-monopoly—public or private—can affect the outcome of an election where everything else seems fair and free.

In Mexico, where things are seldom fair or free, a more outrageous example of the media's misconduct occurred in 1988. Televisa, Emilio Azcarraga's virtual monopoly, had been subservient to official Mexico for decades. In the 1988 campaign, he openly declared his sympathy for PRI candidate Carlos Salinas and stated frankly that on his network Salinas was the people's choice.[24] Electoral legislation stipulated free and equal airtime for all contenders, but other candidates' spots were transmitted late at night or on channels no one watched. That was par for the course in Mexico, but it was surpassed by what happened a few weeks before the election and in the midst of a closing surge by opposition candidate Cuauhtémoc Cárdenas.

For nearly thirty years, Mexico's television audience has watched Jacobo Zabludovsky's nightly newscast. By First World criteria, it is astonishingly mediocre: Soviet-style coverage of Mexican government activities, no teleprompter until recently, incessant editorializing. But even by its own standards, it stooped to a new low. Zabludovsky began his show one evening by introducing two individuals whom he called former president Lázaro Cárdenas's never acknowledged illegitimate

---

24. Azcarraga, not a man to change his mind easily, restated his devotion again in 1991: "Televisa considers itself part of the government system and as such supports the campaigns of PRI candidates. The president of the republic, Carlos Salinas de Gortari, is our maximum leader, and we are happy about that." Marjorie Miller and Juanita Darling, "El Tigre," *Los Angeles Times Magazine*, November 10, 1991, p. 28.

sons, and consequently Cuauhtémoc Cárdenas's half brothers. He then transmitted a scathing attack on the presumed sibling for his betrayal of the PRI and "their" father's heritage. This was then rounded off by the so-called half brothers' assertion that Cárdenas père, Mexico's most admired president of the century, would have frowned on Cuauhtémoc's behavior had he been alive. Zabludovsky never substantiated the men's claims, nor did he allow anyone to reply on Cárdenas's behalf. This was obviously a government maneuver, enthusiastically fulfilled by Televisa. It probably backfired, but underlined how far Mexico had to go before attaining anything like a level playing field, or an undistorted television screen, as it were.

Oversight boards on fairness in newscasting can monitor news shows during campaigns. There must be some means of filing claims of unfairness, cheating, unequal access, and other grievances; an independent electoral entity has precisely that purpose. The fact that a network is privately owned does not justify its biased use of the public's airwaves. Regulation of campaign news coverage, guaranteeing equal time, no-slant coverage, and right of rebuttal, is a necessary ingredient of democratic politics.

Last, a level electoral playing field implies freedom from repression or intimidation for opposition candidates. From the Sandinista *turbas*, or mobs, who broke up opposition rallies and frightened off many rivals in 1984, to the Brazilian countryside and Colombian drug lords and death squads, elections under siege conditions are meaningless. But the most extreme cases, tragic though they may be, are not always the most pernicious. Harassment, intimidation, threats of losing jobs and rights (schools for children, pensions, health care, and land) frequently skew electoral competition much more severely than isolated murder or kidnappings. These other more subtle, indirect distortions seek to instill fear and resignation among opposition candidates and electorates, undermining the viability of alternation in office. When they succeed, physical elimination becomes redundant: the same results are achieved without it. Guaranteeing adequate protection and liberties for candidates and voters against their respective governments is a necessary condition for electoral fairness. It will not be attained unless the left make an issue of it, as the FMLN in El Salvador and the M-19 in Colombia (without great success, in this last case) did in the course of negotiating an end to both nations' civil wars.

The second aspect of democratizing democracy concerns what Fernando Henrique Cardoso has called the worst vice of Brazilian (and by extension, Latin American) democracy: the lack of accountability. This can range from presidents being elected on one platform, then turning around and implementing a diametrically opposed program (what Carlos Saúl Menem, Carlos Andrés Pérez, and Alberto Fujimori are often accused of doing), to rampant corruption, mismanagement, shortsightedness, brazenly political use of public resources, misuse or overexploitation of natural resources (oil, fisheries, forest), and dissipation of foreign currency on military hardware, capital flight, or luxury imports. While there is no quick fix for these endemic woes, a number of reforms can be implemented, and on occasion have been.

The general guiding principle must be the strengthening of the autonomy of different institutions: establishing and reinforcing the separation between state and government. The confusion of the two has been a bane on Latin American politics since time immemorial. Without the distinction between a government that is elected for a determined period and the state, with its permanent institutions, political neutrality, and lasting nature, democratic rule is all but impossible. For multiple reasons—traditions, the patrimonial state, military coups, *caudillismo*, presidentialism—state and government have acted, have been perceived to be, and generally pretend to be one and the same in Latin America. The most experienced and wise politicians of the left know this well, and understand why it has occurred:

> The central problem in the political structure of Latin America has been the patrimonialism of the exercise of public administration. There were no borders between public administration and private patrimony. Back in colonial times, there were only two ways to keep the Crown's envoys under control: to rotate them as soon as possible; and to let them get rich. The criollos always had the money to buy off the colonial authorities; better for officials to get rich at the expense of the Crown than to be bought off by the criollos who were the Crown's chief rivals in controlling the Indians and the colonies' natural resources. The states of Latin America were born with the original sin whereby public office, from Independence onward, permits the acquisition of economic force, which in turn provides political power.[25]

Destroying the symbiosis between public office and private patrimony is the paramount structural reform Latin American democracy requires. It is a monumental task, implying the empowerment of many existing institutions and splitting them off from government.

The first one is the legislative branch. Congress, Parliament, or the National Assembly must be granted the power, but also the resources, moral authority, and technical capability to carry out its lawmaking and

---

25. Porfirio Muñoz Ledo, interview with the author, Mexico City, June 23, 1992.

oversight functions. This includes making it impossible for the executive to get around the Congress through government by decree, or by simply dissolving Congress—as Fujimori did in Peru in 1992. It also signifies broadening congressional authority over the executive by entrusting the legislative body with a series of irrevocable appointments now made solely or jointly by the executive: judges, electoral boards, comptroller's office, etc. But equally important, it obliges the executive to surrender prerogatives, delegating power to other branches.

Several further aspects of the separation of state and ruling government belong on the left's political agenda. Whether devolved to the Congress or to the courts in some cases, the left should seek to establish the self-management or administrative autonomy—i.e., independence from the executive—of four institutions: (1) the central bank, [26] (2) the equivalent of a comptroller's office with supervisory authority and sufficient resources to watch over adequate use of public funds and combat corruption, (3) the tax collection agency, and finally (4) large state-owned enterprises.

These transformations are not devoid of contradictions. Autonomy with respect to the executive makes these institutions less sensitive to electoral demands for change, to the clamor for reform and social pressure: this is not to the left's advantage, and it is not necessarily good for democracy. But the above-mentioned institutions have been so abused in the past and so many excesses and mistakes have been committed in their name that the solutions adopted elsewhere in the world appear preferable, despite their drawbacks. The very real problems these solutions engender—locking in a certain monetary orthodoxy in the central bank, allowing a comptroller to become an obstacle to new laws, making state-owned firms unresponsive to policy changes—are offset by their advantages. The latter include greater accountability to Congress, isolation from political turbulence, fewer prerogatives for the executive branch of government, the strengthening of the institutions in question, and fewer opportunities for abuse and corruption.

The specifics of these reforms are beyond the scope of this work. Some of them are already in place in certain nations—often not by the left's doing. Others have been tried and given up on. The variations are multiple and depend on particular circumstances. In the final analysis, however, it is the gist of the modifications that counts: separating the

---

26. This may sound like a strange goal for the left to pursue, but under existing circumstances—with central banks becoming increasingly responsive only to the international financial community—it is a bold and far-reaching one that institutionalizes an existing state of affairs but guarantees a certain independence of public finance.

state from government and rendering it more accountable, more efficient and just—in a word, more democratic, though not necessarily smaller, sometimes in fact larger.

Other autonomous institutions must be created or reinforced, such as human rights commissions, ombudsmen, or independent media outlets or "watchdog" authorities (like the French "Haute Authorité" set up in 1982). But among the most important reforms of the Latin American state that the left must strive for are those that address two of the region's most severe weaknesses: the lack of a truly independent, functioning judiciary, and of a competent, relatively honest, and more or less permanent civil service. Some countries have had vestiges of both in the past—Chile, Uruguay—and even maintained them during the darkest hours of the dictatorships.

An independent judiciary is of the utmost priority in building and consolidating democratic rule on the continent. Without it, many other advances can either be overturned or crippled. It came as no surprise when, in the course of their arduous negotiations to bring the civil war in El Salvador to a close, the left and the center both insisted on the need for an independent, well-endowed, and well-trained judiciary as a condition for civilized coexistence. In its absence, guarantees against police violence and the authorities' abuses are worthless and elections, accountability, congressional oversight, autonomy for state-owned firms, and an end to corruption are virtually illusory. The very notion of an adequate regulatory framework—in business, trade, finance, labor, capital markets, consumer protection, etc.—is inconceivable without the foundation that framework must rest upon: an independent, honest, and powerful judiciary. Indeed even the conservatives' dogmatic reliance on the market is a pipe dream without the regulatory framework that allows markets to function properly. Nowhere is change really taking place on this count. Certainly not in Mexico, where the corruption and subservience of judges are notorious; not in Brazil, where despite some judges' autonomy in urban areas and on federal issues, the backlands and lower levels remain plagued by graft and local clientelism; not in Colombia or Peru, where drugs and counter-insurgency have smothered any hint of independence, despite notable individual exceptions.

Profound change is also urgent in the case of security and law enforcement. The emergence of civilian police forces with radically different training, funding, and ideology from the past is a widespread aspiration in Latin America. With few exceptions, the police in the region are corrupt, brutal, ineffective, and unaccountable. This is evidently due to the role that has traditionally been assigned to them, and as a result of the ideas they have become imbued with. Separating law enforcement from *government* and from political strife, and subordinating it to the *state* while establishing a semblance of neutrality and accountability, must be on any democratic agenda. Putting an end to impunity through specific reforms is an undertaking that wide swathes of the region's population clamor for. In innumerable polls, security, an honest police, and protection from state-sponsored violence appear as the highest-ranking demands of the population. Again, the Salvadorean Peace Agreements of 1992 are a helpful guide. The importance given to recruitment and the ideology underpinning training, as well as the unification of all security forces and federal law enforcement agencies under a single civilian command are some of the lessons of El Salvador.

The establishment of a civil service in most of Latin America is a task of great urgency and import. Again, there are exceptions to its absence. Itamaratí, the Brazilian Foreign Office, and Tlatelolco, the Mexican Ministry of Foreign Relations, are home to career foreign services renowned for their competence and honesty. The Central Bank and the Ministry of Finance in Mexico enjoy a similar status, as has much of the Chilean bureaucracy, before, during, and after Allende and Pinochet. The military in many nations often functions as a civil service, with standards of permanence, career loyalties, and professionalization, though certainly not with the probity and "apolitical" zeal that is associated with such a corps. But by and large, a full-fledged civil service does not exist in most of Latin America.

The problem with the Latin state is mostly not its magnitude, but its chronic inability to get things done. Not always: the Brazilian and Mexican states, for example, have a long history of economic activity, which, until the current disdain for any state involvement in the economy, was a source of pride for these nations. Highways, dams, oil refineries, thermoelectric plants, airports, and steel mills were all constructed—some with greater success than others—and then managed— more often than not, well managed—by the state. But this was the exception: the rule was that for social policy, tax collection, public education and health, distributing land and controlling prices, and countless other tasks, there was a dearth of administrative capacity, trained and adequately remunerated personnel, honesty and efficiency.

The reasons are well known. Again, the Latin American notion of a patrimonial state is the root of the problem. If the state belongs to an individual, a group, a party or even a *generación* (a term designating more than a university graduating class but less than a generation in English), everything in it comes and goes with its proprietors. The region's presidential system when it worked and its succession of coups, revolts, and revolutions when it didn't, generated nearly every-where a spoils system in spades: everybody came and went.

Repression, populism, governmental precariousness and turbulence made the very idea of a permanent, apolitical, well-paid and competent civil service, with rights, duties, hierarchies, and promotion ladders almost unthinkable. Yet without, it the democratic ideal remains out of reach while many of the tasks of governance are rendered exceed-ingly difficult if not impossible to accomplish. The establishment of such a service in most of Latin America is now feasible. Years of education, training abroad, bureaucratic sedimentation, and experience ensure that at least the higher and middle echelons of personnel exist, and that the knowledge of how to carry out such an undertaking is available. It is essentially a question of political will.

The creation of a civil service is a task the left must place on its agenda. It has everything to gain from its existence: the possibility of alternating in office without having to change every government offi-cial; the confidence that many officials would sympathize with the left opposition if they felt secure in their jobs; the enhanced efficiency of public policies, particularly in the social sphere: education, health, housing, combating absolute poverty, etc. Left-of-center leaders like Porfirio Muñoz Ledo in Mexico have made this a leitmotif of their efforts to reform the state:

> The transition to a modern and democratic state implies the separation among what is public, political, and administrative. The most demo-cratic regimes are those where public administration is carried out with a neutral—or, as some say, lay—character, not in reference to beliefs, but in regard to ideologies, and is nothing more than the execution of decisions made by those elected by the popular vote. The creation of a civil service in this sense is one of the most important tasks for the left in Latin America today, and for any political party.[27]

While right-of-center neoliberal governments have paid lip service to the idea, they have not truly pursued it, for reasons analagous to their refusal to weaken the executive in any way. Their own projects and survival would be at stake. The left would be well served by taking this task to heart: it will not be achieved otherwise, and the rewards for authorship will be considerable.

Many have concluded that the all-encompassing reform Latin America needs to bring all these other institutional modifications to fruition is the shift to a parliamentary system. Scholars like Alfred

---

27. Muñoz Ledo, interview.

Steppan and politicians from Salvador Allende to Lula and Cárdenas have reached the same conclusion: the founding of a "parliamentary republic" is a necessary condition for overhauling the state in the hemisphere. According to this view, only by abandoning the ancient, ever present presidential scheme lifted from the American Constitution can democratic rule be achieved in the region. There is something to be said for this "silver bullet" theory of parliamentary rule.

The first and best argument consists perhaps in its originality. If no nation in Latin America has had a parliamentary system for a significant period of time and the presidential arrangement has never worked quite well, then little can be lost and much gained by trying something new. Secondly, the parliamentary option solves one problem posed by the separation of state and government: ensuring the existence of strong government with a parliamentary majority not needing to use state institutions as crutches for governance.

Often the argument is heard that the region's problems are so overwhelming, the challenges it confronts so daunting, that only a strong executive with a compliant Congress can expect to deal with them effectively. Conversely, if accountability, rule of law, and separation of state and government are ever to be accomplished, a strong legislative branch is indispensable. Parliamentary rule bridges the gap, by providing for automatic lawmaking majorities and allowing the autonomy of many state institutions. Similarly, the establishment of a parliamentary democracy is seen as ensuring the viability of a civil service, as it represents the antinomy of a spoils system. Congressional majorities and the governments they support come and go; the continuity of the state is guaranteed by the stability of an apolitical and honest civil service. If proportional representation without ticket splitting is thrown in for good measure, the mix is appealing and, in any case, innovative for the region.

It would be wrong to make too much of this issue, and the left should not let itself get bogged down in too many institutional debates of this nature. But the scheme is attractive for the left in another way. It lends itself to coalition building and consensus governance—if proportional representation is included—which plays to its strong suit: influencing policy, or participating in its formulation and implementation, without having to govern alone. For this reason, as well as the others, it would appear wise for the left to convince itself fully of the virtues of the parliamentary system, all the more so since it has generally favored this option in the past.

Finally, the left's democratic agenda must include the effort to extend democracy "where it ain't." Throughout the continent, there are vast uncharted territories where democratic practices and ground rules are missing: labor unions, the media, professional and business associations, small towns and villages, squatters' organizations, universities and student associations, women's groups and public service agencies. Sometimes their democratization is an affair of state; on other occasions it is strictly up to these organizations themselves to work out their own guidelines. But they cannot do it if the context—legal, political, financial, administrative—is not propitious.

The media is central. Latin America, despite its poverty and disparities, is now a full-scale media market: television reaches well over 80 percent of the homes in the more populous nations. Because reading traditions are restricted to much narrower segments of society, the contrast between television and the printed press is perhaps more acute than in the industrialized world. And the challenge of democratizing the media and making it both independent and accountable, free and fair is consequently more complicated in Latin America than elsewhere. Where television is private and prosperous—i.e., Brazil, Mexico—it is either subservient to the government or totally lacking in responsibility. Where it is state-owned it is slanted, propagandistic, and even more forbidding to political opposition. But this circle, like so many others in the region, must be squared. Perhaps the type of solution Western Europe adopted during the period when television was spreading to every home in each nation—state-owned media, but regulated to ensure fairness: the BBC, the ORTF, the RAI—is the best choice. Certainly the status quo is unacceptable.

Breaking up corporativist union codes and structures is another typical example. In nations like Brazil until 1980, Argentina through the middle of the decade, and Mexico as late as 1992, labor unions, collective bargaining, the right to strike and organize were codified by archaic labor laws dating back to or inspired by the incorporation process of the 1930s and 1940s. While many of the provisions imbedded in this legislation were originally well intended and have protected workers from the ravages of early capitalism, they became constraints on the extension of basic democratic rights in the workplace. In other cases, such as university autonomy—formally established and largely respected for many years—a broadening of democratic practices is still necessary: election of authorities, more-responsive collegial bodies, more-democratic methods for the tough choices ahead: fees, admission requirements, relations with the private sector.

Finally "new" areas—squatters, women, indigenous movements, gay groups, youth, etc.—require a legal and political framework, as well as financial resources, to flourish. Consumer movements, user networks (of transportation, housing, health clinics, public schools) also need an institutional context in which to thrive and oversight to ensure that whatever rules they adopt are respected. Too much state and these movements wither; not enough regulation and protection can expose them to manipulation and corruption.

Democratic rule has not been a fixture of Latin America's history. The present infatuation may well be as skin-deep as previous ones; there are reasons why Latin America and democracy have not hit it off in the past. In fact, it seems safe to say that if a democratization agenda such as the one spelled out in the preceding pages were implemented, few sitting governments would survive. The corruption scandals, aborted coups, and *autogolpes* of the past few years, together with the rest of the difficulties confronting current regimes, stem largely from this single fact. For the first time in years, despite all the shortcomings described above and the immense road still to travel, authorities in Latin America are facing a degree of accountability, oversight, scrutiny, and dissemination of power; and the result is that governance is not what it used to be. What the Nobel Peace Prize–winning former president of Costa Rica Oscar Arias once said now truly applies to many other countries of the region: "It is very difficult to be a good president in Latin America."[28]

At stake is the nature of the democracy that is finally instituted: that is why the task of democratizing the region is so pressing. The underlying causes for the idea's failures or shortcomings lie in the elitist, socially segregated order of Latin American societies. The right has benefited from this state of affairs; the left has suffered. Thus the democratic imperative: only if Latin American democracy can be fully democratized will it serve the left and the majority of the population; only if the left fights for these reforms will they come about.

---

28. Oscar Arias, speech made at Nobel Jubilee Symposia, Oslo, December 8, 1991.

13

A Latin American Dilemma

■

The economic and social riddle the Latin American left has been obliged to decipher over the past half century is as complex as the challenge of finding an answer to it. The conundrum has been formulated on many occasions. But perhaps two Chileans summed it up best, nearly twenty years apart. Fernando Fajnzylber's empty box and Salvador Allende's provocation introduce the left's debate with itself, and with the rest of Latin American society, in as succinct and sharp terms as possible. All of the left's utopias and illusions, as well as the right's endless denunciations of populism and ineptitude, have not altered the formulations that these two deceased and devoted Chileans drew up, fixing the limits and setting the scope of the left's transformation.

The dilemma posed for the left—and indeed, for all well-meaning citizens of the continent's nations—resides in the empty box of growth and equity conceived by Fajnzylber.[1] The Chilean economist constructed a double-entry matrix for Latin America for both growth and equity. He defined growth as an average annual per capita GDP growth of 2.4 percent or more, that is, the yearly rate at which the advanced countries grew over the past two and a half decades.[2] Equity was also defined as a function of developed-nation standards.[3]

---

1. Fernando Fajnzylber, *Unavoidable Industrial Restructuring in Latin America* (Durham, N.C.: Duke University Press, 1990), Chapter 1.

2. Ibid., p. 1.

3. If in the industrialized nations the earnings of the bottom 40 percent of the population are equal to 0.8 percent of those of the richest 10 percent, then an adequate dose

The results are predictable, but dismal. From 1965 to 1986, some nations in Latin America grew at well over 2.4 percent per capita yearly: Brazil, Colombia, Mexico are the largest ones. Other countries enjoyed an adequate level of equity, where the bottom 40 percent of the population received more than 0.4 percent of the earnings available to the top 10 percent: Argentina and Uruguay. The majority have achieved neither equity nor growth: Bolivia, Chile, Peru, Venezuela, Haiti, and all of Central America. But no country has simultaneously managed growth and equity: the matrix's fourth "box" is empty.[4] With minor changes in the definition of "equity," nations such as Costa Rica, Chile, and Venezuela would enter the equity box, though not the growth one; similarly, a slightly less rigorous definition of growth would enlarge that category's membership but still leave it bereft of equity. No nation in Latin America has been able to attain both growth and equity in recent history, if ever. This simple yet tragic state of affairs defines the nature of the challenge the continent and the left have faced in the past and continue to confront today.

Needless to say, the Chilean economist was not the first to identify the growth-versus-equity trade-off, or the total absence of any combination of the two in Latin American development. Furthermore, his theorem does not hold that poverty has not diminished in Latin America over the past half century. The point of his argument, rather, is that even when growth occurred, and poverty was rolled back in relative—and even in absolute—terms, the distribution of income, wealth, and opportunity remained terribly, unacceptably skewed. Brazil, which has perhaps combined growth and *inequity* in greater doses than any other Latin American nation over the past forty years, is a case in point. Between 1950 and 1980, Brazilian GDP went from $30 billion to $252 billion in 1980 dollars; per capita GDP rose from $570 to $2,080 in constant terms; employment in the low-income primary sector plummeted from 60 percent of the labor force in 1950 to 30 percent in 1980.[5] It is obvious that productivity and income cannot rise simultaneously throughout the economy: some sectors advance more rapidly than others. But if corrective measures are not applied, matters get out of hand, as they did in Brazil: income distribution followed a totally different

---

of equity in Latin America implies that the same poorer 40 percent of the population dispose of 0.4 percent of the earnings obtained by the richest 10 percent. Ibid.

4. Ibid., p. 2.

5. Pedro Malan and Regis Bonelli, "The Success of Growth Policies in Brazil," in Simón Teitel, *Towards a New Development Strategy for Latin America: Pathways from Hirschman's Thought* (Washington, D.C.: InterAmerican Development Bank/Johns Hopkins University Press, 1992), p. 51.

curve. In 1960 the top 5 percent of the population received 27.7 percent of total income; in 1970 it got 34.9 percent, and by 1980 it was obtaining 37 percent. The bottom 50 percent received 17.7 percent of the country's income in 1960; its share fell to 14.9 percent by 1970, and dropped to 13.4 percent in 1980.[6] Hence the difference between combating poverty and promoting equity: by 1980 there were fewer poor in Brazil than twenty-five years before, but the relative status of the remaining poor was worse.

The tragedy is accentuated by the fact that this trade-off has not been a fixture of other regions' development. Fajnzylber shows that there are developing countries that have filled the empty box in recent years: China, Thailand, Hungary, Portugal, the former Yugoslavia, South Korea, and Spain.[7] As Fajnzylber points out, the group "ranges over the entire political spectrum in terms of world trade orientation. The same degree of diversity is observed in the relative significance of the public sector."[8]

All of them had undertaken diverse protection, import-substitution policies, though some with an export emphasis, others not. Some had extensive state control or ownership, others moderate amounts, and still others significantly less, although none were fully privatized, American-style economies. Stranger still, although these nations are now mostly representative democracies, they were not in the past, especially during much of the development period. A combination of historical, cultural, economic, and policy factors contributed to their felicitous outcome.

There are, of course, many ways of dodging or simply obviating the problem of the empty box. One is to postpone equity more or less indefinitely: the solution most Latin American governments, past and present, have chosen. Either by making believe the difficulty is on the way to resolution—even if every statistic indicates the contrary—or by justifying its postponement—through various versions of the trickle-down theory—most Latin regimes over the past half-century have just sidestepped the issue. The failure of the populist regimes, so criticized for not achieving their aims, has led to the plain and simple elimination of their stated objectives from the continental agenda. By straightforwardly removing equity from the list of national priorities, the populists' successors—the neoliberal, free-market ideologues—ensure that the box will remain empty.

6. Ibid., p. 52.
7. Ibid., p. 156.
8. Ibid., p. 157.

The left, for its part, while obviously unable and unwilling to set the problem aside, has in fact neglected or underestimated the growth side of the equation. For reasons that will become more readily apparent below, the left cannot overlook the equity issue: its raison d'être consists precisely in devising an answer to the riddle. It is unfair and inaccurate to pretend, as many critics of populism have, that the left, on the few occasions when it has acceded to power, has been anti-growth. But policies for encouraging growth have promoted injustice and inequality, whereas policies biased in favor of equity have forestalled growth, largely because they have proved inflationary, externally unsustainable, and consequently short-lived.

The heart of the problem lies in the other paradox outlined by Fajnzylber's compatriot Salvador Allende. Just after he took office as president of Chile, in November of 1970, Allende ventured a statement that seemed to confirm most of his opponents' worst apprehensions about what his presidency would entail for the country. Allende declared that while he would of course respect the rights and opinions of all Chileans during his mandate, he was not the president of all Chileans, but of the workers and peasants, of Chile's poor.[9]

It was one of his most controversial statements, perhaps one of the master politician's least prudent or thoughtful reflections, yet it pointed to an undeniable fact. Allende had not been elected by all Chileans, nor on a platform aspiring to benefit all of the country's inhabitants. The parties that supported him were class-based political organizations; the program he ran on was one of deep economic reform and social change. And the social activism and political mobilization backing him were not going to be contented with cosmetic tinkering and maintenance of the status quo. Allende would either govern for his constituency or not govern at all. Yet by remaining faithful to his supporters, he also created the conditions for his own downfall.[10]

---

9. In what many thought was the beginning of a similar process, François Mitterrand first reproduced Allende's stance, then contradicted it, in his inaugural speech on May 21, 1981, in the Elysée Palace: "As I take office today, my mind turns to the millions and millions of women and men of our country who, for over two centuries. . . wrought the history of France without acceding to it other than during brief and glorious crises of our society. Today, the political majority of France has become identified with its social majority. . . . As president of all the French, I wish to bring them together in pursuit of the great causes before us. . . ." François Mitterrand, quoted in Pierre Favier and Michel Martin-Roland, La Décennie Mitterrand (1. Les Ruptures) (Paris: Editions du Seuil, 1990), p. 57.

10. One of the few currently fashionable economic authors who has at least tried to establish a link between social and political conditions on the one hand, and economic

The quandary was plain to see. An economic and social policy that did not respond to the pent-up, long-forestalled demands of the poorer sectors of Chilean society was simply not viable *politically*: equity was an imperative for a democratically elected government brought into office by a minority of the electorate but largely made up of the poorer strata of society, of which it probably represented a majority. Unfortunately, this policy would prove *economically* inviable: the political consequences of its implementation led to the economic and financial chaos that ultimately alienated the middle class.

The dynamic is a well-known one and has affected other left-wing or left-of-center regimes in Latin America, whether they reached power through the ballot box, a mass insurrection, or the barrel of a gun. A new regime takes office and quickly proceeds to implement the policies it promised, those that its constituents clamor for and that its own members' conscience and sincere convictions push them to apply. Wages are raised, both in the public sector—always a considerable proportion of the salaried work force in Latin America—and in the private area of the economy. Social expenditures are rapidly increased, as spending on education, health, housing, and child care skyrockets in response to real demands and the perceived imperative of righting decade or century-old wrongs.

How will it all be paid for? By "expropriating the surplus," that is, by transferring wealth from the rich or the foreigners to the poor: nationalizing natural resources, levying taxes, taking over privately owned, apparently highly profitable businesses. In countries where income and wealth disparities are glaring and ancestral, the temptation to redistribute and place exorbitant hopes on redistribution is not only understandable; it is unavoidable. The rich are so rich, the poor so poor, that soaking the former to improve the lot of the latter is the obvious way to go. Indeed, initially the strategy appears to work.

Thus in Chile in 1971 the economy grew strongly, while Allende's Popular Unity coalition picked up more than 50 percent of the vote in the April 1971 municipal elections. In Peru in 1986, after Alan García's less radical but not insignificant reorientation of economic policy and particularly his reduction of debt service to 10 percent of export earnings, a similar turn of events took place. García's popularity climbed,

policy on the other, without simply reducing "wrong" economic policies to foolishness or ignorance is Jeffrey Sachs, in "Social Conflict and and Populist Policies in Latin America," National Bureau of Economic Research Working Paper 2897, Cambridge, Mass., 1989.

as did output, employment, and confidence during most of 1986 and 1987. This pattern is not totally inapplicable to what has occurred even in advanced countries such as France, for example, be it in 1936 under the Popular Front, or in 1981, after François Mitterrand's election.[11]

But soon there appear inflation, pressure on the external accounts, and capital flight, all of which have been lurking over the horizon from the outset. Wage increases and growing governmental deficits push prices up; domestic supply originally stimulated by rising spending stagnates and is quickly replaced by imports, even in protected economies. The exchange rate is kept nominally stable but appreciates in real terms, as a devaluation is seen as a typical concession to imperialism and economic orthodoxy, and in fact would have devastating inflationary consequences. Together with capital flight, a trade deficit begins to seriously erode foreign reserves, and dollars become scarce. Exchange controls are imposed or strengthened, and a black market surfaces. The mood of the middle classes sours, and the business community disinvests, in turn infuriating unions and radicals, who accuse factory- and landowners of sabotaging the entire experiment, which they argue—often justifiably—was democratically chosen. Land seizures, sit-down strikes, and factory takeovers proliferate, accentuating tensions. Runs on the currency, continuing devaluations, and spiraling prices all rock society. The initial bias against redistribution in the market economy of a highly inequitable society is aggravated by the left's mistakes. The latter is blamed—unfairly—for both the bias and the foul-ups. The business elite begins to conspire with the military and/or the U.S. Embassy, and one of several outcomes becomes inevitable.[12]

In the best of cases, the original economic and social policies are

---

11. Mitterrand began a major program of reforms immediately after his inauguration, which he justified as follows: "Our obligations to the French were as much social as economic. We were not elected to keep *Le Figaro* happy, but to respect through our social policy the authentic part of socialism. . . . Obviously everything would have been perfect if we had done nothing. We would have been considered serious people, but we could not ignore the expectations of those who had taken us to power." Favier and Martin-Roland, op. cit., p. 112. Spending in the first Mitterrand budget was up 27 percent, the minimum wage was raised, a wealth tax on the rich was established, many large firms were nationalized, and six months after his inauguration, Mitterrand's standing in the polls remained spectacularly high. Ibid., p. 159.

12. This sequence has been most recently described in Rudiger Dornbusch and Sebastian Edwards, "The Macroeconomics of Populism," in Dornbusch and Edwards, eds., *The Macroeconomics of Populism in Latin America*, National Bureau of Economic Research Project Report (Chicago: University of Chicago Press, 1991), pp. 11–12, and in the case of Chile, in the World Bank Development Report, 1990, p. 133.

abandoned either by the sitting government—again, the French case in 1983[13]—or by one that replaces it through elections held under varying conditions: the Nicaraguan or Jamaican itinerary. A stabilization program with International Monetary Fund guidance is put in place, and the causes of chaos are gradually erased but not the causes of the causes: the poor remain poor, equity is still far removed, and the attempt to redress ancestral injustice and deprivation is forgotten.[14] International agencies and the foreign press and academia applaud a return to "responsible policies," and promise a bright future after an unavoidable but (what they hope will be) brief period of atonement for past sins.

Another outcome is a military coup of one sort or another—bloody, violent, and drastic, as in Chile or Brazil, or gradual and peaceful, as in Peru after 1972. The constituency for the original reforms shrinks and is reduced to its minimum expression: unions, left-wing political parties, and intellectuals, perhaps the Soviet Union and Cuba standing by. Former left-wing government officials, activists, and sympathizers are persecuted, exiled, or murdered. Unions, political parties, and associations are banned; an international outcry in some quarters is met with steely indifference or outright rejoicing in others, and the entire affair is written off as a mistake with a perfectly predictable outcome.

With variations and exceptions, this is the way things have turned out for the left in office in Latin America. But the prejudicial effect of this infernal logic affects the other sectors of the political spectrum, as well as the left when out of office. The so-called populist experiments are often—and not always accurately—associated with the left's fleeting passages through governance: the Perón years in Argentina, the Echeverría and López Portillo era in Mexico, Alan García's term in Peru, regimes all difficult to classify as left-wing. If one exception to

---

13. In relation to the 180-degree shift put in practice by Mitterrand in March 1983, the two most praised narrators of his years in office said the following: "Instead of openly stating that the left had changed . . . or of trying to convince everyone of the need to forsake the ideals of 1981, Mitterrand preferred to let the French realize for themselves, through the new austerity policy, how necessary a change was, and how imperative it was to take economic realities and the magnitude of the crisis into account." Ibid., p. 492.

14. American historian Paul Drake grasped the underlying paradox: "The problem is how to bridge the gap between the political, electoral logic of speaking to the desperate needs of the deprived majority, and the economic, governing logic of adhering to the requirements of investors and entrepreneurs. . . . Today, most of Latin America is plagued with poverty, not populism." Needless to say, the majority of present-day economists and observers think the opposite: the problem is populism, not poverty. Paul Drake, comment, in Dornbusch and Edwards, op. cit., p. 40.

the rule exists, it is Cuba: the left both remained in power and—until the fall of the Eastern bloc—pursued its own policies, whatever their merits. But this was feasible only thanks to the support of the Soviet Union and in the context of an undemocratic political system.

Stagnation or growth follow, but always under authoritarian rule. Years later, when a democratic transition finally gets under way, virtually the same problems are once again confronted: how to achieve equity with growth, or growth with equity. The dilemma is compounded by incontrovertible, proven truths: a necessary condition for equity *in Latin America* appears to be democratic rule, but democracy seems incompatible with growth under actually existing circumstances. No long-lasting democratic government has produced sustained growth; no government that has generated growth over a significant period of time has established and maintained its democratic credentials (Uruguay and Costa Rica were relative exceptions in the past). The blame for failure is placed on regimes that attempted to modify the underlying causes of the region's problems, never on the causes. The solution that is finally adopted for seemingly intractable problems is to ignore them, hoping that time and the infinite patience of the people will postpone a final reckoning that never comes.

The problem is even more complicated than this rapid presentation suggests. The deep-rooted, historical obstacles to development in Latin America have been explored and described on countless occasions, and the aim here is not to pursue a new approach or discover a different causality. But with regard to the left's problems and challenges, a somewhat broader, more historical and structural description of the impediments to democratic economic and social reform is in order. It springs from an analysis of the almost immovable social structures of Latin America; it rests on the premise that for the region's left, in any case, the status quo remains an unacceptable state of affairs, the simple caretaking and management of which is not a worthy undertaking.

The dilemma begins with the region's social structure, often forgotten or ignored, particularly at times of great euphoria in the rest of the world in relation to experiments or innovation in Latin America. With the relative exception of Argentina and Uruguay, the hemisphere's nations have a typical "Third World" profile: a small wealthy elite, a reduced middle class, and a large, oversized part of the population that is defined as poor. Mostly urban today, with living standards higher than twenty or forty years ago but still low in relation to the rest of society and to the advanced nations, this huge lower or underclass segment is both the largest and neediest sector of society.

In a 1970 survey the United Nations Economic Commission for Latin America attempted to classify social strata in the region, and particularly to determine the size of the upper and middle classes. The countries with the largest upper and middle classes in relative terms were Argentina and Uruguay, with 38 percent and 35 percent of their population respectively. The nations with the smallest middle and upper sectors were Guatemala and Paraguay, with 11 percent and 15 percent each; others included Bolivia with 17 percent, Brazil with 23 percent, Mexico with 24 percent, Chile with 29 percent, and Venezuela with 32 percent.[15] In general terms, what can be called the middle-class, fully incorporated segment of society, enjoying services such as education, health, housing, reasonable incomes and nutrition levels, and "First World" consumption standards and patterns, represents approximately a third of the hemisphere's population.

The question of definition is once again paramount. There are long treatises written about the importance, function, and limits of the middle class in Latin America, and indeed, any calculation of its size depends ultimately on the definition one accepts. Thus if the sociological or political approach is chosen, the middle classes would exclude the industrial working class for example, limiting itself to the professional, clerical, and public sector employees, including perhaps a small minority of the rural sector. Other dividing lines include the formal or informal sector: the division between poorer and middle sectors would overlap with the distinction between the formal sector of the economy and the informal one. This definition is more helpful in urban areas; it is less precise in the countryside. There is also the standard of considering middle class all those whose income is in the vicinity of the median; although this definition is probably better suited to the more homogeneous nations.

For the purposes of the arguments developed here, the economic distinction of income levels, together with the social criterion of inclusion in a modern web of income, services, consumption patterns, educational levels, and citizenship is the more relevant one. Up to a point, the middle and upper classes, defined this way, are the upside-down image of "poor." We have discussed the taxonomical problems that the notion of poverty entails: depending on how it is measured, particularly on whether the poverty line, income, or the lack of satisfaction of basic needs is used, its breadth in Latin America varies

---

15. Economic Commission for Latin America and the Caribbean, *Statistical Yearbook for Latin America and the Caribbean*, 1983 ed. (Santiago, 1984), p. 82. ECLA stopped publishing this specific table after 1986; none of the subsequent yearbooks includes a similar table referring specifically to "upper and middle strata."

significantly. So do the dimensions of the middle and upper classes, if they are defined as those who are not poor.[16]

Suffice it to say that this last definition of the middle class is the most suitable one. It includes consequently the organized, protected, working class of large and resource-based industry; most of the public sector employees, though not the lower levels (chauffeurs, janitors, messengers, doormen, all of whom often receive only the minimum wage); professionals ranging from clerks and secretaries to doctors, lawyers engineers, and university professors, but often excluding primary schoolteachers who make less than two or three times the minimum wage in most countries; in the countryside, the rural middle class is made up of small landowners or providers of services to agriculture. Beyond the middle class, of course, is the upper class, comprising the wealthy: businessmen, high-level government officials, successful artists, etc.

In a nutshell, belonging to the middle and upper classes means having a minimum income and living standard, which generally implies being incorporated into the modern social web of education, health, taxes, consumption, housing. Yet the opposite is not always true: simply belonging to many of these networks—for example, having access to public housing or public education—does not imply inclusion in the middle class. While services have been provided by the state to some sectors, their income levels remain so low that it would be difficult to consider them anything other than poor, even if their children do go to public elementary school and they are entitled in principle to free health care and perhaps housing.

In Mexico, which is situated about at the middle of the Latin American scale,[17] the "middle sector," representing those who earned between two and five minimum salaries per month constituted 25 percent of the population, with only 7.6 percent obtaining more than five minimum wages.[18] A household can unquestionably make more

---

16. For a recent guide to the definitional issues of poverty in Latin America, see Julio Boltvinik, "El conocimiento y la lucha contra la pobreza en América Latina," *Comercio Exterior* (Mexico City), vol. 42, no. 5, May 1992, pp. 483–489.

17. According to the 1992 United Nations Human Development Index, Mexico ranked forty-sixth in the world classification, with nations such as Uruguay, Trinidad and Tobago, Chile, Argentina, Costa Rica, and Venezuela above it, and countries such as Brazil, Colombia, Cuba, Panama, and the rest of Central America below. United Nations Development Program, *Rapport Mondial sur le Développement Humain* (Paris: Economica, 1992), p. 140.

18. Instituto Nacional de Estadística, Geografía e Informática (INEGI), Estados Unidos Mexicanos, *Perfil Sociodemográfico, XI Censo General de Población y Vivienda, 1990*, p. 63. It is perhaps necessary to repeat that all data based on question-and-answer

than the income of its head, and most Mexicans do underreport their income. But the minimum wage in 1990 was equal to only $100 monthly; thus even with two incomes per household, and substantial underreporting, the middle sector according to this measurement would include those who received as little as $400–500 per month per household (the average size of which in Mexico is five). At 1990 prices in Mexico, it is difficult to consider that income level as middle class and not as poor, even if 65 percent of the population obtained less than this amount and only 7–10 percent received more.[19] In Brazil, 65 percent of the population has an income of one or less than one minimum wage, which in late 1991 was equal to approximately $70 per month. This averaged out at about $40 per month.[20]

This is the type of difficulty the issue of defining and escaping from poverty entails. The Latin American official community and the United Nations have recently attempted to measure poverty with greater precision. At a recent meeting held on the subject (in Quito, in 1990) a figure of 62 percent, or 270 million Latin Americans, was arrived at.[21] Conversely, around 35–40 percent of the population can be

---

surveys in Mexico and in most Latin American nations must be taken with a grain of salt. If done at home, they are biased in favor of women respondents, who often do not know what their husbands' income or salary levels are. If done at the workplace, which is often the street, they frequently involve answers by individuals who cannot calculate a weekly, monthly, or yearly income adequately, because they do not earn it in regular, constant, equal installments. All of those statistics must be seen as indications of a general magnitude, as illustrative of trends, in a word, as ballpark figures.

19. If confirmation was needed as to the extent of inequalities in Mexico, and the limited size of the middle class, a National University survey of its own students provided the following evidence. Three surveys were carried out to determine student household incomes: one based on student-volunteered information, one on campus, another at student homes. The three were then merged. The results were shocking: the average family income was $1,100 per month; 81 percent of the 274,000 students came from households with incomes of less than $1,500 per month; 48 percent came from households that earned less than $1,000 per month. It is important to note that these figures are for household incomes, not head-of-household salaries. The National Autonomous University of Mexico is the nation's premier public institution of higher education, and its students, no matter how impoverished or uncompetitive in the job market, continue to represent an elite. With price levels of many goods and services rapidly approaching those in the United States, these figures show the true colors of Mexico's social structure. Prospectiva Estratégica AC, "El nivel del estudiante de la UNAM," 1991.

20. This figure was quoted by Helio Jaguaribe, the country's most renowned social scientist, appointed minister of science and technology in 1992. Helio Jaguaribe, statement at the *Time* Conference on Latin America in the Year 2000, Cartagena, Colombia, October 8, 1991, unofficial transcript provided by *Time* magazine to the author as a participant.

21. United Nations Development Program-Regional Project, "II Conferencia Regional sobre la Pobreza en América Latina y el Caribe, Declaración de Quito," November

considered to belong to the middle and upper classes, remembering always that the lower levels of this group find themselves in a borderline, oscillating situation: middle class one year, poor the next, depending on myriad factors that can affect their standards of living dramatically and very quickly. This breakdown nonetheless can be considered a useful and accurate one for our purposes: under a broad definition of the term, in most countries most of the time, one half to two thirds of the population can be considered "poor." One third can be seen as middle or upper class.

This amounts to a considerable number of people: nearly 30 million in Mexico, more than 50 million in Brazil, perhaps as many as 15 million in Argentina. But in proportional terms, this is exactly the inverse of what occurs in the advanced nations, in which anywhere from 70 to 90 percent of the population is middle- or upper-class, enjoying relative job security, education, housing, health and adequate nutrition, consumption levels generally identified with middle class patterns (automobiles, household durables, clothing, etc.). Poverty and exclusion, needless to say, exist in the First World, and have grown in many industrialized countries over the past decade. And the nuclear or extended family in the poorer nations provides a network of support that rarely exists in the more modern nations, making poverty less unbearable and more manageable. But what remains to be done in terms of providing services, integrating the population, creating jobs, and raising living standards is truly monumental.[22]

Herein lies the first part of the Latin American dilemma. In terms of education, health, housing, nutrition, and social protection the needs of the vast majority are immense, as are the required levels of infrastructure to even begin to meet them: the highways and airports, telecommunications and schools, dams and bridges, ports and hospitals. But the social tax base—i.e., that part of society that belongs to the modern economy, that has income and consumption levels and a degree of inclusion in society that render it taxable—is remarkably small. In addition it is, as everywhere, unwilling to pay for the fulfillment of others' wants. The middle and upper classes are reluctant to

---

20–23, Quito, Ecuador, reproduced in *Comercio exterior* (Mexico City), vol. 41, no. 5, May 1991, p. 463.

22. Another dramatic illustration comes from the following fact: "In the State of São Paulo—the richest in Brazil—the number of abandoned children is approximately equal to that of the number of children enrolled in the public school system." George Reid Andrews, *Blacks and Whites in São Paulo, Brazil 1888–1988* (Madison: University of Wisconsin Press, 1991), p. 240.

finance the satisfaction of the needs of a poor and often unemployed underclass: this is a similar but more drastic problem than the one the advanced countries suffer from.

Even if all members of society agreed that everyone's basic needs must be met rapidly, and if there were a broad consensus on how to achieve this, the question would remain: who will pay? The tax burden of financing the education of millions of poor children, of extending health care to millions of sick and malnourished, of housing millions of homeless, let alone building of miles of highways and dozens of airports and laying countless telephone lines, would be enormous. If in the United States 70 percent of the population refuses to pay for the satisfaction of the far less dire needs of 30 percent, how can 30 percent of the population be persuaded to shoulder the load to pull up the remaining 70 percent?[23]

The problem was solved in the United States through time and immigration. As people arrived, the progressively generated demands for services were gradually attended to. Those who were around from the beginning had to wait longer, and some are still waiting. The newly arrived were willing to wait for a while precisely because they had just disembarked. Almost infinitely abundant natural resources, fertile soil, rivers and lakes helped, to say the least. As with enfranchisement, the problem was managed in Western Europe through gradualism. Taxation rose along with the expansion of the middle class in a virtuous dynamic. As the middle class grew, the tax base expanded; as the tax base was broadened, more services became fundable and available, thus enlarging the middle class.

The fear of social revolution from 1848 onward also contributed to this: better to give the poor schools and hospitals, unemployment insurance and paid vacations than have them rise up and take everything. But just as important, the problem was managed thanks to dramatically slower population growth in Western Europe: as the number of people increased more slowly, greater numbers were incorporated into the middle class. By the mid-1800s population increase in England was 1.1 percent; by 1900 it had stabilized at 1.2 percent. The equivalent figures for France were 3 percent during the middle of the

---

23. A different way of saying the same thing is the following: "In the industrialized nations, taxation takes from the many and distributes to poor, often discriminated minorities; in Latin America, it would have to take from the rich minority and distribute to the poor majority. It rarely does, and when this happens, the money often goes right back to the wealthy minority." João Sayad, University of California, Berkeley "Brazil Today" Conference, April 15–16, 1992.

last century, dropping to 1 percent by 1900; for Germany: 0.9 percent in the mid-1800s, 1.4 percent by the turn of the century; for the United States: 1.7 percent in the mid-1800s, and 1.4 percent by 1900.[24]

Population growth rates in Latin America are still more than twice these levels, and reached three to four times that size in the 1960s and 1970s. Between 1965 and 1980, population growth in Brazil averaged 2.4 percent; in Mexico, 3.1 percent, in Colombia 2.2 percent, in Peru 2.8 percent, in Venezuela 3.5 percent. Only in Uruguay, Chile, and Argentina was it below 2 percent; and of the three, only in Uruguay was it under 1 percent.[25] By 1990 these rates had dropped, but stayed well above the averages for the industrialized countries a century ago. Moreover, although the aggregate population increase did decline significantly from the early seventies onward, the rate of growth of the working-age cohorts remained exceptionally high.

But perhaps the most important reason why Latin America has been unable to solve this dilemma is political. In principle, an unequal social structure subject to democratic governance will self-correct: the poor, who are a majority, will vote for governments and policies that redistribute wealth in their favor, making the poor progressively less poor and more middle class. As this occurs, the tax base expands, more money becomes available, and more wealth is redistributed. While this is not exactly what happened in Western Europe and the U.S.—none of this should be nostalgically idealized—it is not far removed.

In Latin America, however, two factors have blocked this evolution. The first is that democratic governance has been the exception, not the rule, largely because the moneyed classes understood that democracy would have entailed redistribution of one sort or another. Secondly, thanks to capital mobility and support from abroad for authoritarian rule—two mechanisms unavailable in Europe in the late nineteenth and early twentieth centuries—they have been able to get away with opposing democratic rule and redistribution. The internationalization of politics and capital flows have given Latin elites options their predecessors elsewhere did not possess: ask for help, or leave. So the skewed social structure and its ensuing tax structure seem to have become immutable: social inequalities persist because the redistributive role of the state—made possible mainly through taxation but not limited to it—is blocked. The tax structure doesn't change, because transforming it would imply either a democratic con-

24. Simon Kuznets, *Modern Economic Growth: Rate Structure and Spread* (New Haven, Conn.: Yale University Press, 1966), pp. 42–43.

25. World Bank, *World Development Report, 1988* (New York: Oxford University Press, 1989), p. 274.

straint—forcing the rich to pay through the ballot box—or a modification of the social structure: expanding the middle class. When certain changes did take place, during the populist eras, they affected only a middle-class minority; before they reached a broader segment, they were arrested.

Simplistic responses to this dilemma have surfaced, as could be expected. The most accurate and simultaneously the most confounding and policy-resistant can be found in the conventional wisdom regarding Latin America, which, as is often the case, reflects a certain truth. The rich are not simply well-off: they are fabulously wealthy, from the old polo-playing gentlemen of the Argentine pampas to the new Chilean and Mexican stock traders with their submersible cellular phones (necessary if the phone rings while one is swimming in one's pool) or the Venezuelan magnates and their two-sided apartments on Brickell Avenue in Miami, and including the drug lords of Mexico, Colombia, and Rio de Janeiro. The answer then is to soak the rich.

But as many economists and presidents have lamented, the hemisphere is full of rich businessmen with poor businesses. The private sector is nothing to write home about. If the dearth of the middle class, and the ensuing narrowness of the social tax base were alleviated by the existence of a large, domestic business sector of the economy, which could be taxed in lieu of a broad middle stratum, things would be quite different. In this regard also, however, Latin America is not Europe, the United States, or Japan. There are many explanations that justify it, and changes are undoubtedly under way, but the private sector has been traditionally weak, protected, and scantly represented in the economies of most of the region's nations. This has been more true of some countries and times than others. But by and large, since the late nineteenth century, when the industrialization process began and insertion into the world economy and the emergence of national markets got started throughout the continent, the local private sector has tended to be a minor player.

The debate over which came first, the weakness of the private sector or the policies that gave birth to or consolidated its weakness, is as old as the region's multiple dramas. Today's answers are not necessarily more accurate or less simplistic than those of years or decades gone by. But a weak private sector has been a fixture of Latin American reality for more than a century and has become the corollary of another long-standing feature of the hemisphere's economies: the importance of the state-run and foreign-owned portions of the economy. This was the case in the nineteenth century for the resource-based industries, utilities, and railroads. It was true for the manufacturing base that sprang up from the Depression and the Second World War, as the formerly foreign-owned companies were nationalized. It is a fact today as new export sectors surface and old state-owned firms are privatized.

In 1991, as the privatization wave was already well under way, of the ten largest companies in Latin America, six were state-owned, two were foreign-owned, and two belonged to the local private sector.[26] Of the top fifty firms, seventeen were state-run, eighteen were foreign-owned, and just fifteen were part of the domestic private sector. Only as one moved on to the largest hundred businesses did the shares begin to even out: thirty-one state-owned, thirty foreign-owned, the remaining thirty-nine belonging to the domestic private sector.[27] In Mexico in 1991, of the top ten firms, two were state-owned, and four were multinational subsidiaries. In Brazil, the country traditionally blessed with the strongest private sector in Latin America, six of the ten largest companies were state-owned, four were foreign; not one belonged to the private sector.[28]

The current transfer to the private sector of publicly owned assets will undoubtedly mature. Outward-looking growth, export strategies, and the opening to competition from abroad, as well as associations with foreign firms, will make a difference with time. But odds are that at the end of the day, many of the biggest businesses in Latin America will remain largely state- or foreign-owned, or in some cases, paradoxically, both. Many of the privatizations in Argentina, Chile, and Brazil (and to a much smaller extent in Mexico) are taking place in favor of European state-owned companies, from Spanish airlines to Italian phone companies and French banks.[29]

A quick review of the largest exporters in the hemisphere shows that the present emphasis on outward-looking economies, whatever its

---

26. "Las 500 de América Economía," *América Economía* (Santiago), special issue, December 1992, pp. 46–47.

27. Ibid., pp. 46–49.

28. Ibid., p. 90. Of the 500 largest companies, 265 were local privately owned, 134 were in foreign hands, and 101 were state-owned. But if one looks at the sales of each group, the state-owned division generated $129 billion, or 39 percent, while the local, privately held contributed only 36 percent, and foreign companies, 25 percent.

29. Thus, one of two foreign minority buyers of Telmex was France Telecomm, the government-owned French telecommunications group; "Venezuela's airline Viasa was sold to a group headed by the Spanish airline Iberia, and the telephone company CANTV was sold to a group led by GTE and Spain's Telefónica. In a similar way, Argentina sold Aerolíneas Argentinas to Iberia and Argentine investors. Its telephone company ENTEL was split in two and sold to groups headed by Spain's Telefónica and Italy's STET." Miami *Herald*, April 13, 1992. Iberia, Telefónica, and STET are all fully or partly state-owned companies. Likewise, one of the Argentine power utilities sold off in July 1992 was purchased by French and Spanish state-owned electrical companies.

other merits or drawbacks, has not yet significantly altered the traditional structure of Latin business ownership. Of the ten largest exporters in Latin America in 1991, six were state-owned, three were foreign subsidiaries (Chrysler, Ford, and General Motors de México), and only one (Minpeco of Peru) was in private hands.[30] Of the twenty most important exporters, eleven belonged to the state, five were foreign-owned, and four were local firms. Finally, of the hundred largest exporters, twenty-nine were state-owned, thirty-one foreign, and only forty in local private hands.[31] Only in banking has the local private sector occupied a decisive slot.

It is the combination of foreign and state ownership that creates a problem. Taxing state-owned firms—indeed, transforming them into tax cows for the state—is easy, though costly. But it is ultimately an incestuous or perverse process, with one part of the state expropriating resources from another. Foreign ownership, whatever its benefits in some cases, has an essential drawback: too much taxation can drive it out, and in fact, most countries bend over backwards offering tax breaks to attract foreign investors. While multinationals from abroad are good tax citizens in many countries, they frequently are so because the rules they respect have been written specifically for them and are remarkably lenient.

In the case of the domestic private sector, even if it were truly less mobile internationally than foreign corporations, there wouldn't be much to tax anyway. A vicious circle is at work here. The private sector in Latin America—the only sector that could conceivably shoulder a higher tax burden—is actually quite lightly taxed, or in many cases, not at all. One of the reasons is that a sizable chunk of its assets are abroad: stashed away in Miami and Cayman, in Switzerland and New York. In order to entice it to return and invest at home, a series of incentives have to be devised and offered. Among these, fiscal amnesties or their equivalent are often the easiest.

Thereby the paradox. Largely as a result of the extraordinarily high yields local stock exchanges were generating in the early 1990s, substantial amounts of flight capital returned to Mexico, Argentina, and, to a lesser extent, Brazil and Venezuela. But these yields, in some cases over 100 percent in dollar terms per year, went untaxed. There are no capital gains taxes in most of these nations (other than on real estate), and the very mention of them sent shudders through government and

---

30. "Los 100 mayores exportadores de América Latina," *América Economía* (Santiago), December 1992, p. 115.

31. By sales, the state-owned exporters generate four times as many dollars as the local private firms. Ibid., pp. 115–116.

central-bank offices: capital gains taxes would literally kill the proverbial golden egg–laying goose. Fair enough: had such measures been introduced, the money perhaps would not have returned. The lowered after-tax yield, together with the ensuing, necessary public disclosure of ownership and origin of funds, would have undoubtedly deterred capital repatriation.

In Mexico the establishment of a 4 percent "no questions asked," one-time-only levy on returning assets was better than nothing. This was the Mexican equivalent of the *"ventanilla siniestra,"* or drug window, of the 1980s in Colombia, an effective way of keeping hot money or drug money—or sometimes money that was both—at home. But in order to attract money to look away from, immense, untaxed profits had to be available on the Mexico City Bolsa. While some of the repatriated money was eventually invested in industry, agriculture, and modern services, much of it was speculative.

Herein lies another contradiction: while there continues to be broad agreement—even among the most conservative circles—that a substantial part of the development effort and expenditures must be carried out by the state, there is in fact very little money around to fund it. It has often been said that the Latin American state lacked money because it did too many things or wasted the money it had, or because corrupt politicians of the left or right simply stole the money there was. While these assertions are all largely valid, they also miss the point. Beyond anecdotal exaggerations such as state-owned bicycle factories or toy stores—which are useful in the ideological infighting to roll back the state but constitute marginal exceptions—when the state has gotten involved in production in Latin America it has often been for one of three solid reasons. The first two are easily disposed of; the last one concerns us most.

On some occasions, the state has intervened in economic activity to protect existing employment, when private sector companies were about to go out of business for one reason or another. The enormous difficulty of creating jobs, and the overwhelming magnitude of under- and unemployment, together with the absence of a social safety net, made it impossible to simply let existing employment, whatever its macroeconomic cost, go down the tubes.

The state also got involved in productive endeavors because of the need to deliver services or provide goods that, if left to the market and the profit motive, would not be extended to a significant segment of society, or would generate the negative effects of a private monopoly of basic services. Also, the state intervened directly in productive activities as part of the industrialization process, in an effort to build manufacturing complexes, industrial linkages, and synergies in general. This was the case of the steel, refining, and capital goods industries.

But the first and foremost reason for the state to engage in productive activities has been to "expropriate the surplus" by taking over natural resource industries or utilities that actually provided extraordinary, monopolistic rents, or in any case seemed to from a distance. If the state had to educate children, heal the sick, build housing for the homeless and highways for transportation, and there was no money to be found in taxation, then the obvious solution was to take over those economic activities that were highly profitable and capture their rents. The list of natural resources nationalized in Latin America by governments both civilian and military, elected and authoritarian, populist and leftist is lengthy indeed: oil in Mexico in 1938, and in Venezuela in 1976, tin in Bolivia in 1952, copper in Chile in 1971, bauxite indirectly in Jamaica during the mid-seventies, copper and oil in Peru in the late sixties.

A similar, though less direct, process occurred with transportation and utilities, Perón nationalizing Argentina's railways in 1948, Mexico taking over the electric company in two stages and the entire telephone company by the mid-seventies, and Getulio Vargas creating Electrobras in Brazil before his suicide in 1954. On many occasions these takeovers involved issues of national sovereignty or the hope of guaranteeing a cheap and flexible supply of electricity, for example, but their purpose was also partly to capture for the state the monopoly rents they provided. The broader goal was to then place those rents at the service of development as it was understood at the time. One can argue as to whether that use was the most judicious, and it can be reasonably surmised that often the rents were partly stolen or wasted, but that was the logic.

Essentially, then, the state intervened in the economy, and became more and more an agent of economic activity because it needed the money theoretically available in certain sectors to finance expenditures in others. While this may not have been the conscious intention of all forms of state intervention, it was the "unconscious" motivation. Similarly, during certain periods substantial expenditures were fundable through other means: tourism, remittances, aid, or concessional lending. But the striking similarities among virtually all of the region's countries in their economic cycles show that over the long run this pattern affected them all. The rash of natural resource and/or utility nationalizations carried out between the late thirties and early seventies across Latin America all point in this direction. If there were extraordinary rents to be had in these sectors, then the state should be the one to capture them directly. The fact that most of the time previous to nationalization these activities were owned by foreign entities that were particularly hard to tax increased the incentive to take them over and bestowed a nationalist tint to the affair.

But whatever the actual sequence of motivating factors, nationalizations did not address the basic dilemma: the sparsity of state revenues from other sources to finance the cost of development. Because of the vast needs and the skewed social structure outlined above, there remained the problem of low taxation in the face of enormous demands for public expenditures. Expropriating natural resource rents, utilities, or highly profitable businesses was a provisional, sometimes adequate, but by definition limited substitute to raising revenues otherwise: by taxing the wealth there was. As the years went by, the initial effect of taking over resource or monopoly rents wore off, but the funding problem persisted. The great nationalizations from the late thirties to the mid-seventies didn't achieve growth with equity, even if without them the situation would have been far worse. The basic tax structure and its consequences remained untouched.[32] The problem of resource scarcity could certainly not be reduced only through taxation; but short of a different tax structure, it could not be addressed at all. As one scholar and former policy-maker put it:

> It requires an effective state, not reliance on the market alone, to establish expenditure priorities and impose restraint. . . . Magic formulas don't work. They obscure the underlying lack of consensus within Latin American countries and ineffective mobilization of elite opinion that made it impossible to raise taxes early in the debt crisis or adequately cope with a deteriorating fiscal balance in the 1950s and 1960s.[33]

Thus, according to the World Bank, the average tax revenue over GDP ratio in Latin America moved from 16 percent in 1975 to slightly

---

32. This is not to say that tax reforms have not been attempted in Latin America, some with an undeniable, though temporary degree of success. The best examples are the 1967 reform undertaken by the military government in Brazil, which increased revenues over GDP from 15 percent to 26 percent in a decade, only to see them fall again during the 1970s; the Chilean reform of the mid-seventies, which seems to have lasted longer; and the Mexican one of 1978, which was also short-lived. There have also been attempts at improving collection. But long-lasting, deep tax reform, including higher rates and different taxes, are still pending.

33. Albert Fishlow, "The Latin American State," *Journal of Economic Perspectives*, vol. 4, no. 3, summer 1990, p. 69.

under 18 percent in 1985.[34] But the average for the high-income countries for this period rose from 28 percent to 32 percent of GDP.[35] Moreover, these aggregate figures mask large differences between countries in each group of nations and in the composition of the taxes collected in Latin America. Typically, in the industrial countries, the largest components of the total are personal income taxes, social security taxes, and sales or value-added taxes: personal taxes account for 27 percent of total taxes, social security for 31 percent. In Latin America personal taxes account for only 5 percent of total tax revenues.[36] In the middle-income developing nations in general, the largest components are commodity taxes, corporate taxes—often a euphemism for taxing state-owned enterprises—as well as sales and value-added taxes and import fees. That makes their tax structures less progressive and more unfair, despite the fact that their societies are far more unequal and thus have all the greater need for more progressive tax systems. The high dependency on international trade and companies—which are often state-owned—shows both the difficulty of taxing other sectors of economic activity and the relative ease of taxing imports and state-owned companies.

It is far easier to tax a state-owned company than a privately owned one; it is far more convenient to tax transactions than incomes; it is far less troublesome to tax companies than to tax people directly, even if companies are poor and cannot pay much while their owners are rich and could pay a great deal. But a policy that taxes companies more than people creates an incentive for transferring wealth from companies to their owners, almost always family owners. Hence the difference between the tax burden of some advanced nations and that of the larger Latin American countries is dramatic. This is true even of the United States, where the federal tax burden is much lower than almost anywhere else—partly because of state and local taxes and partly because of the reduced level of state intervention in the economy. It is also valid for Japan, where the formal tax burden is lower partly because the Japanese population is much older and Japanese tax statistics exclude social security payments. In countries such as Sweden, France, the UK, Germany, and even Italy, renowned for its citizens' tax evasion proclivities, total taxes average approximately 40 percent of GDP (ranging from 32 percent for Britain to 44 percent for Holland). Direct taxes—

---

34. World Bank, *World Development Report, 1988* (New York: Oxford University Press, 1988), p. 82.

35. Ibid.

36. Ibid.

the more progressive type—hover around 35 percent of all taxes, with France at the bottom of the scale with 18 percent, and Germany near the top with 45 percent.[37] But in Latin America the first rates range from 6 percent in Peru to 23 percent in Chile, with Brazil, Mexico, Argentina, and Colombia bunched in the middle at around 12–14 percent. And direct taxes are in the low 20 percent category, except in countries with large state-owned resource companies, such as Mexico, Chile, and Venezuela.[38]

The nations of Latin America average less than half of the tax burden of Western Europe and about 50 percent less than in the U.S., and the direct-tax share is significantly lower in Latin America than in Europe. This is partly the result of structural considerations: a larger informal economy, more numerous small tax subjects, for example. In the words of the UN Economic Commission for Latin America and the Caribbean: "In fact, the region's direct tax burden is equal to half that of the East Asian nations and a quarter of the direct tax burden of the OECD countries."[39]

Yet the actual tax rates on consumption—indirect taxes on sales, excise taxes, etc.—are similar to those of the industrialized nations. But the responsibilities falling to the state in Latin America are disproportionately large in relation to Europe: health needs, education, housing, infrastructure are all far less developed, poverty is incommensurably more widespread, and the capacity of the private sector to carry part of the load is also much smaller. Hence the contradiction underlined by a former Argentine foreign minister:

> Argentina has almost the same structure as developed countries as far as consumption taxation is concerned, and we have less than 1 percent [fourteen times less] direct taxation. So if you want to have a system which solves the problem of public demands and the need for structural adjustments, if you want to solve the problem of having a free system of social demands and do something about poverty, you have to go into

37. The numbers come from the United Nations–UNDP Rapport Mondial sur le Développement Humain, Paris, 1992, pp. 186–187, 216–217. Compared with other tables or methodologies, there are minor discrepancies, for example regarding whether or not social security receipts are included. Other sources exclude revenues from state-owned companies in direct taxes, though here they are partly included, as is social security; but if the different accounting methods are applied *ceteris paribus*, the result is always the same: the governments of Latin America receive far less money in taxes than their counterparts in the advanced nations.

38. Ibid.

39. Naciones Unidas, Comisión Económica para América Latina y el Caribe (CEPAL/ECLA), "Equidad y transformación productiva: Un enfoque integrado," Santiago, 1992, p. 93.

a very, very deep taxation reform. Otherwise there is no solution. And this point is not being discussed in our countries.[40]

Two examples illustrate this trend. A 1978 study of Argentina—the nation with the most equal distribution of income and, together with Uruguay, with the highest United Nations Human Development Indicator—showed that "80 percent of gross income was not reported and that only 30 percent of 1.6 million people eligible to pay taxes on nonwage income did so."[41] Conversely, in Mexico, a Pemex report issued in 1992 contended that "In 1991 Pemex paid the Mexican federal government a total of almost $15 billion in taxes, including direct taxes on extraction of hydrocarbons, indirect VAT, and a special tax on production and services."[42] This sum was the equivalent of more than 94 percent of Pemex's earnings, and about one third of the government's current revenue. In 1990 in Mexico, only 19 percent of the total number of economic units accounted for in the country were fiscally registered and 13 percent of these accounted for 70 percent of all taxes originating in the private sector.[43] A similar situation exists in Venezuela with oil, in Chile with copper, in Bolivia with tin. By 1992, Mexico, a major exporter of crude oil, was importing nearly 100,000 barrels net per day of gasoline.

The contradictions and perverse effects of the attempts by states to exploit these sources of funding were thus evident, but so were the advantages. These were acknowledged even by the most reluctant statists and the most rabid free-marketeers. It was no coincidence that the two most successful macroeconomic adjustments undertaken during the 1980s in Latin America occurred in Chile and Mexico. In these two countries, thanks to their left-wing predecessors, right-of-center authoritarian regimes enjoyed their own sources of hard currency and were not obliged to shop for dollars in domestic markets to pay off foreign debts. During its fifteen years in power, the Pinochet government—which went on a privatization binge, sometimes even privatizing the same firm or bank twice—never contemplated selling off Codelco. The state-owned copper company set up during the Allende period remained the single most important source of hard currency and revenue for the Chilean state, and for the Chilean armed forces that controlled it. Similarly, thanks to Pemex, Mexico had its own dollars

---

40. Dante Caputo, statement at the *Time* Conference on Latin America in the Year 2000, Cartagena, Colombia, October 8, 1991, unofficial transcript provided by *Time* magazine to the author as a participant.
41. World Bank, op. cit., p. 85.
42. *La jornada* (Mexico City), June 15, 1992.
43. *El financiero* (Mexico City), March 24, 1992, pp. 1, 13.

available and was able to continue servicing its foreign debt without the hyperinflation provoked by the need to offer higher rates of exchange and interest to domestic holders of dollars.[44]

Neither was it a coincidence that the two nations that went through the longest series of unsuccessful adjustment attempts, with economies that otherwise should have fared well, were Brazil and Argentina. There the situation was exactly the opposite: the state had no dollars of its own because all of the export activities—meat, wheat, and corn in Argentina; coffee, the automobile industry, part of the arms sector, shoes, orange juice, and sorghum in Brazil—were in private hands. The two states had to purchase dollars from the private sector to service the foreign debt, spending more cruzeiros and then cruzados, pesos then australes, to buy dollars that the local private sector either wanted for its own consumption, or saved in nest eggs in Miami or Montevideo.

The problem is then obvious. Even if one accepts the small-state theory of the current "Washington consensus," and approves of the reduction of all forms of state intervention to exclusively "market-friendly" actions, the question of where the money will come from remains paramount. Just the financing of the World Bank's small-state agenda constitutes a major obstacle to development:

> Governments need to do more in those areas where markets alone cannot be relied upon. Above all, this means investing in education, health, nutrition, family planning, and poverty alleviation; building social, physical, administrative, regulatory and legal infrastructure of better quality. . . . government intervention to protect the environment is necessary for sustainable development.[45]

Once the Latin American states ran out of natural resources and/or utilities to expropriate, and once the rents from those they took over evaporated, there were only three ways left—outside of raising taxes—to pursue these activities: (1) increasing the fees or prices of goods and services provided by the state, (2) printing money, or (3) borrowing it. The first course was considered politically inviable and, when it was finally tried out of desperation, rapidly proved limited. The state does

---

44. "In the 1980s there were several successful fiscal adjustments. The great efforts carried out by Bolivia, Colombia, Costa Rica, Chile, and Mexico worked because in almost all of those countries the public sector ran a surplus in hard currency, since it was the owner of the main tradeable natural resource, or derived from it a large part of its revenues." CEPAL, op. cit., p. 78.

45. World Bank, *World Development Report, 1991* (New York: Oxford University Press, 1991), p. 9.

not provide that many services or produce that many goods for which it can charge market prices. In addition, this simply tended to increase the amount state-owned companies supplying the goods and services could be taxed for. In the end, it was still the same source of revenue. Except that by raising fees and charges, a more regressive revenue-raising structure was strengthened, as users and purchasers are of all social strata, but public transportation, residential electricity, gasoline, drinking water, and sewage represent a higher share of the poor's spending than of the wealthier.

The other two options—debt and inflation—were the preferred choices.[46] As social demands exploded because of demographic and cultural factors, together with the political implications of modernization, spending without greater revenues began to grow. This was the real origin of the debt crisis, as well as much of the great Latin American inflation. Regardless of the amount of money that was stolen or wasted, and of the unscrupulous behavior or ambitions of many of the region's rulers during the 1970s, any attempt at development beyond the point that had already been reached implied considerable transfers of resources from abroad or a profound redistribution of income at home. The latter seemed simply impossible under existing conditions. Most attempts to increase taxes, given the extremely narrow base on which they were levied in the first place, simply enhanced evasion, underreporting, and capital flight.

But short of raising revenues, and if the effort to keep spending on education, health, housing, infrastructure, and combating poverty was to continue—if only for reasons of self-preservation on the part of authoritarian rulers—the remaining solution was inflation or for someone else to provide the funding. The latter was a task foreign bankers were more than willing to fulfill, at the right price. When the debt grew too large, the debt crisis exploded and the path back to orthodoxy was undertaken, with several perverse effects. But the debt years, although fueling growth and diminishing absolute poverty, did not enhance equity. When credits dried up, Latin America was back where it had started: with no way to fund spending, or of combining growth with equity.

In addition to having lost access to new credits to solve the initial

---

46. Thus "Brazil has long relied on intervention on the foreign exchange system, on foreign sources of finance, and very often, inflationary finance. The recurrent inability to expand the tax base, raise taxes and/or cut government expenditures, partly explains why money creation . . . has been so important." Malan and Bonelli, op. cit., p. 60.

problem, Latin America now had to find the resources to pay interest on the accumulated debt. That meant cutting spending on everything, but inevitably more in politically weaker areas: education, health, children, etc. The reduction of expenditures made a trade surplus and debt servicing possible. But after several years of this, it became apparent that nothing else was feasible—not growth, development, or equity. Austerity had not solved the problem or come anywhere near to dealing with it; something else had to be tried to find money.

But satisfying the conditions for attracting new money, which now had to be of a different nature, since commercial bank lending had come to a halt for the foreseeable future, was no easy chore. Combining that search with economic growth and a degree of equity was even more arduous an undertaking. This was the essential characteristic of the so-called neoliberal scheme implemented in Latin America from the late eighties onward in a virtually generalized, uniform fashion by regimes ostensibly of the right, left, and center. The problem was that the model generated effects at odds with each other, leaving the original problem intact, or accentuating it. The contradictory nature of the model was summed up by a former Mexican finance minister and one of the most influential Latin American economists of the 1960s and 1970s:

> In Latin America the new model implies giving the business community a greater quota of power, even though the advance of democracy would seem to call for greater empowerment of those groups only imperfectly incorporated into modern life; the model implies postponing the satisfaction of social demands at a time when the welfare state is barely reaching an embryonary stage in Latin America; it calls for stronger ties with the rest of the world, when in many cases the process of consolidation of national identities has not been completed; it signifies curtailing state intervention in production when the hemisphere faces the enormous task of reorienting the direction and style of development. . . . this must be done while conserving democracy and the modernization of political regimes.[47]

On the one hand, expenditures had been slashed. Over time this entailed greater inequity. Cutbacks in education, in the fight against poverty, in health, housing, infrastructure, and energy widened the gaps between rich and poor regions and people. But in addition to compounding the initial dilemma, the greater inequalities further

---

47. David Ibarra, *Privatización y otras expresiones de los acomodos de poder entre Estado y Mercado en América Latina* (Mexico City: Universidad Nacional Autónoma de México, 1990), p. 23.

shrank the social tax base.[48] There were a greater number of poor people as a percentage of the total by the early nineties than a decade before, and since spending had been drastically curtailed there was less money to satisfy the needs of a greater number of poor. The more numerous the poor, the greater the expenses needed to catch up and the narrower the resource base for doing so.

On the other hand, the need to attract money from abroad, both to service the debt and to carry out at least minimal development, made it necessary to create the conditions that the said money demanded. Since it was no longer credit but investment of one sort or another that was at stake, this forced governments, among other actions, to entice it by implementing a number of macroeconomic reforms labeled "the right policies," that is, those able to attract capital: selling off assets and reducing taxes as incentives to investors.[49]

Whence the new paradox: in order to make up for falling domestic revenues and a low and declining rate of domestic savings, by attracting money from abroad, states throughout Latin America sold off the companies they had taken over to generate revenues—resource-based enterprises, airlines, banks, utilities. Perhaps because history is cruel, the most flagrant examples were also the most tragicomic. In 1976, Carlos Andrés Pérez nationalized the Venezuelan oil industry to the applause of the entire region and the Socialist International, and to the displeasure of U.S. secretary of state Henry Kissinger. Fifteen years later, Carlos Andrés Pérez began the privatization of the same industry, reaping

---

48. This is as good a stage as any to point out that the tax dilemma had as its corollary the low savings predicament. The continent had traditionally a low savings rate—averaging in the lower 20 percent range, with significant deviations country by country. The debt crisis forced a further reduction, as anywhere from 3 to 6 points of domestic savings were transferred abroad and foreign savings no longer flowed in: the rate fell to 15–16 percent on average. The same social structure that engenders a skewed tax situation implies low savings: the poor can't save and too many of the people are poor. The poorer the population gets, the lower the savings rate; the lower the latter, the poorer the former. The 1980s contributed to a further, long-term drop in savings, beyond the debt crisis, by concentrating income even more and diminishing the number of people who can save. This was compensated for somewhat by having the public sector run budget surpluses, originating in . . . lower spending on social needs.

49. The ensuing public finance quandary has been formulated as follows: "Public finance in the region today also works against distributive equity. On the side of public revenue, taxes on export trade by necessity have to be reduced, while indirect taxes, which can be deducted from the cost of exports, gain in importance; there is also a general effort to adjust the tax structure as much as possible to international standards, with taxes imposed primarily on the income of firms and individuals. Since the taxation of wealth and income is now thought to be excessive in the industrialized countries, the global tendency is to reduce taxes on capital gains and profits, and lower the progressiveness of tax rates." David Ibarra, "Equity and Development," mimeo, June 17, 1992, Mexico City, p. 10.

praise from the rest of the continent, the IMF and World Bank, the Bush administration, and Perez's own consultant Henry Kissinger.

Some of the sold-off state firms had actually become money losers because they had been taxed to death. A few remained highly profitable, and others still were unprofitable but essential to national development. Furthermore, the actual transactions, as well as the new, privately owned corporations, had to be offered tax breaks; if not, the process would simply not get under way. Capital gains on rising stock prices went untaxed, and some of the state-owned firms were sold for a song, or under dubious conditions: insider trading, influence peddling, etc.[50] New money flowed into several Latin American nations but did not translate into a greater and sustained government spending capacity, once the initial, one-time-only sales had been consummated.

Schematically, the states of Latin America were driven to the last resort: selling assets to raise revenues and pay off debts.[51] Some governments actually acknowledged this, flaunting the procedure in the process. President Salinas de Gortari in Mexico went as far as claiming, at the outset of his term when part of Mexicana Airlines was auctioned off, that the proceeds would be destined to provide drinking water to an impoverished slum outside Mexico City. He argued that this was a much more sound use of the state's resources than buying planes for a national airline.

The argument was subsequently reformulated, contending that privatization revenues would pay off domestic debt and consequently reduce outlays necessary to pay interest on it, freeing monies for other purposes. The reasoning was later extended to the foreign debt. In June 1992 the Mexican government announced it was buying back $7 billion of external debt, and that it had used $1 billion from the sale of

---

50. When the Argentine national airline, Aerolíneas Argentinas, was privatized in 1991, congressmen in Buenos Aires calculated that the three Boeing 747s owned by the airline had been sold off for $590,000 each, less than a tenth of their value. An old 707, according to these same sources, went for one dollar and fifty-four cents, less than a toy model of the same plane. "Las ventas de Entel y la línea aérea, llenas de errores," *Excelsior* (Mexico City), March 23, 1991, p. 19-A. The deal was so shady and shaky that the Argentine government was forced to buy back 28 percent of the company in July 1992. *New York Times*, July 31, 1992, p. C5.

51. This is what a renowned American economist wrote back in 1988 about the merits of selling off assets by the United States: "As long as foreigners are willing, we can continue to finance what we owe by borrowing more and by selling off our assets. . . . Selling off our real assets will keep the party going longer. . . . But it will also make the mortgage on our future and the reduction in our standard of living required to meet the payments all the greater. . . . We have always been suspicious of foreign acquisition of American business and property. Twenty-nine states have laws that restrict foreign ownership of farmland. . . ." Benjamin Friedman, *Day of Reckoning* (New York: Random House, 1988), pp. 33, 71.

remaining stock in the telephone company for that purpose. This was precisely and forthrightly what everyone was doing in Latin America: selling assets to pay debt, with the hope that when the sales came to an end, as they inevitably would, someone else would take up the slack, and money from other sources would materialize.

But once yields on stock exchanges stabilized and the fire sales were over, where would the money come from? Would it be possible to keep the hot money still if taxes were levied on capital gains? Would the new Latin American magnates accept higher tax rates and continue to invest in their large corporations despite them? Or would they simply strip their newly acquired businesses and place their money elsewhere? Few of these questions received answers, showing that there was less ideological conviction and more dire necessity to proceed in this fashion than most officials, businessmen, and commentators readily acknowledged. The almost unavoidable result of dozens of governments' virtual bankruptcy was presented as a deliberate, freely adopted policy choice applauded by ideologues in Washington and local beneficiaries. The fact that few of the real problems that gave rise to overindebtedness and the ensuing debt crisis were being addressed was rarely mentioned.

This was also the case for the other, logical consequences of this new funding crutch. Most of the economic adjustment in the nations of the hemisphere came on the spending side.[52] The little that had been done on the revenue side stemmed from higher fees and charges on public goods and services; very little flowed from higher tax receipts.[53] Deficits were cut, and much progress was made in many countries in squaring public accounts and reducing inflation, exchange rate instability, and

---

52. A few cases taken more or less at random: for tax receipts relating to GDP for Uruguay, the numbers went from 19.8 percent in 1972 to 20 percent in 1982, to 21.8 percent in 1985. For Brazil, they varied from 17.7 percent in 1972 to 19.6 percent in 1982, to 16.6 percent in 1985, to 19.3 percent in 1988. Finally for Colombia, the country least affected by the debt crisis, the figures varied from 10 percent in 1972 and 1982 to 12 percent in 1990. Again, it is important to point out that these statistics must be taken as indications of trends and magnitudes, not highly precise numbers. Moreover, they do not correspond entirely with data used in this chapter taken from other sources, since, as was mentioned in Note 37, the exact definition of tax revenues varies from source to source. The important thing here is to note that using the same sources, and roughly similar accounting methods, the changes on the revenue side, during a period when everything else changed in Latin America (ten years of growth with debt, ten years of debt with no growth, half a decade of structural reform) were insignificant. World Bank, *World Development Report* (New York: Oxford University Press, 1992, 1987, 1984), table on Central Government Current Revenues in each edition.

53. "With the exception of the prices of public services or of state-produced goods, the reform efforts on the government revenue side have in general been smaller or have been canceled out by the drop in growth rates." Ibarra, op. cit., pp. 35.

even capital flight. But this was rarely achieved by increasing continuous revenues. In some countries, like Argentina, spending was held constant for a few years while revenues rose. But at the end of the decade, it had fallen again, and taxes returned to their initial levels after having increased as a share of GDP for a brief period.[54]

The greater reliance on the private sector, and on money from abroad, as well as the more intense international competition for capital made it exceedingly difficult to raise taxes or broaden the tax base to the upper middle class, the stock exchange, foreign firms, or the wealthy. The ideological bias against taxation and state involvement in the economy, and a reduction of inequalities, compounded the conundrum. While some Latin American economies were able to grow slightly, and others implemented high-profile programs combating extreme poverty, the gaping injustice of Latin American life became visibly greater. Partial solutions emerged and actually worked, but only exceptionally or with exorbitant costs: much closer ties with the United States in the case of Mexico, together with mass immigration; drugs, in a growing number of countries; the spread of the informal economy as a form of reducing overt, full-time unemployment and supplementing incomes.

And even the simpler pleasures of life were compromised, as demonstrated by the *arrastões*, or waves of teenage vandals that unfurled on the beaches of Rio de Janeiro, from Copacabana to Ipanema, in October of 1992. Literally thousands of young, poor, mostly black *favelados* from Baixada Fluminense swept down on the coast, stealing everything in their wake. A poll taken by a Rio paper a few days later revealed that a good half of all Carioca bathers would find another way

54. In Mexico, for example, taxes—excluding Pemex—averaged 10 percent of GDP from 1979 through 1987; in other words, during the stabilization period of the Mexican crisis, no change took place on the tax side; whatever increases occurred in government revenues—and they were minimal—came from slightly better collection of the value added tax and higher taxes on gasoline sales. From 1988 onward, matters remained the same. According to figures the Mexican government provided to the IMF, tax revenues from 1988 through 1991 remained at 10 percent of GDP and were not expected to rise. The entire Mexican adjustment took place on the spending side. Lower tax rates to equalize Mexican rates with those of the United States did not produce a shortfall, because collection did improve somewhat under President Salinas, but the overall tax burden was unchanged. The figures for 1979–1987 are from CIEMEX–WEFA (Wharton Econometric Forecasting Associates (Bala Cynwyd, Pa.: *Perspectivas Económicas de México*, December 1988), p. 249; those for 1988–1991 are from International Monetary Fund, Mexico: Extended Arrangement Review and Program for the Third Year, Approved by S. T. Beza and Eduard Brau, Washington, D.C., March 25, 1991, p. 34. These figures coincide with those published in the most recent, and insightful, book on the Mexican economy: Nora Lustig, *Mexico: The Remaking of an Economy* (Washington, D.C.: Brookings Insitution, 1992), pp. 100–101.

to cool off and take the sun as the Southern summer arrived.[55] Poverty and delinquency were hitting the beaches, as it were.

Tragically, though, the greater reliance on the market and the above-mentioned cures all had perverse effects. On the revenue side, immigration left tax receipts abroad, and it was practically impossible to tax remittances. Drug-dealing was by definition a highly profitable but untaxable economic activity that diverted capital and labor from taxable ventures. Most of the underground economy was also highly tax-evasive, in addition to its other drawbacks—getting around already weakened social regulations regarding child employment, social security, occupational safety and health, and the environment. This was also the major disadvantage of bestowing a greater role on the market: the market in question, contrasting with the case in Europe or the United States, was an unregulated, rough-and-tumble place. Free markets function correctly with adequate regulatory frameworks, legislation to protect the weak and poor, and socially accepted limits on unintended consequences and externalities. The law of the jungle was given free rein in Latin America; the foreseeable, unavoidable consequences were just a matter of time.

After nearly twenty years of varying solutions, crises and contradictions, Latin American social and economic development was right where it had been decades before. The relative shares of upper and middle classes on the one hand and the poor on the other, were approximately the same or more skewed. The possibility of sustaining lasting high levels of social spending, and expenditures on infrastructure, energy, the environment, etc., without altering these societies' fundamental tax equation loomed as remote as ever. Conversely, the chances of transforming that social structure and significantly reducing the number of poor and substantially and rapidly enlarging the middle class seemed smaller than ever. The failure of the right, center, and left only underlined the complexity of the problem. The attraction of the neoliberal model resided in its novelty: since nothing done before had worked, maybe this new experiment would. It didn't, in the sense that the underlying problems remained without a solution or an answer. The combination of growth and equity seemed as distant as before.

Worst of all, the probability was great that Latin American elites had resigned themselves to the dilemma. Their despair in the face of external constraints, and their largely sincere if not well-founded belief that the availability of foreign funding was to a considerable extent a

---

55. *O Globo*, Pesquisa de Infoglobo, October 24, 1992.

function of their own policies, underscored this resignation. Indeed, the strongest arguments heard in favor of the free-market radicalism of the late eighties and early nineties consisted precisely in the importance of the foreign constraint. Nothing could be done without external resources; these were more sought after than ever; only certain policies and countries would succeed in attracting them, and consequently there was no alternative to the policies that—it was hoped—would attract funding. However, the real situation regarding Latin America's leeway at the end of the Cold War, and the rigidity of the international constraints it faced, was far more complex.

•

On the surface of things, the end of the Cold War reduced Latin America's international margin of maneuver. It apparently strengthened the international economic constraint on the region, as even the illusion of an economic alternative to participation in the Western financial and economic community vanished. In an age when everyone follows the same musical score, the penalty for singing out of tune quickly rises. In the "new world order" characterized by economic globalization, free-market homogeneity, and cutthroat competition for scarce capital and protected markets, the real economic check placed on Latin American autonomy was no longer the fear or reality of retaliation by the United States. Rather, it superficially consisted of the economic, financial, and ultimately political impossibility of straying far beyond the bounds of economic and ideological orthodoxy. The true constraint Latin American governments were up against was the prospect of sources of credit, investment and aid drying up, and markets for exports and sympathy contracting because of policies deemed hostile or unwise. Nationalizing natural resources, emphasizing social spending, or placing restrictions on foreign trade or investment no longer necessarily invited invasion or destabilization. They simply seemed to lead inevitably to financial scarcity and economic ostracism.

But the contradictory nature of world economic trends simultaneously showed that current events were perhaps less unfavorable to change in Latin America than appearances indicated. World capital scarcities and the region's shrinking role in the world economy disputed the relevance of initial impressions of a hardening of the foreign constraint. International penalties for transgressors of orthodoxy exist only if they matter, and if there is a true reward for compliance. The validity of both conditions is open to question.

Many long-term economic forecasts predicted dire consequences for the region as the trend toward capital scarcity began to bite across the world. Low savings rates in the United States, and its economy's unsatiated appetite for foreign capital, along with Japan's greater consumption and investment needs and German preoccupation with Central and Eastern Europe, all contributed to less availability of international capital. The conversion to a market economy in the former Soviet bloc, as well as the free-market reforms in Latin America, caused a severe strain on world capital markets:

> By 1995 Eastern Europe and Latin America are likely to require about $170 billion per year of external financing; about $10 billion of this is for Eastern Europe, and the rest is for Latin America. . . . The conclusions regarding the balance between investment and savings as the potential transfer of resources from the Western countries to the restructuring areas . . . are downright alarming. Japanese capital outflows are likely to continue to contract over time. Instead of exporting capital, Germany is likely to import capital. . . . To satisfy the world's need for extra savings, gross U.S. national savings rates would have to rise from 14 percent of GDP to 18 percent, without growth falling below 2 percent per year.[56]

Once low U.S. short-term rates, induced to bring the country out of a recession in 1992, start going up again, the cost of money worldwide is expected to rise accordingly.[57] Not everyone was so pessimistic: the multilateral agencies were perhaps less gloomy about the prospects for growth and capital availability in the 1990s. But even the World Bank agreed that "The pattern of savings-investment balances across broad country groups is not likely to depart over the medium term from the broad trend established in the past few years."[58] It did emphasize that significant variations would occur country-by-country, and, more importantly, that domestic-policy reform would make a dramatic difference between receiving capital and not. But if every nation in Latin America implemented the same policy reforms, then the competition

---

56. David C. Roche, *The Global Resource Model*, Morgan Stanley, Investment Research UK and Europe, December 13, 1990, pp. 81–82. In a speech in April 1992, José Córdoba, Mexico's second highest official—next only to President Carlos Salinas de Gortari—put the tab on his country's requirements at $15 billion per year for ten years while emphasizing that the world was entering a phase of capital scarcity and greater competition for whatever was available. *El Financiero* (Mexico City), April 29, 1992, p. 1.

57. "The world is short of capital and therefore real interest rates will remain high and there will be piles of new equity issues (particularly privatizations) and less liquidity to buy them with." Ibid., p. 6.

58. World Bank, *World Development Report 1991* (New York: Oxford University Press, 1991), p. 23.

among them, and between the hemisphere and other areas, would remain equal.

At the same time, Latin America, together with Africa and significant parts of Asia, was being increasingly marginalized from the world economy. Most of the factors governing long and mid-term international investment and credit flows had been moving away from Latin America for years. The region, with a few very minor exceptions, had been excluded, for example, from voluntary commercial bank lending since 1982. The economic component of the United States' and the rest of the world's Latin stake was dwindling. In 1980, 18 percent of U.S. direct foreign investment was located in Latin America; by 1989 the proportion had fallen to 16 percent. In 1980 Latin America received 16.3 percent of U.S. exports; by 1990, only 12.4 percent.[59]

In 1982 the hemisphere generated 7.1 percent of the world's gross "domestic" product; by 1989 the figure had fallen to 4.4 percent.[60] In 1960, Latin America's share of world exports stood at 6.4 percent. By 1980 it had dipped to 5.5 percent, and by 1990 it had shrunk to only 3.8 percent. On the import side the decline was more precipitous, from 7.7 percent in 1960 to 5.4 percent in 1970, to 4.7 percent in 1980, and 4.5 percent by 1990.[61] Its part of foreign investment in the developing countries plummeted from 40 percent in 1970 to 28 percent in 1989.[62]

These trends led several authors to speculate about a "North-North" circuit of investment, credit, and trade incorporating the former socialist economies and parts of China and excluding the Third World and specifically Latin America, with the exception of a few "buffer states" like Mexico, Morocco, and perhaps Iran.[63] Trade, investment, and credit would all become concentrated in the Northern Hemisphere. The fading interest in Latin America by the developed world's universities, press, business, and politicians sprang from this prospect.

Paradoxically, after so many years of worrying about excessive American involvement in the region, Latin America would now suffer

---

59. *Statistical Abstract of the United States, 1991* (Washington, D.C.: U.S. Dept. of Commerce), pp. 797, 806.

60. International Monetary Fund, *International Financial Statistics, Direction of Trade* (Washington D.C., 1992).

61. Ibid.

62. United Nations–UNDP Rapport Mondial, op. cit., p. 41.

63. See, for example, Peter Smith, "La Nueva Relación entre México y Estados Unidos," *Nexos* (Mexico City), February 1990. The point was also made in a study by the United Nations Center on Transnational Corporations, "World Investment Report: The Triad in Foreign Direct Investment," quoted by *Courier International* (Paris), September 5, 1991, p. 6.

from U.S. indifference, compounded by the rest of the world's traditional relative disinterest. This "benign" neglect could actually do the
region a substantial bit of good, were it to materialize. In the short
term, however, it has frightened elites accustomed to attention and
masses avid for aid. And yet, superficial trends and sentiments notwithstanding, the transformation of the modern world into watertight
compartments devoid of any significant influence of one upon the
other was not a viable scenario. In the same way that Europeans, for
example, were rapidly—and sometimes fearfully—grasping how inter-
woven their societies had become with those of North and sub-Saharan
Africa, the United States had to acknowledge its bonds with Latin
America. The rise of Islamic fundamentalism in North Africa and the
Middle East became a European issue only when it became apparent
that millions of actual and potential Algerian, Tunisian, and Moroccan
immigrants were deeply immersed in the ideological trends sweeping
their former or present-day homelands. Racism in Europe and civil
strife and poverty in the Maghreb or sub-Saharan Africa suddenly appeared as clearly linked phenomena. Whatever illusions Western European elites harbored regarding their nations' hypothetical insulation
from trends across the Mediterranean were quickly dispelled by the
realization that the European Community was also becoming a Mediterranean community. The globalization of the world economy and
environment, of financial and trade flows, was not limited to the cross-
currents the industrialized nations preferred: capital, high-tech, competitive goods, and efficiently provided, high-quality services. The new,
worldwide flows included drugs and immigration, global warming and
ozone depletion, biodiversity conservation and sustainable development, poverty and cultural habits, from loud music at night to spicy
food and different sexual mores.

The United States can isolate itself far less from the welfare of the
Peruvian highlands' peasants, civil wars in Central America, wage
levels in Mexico and the Dominican Republic, the spread of AIDS in
Brazil or Haiti or cholera in Ecuador, than Europeans can feign indifference to Algerian election results or Tanzanian environmental
problems. The direct U.S. economic stake in Latin America today
may be less important than before—although even this is arguable,
given enduring U.S. energy dependence and the precarious nature of
Middle East sources. But the noneconomic effect of Latin America
affairs on the U.S.—the so-called "intermestic" issues—seems greater
than ever.

In any case, capital shortages and decreasing relevance in world
markets served to nuance the economic constraint on the region.

Money flowed into some countries—as long as certain policies were followed and yields remained high—and then moved on to the next nation. Individual countries found niches or windfalls, but the region as a whole faced a capital crunch. The payoff for orthodoxy was real, but relative and generally short-lived; the penalty for deviation was all the lighter.[64] The region's narrowing leeway was undisputed but it was enhanced by countervailing economic trends that moderated its impact.

The challenge facing the continent and its left, then, is to finally achieve the combination of economic growth with social equity. It is an almost insurmountable challenge because the resources involved are enormous and the resistances to providing them, either internally or abroad, are also immense. The rich and middle classes in Latin America fiercely refuse to pay taxes for many reasons, most of them selfish and unacceptable, but also for a very good one: they believe that their taxed pesos or cruzeiros will be misspent, stolen, or wasted by undemocratic, unresponsive, or unaccountable governments. Taxpayers in the United States and Western Europe do not want to pay for the reduction of inequalities in their own nations, let alone in countries they have a dismal opinion of, sometimes not without justification.

The fact that the right and center, which have been governing most of Latin America for the last half century, have not proved up to the task, does not mean that the left has the benefit of its adversaries' failure or that the task is unfulfillable. It simply means that there is a great deal of work to be accomplished.

---

64. Thus the paradox: Brazil, the black sheep of neo-liberal reform in the early nineties, was receiving as much speculative investment as "model reformers"; but no one was managing to sustain high growth rates.

14

A Grand Bargain for
the Millennium

■

Wherever there is a left today, it seems intractably confronted with a central problem: devising a viable and substantively different alternative to the status quo. In the United States, liberal democrats are excoriated for "not having an alternative"; in Western Europe, socialists and "greens" are chastised for dreaming or adopting the stances and policies of their adversaries. In Latin America the center-right, with its overwhelming support and sympathy from the international financial community and media, is deemed irreversibly successful because of its sheer existence and because it has implemented the "right" policies, regardless of their consequences or the prevailing correspondence between goals and results.[1]

Despite the drawbacks, in contemporary politics and economic globalization, refusing to play on the same playing field, no matter how tilted, amounts to condemning oneself to marginality. The left must have a program; an alternative is necessary not so much because of its own intrinsic desirability, but because it's like a scorecard at a ball

---

1. One of the stranger mechanisms at work in the neoliberal wave is the way success is gauged. As three analysts have noted:"There are several ways to think about success. One (used by some conservative authors) is to define it merely in terms of a continued implementation of reform measures, whatever they may be: they gave up on using economic criteria to evaluate the success of reforms and decided to explain instead the degree to which policy decisions were carried out rather than economic outcomes of the measures taken." Luis Carlos Bresser Pereira, José Mará Maravall, and Adam Przeworski, "Economic Reforms in New Democracies: A Social-Democratic Approach" presented at the Conference on Democracy, Markets and Structural Reforms in Latin America, Buenos Aires, March 25–27, 1992, p. 4.

game: you can't tell the players without one. But this path leads to another dilemma: the painful choice between erecting a different model—as socialism was for over a century—or bending and molding existing ones into something new, yet not totally opposed to the status quo. The first option has the advantage of contrast and attacking the root causes of the prevailing state of affairs. It has the disadvantage of seeming illusory in today's world. The second choice's main weakness lies in its reformist idealism: changing effects without dwelling on causes. Its strength, though, resides in its viability: a reformist platform is realistic, as remote as its realization may seem.

The line between the two is a fine one: Marx himself described his "scientific socialism" as originally being nothing more than a patchwork quilt of English political economy, German philosophy and French utopian socialism, becoming a new alternative only when it was socialized and assimilated by parts of the labor movement. What starts out as a Chinese restaurant menu—one from column A, two from column B—ends up being a full-fledged paradigm. In this particular instance, the tilt is toward the hodge-podge solution: rather than attempting to formulate a completely different paradigm, the pages that follow seek to pick and choose that which can be salvaged from existing ones. This procedure can provide nothing more than an incipient foundation, and is open to criticism for being insufficiently ambitious. It is, however, what the traffic will bear in the present juncture.

The left's alternative has to rest on three pillars, all of which imply taking the utmost advantage of the principal changes the world and the region have recently undergone. First, the left must maximize the differences among existing market economies and models, now that the overriding opposition between socialism and the market has virtually vanished. Second, the left must put to good use the greater leverage granted by changes in the international situation, as the globalization of economic flows increasingly implies the globalization of the consequences of Third World poverty. Finally, the left's proposal must part from the principle that the conservative policies implemented in Latin America in the aftermath of the debt crisis have so widened the gap between rich and poor that a social explosion becomes again imaginable. There is beginning to be a greater evil once again, enhancing the moderate left's only true leverage: being a lesser evil.

In recent years, the mainstream debate about policy, growth, and development in Latin America has centered on a series of Manichaean oppositions: state versus market, protectionism versus free trade, growth versus distribution, domestic reform versus external cooperation. All of these dichotomies are real and important. But they have also served to sublimate another contrast that in the last analysis determines the others: the difference between rich and poor. How much market? how much state? how much protection and free trade? even how much growth and distribution? are all questions whose answers stem from the chief query: how many poor can the region tolerate, and how rich should the rich be?

The following pages rest on the premise that there must be a fundamental shift in resources and policy emphasis from the rich to the poor in order to solve the region's problems. This is not tantamount to eliminating the rich or impoverishing them, to equalizing income downward, or carrying out any of the terrible things' the rich have traditionally been terrorized by in any suggestion of reform. But it does mean limiting their wealth and asking for sacrifices on their part. To redress the inequitable sharing of the pie by hoping to make it bigger is as foolhardy a quest and as historically an improbable expectation as the opposite: redistributing the pie by making it smaller. Either it grows and is split up differently or it stays the same.[2]

•

The end of the Cold War and the dissolution of the socialist bloc have had a paradoxical effect on world ideological trends. Numerous authors in Europe and the United States have pointed out how, as the socialist glue evaporated, the capitalist camp became unstuck. Where before the rivalry between the United States and the Soviet Union and between centrally planned and market economies smothered the differences among the latter, today those distinctions stand out as they did not before. Where they seemed marginal or irrelevant in the face of the overpowering confrontation between communism and capitalism, they now appear far-reaching.

Similarly, competition—now economic—dividing the remaining great powers—the United States, a German-dominated Europe, Japan—has replaced the military and ideological confrontation that previously

---

2. On the issue of these very same options, one of the more insightful and recent collections of essays included an enlightening passage: "One of the fundamental dichotomies of Latin American development is that intelligent people who know the facts divide into camps on very basic issues, either eschewing those who disagree as incoherent populists if they themselves are concerned mainly about growth, or disdaining concern for efficiency and macroeconomic balance if they are mainly concerned with inequality." John Sheahan, "Development Dichotomies and Economic Strategy," in Simón Teitel, *Towards a New Development Strategy for Latin America: Pathways from Hirschman's Thought* (Washington, D.C.: Interamerican Development Bank/Johns Hopkins University Press, 1992), p. 40.

opposed the "West" and the Warsaw Pact. Until now, the contrasts separating the powers of the advanced world have not converged: the trade and economic confrontation among the three regions and the different types of capitalism prevailing in each one have not translated into a single overall rivalry opposing different trade blocs, military powers, and ideological paradigms.

But there is every reason to believe that as an era characterized by one type of contradiction comes to a close, it will be followed, as in the past, by a new era featuring different rivalries. At present, there is no German-European or Japanese ideological paradigm: there is a Rhineland and Nippon *example*, together with looming trade disputes and competition between the dollar, the mark, and yen zones. But with time, a clash of paradigms will come to the fore.[3] There is no economic power that doesn't reach beyond its own limits, spilling over into other domains: this is what history teaches. Where the difference between a paradigm and a mere example may first surface could well be within the institutions that play the most important role in managing international economic relations today: the World Bank and the International Monetary Fund.

Until now, Japan and Germany have not acted their age, so to speak, in these two agencies. Until 1992 they readily accepted the United States' leadership not only in actual decision-making but, most important, in ideological or policy-setting realms.[4] Thus Germany and Japan voiced scant disagreement with World Bank documents or IMF recommendations that ran directly counter to their own experience, or that vaunted American behavior that their own societies had rejected and criticized. But by the early 1990s this began to change, particularly as Japan started questioning the wisdom of the World Bank's constant criticism of protectionism and exultation of free trade. The least one could say was that the Japanese precedent was not quite consonant with that view and was certainly as valid a model of development as

---

3. "They (the distinctions between the German, Japanese and American versions of capitalism) will be the source of increasingly fierce disputes over trade and investment, to be sure, but the different economic and social systems will become rivals for the allegiance of other nations in Latin America, Eastern Europe and Southeast Asia, and they will produce conflicting policies in the UN, the IMF and the GATT." Jeffrey E. Garten, *A Cold Peace: America, Japan, Germany and the Struggle for Supremacy* (New York: Times Books, 1992), p 16.

4. "Because of Japan's and West Germany's deference to American leadership, there has been a remarkable lag in the relative influence of nations within the councils of the IMF and World Bank. It is as if the clock had stopped and the degree of financial weight had frozen in the 1960s." Robert Kuttner, *The End of Laissez-faire: National Purpose and the Global Economy after the Cold War* (New York: Knopf, 1991), p. 241.

any other example. For the moment, the two Bretton Woods institutions continued to act as if there were only one type of market economy, which all others more or less faithfully mimicked, and that looked, smelled, and sounded a great deal like the Anglo-Saxon, Reagan-Thatcher model of free-market radicalism.[5] The Bank and the Fund could become the last redoubt of the conservative paradigm.[6] Undoubtedly, these are not the only transformations occurring in the world today. The emergence of new economic blocs is an important addition, as is the growing weight of multinational firms and their increasing tension with national sovereignties.

Existing economic rivalries will soon meld into a paradigmatic competition, opening new alternatives across the globe—tradewise, perhaps militarily, and certainly ideologically. As one of the leading French exponents of the emerging conflict among contending capitalisms has phrased it:

> This will be a subterranean war, violent and with no quarter, but subtle and hypocritical, like conflicts among chapels of the same Church. It will be a war of enemy brothers armed with two models emanating from a common system, inspired by the two antagonistic logics of capitalism operating within the same liberal creed.[7]

The left's alternative must take advantage of and build on these rapidly sharpening differences. While the left can no longer expect to convince a majority of the population that the extinct socialist model is an aspiration worth pursuing, it can reasonably hope to persuade

---

5. It may be that for a while after the entire world has abandoned the radical free-market notion, the World Bank and the Fund will continue to emphasize it. This would be logical: the corrections imposed on the market by suffrage and society take far longer to work their wonders in supranational institutions, which are by definition unaccountable to voters or civil society and have acquired a certain autonomy in relation to their member governments.

6. This was exemplified by the tragicomic brouhaha surrounding World Bank chief economist Lawrence Summers's notorious February 1992 memo regarding the institution's stance on the environment: "I think the economic logic behind dumping a load of toxic waste in the lowest wage country is impeccable and we should face up to it. . . . Under-populated countries in Africa are vastly under-polluted. . . . Only the lamentable facts that so much pollution is generated by non-tradable industries and that the unit transport costs of solid waste are so high prevent world welfare enhancing trade in air pollution and waste." Quoted in *BankCheck*, Berkeley, winter 1992, p 1. Summers subsequently claimed he was misunderstood and only trying to stimulate debate within the Bank; the fact is, his views were the logical corollary of World Bank policy and the underlying inspiration for conservative, unregulated free-trade agreements: let those countries that wish to, import pollution or waste, and be paid for doing so.

7. Michel Albert, *Capitalisme contre capitalisme* (Paris: Editions du Seuil, 1991), p. 26.

millions of Latin Americans that another type of market economy, contrasting starkly with the one currently being hailed throughout Latin America, is preferable to the status quo. A clarification is in order at this stage: adopting a paradigm does not mean engaging a trade partner. A nation does not have to enter the Japanese or European economic sphere of influence to latch on to their respective paradigms on economic policy and social organization; nor does it have to leave the U.S. trade and credit sphere in order to abandon the U.S. paradigm (which, coincidentally, may be undergoing its own wrenching transformation). After the Cold War, a country can assimilate ideas without indiscriminately purchasing the guns or butter that go with them. Conversely, it can import the latter without adopting the ideas that accompany them. Ideological affinity with the paradigm does not necessarily entail closer, let alone exclusive, trade, financial, and military ties. The fact that frequently most of the facets of great power behavior go together does not mean that they must always do so.

By formally and sincerely accepting the logic of the market, and then immediately and equally sincerely endorsing the variations, regulations, exceptions, and adaptations the European and Japanese market economies have adopted over the years, the Latin American left can set the stage for the construction of a paradigm that is substantively different from the present state of affairs. This is a widening, but still reluctant, sentiment within the Latin American left, as witness the advice of the Brazilian sociologist Francisco Weffort to his colleagues:

> Socialists must learn to live with the most advanced forms of capitalism . . . But they need not be identified, in their values or their movements, with the "soul" of capitalism. Socialists should marry democracy out of love, but their union with the market need be no more than a "marriage of convenience."[8]

Moreover, by doing so the left will have taken the first step in building a model that is viable and credible and that passes the test of the finger and the globe. This test, as devised once by a Salvadorean guerrilla leader, is simple. It consists in defining a model by its materialization on the globe: if one can't point to a country where the scheme one hopes to emulate actually exists, the model is dysfunctional. Conversely, if a spot on the globe can be found where it exists and thrives, ipso facto it is a valid and useful one.

---

8. Francisco Weffort, "The Future of Socialism," *Journal of Democracy*, July 1992, Washington, D.C., p. 98.

Accepting the market can be a matter of conviction, of convenience, or both. For the left, it is not an easy step to take. For years—in fact forever—it has frowned upon the principle of the market, largely because in Latin America it has been associated with all the vices and horrors of the past. Moreover, U.S. insistence on it, and the way Washington has simplistically identified market mechanisms with both political freedom and social equality, in a region where the three have never gone together, has not made matters any easier. As recently as the 1980s, those sectors of the left that gladly accepted the priority of democratic rule quite rightly retained a theoretical distinction between the market and democracy.[9] They also distinguished—less persuasively—between the need to incorporate one and the desirability of still rejecting the other. But the end of socialism offers wide possibilities of differentiation and competition among market options.

What makes these options available to Latin America is precisely the difference between its economies and the command economies of Eastern Europe and the former USSR. A conservative Czech finance minister once said that "the third way is the fastest way to the Third World."[10] The proposition is arguable in theoretical terms—the reasons are probably more political than economic—but it seems undeniable that the formerly socialist economies had in fact no choice but to rush toward the ravages of the unfettered free market, whatever social-democratic dreams many of the original opponents of the *anciens régimes* may have nurtured.

But the economies of Latin America never were socialist command structures. They all had markets, prices, private property, unemployment, moving wage scales, financial intermediation, more or less convertible currencies. They were protected, subsidized, and in some cases inefficient economies, but not socialist ones. Thus the transition is not one from socialism to the market, but from one type of market economy to another: to the Anglo-Saxon, individualistic market economy, or to a European-style social-market economy, or a Japanese version. This is not to say that this transition is a benign one: it implies an

---

9. "Within the Latin American left, criticism of the State is much more the defense of political democracy than the defense of the market. Accepting capitalism as a reality does not mean accepting the market as a value. . . . If Latin American [left-wing] intellectuals accept today the reality of the market, they do not love it." Francisco Weffert, "Latin America–United States Relations," paper prepared for the Inter-American Dialogue Workshop on the Changing Global Context for U.S.–Latin American Relations, Airlie House, May 23–25, 1990, p. 12.

10. Vaclav Klaus, "Transition—An Insider's View," Problems of Communism, 40th Anniversary Conference Proceedings, January–April 1992, p. 73.

excruciatingly painful relinquishing of sovereignty, as well as domestic transfers of power and wealth. But the difference is important: difficult as they are, these transitions allow halfway solutions; the others apparently do not.

The variations among market economies have been eloquently spelled out in recent times by authors on both sides of the Atlantic, and by observers of Japanese and East Asian capitalism.[11] They range from the features of the Rhineland, social market economy of most of Western Europe, to the type of state-business relationship prevalent in Japan and Korea:

> Japan, Korea and other economically vigorous Asian nations use an explicitly developmental state. . . . they certainly do not have free markets in the Western sense. . . . The European Community practices a mix of managed and free markets. . . . Even the most "conservative" nation of the EC [Germany] spends nearly half its its gross national product in the public sector and offers its citizens generous universal welfare-state support. . . . The coming of age of Japan and the European Community increases the influence of forces that neither preach nor practice U.S.-style classical liberalism. . . .[12]

Building from these distinctions, the left can begin to craft a paradigm for the future by blending the social corrections imposed upon the market by Western European capitalism, with the business-government complement to the market developed by Japanese capitalism.

Socially, the broad contours of the model are well known. They shape the cradle-to-grave welfare state that Europeans have built in the course of the last century—dating back to the first Bismarckian social reforms of the 1880s—and that they continue to support and pay for, despite the rising costs and the ideological war waged against it since the early 1980s. A high tax burden, shared as equitably as possible by

---

11. Among them are: Alain Lipietz, *Choisir L'Audace. Une Alternative pour le XXIe siècle* (Paris: Editions La Découverte, 1989); Michel Albert, op. cit.; Lester Thurow, *Head to Head: The Coming Economic Battle Among Japan, Europe and America* (New York: Morrow, 1992); Robert Kuttner, op. cit.; John Kenneth Galbraith, *The Culture of Contentment* (Boston: Houghton Mifflin, 1992): Jeffrey E. Garten, op. cit.; Robert Wade, *Governing the Market: Economic Theory and the Role of Government in East Asian Industrialization* (Princeton, N.J.: Princeton University Press, 1990); Fernando Fajnzylber, *Unavoidable Industrial Restructuring in Latin America* (Durham, N.C.: Duke University Press, 1990); David Ibarra, *Privatización y otras expresiones de los acomodos de poder entre Estado y Mercado en América Latina* (Mexico City: Universidad Nacional Autónoma, 1990). We draw heavily on them in the pages that follow.

12. Kuttner, op. cit., pp. 7–8.

all those able to pay, ensures considerable social expenditures in decisive areas: education, health, housing, unemployment insurance, professional training, infrastructure.

Another feature of the Rhineland model, though not of all Western Europe necessarily, can be found in the high levels of labor force unionization as well as the involvement of workers in production processes and the administration of large business conglomerates. In the United States, in addition to the extremely low unionization rate (15–17 percent in recent years) a social stigma has surfaced in relation to labor unions. They are often seen as obstacles to sound business, competitiveness, and modernity; in the best of cases as an unavoidable legacy of the past. In Germany, the rate of unionization is 42 percent, including public sector contingents. In Japan it is above 30 percent, though concentrated in what are in fact company unions. But in addition to the obvious implications of greater unionization for collective bargaining, higher wages and fringe benefits, the lowering of income differentials, and the existence of representative interlocutors for business and government, the German and Japanese systems also allow for the growing participation of workers in the production process. And, just as important, it provides for far greater job security.

Through the German *Mitbestimmung* system of co-management or co-responsibility, union representatives sit on the boards of all companies with more than 2,000 employees. This arrangement provides for union participation in training, layoffs, schedules, work organization, and salary disbursement schemes. While these mechanisms should not be idealized—companies are still run by their owners—and could not be set up in the absence of the broad social consensus that them, they have contributed greatly to the source of the German model.

Worker involvement constitutes a radical departure from the American-style, Taylorite form of worker-management organization, permitting what French economist Alain Lipietz has labeled the "implication" of workers in the production process. This post-Taylorite model of labor-management relations increases productivity, competitiveness, and stability by involving workers in the production process, instead of excluding them and limiting their participation to Taylor-like time and movement mechanics, separating intellectual labor from manual labor. The battle of the two (or three) market economies is also a fight to exit from the no longer functioning Taylor-Ford compromise, where in exchange for the welfare state and growing levels of consumption on the part of workers, the latter abdicated any participation or "implication" in the production process.[13] According to Lipietz, there were two exits from the crisis of the existing compromise: a neo-Taylorite solution, where flexibility in hiring and firing characterizes an overall flexibilization of the wage-earning relationship. Or a "Kalmarian" solution, named after the Swedish town where Volvo began experimenting with the other course in the 1970s, and applied in Japan, Germany, and Northern Italy, with workers actively involved in the productivity learning curve, the quest for quality, and the management of productive processes.

Thanks to the welfare state and the role of unions and different labor-management relations, income inequalities are much smaller in these market economies than in the United States. Citizens pay far more in taxes, but they also receive more; the redistributive function of taxation is respected. In the past this may have led to less dynamic, mobile, and enterprising societies; it also entailed fairer, more homogeneous communities with greater solidarity among their members.[14] Once a given overall standard of living is reached, the model may require corrections as the income distribution pattern becomes too narrow for the proper functioning of capitalism and the tax burden becomes too heavy. That may have occurred already in some of the most prosperous nations that have social market economies, like Sweden; Latin American is still light-years away.

Finally, with regard to the social aspects of this Rhineland capitalism, it implies a regulatory framework that is an intimate ingredient of the entire arrangement. Regulation by the state and society, be it of a decentralized nature—as in Germany—or a more Jacobin type, as in France—is accepted and welcomed by society's members, even if on occasion they complain bitterly about it or consistently try and get around it. But a broad consensus prevails that the market must be regulated. The unfettered activity of the free market is not the ideal of this form of social organization, nor is "market-friendliness" the key element in ascertaining whether certain regulations are positive or not. The central criterion is whether they achieve the purpose they set

---

13. Lipietz, op cit., p 25.

14. "The Rhineland countries are relatively egalitarian. . . . The middle class is statistically more important than in the United States, even though the latter was the middle-class country *par excéllence*. If we define the middle class as the group of people whose income is close to the national average, it represents only 50 percent of the population in the U.S., versus 75 percent in Germany and 80 percent in Sweden and Switzerland. In Japan, surveys show that 89 percent of the population considers itself middle class: a subjective but significant indication." Albert, op. cit., p. 177.

themselves. These societies readily accept that there are economic costs to this regulatory maze, and that they are worth paying.

This type of market economy depends on a basic consensus regarding the maintenance of the welfare state, the role of unions and associations, the tax burden and the regulatory framework. It cannot function if one part of society rejects it, if the rich and prosperous refuse to be taxed and regulated, if the poor and less advantaged insist on changing the rules of the game or the overall arrangement if given the chance. After the lengthy, turn-of-the-century debates on the choice between reform and revolution in the European labor movement, it is obvious today that there was somewhat of a trade-off between the two options. The consensus achieved in nations like Germany after 1959 or Austria and the Netherlands in the fifties and sixties, rests—as in Sweden since the 1930s—on an underlying agreement among the majority of the inhabitants of these nations. The best proof of this solid consensus is that the basic features of the social market economy have remained essentially unaltered through successive changes in government, particularly in Germany. Indeed, the social market economy, or Rhineland capitalism, is no longer identified with one country or political current.

This also true of the extensive state involvement in the economy that has often been associated with the Japanese model of growth and development, but which in fact is almost as characteristic of Europe as of East Asia. Its features include an important role for the state in production itself at different stages of development, as well as a special symbiosis between the state and the business community, forging an industrial policy and planning for the future. It also serves to protect those sectors of the economy from foreign competition, ensuring that high-wage, high-skill employment remains at home instead of being transferred abroad through unfavorable trading patterns, no matter how "free" they may seem in the textbooks. There is growing support for these policies in the United States as well as increasing awareness of their advantages for developing countries.

In most of Western Europe, as in Japan to a lesser extent, the state does not provide only the regulatory framework, the infrastructure and social spending on housing, education, and health that are generally considered "acceptable" or market-friendly forms of state intervention. In France, the state continues to run the largest automobile firm, the railroads and subway, the electrical and telecommunications utilities, part of the gas and oil industries, a large part of the banking sector, and many of the nation's largest industrial conglomerates. Likewise in Italy, perhaps even on a broader scale. In Spain, where according to conventional wisdom free-market radicalism has been all the rage since a Socialist government was elected in 1982 and led the country into the Common Market in 1986, more than half the gross domestic product is generated by government-owned firms. In Germany, the most productive, prosperous, and efficient economy in the world, where no privatizations took place during the 1980s and early 1990s, even under a right-of-center Christian Democratic administration:

> German governments [state and federal] own more shares in more industries [airlines, autos, steel, chemicals, electric power, transportation—some outright, some partially] than any noncommunist country on the face of the globe.[15]

In Japan, the situation is analogous, though with important nuances. The intervention of the state, while less proprietary than in Europe, is no less pervasive, and perhaps more intrusive than in the previously mentioned cases. It is a long-standing affair. According to E. Herbert Norman:

> Japan's formative years of industrial development following three centuries of cultural isolation were characterized by a unique feature of Japanese industrialization: state control of strategic industries. These industries were considered strategic either because of their connection with naval and military defense or because of their importance in export industries competing against foreign products and requiring subsidy or protection.[16]

The fundamental difference between state ownership in these countries and in the former socialist economies lies in the way in which they are managed and the context in which it takes place. Management autonomy, adherence to market principles, accountability to democratically elected or appointed oversight authorities, scrupulous honesty and exposure to competition make the majority of state-owned firms efficient and competitive. Their privatization, when it occurs—for example, during the cohabitation period in France in 1985–88, when the right-of-center Gaullist Jacques Chirac was prime minister, or in Britain under Margaret Thatcher—is much more due to ideological considerations than to economic factors. In Latin America, however,

---

15. Thurow, op. cit., p. 36.
16. E. Herbert Norman, *Origins of the Modern Japanese State* (New York: Random House, 1975), p. 211.

precedents point in different directions. Often the inefficiency or un-profitability of state-owned firms stemmed from their function: launching heavy industry, creating development poles, subsidizing the private sector or consumers.

Furthermore, these nations reserve a very specific and broad role for the state in regulating the market. In Japan, Korea, and much of West-ern Europe, industrial policy, protection of given sectors, long-term planning, subsidies and state-sponsored market reserves or conquests are the rule. Few things are left only to the market. In Japan and in Europe it is only under exceptional circumstances that the market picks winners and losers. Natural comparative advantage is not the final determinant of trade policy; capturing advantages through man-made factors—education, investment, protection, subsidies, national security considerations—and arbitrariness is a more important consid-eration. The involvement of the state in the Japanese market economy extends into the present and future. Japan became the first develop-mental state: the state not only regulates and creates incentives; it directly decides matters of economic policy.[17]

The Korean example is very similar. But the Korean praetorian state owned a far greater share of the economy from the outset, and is much more of a "command capitalism," although other analogies are re-markable. In 1961, just after the military coup that brought Park Chung-Hee to power, and where he stayed until his assassination in 1979, the government nationalized the entire commercial banking sys-tem, of which it retained 96 percent until it began selling it off in 1983. Where the Korean model does follow the Japanese example is in its strategic planning and state-led growth: "Korea is one of the few suc-cessful cases of state-led economic growth in the postwar-period,

---

17. A more recent student of Japanese affairs summarized Chalmers Johnson's chief conclusions regarding the state's intervention in the market with the following "five strategic concepts: (1) instituting new forms of government-business interaction, based on cooperation rather than confrontation, that link long-term incentives to the mainte-nance of domestic competition while encouraging a cooperative internal stance against all foreigners; (2) making a commitment to export-oriented growth, which looks out-ward in search of global standards against which to measure product prices, product quality, and performance; (3) encouraging extremely high rates of savings and invest-ment through massive strategic incentives from the Ministry of Finance, which lead to a primacy of production over consumption; (4) establishing an equitable system of in-come distribution across all industries and classes and egalitarian access to high-quality education as a national priority; and (5) emphasizing small, frequent incremental en-hancements in Research and Development technology. . . ." Chalmers Johnson, quoted by Steven Schlossstein, *The End of the American Century* (New York: Congdon and Weed, 1989), p. 28.

where presidential command supplanted the market as the main motor of economic development."[18]

The most interesting aspect of the Korean experience, from the perspective of the state's involvement in the economy, was the export drive: how from the mid-sixties onward the country's export-led growth was also state-led growth. The large Korean conglomerates and the state jointly determined the sectors and stages where they would concentrate their efforts. Export subsidies, cheap credit, and special tax breaks were all put in place. Research and development spending, along with higher educational expenditures, was also planned and implemented with a strategic purpose. The coercion applied to the labor and student movements and the rates of exploitation common in agriculture and industry were undoubtedly unacceptable by other nations' standards. But all of this was accomplished with a far better distribution of income than in Latin America.

These nations have all enacted legislation restricting foreign investment in certain areas, protecting certain industries, and all practice managed trade while subsidizing their exports. They carve out markets for themselves, develop joint projects among them, and openly or overtly, fairly or not so fairly, attempt to capture market shares that they do not have. When their competitors or trade rivals cry foul and complain, they stonewall, negotiate, and eventually give in, but only at the end of the day and never on the basis of ideological adherence to sacrosanct principles.

In Robert Wade's fortunate phrase, they "govern the market":

> Governing-the-market policies have aimed to channel resources into industry based within the national territory . . . By means of politically determined constraints and rigged prices, they have steered the competitive process into higher wage, higher technology alternatives . . . The policies include: maintenance of a post-land reform ceiling on agricultural land ownership . . .; control of domestic and cross-border sources of credit, so that finance remains subordinate to industry and amenable to government direction; stabilization of the main macroeconomic parameters of investment choice; modulation of international competitive pressure on parts of the domestic economy; export promotion; investment in technological capacity, and assistance to specific industries. Under all these headings the governments [of East Asia]

---

18. Walden Bello and Stephanie Rosenfeld, *Dragons in Distress: Asia's Miracle Economies in Crisis*, (San Francisco: Food First, Institute for Food and Development Policy, 1990), p. 48.

have gone well beyond the limits of what would be sanctioned by free-market approaches . . .[19]

In some cases high levels of protection are compensated for by intense domestic competition. On other occasions, competition from abroad is fostered, although domestic monopolies or cartels are officially accepted and supported. The state plays a multifaceted role, either through legislation and regulation or by coordinating efforts among social partners. It tempers the short-range anxieties of shareholders and the market by stressing the long term. It moderates the power of the bottom line by insisting on the importance of market share. It promotes trade-offs among different sectors of society, regions, and objectives.

■

None of these forms of state intervention in the economy are unproductive, inefficient, or socialist. They are examples of corrections, incentives, and restraints placed on the market by societies that have evolved over time from radical free-market abstract principles to greater practical regulation and constraints. They imply protection without full-scale protectionism, regulation without stifling the market, state ownership without a command economy, competition without savage capitalism. They enjoy the support of broad political majorities, as governments of the right and left sustained them over the years. They were born long ago, yet seem to be acquiring a new life through higher stages of supranational cooperation. As one American admirer of the European scheme has put it:

> The first moves toward economic integration, via the European Coal and Steel Community, entailed a blend of state ownership and negotiated shares of European steel and coal capacity. . . . As Europe moved to a single market, the exercise included a high degree of national economic planning, strong welfare-state guarantees, and a collective refusal to let Japanese or American competition push them out of key industries simply because the gospel of laissez-faire awarded the entire market to this year's low-cost producer.[20]

The adaptation of these traits of European and Japanese capitalism to Latin American reality is obviously not easy. Although it would be

---

19. Robert Wade, *Governing the Market: Economic Theory and the Role of Government in East Asian Industrialization* (Princeton, N.J.: Princeton University Press, 1990), pp. 297–298.

20. Kuttner, op. cit., pp. 51, 136.

consonant with the region's tradition of importing ideologies and solutions from the rest of the world, it would also seem out of custom:
Latin America has always imported the most fashionable notions, not
the more meaningful but less trendy ideas. Indeed, this is what it is
largely doing today as it tries to construct not *a* market economy, but
one particular type of market economy: the Anglo-Saxon, deregulated,
"leave-it-to-the-market" model.

In a sense, one could say that together with its military power and
cultural hegemony, the last remaining bastion of U.S. supremacy in
the world is its paradigmatic prowess in the Third World (and, up to a
point, in Europe also). As Michel Albert has put it: "how is it that the
defeated, uncompetitive, and unperforming market economy has ideologically triumphed over competing paradigms that unquestionably
are performing better today?"[21] The United States' last act of nonmil-
itary hegemonic existence may well be its effort to cling to the vestiges
of trade and ideological domination in the same region where it walked
its first steps as a world power: Latin America. Its insistence on signing
free-trade pacts up and down the hemisphere synthesizes its down-
sized ambition: selling a dysfunctional (ideological) paradigm and damaged (trade) goods, the latter thanks to the former, to clients that have
apparently no choice but to buy.

That the "halfway" version of capitalism performs better and is
more humane seems undeniable today, as it would appear beyond dispute that the reason it works better is the same one, as Joseph Schum-
peter said, that explains why cars can go fast: because they have brakes.
It is precisely the sum of regulations and corrections which make this
type of market economy more productive and fairer, that will also, in
time, render it more attractive to the peoples of Latin America. But
this superiority should not conceal the fact that this capitalism too has
fallen prey today to two serious dilemmas.

The first one is rollback. In its very bastions, the merits and desirability of this scheme of things are subject to severe questioning.
Taxation is being disputed, some state firms are being privatized,
regulation is decried, and the U.S. model is touted as the ultimate
expression of perfection. This may not be a lasting trend; furthermore,
it could be more rhetorical than institutional. But it is occurring, and
it would be naïve to ignore it. The second, more substantive problem
is Marx's greatest contribution to the understanding of capitalism: it is
inherently and permanently contradictory, encountering new problems in the process of solving old ones. The corrections imposed on the

---

21. Albert, op. cit. p. 217.

market by more than a century of social strife, state regulation, international conflict and coexistence, and ideological alterations have diminished many of the market economies' most lacerating defects. But they have not eliminated their self-contradictory nature and proclivity for generating new injustices and excesses. German or Swiss capitalism is not always a pretty postcard, nor is it that for everyone. It alienates its youth, mistreats its *gastarbeiters*, creates new pockets of poverty, violence, and racism, and bores many of its greatest beneficiaries to tears. It is a far better deal than anything else existing on the planet, but it is not the marvelous model to be blindly emulated that it sometimes seems.

The task of crafting an endogenous Latin American paradigm loosely based on the European and Japanese schemes in the post–Cold War world is a worthy challenge for the left in Latin America today. But the piecemeal approach outlined above can be only a starting point. It is the only option available, and it is an attractive and viable one that can be made to work in Latin America. Not by itself: it must be accompanied by reforms on the democratization front and a major updating of Latin American nationalism. But it also demands extensive support from abroad.

Obtaining it means maximizing the new spaces opened up by changes in the world arena. The conventional consensus is that the North-South agenda is out of time and touch: the era of generosity and worldwide policies or arrangements in support of the Third World is over—as if it had ever begun. The market takes over where whining left off: those nations who can make it on their own will, those who can't won't. Yet there are sounder motives today than ever for the wealthier nations to spend money on the poorer ones, or to extend advantages to them that will enhance their possibilities of development. The reason is simple: global interdependence gives the poorer nations of the South leverage they never had before. And competition among the Northern powers is also more intense, as the disappearance of the Soviet Union dislocates the Western bloc and loosens the ties among its members.

The South's leverage is not yet sufficient to bring about radical changes in North-South relations, but it is growing. If pushed along by significant changes in Southern attitudes, a decisive transformation of North-South relations becomes conceivable, and a Grand Bargain between North and South becomes possible. On the one hand, for the first time in history, there are important interests the advanced nations want to see protected and addressed in the poorer nations, and that can be dealt with only through the poorer region's governments' and societies' acquiescence.[22] On the other hand, most Southern nations have a specific agenda for their dealings with the North that can now be addressed. The fact that both sets of countries have real and specific agendas, mutual leverage, and a growing awareness of their interdependence is the basic condition for a deal.

In this respect, the 1992 Rio de Janeiro Earth Summit was a true watershed in North-South relations, even if its expectations were not fully met. It did not quite amount to a Grand Bargain, although many of its achievements point in this direction, and that was its goal. But it may well have ushered in a new era, for many reasons. First, both sides of the globe had an agenda: the North sought Southern cooperation on protection of forests and access to biological resources, and on the broader issue of sustainable development.[23] If the nations of the South did not take environmental considerations into account in their economic development, there was simply no way of addressing any international environmental concerns. The developing nations' agenda was equally concrete: funding from the North for sustainable development in general, for next century's Agenda 21 cleanup program, through implementation of the principle that the polluter pays, and for sharing proceeds from the South's biodiversity more equitably.

While the actual trade-off did not jell, the complementarity of the two sets of demands was evident. As was the fact that although the United States rejected most of the developing nations' demands due to domestic political reasons and ideological objections, Europe and Japan accepted many of them. The Japanese from the outset used the Rio Conference as a first occasion to advance their position as an emerging great power. In the course of the preparatory work on the different conference treaties and documents, they offered credits, technology, and ideas, as well—and most importantly—as leadership.[24] They did

---

22. Another way of saying the same thing, and in relation to the debt crisis, is what author Susan George has called the debt boomerang. She outlines six specific effects of the South's debt crisis on the nations of the North: the environment, drugs, how northern taxpayers bail out the banks, lost jobs and markets, immigration, and conflict and war. See Susan George, *The Debt Boomerang: How Third World Debt Harms Us All* (London and Amsterdam: Pluto Press with the Transnational Institute, 1992).

23. In the words of a French "Green" activist who participated in the Preparatory Commission meetings and at the Rio Summit itself: "Nonetheless the Southern countries felt they had some real cards to play. The North is in the role of asking for things. It senses a coming ecological crisis, for which it bears the main responsibility, but knows the South must make some sacrifices. The new division within the North takes over where the East-West rivalry left off." Alain Lipietz, *Berlin, Baghdad, Rio* (Paris: Quai Voltaire-Edima, 1992), pp. 28–29, 118.

24. A long analysis of the Rio Conference quoted an important Japanese figure involved in his country's preparation of the conference: "We tend to see Rio and the

not entirely follow through at the conference itself, but for the first time a Northern nation with money, technology, and a "song to sing" was willing to deal directly with the South, in open defiance of the United States.[25]

The Europeans had a lower profile during the preparatory conference, largely because they still lacked the unity and capability of acting as a great power with a message. But at the conference itself, by agreeing to sign the Biodiversity Treaty and committing themselves to greater sums of money for the Third World than would have been imaginable scant years before, they broke with the United States. The Europeans had, of course, ulterior motives:

> The EEC sketched out an ambitious project: to take advantage of its technological and economic lead over the United States to propose to the developing world a new "social-ecological democratic" compromise, firstly for domestic consumption, then to gain world hegemony, vis-à-vis the South, on the issue of the environment. Europe would thus repeat the "double dip" coup that the Roosevelt New Deal accomplished for the United States in the 1940s, when it offered both a new compromise between capital and labor and a model—*the American way of life*—for all nations.[26]

The widening of the great-power spectrum allows for much greater Latin American paradigmatic leeway. For obvious reasons, Latin America's chief interlocutor will doubtless remain the United States, but under very different circumstances. As the other powers make their voices heard throughout the institutions and meeting points of inter-

---

environment as offering Japan a key leadership role. It is tied directly to what we call *kokusaika*—the internationalization of policy. . . ." According to John Newhouse: "Japan's MITI began to envision a huge market for pollution-control hardware; the Third World part of the market would be financed with Japan's foreign aid. As the Foreign Ministry saw it, Japan would acquire a stronger presence in various countries—show them how to go about their own development and how to manage the environmental consequences. As MITI saw it, pushing Japan's environmentally benign energy-saving technology even harder would reap still greater rewards in energy efficiency, and these in turn would sustain Japan's competitive edge over Europe and America. . . . Briefly, a world community that decides to save itself by saving the global environment will be promoting many large Japanese interests." John Newhouse, "The Diplomatic Round: Earth Summit," *The New Yorker*, June 1, 1992, pp. 68–69.

25. The United States delegation was of course aware of this: "Mostly, though, the Americans [in Rio] fought critics with fire. U.S. briefers accused Germany and Japan of falling prey to 'guilt-developed world logic' which dictates that the rich 'owe the rest of the world.' That stunned officials in Bonn and Tokyo, and didn't score many points with Third World delegates either." "The Road from Rio," *Newsweek International*, June 22, 1992, p. 11.

26. Lipietz, op. cit., p. 124.

national relations, the change will be all the more important. The only possibility for the Latin American left's alternative to function lies in having a viable international agenda, and some degree of cooperation from abroad beyond rhetoric and sympathy. Today, the region has an agenda with the United States and the rest of the industrialized world, but more importantly, the United States has a specific agenda for Latin America.

The left's agenda calls for what could be labeled paradigmatic autonomy—i.e., that the United States be neutral in its support for one economic and social program or another—far-reaching debt relief (virtual condonement, in fact), international cooperation on tax reform, access to markets without draconian reciprocity, and significant transfers of resources for sustainable development: quite a package. The United States' agenda is not a pleasant one either: drug enforcement, often of a highly intrusive nature; environmental protection, frequently to the detriment of immediate local interests and objectives; immigration deterrence, occasionally with nasty domestic legal and political ramifications, and acceptance of norms that restrain job displacement from North to South. Each agenda includes items that must be discarded: inviolate national sovereignty for Latin America, an exclusive free-trade hemispheric zone for the United States. Both agendas require major concessions and changes in outlook; that is what makes a compromise possible. Without a significant ideological shift in the United States—from the Reagan-Bush conservative dogma to a more European-style approach—little can be accomplished. More than ever, the prospects for change in the region depend on significant modifications in the mainstream American outlook on economic and social matters.

But there is also a domestic Grand Bargain that must be struck in each individual country in Latin America, without which the left's program cannot prosper. The road to the region's modernity must lead to a special government-business relationship and social compensation for the ravages of the market. The business community must be convinced that a compromise of this sort is in its interests and that the alternative is worse.

With the exception of the thirties and forties in Mexico, Brazil, and Argentina, the fifties in Costa Rica, and the sixties again in Chile, the private sector in Latin America has never truly found itself in a situation where in exchange for significant sacrifices on its part, other sectors would also make concessions and generate national synergies. There has in fact been scant incentive for the business community to do so: it had little to gain from new sacrifices, and little to lose from the conservation of the status quo.

Today, for the first time in decades, and largely as a result of the changes wrought by the debt crisis, the adoption of the Reaganite, free-market model, and its effects on Latin American business and society, there begins to be a tiny insinuation of an incentive for change on the part of the business community and a significant cost for sustaining the status quo. Overwhelming competition from abroad is devastating entire swaths of the Latin American private sector, as trade liberalization without any form of financial cushion is introduced cold turkey. Along with it, frightful social inequalities are transforming vast areas of cities into war zones, begetting fundamentalisms of one sort or another across the continent.

The divergences between the private sector and the conservative model are not ideological. With the exception of Brazil, most of the business communities in the continent initially supported trade liberalization in principle, but requested waivers and waiting periods in practice. Furthermore, the region's entrepreneurs are also being pushed by external competition to drive down wages and employment, and by imported neoliberalism toward ever more exclusionary social compacts. But as time goes by, it becomes increasingly evident to them that without an entirely different scheme, including partial protection and subsidies, support from unions and government, as well as greater investment in infrastructure and education, most firms cannot compete with foreign firms, notably American ones. Either natural comparative advantage becomes the solution—Chilean grapes, kiwis, and salmon, Colombian flowers, and Mexican melons—or entire domestic markets will be lost to foreign producers that are far more productive and efficient and enjoy huge leads in resources, economies of scale, etc. Many firms will in all likelihood sell out to foreign competitors and eventually disappear or become subcontractors for low-wage-seeking multinationals. They can fight back, but only if a new bargain is struck between business, labor, and government regarding national strategies and mutual compromises. It is no surprise that the first hint of this solution has surfaced in Brazil, where business and labor are stronger than elsewhere in Latin America and the notion of a national strategy is the most firmly rooted.

As the intrinsic advantages of a compromise gradually appeared, the exorbitant costs of the status quo also surfaced. The new, sprawling urban poverty in Latin America and its economic and political consequences started to have an impact: uncontrolled, apolitical violence, from looting in Caracas to *arrastões* in Rio; fanatical, highly politicized, fundamentalist violence; glaring inequalities that make life unpleasant at best, intolerable at worst; reactions to inequalities and violence from all quarters: the military, authoritarian caudillos, ethnic groups, foreign investors. Perhaps because the United States was becoming a two-tier society, Latin Americans were beginning to see their own reality more clearly. The description of a hypothetical future of U.S. society provided by a member of President Clinton's cabinet—no radical, left-wing extremist—fitted the current situation of the countries south of the Rio Grande to a T:

> Distinguished from the rest of the population by their global linkages, good schools, comfortable lifestyles, excellent health care, and abundance of security guards, symbolic analysts [the winning, wealthiest one-fifth of the population] complete their secession from the union. The townships and urban enclaves where they reside, and the symbolic-analytic zones where they work, will bear no resemblance to the rest of America; nor will there be any direct connections between the two. America's poorest citizens, meanwhile, will be isolated within their own enclaves of urban and rural desperation; an ever-larger proportion of their young men will fill the nation's prisons. The remainder of the American population, gradually growing poorer, will feel powerless to alter any of these trends.[27]

But lesser evils can function only in reference to greater ones; they require a clear and present danger to be credible. Thus the condition for the renewed viability of reformism in Latin America—of any persuasion, but mainly in consonance with the social-democratic paradigm—lies inevitably in the threat of something worse. Since it cannot be revolution as such—the way Cuba was for nearly twenty years—it must be different, yet terrifying nonetheless. This is the syndrome of Sendero Luminoso.

The Shining Path, while peculiar to Peru in many ways and part of the region's past in many others, still relays a relevant message to the rest of Latin America. Sendero possesses sufficient characteristics common to the entire region that while it cannot become an alternative to compete against, it can certainly instill fear in the hearts and minds of many. Sendero reflects the new bane of Latin America: the overwhelming poverty of the immense belts of hopelessness surrounding its cities. The social disintegration of which Sendero, the violence in Rio, military unrest in Venezuela, and the drug trade in Colombia represent

27. Robert Reich, *The Wealth of Nations* (New York: Knopf, 1991), p. 303.

nothing more than symptoms, is the new greater evil that might make reformism a going concern again in Latin America. Without the fear inspired by the prospect of losing everything, the wealthy and middle class will prefer to lose nothing.

This is the way it has always been in Latin America. The oligarchy and business elites in the past never looked favorably on reforms; they resigned themselves to their implementation only when forced to. The great inclusionary reforms of the 1930s and 1940s in Latin America came about this way: the threat of Communism and generalized revolt accentuated by the effects of the Depression, made the minimum wage, collective bargaining, social security and public works less horrifying than before.

Cárdenas, Perón, the first and second Vargas did not persuade the private sector and what there was of a middle class of the intrinsic merits of their reforms. Nor did they impose them brutally. But the Communist menace focused the minds of the wealthy as nothing else could. In Argentina it was exemplified by the growing influence of the Communist and Socialist parties in the CGT unions during the 1930s.[28] In Brazil it was reflected in the Communist mobilization and putsch attempt in 1935, with a backdrop of rapidly enhanced left-wing presence in the labor movement and middle class.[29] In Mexico the fear of the "*México bronco*" was fired up by the founding of the CTM labor union and the legalization and influence of the Communist Party in the labor movement and its support for the Cárdenas government.[30]

---

28. "Peron's political agenda must be seen within the context of growing concern with the 'social question' and with the issues linked to that concern: class conflict and the role of the State in mitigating such conflict; fear of revolution in the face of the growing influence of the Communist sector of the labor movement. . . . When speaking before business audiences, Perón continuously returned to the themes of revolution and the threat of communism, arguing that this threat should be averted by a systematic state effort to organize the labor movement and channel social conflict." Ruth Berins Collier and David Collier, *Shaping the Political Arena* (Princeton, N.J.: Princeton University Press, 1991), p. 332.

29. "On the left, one faction of the Communist Party organized a popular-front movement (the Aliança Nacional Libertadora, ANL). Although the movement depended heavily on Communist Party organization, it succeeded in reaching large numbers of perplexed middle class voters. . . . Suddenly it appeared that the left had come to life. More than 1600 local branches of the ANL had sprung up by the end of May, 1935. The 'progressive' elements within the middle class were at last joining with the militant labor unions to support a radical program." Thomas Skidmore, *Politics in Brazil 1930–1964: An Experiment in Democracy* (New York: Oxford University Press, 1967), pp. 20–21.

30. "Not only did the alliance with Cárdenas give the Communists unprecedented opportunities to recruit in labor unions and peasant organizations, but it also increased the party's prestige, and opened the government agencies to Communist infiltration. . . .

The three large reform movements were grudgingly accepted (and just barely) by the elites for these reasons. Their acceptance paid off: the Communist Party and the left in general would never regain their working-class base (in Mexico and Argentina) or do so only after half a century had elapsed (in Brazil).

In a similar fashion, as the initial fascination with the Latin American fire sale of assets wears off and short-term, high-yield portfolio investment peaks without a real increase in physical investment, the business sector will have to address one of the foreign investor's chief long-term concerns: are the social structures of Latin America—as opposed to those of other zones—truly conducive to long-term profits, stability, and growth? Can any region sustain such gaping inequalities, such sharp racial and ethnic tensions, and such widespread economic hardship for so large a share of the population? Until the late eighties, poverty was a nonissue; at the beginning of the nineties, it rose to the fore, though wishful thinking about how the market would solve all problems endured. But as problems worsened, it became increasingly evident that without a sustained economic and social effort the continent would never become an attractive destiny for investment, credit, or anything else. Political charity to mitigate the immediate, explosive effects of extreme poverty through special programs like those set up in Mexico and Chile, while effective in the immediate term, were not enough.

The above changes notwithstanding, Latin American oligarchies have always had a way out, which their peers elsewhere cannot necessarily resort to: picking up their marbles and going to . . . Miami. For the rich and the powerful, the logic of reformism or economic and social change other than revolution is that it implies both an incentive and a sanction. The incentive is that every now and then, it is advisable in order to continue doing business as usual; or even better, it is that concessions are imperative. The sanction is that short of those concessions there is no choice but exile and the end of a way of life: such was the fate of the White Russians in Paris after 1917, the Kuomintang warlords on Taiwan since 1949, the Cuban magnates in Florida after 1959. When there is a possibility of resisting reform simply by moving money and family to Miami—and moving not only does not entail a painful exile or a change of life-style but in fact means more of the same life-style, only nicer—the sanction's impact shrinks.

The Party grew rapidly, attaining perhaps a maximum strength of 30,000 in 1939. . . ."
Karl M. Schmidt, *Communism in Mexico: A Study in Political Frustration* (Austin: University of Texas Press, 1965), p. 19.

For much of the private sector, the alternative to the status quo is not reform but capital flight and geographical mobility. The gradually emerging difference, however, is that not everyone can move to Miami, nor can everyone transfer funds abroad. The consequences of Latin America's social crisis are affecting the entire affluent sector of society, not just the very rich. Upper-middle-class, midsize businessmen with new export-led firms are just as subject as anyone to urban violence and kidnapping, military uprisings, an incredibly deteriorated environment, and thousands of homeless children on street corners selling everything from microwave ovens to crack and sex.

But they cannot all move to Miami or Los Angeles, and chances are that those who do will find the same children and violence, the very racial, ethnic, and social barriers and hatred there that they fled from at home. Globalization works both ways: many more can flee the horrors of Latin America's megalopolis, but among them are the poor, chasing the oligarchs and *jeunesse dorée* all the way to Melrose and Coconut Grove. And in the end, this is what will make or break the chances for reform in Latin America, and will determine whether a compromise is indeed a viable proposition.

·

The opportunities provided by change in the world and the region are necessary and sufficient conditions for the left to propose an alternative that is different and realistic, viable and attractive to most of Latin America's inhabitants. The left has its work cut out for it. It must struggle for a social market economy that reduces inequalities and improves living standards for everybody, but much more for the poor than for the rest. It has to construct a business-government relationship that plans for the future, sets national strategies, and promotes competitiveness abroad by capturing comparative advantages that are chosen, not laid down by nature, geography, and low wages. The effort must be above all domestic, but entails a substantial, foreign component of money and political backing.

There are three broad directions in which the left's platform should reach: first, the establishment of an authentic Latin American welfare state that extends its protection to a majority of the population; second, funding this goal through profound tax reform, massive debt relief, and major cuts in military spending; finally, laying the basis for the long-term viability of the first two objectives through a nationally devised strategy for export-led, environmentally sustainable industrializing growth. This strategy implies deep involvement by the state in concentrating the strengths and talents of the private sector, but also entails overhauling—not privatizing—state-owned enterprises.[31] These axes do not constitute an entire economic policy plan; this can be drawn up only country by country; they suggest the broad outline of a modern paradigm.

It is best to begin with the problem of resources to fund the welfare state. The first item on the left's economic and social agenda must be tax reform.[32] Some countries need it more than others, there are greater possibilities of achieving it in some nations than elsewhere, but nothing in Latin America can be done without a major overhaul of the tax system. Corporate taxes must be increased substantially, taxes on wealth must be levied, capital gains taxes on financial markets must be established, collection must be dramatically improved, and income taxes must be enforced on prosperous professionals and the upper middle class, as well as on corporate and personal assets held abroad. Just about all of the crutches have been tried: monopoly and natural resource rents, foreign lending, higher tariffs of publicly provided goods and services, selling off assets. There is no other option than tax reform. It is not sufficient: as many Brazilian social scientists and politicians have often emphasized, tax reform without changing the social and income distribution structure would redistribute the new revenues the same way. But is is a necessary condition: without raising revenues and devoting them to reducing social disparities, the social structure will not change.

---

31. This is a similar outline to what many sectors of Latin America reformist thought are contemplating, most notably, the UN Economic Commission on Latin America, which for years was a guiding light in Latin America but was somewhat sidelined by the debt crisis and the preeminence assumed by other international institutions. In a lengthy document published in 1992, it laid out objectives not unlike the ones emphasized here: "(1) Tax reform; (2) spending reforms with the purpose of ensuring levels of social and public spending; (3) reforms of state-owned companies; (4) policy reform aimed at reducing external indebtedness and liberating resources for social purposes. . . ." Comisión Económica para América Latina y el Caribe, *Equidad y transformación productiva: Un enfoque integrado* (Santiago, 1992), p. 88.

32. There is a growing awareness among liberals in the United States that the problem is not dissimilar, even if solving it often seems impossible: "One response is to offset the polarizing tendencies of the new global economy through a truly progressive income tax, coupled with the closure of gaping tax loopholes. . . . There have been times in our nation's history when the idea of a progressive income tax was not considered especially radical. . . . Today the ideal of tax progressivity seems fairly quaint. . . . Were the tax code as progressive as it was even in 1977, symbolic analysts would have paid approximately $93 billion more in taxes than they in fact paid in 1989. . . . To improve the economic position of the bottom four fifths will require that the fortunate fifth share its wealth and invest in the wealth-creating capacities of the other Americans. Yet as the top becomes ever more tightly linked to the global economy, it has less of a stake in the performance and potential of its less fortunate compatriots." Reich, op. cit., pp. 245, 246, 260, 301.

In a real tax reform, direct taxes must be favored over indirect ones; and within direct taxes, those on privately owned corporations or wealthy and upper-middle-class individuals must be raised more. A wealth tax in Latin America, on both property and other assets, must be imposed, as has been done in many countries in Western Europe. The geographical location of the wealth should not be the sole criterion for taxing it. The nationality and residence of asset owners should also be taken into account: nationals of Latin American countries must be taxed by their respective governments, wherever their assets are situated. Upscale professionals in Latin America must also be taxed heavily, through much more effective collection schemes and higher rates. Some progress has been recently made in this area in a few nations, like Chile and Mexico, but it is far from sufficient.

The informal economy must be incorporated into the tax base. Often, street vendors and sidewalk store owners or employers are not really the budding entrepreneurs glorified by Hernando de Soto and other supporters of the underground economy. Frequently, they are paid employees of large chains or medium-size retail outlets that prefer to sell on sidewalks to evade taxes. The immense transfer of economic activity from the formal to the informal economy in recent years has narrowed the tax base in countries where it was already dreadfully small.

There is a social and electoral constituency for tax reform in Latin America, because the United States electoral-fiscal paradox is not yet at work in the region. In the U.S., as John Kenneth Galbraith has put it:

> The fortunate pay, the less fortunate receive. The fortunate have political voice, the less fortunate do not. It would be an exercise in improbably charitable attitude were the fortunate to respond warmly to expenditures that are for the benefit of others.[33]

In Latin America, as representative democracy has taken hold and engendered mostly high voter turnouts, the bias in favor of upscale electorates is often absent. A huge majority of voters are lower middle class and poor, harboring few illusions about becoming rich quickly. This is not to say there are no impediments: the informal economy is one; another is the penchant for tax evasion, strengthened by the widespread belief that government steals whatever is handed over to it—a far from unjustified sentiment. Without the previously described po-

---

33. John Kenneth Galbraith, *The Culture of Contentment* (Boston: Houghton Mifflin, 1992), p. 46.

litical and "national" reforms and a profound "democratization of democracy," including the creation of independent, scrupulously honest state agencies, tax reform is impossible.

There is also an international constraint on tax reform: capital mobility. Which is why domestic efforts must have a foreign corollary, the grounds of which have already been argued: the United States and the industrialized nations now have a vested interest in social reform in Latin America and consequently should be willing to cooperate and make minor sacrifices to make it possible. The problem is simple and well known. If the rich are taxed, many say—and historical experience bears them out—they will simply take their money out of the country.

No solution to the Latin American fiscal crisis can occur without some sort of international agreement whereby foreign-held assets and income in the United States or elsewhere would be taxed at the rate of the country that taxes most, with the revenues going to the country of which the asset holder is a resident and citizen. Though this can be partly solved through traditional double-taxation treaties—like those several nations have signed with the U.S.—often these are insufficient and/or unnecessary for this specific purpose. Special agreements whereby flight capital is taxed and reported back to the originating country are an indispensable component of tax reform in Latin America. This is less utopian or wild-eyed than it seems. In American Treasury Under Secretary Harry Dexter White's initial proposal for conditions of membership to the IMF at the Bretton Woods Conference in 1945, "Nations had to agree not to accept or permit deposits or investments from any member country except with the permission of the government of that member country."[34]

Tax reform must not only be quantitative and for the federal government, though. Resources must be left to municipal and state authorities to ensure the success of decentralization, municipal autonomy, and the democratization of local governments. The only way to spread tax monies around, though, and allow local entities to both raise revenues and keep them is through a deep reform that increases the available resources and permits towns and states to tax for themselves and to keep what they realize.

Reforms would also lighten the load on the state-owned tax cows in many Latin American countries. Pemex, Telmex until recently, Codelco, Pedevesa, Petroperu, and other state-owned companies are being taxed to death or sold off because they cannot muster enough revenues for investment. They actually generate bountiful revenues

---

34. Quoted in Kuttner, op. cit., p. 38.

but do not dispose of them as they see fit. If Pemex were to keep a share of its profits, plow them back into investment, maintenance, security, and training, it would not need as much foreign credit or higher gasoline prices. But then the Mexican state would have to tax others to make up the difference.

Taxation is the best way to obtain money for the state, but in Latin America it has been the least favored way.[35] In addition to its other virtues, taxation provides governance with instruments most regimes lack in reality: tax incentives or breaks. If firms and households do not pay taxes, or pay very little, reducing their burden is not much of an incentive to behave differently. Although this should be of interest to any regime, only the left will truly push to make it happen. The right will not do it of its own accord: either it will be forced to by pressure from the left, or tax reform will occur in the context of vast national left-right alliances seeking to right Latin America's wrongs. Moreover, present trends run directly counter to this scheme: the tendency is toward lower taxation to compete for capital, not in the direction of higher taxes. But that is what being on the left means: proposing alternatives that may not be fashionable today but might appear so tomorrow.

Yet taxation alone will not be sufficient. Resources must spring from two other sources: reductions in military spending and debt relief. Conventional wisdom and ideological policy recommendations from the Washington consensus are possibly exaggerating its importance, transforming reduced military spending into a new silver bullet. And in fact, with the exception of Cuba, Nicaragua, El Salvador, Peru, and Bolivia, Latin American nations have very low military spending over GDP ratios, of generally less than 5 percent according to their national budgetary accounts. The larger countries—Brazil, Mexico, Argentina—allocate a small share of their expenditures to defense. But often expenses are hidden elsewhere—for example, the presidency—or go unreported. So in fact there is probably somewhat more fat to cut than is readily apparent.

However, very little of what is spent is necessary, and much can be easily transferred to other areas. In those countries where military spending is 4 percent or higher, slicing it in half would represent the equivalent of reducing the 1980s debt burden by 50 percent (the entire debt crisis rarely implied a net negative transfer of resources of more than 4 percent of GDP). This would constitute an enormous injection

---

35. There is nothing very radical or original about this view: it is good, old-fashioned, bread-and-butter reformism: "The only effective design for diminishing income inequality inherent in capitalism is the progressive income tax." Galbraith, op. cit., p. 179.

of money into social spending, and while there are constraints and externalities—layoffs of troops, etc.—it is a significant and relatively painless source of funding. It simply requires the most scarce and precious commodity of all: political will.

Finally, money must come from the place everyone in Latin America has pointed to for a decade: debt relief. The hemisphere requires and deserves major debt relief, which can come only from debt forgiveness. According to the United Nations Economic Commission for Latin America, the region owed $426 billion at the end of 1991.[36] But this figure was calculated without taking into account two of the new trends emerging in Latin American finance: the reentry of the private sector into international bond markets, and growing foreign holdings of Latin American government securities.

Thus while ECLA estimated Mexico's year-end debt at $100 billion,[37] the Institute of International Finance in Washington, which produces data for many of the world's banks, put it at $127 billion.[38] Although the difference is greater for Mexico than for other nations, it is pervasive: the continent's foreign debt was probably closer to $500 billion at the end of 1991. Rising international reserves partially offset this increase, though the volatility of much of the region's accumulation of reserves casts a doubt on whether actual indebtedness remains equal to gross debt minus reserves.

On the debt service front, while in 1991 the region experienced a positive transfer for the first time since 1981, it still paid out nearly $30 billion in interest payments, despite low interest rates and the fact that Brazil, Argentina, and Peru had not yet renewed service of their commercial bank debt. Any increase in interest rates or a resumption of debt service payments by the larger debtors in arrears would have wiped out the positive transfer. Even countries that renogotiated their debt—receiving some debt relief and securitizing the remainder—continued to dole out high levels of service, only marginally reduced (by 10–15 percent) in relation to the past. Ratios of debt to gross domestic product did drop, as did debt service in relation to exports, but even this has to be qualified. GDP in nominal terms tends to be exaggerated after long periods of exchange rate stability, and persisting high inflation: the two together generate yearly

---

36. Comisión Económica para América Latina y el Caribe, *Balance Preliminar de la Economía de América Latina y el Caribe* (Santiago, 1992), p. 54.

37. Ibid., p. 54.

38. Institute of International Finance, quoted in *El Financiero* (Mexico City), June 15, 1992), p. 5.

nominal growth rates of 20 or 30 percent. Debt-to-GDP ratios did fall, but any eventual devaluation of the currency would quickly erase the gains.[39]

Under these conditions it is virtually impossible for Latin America's economies to grow at sufficient rates for a sustained period of time. The debt crisis is not over, even if for U.S., Japanese, and European banks it now belongs to the past. All the more reason for debt forgiveness: if it would have exclusively beneficial consequences for the economies of the region and no negative ones for the world banking community, it should be done. Government funding would have to come from the industrialized nations. They have provided money for Egypt, Poland, and Russia for geopolitical considerations and should do it for others. Few authors have summed up the problem and its solutions more succinctly than Lester Thurow:

> One can argue over which party is most to blame for these debt problems [the borrowers or the lenders], but that argument is now irrelevant. The debts exist and have to be dealt with regardless of fault. The solution to the debt problem lies in the developed world. It has to forgive the debts. Latin America and Africa have to get themselves organized to prevent a repetition of their debt problems, but they cannot solve the existing problem. Only the taxpayers in the wealthy industrial countries can forgive what must be forgiven.[40]

The money raised through tax reform, cutbacks in military spending, and debt relief, must be channeled to promote the social policies that Latin America requires. The application of the Rhineland model in Latin America means first building, then extending, a true welfare state to the region's poor and excluded. The belief that yesterday's populist-built assistance programs—or today's social charity programs—are the local equivalent of the European welfare state is way off the mark. Latin America does not yet have a welfare state, but it is high time it did. The safety net built up since the 1930s and 1940s fulfilled its function: incorporating the urban, organized working class and the lower middle class into the market, employment, and minimum standards of living. But today the construction of the welfare state means extending it to those who do not enjoy its benefits: those

---

39. Thus in the case of Mexico, for example, while the debt-to-GDP ratio fell in nominal terms, in constant 1985 dollars it barely budged. According to one estimate, in mid-1992, when theoretically the Mexican debt crisis had been left behind, the debt/GDP ratio was identical in real terms to that in 1981—just months before it began. Vladimiro Brailovsky, *Cuaderno de Nexos* (Mexico City), August 1992, p. VIII.

40. Thurow., op. cit., p. 215.

without formal employment or with seasonal or part-time jobs, mainly the urban poor but also the rural misbegotten. Thus land reform, while no longer the central issue facing the hemisphere, is still paramount in many nations, or in specific areas (Guatemala, El Salvador, and Brazil chiefly). There is no question that raising living standards for the very poorest in these nations requires land reform, accompanied by the rural equivalent of an urban welfare state and spending.

But poverty and inequality affect increasingly the urban masses in most of the region. A majority of the peasantry is poor, but a majority of the population is urban. And that is where the basic thrust of the welfare state should be focused. Money should be spent first on the obvious: education, health, housing and basic needs like sewage, drinking water, and urban mass transportation. Many governments say they aim to do this or that they are doing it: virtually none meets any of the international targets generally agreed upon as minimum spending thresholds (such as 8 percent of GDP on education). Most of them accept rationalizations about spending cuts, making necessity and imposition a virtue. Thus, since there is not enough money for education, regimes throughout Latin America appropriate the World Bank's dictums that only elementary education should be bothered with.

Given the limits on educational expenditures set by present tax structures and spending constraints, it is probably preferable to allocate what little money there is to elementary schooling. But the largest and most rapidly growing segments of the population are adolescents and young people, and remedial education for them is as necessary as concentrating on small children. Moreover, formal higher education will remain for years the functional equivalent of high school in the developed countries: abdicating the responsibility of public higher education condemns most of the population to a junior high school–level education at best, reducing competitiveness and wages.

Likewise, focusing on certain types of health care in contrast to other, more costly ones, while inevitable if resources to do both are insufficient, makes sense only if the constraints on spending are set in concrete. Extending minimal education and health care to the entire population is something that Latin America must accomplish. The prodigious significance of making headway in this domain can be seen in the Cuban example: when ample resources, attention, and political will are dedicated to this objective, it can be reached. Cuba in 1959 was not the most backward of Latin America nations in this realm; it was not the most advanced either. Thirty years of sustained effort extended K–12 education and basic health care to everyone. A hefty transfer of resources, domestically and from abroad, made it possible.

Housing is another area that cries out for support. Demographic growth, low savings rates, and lack of public funding have created a housing nightmare. From *Black Orpheus* and *Los Olvidados* to Sendero Luminoso and the Caracazo, the teeming, sprawling shantytowns outside and within every Latin American city testify to the extent of the region's current and past housing crisis. In Europe it was largely public housing that solved the problem over the years: HLMs in France, public individual housing in Britain, Soviet-style *urbanizaciones* in Franco's Spain. Gray and depressing, dangerously delinquent, and mostly shabby, the huge public housing complexes outside the larger European capitals may not seem like much today, but from a Latin vantage point they would represent a phenomenal improvement. In Latin America, given deficient private savings and the sheer magnitude of the ill-housed or homeless population, only state-financed systems seem conceivable. Credit and tax incentives appear quixotic: in some areas, the lower middle class might be able to obtain housing, but the urban poor are neither creditworthy nor responsive to tax incentives: they pay no taxes because they barely have income.

Unemployment insurance is another area of the welfare state that needs to be created. With a few exceptions, Latin America does not have unemployment compensation systems. For years various substitutes filled in: high severance pay and drastic rigidity in layoffs. But economic stabilization and adjustment, together with the changes most of the region's economies underwent, rendered these traditional replacements dysfunctional. Hundreds of thousands of workers are being laid off today in Latin America, as imports, recession, privatization and modernization shut down plants and transfer jobs. It is difficult to imagine what would happen if similar adjustment processes took place in the industrialized nations without the unemployment benefits institutionalized since the Depression.

A welfare state for the poorer sectors of society, while not necessarily implying a drop in the living standards of those presently protected by the safety net, inevitably entails a freeze on their benefits and a decline in their standing in relation to other sectors. The industrial working class, as impoverished as it may have become over the past decade, cannot be the prime beneficiary of more and better spending. It may even have to pay higher taxes, although its share of a greater burden should not be significantly increased. The question then is: what can the workers get out of such reform?

The answer lies in traditional responses and newer ones. In countries where urban and social services are shoddy at best and often nonexistent, large-scale improvement or enhancement of those services benefits all of its users, not only the targeted ones. Better schools, health clinics and hospitals, sewage and drinking water, paved and lighted streets, improved urban transportation and housing, parks and sports facilities are to every class's advantage. The working class, although it has moved up into the social service network, still has long-accumulated demands for better services, or new ones until now unavailable. While higher wages and fringe benefits for the industrial proletariat are not the utmost priority on any agenda today in Latin America, there are huge advantages awaiting this sector from the extension of the welfare state to those who so far have been excluded from everything.

Secondly, new forms of labor involvement at the workplace can be of great satisfaction to many urban, skilled workers in Latin America. People can draw pleasure and rewards from being taken seriously and having their main occupation cease to be an isolated, mechanical repetition of movement and become a more collective, reflective, and responsible endeavor. Participating in production and quality control, in searching for and finding ways to make better products more efficiently, in transmitting experience and training to younger workers, and in seeing the benefits of higher productivity and competitiveness appear in the paycheck, fringe benefits or a shorter work week is nothing to sneer at. This is an imperative component of the domestic Grand Bargain that must be struck in Latin America. Where a new labor movement has begun to surface, radical and combative but less bureaucratic and aristocratic than before, it can happen.

It is highly dubious that the private sector has ever provided any of the above-mentioned services anywhere; there are no grounds for believing that it can or will do so in contemporary Latin America. If all of this sounds a great deal like what Ronald Reagan called the "tax and spend" policies of the past, it's for a good reason. "Tax and spend" is what the United States and much of Europe did for nearly a century in order to become what they are: middle-class societies where the fundamental necessities of life, as well as dignified living standards, are afforded to a majority of the population. As a former Brazilian finance minister has said:

> The role of government in Brazilian society cannot be overestimated. Ours is a society of masters and slaves that needs to bring huge shares of its population into the market and citizenship, expenditures on education, urban and general infrastructure like sewage and water supply, housing and public transportation. All of them represent huge amounts of income distribution—"the modern" part of the country paying taxes

and giving credit to investments that only in the very long run can produce positive rates of return.[41]

Once Latin America taxes and spends itself into modernity, it can decide, like Ronald Reagan, if it went too far, taxed too much, and overspent.[42]

In the long-term, even if resources from tax reform, defense, and debt are available today, only sustained economic growth can support the redistributive social policies outlined above. There is no miracle in sight: Latin America will not soon recover the extraordinarily high rates of growth of the 1940–1980 period for years to come, if at all. But sound, continued expansion is possible—if there is a national consensus behind it, and if its contours are designed on the basis of national priorities, not ideological imposition from without. Here the left must provide a Japanese answer, in the same way that its social response must be a German one, so to speak.

The left's blueprint for the region's future economic growth must combine lessons from and major breaks with the past, as well as with current dogma. Latin America must continue to pursue a single-minded industrialization effort, but through export-led growth. Its thrust should not be left to the market, but to a national strategy in which the state, business, and labor, thanks to a long-term industrial policy, choose the niches in which each country will specialize, and together map out a plan for capturing the markets they choose.

Walking down this path implies a major revision of age-old beliefs for the left, while simultaneously confirming parts of its traditional mind-set. The idea that the state must continue to play a leading role in the industrialization drive is something that the left has always subscribed to. That not everything should be left to the market is equally a fixture in the left's thought and practice. But to bestow a central role also on the private sector, and to accept that the market should have a dominant function in the process, represents a major

---

41. João Sayad, "Monetary Order and Brazillian Inflation," paper presented at a University of California, Berkeley, Conference on Brazil Today, April 15–16, 1992, p. 21.

42. A program of this sort would also be dismissed as technically out of touch, as if this were a technical issue: "There is a highly ideological agenda concealed in this seemingly technical formula [recommended by the IMF]. A left-of-center government that might have been elected on its promise of a development program via, say, public-works spending, land reform, social welfare, domestic industrial development, redistributive taxation, and controls on capital exports—just what Western Europe did in the 1950s—would be judged technically incompetent by the IMF technicians and denied funds." Kuttner, op. cit., p. 255.

break for the left, one that few would find desirable, or that would have occurred if recent events in the world had not taken the turn they did.

But regardless of the original motivations for such a shift, the condition today for the left's formulation of a model that is viable and different from the free-market dogma being rammed down the throats of Latin American societies and economies is to adopt the market. For the left to assimilate an industrialization model that emphasizes the private sector and calls for a long-term alliance between the business community and the state is a sea change. It is the inevitable price to pay for a new paradigm, as excessive as it may seem.

Industrialization has been the centerpiece of the continent's economic development over the past fifty years, and whatever inefficiencies and costs it has incurred do not invalidate this purpose. On this there is broad agreement in the left, even among those sectors that have taken the greatest steps to "modernize" themselves, such as Colombia's M-19:

> It sounds a bit strange, but Colombia has to be industrialized. Without industrialization, it is impossible for this country to have a development model for the twenty-first century. If we keep exporting flowers, bananas, and coffee, plus some oil and coal, we will always be screwed. Because we have too little value-added in our exports, we keep exporting raw materials, and we lose the chance to create employment for the people, we lose the chance for technological and scientific development, we lose the chance to have a future. That model of development was tried once in Latin America and it failed.[43]

Despite its efforts, however, Latin America still lags far behind in generating value-added activities on a scale consonant with its population and economic dimensions. In the mid-1980s Latin America accounted for 8 percent of the world's population and 7 percent of its GDP, but only 6 percent of its manufactured products, 3 percent of its capital goods, 2.4 percent of its engineers and scientists, and 1.8 percent of its manufactured exports.[44] With an adequate level of industrialization, Latin America should have an equal share of manufactures and manufactured exports as it does of GDP or population. The region can, on the one hand, accept the lag and devote itself to low-value-added activity, determined by natural comparative advantage: seasonal agriculture, raw materials, and the production of some cheap-

---

43. Antonio Navarro Wolff, interview with the author, Cartagena de Indias, October 6, 1991.
44. Fajnzylber, op. cit., pp. 3–4.

labor, environmentally unfriendly goods. Or, on the other hand, it can undertake a deliberate long-term effort to develop higher-value-added activities.

The option is much more political and ethical than technical.[45] Industrialization can be achieved, even this late in the game. Other nations have done so in recent years. Important areas of Latin America are industrial regions: São Paulo, Monterrey, Medellín. When state, business, and labor in the hemisphere, or any combination of the three, have put their minds and shoulders to the task, much has been accomplished. But the first necessary ingredient is the political will to do so, and it is sadly lacking today, as free trade and static comparative advantages are all the rage. The greater the reason for the left to raise the banner of industrialization, but to do so differently than in the past.[46]

The region requires export-led industrialization, as opposed to the previous drive for import-substitution industrializing (ISI). Foreign and domestic demand together must be the locomotives of economic growth. Export sectors must adjust to market principles to be competitive, and they must compete in international markets to capture market shares. On this point, the left has to accept that the past is no longer the wave of the future. Moreover, it should remember that for years it was the left that denounced the vices of ISI: its inefficiencies, injustice, and protected rents. But the left cannot abdicate, as the right and center seem to have done, the principle of industrialization, or that of an industrial policy that chooses the sectors in which industrialization will take place and competitiveness will be sought.[47]

45. There are, however, technical arguments in favor of industrialization and against relying on agriculture and natural resources. The main one, of course, is that the long-term prices of both raw materials and agricultural exports tend to fall, while those of manufactured, high-value added ones tend to rise, at least in relative terms. More and more Chilean kiwis, salmon and copper will be needed to purchase the same amount of American or Japanese computers, cars and VCRs. As one impeccably pro-market voice put it: "Given long-term trends in the natural-resource prices and usage, there are unlikely to be additions to the list of the twenty wealthiest countries in the century ahead simply as a result of abundant natural resources. . . There will be increasing demands for the Southern Hemisphere's fresh fruits and vegetables during the Northern Hemisphere's winter. But traditional agriculture is not a growth area that can support economic development." Thurow, op. cit., p 207.

46. The setbacks of the past were a poor excuse for eschewing a voluntaristic approach: "Even if there has been implementation failure in Latin America, that is an argument for correcting it, not for pursuing a second-best policy of laissez-faire . . . In the absence of state capacity, concentrated market and political power and other imperfections may make laissez-faire an nth-best choice." Albert Fishlow, "The Latin American State," *Journal of Economic Perspectives*, vol. 4, no. 3, summer 1990, p. 66.

47. As many authors have pointed out, every industrial nation has an industrial policy, including the United States. The latter simply does not acknowledge how, for

The left must acknowledge that a series of external constraints need to be respected to broaden the tax base and finance the welfare state that must be created. But where the left has a wide margin of differentiation available to it in relation to the current free-market, neoliberal model is in how to attain that export-led growth, and how the sacrifices and benefits it entails will be shared.[48] Leaving the choice of winners and losers to the market, and acting as if the world market were truly free, is one of the great intellectual distortions of modern times. No one has captured markets or attained international competitiveness exclusively by opening up economies and letting the chips fall where they may. Britain in the nineteenth century and the United States after World War II were free-traders because they were the world's most efficient producers of the highest value-added goods. They did not become so through free trade; they protected themselves for decades in order to achieve that end.[49]

Latin America today can devise a long-term strategy for export-led growth dramatically different from the free-trade, leave-it-to-the-market approach. Export industries would be forced to compete abroad but would be protected at home as long as they made significant gains in competitiveness. Domestic markets would remain protected when necessary, and open in those areas where either competitive local firms were already active or where the attempt to develop a national or regional industry was patently idealistic or foolish. Credits, subsidies, R&D, duty-free imports would be made available for those industries

---

instance, "The revealed strategy of national science and technology policy was to remain ahead of the Soviet Union." Otis L. Graham Jr., *Losing Time: The Industrial Policy Debate* (Cambridge, Mass.: Harvard University Press, 1992), p. 180.

48. It must be pointed out that there is inevitably a vast space between the prescriptive discourse generated by international financial institutions and the actual policies its officials try to foist upon borrowing governments. There is then a subsequent distance between what even the most ideological World Bank and IMF officials suggest, and what many governments actually do to ingratiate themselves with such institutions. Thus the Bank and others can accept that "infrastructure" should be built by the state, but its officials press for the privatization of railroads, highways, and telecommunications, and governments go as far as trying to privatize water delivery systems for large cities. The Bank as an institution insists on the state's role in social matters such as health and education; its officials often promote the idea of privatizing sectors of these two areas; finally governments are now seeking to privatize significant chunks of social security and higher public education.

49. "For Britain, the industrially most advanced of countries, free trade was of obvious advantage, and like laissez-faire, it acquired a strong theological aura. In Germany and the United States, on the other hand, economic interest was better served by tariffs. Accordingly, the most respected economists in those countries—the noted Friedrich List in Germany, the eloquent Henry Carey in the United States—spoke vigorously for protection for their national 'infant industries,' protection, in fact, from the products of the British colossus." Galbraith, op. cit., p. 80.

that were making headway on export markets, and unavailable for those that were not. The role of the state would remain paramount in infrastructure, support services, and certain public investment programs to consolidate dynamic comparative advantage.

The choice of markets, productive niches, and strategies would be left not to the market but to MITI-like government-business negotiations and agreements, with long-term goals and timetables. Where the private sector thought it could carry the entire load—requiring only protection and subsidies from the government, for instance—in negotiating with other countries for nonreciprocal access to markets, the state would not get involved in production. It would retreat from previously occupied areas, limiting itself to establishing state-run supplier networks, for example, in order to ensure backward linkages during an infancy stage.

In some cases, the comparative advantage bestowed by natural resource endowment would be part of the criteria determining which niches Latin America would specialize in. On other occasions, historical patterns or links to markets would be dominant. When possible, regional integration would play a key role by having various nations decide collectively which niches they would seek and what dynamic comparative advantages they would attempt to capture. Inefficiencies would undoubtedly arise, and errors would have to be corrected: planners, just as markets, do not always get it right, and as in Korea or Japan, the state would have to pick up the broken dishes. Mistakes notwithstanding, many successes—and the hope of achieving both competitiveness and high value-added exports, growth and equity—make this a better option than leaving everything exclusively to the market.

There are two objections to this option generally addressed in the Latin American case. The first has to do with the difficulty of withdrawing subsidies and protection from interest groups and industries once they are put in place. The second objection concerns the broader issue of the presumed ineptitude of the state: if it cannot collect garbage or deliver the mail, how can it be expected to coordinate and promote biotechnology exports, among other marvels? Both reservations beg the question of the overall context of reform in the continent. Without democratic and regional reforms, the possibilities of implementing the ones laid out in this chapter are unquestionably remote. Conversely, a democratic, strong, and reformed Latin American state, at least minimally accountable and responsive, could quite well provide subsidies and protection and subsequently resist "hijacking" and withdraw them if the results do not conform to expectations. The problem is essentially political, not economic.

As for the blanket incompetence of the Latin state, that is a highly arguable proposition. In fact, the Chilean, Brazilian, and Mexican states have a long-term track record of quite adequate economic management, and of impressive results to show for it. Growth and investment rates have been high, infrastructure constructed, and state-owned firms generally successful. The social administration has been far less praiseworthy, but again, the reasons have been much more political than technical. It is not clear that building the Amazon highway or setting up the Mexican administrative, educational, communications, and health system is that much easier than promoting exports. In fact, in most Latin American nations, among the few things that work at all are those involving the state. And indeed, many Latin states are quite capable of collecting garbage and delivering the mail, even under highly adverse circumstances.

The basic difference between this approach and the current free-trade focus is that it stresses export promotion and subordinates other considerations to that end, while free trade emphasizes the virtues of trade liberalization and supposes that exports will automatically grow as a result. This difference explains why a nation like Korea (not to mention Japan) remains, even today, a very closed market to goods and services from abroad, while at the same time allowing imports for reexport duty-free and becoming highly competitive. On the contrary, countries like Mexico and Chile have almost totally open economies but remain far less competitive than the East Asian nations. In fact, in these two countries and the rest of Latin America presently undergoing trade liberalization, the approach is as much an antiinflationary policy, and in response to American exhortations, as an instrument to promote exports and competitiveness. Otherwise, it would not have been comprehensive and applied overnight, but selective and applied gradually, depending on the sectors the nation wanted to encourage and support and those it had decidedly cast aside.

This brings us to the international corollary that this axis of the left's program must have. Latin American nations must be able to cajole, pressure, and drag the United States, Japan, and Europe into a Grand Bargain on international trade. The agreement must entail a return to nonreciprocal policies and differentiated market access, in compensation for the implementing of environmental and social policies in the Third World that deter jobs from fleeing en masse from the high-wage countries to the low-wage ones, while at the same time ensuring more job creation and investment in the Third World countries than would occur otherwise. This is not an easy bargain to strike, but its absence would probably be more prejudicial to both parties than any agreement would be.

Many Latin American countries have opened their trade doors indiscriminately and abandoned any pretense of nonreciprocity, asymmetrical treatment, or differential market access. They did so partly out of conviction, partly because the pattern of the past stopped functioning, and partly out of imposition from abroad. But they all expected to obtain greater access to industrialized markets, and particularly the U.S. market, in return. Few have. It should be the other way around: full access granted to the poorer economies, limited entry to the more advanced ones. It will not be easy to move back from unfair arrangements, particularly as international agreements are being constantly signed to lock these measures in forever. But a deal can be struck.

Its shape is plain to see. For Latin American economies to generate competitive, high value-added export sectors other than fruit, vegetables, flowers, or fish, they need protection, subsidies, planning, R&D, tax breaks, cheap credits, etc. They also require foreign exchange flexibility. Latin American nations will not be able to develop an export sector if they begin to run huge, prolonged trade deficits of well over 2 or 3 percent of GDP. In order for the transfer of jobs from the North to the South to take place in an orderly and, one would hope, painless fashion, it must be done slowly, carefully, and without major disruptions. Otherwise political pressures in the North or dislocations and immigration from the South will render it intolerable. Environmental damage in the South means environmental damage in the North, whether it be directly on the U.S.-Mexican border or more indirectly though global warming, ozone depletion, etc.

In exchange for not leaving their markets totally unprotected, and eliminating their own subsidies, dismantling their own industrial policies, and other forms of support for their exports, the nations of Latin America should establish social and environmental controls in their export sectors conforming to norms followed in the industrialized nations. Exports would grow at a reasonable pace, domestic markets would remain protected in some areas, and not so many jobs would be displaced from North to South. The added benefit of such a compromise is that it might make sustainable development possible.

The Chinese motor scooter paradox sums up the sustainable-development dilemma best, perhaps: "If every citizen of China had a motor scooter, the world would blow up." The logic is impeccable: given prevailing technologies, the CO_2 emissions, energy consumption, resource depletion, and global warming resulting from approximately a billion more scooters tearing around Shanghai and Beijing, would destroy the world's fragile ecological balance. The poor-country response to the paradox is also well known: why should the Chinese be deprived of motor scooters, if Americans have two cars and Europeans have consumed energy and resources from the Third World for several centuries now?

The only acceptable answer to these stances is that with prevailing technologies and consumption patterns, the South cannot raise living standards and incomes without blowing up the ecosystem,[50] but with different, environmentally sound and resource-saving technologies, it certainly can, as history has proved on many occasions. The issue then becomes whether the North will pay for and the South will accept the changes in policies and traditions that this implies. Energy-saving, resource-protecting and environmentally restrictive economic policies and technologies exist, but implementing them costs money and political will. This entails universal application of the polluter-pays principle, be it on country-scale or within each nation and society. The viability of such a measure is far less remote than imagined; it is well on the way to entering the mainstream of environmental theory and practice. It means renouncing the option of attracting jobs as the rich countries' toxic-waste dumps—the Mexican solution—and taking tough measures against "poor environmental predators": slash-and-burn farmers, wood burners, strip miners, etc. Not only do international compacts incorporating environmental conditions bring money to the South and respite to the North; they can contribute to bringing sustainable development to the South.

Beyond the environment, the United States would benefit from an international Grand Bargain in that while perhaps not realizing access to markets that were not as open as it hoped, the markets it would gain partial access to would be larger and more dynamic, expanding U.S. exports at a more moderate but realistic rate, and would make a greater contribution to the development of the societies and economies of Latin America. Under the Reagan and Bush administrations this type of bargain was inconceivable, and will undoubtedly remain so until the free-market radicalism that swamped the United States since 1981 has finally passed from the scene.[51]

---

50. Lipietz, *Berlin, Baghdad, Rio*, op. cit., p. 140.

51. Far-reaching compromises similar to the one outlined have been floating around for some time: "A new Great Compromise would promote the integration of developing economies into the global system. The industrial countries would commit to providing . . . a megaeconomic climate much more suited to the needs of the developing countries. In return, developing countries would agree to measures aimed at stabilizing their ex-

But in addition to being export-led and environmentally sustainable, growth in Latin America must rest partly on a modern, efficient, and accountable state-owned sector of the economy. The left, almost by definition, has stressed the importance of a strong state-owned sector of the economy. Even the British social-democratic left in the forties, fifties, and sixties was "statist," and for good reason: state ownership allows for better contracts providing for higher wages, larger fringe benefits, and greater job security. The Latin American left in particular has pinned a great many hopes—too many, undoubtedly—on state-run enterprises. They were wrongly seen as a panacea for many of the region's ills; nevertheless, they are indispensable.

The left has to continue to be a firm defender of parastatal companies in Latin America. There is nothing wrong with them intrinsically, and much that is positive. In nations with the historical characteristics of Latin America, they are an indispensable part of any development process. In key natural resources, or in areas where long lead times, low rates of return, and other specific obstacles prevail, publicly owned companies are necessary and desirable. As real or potential leaders in social and environmental policy (they can also be exactly the opposite: focal points of authoritarian, ecologically criminal behavior), they set standards and establish guidelines. They maintain strategic sectors under public control and provide governments with instruments of policy that they would otherwise lack. The fact that they sometimes abuse this prerogative is another story. Every industrialized nation in the world, other than the U.S., as well as the successful newly industrializing nations, have large, publicly owned sectors of their economies.

There are, however, excesses and inefficiencies and mainly major changes that must take place. Yet instead of reforming state-owned firms, most of Latin America is selling them, thereby once again not only throwing the proverbial baby out with the bathwater, but transforming publicly owned, corrupt, inefficient monopolies into equally inefficient, corrupt private ones. In country after country the necessary reforms of large parastatals are not only not taking place but are being forsaken with the hope that privatization will solve the problems on its own. It doesn't.

The left must take up the banner of reforming parastatals and making them, once again, symbols of national pride and showcases of what

---

change rates and to a move from Victorian to Fordist principles . . . Developing countries would accept substantial compliance with international norms on a variety of issues. . . . They would be expected to meet agreements upon social goals such as minimum-wage levels. . . ." Walter Russell Mead, "The United States and the World Economy," reprinted from *World Policy Journal,* summer 1989, pp. 540–451.

Latin America can do, instead of being oft-cited examples of what's wrong—and worse—in the region. The reforms must have several facets, and will vary from country to country. Moreover, they cannot be separated from other important changes, particularly those involving the democratization of the Latin state. With these caveats the three faces of reform are management autonomy, accountability and oversight, and submission to the market, up to a point.

One of the main woes afflicting these firms has been their ancestral lack of management autonomy. Two aspects overshadow the others but are not the only expression of these ills: overtaxation and subjection to macroeconomic policy. Since the state owns these firms and their executive officers are government-appointed, nothing is easier than to burden them with exorbitant tax loads. When macroeconomic targets agreed upon with international lending agencies can be met only thanks to given microeconomic behavior by the larger parastatals, the latter do what they are told.

The first change that must take place in the way parastatals are managed is to grant them full management autonomy even if they are assigned an overall role to play in a long-term strategy of national development. Their tax burden should be lowered, though perhaps not to the same level as their competitors abroad or to what similar-sized firms pay domestically. There is a logic to having a state-owned monopoly that owns a major national resource transfer part of the earnings derived from the exploitation of that resource to society as a whole. State-owned firms should be subject to a tax code that stimulates investment and guarantees an adequate share of earnings to plow back into the company itself.

Parastatals must not be submitted to the day-to-day vicissitudes of macroeconomic policy, even if they will logically be subject to overall fiscal and monetary policy and the business cycle, like any firm. While chosen by the government, their managers should be appointed for fixed terms and not be removable or exposed to political strife. State-owned firms should be accountable and held in check through strict oversight on matters different from everyday management. There are many ways of doing this, ranging from congressional oversight, which should be the central feature of accountability, to an independent comptroller's office supervising their finances, procurement, labor and environmental behavior, and, most of all, their honesty.

But additional forms of oversight and accountability can be established for certain parastatals. These include labor unions and user associations—or neighborhood committees in the case of companies with significant environmental impacts—and municipal and state authorities. Unions themselves must be reformed in many parts of Latin America, but where a new, democratic labor movement has emerged, it is of the utmost importance that the representatives of its rank and file be involved in the supervision of large publicly owned firms.

There are unquestionable difficulties involved in exposing the management of enormous and, one would hope, world-class oil companies, electric power utilities, airlines, or steel mills to endless union hall debates. Limits have to be set. But together with user associations and local governments, the involvement of civil society in the oversight of parastatals can represent a major innovation in traditional rules of accountability in Latin America. It would constitute a typical form of democratization of the state where it counts: in its direct contact with citizens in everyday life. Responsible restrictions must be established, however, to avoid a new horror story of market-unfriendly aberrations.

The third and final feature of reform has to be adherence to the discipline of the market. One of the main attractions and redeeming features of state-owned firms is precisely that they don't behave like private ones. If they did, their very existence would be meaningless. But when they act in total disregard of the market, their existence becomes untenable, as consumers, clients, and society as a whole begin to clamor for their disappearance and/or privatization. Subjection to the market does not mean abandoning all social, national, or environmental standards that private firms would not respect. But it does imply that levels of efficiency, productivity, salaries, and employment must be vaguely consonant with what the market determines. Subsidies to consumers of state-provided inputs, differential price scales, regional incentives are all necessary and logical. But they should remain exceptions, be as transparent as possible, and fit into the broad scheme of an industrial policy.

■

In principle, these various realms of reform—social and economic, macro- and microeconomic, on trade and on the public-private dichotomy—are all mutually compatible, self-reinforcing, and form a coherent whole. In the abstract, the international corollaries of the domestic agenda laid out here make it possible and reduce the costs of implementation. The European welfare-state aspects correct the feudal, command capitalism facets of the Asian model that are unacceptable in Latin America—or anywhere else, for that matter. In the real world, however, matters are much more complicated. Which is why the key to the left's economic and social platform must be found in its political underpinnings. The left's program has to be different from what other sectors of the political spectrum are proposing. Virtually everything spelled out here is distinct, and as a self-contained whole has not figured on other agendas. However, nearly all of these concrete proposals have been tabled one by one on several occasions, in various countries. The chief problem is often not to formulate an alternative agenda, but to build the coalition that could make it work.

Although large parts of the business community throughout the region have still not convinced themselves of Henry Ford's dictum that you can't make a profit manufacturing cars without laborers who can buy them, certain sectors are coming around. Some still believe that the solution lies in export markets: pay Mexican or Brazilian workers a pittance and peddle your wares to German or American consumers. It is becoming increasingly clear, however, that this is not a long-term solution. Agreements such as the April 1992 deal signed in Brasilia are not only the wave of the future; they constitute the only possibility for a real way out of the region's current and long-standing dilemma.

After President Fernando Collor de Mello plunged his country into a deep recession in 1990, the labor movement and business sector were slow to react and the government remained largely paralyzed. Inertia, continued hyperinflation, an on-dragging debt renegotiation, and political gridlock seemed to make it impossible for Brazil to emerge from its crisis. In fact the Brazilian economy remained stronger than others, with firmer grounds for growth and competitiveness. Its political difficulties, moreover, stemmed from the far more democratic institutions and procedures that it gave itself in the 1980s. They also sprang from the much more vibrant and extensive civil society it developed during that period.

By early 1992, automobile manufacturers, constituting the nation's most important industry, producing both for the domestic market and for export, had seen their business drop through the floor. In relation to mid-1990, sales were down nearly 70 percent; losses for the Volkswagen-Ford Autolatin consortium and General Motors were skyrocketing. Not much could be done on the labor side: the most important auto unions, the São Bernardo and Diadema Sindicato dos Metalúrgicos, a PT bastion where Lula had founded the new Brazilian labor movement, were among the strongest and most radical in the country.

But thanks to the crisis, the government's patience, and a healthy sense of self-preservation, in April of 1992 the three sectors—the car firms, the unions, and the state of São Paulo and federal government—singed a historic compact. For ninety days, renewable, the unions agreed to postpone already negotiated salary increases in exchange for keeping their jobs, and partly attributing to themselves a reduction in car prices, the manufacturers slashed prices by 22 percent; the state and federal governments agreed to give up 12 percent in sales taxes. Everyone surrendered something, to bring prices down, shore up sales, and maintain employment. As the Brazilian magazine *Veja* put it:

> The agreement was signed by a group of frightened partners. . . . As ironic as it may seem, the power of fear present in the auto agreement could be an indication that the dream of a general pact to put the Brazilian economy back on the road to growth has failed only because there wasn't a threat of sufficient magnitude to give the country a collective fright.[52]

The agreement alone could obviously not solve the rest of the country's problems. By once again reducing the federal and state government's revenues, it could actually threaten long-term fiscal stability and the possibility of increasing spending where necessary. But the interesting aspect of it was that the most radical left-wing unions, led by a new PT labor leader, Vicente Paulo da Silva ("Vincentinho"), the largest industry in Brazil, and the state and federal governments were together able to achieve a compromise that would have previously been unimaginable. Fear of the alternative was the incentive; legitimacy and flexibility were the condition for success; the knowledge that sacrifices were indispensable in order to help the rest of society and that they could be equitably shared—all these factors combined to make this deal an incipient model for a new coalition.

This new coalition must include ample sectors of the political spectrum that do not identify with the left and would not even remotely accept the label. Herein lies the underlying, foremost lesson of the last thirty years. The monumental changes called for in Latin America to create modern, just societies, require the conscious support of much more than half the electorate, or a far greater segment of the population than what recognizes itself to be in a revolutionary vanguard, as popular as it might be. Salvador Allende in Chile tried to execute a program of deep reform with anywhere between 34 and 43 percent of the vote; he failed. The Sandinistas in Nicaragua attempted to make a revolution originally with vast popular backing, but later with not much more than half the population and perhaps, toward the end of

52. *Veja* (São Paulo), April 1, 1992, p. 72.

their stay in power, considerably less. The central political hurdle facing the left in Latin America—or any party, movement, or ideological current—is to build a far broader coalition than an electoral majority or the supporters of a popular uprising after its initial euphoria.

After years of seeking vanguards and justifiably engaging in confrontational activism, the left must move on to a politics of broad coalitions, or historical compromises. It should strive to extend the backing for its program to as much as two thirds of the electorate and political forces of any given nation. Its program must consequently be strictly reformist, yet sufficiently radical to make a difference.

The natural constituency of the left and reform has to be the enormous mass of excluded urban poor; any coalition must include a substantial part of the middle class as well as a significant chunk of the business community. Short of these two sources of support, no program is viable. But its basis must be to bring into society the millions of unemployed, marginalized, and misbegotten, who lack education, health care, housing, basic services, and even food.

A new social pact must be drawn up, fundamentally different however, from the social contracts of the thirties and forties. Those to be included this time around are those left out before: the new urban poor, the remaining rural destitute, the lower middle class, which has grown exponentially in recent decades without the benefits its predecessors enjoyed nearly half a century ago. Moreover, and decisively, the pact this time requires a democratic sanction and legitimacy. People must vote for the rulers who will make it happen, and must be able to vote them out if they do not deliver on their promises.

The constituency then for the left's economic and social alternative is a hodgepodge of society and, at the same time, the sum of those with a vested interest in changing the status quo. Perhaps the greatest loss derived from the disappearance of the socialist paradigm consists of the concomitant elimination of its built-in constituency. Socialism was the model; the working class or (in the Third World) the national liberation coalition were its congenital and always willing protagonists. The problem with constructing substitute paradigms is finding them a mass base; without one, they will never prosper. Yet only socialism, thanks to the Marxist notion of class struggle, provided an automatic constituency for its vision of social change. Socialism is no more.

The new constituency includes first and foremost the poor, for whom the status quo is unacceptable, and labor, who must make sacrifices but can obtain in exchange significant advances regarding involvement in production, job stability, social benefits for families, and even a reduction in the work week if this allows others to find employment. It incorporates the middle class, which will have to make greater sacrifices than labor but will get more in return: a decent country to live in, an end to the growing fear of violence, drugs, and social disintegration, and real participation in the nation's affairs, through the strengthening and preservation of a democratic system that is untenable without social reform. Finally it needs the business community, which can expect significant concessions on the part of labor, rising profits domestically from broader markets, and greater government support to conquer foreign markets, if it is willing to act as an entrepreneurial class and not simply as rich Mexicans or Brazilians. The idealistic ring to this scheme is undeniable: without it, there is scant hope of pulling Latin America out of its years of solitude and suffering.

•

We reach here the end of the long and winding road leading from the left's past and fall to its future promise. If a simple but penetrating question has struck the reader intermittently throughout these pages, it is for good reason: Why should the agenda laid out for the left be exclusive to it? It shouldn't, and the only explanation for it appearing so in these chapters is because that is the subject of the book, and the left is in dire need of an agenda. But indeed, the goals—and ways to achieve them—as spelled out here are not meant, nor can they be, the property of one segment of the political spectrum. They constitute aims and aspirations for all Latin Americans, and will never come to fruition unless all sectors appropriate them. It is unlikely that every sector of the regions' societies could one day subscribe to this vision; it is impossible for it to come true if only the left raises high its banner. Hence the answer to the riddle: the pages that precede this conclusion are not a program for the left alone; they are, instead, an outline of a better future for Latin America as a whole.

The left can contribute in may ways to bringing the dream about. In some countries, now and then, through governance: by getting elected to high office and implementing a program analogous to the one sketched out here. But it can also leave its mark by joining broad coalitions it does not lead, or participating as an equal with other partners: this option is viable and attractive, and perhaps the most likely. Finally, it can push for change from below and from without: by mobilizing the enormous energies of civil society and providing the proliferating popular movements of the continent with an agenda, a vision, and instruments to realize them. Municipal and state governance, unions and students, women and squatters, peasants and intellectual can all look to the left to channel their protest and aspirations into broader blueprints for lasting change. Power, the left has learned, is not quite everything, although it is a lot. Mainly, it is everywhere: in the streets and shantytowns, in schools and city halls, in books and newspapers and on television, and in the factories and fields. Without power nothing can be accomplished; but there are many shapes and sizes of it, and they are all conducive to the purposes pursued. The main thing is to know what to do with it, and what not. This is the lesson the Latin American left has learned, and that can set it on the right track as the century comes to a close.

Index

■

Printed in the United States
by Baker & Taylor Publisher Services